THE PRACTICE OF FISCAL FEDERALISM

A GLOBAL DIALOGUE ON FEDERALISM
A Joint Program of the Forum of Federations and
the International Association of Centers for Federal Studies

EDITORIAL BOARD

CO-CHAIRS
Raoul Blindenbacher, Canada/Switzerland
Cheryl Saunders, Australia

SENIOR EDITOR, BOOK SERIES
John Kincaid, United States

David Cameron, Canada
J. Isawa Elaigwu, Nigeria
Thomas Fleiner, Switzerland
Fernando Rezende, Brazil
Horst Risse, Germany
Nico Steytler, South Africa
Ronald L. Watts, Canada

www.forumfed.org
www.iacfs.org

A Global Dialogue on Federalism publications available
BOOK SERIES
Constitutional Origins, Structure, and Change in Federal Countries (2005), Volume 1
Distribution of Powers and Responsibilities in Federal Countries (2006), Volume 2
Legislative, Executive, and Judicial Governance in Federal Countries (2006), Volume 3
BOOKLET SERIES
Dialogues on Constitutional Origins, Structure, and Change in Federal Countries (2005), Volume 1
Dialogues on Distribution of Powers and Responsibilities in Federal Countries (2005), Volume 2
Dialogues on Legislative, Executive, and Judicial Governance in Federal Countries (2006), Volume 3
Dialogues on the Practice of Fiscal Federalism: Comparative Perspectives (2006), Volume 4
Dialogues on Foreign Relations in Federal Countries (2007), Volume 5
Dialogues on Local Government and Metropolitan Regions in Federal Countries (2007), Volume 6

Select Global Dialogue publications are available in other languages, including Arabic, French, German, Portuguese and Spanish. For more information on what is available, please visit www.forumfed.org.

A Global Dialogue on Federalism
Volume IV

THE PRACTICE OF FISCAL FEDERALISM: COMPARATIVE PERSPECTIVES

EDITED BY ANWAR SHAH

SENIOR EDITOR JOHN KINCAID

Published for

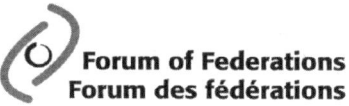

Forum of Federations
Forum des fédérations

and

iacfs
INTERNATIONAL ASSOCIATION OF
CENTERS FOR FEDERAL STUDIES

by

McGill-Queen's University Press
Montreal & Kingston · London · Ithaca

© McGill-Queen's University Press 2007
ISBN 978-0-7735-3301-1 (cloth)
ISBN 978-0-7735-3302-8 (paper)

Legal deposit fourth quarter 2007
Bibliothèque nationale du Québec

Printed in Canada on acid-free paper that is 100% ancient forest free (100% post-consumer recycled), processed chlorine free

This book has been published with generous financial support from the Government of Canada, the Swiss Agency for Development and Cooperation, the World Bank.

McGill-Queen's University Press acknowledges the support of the Canada Council for the Arts for our publishing program. We also acknowledge the financial support of the Government of Canada through the Book Publishing Industry Development Program (BPIDP) for our publishing activities.

Library and Archives Canada Cataloguing in Publication

The practice of fiscal federalism: comparative perspectives / edited by Anwar Shah; senior editor John Kincaid.

(A global dialogue on federalism; v. 4)
Includes bibliographical references and index.
ISBN 978-0-7735-3301-1 (bnd)
ISBN 978-0-7735-3302-8 (pbk.)

1. Federal government. 2. Federal government – Economic aspects. 3. Comparative government. I. Shah, Anwar II. Kincaid, John, 1946– III. International Association of Centers for Federal Studies IV. Forum of Federations V. Series: Global dialogue on federalism; v. 4

HJ141.P69 2007   321.02   C2007-902348-7

This book was typeset by Interscript in 10/12 Baskerville.

Contents

Preface vii

Introduction: Principles of Fiscal Federalism ANWAR SHAH 3

Commonwealth of Australia ALAN MORRIS 43

Federal Republic of Brazil FERNANDO REZENDE 73

Canada ROBIN BOADWAY 98

Federal Republic of Germany LARS P. FELD / JÜRGEN VON HAGEN 125

Republic of India GOVINDA RAO 151

Malaysia SHANKARAN NAMBIAR 178

Federal Republic of Nigeria AKPAN EKPO 204

Russian Federation ALEXANDER DERYUGIN / GALINA KURLYANDSKAYA 235

Republic of South Africa BONGANI KHUMALO / RENOSI MOKATE 262

Kingdom of Spain JULIO LÓPEZ-LABORDA / JORGE MARTÍNEZ-VÁZQUEZ / CARLOS MONASTERIO 287

Swiss Confederation GEBHARD KIRCHGASSNER 317

United States of America WILLIAM FOX 344

Comparative Conclusions on Fiscal Federalism ANWAR SHAH 370

Contributors 395
Participating Experts 401
Bibliography 409
Index 427

Preface

This volume on the practice of fiscal federalism in twelve federal countries is the fourth contribution to a series of practical books on federalism being published as a part of the program "A Global Dialogue on Federalism." The goal of this Global Dialogue is to engage experts from around the world in comparative conversations and debates about core themes and issues of federalism, with the aim of building an international network that enables practitioners, students, scholars, and others to learn from one another, share best practices, and enhance their understanding of the prospects as well as the problems of federalism as a mode of governance in today's world, especially in relation to democracy, freedom, prosperity, and peace.

The Global Dialogue is a cooperative program created and conducted jointly by the Forum of Federations and the International Association of Centers for Federal Studies (IACFS). The Forum is an international network on federalism that seeks to strengthen democratic governance by promoting dialogue on, and understanding of, the values, practices, principles, and possibilities of federalism. The IACFS is an association of centres and institutes throughout the world that maintain a research and teaching focus on political systems that have federal features.

The work of the Forum of Federations and the IACFS is part of a broader endeavour to build and strengthen democracy through federalism when and where appropriate. As a mode of governance that seeks to combine self-rule for regional and minority interests with shared rule for general and common purposes, federalism is necessarily of interest to advocates of democracy. This is particularly true in a world in which the vast majority of nation-states are multinational, multilingual, multireligious, and/or multicultural. Indeed, there has been a tremendous upsurge of interest in federalism since the emergence of a new wave of democratization in the late 1980s. This worldwide interest in federalism is linked directly to movements promoting greater democracy and decentralization and to the simultaneous trends towards globalization and regionalization evident throughout today's world.

Given the dominance of statist ideologies during the past two centuries, however, federalism has often been viewed as a stepchild less worthy of attention and cultivation than the seemingly natural children of modern nationalism. Consequently, while there is a long history of federal-democratic experience in a few countries, such as Australia, Canada, Switzerland, and the United States, there is little practical experience with democratic federalism in most countries, and there are problematic experiences in a number of fledgling federal democracies. In turn, there is a paucity of accessible literature and information on comparative federalism and a dearth of intellectual capital available for investment in research and teaching about the many varieties of federalism worldwide.

This series of books, being published as one important product of the Global Dialogue program, seeks to create informational capital and to fill gaps in our comparative knowledge by providing as balanced a view as possible of theories and practices of federalism in various countries around the world. The series does this by exploring comparative and contrasting theoretical and practical perspectives, with each volume focusing on a particular aspect of federalism through the examples of selected countries that reflect federalism's diversity, including its strengths and weaknesses.

Our aim is to produce books that are accessible to interested citizens, political leaders, government practitioners, and students and faculty in institutions of higher education. Each chapter in this volume, therefore, seeks to provide an overview of its country's fiscal arrangements, institutions, and practices in a way that covers all relevant, important information without overwhelming the reader in detail, while also providing some analysis of the rationales and workings of fiscal federalism and indicating how well or poorly the fiscal arrangements and institutions function in relation to their constitution and their society. Revenue is the lifeblood of all governments, but this is even more the case in federal countries where revenue and expenditure responsibilities must be both divided and shared, and where revenues must be transferred between governments for various capacity and equity purposes.

The first volume, *Constitutional Origins, Structure, and Change in Federal Countries* (2005), began the series with an exploration of the constitutional systems of twelve federal countries. The second volume, *Distribution of Powers and Responsibilities in Federal Countries* (2006), examines the various practices and dimensions of power distribution in eleven federal countries. The third volume, *Legislative, Executive, and Judicial Governance in Federal*

Countries (2006), examines the dynamics and interactions of the multiple legislatures, executives, and courts that operate in federations. Future volumes will be devoted to foreign affairs in federal countries, local government and metropolitan regions, diversity and unity in federal countries, and other important themes, with a somewhat different mix of countries being represented in each volume. The Global Dialogue program also produces a booklet series that provides an entry point to each corresponding book by highlighting the insights, key issues, and items of international interest that arose at the country and international roundtables. In keeping with their educative and accessible format, the booklets also include a glossary of country-specific terminology. The corresponding booklet to this book is available; indeed, the more limited scope of the booklet allows it to be published quickly, in multiple languages, and reproduced as changes in the federal countries warrant.

The conceptual framework of the program can be found in the first volume, *Constitutional Origins, Structure, and Change in Federal Countries*, edited by John Kincaid and G. Alan Tarr. The key idea of the Global Dialogue is to draw on the wealth of others' experiences in order to learn from one another. The program entails a comparative exploration of a dozen core themes in federal governance. Through a series of themed roundtables, participants representing diverse viewpoints in a representative and diverse sample of federal countries search for new insights and solutions. The new information emanating from the roundtables is used to produce comparative materials for worldwide distribution.

Each theme exploration entails a multiple-staged process. First, a "theme coordinator" is chosen, who makes use of the most current research on the theme to create an internationally comprehensive set of questions covering institutional provisions and how they work in practice. This set of questions, or "theme template," is the foundation of the program as it guides the dialogue at the roundtables and forms the outline for the theme book. The theme coordinator also selects a representative sample of federal countries and recommends, for each featured country, a "country coordinator" – each of whom is the author of a country chapter in this volume.

Next, each country coordinator invites a select and diverse group of expert practitioners and scholars to participate in a roundtable in his or her country, guided by the theme template. The goal is to create the most accurate picture of the theme in each country by inviting experts with diverse viewpoints and experiences who are prepared to share with and learn from others in a non-politicized environment.

At the end of the day, the coordinators are equipped to write a short article that reflects the highlights of the dialogue from each country roundtable. The booklet articles are generated from such exchanges.

Once each country has held its roundtable, representatives gather at an international roundtable. The representatives are experts who share their varied experiences and perspectives, as well as the knowledge gained from their country's roundtable, in order to identify commonalities and differences and to generate new insights.

To ensure that the knowledge gained at these events does not end with only those who participated in them, the final stage integrates the reflections from the country roundtables and new insights from the international event into book chapters, thus building on the progress already made and creating opportunities to use the material for further events. The chapters reflect the fact that their authors were able to explore the theme from a global vantage point, resulting in a more informed comparative analysis of the topic.

Given the extent of the Global Dialogue program, we have many people and institutions to thank. Special appreciation is owed to the World Bank and the Canadian International Development Agency for their generous support of this volume. We offer thanks to the editor of this book, Anwar Shah of the World Bank, for his invaluable help in organizing and launching this volume. We also thank Sandra Gain, consultant to the World Bank, for her initial copyediting of this book. We wish to acknowledge the contributors to this volume and their institutions for their dedication in hosting events, writing the chapters, and helping us to uphold the excellence of the program. Thanks are due also to participants in the twelve-country roundtables, and in the international roundtable, whose input helped to shape the content of the chapters.

We wish to thank, as well, colleagues who read and critiqued drafts of the chapters contained in this book: José Roberto R. Afonso, Banco Nacional de Desenvolvimento Economico e Social, Brazil; Robert Agranoff, Indiana University-Bloomington, United States; Luis Ortega Alvarez, Universidad de Castilla-La Mancha, Spain; Chiichii Ashwe, Federal Capital Territory, Abuja, Nigeria; Chan Huan Chiang, Universiti Sains Malaysia; David Collins, Macquarie University, Australia; Brian Dollery, University of New England, Australia; Harley Duncan, Federation of Tax Administrators, United States; Isawa Elaigwu, Institute of Governance and Social Research, Nigeria; Gisela Färber, Deutsche Hochschule für Verwaltungswissenschaften Speyer, Germany; Patrick Fafard, University of Ottawa, Canada; Thomas Fleiner, Université de Fribourg, Switzerland; Bhajan Grewal, Victoria University, Australia; Merl Hackbart, University of Kentucky, United States; Mary Harris, Cabrini College, United States; Rakesh Hoooja, Indian Administrative Service, India; Daphne A. Kenyon, Kenyon and Associates, United States; Harry Kitchen, Trent University, Canada; Hanspeter Kriesi, Universität Zürich, Switzerland; Akhtar Majeed, Hamdard University, India; Christina Murray, University of Cape Town, South Africa; Suresh Narayanan, Universiti Sains

Malaysia; Phang Siew Nooi, Universiti Malaya, Malaysia; Eghosa Osagie, Ben Idahosa University, Nigeria; Michael A. Pagano, University of Illinois-Chicago, United States; Jonathan Pincus, Commonwealth Government, Australia; Paul Posner, George Mason University, United States; Wolfgang Renzsch, Otto-von-Guericke-Universität Magdeburg, Germany; Horst Risse, Bundesrat, Germany; Sandra Roberts, Syracuse University, United States; David Samuels, University of Minnesota, United States; Sandeep Shastri, MATS University, India; Celina Souza, Universidade Federal da Bahia, Brazil; D.K. Srivastava, Madras School of Economics, India; Nico Steytler, University of the Western Cape, South Africa; François Vaillancourt, Université de Montréal, Canada; Joachim Wehner, London School of Economics and Political Science, United Kingdom; Sam Wilson, University of Alberta, Canada; Kenneth Wiltshire, University of Queensland, Australia; and Ildar Zulkarnay, Bashedu University, Russia. The assistance of these individuals is much appreciated, although they are, of course, not responsible for any deficiencies in the chapters.

We also thank our colleagues and associates at the Forum of Federations and at the International Association of Centers for Federal Studies. The program and the present book could not exist without their assistance and expertise. We wish to acknowledge the work of the entire Forum of Federations staff and, in particular, the Global Dialogue staff: Abigail Ostien Karos, program manager; Nicole Pedersen, program assistant; Rhonda Dumas, program assistant; Chandra Pasma, interim program manager; Rod Macdonell, senior director of communications; and Chris Randall for technical support. Thanks are due also to David Stamm, undergraduate EXCEL scholar, and to Terry A. Cooper, administrative assistant, for their work on behalf of this volume at the Robert B. and Helen S. Meyner Center for the Study of State and Local Government at Lafayette College, Easton, Pennsylvania. Finally, we thank the staff at McGill-Queen's University Press for all of their assistance in producing the volume and for working with us to ensure the success of this fourth book in the Global Dialogue series.

On behalf of the Global Dialogue Editorial Board
John Kincaid, Senior Editor

THE PRACTICE OF FISCAL FEDERALISM

Introduction:
Principles of Fiscal Federalism

ANWAR SHAH

A large and growing number of countries are re-examining the roles of various orders of government and their partnerships with the private sector and civil society in order to improve their ability to serve their people more effectively and efficiently. This rethinking has led to a resurgence of interest in the principles and practices of fiscal federalism. Federal systems are seen to provide safeguards against the threat of centralized exploitation as well as decentralized opportunistic behaviour while bringing decision makers closer to the people. The principles of fiscal federalism are concerned with the design of fiscal constitutions – that is, how taxing, spending, and regulatory functions are allocated among governments and how intergovernmental transfers are structured. These arrangements are of fundamental importance to the efficient and equitable provision of public services.

This chapter begins by reviewing basic concepts in federalism. This is followed by a discussion of the conceptual underpinnings of federal fiscal constitutions. The principles of fiscal federalism outlined in this chapter are primarily based on economic premises; hence, they are limited in their application to economic criteria. Some nations may well consider political, sociological, and historical criteria of greater relevance in their circumstances.

A discussion of the conceptual basis of expenditure assignment is followed by a review of the theory of tax assignment. Tax-base and revenue-sharing concepts and transfer mechanisms are then introduced briefly. A concluding section brings together the main themes of the fiscal federalism literature.

BASIC CONCEPTS OF FEDERALISM

Constitutional divisions of powers among various orders of government fall into three categories: unitary, federal, and confederal.

Unitary Government

A unitary country has a single or multi-tiered government in which effective control of all government functions rests with the central government. A unitary form of government facilitates centralized decision making to further national unity. It places a greater premium on uniformity and equal access to public services than it does on diversity. An overwhelming majority of countries (148 of 193 countries in 2006) have a unitary form of government. The city-states of Singapore and Monaco are single-tiered unitary governments. China, Egypt, France, Indonesia, Italy, Japan, Korea, New Zealand, Norway, the Philippines, Portugal, Sweden, Turkey, and the United Kingdom have multi-tiered governments based on unitary constitutions. As a result, some unitary countries (e.g., China, Denmark, Norway, and Sweden) are more fiscally decentralized than are some federal countries, such as Australia and India.

Federal Government

A federal form of government has a multi-order structure, with all orders of government having some independent as well as shared decision-making responsibilities. Federalism represents either a "coming together" or a "holding together" of constituent geographic units to take advantage of the greatness and smallness of nations in a flat (globalized) world in which many nation-states are too large to address the small things in life and too small to address large tasks.[1] Subscribing to the "coming together" view of federalism, Daniel J. Elazar pointed out and elaborated that the word "federalism" has its roots in the Latin *foedus*, meaning "league," "treaty," or "compact."[2] More recently, Robert Inman noted that "the word 'federal' has come to represent any form of government that brings together, in an alliance, constituent governments each of which recognizes the legitimacy of an overarching central government to make decisions on some matters once exclusively the responsibility of individual member states."[3] "Coming together" has been the guiding framework for mature federations such as the United States, Canada, and, more recently, the European Union. The alternative "holding together" view of federalism, also called "new federalism," represents an attempt to decentralize responsibilities to state-local orders of government with a view to overcoming regional and local discontent with central policies. This view is the driving force behind the current interest in principles of federalism in unitary countries and in relatively newer federations such as Brazil and India and emerging federations such as Iraq, Spain, and South Africa.

A federal form of government promotes decentralized decision making and, therefore, is conducive to greater freedom of choice, diversity of preferences in public services, political participation, innovation, and accountability.[4] It is also better adapted to handle regional conflicts. Such a system, however, is open to a great deal of duplication and confusion in areas of shared rule and requires special institutional arrangements to secure national unity, ensure regional equity, and preserve an internal common market.

Federal countries broadly conform to one of two models: *dual federalism* or *cooperative federalism*. Under dual federalism, the responsibilities of the federal and state governments are separate and distinct. According to William H. Riker, under such a system, "two levels of government rule the same land and the people, (2) each level has at least one area of action in which it is autonomous, and (3) there is some guarantee ... of the autonomy of each government in its own sphere."[5] Under cooperative federalism, the responsibilities of various orders are mostly interlinked. Under both these models, fiscal tiers are organized so that the national and state governments have independent authority in their areas of responsibility and act as equal partners. National and state governments often assume competitive, non-cooperative roles under such an arrangement. Dual federalism takes either the *layer cake* or *coordinate-authority* approach. Under the layer-cake model, practised in Mexico, Malaysia, and Russia, there is a hierarchical (unitary) type of relationship among the various orders of government. The national government is at the apex, and it has the option to deal with local governments either through state governments or more directly. Local governments do not have any constitutional status: they are simply extensions of state governments and derive their authority from state governments. In the coordinate-authority model of dual federalism, states enjoy significant autonomy from the federal government, and local governments are simply handmaidens of the states and have little or no direct relationship with the federal government. The working of the federations of Australia, Canada, India, Pakistan, and the United States resembles the coordinate-authority model of dual federalism.

The *cooperative federalism* model has, in practice, taken three forms: interdependent spheres, marble cake, and independent spheres. In the interdependent spheres variety as practised in Germany and South Africa (a unitary country with federal features), the federal government determines policy, and the state and local governments act as implementation agents for federally determined policies. In view of federal domination of policy making, in this model, state/provincial governments have a voice in federal policy making through a second chamber (the upper house of the Parliament). In Germany and South Africa, the second-order (state) governments are represented in the upper house of the national parliament (the *Bundesrat* and the Council of the Provinces, respectively). In the marble cake model of cooperative federalism, various orders of government have overlapping and shared responsibilities, and all constituent governments are treated as equal partners in the federation. Belgium, with its three territorial and four linguistic jurisdictions, has a strong affinity with this approach. Finally, in a model of cooperative federalism with independent spheres of government, all orders of government enjoy autonomous and equal status and coordinate their policies horizontally and vertically. Brazil is the only federation practising this form of federalism.

The *competitive federalism* model is a theoretical construct advanced by the fiscal federalism literature and not yet practised anywhere in its pure form. According to this construct, all orders of government should have overlapping responsibilities, and they should compete both vertically and horizontally to establish their clientele of services.[6] Some analysts argue that such a competitive framework would create leaner and more efficient governments that would be more responsive and accountable to people.

Countries with a federal form of government vary considerably in terms of federal influence on subnational governments. Such influence is very strong in Australia, Germany, India, Malaysia, Mexico, and Pakistan; moderately strong in Nigeria and the United States; and weak in Brazil, Canada, and Switzerland. In the last group of countries, national control over subnational expenditures is quite limited, and subnational governments have considerable authority to determine their own tax bases and tax rates. In centralized federations, conditional grants by the federal government play a large role in influencing the priorities of the state and local governments. In Australia, a centralized federation, the federal government is constitutionally required to follow regionally differentiated policies.

Federal countries also vary according to subnational influence on national policies. In some countries, there is a clear separation of national and subnational institutions ("executive" or "interstate" federalism), and the two orders interact through meetings of officials and ministers, as in Australia and Canada. In Germany and South Africa, state/provincial governments have a direct voice in national institutions ("interstate" federalism). In the United States, regional and local coalitions play an important role in the Congress. In some federal countries, constitutional provisions require that all legislation recognize that ultimate power rests with the people. For example, all legislation in Canada must conform to the Canadian Charter of Rights. In Switzerland, a confederation by law but a federal country in practice, major legislative changes require approval by referendum. Such direct-democracy provisions indirectly reinforce the decentralized provisions of public services. In all federal countries, local government influences on the federal and state governments remain uninstitutionalized and weak.

Asymmetric Federalism Countries with a federal form of governance do not necessarily treat second orders of government in a uniform manner. They often offer flexibility in accommodating the special needs or demands of constituent units or impose a federal will in certain jurisdictions. This may take the form of treating some members as less equal than others. For example, Chechnya in Russia and Kashmir in India enjoy lesser autonomy than do other oblasts and states. Or the federation may treat some members as more equal than others by giving them wider powers, as is the case with Sabah and Sarawak in Malaysia and Quebec in Canada. Some federations offer constituent units freedom of choice to be unequal or more equal than others through opting-in or opting-out of federal arrangements. Such options are part of the arrangements offered by Canada, Spanish agreements, and the European Union's treaty exceptions for the United Kingdom and Denmark.[7]

Market Preserving Federalism   Barry Weingast has advanced a theoretical concept for comparative analyses of federal systems.[8] Market-preserving federalism is put forth as an ideal form of federal system in which (1) multiple governments have clearly delineated responsibilities; (2) subnational governments have primary authority over public goods and services for local autonomy; (3) the federal government preserves the internal common market; (4) all governments face the financial consequences of their decisions (hard budget constraints); and (5) political authority is institutionalized.

Confederal Government

In a confederal system, the general government serves as the agent of the member units, usually without independent taxing and spending powers. The United States had a confederal system from 1781 to 1787. The United Nations, the European Union, and the Commonwealth of Independent States (CIS), which now consists of 11 of the former republics of the Union of Soviet Socialist Republics (USSR), approximate the confederal form of government. A confederal system suits communities that are internally homogeneous but, as a group, completely heterogeneous. The European Union, however, over time has consistently moved to assume a federal role.

THE GENESIS OF FISCAL FEDERALISM

Several accepted theories provide a strong rationale for decentralized fiscal constitutions on the grounds of efficiency, accountability, manageability, and autonomy.[9]

Home Rule

George Stigler identifies two principles of jurisdictional design:[10] (1) a representative government works best the closer it is to the people, and (2) people should have the right to vote for the kind and amount of public services they want.

These principles suggest that decision making should occur at the order of government closest to the people consistent with the goals of allocational efficiency. Thus the optimal size of a jurisdiction would vary with specific instances of economies of scale and benefit-cost spill-outs.

Fiscal Equivalency

A related idea on the design of jurisdictions has emerged from the public choice literature. Mancur Olson argues that, if a political jurisdiction and benefit area overlap, the free-rider problem is overcome and the marginal benefit equals the marginal cost of production, thereby ensuring the optimal provision of public services.[11] Equating the political jurisdiction with the benefit area is called the "principle of fiscal equivalency" and requires a separate jurisdiction for each public service. Wallace Oates proposes a related idea, the so-called "correspondence principle."[12] According to this principle, the jurisdiction determining the order of provision of each public good should include precisely the set of individuals that consume it. This generally requires a large number of overlapping jurisdictions.

The Decentralization Theorem

According to the "decentralization theorem" advanced by Oates, "each public service should be provided by the jurisdiction having control over the minimum geographic area that would internalize the benefits and costs of such provision."[13] The practical implications of this theorem require a large number of overlapping jurisdictions. Bruno Frey and Reiner Eichenberger have extended this idea to define the concept of functional, overlapping, and competing jurisdictions (FOCJ). They argue that jurisdictions can be organized along functional lines while overlapping geographically and that individuals and communities could be free to choose among competing jurisdictions. Revenues are raised from members in return for delivery of services to them. The school communities of the Swiss canton of Zurich and special districts in North America follow the FOCJ concept.[14]

The Subsidiarity Principle

According to the subsidiarity principle advanced by the European Union, taxing, spending, and regulatory functions should be exercised by the lowest order of government (the government closest to the people) unless a convincing case can be made for assigning these to higher orders of government.

ALLOCATION OF RESPONSIBILITIES

The "assignment problem," or the allocation of expenditure, regulatory, and tax functions to various orders of government, is the most fundamental issue in a federation. The literature on fiscal federalism argues that finance should follow function. In other words, assigning responsibilities for spending, including the exercise of regulatory functions, must precede the assignment of responsibilities for taxation because tax assignment is generally guided by the spending requirements of the different orders of government and cannot be determined in advance. It may be desirable to decentralize taxation at the same time as decentralizing spending, so that subnational governments will not have to rely exclusively on grants from the national government. If subnational governments are not responsible for raising at least some level of their own revenues, they may have too little incentive to provide local public services in a cost-effective way. If subnational governments are assigned more revenues than their spending requires, they may have an incentive to reduce taxes or increase public-sector wages.

Principles of Expenditure Assignment

The fiscal federalism literature provides broad guidance in delineating expenditure and regulatory responsibilities among member units in a federation. The basic principles enunciated by this literature are relevant even for unitary states in which subnational governments are simply extensions of higher-order governments. By following these principles, the central government's agents face just the right incentives for an efficient and equitable delivery of public services. These principles are discussed below, and, where appropriate, qualifications for unitary governments are stated.

Efficient Provision of Public Services Public services are provided most efficiently "by the jurisdiction having control over the minimum geographic area that would internalize benefits and costs of such provision," because:[15]

- Local governments understand the concerns of local residents.
- Local decision making is responsive to the people for whom the services are intended, encouraging fiscal responsibility and efficiency, especially if financing of services is also decentralized.
- Unnecessary layers of jurisdiction are eliminated.
- Interjurisdictional competition and innovation are enhanced.

A decentralized system ideally ensures an order and combination of public services consistent with voters' preferences, while providing incentives for efficient provision of such services. Nevertheless, some degree of central control or compensatory grants may be warranted in the provision of services when the following considerations apply:

- *Spatial externalities.* Spatial externalities arise when the benefits and costs of public services are realized by non-residents. In the case of benefit spill-outs, the jurisdiction providing the service does not consider the proportion of benefits of a public service accruing to non-residents and therefore underprovides such a service. The reverse result is obtained in the case of cost spill-outs, where the public service could not be financed by exporting taxes to other jurisdictions. There are also public services whose benefits are considered national in scope, such as defence and foreign affairs. As a corollary, these services would be best provided by the federal government.
- *Economies of scale.* Certain services require areas larger than a local jurisdiction for cost-effective provision, for example, public transportation and sewerage in metropolitan areas.
- *Administrative and compliance costs.* Centralized administration generally leads to lower administrative costs associated with financing public services.

Fiscal Efficiency Decentralized decision making in a federation results in differential net fiscal benefits (imputed benefits from public services minus tax burden) being realized by citizens depending on the fiscal capacity of their place of residence. A richer jurisdiction can provide a higher level of public services at a lower tax rate than can a poorer jurisdiction. It is argued that such differential net benefits (NFBs) would encourage people to move to a resource-rich area, although appropriate economic opportunities may not exist there. Thus, resource allocation would be inefficient because people in their relocation decisions would compare gross income (private income plus net fiscal benefits minus cost of moving) at new locations, whereas economic efficiency considerations warrant comparing private income minus moving cost. It is argued that the national government should have a role in correcting such a "fiscal inefficiency."[16]

Regional (Horizontal) Equity Differential net fiscal benefits across jurisdictions also lead to unequal treatment of citizens with identical private incomes depending on their place of residence. This is because their after-tax income inclusive of NFB would be different depending on their residence. This calls for the national government to play a role in dealing with these fiscal inequities.

The Redistributive Role of the Public Sector It is commonly argued that effective redistribution is possible only through national programs (i.e., progressive income taxes and transfers to persons), suggesting that local jurisdictions attempting to carry out redistributive policies are likely to drive out the rich.

While such arguments have merit, they leave a number of questions unanswered. National governments often prefer to strengthen their own power bases rather than to benefit citizens at large. In such situations, the national government may not redistribute from the rich to the poor in a symmetric fashion in the nation as a whole. Furthermore, views on standards for equity and methods to achieve such standards are likely to vary across a nation, making subnational government involvement critical to determining policies appropriate for each area. While the centre may assume a dominant role in pursuit of vertical equity, the involvement of subnational governments in implementing specific programs can be tailored to meet the circumstances of individual jurisdictions.[17]

Provision of Quasi-Private Goods Modern governments provide many services that, by virtue of their technologies, are essentially private goods – for example, health, education, and social insurance. Public provision of these private services is justified on equity grounds. Given that benefits accrue mainly to residents of separate jurisdictions, such services would be better provided by subnational governments. The national government's involvement is nevertheless justified to ensure horizontal and minimum standards of service in all jurisdictions. Except for minimum standards in environmental protection – the absence of which would not adversely affect interregional trade – such standards for most services encourage the free flow of goods and services throughout the nation as a whole.

Preservation of the Internal Common Market Preservation of an internal common market remains an important area of concern to most nations undertaking decentralization. Subnational governments, in their pursuit of labour and capital, may indulge in beggar-thy-neighbor policies and, in the process, erect barriers to goods and factor mobility. Thus, decentralization of government regulatory functions creates the potential for disharmonious economic relations among subnational units. Accordingly, the regulation of economic activity such as trade and investment is generally best left to national governments. It should be noted, however, that national governments themselves may pursue policies detrimental to the internal common market. Therefore, as suggested by Robin Boadway, constitutional guarantees for the free domestic flow of goods and services may be the best alternative to assigning regulatory responsibilities solely to the national government.[18]

Economic Stabilization It is customary to argue that the federal government should be responsible for stabilization policies because such policies cannot be carried out effectively by local jurisdictions. Local pursuit of such fiscal policies leads to much of the gains being lost to outside jurisdictions. Monetary policy has little scope for being carried out by the local governments. Guidelines for centralized fiscal policy have, however, only limited relevance for a country with a decentralized constitution.

Decentralized fiscal policies have worked well in highly decentralized federations such as Canada, Switzerland, and the United States, but the concept of a decentralized monetary policy does not exist. The proposition that monetary authority should be independent of any order of government conflicts with a parliamentary system of government. In both Canada and Switzerland, the monetary policy function is delegated by the federal government to an independent central bank, while fiscal policy is a responsibility shared by all orders of government. The federal governments in these countries use their powers of the purse (transfers) and moral suasion through joint meetings to induce a coordinated approach. The Swiss practice of allocating a portion of the profits of the central bank (seigniorage) to cantons promotes a wider sense of ownership of the monetary authority and could be a useful policy for other countries. An independent central bank should have exclusive jurisdiction in monetary policy. The national government should ensure fiscal policy flexibility by appropriately structuring tax assignments and by coordinating fiscal policy through regular meetings of officials of the national and subnational governments.

Monetary policy plays a critical role in ensuring a stable macroeconomic environment for growth. Empirical evidence supports the view that an independent central bank with a singular focus on price stability is essential for keeping inflation in check. Evidence on this practice confirms that such independence is more likely granted in federal systems in view of the presence of multiple orders of government with diverse and conflicting interests. The politics of federalism dictates such an independence. There are no such political imperatives in a unitary country unless there is an unstable coalition in power. Thus, while monetary policy issues are mainly governed by central bank behaviour, central bank governance is influenced by the fiscal constitution of the country.

Federal fiscal constitutions appear to exert positive influence in this regard. Fiscal policy coordination represents an important challenge for federal systems. In this context, fiscal rules and institutions provide a useful framework for, but not necessarily a solution to, this challenge. Fiscal rules binding on all orders can help sustain political commitment in countries having coalitions or fragmented regimes in power. Coordinating institutions help in the use of moral suasion to encourage a coordinated response.

The experiences of industrialized countries also show that, typically, unilaterally imposed federal controls and constraints on subnational governments do not work; instead, societal norms based on fiscal conservatism, such as the Swiss referenda and political activism of the electorate, play important roles. Ultimately, capital markets and bond-rating agencies provide more effective discipline on fiscal policy. In this context, it is important for the national government not to backstop state and local debt and not to allow ownership of the banks by any order of government. Transparency of the budgetary process and institutions, accountability to the electorate, and general availability of comparative data encourage fiscal discipline.

Fiscal federalism poses significant challenges for macroeconomic management. These challenges require careful design of monetary and fiscal institutions to overcome the adverse incentives associated with "common property" resource-management problems or with rent-seeking behaviours. The experiences of federal countries indicate significant learning and adaptation of fiscal systems to create incentives compatible with fair play and to overcome incomplete contracts. This explains why decentralized fiscal systems appear to do better than centralized fiscal systems on most aspects of monetary and fiscal policy management and transparent and accountable governance.[19]

Spending Power In a federation, there is always some degree of conflict among the priorities established by the various orders of government. One way to induce state and local governments to follow the priorities established by the national government is for the latter to use its powers of the purse, its so-called spending power. Matching transfers are often used to influence state and local priorities. Both national and state governments could legitimately pursue such policies; that is, state governments can also pursue such policies with respect to their local government.

Besides having exclusive authority to carry out monetary policy and to provide public services that are national in scope, the federal government has a role in correcting the fiscal inefficiencies and regional inequities arising from the differential fiscal capacities of various jurisdictions. It also exercises a redistributive role through a tax and transfer system or through the joint provision of such public services as education and health, which are "transfers in kind."[20] The federal government may also provide compensatory grants to cover the spillovers from provincial services.

Both the national and provincial governments could provide matching transfers to influence state and local priorities to further their own objectives. All other services are best provided by local governments, with the national and provincial governments defining minimum standards. Table 1 presents a representative assignment of major public services based on the theoretical considerations discussed above. It shows that a significant number of major services would be suitable for concurrent assignment to two or more orders of government. For such services, in order to avoid duplication and confusion and to ensure accountability to the electorate, it is important to specify as clearly and as precisely as possible the roles of the various orders of government. Such precise specification is critical for infrastructure and social services in most developing countries.

Table 1
Representative assignment of expenditure responsibilities

Function	Policy, standards, and oversight	Provision and administration	Production and distribution	Comments
Interregional and international conflicts resolution	U	U	N,P	Benefits and costs international in scope
Protection of fundamental rights	U,N	N	N,P	Has national and global dimensions
External trade	U	U,N,S	P	Benefits and costs international in scope
Telecommunications	U, N	P	P	Has national and global dimensions
Financial transactions	U,N	P	P	Has national and global dimensions
Environment	U,N,S,L	U,N,S,L	N,S,L,P	Externalities of global, national, state, and local scope
Foreign direct investment	N,L	L	P	Local infrastructure critical
Defence	N	N	N,P	Benefits and costs national in scope
Foreign affairs	N	N	N	Benefits and costs national in scope
Monetary policy, currency, and banking	U, ICB	ICB	ICB, P	Independence from all orders essential; some international role for common discipline
Interstate commerce	Constitution, N	N	P	Constitutional safeguards important for factors and goods mobility
Immigration	U,N	N	N	U because of forced exit
Transfer payments	N	N	N	Redistribution
Criminal and civil law	N,S	N,S	N,S	Rule of law, a national concern but states may have special concerns such as the French Civil Law in Quebec
Industrial policy	N	N	P	Intended to prevent "beggar thy neighbor" policies

Table 1
Representative assignment of expenditure responsibilities (*Continued*)

Function	Policy, standards, and oversight	Provision and administration	Production and distribution	Comments
Regulation	N,S,L	N,S,L	N,S,L,P	N for Internal common market, S,L for regional and local concerns
Fiscal policy	N	N,S,L	N,S,L,P	Coordination possible
Natural resources	N	N,S,L	N,S,L,P	Promotes regional equity and internal common market
Education, health, and social welfare	N,S,L	S,L	S,L,P	Transfers in kind
Highways	N,S,L	N,S,L	S,L,P	Benefits and costs vary in scope
Parks and recreation	N,S,L	N,S,L	N,S,L,P	Benefits and costs vary in scope
Police	S, L	S,L	S,L	Primarily local benefits
Water, sewer, refuse, and fire protection	L	L	L,P	Primarily local benefits

Sources: Anwar Shah, *The Reform of Intergovernmental Fiscal Relations in Developing and Emerging Market Economies* (Washington, DC: World Bank, 1994); Anwar Shah, "Fiscal Decentralization in Transition Economies and Developing Countries," in *Federalism in a Changing World: Learning from Each Other*, ed. R. Blindenbacher and A. Koller, 432–60 (Montreal and Kingston: McGill-Queen's University Press, 2003).

Note: U = supranational responsibility, ICB = independent central bank, N = national government, S = state or provincial government, L = local government, and P = nongovernmental sectors or civil society.

Roles and Responsibilities of Local Governments

The fiscal federalism approach treats local government as a subordinate order in a multi-tiered system and outlines principles for defining the roles and responsibilities of the orders of government. Hence, in most federations, as in Canada and the United States *(dual federalism)*, local governments are extensions of the state governments. In a few isolated instances, as in Brazil (*cooperative federalism*), they are equal partners with the national and state governments. And, in an exceptional case, Switzerland, communes are the main source of sovereignty and have greater constitutional significance than does the federal government. Thus, depending on the constitutional and legal status of local governments, state governments in federal countries assume varying degrees of oversight with regard to the provision of local public services. That is why there is an insignificant role for local governments in Australia but an expansive role in Brazil and Switzerland.

The fiscal federalism literature, however, does provide a normative framework for assigning responsibilities to local governments. The assignment of public services to local governments or to metropolitan or regional governments can be based on considerations such as economies of scale, economies of scope (appropriate bundling of local public services to improve efficiency through information and coordination economies, and enhanced accountability through voter participation and cost recovery), cost-benefit spillovers, proximity to beneficiaries, consumer preferences, and budgetary choices about the composition of spending. The particular order of government to which a service is assigned determines the public or private production of the service in accordance with considerations of efficiency and equity.

Large metropolitan areas with populations in excess of one million could be considered for subdivision into a first tier of municipal government of smaller size responsible for neighbourhood-type services and a second tier of metropolitan-wide government responsible for area-wide services. The first-tier governments could be directly elected, and elected mayors of these governments could form the metropolitan council at the second tier. Two-tier structures for metropolitan governance have been practised in Melbourne, Australia; Vancouver, Canada; Allegheny County, Pennsylvania, United States; and Stockholm, Sweden.

In mature federations, special-purpose agencies or bodies deliver a wide range of metropolitan and regional public services, including education, health, planning, recreation, and environmental protection. Such bodies can include education and library boards; transit and police commissions; and utilities providing water, gas, and electricity. These agencies deal with public services whose delivery areas transcend political jurisdictions and that are better financed by loans, user charges, and earmarked benefit taxes, such as a supplementary mill rate on a property tax base to finance a local school board. If kept to a minimum, such agencies help fully exploit economies of scale in the delivery of services where political boundaries are not consistent with service areas. A proliferation of these agencies can undermine accountability and budgetary flexibility in the local arena. Accountability and responsiveness to voters are weakened if members of special-purpose bodies are appointed rather than elected. Budgetary flexibility is diminished if a majority of local expenditures fall outside the control of local councils.

Table 2 provides a subjective assessment of how various allocation criteria favour local or metropolitan assignment and whether public or private production is favoured for efficiency or equity. The criteria and the assessment

Table 2
Assignment of local public services to municipal and regional/metropolitan governments

Public service	Allocation criteria for provision							Allocation criteria for public vs. private production			
	Economies of scale	Economies of scope	Benefit-cost spillout	Political proximity	Consumer sovereignty	Economic evaluation of sectoral choices	Composite	Efficiency	Equity	Composite
Fire fighting	L	L	L	L	L	M	L	P	G	P
Police protection	L	L	L	L	L	M	L	P	G	G
Refuse collection	L	L	L	L	L	M	L	P	P	P
Neighbourhood parks	L	L	L	L	L	M	L	P	G	G
Street maintenance	L	L	L	L	L	M	L	P	P	P
Traffic management	L	M	L	L	L	M	L	P	P	P
Local transit service	L	M	L	L	L	M	L	P	P	P
Local libraries	L	L	L	L	L	M	L	G	G	G
Primary education	L	L	M	M	L	M	M	P	G	P,G
Secondary education	L	L	M	M	L	M	M	P	G	P,G
Public transport	M	M	M	L,M	M	M	M	P,G	G	P,G
Water supply	M	M	M	L,M	M	M	M	P	G	P,G

Table 2
Assignment of local public services to municipal and regional/metropolitan governments (Continued)

Public service	Allocation criteria for provision							Allocation criteria for public vs. private production		
	Economies of scale	Economies of scope	Benefit-cost spillout	Political proximity	Consumer sovereignty	Economic evaluation of sectoral choices	Composite	Efficiency	Equity	Composite
Sewage disposal	M	M	M	M	M	M	M	P,G	P,G	P,G
Refuse disposal	M	M	M	M	M	M	M	P	P	P
Public health	M	M	M	M	M	M	M	G	G	G
Hospitals	M	M	M	M	M	M	M	P,G	G	P,G
Electric power	M	M	M	M	M	M	M	P	P	P
Air and water pollution	M	M	M	M	M	M	M	G	G	G
Special police	M	M	M	M	M	M	M	G	G	G
Regional parks	M	M	M	L,M	M	M	M	G	G	G
Regional planning	M	M	M	L,M	M	M	M	G	G	G

Note. L = local government, M = regional/metropolitan government, and G = sector.

presented in this table are arbitrary; practical and institutional considerations should be applied to this analysis, and the reader may well reach different conclusions using the same criteria. Further, in recent years, globalization and the information revolution appear to place a premium on the role of local government as facilitator of a broad network of service providers in a local area to further local economic development goals and to improve economic and social outcomes for local residents.[21]

Private-sector participation can also take a variety of forms, including contracting through competitive biddings, franchise operations (local government acting as a regulatory agency), grants (usually for recreational and cultural activities), vouchers (redeemable by local government with private providers), volunteers (mostly in fire stations and hospitals), community self-help activities (for crime prevention), and private nonprofit organizations (for social services). Thus, a mix of delivery systems is appropriate for local public services, with local government acting as a purchaser, regulator, or financier but not necessarily as a provider of local public services. In most developing countries, the financial capacities of local governments are quite limited. Fostering private-sector participation in the delivery of local public services thus assumes greater significance. Such participation enhances accountability and choice in the local public sector. However, assigning responsibility for the provision of a service to a specific order of government does not imply that government should be directly engaged in its production. It may simply finance, purchase, or regulate such a service. Limited empirical evidence suggests that public-private competition and/or private production of some services promotes efficiency and equity.

Principles of Tax Assignment

The division of revenue sources among federal and subnational governments constitutes the tax assignment problem. Once expenditure and regulatory assignments have been agreed on, tax assignment and the design of transfers become critical elements in matching expenditure needs with revenue means at various orders of government. Although tax assignment can be undertaken independently of expenditure assignment – a common practice in developing countries – the advantages of a centralized tax administration and a decentralized provision of public services become apparent when tax assignment reflects anticipated spending. Such arrangements prevent an overdependence by state and local governments on intergovernmental transfers, which can otherwise distort local spending priorities. Where theoretical guidance on tax assignment is unclear, expenditure assignment can provide a powerful argument for assigning responsibility to the government with the greatest need for more money. Efficiency and equity arguments have to be tempered by administrative considerations, and the exact assignment depends on informed judgment. We can, however, outline the economic principles that come into play in deciding which taxes to assign to what order of government.

Four general principles require consideration in assigning taxing powers to various governments. First, the *economic efficiency* criterion dictates that taxes on mobile factors and tradable goods that have a bearing on the efficiency of the internal common market should be assigned to the national government. Subnational assignment of taxes on mobile factors may facilitate the use of socially wasteful beggar-thy-neighbour policies to attract resources to own areas by regional and local governments. In a globalized world, even the national assignment of taxes on mobile capital may not be very effective in the presence of foreign tax havens and the difficulty of tracing and attributing incomes from virtual transactions to various physical spaces.

Second, *national equity* considerations warrant that progressive redistributive taxes should be assigned to the national government. This assignment limits the possibility of regional and local governments' following perverse redistribution policies using both taxes and transfers to attract high-income people and to repel low-income ones. Doing so, however, leaves open the possibility of supplementary, flat-rate, local charges on residence-based national income taxes.

Third, the *administrative feasibility* criterion (lowering compliance and administration costs) suggests that taxes should be assigned to the jurisdiction with the best ability to monitor relevant assessments. This criterion minimizes administrative costs as well as the potential for tax evasion. For example, property, land, and betterment taxes are good candidates for local assignment because local governments are in a good position to assess the market values of such assets.

Fourth, the *fiscal need*, or *revenue adequacy*, criterion suggests that, to ensure accountability, revenue means (the ability to raise revenues from own sources) should be matched as closely as possible to expenditure needs. The literature also argues that long-lived assets should primarily be financed by raising debt so as to ensure equitable burden-sharing across generations.[22] Furthermore, such large and lumpy investments typically cannot be financed by current revenues and reserves alone.

These four principles suggest that user charges are suitable for use by all orders of government, but the case for decentralizing taxing powers is not as compelling as is that for decentralizing public service delivery. This is because regional (province/state) and local taxation can introduce inefficiencies into the allocation of resources across the federation and cause inequities among people in different jurisdictions. In addition, collection and compliance costs can increase significantly. These problems are more severe for some taxes than for others, so the selection of which taxes to decentralize must be made with care, balancing the need to achieve and sustain fiscal and political autonomy and accountability at regional and local orders of government against the disadvantages of having a fragmented tax system. The trade-off between increased accountability and increased economic costs from decentralizing taxing responsibilities can be mitigated by fiscal arrangements that permit joint occupation and harmonization of taxes to overcome fragmentation. In addition, fiscal equalization transfers can reduce the fiscal inefficiencies and inequities that arise from different fiscal capacities across regional and local governments.

Table 3 shows the assignment of major taxation instruments to various orders of government based on the criteria discussed earlier. Box 1 presents guidance on local finances.

INSTRUMENTS OF INTERGOVERNMENTAL FINANCE

Instruments of intergovernmental finance have an important bearing on efficiency, equity, and accountability in federal systems.

Tax-Base and Revenue-Sharing Mechanisms

Tax-base and revenue-sharing mechanisms are customarily used to address fiscal imbalances or mismatched revenue means and expenditure needs arising from the constitutional assignment of taxes and expenditures to different orders of government. Tax-base sharing means that two or more orders of government levy rates on a common base. Tax-base determination usually rests with the national or state government, with the state and local governments levying supplementary rates on the same base. Tax collection is by one order of government, generally the national government in market economies and the local government in centrally planned economies, with proceeds shared downward or upward depending on revenue yields. Tax-base sharing is quite common in mature federations and almost nonexistent in newer federations in developing countries.

A second method of addressing vertical fiscal imbalances is revenue sharing, whereby one order of government has unconditional access to a specified share of revenues collected by another order. Revenue-sharing agreements typically specify how revenues are to be shared among the federal government and the state and local governments, with complex criteria for allocation and for the eligibility and use of funds. Such limitations run counter to the underlying rationale of unconditionality. Revenue-sharing mechanisms are quite common in developing countries. They often address multiple objectives, such as bridging the fiscal gap, promoting fiscal equalization and regional development, and stimulating tax efforts by state and local governments.

Table 3
Representative assignment of taxing powers

Type of tax	Determination of		Collection and administration	Comments
	Base	Rate		
Customs	N	N	N,P	International trade taxes
Corporate income	N,U	N,U	N,U	Mobile factor, stabilization tool
Resource taxes				
Resource rent tax (profits, income)	N	N	N	Highly unequally distributed tax bases
Royalties, fees, charges, severance taxes;	S,L	S,L	S,L,P	Benefit taxes/charges for state-local services
Conservation charges	S,L	S,L	S,L,P	To preserve local environment
Personal income	N	N,S,L	N	Redistributive, mobile factor; stabilization tool
Wealth taxes (taxes on capital, wealth, Wealth transfers, inheritances, and bequests)	N	N,S	N	Redistributive
Payroll	N,S	N,S	N,S	Benefit charge, e.g., social security coverage
Multistage sales taxes (value-aided tax [VAT])	N	N,S	N,S	Border tax adjustments possible under federal assignment; potential stabilization tool
Single-stage sales taxes				
(manufacturer, wholesale, retail)				
Option A	S	S,L	S,L	Higher compliance cost
Option B	N	S	N	Harmonized, lower compliance cost
"Sin" taxes				
Excises on alcohol and tobacco	N,S	N,S	N,S,P	Health care a shared responsibility
Betting, gambling	S,L	S,L	S,L,P	State and local responsibility
Lotteries	S,L	S,L	S,L,P	State and local responsibility
Race tracks	S,L	S,L	S,L,P	State and local responsibility

Table 3
Representative assignment of taxing powers (*Continued*)

Type of tax	Determination of Base	Rate	Collection and administration	Comments
Taxation of "bads"				
Carbon	N,U	N,U	N,U	To combat global/national pollution
BTU taxes	N,S,L	N,S,L	N,S,L,P	Pollution impact may be national, regional, or local
Motor fuels	N,S,L	N,S,L	N,S,L,P	Tolls on federal/provincial/local roads
Effluent charges	N,S,L	N,S,L	N,S,L,P	To deal with interstate, inter-municipal or local taxes
Congestion tolls	N,S,L	N,S,L	N,S,L,P	Tolls on federal/provincial/local roads
Parking fees	L	L	L,P	To control local congestion
Motor vehicles				
Registration, transfer taxes, and annual fees	S	S	S	State responsibility
Driver's kitchen and fees	S	S	S	State responsibility
Business taxes	S	S	S	Benefit tax
Excises	S,L	S,L	S,L	Residence-based taxes
Property	S	L	L	Completely immobile factor, benefit tax
Land	S	L	L	Completely immobile factor, benefit tax
Frontage, betterment	S,L	L	L	Cost recovery
Poll	N,S,L	N,S,L	N,S,L	Payment for services
User charges	N,S,L	N,S,L	N,S,L,P	Payment for services received

Note: U = supranational agency, N = national/federal, S = state or province, L = municipal or local, and P = private.

Box 1
Key considerations and tools for local government finances

KEY CONSIDERATIONS

The overall objective of local governments is to maximize social outcomes for residents and to provide an enabling environment for private-sector development through efficient provision of public services. This requires that local financing should take into account the following considerations:

- Local government should limit self-financing of redistributive services.
- Business should be taxed only for services to businesses and not for redistributive purposes.
- Current period services should be financed out of current year operating revenues, and future period services should be financed by future period taxes, user charges/fees, and borrowing.
- Residential services should be financed by taxes and fees on residents.
- Business services should be financed on site/land value taxes and user charges. Profit, output, sales, and moveable asset taxes may drive business out of the jurisdiction.

TOOLS FOR LOCAL FINANCE

- *Local taxes* for services with public goods characteristics – streets, roads, street lighting
- *User charges* for services with private goods characteristics – water, sewerage, solid waste
- *Conditional, non-matching, output-based grants* from national/state-order governments for merit goods: education and health
- *Conditional matching grants* for spillovers in some services
- *Unconditional grants* for fiscal gap and equalization purposes
- *Capital grants* for infrastructure if fiscal capacity is low
- *Capital market finance* for infrastructure if fiscal capacity is high
- *Development charges* for financing growth with higher charges for developing land on local government boundaries
- *Public-private partnerships* for infrastructure finance but keeping public ownership and control of strategic assets
- *Tax increment financing districts* to deal with urban blight. For this purpose, the area should be designated for redevelopment and annual property tax revenues frozen at pre-vitalization levels. For a specified period, say fifteen to thirty-five years, all tax revenues above base are used for redevelopment. Capacity improvements are undertaken through municipal borrowing/bonds against expected tax increments.

Source: Robert P. Inman, "Financing Cities," NBER Working Paper 11203, National Bureau of Economic Research, Cambridge, MA, 2005; and Anwar Shah, ed., *Local Governance in Developing Countries* (Washington, DC: World Bank, 2006).

Intergovernmental Transfers

Intergovernmental transfers, or grants, can be broadly classified into two categories: general-purpose (unconditional) and specific-purpose (conditional or earmarked).

General-Purpose Transfers General-purpose transfers are provided as general budget support, with no strings attached. These transfers are typically mandated by law, but occasionally they may be ad hoc or discretionary. Such transfers are intended to preserve local autonomy and to enhance interjurisdictional equity. That is why Article 9 of the European Charter of Local Self-Government advocates such transfers: "As far as possible, grants to local authorities shall not be earmarked for the financing of specific projects. The provision of grants shall not remove the basic freedom of local authorities to exercise policy discretion within their own jurisdiction."[23]

General-purpose transfers are termed block (also "bloc") transfers when they are used to provide broad support in a general area of subnational expenditures (such as education), while allowing recipients discretion in allocating the funds among specific uses. Block grants are a vaguely defined concept. They fall in the grey area between general-purpose and specific-purpose transfers as they provide budget support with few strings attached in a broad but specific area of subnational expenditures. The Community Development Block Grant for poor municipalities in the United States is one example.

General-purpose transfers simply augment the recipient's resources. Because the grant can be spent on any combination of public goods or services or can be used to provide tax relief to residents, general non-matching assistance does not affect relative prices. Formula-based general-purpose transfers are very common. The federal and state transfers to municipalities in Brazil are examples of grants of this kind. Evidence suggests that such transfers induce municipalities to underutilize their own tax bases.[24]

Specific-Purpose Transfers Specific-purpose, or conditional, transfers are intended to provide incentives for governments to undertake specific programs or activities. These grants may be regular or mandatory in nature or they may be discretionary or ad hoc.

Conditional transfers typically specify the type of expenditures that can be financed (input-based conditionality). These may be capital expenditures, operating expenditures, or both. Conditional transfers may also require attainment of certain results in service delivery (output-based conditionality). Input-based conditionality is often intrusive and unproductive, whereas output-based conditionality can advance grantors' objectives while preserving local autonomy.

Conditional non-matching transfers provide a given level of funds without local matching as long the funds are spent for a particular purpose. Conditional non-matching grants are best suited for subsidizing activities considered high priority by a national or state government but low priority by local governments.

Conditional transfers may incorporate matching provisions, requiring grant recipients to finance a specified percentage of expenditures using their own resources. Matching requirements can be either open-ended (meaning that the grantor matches whatever level of resources the recipient provides) or closed-ended (meaning that the grantor matches recipient funds only up to a pre-specified limit).

Matching requirements encourage greater scrutiny and local ownership of grant-financed expenditures; closed-ended matching is helpful in ensuring that the grantor has some control over the costs of the transfer program. Matching requirements, however, represent a greater burden for a recipient jurisdiction with limited fiscal capacity. In view of this, it may be desirable to set matching rates in inverse proportion to the per capita fiscal capacity of the jurisdiction in order to allow poorer jurisdictions to participate in grant-financed programs.

Conditional open-ended matching grants are the most suitable vehicles through which to induce state and local governments to increase spending on the assisted function. If the objective is simply to enhance the welfare of local residents, general-purpose non-matching transfers are preferable as they preserve local autonomy. To ensure accountability for results, conditional non-matching output-based transfers are preferable to other types of transfers. Output-based transfers respect local autonomy and budgetary flexibility while providing incentives and accountability mechanisms to improve service-delivery performance.

Designing Fiscal Transfers: Dividing the Spoils or Creating a Framework for Accountable and Equitable Governance?

The design of fiscal transfers is critical to ensuring the efficiency and equity of local service provision and the fiscal health of subnational governments.[25] A few simple considerations can be helpful in designing these transfers:

Guidelines for Grant Design

1 *Clarity in grant objectives.* Grant objectives should be specified clearly and precisely.
2 *Autonomy.* Subnational governments should have complete independence and flexibility in setting priorities. They should not be constrained

by the categorical structure of programs and uncertainty associated with decision making by national officials. Tax-base sharing – allowing subnational governments to introduce their own tax rates on national bases, formula-based revenue sharing, or block grants – is consistent with this objective.
3. *Revenue adequacy.* Subnational governments should have adequate revenues to discharge designated responsibilities.
4. *Responsiveness.* The grant program should be flexible enough to accommodate unforeseen changes in the fiscal situation of the recipients.
5. *Equity (fairness).* Allocated funds should vary directly with fiscal-need factors and inversely with the tax capacity of each jurisdiction.
6. *Predictability.* The grant mechanism should ensure predictability of subnational governments' shares by publishing five-year projections of funding availability. The grant formula should specify ceilings and floors for yearly fluctuations. Any major changes in the formula should be accompanied by hold harmless or grandfathering provisions.
7. *Transparency.* Both the formula and the allocations should be disseminated widely in order to achieve as broad a consensus as possible on the objectives and operation of the program.
8. *Efficiency.* The grant design should be neutral with respect to subnational governments' choices of resource allocation to different sectors or types of activity.
9. *Simplicity.* Grant allocation should be based on objective factors over which individual units have little control. The formula should be easy to understand so as not to reward grantsmanship.
10. *Incentive.* The design should provide incentives for sound fiscal management and should discourage inefficient practices. Specific transfers should not be made to finance subnational government deficits.
11. *Reach.* All grant-financed programs create winners and losers. Consideration must be given to identifying beneficiaries and those who will be adversely affected in order to determine the overall usefulness and sustainability of the program.
12. *Safeguarding the grantor's objectives.* The grantor's objectives are best safeguarded by having grant conditions specify the results to be achieved (output-based grants) and by giving the recipient flexibility in the use of funds.
13. *Affordability.* The grant program must recognize donors' budget constraints. This suggests that matching programs should be closed ended.
14. *Singular focus.* Each grant program should focus on a single objective.
15. *Accountability for results.* The grantor must be accountable for the design and operation of the program. The recipient must be accountable to the grantor and its citizens for financial integrity and results

(i.e., improvements in service delivery performance). Citizens' voice and exit options in grant design can help advance bottom-up accountability objectives.

Some of these criteria may be in conflict with others. Grantors may therefore have to assign priorities to various factors in comparing design alternatives.[26]

As noted earlier, for enhancing government accountability to voters, it is desirable to match revenue means (the ability to raise revenues from own sources) as closely as possible with expenditure needs at all orders of government. However, the national and state governments must be allowed greater access to revenues than is needed to fulfill their own direct service responsibilities. This is so that they are able to use their spending power through fiscal transfers to fulfill national and regional efficiency and equity objectives.

Six broad objectives for national fiscal transfers can be identified. Each of these objectives may apply to varying degrees in different countries, and each calls for a specific design of fiscal transfers. Lack of attention in these designs to specific objectives leads to negative perceptions of these grants.

Bridging Vertical Fiscal Gaps   The terms *vertical fiscal gap* and *vertical fiscal imbalance* have been mistakenly used interchangeably in recent literature on fiscal decentralization. A vertical fiscal gap is defined as the revenue deficiency arising from a mismatch between revenue means and expenditure needs, typically of state and local orders of government. A national government may have more revenues than warranted by its direct and indirect spending responsibilities, while regional and local governments may have less revenues than their expenditure responsibilities.

A vertical fiscal imbalance occurs when the vertical fiscal gap is not adequately addressed by the reassignment of responsibilities or by fiscal transfers and other means. Boadway argues that vertical fiscal imbalance incorporates an ideal or optimum view of expenditures by different orders of government and is therefore difficult to measure.[27]

A vertical fiscal gap may arise due to (1) inappropriate assignment of responsibilities; (2) centralization of taxing powers; (3) pursuit of beggar-thy-neighbour tax policies (wasteful tax competition) by subnational governments; or (4) lack of tax room at the subnational orders due to heavier tax burdens imposed by the national government. To deal with the vertical fiscal gap, it is important to deal with its sources through a combination of policies such as the reassignment of responsibilities, tax decentralization or tax abatement by the centre, and tax-base sharing (by allowing subnational governments to levy supplementary rates on a national tax base). Only as a last resort should revenue sharing, or unconditional formula-based transfers, all of which weaken accountability to local taxpayers, be considered in order to deal with this gap.

Bridging the Fiscal Divide through Fiscal Equalization Transfers Fiscal equalization transfers are advocated to deal with regional fiscal equity concerns. These transfers are justified on political and economic considerations. Large regional fiscal disparities can be politically divisive and may even create threats of secession.[28] This threat is quite real. Since 1975, about forty new countries have been created by the break-up of existing political unions. Fiscal equalization transfers could forestall such threats and create a sense of political participation, as is demonstrated by the impact of such transfers on the separatist movement in Quebec, Canada.

Decentralized decision making results in differential net fiscal benefits (imputed benefits from public spending minus tax burden) for citizens depending on the fiscal capacities of their place of residence. This leads to both fiscal inequity and fiscal inefficiency in resource allocation. Fiscal inequity arises as citizens with identical incomes are treated differently depending on their place of residence. Fiscal inefficiency in resource allocation results from people in their relocation decisions comparing gross income (private income plus net public-sector benefits minus cost of moving) at new locations; economic efficiency considerations warrant comparing private income minus moving costs, only without any regard to public-sector benefits. A nation that values horizontal equity (the equal treatment of all citizens nationwide) and fiscal efficiency needs to correct the fiscal inequity and inefficiency that naturally arise in a decentralized government. Grants from the national government to states and/or local governments can eliminate these differences in net fiscal benefits if the transfers depend on the tax capacity of each state relative to others and on the relative need for and cost of providing public services. The more decentralized the tax system is, the greater the need for equalizing transfers.

The elimination of net fiscal benefits requires a comprehensive fiscal equalization program that equalizes fiscal capacity (the ability to raise revenues from own basis using national average tax rates) to a national average standard, and it provides compensation for differential expenditure needs and costs due to inherent cost disabilities rather than differences that reflect different policies.

Fiscal equalization programs, especially if they are too generous, can have some adverse unintended consequences for interjurisdictional factor mobility and the economic well-being of disadvantaged regions. To the extent such programs discourage factor mobility and dampen market adjustment mechanisms, they can create "transfer dependencies"; that is, incentives and magnitudes of transfers serve to counteract the natural forces of adjustment or lead to decisions that are not in the economic interests of fiscally disadvantaged regions. Transfer dependency symptoms include a persistent interregional trade deficit, a regional unemployment rate persistently higher than the national average, wages in the depressed regions greater than productivity, and personal income in a depressed region higher than its GDP. Such symptoms create a widow's curse for the depressed regions, whereby the generosity of fiscal transfers and regionally differentiated expenditure policies retard natural adjustment processes and prevent regional economic convergence. Some economists also argue that, if public-sector tax burdens and service benefits are fully capitalized in property values, then the case for fiscal equalization transfers is weaker as residents in rich states pay more for private services and less for public services (and vice versa in poorer states). According to this view, as argued by Oates, fiscal equalization is a matter of political taste.[29] This view has gained currency in the federal government in the United States and helps to explain why there is no federal fiscal equalization program there. In contrast, local fiscal equalization drives most state assistance to local governments in the United States, especially school finance.

Setting National Minimum Standards Setting national minimum standards for regional and local services may be important for two reasons. First, there is an advantage to the nation as a whole from such standards, which contribute to the free flow of goods, services, labour, and capital; reduce wasteful interjurisdictional expenditure competition; and improve the gains from trade from the internal common market. Second, these standards serve national equity objectives. Many public services provided by the subnational governments, such as education, health, and social welfare, are redistributive in their intent, providing in-kind redistribution to residents. In a federal system, state and/or local provision of such services – while desirable for efficiency, preference matching, and accountability – creates difficulty fulfilling federal equity objectives. Factor mobility and tax competition create strong incentives for state and local governments to underprovide such services and to restrict access to those most in need, such as the poor and the old. Attempts to exclude those most in need are justified by their greater susceptibility to disease and potentially greater risks for cost curtailment.

Such perverse incentives can be alleviated by conditional non-matching grants, in which the conditions reflect national efficiency and equity concerns and there is a financial penalty associated with failure to comply with any of the conditions. Conditions are thus imposed not on the specific use of grant funds but on attainment of standards in quality, access, and level of services. Such output-based grants do not affect local government incentives for cost efficiency, but they do encourage compliance with nationally specified standards for access and level of services. Properly designed conditional non-matching output-based transfers can create incentives for innovative and competitive approaches to improved service delivery. Input-based grants fail to create such an accountability environment.

In conclusion, while output-based (performance-oriented) grants are best suited to the grantor's objectives and are simpler to administer than are traditional input-based conditional transfers, they are rarely practised. The reasons have to do with the incentives faced by politicians and bureaucrats. Such grants empower clients while weakening the sphere for opportunism and pork-barrel politics. The incentives they create strengthen the accountability of political and bureaucratic elites to citizens and weaken their ability to peddle influence and build bureaucratic empires. Their focus on value for money exposes corruption, inefficiency, and waste. Not surprisingly, this type of grant is blocked by potential losers.

Compensating for Benefit Spillovers Compensating for benefit spillovers is the traditional argument for providing matching conditional grants. Regional and local governments will not face the proper incentives to provide the correct levels of services that yield spillover benefits to residents of other jurisdictions. A system of open-ended matching grants based on expenditures giving rise to spillovers will provide the incentive to increase expenditures. Because the extent of the spillover is usually difficult to measure, the matching rate will be somewhat arbitrary.

Influencing Local Priorities In a federation, there is always some degree of conflict among priorities established by various orders of government. One way to induce state and local governments to follow priorities established by the national or state government is for the national or state government to use its spending power by providing matching transfers. The national or state government can provide open-ended matching transfers with a matching rate that varies inversely with the recipient's fiscal capacity. The use of ad hoc grants or open-ended matching transfers is inadvisable. Ad hoc grants are unlikely to result in behavioural responses that are consistent with the grantor's objectives. Open-ended grants may create budgetary difficulties for the grantor.

Dealing with Infrastructure Deficiencies and Creating Macroeconomic Stability in Depressed Regions Fiscal transfers can be used to serve national government objectives in regional stabilization. Capital grants are appropriate for this purpose, provided funds for future upkeep of facilities are available. Capital grants are also justified to deal with infrastructure deficiencies in poorer jurisdictions in order to strengthen the common economic union.

Capital grants are typically determined on a project-by-project basis. Indonesia took a planning view of such grants in setting a national minimum standard of access to primary school (within walking distance of the community served) for the nation as a whole. The national government provided for school construction, while local governments provided land for the schools. Experience with capital grants shows that they often create facilities that are not maintained by subnational governments, which either remain unconvinced of their utility or lack the means to provide regular upkeep.

Special Issues in Transfers from States/Provinces to Local Governments

General-purpose transfers to local governments require special considerations as local governments vary in population, size, area served, and type of services offered. In view of this, it is advisable to classify local governments by population size, municipality type, and urban/rural character, creating separate formulas for each class of municipality. The national or state government could adopt a representative tax system-based fiscal capacity equalization system and set minimum standards grants for each class and type of municipality. Where the application of a representative tax system is not feasible due to a lack of significant tax decentralization or poor local tax administration, a more pragmatic but less scientific approach to general-purpose grants could be used. Some useful components in these grant formulas are an equal per municipality component, an equal per capita component, a service-area component, and a fiscal capacity component. Grant funds should vary directly with the service area and inversely with fiscal capacity.[30] South Africa has applied a variant of this approach in central-local transfers.

Having a formal, open, contestable, and deliberative process for municipal incorporation, amalgamation, and annexation should be a prerequisite for introducing an equal per municipality component in grant finance. The lack of such a process can create a perverse incentive for the break-up of existing jurisdictions so as to qualify for additional assistance, as is demonstrated by the experience in Brazil.[31]

Lessons from International Practice in Intergovernmental Fiscal Transfers

Review of international practice yields a set of practices to avoid and a set of practices to emulate. A number of important lessons also emerge (Table 4).

Negative Lessons: Types of Transfers to Avoid Policy makers should avoid designing the following types of intergovernmental grants:

1. Grants with vaguely specified objectives.
2. General revenue-sharing programs with multiple factors that work at cross purposes, undermine accountability, and do not advance fiscal efficiency or fiscal equity objectives. Tax decentralization or tax-base sharing offer better alternatives to a general revenue-sharing program because they enhance accountability while preserving subnational autonomy.

Table 4
Principles and better practices in grant design

Grant objective	Grant design	Examples of better practices	Examples of practices to avoid
Bridge fiscal gap	Reassignment of responsibilities, tax abatement, tax-base sharing	Tax abatement and tax-base sharing (Canada)	Deficit grants, wage grants (China), tax by tax sharing (China)
Reduce regional fiscal disparities	General non-matching fiscal capacity equalization transfers	Fiscal equalization with explicit standard that determines total pool as well as allocation (Canada, Denmark, and Germany)	General revenue sharing with multiple factors (Brazil and India); fiscal equalization with a fixed pool (Australia, China)
Compensate for benefit spillovers	Open-ended matching transfers with matching rate consistent with spill-out of benefits	Grant for teaching hospitals (South Africa)	Closed-ended matching grants
Set national minimum standards	Conditional non-matching output-based block transfers with conditions on standards of service and access	Road maintenance and primary education grants (Indonesia before 2000) Education transfers (Brazil, Chile, Colombia), Health transfers (Brazil, Canada)	Conditional transfers with conditions on spending alone (most countries), pork barrel transfers (USA e.g., $200 million earmark in 2006 for a "bridge to nowhere" in Alaska), ad hoc grants
	Conditional capital grants with matching rate that varies inversely with local fiscal capacity	Capital grant for school construction (Indonesia before 2000), highway construction matching grants to states (United States)	Capital grants with no matching and no future upkeep requirements
Influence local priorities in areas of high national but low local priority	Open-ended matching transfers (preferably with matching rate varying inversely with fiscal capacity)	Matching transfers for social assistance (Canada before 2004)	Ad hoc grants
Provide stabilization and overcome infrastructure deficiencies	Capital grants, provided maintenance possible	Capital grants with matching rates that vary inversely with local fiscal capacity	Stabilization grants with no future upkeep requirements

Source: Anwar Shah, "A Practitioner's Guide to Intergovernmental Fiscal Transfers," in *Intergovernmental Fiscal Transfers*, ed. Robin Boadway and Anwar Shah, 1–53 (Washington, DC: World Bank, 2007).

3 Grants to finance subnational deficits, which create incentives for running higher deficits in the future.
4 Unconditional grants that include incentives for fiscal effort. Improving service delivery while lowering tax costs should be public-sector objectives.
5 Input- (or process-) based or ad hoc conditional grant programs, which undermine local autonomy, flexibility, fiscal efficiency, and fiscal equity objectives.
6 Capital grants without assurance of funds for future upkeep, which have the potential to create white elephants.
7 Negotiated or discretionary grants in a federal system, which may create dissention and disunity.
8 One-size-fits-all grants to local governments, which create huge inequities.
9 Grants that involve abrupt changes in the total pool and its allocation.

Positive Lessons: Principles to Adopt

Policy makers should strive to respect the following principles in designing and implementing intergovernmental transfers:

1 Keep it simple. In the design of fiscal transfers, rough justice may be better than full justice if it achieves wider acceptability and sustainability.
2 Focus on a single objective in a grant program and make the design consistent with that objective. Setting multiple objectives in a single grant program runs the risk of failing to achieve any of them.
3 Introduce ceilings linked with macro indicators and floors in order to ensure stability and predictability in grant funds.
4 Introduce sunset clauses. It is desirable to have the grant program reviewed periodically – say, every five years – and renewed (if appropriate). In the intervening years, in order to provide certainty in budgetary programming for all governments, no changes should be made to the grant program.
5 Equalize per capita fiscal capacity to a specified standard in order to achieve fiscal equalization. Such a standard would determine the total pool and allocations among recipient units. Calculations required for fiscal capacity equalization using a representative tax system for major tax bases are possible for most countries. In contrast, expenditure-need equalization requires difficult and complex analysis, inviting much controversy and debate; as desirable as it is, it may, therefore, not be worth doing. In view of this practical difficulty, it would be best to deal with fiscal-need equalization through output-based sectoral grants that also enhance results-based accountability. A national consensus on the standard of equalization is critically important for the sustainability of any equalization program. The equalization program must not be looked at

in isolation from the broader fiscal system, especially conditional transfers. The equalization program must have a sunset clause and provision for formal review and renewal. For local fiscal equalization, one size does not fit all.
6 For specific-purpose grants, impose conditionality on outputs or standards of access and quality of services rather than on inputs and processes. This allows grantors to achieve their objectives without undermining local choices on how best to deliver such services. Most countries need to establish national minimum standards of basic services in order to strengthen the internal common market and economic union.
7 Recognize the population size, class, area served, and the urban/rural nature of services in making grants to local governments. Establish separate formula allocations for each type of municipal or local government.
8 Establish hold harmless or grandfathering provisions that ensure that all recipient governments receive at least what they received as general-purpose transfers in the pre-reform period. Over time, as the economy grows, such a provision would not delay the phase-in of the full package of reforms.
9 Make sure that all stakeholders are heard and that an appropriate political compact on equalization principles and the standard of equalization is struck. Politics must be internalized in these institutional arrangements. Arm's-length institutions, such as independent grant commissions, are not helpful as they do not allow for political input and therefore tend to opt for complex and nontransparent solutions.

Moving from a public-sector governance culture of dividing the spoils to an environment that enables responsive, responsible, equitable, and accountable governance is critical. Doing so requires exploring all feasible tax decentralization options, instituting output-based operating and capital fiscal transfers, establishing a formal fiscal equalization program with an explicit standard of equalization, and ensuring responsible access to borrowing.

Institutional Arrangements for Fiscal Relations

Who should be responsible for designing the system of federal-state-local fiscal relations? There are various alternatives.[32] The first and most commonly used practice involves the national government deciding on it alone. The most obvious practice is to make the federal government solely responsible, on the grounds that it is responsible for the national objectives that are to be delivered through the fiscal arrangements. In many countries, this is the norm, and one or more federal government agencies assume exclusive responsibility for the design and allocation of fiscal transfers. A potential problem with this approach is the natural tendency of the federal government to be overly involved with state decision making and not to allow the full benefits of decentralization to occur. This biases the system towards a centralized outcome, despite the fact that the grants are intended to facilitate decentralized decision making. To some extent, this problem can be overcome by imposing constitutional restrictions on the ability of the federal government to override state and local decisions. In India, the Union government is solely responsible for Planning Commission transfers and centrally sponsored schemes. These transfers have strong input conditionality with the potential to undermine state and local autonomy. The 1988 Brazilian Constitution provides strong safeguards against federal intrusion by enshrining the transfers' formula factors in the Constitution. These safeguards represent an extreme step as they undermine the flexibility of fiscal arrangements to respond to changing economic circumstances.

Alternatively, a separate body could be involved in the design and ongoing reform and enforcement of fiscal arrangements. This could be an impartial body or a body made up of both federal and state representatives. It could have true decision-making authority or be purely advisory. Whatever body is responsible, in order to be effective it needs to be able to coordinate decision making by the two orders of government. Three commonly practised options are (1) an independent grants commission, (2) an intergovernmental forum, or (3) an intergovernmental-cum-civil-society forum.

Some countries set up a quasi-independent body, such as a grants commission, to design and reform the fiscal system. Such commissions can have a permanent presence, as in Australia or South Africa, or they can be brought into existence periodically to make recommendations for the next five years, as in India. India has also instituted independent grants commissions in the states as advisory bodies for state-local fiscal transfers. These commissions have proven ineffective in some countries, largely because many of their recommendations have been ignored by the government and not implemented, as in South Africa. In other cases, the government may have accepted and implemented the commission's recommendations but been ineffective in reforming the system due to self-imposed constraints, as in India. In some cases, these commissions become too rigorous and academic in their approaches, contributing to the creation of an overly complex system of intergovernmental transfers. This has been the case with the Commonwealth Grants Commission in Australia.

A few countries use intergovernmental forums or executive federalism or federal-provincial committees to negotiate the terms of the system, as do Canada and Germany. In Germany, this system is enhanced by having state governments (*Länder*) represented in the *Bundesrat*, the upper house of the Parliament. This system allows for explicit political input from the jurisdictions involved and attempts to develop a common consensus. Typically, such forums opt for simplicity in design so as to make the system transparent and politically acceptable.

Finally, a variant of the above involves using an intergovernmental cum legislative cum civil society committee with equal representation from all constituent units, chaired by the federal government, to negotiate changes in federal-provincial fiscal arrangements. The Finance Commission in Pakistan is an example of this model, which is constituted periodically to determine allocations for the next five years. Pakistan also follows the same approach by having provincial finance commissions for designing and allocating provincial-local fiscal transfers. An advantage of this approach is that all stakeholders – donors, recipients, civil society, and experts – are represented on the commission. Such an approach keeps the system simple and transparent. An important disadvantage of this approach is that, due to the unanimity rule, such bodies may be permanently deadlocked, as has recently been witnessed at the federal order in Pakistan.

SELECTED ISSUES IN FISCAL FEDERALISM

This section addresses three topical issues in fiscal federalism: regional equity, horizontal competition, and corruption.

Federalism and Regional Equity

Regional inequalities represent an ever-present development challenge in most countries, especially those with large geographic areas under their jurisdiction. Globalization heightens these challenges as it places a premium on skills. With globalization, skills rather than the resource base of regions determine their competitiveness. Skilled workers gain at the expense of unskilled ones. As typically rich regions also have better educated and better skilled labour than do poor regions, the gulf between the former and the latter widens. Large regional disparities represent serious threats in federal countries as the inability of the government to deal with such inequities creates a potential for disunity and, in extreme cases, for disintegration. Although the policy challenges in reducing regional disparities are large, federal flexibility in the choice of instruments is curtailed by the division of powers in a federation. In contrast, central governments in unitary states are relatively unconstrained in their choice of policies and instruments.

Under these circumstances, there is a presumption in development economics that a decentralized fiscal constitution leads to ever-widening regional inequalities. However, empirical evidence refutes this presumption. Raja Shankar and Anwar Shah show that regional development policies have failed in almost all countries – federal and unitary alike – as regional convergence is largely attributable to removing barriers to goods and factor mobility and securing a common economic union, as demonstrated by the successful experience of the United States in reducing regional income inequalities.[33] Federal countries do better in restraining regional inequalities because widening regional disparities pose a greater political risk. In such countries, inequalities beyond a threshold might lead to calls for separation by both the richest and the poorest regions. While the poorest regions might consider such inequalities a manifestation of regional injustice, the richest regions might view a union with the poorest regions as, in the long run, possibly holding them back in their drive for prosperity.

Federalism and Horizontal Competition

Preserving interjurisdictional competition and decentralized decision making are important for responsive and accountable governance in federal countries. Beggar-thy-neighbour policies have the potential to undermine these gains from decentralized decision making. Short of federal intervention, a number of solutions are possible. Competing jurisdictions could reach mutual agreements on the rules of the game and a coordination strategy. There might be high coordination costs for reaching such agreement and developing enforcement mechanisms. In the end, such agreements could prove ineffective on issues with higher stakes for the competing jurisdictions. Alternately, constitutional prohibitions against local impediments to factor mobility may be helpful. But interpretations of these provisions by the courts may not serve federalism well because they may unduly restrain the powers of subnational governments.

There is no consensus as to the federal role in preserving horizontal competition while overcoming some of the negative side effects associated with this competition. Federal government oversight of horizontal competition may prove too obtrusive to respect local autonomy. However, a federal government role in using its spending power to secure a common economic union appears promising.

This leads us to conclude that a partnership approach that facilitates an economic union through free mobility of factors by ensuring common minimum standards of public services and dismantling barriers to trade, plus wider information and technological access, offers the best policy alternative for regional integration and internal cohesion within federal nations. The question is not how to compete or how to cooperate but, rather, how to make sure that all parties compete but do not cheat.[34]

Federalism and Corruption

Power corrupts and absolute power corrupts absolutely. Federalism helps to break the monopoly of power in the national order by bringing decision making closer to people through localizing it. Localization strengthens government accountability to citizens by involving them in monitoring government performance and demanding corrective actions. Localization, as a means of making government responsive and accountable to people, can help to reduce corruption and to improve service delivery. Efforts to improve service delivery usually force the authorities to address corruption and its causes. However, one must pay attention to the institutional environment and the risk of local capture by elites. In the institutional environments typical of some developing countries – when, in a geographical area, feudal and industrial interests dominate, institutions of participation and accountability are weak or ineffective, and political interference in local affairs is rampant – localization may increase opportunities for corruption. This suggests a pecking order of anti-corruption policies and programs. Thus the rule of law and citizen empowerment should be the first priority in any reform. Localization in the absence of the rule of law may not be a potent remedy for combating corruption.[35]

WHY FISCAL FEDERALISM? SOME CONCLUSIONS

Federal fiscal constitutions have been recommended for large and diverse countries because they create incentives for multiple orders of government to provide services to their citizens in a competitive, efficient, equitable, and responsible manner. This is accomplished while respecting diversity in local identities and preferences. Federal fiscal constitutions pay special attention to regional economic and digital divides to ensure a level playing field and to strengthen the economic union. A review of comparative practices shows that federal countries do better than unitary countries on all aspects of public governance – citizen participation, political freedom, political stability, rule of law, bureaucratic efficiency, absence of corruption, human development, egalitarian income distribution, and fiscal and economic management.[36] This is because, as elaborated in this chapter, federal fiscal constitutions pay a great deal of attention to clarifying the roles, responsibilities, and accountabilities of various orders of governments and designing fiscal institutions compatible with responsive, responsible, and accountable results-based governance. The synthesis of the principles of fiscal federalism documented in this chapter will, I hope, assist policy makers and practitioners in reforming their fiscal systems.

NOTES

Author's note: The author is grateful to John Kincaid for his helpful comments.

1 Anwar Shah, "Fiscal Decentralization and Macroeconomic Management," *International Tax and Public Finance* 13, 4 (2006): 437–62.
2 Daniel J. Elazar, "The Political Theory of Covenant: Biblical Origins and Modern Developments," *Publius: The Journal of Federalism* 10 (1980): 3–30.
3 Robert Inman, "Why Federalism?" unpublished paper, Wharton School, University of Pennsylvania, Philadelphia, September 2006.
4 Not all federal countries are decentralized and not all unitary countries are centralized. For example, Canada is highly decentralized, but Australia and Germany are centralized federations, as is indicated by the share of subnational expenditures in consolidated public expenditures. Nordic unitary countries are more decentralized than are Australia and Germany.
5 William H. Riker, *Federalism: Origin, Operation, Significance* (Boston, MA: Little-Brown, 1964), 11.
6 See Pierre Salmon, "Horizontal Competition among Governments," in *Handbook of Fiscal Federalism*, ed. Ehtisham Ahmad and Giorgio Brosio, 61–85 (Cheltenham, UK: Edward Elgar, 2006); and Albert Breton, "Modeling Vertical Competition," in *Handbook of Fiscal Federalism*, ed. Ehtisham Ahmad and Giorgio Brosio, 86–105 (Cheltenham, UK: Edward Elgar, 2006). See also Daphne A. Kenyon and John Kincaid, eds., *Competition among States and Local Governments: Efficiency and Equity in American Federalism* (Washington, DC: Urban Institute Press, 1991).
7 See Ronald L. Watts, *Comparing Federal Systems* (Montreal and Kingston: McGill-Queen's University Press, 1999).
8 Barry Weingast, "Second Generation Fiscal Federalism: Implications for Decentralized Democratic Governance and Economic Development," discussion draft, Hoover Institution, Stanford University, 2006, 6.
9 This refers to civic republics as termed by John Kincaid, "Municipal Perspectives in Federalism," unpublished paper, cited in Ann O. Bowman and Robert C. Kearney, *State and Local Government* (Boston, MA: Houghton Mifflin Company, 1990).
10 George Stigler, "The Tenable Range of Functions of Local Government," in *The Economics of Fiscal Federalism and Local Finance*, ed. Wallace E. Oates, 3–9 (Cheltham, UK: Edward Elgar, 1998).
11 Mancur Olson, "The Principle of Fiscal Equivalence: The Division of Responsibilities among Different Levels of Government," *American Economic Review* 59, 2 (1969): 479–87.
12 Wallace Oates, *Fiscal Federalism* (New York: Harcourt Brace Jovanovich, 1972).
13 Ibid., 55.
14 Bruno Frey and Reiner Eichenberger, *The New Democratic Federalism for Europe: Functional Overlapping and Competing Jurisdictions* (Cheltenham, UK: Edward Elgar, 1999).

15 Ibid., 55.
16 Robin Boadway and Anwar Shah, "Fiscal Federalism in Developing/Transition Economies: Some Lessons from Industrialized Countries," paper presented at the National Tax Association Meetings, St. Paul, Minnesota, November 1994; *National Tax Journal*, proceedings issue, April 1994, 64–71; Robin Boadway, Sandra Roberts, and Anwar Shah, "The Reform of Fiscal Systems in Developing and Emerging Market Economies: A Federalism Perspective," Policy Research Working Paper 1259, World Bank, Washington, DC, 1994; Robin Boadway, Sandra Roberts, and Anwar Shah, "Fiscal Federalism Dimension of Tax Reform in Developing Countries." in *Fiscal Reform and Structural Change in Developing Countries*, vol. 1, ed. G. Perry, J. Whalley, and G. McMahon, 171–200 (London: Macmillan, 2000).
17 Robin Boadway, *The Constitutional Division of Powers: An Economic Perspective* (Ottawa: Economic Council of Canada, 1992).
18 Ibid.
19 Anwar Shah, "Fiscal Decentralization and Macroeconomic Management," *International Tax and Public Finance* 13, 4 (2006): 437–62; and Anwar Shah, "Corruption and Decentralized Public Governance," in *Handbook of Fiscal Federalism*, ed. Ehtisham Ahmad and Giorgio Brosio, 478–98 (Cheltenham, UK: Edward Elgar, 2006).
20 Robin Boadway, *The Constitutional Division of Powers: An Economic Perspective* (Ottawa: Economic Council of Canada, 1992).
21 See Anwar Shah with Sana Shah, "The New Vision of Local Governance and the Evolving Roles of Local Governments." In *Local Governance in Developing Countries*, ed. Anwar Shah, 1–46 (Washington, DC: World Bank, 2006), 1–46.
22 Robert P. Inman, "Financing Cities," NBER Working Paper 11203, National Bureau of Economic Research, Cambridge, MA, 2005.
23 Izabella Barati and Akos Szalai, "Fiscal Decentralization in Hungary" (Center for Public Affairs Studies, Budapest University of Economic Sciences, 2000), p. 21.
24 Anwar Shah, "The New Fiscal Federalism in Brazil," Discussion Paper 124, World Bank, Washington, DC, 1991.
25 For a comprehensive treatment of the economic rationale for intergovernmental fiscal transfers, see Robin Boadway and Anwar Shah, eds., *Intergovernmental Fiscal Transfers* (Washington, DC: World Bank, 2007); and Anwar Shah, "A Practitioner's Guide to Intergovernmental Fiscal Transfers," in *Intergovernmental Fiscal Transfers*, ed. Robin Boadway and Anwar Shah, 1–53 (Washington, DC: World Bank, 2007).
26 Anwar Shah, *The Reform of Intergovernmental Fiscal Relations in Developing and Emerging Market Economies* (Washington, DC: World Bank, 1994); Government of Canada, *Achieving a National Purpose: Putting Equalization Back on Track* (Ottawa: Department of Finance, 2006); Government of Canada, *Restoring Fiscal Balance in Canada* (Ottawa: Department of Finance, 2006); and Anwar Shah, "A Practitioner's Guide to Intergovernmental Fiscal Transfers," in *Intergovernmental Fiscal Transfers*, ed. Robin Boadway and Anwar Shah, 1–53 (Washington, DC: World Bank, 2007).

27 Robin Boadway, "The Vertical Fiscal Gap: Conceptions and Misconceptions," paper presented at Canadian Fiscal Arrangements: What Works, What Might Work Better, Winnipeg, Manitoba, 16–17 May 2002.

28 Raja Shankar and Anwar Shah, "Bridging the Economic Divide within Nations: A Scorecard on the Performance of Regional Development Policies in Reducing Regional Income Disparities," *World Development* 31, 8 (2003): 1421–41.

29 Wallace Oates, *Fiscal Federalism* (New York: Harcourt Brace Jovanovich, 1972). For a more elaborate discussion of absence of fiscal equalization in the United States, see Daphne A. Kenyon and John Kincaid, "Fiscal Federalism in the United States: The Reluctance to Equalize Jurisdictions," in *Finanzverfassung im Spannungsfeld zwischen Zentralstaat und Gliedstaaten,* ed. Werner W. Pommerehne and George Ress, 34–56 (Baden-Baden: Nomos Verlagsgesellschaft, 1996).

30 On examples of state-local transfers from Australia, Brazil, and Canada, see Anwar Shah, *The Reform of Intergovernmental Fiscal Relations in Developing and Emerging Market Economies* (Washington, DC: World Bank, 1994).

31 Anwar Shah, *The New Fiscal Federalism in Brazil* (Washington, DC: WORLD BANK, 1991).

32 For an evaluation framework and comparative reflections on alternate institutional arrangements, see Anwar Shah, "Institutional Arrangements for Intergovernmental Fiscal Transfers and a Framework for Evaluation," in *Intergovernmental Fiscal Transfers,* ed. Robin Boadway and Anwar Shah, 293–317 (Washington, DC: World Bank, 2007).

33 Raja Shankar and Anwar Shah, "Bridging the Economic Divide within Nations: A Scorecard on the Performance of Regional Development Policies in Reducing Regional Income Disparities," *World Development* 31, 8 (2003): 1421–41.

34 See Anwar Shah, "Interregional Competition and Federal Cooperation: To Compete or to Cooperate – That Is Not the Question," paper presented at the International Forum on Federalism in Mexico: Local and Global Challenges, held in Veracruz, Mexico, 14–17 November 2001.

35 Anwar Shah, "Corruption and Decentralized Public Governance," in *Handbook of Fiscal Federalism,* ed. Ehtisham Ahmad and Giorgio Brosio, 478–98, (Cheltham, UK: Edward Elgar, 2006).

36 Anwar Shah, "Balance, Accountability, and Responsiveness: Lessons about Decentralizations," Policy Research Working Paper Number 2021, World Bank, Washington, DC, 1998; Anwar Shah, "Fiscal Decentralization and Macroeconomic Management," *International Tax and Public Finance* 13, 4 (2006): 437–62; and Robert Inman, "Why Federalism?" unpublished paper, Wharton School, University of Pennsylvania, Philadelphia, 2006.

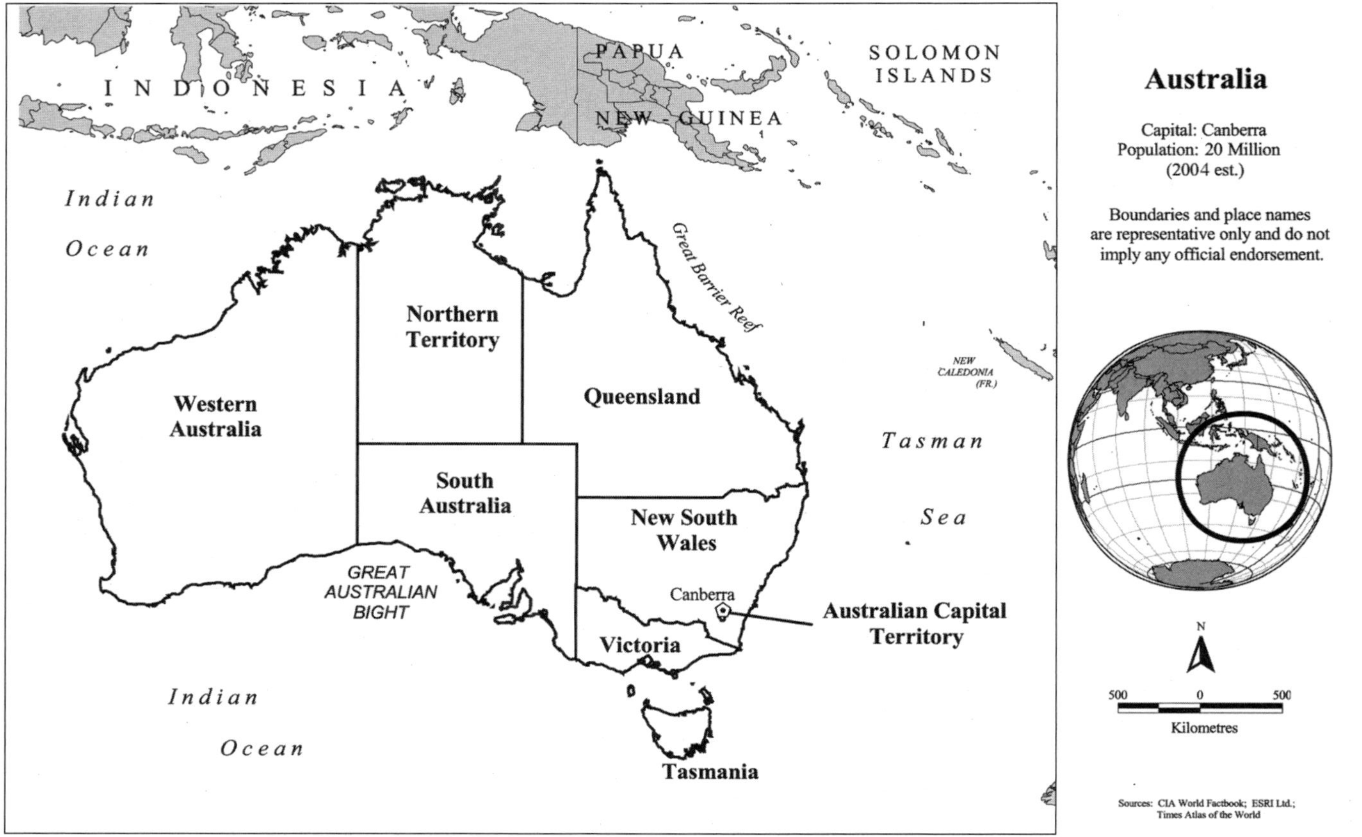
Australia
Capital: Canberra
Population: 20 Million
(2004 est.)
Boundaries and place names
are representative only and do not
imply any official endorsement.
INDONESIA
PAPUA
NEW - GUINEA
SOLOMON
ISLANDS
Indian
Ocean
Great Barrier Reef
NEW
CALEDONIA
(FR.)
Northern
Territory
Western
Australia
Queensland
South
Australia
New South
Wales
Tasman
Sea
GREAT
AUSTRALIAN
BIGHT
Canberra
Australian Capital
Territory
Victoria
Indian
Ocean
Tasmania
N
500
0
500
Kilometres
Sources: CIA World Factbook; ESRI Ltd.;
Times Atlas of the World

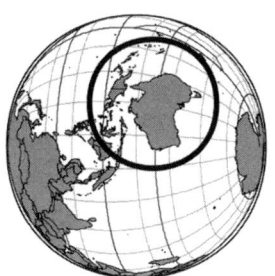

Commonwealth of Australia

ALAN MORRIS

The Australian Federation, which today comprises the federal government, six states, and two internal self-governing territories, was formed by the coming together of six self-governing British colonies in 1901. The foundations of the federation were enshrined in the Australian Constitution adopted at that time. The Constitution set out the basis on which the states would federate – including the powers and responsibilities of the newly created Commonwealth of Australia (the federal government) and those of the states, and the financial powers and responsibilities of each order of government – and guaranteed the sovereignty of the states.[1] In broad terms, and in line with most federations, the Commonwealth was vested with responsibility for national functions such as immigration; trade; foreign relations; postal, telegraphic, and telephonic services; currency; and defence. The states retained responsibility for the functions not specifically vested in the Commonwealth, including such large service-delivery areas as health, education, law enforcement, transportation, and most infrastructure.

In political terms the federation today also comprises some 720 local government bodies, but the Constitution itself makes no reference to local government. Local government bodies are established by the states and territories under state/territory legislation.

In a constitutional and legal sense, the Australian Federation began as a partnership of equals, with clear and separate constitutional roles, responsibilities, and powers for the two higher orders of government. But in the years since Federation, much has changed. Largely reflecting the increasing fiscal strength of the federal government, there have been significant changes in the de facto roles and responsibilities of the federal government and the states, with the former using its fiscal strength to take significant policy and funding roles in areas for which the latter has constitutional responsibility. This is done mainly by offering additional financial incentives for the states to commit to "national objectives and priorities" as articulated by the federal government.

THE AUSTRALIAN FEDERATION

National Characteristics

Australia is the sixth largest country in the world, with an area of 7.7 million square kilometres. The total population numbers just over 20 million, most of whom occupy a relatively narrow strip of land around the southeast coastline. While the average population density makes Australia one of the most sparsely populated countries in the world, somewhat paradoxically, it is also one of the most highly urbanized. Indigenous Australians make up about 2.4 percent of the total population.

Since the Second World War, Australia has supported a vigorous immigration program, and now almost one-quarter of Australia's population were born overseas. One clear feature of Australia's demographics is the aging of its population. The median age has increased by six years in the last twenty years.

State and Territory Characteristics

As indicated in Table 1, the Australian states and territories vary significantly in terms of size, population, and economic significance. The Australian Capital Territory has an area of 2,358 square kilometres, while Western Australia covers some 2,530,000 square kilometres. State populations range from 200,000 in the Northern Territory to 6.7 million in New South Wales, while per capita gross state product ranges from $US35,800 in the Australian Capital Territory to $US22,350 in Tasmania.

New South Wales and Victoria dominate in terms of the level and range of economic and business activity generally, while mineral and resource wealth is concentrated in Western Australia and Queensland and, to a lesser extent, the Northern Territory. These differences are important drivers of the particular outcomes of Australia's fiscal federalism.

Structure of Government

Australia is a constitutional monarchy, with the queen as titular head of state. The queen is represented in Australia by a governor general, who is appointed by the queen on the advice of the prime minister.

The system and structure of government in Australia essentially follow the Westminster model. All three orders of government – federal, state/

Table 1
State and territory characteristics

State/territory	Area (sq km)	Population	GSP ($US billion)	GSP per capita ($US)
New South Wales	800,000	6.7 million	212	$31,500
Victoria	227,000	4.9 million	154.5	$31,350
Queensland	1,730,000	3.8 million	105	$27,450
Western Australia	2,530,000	1.9 million	66.75	$33,850
South Australia	983,000	1.5 million	40.5	$26,400
Tasmania	68,400	480,000	10.65	$22,350
Australian Capital Territory	2,358	325,000	12.2	$37,800
Northern Territory	1,349,000	200,000	7.13	$35,837

territory, and local – operate as parliamentary democracies, with universal adult suffrage and compulsory voting.

The federal Parliament is a bicameral chamber. The lower chamber, known as the House of Representatives, comprises 150 members. The federal government is formed by the political party that secures a majority in the lower chamber. The House of Representatives is dominated by two major political parties. The current federal government has been in office since 1996.

The Upper House, known as the Senate, comprises 76 members. The Senate was designed as both a house of review and as the states' house. However, in practice, voting in the Senate generally follows party rather than state lines. Senate representation is also characterized by two major parties, with third parties or independents often having the balance of power.

The Executive, known as the Cabinet, is drawn from members of the governing parties from either parliamentary chamber, but the prime minister must be a member of the Lower House.

State parliaments are constitutionally sovereign. In keeping with the formal structure of a constitutional monarchy, states have governors, appointed by the queen on the advice of the state premier. All states have bicameral parliaments, except Queensland, which has a unicameral parliament (as do the two territories).

The two territories occupy a different constitutional position than do the states. They have been established under legislation of the federal Parliament and do not enjoy the same constitutional protection as do the states. For purposes of broad intergovernmental fiscal arrangements, however, the two territories are treated as though they are states, and their principal fiscal transfers are taken from the same pool as are those for the states (and according to the same principles).

Local government bodies in Australia are not established by or under the Constitution; rather, they are established under legislation of the relevant state or territory parliament. Local governments are elected through direct elections, but the party system is not as prevalent at this level as it is at the federal level. Local government receives some limited financial support from both federal and state governments, but it does not share in the principal intergovernmental fiscal transfers.

The judiciary is independent of government in Australia in terms of its constitutional position, legislative basis, and custom and practice. The structure of the judiciary comprises a hierarchy of both federal and state/territory courts. The High Court of Australia is the highest court of appeal.

Government Accountability

The Australian Constitution does not include or provide for a bill of rights. Parliaments remain the arbiters of matters that, in other federations, may be provided for under a bill of rights and, of course, the High Court also plays a role. The Constitution makes provision for constitutional change through a referendum of the Australian people. For a referendum to succeed, it must receive the support of a majority of Australians and a majority in a majority of states. Since 1901, there have been forty-four referendum questions put, with only eight of these being approved.

A number of commissions and tribunals have been established at both the federal and state/territory levels to promote transparency and accountability. All jurisdictions have auditors-general that report directly to their parliaments. Other accountability bodies include ombudsmen, administrative appeals tribunals, and various review bodies as well as commissions charged with protecting the interests of particular groups, including a human rights commission and commissions with particular responsibilities for women and ethnic minorities.

Economy

Australia's gross domestic product is $US600 billion. Economic growth has been strong over the past decade, with a current growth rate of GDP of just under 3 percent. The growth rates of the states and territories vary, with the resource-rich states of Western Australia, Queensland, and the Northern Territory currently exhibiting the strongest growth. Inflation is historically low and the national unemployment rate of around 5 percent is also low by historical standards.

Historically, the Australian economy has been dominated by primary industry, particularly agriculture and natural resources, but over recent decades the services sector has contributed increasingly to GDP and employment. The economy is highly open, and international trade constitutes a significant proportion of overall economic activity. Tertiary activities are increasing in importance.

There has been substantial growth in Australia's foreign debt over the past decade. Net foreign debt is now equivalent to just under 50 percent of national GDP. This reflects the traditional pattern of Australia's external accounts, with large deficits on the current account of the balance of payments, supported by capital inflow.

Public-sector debt reveals a different picture. The Australian government's net debt is presently around $US12.3 billion (or 1.9 percent of GDP), down from $US72 billion (19 percent of GDP) in 1995–96. State debt has similarly fallen over the last decade, although there are indications that the states may turn to some debt financing in the years ahead.

STRUCTURE OF GOVERNMENT AND DIVISION OF FISCAL POWERS

Common Economic Union

The Constitution provided for a uniform external tariff barrier for the newly formed Commonwealth of Australia, and it required the removal of the internal tariffs between the colonies that existed at the time of Federation. There are no limitations on mobility of capital or labour within the Federation and no internal barriers to trade. An aggressive microeconomic reform agenda has been instituted by the Council of Australian Governments (the heads of government of the federal, state, and territory governments) to bolster national productivity and efficiency and to eliminate any remaining barriers to competition, including with respect to the operation of government business enterprises.[2]

There is a strong commitment to market solutions at all orders of government, and the role of government in economic activity has steadily contracted over recent decades. Most government business enterprises have been fully or partially privatized. There is also increasing interest in public/private partnerships at both the federal and state/territory levels for infrastructure development, including toll roads, hospitals, schools, and so on.

The Evolution of Federal-State Financial Arrangements

Prior to Federation in 1901, the most important revenue source for the six colonies was customs and excise duties. At Federation, this important source of revenue was transferred to the new Commonwealth (federal) government, with a condition that for ten years after Federation at least three-quarters of the customs and excise revenue would be returned to the states to enable them to meet their expenditure obligations. Payments from the Commonwealth to the states in the first three decades after Federation were made on an equal per capita basis, with additional payments to Western Australia, Tasmania, and South Australia, which were judged to be in need of additional assistance.

The Commonwealth Grants Commission was established in 1933 to consider claims from the states for additional financial assistance. This was done under Section 96 of the Australian Constitution, which provides that the federal Parliament "may grant financial assistance to the states on such terms and conditions as the Parliament thinks fit." In 1942, the federal government became the sole authority levying income tax.[3] To compensate for the loss of revenue, each state received annual payments equal to its average annual income tax collections in the recent past. If a state felt that the payments under this arrangement were insufficient to meet its revenue requirements, it could apply for financial assistance through the Commonwealth Grants Commission.

In 1959, the tax reimbursement grants were replaced by financial assistance grants. These grants remained the basis of the federal government's general revenue payments to the states until the mid-1970s. The method of allocating funds to each state had population as its base, but a large number of ad hoc adjustments were made in response to state submissions. A third source of federal payments to the states, specific purpose payments (SPPs), was also growing in importance. These grants could be spent only for the purposes for which they were allocated.

In the mid-1970s, concerns on the part of the two largest states, New South Wales and Victoria, that their needs were being ignored, combined with the need to rationalize the number of channels through which the states received funds from the federal government, led to a significant change. Agreement was reached that assessments would be made for all of the states. Since that time, this approach to intergovernmental financial arrangements has been broadly followed. With self-government in the Northern Territory (1978) and the Australian Capital Territory (1989), these jurisdictions were also included in the process.

The importance of fiscal transfers to the states and territories has also been increased over the years by a series of High Court decisions that have restricted the powers of the states/territories to raise particular types of taxes, such as a range of stamp duties and levies on sales of tobacco, petroleum, and alcohol products. Federal-state financial relations underwent a further major change with the introduction of the goods and services tax (GST) in Australia in 2000. Under the Intergovernmental Agreement on the

Reform of Commonwealth-State Financial Relations (IGA),[4] all the revenue collected under the GST was to be allocated to the states and territories under horizontal fiscal equalization principles (replacing the previous financial assistance grants, which were transfers from the federal budget). In return, the states agreed to abolish a number of taxes, including financial institutions' duties and a range of stamp duties. In the short run, because some states could be financially worse off from the reform package, the IGA provided for transitional arrangements so that no state would be worse off than it would have been had the previous arrangements continued.

The constitutional arrangements would suggest that the assignment of expenditure responsibilities between the federal and state/territory governments is relatively clear cut. In practice, however, largely because of the growing intrusion of the federal government into key areas of service delivery – traditionally the responsibility of the states – this is increasingly less the case. As Table 2 indicates, the federal government is responsible for spending in areas such as defence (it spends 100 percent of total public sector expenditure in this area) and most social security and welfare (it spends 92 percent). The federal government is also a significant contributor to total public-sector expenditure in areas of state and territory responsibility, such as education (30 percent) and health (around 60 percent).

Consistent with their constitutional responsibilities, the expenditure of state and territory governments is focused on major service delivery areas, particularly health, education, and law and order (which together account for over two-thirds of total state/territory expenditures). As a constitutional matter, where the powers of the federal and state/territory governments are concurrent, if there is any inconsistency between federal and state laws, federal legislation prevails. Beyond this, and provided that the provisions of Section 92 of the Constitution are not involved, there is no direct intervention in the sense that one level of government can impose a particular policy on another or intervene directly in its spending decisions.

Increasingly, however, the federal government has used its greater fiscal strength to direct some areas of state/territory activity through the provision of additional funding, which is tied to specific objectives or purposes. This has become increasingly evident over the last twenty to thirty years. As Table 3 indicates, the federal government has supported its priorities and objectives in such areas as health, education, housing, and so on. Improving outcomes for indigenous Australians in these areas comprises a large proportion of these payments. In total, these additional payments (known as specific purpose payments) are large; in 2005–06 they totalled nearly $US14.6 billion.

Table 2
Legislative responsibility and actual provision of services by different orders of government

Legislative responsibility (de jure)	Public service	Actual allocation of function (de facto)
Federal	Defence	Federal
Federal	Social security and welfare	Federal
Federal	Foreign Affairs	Federal
Federal	Customs	Federal
Federal	Immigration	Federal
Federal	Post and telecommunications	Federal
State/territory	Education	State (Federal financial support to support national objectives)
State/territory	Health	State (federal financial support to support national objectives)
State/territory	Public order and safety	State
State and local	Housing and community amenities	State and local
State and local	Recreation and culture	State and local
Federal/state (state responsibility for regulation)	Agriculture, forestry, fishing, mining, manufacturing, construction	Federal/state
Federal (e.g., national highways), state (e.g., arterial roads), local (e.g., local roads)	Transport and infrastructure	Federal/state/local

Table 3
Direct expenditures by function and level of government

Function	Federal (%)	State or provincial (%)	Local (%)	All (%)
Defence	100			100
Debt servicing	64	31	5	100
General administration	58	27	15	100
Law and order	17	80	3	100
Economic services	59	34	7	100
Social services	92	7	3	100
Health	61	38	1	100
Education	30	70		100
Subsidies				100
Total				100
Local Public Services*	40	56	4	100

* Let "local public services" include: Primary and preschool education, secondary education, public health, hospitals, urban highways, urban transportation, drinking water and sewerage, waste collection, electric power supply, fire protection, public order and safety, police.

FISCAL FEDERALISM AND MACROECONOMIC MANAGEMENT

Broad macroeconomic policy setting and economic management in Australia is the responsibility of the federal government; the states and territories play no direct role in this area. There is limited opportunity for discussion and debate about macroeconomic issues through federal and state/territory participation in a range of ministerial councils, including the Ministerial Council of Treasurers, but these have no decision-making authority.

Each state and territory government is free to determine its own approach to economic and financial policy within its jurisdiction, although the extent of its reliance on federal financial support establishes some strong de facto constraints to the exercise of significant real discretion. Federal and state/territory governments are individually responsible for their revenue and expenditure decisions, and their budgets are developed independently (but again, in the case of the states and territories, within the constraint of a heavy reliance on transfers from the federal government).

Previous Australian Loan Council arrangements, under which federal and state governments collectively agreed on public-sector borrowing ceilings as well as on shares, no longer apply. The present loan council arrangements operate on a voluntary basis and emphasize transparency of public-sector borrowing rather than adherence to strict borrowing limits. These arrangements are designed to enhance financial market scrutiny of public-sector borrowing and to facilitate judgments about each government's financial performance.

The conduct of monetary policy in Australia rests with the country's central bank – the Reserve Bank of Australia. The Reserve Bank was established under its own (federal) legislation and is independent of government control or influence. The states have no role either in the functions of the Reserve Bank or in its composition (including appointments of the governor or the board). The charter of the bank is broad and requires that its banking policy be directed towards the greatest advantage of the people of Australia, with the specific objectives of currency stability, maintenance of full employment, economic prosperity, and the general welfare of the people of Australia. In 2003, the Reserve Bank adopted an inflation target as a key element in its objective of medium-term price stability.[5]

REVENUE RAISING RESPONSIBILITIES

Structure of Taxation Arrangements

A feature of revenue-raising assignments in Australia is that there is very little sharing of tax bases across the tiers of government. Most tax bases are available to just one tier of government, and there is no tax piggybacking.

As Table 4 indicates, at the federal level, 100 percent of the income tax on individuals and companies, 100 percent of the excise duties and levies, and 100 percent of the taxes on international trade are raised by the federal government (accounting for 64 percent of total public-sector revenue). The federal government also collects all GST revenue (accounting for 13 percent of total public-sector revenue), but it does not include this as a federal tax.

The states and territorial governments raise 74 percent of total payroll tax collections and 100 percent of land taxes, financial and capital transactions taxes, taxes on gambling, taxes on insurance, and taxes on motor vehicles (accounting for 16 percent of total public-sector revenue). Mining revenue, in the form of royalties, is collected by state and territory governments, except for some taxes on offshore oil and gas. In total, it comprises less than 1 percent of total public-sector revenue, but its distribution across states is very uneven. Western Australia and Queensland receive the most revenue through mining royalties.

Local government bodies raise 100 percent of municipal rates (accounting for 3 percent of total public-sector revenue). In recent years,

Table 4
Tax assignment for various orders of government

	Determination of		Tax collection and administration	Shares in revenue (%)			
	Base	Rate		Federal	State/province	Local	All orders
Federal							
Income tax			Federal	100			100
Enterprise (company) tax			Federal	100			100
Sales tax			Federal	100			100
Goods and services tax			Federal	100			100
Commonwealth excise tax			Federal	100			100
Agricultural production excise			Federal/state	99	1		100
Taxes on international trade			Federal	100			100
State or provincial							
Payroll tax			State/federal	25	75		100
Land tax			State		100		100
Financial and capital taxes			State		100		100
Other property taxes			State	0.6	99.4		100
Taxes on gambling			State		100		100
Taxes from public enterprises			State		100		100
Taxes on insurance			State		100		100
Motor vehicle taxes			State		100		100
Franchise fees			State		100		100
Mining revenue			State		100		100
Local							
Municipal rates			Local			100	100

user charges have become an important source of revenue for some local government bodies, but the capacity of local governments to raise user charges varies widely.

State governments are free to impose taxes, at whatever rates they choose, on all tax bases that are not reserved to other tiers of government by the Constitution or by subsequent legislative or judicial decisions. The principal tax bases available to state and territory governments include taxes on land and property, such as land tax and stamp duties; taxes on financial and capital transactions; taxes on activities and the use of goods, such as motor vehicle taxes; taxes on mining; and taxes on gambling and insurance. States and territories have established their own revenue offices and are responsible for administration and collection from their own tax bases as well as taxation policy.

In practice, there is little real tax competition among the states and territories. In part, this reflects a recognition of the futility of beggar-thy-neighbour policies, and, in part, it is influenced by the process of fiscal equalization, with its "all-state standard" approach to the assessment of revenue capacities. There is a view that state tax bases have been corrupted over the years and that states and territories have not optimized the revenue available from their own tax bases.

FISCAL EQUITY AND EFFICIENCY CONCERNS AND INTERGOVERNMENTAL FISCAL TRANSFERS

Vertical Fiscal Imbalance

Table 5 indicates the extent of vertical fiscal imbalance across the three orders of government in Australia. The federal government raises about 80 percent of total public-sector revenue in Australia. This partly reflects the tax powers embedded in the Constitution and partly reflects subsequent history, legislation, and judicial decisions. But the federal government requires only about 61 percent of total public-sector expenditure to meet its own-purpose obligations.

State and territory governments, by contrast, raise about 17 percent of total public-sector revenue from their own revenue sources but require some 33 percent of total public-sector expenditure to meet their obligations. Local governments raise about 3 percent of total public-sector revenue and account for about 6 percent of total public-sector expenditure.

This mismatch between revenue-raising capacity and expenditure obligations produces a very large vertical fiscal imbalance across the two orders of government. Many consider the extent of vertical fiscal imbalance in Australia to be undesirably large and, in several important respects, to impose constraints on appropriate actions. It is sometimes said that it hampers reform

Table 5
Vertical fiscal gaps

	Total revenue collected (in current US$ – 2006–07)	Total revenue available, including net transfers for that level of gov't (in current US$ – state year)	Expenditures (in current US$ – state year)
National	$174b		$164.6b
Subnational			
State/provincial	$40b	$85b	$90b (2004–05)
Local	$13.4b (2003–04)	$15.4b (2003–04)	$13.6b (2003–04)
All orders			

and takes away motivation for fiscal reform on the part of the states and territories. A significant proportion of funding from the federal government to the states and territories comes with strings attached, and some see this as undermining the benefits of federation (i.e., undermining genuine subsidiarity, competitive federalism, and the states' and territories' ability to develop more efficient ways of funding and delivering services). It is also sometimes said that the large vertical fiscal imbalance has negative implications for the accountability of state and territory governments.

Most observers agree that a reduction in the extent of vertical fiscal imbalance in Australia would be desirable. Suggestions for how this might be achieved include allowing the states and territories to levy an income tax by piggybacking on the federal government (with the federal government making room by reducing its own tax rate) and reforming state tax bases, particularly in the area of land tax.

But it is generally agreed that, while the vertical fiscal imbalance in Australia is undesirably large, some degree of imbalance *is* desirable. Some degree of centralization of tax powers is considered essential in order to provide national fiscal capacity to undertake national objectives and priorities.

Fiscal Transfers and Horizontal Fiscal Equalization

The large vertical fiscal imbalance requires a process by which funds are transferred from the federal government to the states and territories to enable them to meet their expenditure needs. At the present time, these transfers total about $US 48.6 billion a year, comprising both general purpose (or untied) transfers (just under $US 30 billion) and specific-purpose transfers, which are tied to particular objectives (nearly $US20 billion, including nearly $US6 billion in health care grants).

Federal transfers are extremely significant to the states and territories. Total untied and tied grants currently comprise, on average, over 50 percent of state and territory budget revenues.[6] Fiscal transfers to the states and territories are also a significant element in the federal budget. They represent about 25 percent of total federal government tax revenue – about 16 percent in the form of untied grants and 9 percent as SPPs.

Until 2001, the actual total amount of the untied transfers (the "pool") was determined by the federal government (subject to certain guarantees) and paid to the states and territories under equalization arrangements as financial assistance grants. Since 2001, under the Intergovernmental Agreement (IGA) accompanying major tax reform, all revenue collected under the newly introduced GST (a value-added tax) has been distributed to the states and territories as untied grants, replacing the financial assistance grants. These transfers continue to be untied, and the IGA states that the distribution across the states and territories is to be based on the principle of horizontal fiscal equalization. Under the IGS, the federal government agreed to cease applying wholesale sales tax, while the states agreed to remove a range of taxes such as financial institutions duty, stamp duty on marketable securities, and debits tax. Agreement has been reached to phase out a range of other state taxes over the next few years. Thus, the composition of the pool of fiscal transfers has changed, but the principles for its distribution to the states have not.

The states and territories were attracted to the new tax arrangements (particularly the GST) because it offered them access to a substantial growth tax. In this regard, their aspirations have been met (although the states and territories have not all benefited equally under the new arrangements). The GST/HCG (health care grants) pool has grown from $US18.2 billion in 2000–01 to an anticipated $US35.7 billion in 2006–07. By way of comparison, the financial assistance grant pool, prior to the introduction of the new arrangements, was just over $US6 billion in 1981–82, and it was $US12.9 billion in 1993–94.

Horizontal Fiscal Equalization

Untied intergovernmental fiscal transfers in Australia are based on the principle of horizontal fiscal equalization, such that:

State (and territory) governments should receive funding from the pool of GST revenue such that, if each made the same effort to raise revenue from its own sources and operated at the same level of efficiency, each would have the capacity to provide services at the same standard.[7]

This principle is implemented under a comprehensive assessment of state and territory revenue-raising capacities and expenditure needs undertaken by the Commonwealth Grants Commission. Rather surprisingly, given the significance and very comprehensive nature of fiscal equalization in Australia, the principle of horizontal fiscal equalization is neither enshrined in the Constitution nor set out in legislation. The current definition has been developed by the Commonwealth Grants Commission, and, for all practical purposes, the basis upon which equalization is implemented has remained essentially unchanged since the mid-1970s.

The Australian states and territories differ in size, population, geography, history, demographics, level of development, and resource endowment. A dollar in the hands of one state cannot always be transformed into the same level of services in the hands of another. Giving all states and territories the same per capita amount would result in quite different levels of capacity for service delivery, even if they followed the same policies. Therefore, the transfer system focuses on distributing the pool so as to equalize the fiscal capacities of the states and territories.

The Three Pillars

"The current approach to fiscal equalization in Australia rests on three conceptual pillars – capacity equalization, policy neutrality, and internal standards."[8] Capacity equalization is particularly important because it establishes the fundamental objective of equalization. Equalization of the budget capacities of the state and territory governments is intended to provide them with the capacity to provide an equivalent range and standard of services to their constituents.

The Australian approach to equalization is not directed towards outcome equalization. The objective of funding distribution is not to provide equal access to public services for all citizens, irrespective of where they live. The states and territories themselves do not do this; people in rural and remote locations cannot gain access to the same range of services as do people in metropolitan areas. In the interest of policy neutrality, the Australian approach to equalization seeks to establish policy standards based on the average of the policies actually adopted by the states. This approach recognizes that policy choices influence all areas of taxing and spending and that an approach that sought to establish policy-free standards cannot be constructed.

For the use of internal standards, the financial benchmarks are the all-state average of revenue raised under the various tax heads, along with expenditure across the various recurrent functions of state and territory governments. External standards or standards (benchmarks) that reflect some concept of best practice are not applied. The assessment of differential per capita revenue capacities or expenditure needs is made only with regard to those influences judged to be beyond the control of individual states and territories.[9] States and territories are not compensated for differences that result from policy choices. A state or territory that chooses to spend more than the average on a particular function does not receive additional funding. It still gets only its assessed need for that function, based on the standard and an assessment of its non-policy disabilities. A state that chooses a high taxation regime keeps the additional revenue it raises, and its grant share is not reduced. So there are no incentives or rewards to encourage "good policies," and there are no penalties for "poor policies." But equally, there is no compensation for states that choose, for example, to have higher than average levels of expenditure or to make a less than standard revenue-raising effort.

The end result of calculating disabilities across the range of expenditure and revenue categories is a measure that is referred to as the state or territory's relativity – that is, its overall financial need relative to that of the other states.

In order to avoid year-on-year volatility in the relativities and grant shares, the calculation of relativities is based on a moving five-year average (i.e., averaging the relativities for each year of a five-year period), using the latest available data. No attempt is made to anticipate relativities or grant shares based on forward projections. This means that the effect of changes in the relative fiscal circumstances of the states and territories is reflected in the relativities and grant shares only with a considerable lag.

Relativities across Australia sum to one (i.e., the per capita relativities for each state and territory, when weighted for population share, will sum to one). The range for 2005–06 is from just under 0.9 for Victoria and New South Wales, to just over 4.3 for the Northern Territory.[10] A relativity of less than one means that a state will receive less than an equal per capita share of the pool to be distributed; a relativity greater than one means that a state will receive more than an equal per capita share.

In 2004–05, the variation between the equalization distribution and an equal per capita distribution was about \$US2.4 billion, equal to about 7.7 percent of the total pool of funds to be distributed.[11] New South Wales and Victoria received about \$US195 per head less than their equal per capita share; all other states and territories received more, ranging from \$US45 per head more than its equal per capita share for Western Australia to \$US825 more for Tasmania and \$US4,755 per head more for the Northern Territory (reflecting its very much greater expenditure disabilities). A little over two-thirds of the equalization distribution results from assessed differences in expenditure needs, and a little under one-third results from differences in assessed revenue capacities.

Western Australia (because of its access to royalties from natural resources) and New South Wales (because of its high asset values, particularly land and property values in Sydney) are assessed to have revenue-raising capacities above the all-state average, while Tasmania and South Australia have the weakest revenue-raising capacities. The Northern Territory has an assessed expenditure need that is more than twice the all-state average (reflecting the greater costs of service provision associated with its large area, generally inhospitable climate and terrain, small population, and the costs of delivering services to the relatively large indigenous population, particularly the large numbers living in small, scattered communities in remote locations). By contrast, Victoria has an assessed expenditure need below the all-state average, reflecting its relatively concentrated population and less demanding geographic and climatic conditions, allowing most services to be delivered at lower cost.

A major driver of the equalization redistribution are the assessments made to address the greater-than-average costs of providing services to indigenous Australians (which account for about one-third of the total redistribution). About two-thirds of the resulting total redistribution goes to support the assessed needs of the Northern Territory and Tasmania.

The comprehensive nature of equalization provides for an assessment of all circumstances and factors that affect the relative cost differences facing the states and territories in delivering standard services. These circumstances include the additional costs facing governments in meeting the requirements of large cities as well as those stemming from delivering services in rural and remote areas.

Australia's equalization process is dynamic. The cycle of periodic reviews of methods and annual updates is designed to keep the relativities up to date in reflecting changes in the relative revenue-raising capacities of the states and territories and their use and cost of services over time. The relativities recently assessed for application in 2006–07 show a particularly clear trend, tracking the changes in the relative circumstances of the states and territories. Reflecting the strengthening of their fiscal positions (due to strong revenue growth from resource royalties and property markets), the relativities of Queensland and Western Australia have fallen, particularly over the last two years of the five-year assessment period. The relativities of New South Wales and Victoria have increased, reflecting the cooling of the property boom in these states and their lesser natural resource bases. The immediate impact of these changes on overall relativities and grant shares is dampened by the five-year averaging process. The proportion of the pool redistributed by equalization has shown a long-term decline between 1981–82 (nearly 12 percent) and 2006–07 (just under 7 percent).

Specific Purpose Payments

In addition to the untied pool of funds distributed under fiscal equalization arrangements, additional payments are made available by the federal government to the states and territories in specific areas. These are called specific purpose payments (SPPs). These payments are intended to support the implementation of particular national priorities. They are conditional payments, requiring the states to commit to undertake particular policies or programs, and sometimes requiring matching contributions by the states.

These payments currently constitute about 45 percent of total federal assistance to the states and territories. This proportion has varied from about 25 percent of total federal assistance in the early 1970s to just over 50 percent in the mid-1990s. These tied grants totalled $US14.6 billion in 2005–06 (up from $US12.37 billion in 1998–99). They predominantly relate to areas that are the responsibility of the states and territories but that are also areas where the federal government wants the states and territories to support specific national objectives. The largest SPPs are in the areas of education, health, social security and welfare, transportation, and housing. SPPs for capital purposes totalled around $US2.25 billion in 2005–06.

The majority of SPPs are tied, meaning they are subject to conditions set by the federal government – conditions that are designed to ensure that national objectives are achieved. These conditions include general policy conditions, requirements that payments be expended for a designated purpose only, state maintenance of effort and matching funding arrangements, and reporting of financial and performance information.

The first-round distribution of these tied grants to states and territories is determined by the specific nature of the intergovernmental negotiations in each case. Some are determined on the basis of bilateral negotiations between the federal government and individual states or territories, while others are determined multilaterally between the federal government and all the states and territories together, typically in the context of the relevant Ministerial Forum of Federal and State/Territory Ministers.

The treatment of SPPs under current equalization arrangements, however, is not well understood. Where an SPP relates to a function of state/territory expenditure for which needs are assessed by the Commonwealth Grants Commission, the services funded by the SPP and the SPP revenue available to the state/territory are included in the scope of the commission's assessments. Since the SPP contributes to state/territory revenue, the effect of this treatment is that, other things being equal, a state/territory with a higher than equal per capita share of the SPP than the commission's corresponding assessment receives a lesser share of untied grants. This approach is taken with regard to all SPPs that are relevant to the scope of the equalization assessments, except those that are excluded by the terms of reference. In practice, very few SPPs are excluded.

The Commonwealth Grants Commission

The Commonwealth Grants Commission plays a central role in the fiscal equalization process in Australia. It is an independent body established under federal legislation, its purpose being to provide recommendations, in the form of relativities, that reflect the fiscal circumstances of the states and territories. This is to be the basis for fiscal transfers whose purpose is to achieve horizontal fiscal equalization in the Australian Federation. The commission responds to terms of reference from the federal government. By convention, the states and territories are consulted on these terms of reference. The commission does not initiate its own inquiries.

The commission exists under the administrative umbrella of the federal government, but its key stakeholders are understood to be the states and territories, and there is extensive consultation and interaction between the former and the latter. While the commission makes recommendations on state/territory relativities, consideration of these recommendations is undertaken by the Ministerial Council of Treasurers, with the formal decisions being made by the federal treasurer.

The commission does not determine the quantum of funds to be distributed (i.e., the size of the pool). Its recommendations relate only to the distribution of the pool among the states. Under the GST arrangements, the quantum of funds available in the pool is whatever is raised through the GST.

Fiscal Federalism beyond Equalization

Horizontal fiscal equalization, including the distribution of the GST pool (i.e., explicit equalization) and SPPs, is only one element of overall fiscal federalism in Australia. Substantial implicit equalization of individuals takes place through other transfers, such as social security and health care arrangements, and other federal own-purpose outlays. In terms of the total amount redistributed, this implicit equalization is larger than is explicit equalization.

National Competition Policy, designed to promote a more competitive domestic market, also provides a further source of transfers from the federal government to the states and territories. Under National Competition Policy, states and territories have committed to review legislation that restricts competition, to apply competitive neutrality to government business activities, and to introduce specific competitive reforms in electricity, gas, water, and road transport. Subject to the National Competition Council's finding that states and territories are complying with these requirements, payments are made to them to compensate them for the costs of these reforms. In 2005–06, these payments totalled about $US600 million.

Issues in Fiscal Federalism

While there continues to be general agreement in Australia that the financially weaker states and territories should receive additional financial assistance, there is a growing political debate about both the existing principle of horizontal fiscal equalization and its implementation. Not surprisingly, as the size of the GST pool has increased, this debate has become more vigorous. Some, particularly in the more populous states, argue that the current concept of fiscal equalization is no longer appropriate because equalization distorts efficiency, drives mediocrity rather than efficiency, and is not consistent with the contemporary wider public policy framework in Australia.

The limited research on this issue does not clearly support a conclusion in either direction.[12] Equalization potentially imposes efficiency costs, but it also has economic as well as social benefits. Some commentators have also noted that it is not the primary purpose of equalization to promote efficiency for the sake of national production.

Equalization is also criticized because it does not do what most people would naturally assume that it does. It is natural to think of equalization in terms of equity for individuals or communities – people being treated equally in terms of access to and quality of services, irrespective of where they live. The approach to equalization in Australia is not designed to achieve equality of outcomes for individuals or communities; rather, its objective is to achieve equality in the financial capacity of state and territory governments to deliver services of a comparable standard.

Supporters of equalization argue that it is a necessary condition for interpersonal or intercommunity equity. They contend that, without the current equalization arrangements, the fiscal system would be even further away from treating individuals equally. Groups with particular interests are critical of the existing approach on the grounds that the states and territories are not obviously spending money in areas for which they "receive grants." More widely, there are concerns about the level of detail and complexity associated with the current process of implementation of fiscal equalization, including the use of data and judgment. The Australian approach to equalization generates enormous requirements for comparable and consistent data across all states and territories at high levels of disaggregation. There are questions about the adequacy of some data and the way they are used, and whether, in these circumstances, a comprehensive and highly disaggregated approach can clearly be said to produce a stronger equalization outcome.

Reflecting on the very comprehensive nature of equalization in Australia, some argue that horizontal fiscal equalization should be a safety net rather than a process requiring equalization of everything all the time. Some argue that the scope of equalization should be limited, for example, to the provision of "merit goods." Others argue, in quite the opposite direction, that equalization should be extended to cover areas of state expenditure not currently differentially assessed.

A further criticism of the current approach involves using internal standards (i.e., what states do) rather than assessing needs and disabilities based on standards that reflect best practice in service delivery or revenue collection. This criticism reflects the importance of optimizing state and territory revenue-raising and expenditure policies and practices, particularly with respect to administrative efficiency. Proponents of this view often associate best practice standards with the principle of mutual obligation: states and territories that receive above average per capita grants should be accountable for the use of the additional funds.

The current approach to "policy neutrality" is also contentious, particularly given the range of adjustments that are made in the assessment process in order to reflect disabilities. The criticism is made that the current process attributes too much of the differences between states and territories regarding the costs of providing services or revenue raised to effects of disabilities, thus understating the effects of policy differences on different costs of service provision and revenue capacities.

Others strongly support the current approach, arguing that it reflects the broad and long-established political consensus concerning the objectives of equalization, which constitute an integral part of the fabric of the Federation. It has been the long-standing position of the Australian government, indeed of both major political parties in the federal arena, to support horizontal fiscal equalization as appropriate to the circumstances of the Australian Federation.

Recent Developments

Under the normal review cycle of fiscal equalization, comprehensive reviews of the methodology for determining relativities (and hence grant shares) are undertaken every five years. These have been limited to a review of the equalization methodology rather than of the principles and objectives of equalization. These reviews have not, therefore, provided a forum for those seeking to modify the principles of equalization in order to argue their case (to their increasing frustration).

In its 2004 report on state relativities, the Commonwealth Grants Commission made a number of observations about equalization and its implementation.[13] It expressed the view that it would be beneficial to review the equalization principles but noted that whether or not such a review was initiated was a matter for governments to decide. It recommended that, in the next review, states and territories agree to consider several matters relating to the implementation of equalization. These included the scope of equalization (whether the present approach, based on a comprehensive assessment of virtually all receipts and expenses in states' operating statements, was appropriate and necessary), the size and trend of the redistributions, whether the process could be simplified (with a higher level of aggregation and fewer adjustments), and examination of the robustness and comparability of key data sets and likely future data availability.

For its 2010 review, the Commonwealth Grants Commission has been given terms of reference directing it to simplify its methods and to regularly report to the Ministerial Council of Treasurers on aspects of simplification. The Ministerial Council has not endorsed a more fundamental review of equalization, including its underlying principles and objectives.

Local Government

There are about 720 local government bodies in Australia, and they vary considerably in size and complexity. Populations vary from around 150 to nearly one million, while areas vary from two square kilometres to over 378,000 square kilometres. Functions also vary – for example, water supply and sewerage is a local government function in some states but not in others.

There are large differences in the range of services provided by councils in capital cities, metropolitan areas, regional centres, rural communities, and remote areas. There are also large differences both in how they raise revenue and in their capacity to do so. Services provided by local government bodies typically include engineering services (roads, bridges, drainage, etc.), community services (elderly care, childcare, fire prevention, etc.), environmental services (waste management and environmental protection), regulatory services (buildings, restaurants, and animals), and cultural services (libraries, art galleries, and museums).

Local government is the responsibility of the states and territories. They provide the legislative framework in which local government bodies operate, and they oversee their operations. As creatures of the states and territories, local government bodies are subject to regulation by state and territory governments and to legislation that may be amended by state/territory parliaments. A degree of autonomy for local government bodies is generally respected, but state and territory governments do have authority to intervene in local government fiscal matters (such as revenue decisions by councils) and, in some states, they have done so (e.g., by imposing rate capping). State governments also impinge on local government autonomy in areas such as local development and planning decisions. Local government functions have expanded over the last thirty years, and the composition of expenditure has changed markedly. Some of the larger changes over this period have been the following: a movement away from property-based services to human services; a decline in the relative importance of expenditure on roads; an increase in the relative importance of recreation and culture as well as housing and community amenities; and an expansion of education, health, welfare, and public safety services.

As a sphere of government in Australia, local government is small financially, and its relative importance has been declining. In 1961–62, local government was responsible for 8 percent of total government outlays, but by 1997–98 its share had declined to 5 percent. Local governments have limited revenue powers; the major source of revenue for local government in all states is taxes on properties (rates), which comprises about 50 percent of revenue on average. User charges are increasing in importance as a source of revenue, but the capacity of local government bodies to levy them varies considerably.

Historically, local government expenditures have exceeded the revenue available from their own sources. Prior to 1974, the states were the main source of additional financial assistance for local government. In 1974, the federal government introduced a program of untied financial assistance through the states (and, subsequently, the territories) to local government. The reasons cited involved making the third tier of government a genuine partner in the federal system and giving local government access to the nation's finances. Subsequent federal governments have maintained and extended the program of financial assistance for local government. The level of financial assistance from the federal government (in the form of financial assistance grants) currently amounts to just over $US1.1 billion. On average, this equates to almost $US53.00 per capita, but reflecting the diversity of local government, the amount individual councils receive varies from about $US15.00 per capita to over $US5,250.00 per capita.

Federal transfers to local government are allocated to the states and territories on an equal per capita basis.[14] Local government grants commissions are required to be established in each state and territory, and to allocate the funds received by the state to local government bodies within the jurisdiction on an equalization basis, subject to the qualification that every local government body in a state is entitled to receive an equal per capita allocation of 30 percent of the total state pool (to reflect the principle that all councils should share in the grant process).

Federal funding also includes a separate road pool, which is distributed to local councils on the basis of their relative need to maintain a local road network. This arrangement reflects the importance of local roads to local government. An inquiry to examine the interstate distribution of local road funding is currently being conducted.

Funding received by local government bodies under these financial assistance arrangements is untied, but it is expected to be applied in a manner that is consistent with the national principles set out in the legislation. Local government bodies also receive some financial assistance from the federal government in the form of SPP. These totalled around $US330 million in 2005–06.

Since the introduction of the federal grants, local government revenue from all sources has grown on average by just over 10 percent per annum. The fastest-growing revenue source has been user charges (13 percent per annum). Federal assistance has increased at around 10.8 percent per annum and municipal rates at 9.4 percent. State assistance has grown more slowly, at 6.6 percent per annum. In total, financial assistance grants from the federal government to local government bodies contribute around 10 percent of local government revenue. (The figure is much higher in the Northern Territory, where there is less ratable land.)

State grants to local government have increased in absolute dollar terms but have declined in relative importance from about 15 percent of total local government revenue in 1974 to around 7 percent in recent years.

Financing Capital Investment

The assessment of state and territory needs for equalization transfers (and most SPPs) is based only on their need for recurrent budget assistance. (Since the equalization transfers are untied grants, states and territories may use these grants for capital purposes.) State, territory, and local governments are free to borrow to support capital investment, subject only to their ability to gain access to capital markets on acceptable terms.

Most states have modest borrowings, including foreign borrowings, which, typically, are undertaken through treasury corporations. All states have received credit ratings from the major credit ratings agencies, with most currently holding AAA ratings.

The previous Australian Loan Council arrangements, which restricted and regulated state borrowings, has been replaced by arrangements that operate on a voluntary basis and that emphasize the transparency of public-sector financing rather than adherence to strict borrowing limits. These arrangements are designed to enhance financial market scrutiny of public-sector borrowing and to facilitate informed judgments about each government's financial performance.

Fiscal Federalism Dimensions of the Public Management Framework

Public-sector management is autonomous within all orders of government. Public-sector staffing and management responsibilities are separate and distinct in all governments (except for the very rare instance in which, when serious misadministration has occurred, a state government has appointed an administrator to replace a local government). Public servants in each jurisdiction are responsible to the relevant jurisdiction minister, and there is no involvement or interference in public-sector appointments or public-sector management generally from one tier of government to another. Each tier of government is free to determine its own size and the structure of public service.

The exercise of executive powers within the states and territories is completely autonomous. Constitutionally, it can be argued that the position of the territories is different from that of the states in that their status and operations can be overridden by the federal Parliament. In practice, however, the territories are treated as states, and this overriding has occurred only in the most exceptional circumstances.

There is more scope for intervention by states and territories in the activities of local governments than in the activities of the federal government. However, while intervention does occur, it is on an exceptional rather than a routine basis and is associated only with instances of serious mismanagement. In some states, the state government has legislated to require local government amalgamations or to impose ceilings on the rate increases that local governments can introduce from year to year. However, at a practical level, the federal government has made considerable use of its fiscal strength to achieve particular objectives. Corruption is not seen as a serious issue in any order of government in Australia. There are comprehensive and rigorous requirements for audits of all agencies, and there is parliamentary oversight for all governments. All states and territories have established ombudsmen commissions and a range of review and appeal mechanisms.

THE WAY FORWARD

The structure of intergovernmental financial arrangements in Australia is well established and comprehensive. It reflects both the constitutional structure of the Australian Federation and the results of political and judicial decisions taken over the years since Federation. Significantly, it also reflects the strongly egalitarian outlook in Australia expressed in the notion of equitable treatment of all citizens. The arrangements focus on federal, state, and territorial governments, with local government occupying a very minor role.

Fiscal federalism in Australia is characterized by a high level of vertical fiscal imbalance between the federal and subnational governments. The extent of vertical fiscal imbalance is larger in Australia than it is in most federations. A unique feature of Australian taxation is that tax bases are available almost exclusively to one order of government, with the federal government having access to the major tax bases.

Most commentators consider the extent of vertical fiscal imbalance in Australia to be undesirably large, imposing constraints on desirable reforms within the states and territories. Notwithstanding this, some degree of vertical imbalance is generally seen as desirable. Some degree of centralization of tax powers provides national fiscal capacity to undertake national objectives and priorities. When the federal government announced a benchmark study of Australia's taxation structure, there was no suggestion that the extent of vertical fiscal imbalance was a matter for review (or even of any concern).

The high degree of vertical fiscal imbalance places considerable focus on the process for transferring funding to the states and territories. In Australia, this is done under the principle of horizontal fiscal equalization, which aims to provide state and territory governments with equal fiscal capacity to provide services to their constituents. This process, which is undertaken through a comprehensive assessment of the relative revenue-raising capacities and expenditure needs of state and territory governments, has in the past generally had a high level of acceptance. However, within the context of budget constraints, and as the circumstances of the states change and the scale of these transfers increases, a number of stakeholders are now questioning this process.

The increasing criticism of horizontal fiscal equalization, particularly from the "donor" states, is directed at both its principle and its implementation. As an issue of principle, it is said that equalization presents an impediment to efficiency. There are clearly trade-offs between equalization and a strict notion of efficiency, but the limited research on this question in the Australian context does not clearly support an argument in either direction. There are also increasing calls to limit the redistribution to only the weakest states or territories rather than to seek equalization across all.

Many people in the larger states have also begun to argue that GST revenue should be distributed on a derivation basis – that is, that it should be returned to the jurisdiction in which it was generated. If implemented, this would lead to massive changes in its distribution and would clearly leave the states and territories in unequal fiscal circumstances. The larger, donor states argue that, under the current approach, the size of the redistribution away from them is becoming unsustainable.

An issue of principle is that the existing equalization processes are not well understood, and there are common misconceptions – in particular, that it seeks to achieve interpersonal or intercommunity equity. It is clearly not a good thing that such an important element of the architecture of the Federation is not well understood.

Criticisms of the implementation of equalization in Australia focus primarily on its complexity. The methodology, which seeks to establish non-policy differences across states and territories over the range of their revenues and expenditures, is extremely comprehensive. Criticisms note its use of data and reliance on judgment. Most commentators agree that, for some assessments, data are used in a manner that contravenes appropriate levels of confidence. The current implementation of equalization is also criticized for using internal standards (i.e., what states do) rather than best-practice standards to determine appropriate benchmarks for revenue capacity and expenditure need. Not surprisingly, the smaller, recipient states are generally supportive of the current approach to equalization.

There has been reluctance to review the principles underlying horizontal fiscal equalization in Australia. Many see it as an essential element of the Federation and one that has served it well. Because it regards the GST as a state/territory tax, the federal government has consistently indicated that such a review would only be considered with the unanimous support of the states and territories.

In contrast with other federations, such as Canada, where there is lively debate over federalism, the limited wider interest in these issues in Australia, including the lack of academic interest in and research on fiscal federalism, means there is very little empirical evidence regarding the implications of equalization for the Federation.

While governments have consistently been unable to agree that the principles of horizontal fiscal equalization should be reconsidered, they have recently agreed to review aspects of its implementation. This review is to be conducted by the Commonwealth Grants Commission as part of its next major review of methodology. The terms of reference given to the commission direct it to simplify its assessments, with particular and early focus on such elements as the materiality of assessments (i.e., whether a particular assessment has a material impact on the relativities and grant shares), the reliability of assessment methods, the scope for more aggregated assessments, and the use of data. It is not clear where these debates will lead in the years ahead. On the basis of current trends, there will be four "donor" states in the next few years, signalling, at the political level, a potential shift in the balance of opinion regarding equalization principles and objectives. The two largest states, while expressing continuing support for the broad principles of equalization, are already arguing vigorously for a new approach that would reduce the extent to which they "subsidize" the smaller states. The federal government has begun to express strong views that the states and territories have not used the increased grants that have resulted from the introduction of the GST to effectively improve service delivery. It seems likely that the Council of Australian Governments will have the issue of fiscal federalism on its agenda in the coming days. It is too early to say where this might lead.

NOTES

1. The functions of the federal government are set out in Sections 51–52 of the Australian Constitution, while Chapter 5 of the Constitution outlines the broad functions of the states.
2. In 1995, a range of initiatives were agreed by all Australian governments designed to enable and encourage competition in the interests of the well-being of all Australians and the long-term sustainability of Australian industry. These initiatives were collectively termed National Competition Policy. The principal elements of National Competition Policy were the introduction of competitive neutrality to enable privately owned businesses to compete with government enterprises on an equal footing; the development of a national access regime to enable competing businesses to use nationally significant infrastructure; and specific reforms in the gas, electricity, water, and road transport industries.
3. Following the bombing of Darwin during the Second World War, uniform income taxation legislation was enacted by the federal government, beginning on 1 July 1942, to enable the Commonwealth to meet expenditure needs during the war. The intention was that the Commonwealth would continue collecting income tax until one year after the end of the war. This legislation remains in force.
4. The Inter-governmental Agreement on Reform of Commonwealth-State Financial Relations came into force on 1 July 1999. Among other things, it introduced a goods and services tax. The Commonwealth and the states also agreed to the abolition of a range of taxes. The goods and services tax was to be collected by the federal government at a uniform rate. The agreement provided that the revenue raised by the goods and services tax would be transferred to the states and territories under horizontal fiscal equalization principles.
5. A Second Statement on the Conduct of Monetary Policy was issued by the federal treasurer and the governor of the Reserve Bank of Australia in July 2003. It set out the agreement between the treasurer and the governor on their respective roles and responsibilities in the operation of monetary policy in Australia. The statement confirmed the independence of the bank and the objectives of monetary policy, including medium-term price stability.
6. The relative importance of federal transfers to the states and territories varies. At the upper end, federal transfers constitute about 85 percent of total government revenue in the Northern Territory, while at the lower end the figure is about 45 percent in New South Wales.
7. Commonwealth Grants Commission, *Report on State Revenue Sharing Relativities, 2004 Review* (Canberra, February 2004), 4.
8. Ibid., 5.
9. The Commonwealth Grants Commission terms these influences "disabilities." The nature of disabilities, and how they are assessed, is provided in each review or update report of the commission. For example, see Commonwealth Grants Commission, *Report on State Revenue Sharing Relativities 2004, Review* (Canberra, February 2004), 7.

10 Commonwealth Grants Commission, *Report on State Revenue Sharing Relativities, 2006 Update* (Canberra, February 2006), 19.
11 Commonwealth Grants Commission, *Report on State Revenue Sharing Relativities 2004* (Canberra, February 2004), 21. Over subsequent *Updates,* the proportion of the GST pool redistributed has decreased, and for 2006–07 it is anticipated that it will be less than 7 percent.
12 Modelling undertaken for the *Review of Commonwealth-State Funding,* commissioned by the states of New South Wales, Victoria, and Western Australia, found that replacing the Commonwealth Grants Commission's recommended allocations to the states and territories with an equal per capita grant distribution would increase national welfare by USD$126 million. See R. Garnaut and V. Fitzgerald, *Review of Commonwealth-State Funding Final Report August 2002* (Melbourne), 143. Using different assumptions, the same model found a welfare gain from horizontal fiscal equalization on the order of US$106 million. See Mark Picton and Peter B. Dixon, *Issues Involving Modelling by COPS of the Efficiency Effects of Commonwealth State Funding: Report to Queensland Treasury* (Melbourne, Centre of Policy Studies, Monash University, March 2003).
13 Commonwealth Grants Commission, *Report on State Revenue Sharing Relativities 2004 Review* (Canberra, February 2004), chap. 7.
14 The basis of these transfers and their purposes are set out in the Commonwealth Local Government (Financial Assistance) Act, 1995.

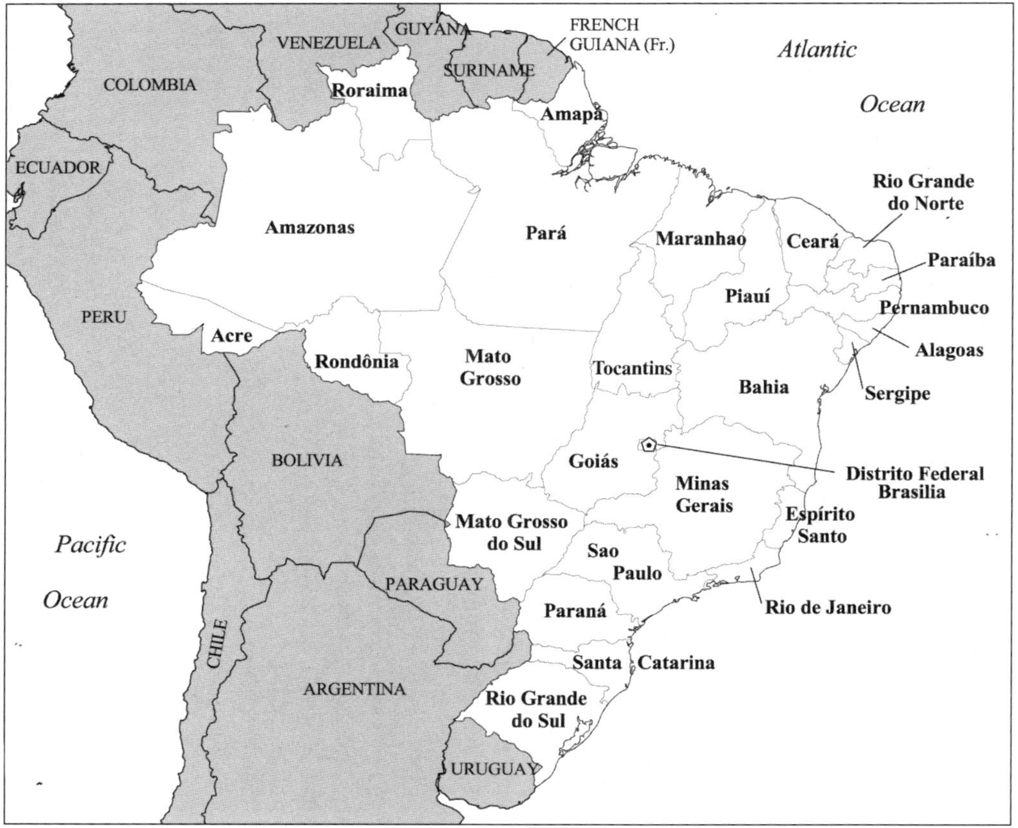

Brazil

Capital: Brasilia
Population: 178 Million
(2004 est.)

Brasilia, the Capital, is situated within the Distrito Federal.

Boundaries and place names are representative only and do not imply official endorsement.

N

500 0 500

Kilometers

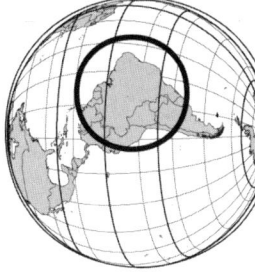

Sources: ESRI Ltd.; CIA World Factbook; Times Atlas of the World

Federal Republic of Brazil

FERNANDO REZENDE

The Federal Republic of Brazil covers 8.5 million square kilometres – about half the total area of South America. Its 184 million inhabitants are unequally dispersed among twenty-six states and the federal district, or 5,558 municipalities (see Table 1 for basic data). Most of the population is located in the six southern states, where the demographic density reaches sixty inhabitants per square kilometre. Although the centre-west and the Amazon regions represent more than 60 percent of the territory, they account for only 15 percent of the population. Population density is also high in the nine poor northeast states on the coast, where nearly 18 percent of the population resides within a perimeter of 1.5 million square kilometres

Africans brought in during the slavery era and a large inflow of migrants from every corner of the world, especially in the late nineteenth and early twentieth centuries, contributed to the multiple faces that characterize Brazil's population nowadays. Despite this, intermarriage and cultural assimilation has produced a quite homogeneous society. Everyone speaks Portuguese, the official language, and cultural values do not differ to a significant extent.

The demographic concentration mirrors the concentration of economic activity. The six southern states account jointly for three-fourths of the gross domestic product (GDP), which reached about US$800 billion in 2005 (1,580 billion in purchasing power parity dollars), placing Brazil among the leading countries in the world in terms of economic size. The country's modern agribusiness and growing modern service economy contribute to a better balanced composition of domestic output. Recent data (2004) point to an economic structure akin to those of modern industrial countries, with the dominance of services (about half of GDP) and a sizable manufacturing sector (about one-fourth of GDP). A still

Table 1
Basic information

Official name: Federative Republic of Brazil	
Population: 184 million inhabitants	
Area (square kilometres): 8.5 million square kilometres	
GDP per capita in US: $ 4,323 (2005)	
Constitution: 1988, Republican	
Orders of government: Three	
Constitutional status of local government: independent units of the federation	
Official language: Portuguese	
Number and types of constituent units: 26 states, the Federal District, and 5,558 municipalities	
Population, area, and per capita GDP in US$ of the largest constituent unit: São Paulo – 38.7 million inhabitants; 248,200 square kilometres; GDP pc = US$4,163	
Population, area, and per capita GDP in US$ of the smallest constituent unit: Roraima – 357,300 inhabitants; 224,300 square kilometres; GDP pc = US$1,529	

important agriculture sector (10 percent of GDP) reflects the recent expansion of highly productive farms that emerged from the incorporation of modern technologies into rural areas.

From a regional standpoint, due to a bias in regional representation in the National Parliament in favour of the less developed north, northeast, and centre-west regions, economic size does not translate directly into political influence on national policies. These regions have sparsely populated states, which are entitled to a minimum of eight representatives in the Lower House, while the highly populated states in the south have a maximum of seventy representatives. Thus, the less populous states exert a strong influence on decision making pertaining to issues related to fiscal and intergovernmental relations.[1] The political imbalance in the representation of the states in the Lower House is reinforced by the equal representation in the Federal Senate (three per state). Although this is a common federal feature, the extended role of the Senate in the Brazilian Federation – all legislation, not only that directly related to federal issues, has to pass through both legislative houses before being sanctioned by the president – creates additional difficulties.[2]

Imbalances in political representation result from the dominance of the regional issue in the formation and consolidation of the Brazilian Federation. The federal regime put into place by the first republican Constitution in 1891 empowered the states with a substantial degree of autonomy and sowed the seeds for the autonomy of local government. Since then, subnational autonomy and regional balance have become intertwined issues, and a proper balance between them has been seen as essential in maintaining internal cohesion in an economically and socially unequal society.[3]

Inequality is, therefore, one of the main features of the country. Parts of the south and the southeast – particularly the state of São Paulo – present indicators of economic development akin to those of modern industrial countries: a high level of per capita income, a high degree of urbanization, diversification in industrial production, and satisfactory social conditions. At the same time, large portions of the country – especially in the north and northeast – still show the classic signs of underdevelopment: low per capita income, poor sanitary conditions, and widespread poverty. It is worth noting, however, that the incidence of poverty is not associated with regional imbalances in economic development. This is because the developed regions have attracted and retained a large number of people below the poverty line.

With the exception of intermittent periods of authoritarian rule, democracy evolved over time and achieved high standards after the mid-1980s. A multi-party system allows for a fairly diversified composition with respect to the distribution of political power in the federation. Despite this, governability is achieved by means of coalitions that, in national politics, contribute to increasing the weight of small political parties beyond what is indicated by their actual size. The practice of forming coalitions has contributed to the stability of the Brazilian democracy, which recently passed two important tests: (1) the impeachment of the president who was elected in 1989 and (2) the 2003 hand-over of the federal government to the first leftist president to be elected in the entire republican period.

A stable democratic regime and sound institutional arrangements have contributed to helping the Brazilian economy muddle through the turbulence generated by the sequence of external financial crises that have hit emerging economies worldwide since the mid-1990s. Yet the macroeconomic policies the country adopted to attenuate the impact of this turbulence severely hampered economic growth, which showed a meager 2.4 percent annual average rate of increase between 1995 and 2004. These policies also impinged upon the subnational autonomy envisaged by the 1988 Constitution.

Being a creature of the transition from authoritarianism to democracy, the 1988 Constitution reacted to two strong forces: (1) the demand for greater autonomy for subnational governments and (2) calls from organized pressure groups for more and better access to state-sponsored social protection. In so doing, it installed a dual fiscal regime. On one hand, the states and municipalities acquired greater power to tax and a greater share of traditional federal revenues; on the other hand, a distinct set of compulsory levies – the so-called social contributions – was assigned to the federal government to finance pensions and free access to health care and social services for every Brazilian citizen regardless of previous contribution to the social security system. Because the extended social rights depended on the federal government's ability to raise enough money to meet a steep rise in social spending, in addition to large surpluses in the public accounts to keep inflation at bay, recourse to social contributions fed a process that reversed the fiscal decentralization intended by the 1988 Constitution.

Over time, equality, autonomy, efficiency, and growth objectives collided. Increasing reliance on federally collected social contributions eroded subnational autonomy. It also worked against promoting efficiency and accountability in public policies through decentralization as earmarked grants from the federal government, supported by revenues from such contributions, became necessary to finance the provision of social services by state and local governments. At the same time, vertical and horizontal imbalances increased in so far as the basis of equalization funds lost importance over time. In addition, inefficient social contributions created further obstacles to economic growth. Therefore, an overhaul of the Brazilian fiscal federalism system is desperately needed.

STRUCTURE OF GOVERNMENT AND DIVISION OF FISCAL POWERS

Brazil is a three-tier federation. According to the 1988 Constitution, states and municipalities are independent units of the Brazilian Federation. Both have independent taxing powers and share with the federal government responsibilities for public services and development policies. A growing direct relationship between the federal and local governments is a source of intergovernmental conflicts and increasing complexity in fiscal relations.

The formal assignment of expenditure responsibilities follows the subsidiary principle. Thus, the Constitution assigns the provision of basic urban and social services (urban roads, water supply and sewerage, public transportation, streetlights, primary education, and basic health and social assistance services) primarily to local governments. These local governments count on technical and financial assistance from the federal and state governments to carry out these responsibilities (see Table 2). Following the usual pattern, the federal government is solely responsible for the armed forces, foreign relations, international trade, and monetary control.[4]

In practice, however, due to high economic and social inequalities, most of the responsibilities are shared in the federation. Responsibility for law and order is mainly in the states' hands, but organized crime, drug trafficking, weapons smuggling, money laundering, and other illegal activities are in the federal jurisdiction. In the social area, with the exception of social protection for private-sector workers (pensions and related benefits),

Table 2
Legislative responsibility and actual provision of services by different orders of government

Legislative responsibility (de jure)	Public service	Actual allocation of function (de facto)
Federal	Defence	Federal
Federal/state	Law & order	Federal/state
Federal/state	Basic Education	State/local
Federal/state	Higher education	Federal/state
Federal	Health	State/local
Federal	Social assistance	Local
Local	Water and sewerage	State/local
State	Police	State
Federal	Environmental protection	Federal/state
Local	Street cleaning and lighting	Local
Local	Public transportation	Local
Local	Urban infrastructure	Local
Local	Waste collection	Local
State	Fire Protection	State

which is the sole responsibility of the federal government, provision of basic education, health care, and other social services is split among states and local governments on a more or less equal basis (see Table 3). The federal government intervenes directly in higher education and in more sophisticated health services.

The absence of a clear definition of the functions to be performed by each order of government is a major source of continuing conflicts. On the tax side, conflicts come up whenever measures adopted by the federal government reduce revenues from the income and manufacturing taxes that form the basis of the present revenue-sharing system. Conflicts also arise when federally sponsored legislation interferes with subnational tax autonomy, for example by granting exemptions from the state value-added tax (VAT) for exports. In such cases, demand for financial compensation becomes a permanent focus of conflict because the compensation has to be negotiated annually during the regular budgetary process. On the expenditure side, changes in rules governing federal financial aid to social programs carried out by the subnational governments are also a source of intermittent conflict.

Table 3
Direct expenditures by function and level of government (percent)

Function	Federal (%)	State (%)	Municipal (%)	Total (%)	% of GDP
Defence	99.8	–	0.2	100.0	0.9
Debt servicing	85.4	12.0	2.6	100.0	10.4
General administration	46.1	28.9	25.0	100.0	5.3
Law and order	26.2	71.5	2.4	100.0	3.2
Economic services[1]	53.7	33.9	12.4	100.0	3.3
Social services	51.9	25.3	22.8	100.0	23.6
Health	26.5	33.6	39.8	100.0	3.8
Education	15.6	49.8	34.6	100.0	5.3
Old age	85.5	11.3	3.3	100.0	10.7
Other social services	32.6	22.6	44.8	100.0	3.7
Subsidies[2]	...	...	...	...	...
Total	58.0	26.1	15.9	100.0	46.7
Local Public Services	13.6	43.3	43.0	100.0	10.1
Primary and secondary education[3]	1.7	43.5	54.9	100.0	3.2
Health	26.5	33.6	39.8	100.0	3.8
Housing and community amenities[4]	3.9	14.3	81.9	100.0	1.2
Environmental protection[5]	14.6	42.8	42.5	100.0	0.3
Police services	10.1	87.1	2.8	100.0	1.6

Notes
The functional classification of expense basically follows the IMF/GFS 2001 methodology.
1. Includes general economic and commercial affairs, agriculture, forestry, fishing and hunting, fuel and energy, transport, communications, R&D, and economic affairs.
2. Amounts related to subsidies are not broken down.
3. Amounts were estimated to exclude outlays other than for primary and preschool and secondary education.
4. Includes housing development, expenditures related to urbanism – street paving and lighting, waste collection, traffic and other urban services.
5. Includes waste water management, water supply, and sewerage.

Conflicts among the states and their municipalities are also noteworthy. The 1988 Constitution granted state legislators the authority to set the criteria for dividing one-fourth of the proceedings of the state VAT that belongs to the municipalities. Quite often, such changes prove contentious because they may be seen to favour political allies or to create losses for some municipalities.

A council of the states' finance ministers was created in the 1970s and was the sole attempt to provide an institution that would be in charge of mediating conflicts. The federal finance minister presided over the council, which worked properly during the authoritarian regimes for obvious reasons. After redemocratization, the federal government could no longer impose rules that had to be obeyed by all, and the council, albeit still formally in existence, was deprived of any power to harmonize states' tax policies. The council lost credibility and became unable to enforce legislation prohibiting special tax concessions by any state without the unanimous approval of all twenty-six states and the federal district.

A long tradition of applying symmetric arrangements to asymmetric situations makes it difficult to avoid conflicts or to find proper solutions. In the fairly heterogeneous Brazilian Federation, symmetric arrangements cannot lead to a proper equilibrium among subnational government units. Symmetry is reflected in equal powers being granted by the Constitution to every state or municipality whatever its size, region, and economic and social characteristics. Well-developed industrialized states and frontier states have to abide by the same rules with regard to administrative organization, tax powers, and expenditure responsibilities. The same goes for large metropolitan cities and small rural municipalities, where differences are even greater. Both have similar organizational structures, a directly elected legislative body, and direct access to federal funds.

Although subnational governments enjoy a great degree of constitutional autonomy, the amplitude of the legislative power of the federal government, in fiscal and regulatory matters, has curtailed the decision-making power of the former. By means of complementary laws to the Constitution, the federal government defines the framework within which states and local governments can set norms for imposing and collecting their own taxes. Federal legislation also establishes detailed provisions concerning the elaboration and execution of subnational budgets. With regard to regulation, the detailed rules of the federal laws leave almost no room for the states in areas such as public utilities, environmental protection, and the exploration and exploitation of natural resources.

In fact, local governments have more autonomy than do the states in so far as the former are entitled to regulate the use of municipal land and the provision of urban services, impose user charges, and define norms for collecting property taxes. In general, local governments also have a reasonable degree of autonomy over their budget because, on average, about 40 percent of their revenues come from general-purpose grants.

Through earmarked grants and control of the subnational debt, the federal government has increased its influence on subnational policies. Coupled with hard budgetary constraints that were put in place to sustain macroeconomic stability, the degree of freedom of state governors to allocate budgetary resources has been curtailed significantly. The situation is somewhat better at the local level, the large metropolitan cities aside, because the criteria applied to divide the municipal share of federal taxes is biased towards smaller municipalities and penalizes the states' capital cities. The state capitals generate one-third of GDP and house one-fourth of the population but get only 10 percent of this pie.

Conversely, subnational governments can interfere in national policies only by means of their representatives' actions in the national Congress. That happens when proposals for federal regulation on the use of natural resources, the provision of public services, or the exercise of tax powers by state and local governments affect state and local government interests. However, due to the fragmentation of political parties and the nature of the electoral process, representatives from the states in the Lower House and the Senate do not always act in accordance with the wishes of state governors, weakening subnational influence on national politics.

FISCAL FEDERALISM AND MACROECONOMIC MANAGEMENT

The success of a monetary stabilization plan adopted in 1994 to close an era of high inflation had important consequences for federal finance. For decades, inflation made it easy to curb budgetary deficits as tax revenues were fully indexed and most expenditure items were not. Thus, through postponing payments and adjusting nominal salaries and pensions only once a year, fiscal disequilibria were easily corrected.

A stable currency brought structural imbalances to light. Expenditure on personnel and social security benefits showed the real effect of a paternalistic approach to past policies concerning employment and pensions across the federation. At the same time, a tight monetary policy to protect the Brazilian economy from external shocks raised the amount of money required to service the public debt.

In the beginning of this new era, price stability was anchored to the overvaluation of the new currency – the real. But the successive external financial crises that hit emerging economies in the second half of the 1990s – Mexico (1995), Southeast Asia (1997), and Russia (1998) – forced the Brazilian government to abandon its policy to control the exchange rate in 1999 and, instead, to let the national currency float. Thus, monetary stability came to depend on responsible management of the fiscal accounts, and fiscal discipline took the place of the exchange rate as the anchor for averting inflation.

The new inflation targeting regime, adopted in 2000, relies on properly functioning monetary and fiscal policies. The National Monetary Council formed by the finance and planning ministers and the president of the Central Bank not only set targets for the inflation rate for two years in a row but also set the interval within which the actual result could differ from the desired outcome. The Central Bank is in charge of bringing inflation as close to the mark as possible, making use of the interest rate to adjust expectations and force convergence towards the target. To that end, the Central Bank has enjoyed a fairly large degree of autonomy, although it does not have formal independence from the national government.

In the fairly decentralized Brazilian Federation, the enforcement of fiscal discipline required important institutional changes. The Fiscal Responsibility Law (FRL), inspired by the highly praised New Zealand experience, was enacted in 2000. This law enforces fiscal discipline at the federal, state, and local government levels through the imposition of objective and clear rules for administering revenue and expenditure policies, the public debt, and government assets. It emphasizes transparency in the public administrator's use of the resources extracted from taxation. Among the norms set by the FRL, the following are worth noting:

1 Limits on spending for personnel. Remuneration of public employees shall not exceed 50 percent of net current revenues at the federal level and 60 percent at the subnational level.
2 Indebtedness limits. Outstanding debts cannot exceed two times current revenues for the states and 1.2 times for local governments. With regard to debt service, annual payments cannot surpass 11.5 percent of current revenues in both cases. In addition, resources from new loans cannot exceed 16 percent of current revenues in any fiscal year.
3 Provision for recurrent expenditures. Public authorities cannot take actions that create future expenses lasting more than two years without identifying a source of financing or a compensating cut in other expenses.
4 Special provision for electoral years. The law prohibits outgoing governors and mayors (in their last year in office) from using tax revenues to provide short-term loans, increase wages, or contract new public servants.

Failure to fulfill obligations imposed by the FRL leads to several administrative penalties, to which personal incriminations included in an additional law may be added. More serious misbehaviours may be punished with the loss of the mandate, ineligibility for employment in the public service, fines, and imprisonment. It is worth emphasizing that all levels of government, federal included, have to abide by the conditions established in the FRL.

To make it possible for states and large municipalities to adhere to the new rules concerning the public debt, previous debts with the federal government were refinanced on favourable terms for a period of thirty-five years. However, unlike previous bailouts, the beneficiaries of such renegotiations were prohibited from issuing new bonds and were required to transfer between 11 percent and 13 percent of their current revenues to the federal treasury on a monthly basis for the duration of these contracts. Together with limits set by the Central Bank on the exposure of public and private banks to public clients, control over subnational government indebtedness was duly enforced. To ensure enforcement, debt-refinancing contracts entitled the federal government to sequester state and local government revenues from federal transfers in the case of failure to comply with the agreed-upon rules.

The hard budgetary constraints put into place by the Fiscal Responsibility Law brought control to public finance. Since its inception, the public sector as a whole has saved a sizable amount of money and reversed the ascending trajectory of the total public-sector debt-to-GDP ratio. The primary surplus – that is, the balance between total revenues and non-financial expenditures – rose steadily between 1999 and 2005, with states and local governments contributing approximately one-tenth of the overall result. Thus, after having reached 7.5 percent of GDP in 1998, the public-sector debt ratio dropped to 2.7 percent in 2004 despite a tight monetary policy that sustained high interest rates.

Conditions built into subnational government debt contracts became a good substitute for macroeconomic fiscal coordination. The revenue sequestration mechanisms adopted, as well as the forced privatization of state-owned banks, worked as a tool to force fiscal discipline at the subnational level. Together with the limits set in the FRL for personnel spending and debt financing, previous windows for irresponsible management of subnational government accounts were duly closed.

As time goes by, incumbent and opposition leaders alike perceive that the culture of fiscal discipline is an important political asset. Yet, present concerns point to the consequences of a lengthy period of public spending restraints on economic growth and income inequality. As public investment plunged, notably at the federal level, road construction and maintenance suffered a severe setback, creating an important handicap for growth in exports of goods. In the social area, difficulties in improving the quality of education and health services will increase the problems faced by low-income people in gaining access to better-paid jobs and escaping the poverty trap.

ISSUES IN REVENUE-RAISING RESPONSIBILITIES

The 1988 Constitution is the basis of the current assignment of taxing powers in the Brazilian Federation (see Table 4). The federal government is solely responsible for imposing taxes on income (corporate and personal), foreign trade, and rural property as well as on payroll. The federal government can also make use of contributions intended to intervene in the economic domain and of any other potential tax source not explicitly attributed to the state or local governments by the Constitution (residual powers).

Federal and state governments have overlapping powers for taxing goods and services. The former is entitled to taxes on manufacturing goods and the social contributions earmarked to finance pensions, health, and social assistance. The states are empowered to levy a VAT type of tax on goods, which is also applied to transportation and telecommunications services. In addition to taxing general services, local governments are entitled to tax ownership and sales of urban property and to apply user charges. An inheritance property tax and a motor vehicle tax are also under the states' jurisdiction.

Despite the constitutional separation of tax powers, subnational governments do not have total autonomy to apply their most important taxes. As mentioned before, complementary laws to the Constitution set the basic rules to be followed by states and municipalities with regard to the state value-added tax (the ICMS) and the municipal services tax (the ISS). These laws narrow the scope of state and local government legislators with regard to the definition of the tax basis but do not interfere with rates. Rates of the states' VAT are only constrained by a constitutional provision that prohibits internal transactions from being taxed at a rate lower than the smallest rate applied to interstate sales.

Restrictions imposed on the subnational governments' ability to implement their most important taxes do not mean that the tax system is harmonized. The residual legislative powers of state governments allow for great differences with regard to the rates applied to each category of goods, ways to reduce the effective tax burden (reduction in the tax base, for instance), special regimes for small businesses, criteria adopted for the utilization of tax credits paid on inputs used to produce exempted export goods, and preferred tax rates for food and other essential consumption items.

Another source of differences in the tax burden imposed on the same goods across the federation arose out of demands from less developed states to apply a reduced rate on goods shipped from the more industrialized south and southeast states to the north, northeast, and centre-west regions to allow consumer states to reap part of the revenues from interstate sales. As a result, a 7 percent rate applies to shipments from the south/

Table 4
Tax assignment for various orders of government
F = Federal; S = State; L = Local; R = Regional

	Determination of		Tax collection and administration	Shares in revenue (%)				
	Base	Rate		F	S	L	R[1]	All orders
Federal								
TAXES								
Import tax – II	F	F	F	100.0				100.0
Export tax – IE	F	F	F	100.0				100.0
Rural territorial tax – ITR	F	F	F	50.0		50.0		100.0
Income tax – IR	F	F	F	53.0	21.5	22.5	3.0	100.0
Tax on manufactured goods – IPI	F	F	F	43.0	29.0	25.0	3.0	100.0
Tax on financial operations – IOF				100.0				100.0
Financial operations dealing with gold – IOF-Ouro	F	F	F		30.0	70.0		100.0
Other taxes and fees	F	F	F	100.0				100.0
CONTRIBUTIONS								
Social contributions								
On sales of goods and services	F	F	F	100.0				100.0
On financial transactions – CPMF	F	F	F	100.0				100.0
On net profit – CSLL	F	F	F	100.0				100.0
On payroll – employee/employer	F	F	F	100.0				100.0
On payroll earmarked to primary education	F	F	F	Shared under special legislation[2]				
Other contributions	F	F	F	100.0				100.0
Royalties – oil and hydroelectric dams	F	F	F	Shared under special legislation[3]				
Contribution on production and imports of oil – CIDE	F	F	F	71.0	21.8	7.2		100.0

Table 4
Tax assignment for various orders of government
F = Federal; S = State; L = Local; R = Regional (*Continued*)

	Determination of			Shares in revenue (%)				
	Base	Rate	Tax collection and administration	F	S	L	R[1]	All orders
State or provincial								
TAXES								
IRRF withheld on state civil servants' wages[4]	F	F	S		100.0			100.0
Motor vehicle property tax – IPVA	S	S	S		50.0	50.0		100.0
Tax on inheritance and gifts – ITCD	S	S	S		100.0			100.0
Tax on circulation of goods and services – ICMS	F, S	F, S	S		75.0	25.0		100.0
CONTRIBUTIONS								
On employees' wages earmarked to pensions	S	S	S		100.0			100.0
Local								
TAXES								
IRRF withheld on municipalities' civil servants' wages[4]	F	F	L			100.0		100.0
Urban land and territorial tax – IPTU	L	L	L			100.0		100.0
Tax on real estate ownership transfer – ITBI	L	L	L			100.0		100.0
Tax on services – ISS	F	F, L	L			100.0		100.0
Betterment taxes	L	L	L			100.0		100.0
CONTRIBUTIONS	L	L	L			100.0		100.0
On employees' wages earmarked to pensions	L	L	L			100.0		100.0

Primary sources: Federal Constitution and Federal Revenue Service.
1. Amount channelled into a regional development fund.
2. Two-thirds goes to the states on a derivation basis. States and municipalities can have access to the other one-third on a project basis.
3. Royalties: states and municipalities receive compensation for the exploration of petroleum, gas, hydroelectricity, and other mineral resources inside their territory or in the adjacent maritime platform.
4. Income tax withheld on the earnings of state and local government public servants.

southeast to the north/northeast/centre-west regions, whereas a 12 percent rate applies to interstate sales flowing in the opposite direction. The same 12 percent rate applies to interregional transactions. This mixed origin-destination principle caused distortions in resource allocation and provided a strong incentive for tax evasion. It also led to the main weapon used in the so-called fiscal war in which Brazilian states have been engaged in order to attract investments and new industries to their jurisdictions.[5]

With respect to the municipal tax on services, a recent constitutional amendment exempted exports from this tax and allowed for the imposition of a ceiling and a floor on rates by way of a complementary law whose purpose was to avoid great variation and to curb harmful competition in metropolitan areas.[6] However, other less visible means for providing fiscal benefits, such as reducing the tax base and providing better terms for payment, may compensate for that.

Fiscal competition among the states in Brazil gained new impetus in the mid-1990s in a bid to attract a new wave of foreign direct investment in the Brazilian automotive sector away from the São Paulo metropolitan region. Due to the mixed origin-destination principle applied to the state VAT, neighbouring states could shift the burden of the fiscal incentives offered to foreign investors to the state of São Paulo, which houses the most important consumer market. In what came to be known as a fiscal war, southern states (mainly Parana, Rio de Janeiro, and Rio Grande do Sul) succeeded in luring investors to locate new plants in their territories. They did this by providing additional benefits, such as infrastructure and training programs for the labour force, to the more usual tax concessions. In one case only, the federal government intervened to move the location of an automotive plant to the northern state of Bahia. Several studies pointed to the irrationality of a fiscal war for attracting investment. However, politicians and public administrators thought it was a good response to the absence of a federal policy to discourage even greater concentration in the already highly concentrated manufacturing activities in a few locations in the country.[7]

Of course conflicts arose out of the fiscal war, making it very difficult to implement any proposal for harmonizing the tax system and propelling tax administrators to cooperate. Cooperation is also hampered by conflicts related to the taxation of natural resources – oil in particular. For oil, as well as for electricity generation, the 1988 Constitution adopted a destination principle for the states' VAT so that producer states would not reap all the revenues from these important tax bases. However, as revenues from oil and electricity came to represent a sizable portion of the taxes collected by the state treasuries, producer states claimed that this exception to the general rule did a lot of harm to their finances. In recent years, states have recognized the cost of this fiscal war and are currently engaged in serious negotiations in an attempt to bring an end to wasteful tax competition.

FISCAL EQUITY AND EFFICIENCY CONCERNS AND INTERGOVERNMENTAL FISCAL TRANSFERS

Despite the tax powers assigned to states and local governments by the Constitution, data on tax collections by each order of the federation show a remarkable degree of vertical imbalance. The federal government obtains a little less than 70 percent of all the money extracted from businesses and households through various taxes. The states collect about 25 percent of total tax revenues, and local governments account for the rest.

Three distinct regimes attempt to address the vertical disequilibria: (1) a conventional revenue sharing system, (2) separate rules concerning the share of state and local governments in revenues from specific taxes, and (3) conditional transfers.

The pillar of the revenue-sharing system is the participation of states and local governments in sharing the proceeds of federal income and manufacturing taxes. According to the 1988 Constitution, 21.5 percent of federal revenues from these taxes goes to the states and 22.5 percent to the municipalities. At the same time as the Constitution more than doubled the share of federal taxes going to states and municipalities, it asked for a revision of the apportionment formula. But implementing this provision became impossible due to conflicts that arose over attempts to carry out the revision. Consequently, quotas for each state and municipality were frozen on the basis of the coefficients prevailing at the time the Constitution was promulgated, and the previous practice of making adjustments in light of updated income and population estimates was abandoned.[8]

Another important component of the revenue-sharing system is the 25 percent share of local governments in their states' VAT collections. Three-fourths of the municipal share is distributed according to the value added in each local jurisdiction; the rest follows rules set by the respective state legislators. Municipalities with a strong economic base benefit from the first criteria, whereas the formulas adopted by the states tend to favour political allies and are subject to frequent changes. Local governments also get 50 percent of revenues from the rural property tax collected by the federal government and from the motor vehicle tax applied by the states.

States and local governments are entitled to keep revenues from the income taxes withheld from their own employees, to receive 100 percent of the proceeds from the federal tax on financial operations in gold (30 percent for the states and 70 percent for the municipalities), to participate in a compulsory levy on the wage bill (earmarked for basic education), to share in federal revenues from a compulsory levy on oil imports, and to receive compensation for exempting exports from the states' VAT. These other sources of subnational revenues are not important in global terms.[9]

Table 5
Vertical fiscal gaps, 2003[1]

Percentage of GDP

Level	Total revenue collected[2]	Total revenue available, including net transfers for that level of government	Expenditures[3]
National	28.8	23.3	31.7
Subnational	13.3	18.7	21.1
State/provincial	10.6	11.3	13.5
Local	2.7	7.4	7.6
All orders	42.1	42.1	52.8

Percentage of total

Level	Total revenue collected[2]	Total revenue available, including net transfers for that level of government	Expenditures[3]
National	68.4	55.4	60.1
Subnational	31.6	44.6	39.9
State/provincial	25.3	26.9	25.6
Local	6.4	17.7	14.4
All orders	100.0	100.0	100.0

US$ millions

Level	Total revenue collected[2]	Total revenue available, including net transfers for that level of government	Expenditures[3]
National	145,777.8	118,239.0	160,667.9
Subnational	67,462.1	95,000.9	106,823.7
State/provincial	53,878.2	57,312.3	68,376.9
Local	13,583.9	37,688.5	38,446.8
All orders	213,239.8	213,239.8	267,491.6

Primary source: National Treasury Secretariat, Federal Finance Minister.
1. 2003 average exchange rate: US$ 1 = R$ 3.07.
2. Current and capital revenues. Does not include loans.
3. Current and capital expenses. Capital expenses exclude debt refinancing.

Royalties from the exploration of natural resources should also be mentioned. Federal legislation establishes the rules for compensating states and municipalities for the extraction of oil, mining, and loss of land due to inundation provoked by hydroelectric dams. Municipal governments are the main beneficiaries of these royalties. The most important distortions in the distribution of royalties are found in the extraction of oil in the maritime plateau in the northern coast of the state of Rio de Janeiro.

With the exception of a constitutional mandate to earmark 25 percent for basic education, resources channelled to state and local government coffers under the revenue-sharing system do not carry any provisions concerning their use. The same applies to the shares of the specific taxes listed above, with the sole exception of the one earmarked for basic education.

Among the conditional transfers, the most important is the health transfer system. A recent constitutional amendment established that the money allocated in the federal budget to finance health spending should increase in line with GDP growth on the basis of the amount spent in the previous year.[10] There is no fixed amount to be transferred to subnational governments. One portion is allocated to state and local governments on a per capita basis to cover basic health care services. Another is distributed on a service provision basis and so follows the spatial distribution of the health service network. Financial cooperation in health care is assured by earmarking 12 percent of state revenues and 15 percent of municipality revenues for health care spending. On the whole, the federal government covers about 60 percent of the health care bill. States and municipalities split the rest on a more or less equal basis. Given the concentration of sophisticated health care facilities, in larger municipalities resources from the health transfer system are more important than is the share of federal government revenues.

The abandonment of the original formula conceived for the revenue-sharing system and the proliferation of other transfers led to the absence of any criteria guiding the intergovernmental flow of resources in the federation. The outcome of such a situation is a hazardous process of redistributing the fiscal pie. On the vertical perspective, the big winners are the municipalities, who have seen their share of the fiscal pie more than treble in relation to own revenues (after taking into account all kinds of intergovernmental money transfers), while the increase for the states has been only 40 percent. As a result, total disposable revenues are roughly split in the following manner: 50 percent to the federal government, 30 percent to the states, and 20 percent to the municipalities. Besides passing on about 30 percent of what it collects to subnational governments, the federal government has lost discretion over more than half its available revenues as it increasingly depends on taxes earmarked for social spending.[11]

Worse still is the outcome regarding the horizontal distribution of fiscal resources. Of the total amount collected by the states, nearly three-fourths belongs to the seven states that comprise the south and southeast region. Among the municipalities, the twenty-six more important metropolitan cities raise more than 60 percent of total local government own-source revenues. Moreover, as each specific transfer follows its own logic to distribute money across the twenty-six states, the federal district, and nearly 5,558 municipalities, an enormous horizontal disparity arises in the distribution of fiscal resources across the federation.[12]

Data on the per capita revenues of the states and municipalities illustrate the size of these imbalances. Current budgetary per capita revenues can be as much as twenty to thirty times greater in small municipalities located in thinly populated regions than they are in the more populous municipalities. Among states, disparities are less severe but still significant. In this case, the low population density of the newly created states in the Amazon and centre-west regions means that the per capita revenues of these states are more than three times higher than the national average. More densely populated states in the northeast, with the single exception of Sergipe, are among those with the lowest per capita revenues.

Inequalities are particularly severe in metropolitan areas, where the outcome is determined by the manner in which economic activity and population are distributed geographically. In general, due to their share in state tax collections, municipalities with an important manufacturing sector and a small population have per capita budgets several times higher than the regional average. At the other extreme, municipalities with a very large population and a fragile economy, usually functioning as a dormitory city, are severely underfinanced, having per capita budgets well below the regional average.

One undesirable consequence of expanding transfers to municipalities without a concomitant revision of the distribution formula was the proliferation of new units. More than one thousand municipalities were created after 1988 because the distribution formula rewarded districts that decided to "emancipate" themselves. They were rewarded either because they housed major industries, in which case they would receive a high quota of the state ICMS, or because they had few people, in which case they would benefit from the apportionment under the Municipal Participation Fund. The combination of these two factors provided an ideal opportunity for demanding autonomy because, in the case of secession, the rules at the time did not require the approval of residents in other parts of the municipality.

Lack of a well-designed institutional arrangement to provide a rationale for the system and to mediate conflicts of interest is a large handicap for better functioning intergovernmental fiscal relations. Brazil does not have a formal fiscal equalization transfer program but, rather, a constitutionally mandated revenue-sharing mechanism that automatically delivers a fixed proportion of income and federal manufacturing tax revenues, plus other minor taxes, to states and local governments on the basis of predetermined fixed rates.[13] Coupled with specific purpose grants, the absence of an equalization thrust in the general-purpose transfers is responsible for a fairly high degree of horizontal disequilibria in the distribution of fiscal resources in the Brazilian Federation, and this adds to the difficulties faced in achieving cooperation in public policies.

FINANCING CAPITAL INVESTMENT

A very low degree of budgetary flexibility – due to excesses in earmarking revenues and a large interest and pension bill – led to insignificant levels of public savings throughout the federation. Data for the public sector as a whole point to a current account surplus of a meager 2.06 percent of GDP, with the federal government showing zero savings and the states as a whole only 0.9 percent of GDP. Conversely, the municipalities show healthier figures. About two-thirds of local governments' investments are financed by savings. Municipalities, on average, show a savings ratio of 1.12 percent of GDP.

Coupled with high indebtedness ratios, the fall in public savings brought public investment along with it. The average rate of public investment was around 3 percent of GDP in the early 2000s, down from the already low 4.2 percent registered in the second half of the 1990s, and shows no sign that it will improve to a significant degree in the short run. Contrasting with the situation that prevailed in the 1970s, when the public sector accounted for a sizable part of total gross capital formation in the Brazilian economy, the state now accounts for less than 20 percent of the annual rate of capital accumulation in the country.

In theory, lack of savings could be compensated by an increase in borrowing. The Brazilian Constitution grants autonomy to federal, state, and local governments with respect to access to the financial market. The only restriction is the requirement of Senate approval for state and local government access to money from external sources.

In practice, however, the situation is much different. As mentioned earlier, the Fiscal Responsibility Law put into place tough limits for the outstanding debt of states and local governments as well as for the amount of their current revenues that can be used yearly for debt servicing. Moreover, Central Bank regulations impose a severe limit on the exposure of public and private financial institutions to public entities, with the result that even financially sound subnational public entities cannot get extra money for financing capital investments. As for the federal government, although limits demanded by the FRL have not yet been put in place, the already high debt-to-GDP ratio imposes a natural barrier to borrowing.

Restrictions on capital financing could be relaxed by reducing the earmarking of government revenues at all levels and going forward with institutional reforms to alleviate the pressures that pension systems put on public budgets. This would allow for the restoration of public savings. Proposals to deal with this situation have been put forward recently, but politicians do not look favourably on the very sensitive issue of cutting pensions or erasing the guarantees to their financing. The proposals also face strong resistance from labour unions and better organized lobbies.

The low level of public investment generates problems for economic growth and inequalities in income distribution, and this has led to a search for alternative means of investment financing. A new federal law, along with similar laws adopted in some states, has been enacted to open room for the formation of partnerships between public and private organizations aimed mainly at gathering resources to finance infrastructure projects. These new institutional arrangements have not had enough time to show how much can be expected from them. The still low degree of confidence in the capabilities of the regulatory agencies and the public bureaucracy's lack of familiarity with such arrangements mean that this alternative may take some time to show its full potential.

Whatever the possibility of exploring alternatives, the need to restore public investment is compelling. In less developed regions, privatization or partnerships will not meet the needs of infrastructure modernization. In metropolitan areas, the absence of public investment means that many low-income families do not have access to good basic urban services, and many newcomers have no access at all. At the same time, health and education infrastructure deserves more attention, especially from state governments.

FISCAL FEDERALISM DIMENSIONS OF THE PUBLIC MANAGEMENT FRAMEWORK

Subnational governments exercise almost complete discretion with respect to the management of their internal affairs. State and local governments alike are free to set rules governing the careers of public servants, hire personnel, set wages and salaries, and establish employee pension systems. In matters related to their own workforce, they are only constrained by the constitutional provisions that require candidates to pass exams in order to obtain permanent positions in the public sector, the federal government included, and that prohibit public administrators from firing public servants without justifiable cause. To circumvent the rigours of the rules concerning public-sector employment, menial jobs – such as security, cleaning, transportation, and low-level administrative tasks – are contracted out to private firms selected by special auction procedures. This introduces some flexibility into areas where it is most needed. The FRL has established limits on personnel costs, which have also induced the substitution of private services for direct public employment.

Health care provides the main example of private agents being actively engaged in service provision under special agreements. The national health system joins the financial, managerial, and human resources of the federal, state, and local governments to give free access to every Brazilian citizen to basic health care as well as to more complex procedures carried out at public and private hospitals. The health care model has been extended to social assistance, and proposals have been floated for adopting a similar approach in the case of public safety. The health system is the most important attempt to improve efficiency and efficacy in public management by means of coordinating policies throughout the federation.

Coordination of public investment and services provision by local governments is impaired by the inability of state governments to organize production of urban and social services across the limits of local jurisdictions. This is particularly important in metropolitan regions and other urban agglomerations. In so far as the states cannot interfere in municipal autonomy, they lack the legislative power and administrative capability to enforce metropolitan policies. In addition, the increasingly direct relationship between the federal government and the municipalities, with high amounts of federal funds being channelled directly into the local purse, undermines the ability of the states to control activities that take place in their territory. Superimposition of programs and lack of integration and coordination lead to waste of resources, higher costs, and uneven access to public services – that is, poor people in less endowed municipalities may receive fewer benefits than the less poor in financially rich municipalities. Attempts to achieve coordination by means of a consortium of municipalities to deal with issues of common interest have proved to be unsatisfactory because the volatile political alignment of mayors contributes to the instability of such arrangements.[14]

Excessive dependence on transfers can be blamed for the non-materialization of the expected benefits from fiscal decentralization. As transfers become the major source of revenues for half the states and the majority of municipalities, efficiency in the use of resources at the subnational level is impaired and accountability cannot be properly exercised. Less reliance on own taxes makes individuals less conscious of the consequences of the expenditure decisions of governors and mayors. And lack of accountability adds to inefficiency and facilitates misconduct in dealing with the public money.

THE WAY FORWARD

Most of the flaws in Brazil's fiscal federalism observed in recent years are the direct result of the dual fiscal regime that was adopted in the 1988 Constitution and of the lack of will to pursue thorough reform thereafter.

Coupled with the dominance of macroeconomic issues in the fiscal policies designed in past decades, this duality led to a reversal of the fiscal decentralization envisaged at that time. There has been backward movement in the quality of the tax system, and increasing constraints on the actual exercise of the fiscal autonomy formally granted to states and local governments, with deleterious impacts on the efficiency and efficacy of public policies.

Nonetheless, politicians and policy makers alike do not see reform as a high priority. Conflicts of interest among developed and less developed states as well as among large and small municipalities may be one of the reasons for that. Another is the fear expressed by federal authorities that any reform proposal could reduce federal revenues and so jeopardize the sustainability of macroeconomic fiscal targets. In addition to more objective reasons for immobilization, it seems that politicians as a whole, mainly those from less developed regions, might be stuck in the view that the present system works to benefit their constituencies. In fact, everyone fears that any movement could lead to unexpected results and so could undermine their particular interests.

An opportunity to reform the entire system was lost in 1993, when the federal Constitution opened a window for a complete reform to be carried out under favourable terms.[15] After that, federal authorities opted for a narrow focus, directed only at minor issues related to taxation, reasoning that any attempt to pursue a broader reform, including changes in the revenue-sharing system, could endanger macroeconomic stability. Meanwhile, successive ad hoc measures have helped to exacerbate distortions and to increase conflicts in the federation.

A consensus among pundits about the need to go for a thorough reform of the Brazilian fiscal federalism model is being formed, but public authorities and politicians are still far from endorsing this view. In the midst of strong antagonisms, every federal entity fears that a structural reform could run against its particular interests. To make matters worse, private business is now very active in the fiscal policy arena and lobbies against any change that might be prejudicial to its interests. On the positive side, society at large has a general aversion to further increases in taxation; this may help to convince political leaders that a complete reform is long overdue.

These are positive signs, but large challenges must be faced in order to achieve a broad understanding of proposals for a new fiscal federalism. A new model will have to be able to reconcile tax harmonization, macroeconomic fiscal discipline, subnational autonomy, and governments that are efficient in the use of fiscal resources and accountable to their citizens. Moreover, the likelihood of an increase in regional disparities in the wake of higher rates of economic growth is not conducive to a reduction in antagonisms that block the search for structural changes.

Nevertheless, the main impediment to reform is the still uncertain situation concerning the vulnerability of the Brazilian economy to external shocks. In the event of an international crisis, macroeconomic pressures may be conducive to renewed resistance on the part of the federal government to changing the present system, thus postponing the reconciliation of Brazil's fiscal federalism with the challenges of economic globalization and monetary stability.[16]

In the meantime, efforts should be made to expose in a clear and understandable way the present system's lack of economic and political rationale. Empirical evidence contained in recent studies has to be translated into terms that can be easily perceived by regional and local leaders throughout the federation so that the need for a thorough reform can be clearly stated and understood.

A forum to discuss the present system and to appraise alternatives to improve federal cohesion and efficiency in public services provision would be of much help. To that end, thirteen states have taken an important first step by creating the Fiscal Forum of the Brazilian States, which has just begun to explore the main issues involved as a prelude to the preparation of a package of reform proposals. Such a process could create a window of opportunity for fundamental reform of the fiscal system in Brazil.

NOTES

1 On imbalances in political representation, see José Serra and José Roberto Afonso, "Federalismo Fiscal à Brasileira: Algumas Reflexões," *Revista do BNDES* (Rio de Janeiro) 6, 12 (1999): 3–30.
2 This particular aspect led Alfred Stepan to consider Brazil an extreme case of a democratically constrained federation. See Alfred Stepan, "Toward a New Comparative Analysis of Democracy and Federalism: Demos Constraining and Demos Enabling Federations," mimeo, Coréia do Sul, 1997.
3 On the importance of the regional issue, see Celina Souza, "Constitutional Aspects of Federalism in Brazil," in *A Global Dialogue on Federalism*, vol 1: *Constitutional Origins, Structure and Change in Federal Democracies*, ed. John Kincaid and G. Alan Tarr, 77–102 (Montreal and Kingston: McGill-Queen's University Press for the Forum of Federations, 2005).
4 For a detailed account of the division of responsibilities in the Brazilian Federation, see Marcelo Piancastelli, "The Federal Republic of Brazil," in *A Global Dialogue on Federalism*, vol 2: *Distribution of Powers and Responsibility in Federal Countries*, ed. Akhtar Majeed, Ronald L. Watts, and Douglas M. Brown, 67–90 (Montreal and Kingston: McGill-Queen's University Press for the Forum of Federations, 2006).
5 See Ricardo Varsano, "Subnational Taxation and Treatment of Interstate Trade in Brazil: Problems and a Proposed Solution," ABCD-LAC Conference, Valdivia, Chile, 1999.

6 Constitutional Amendment 37/2002. A top rate of 5 percent was imposed afterwards.
7 For details on fiscal competition in Brazil, see Ricardo Varsano, "A Guerra Fiscal do ICMS: Quem Ganha e quem perde," IPEA Discussion Paper, Brasília, 1997.
8 The shares of each state were established by CONFAZ. A percentage was set for all municipalities within each state in order to prevent the creation of new municipalities from having outside effects.
9 For the municipalities as a whole, these other revenue sources represent about 6 percent of total revenues.
10 Constitutional amendment 29/2000.
11 By means of transitory amendments to the Constitution, the federal government regained discretionary spending power over 20 percent of revenues from contributions earmarked for social spending.
12 The extent of the fiscal gaps can be seen in Sergio Prado, Waldemar Quadros, and Carlos Cavalcanti, "Partilha de Recursos na Federação Brasileira," FUNDAP, São Paulo, 2003.
13 The 1967 original formula established that the state quotas would be directly related to population and inversely related to per capita income, whereas the municipal quotas would grow with population size but at a decreasing rate.
14 See Fernando Rezende and Sol Garson, "Financing Metropolitan Areas in Brazil: Political, Institutional, Legal Obstacles and Emergence of New Proposals for Improving Coordination," *Revista de Economia Contemporânea* (Rio de Janeiro) 10, 1 (2006): 5–34.
15 The 1988 Constitution called for an entire revision to be carried out five years after its promulgation under special procedures that included approval by single majority in a joint parliamentary session.
16 These challenges are the subject of Fernando Rezende and Jose Roberto Afonso, "The Brazilian Federation, Facts, Challenges and Perspectives," in *Federalism and Economic Reform: International Perspectives*, ed. Jessica Wallack and T.N. Srinivasan, 143–88 (New York, NY: Cambridge University Press, 2006).

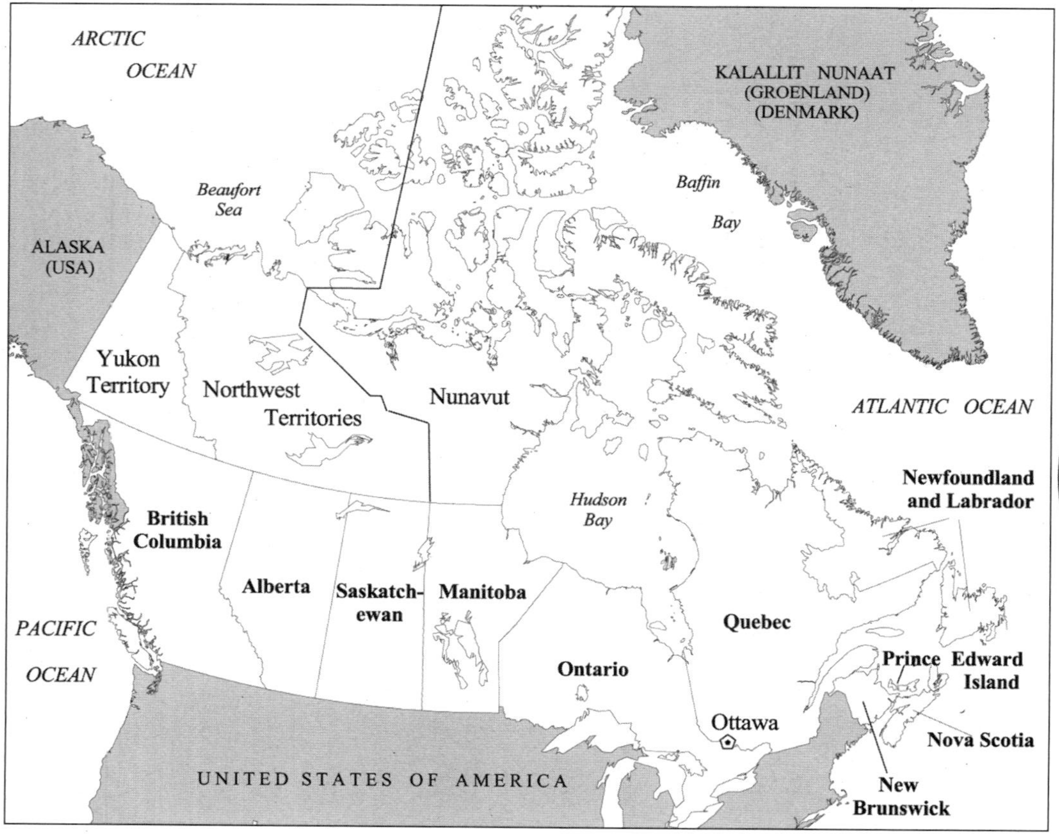

Canada

Capital: Ottawa
Population: 31.5 Million

Boundaries and place names are representative only and do not imply official endorsement.

The three northern territories, while adminstrative divisions, are not provinces.

N

500 0 500
Kilometers

Sources: ESRI Ltd.; National Atlas of Canada; Times Atlas of the World

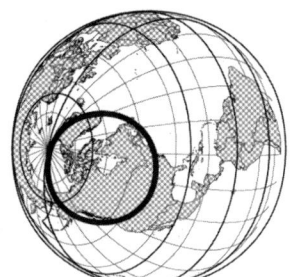

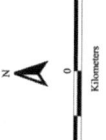

Canada

ROBIN BOADWAY

The Canadian federal system represents the textbook best-practice system of fiscal federalism. Autonomous provincial and municipal governments are responsible for the provision of many important public services. They share with the federal government unrestricted access to all the major tax sources and are responsible for raising a high proportion of their own revenues. Federal transfers to the provinces are only as intrusive as is necessary to achieve national objectives. The two main forms of transfers – unconditional equalization transfers and equal per capita bloc transfers to support provincial social programs – facilitate effective decentralized decision making by ensuring that provinces have comparable fiscal capacities for delivering important public services and by encouraging them to provide health, welfare, and postsecondary education programs that meet minimal nationwide standards. Federal-provincial agreements have led to enviable forms of income tax and sales tax harmonization that provinces are free to adopt, and have established the rules of the game for an efficient internal economic union and for a fair and equitable social union. This chapter reviews the main features of the Canadian federal system and recounts some of the pressures that have arisen recently.

Table 1 summarizes the basic features of Canada. It is the second largest country in the world, covering 9,984,670 square kilometres, but with a population of just 32.3 million. A high proportion of the population lives within 100 kilometres of the border with the United States in an east-west direction. There are ten provinces that run from east to west, and three sparsely populated territories located north of these provinces. The largest province, Ontario, with a population of 12.5 million, covers 1,076,395 square kilometres and has a per capita GDP of US$35,400. The smallest province, Prince Edward Island, with a population of 138,100, covers only 5,660 square kilometres and has a per capita GDP of US$24,994. The nationwide per capita GDP is US$34,710. Roughly speaking, per capita incomes are highest in the west and lowest in the east.

Table 1
Basic political and geographic indicators

Official name: Canada
Population: 32,270,000
Area (square kilometres):9,984,670
GDP per capita in US$ (year): $34,710
Constitution: 1867, Constitutional monarchy
Orders of government: federal, provincial and territorial, and local
Constitutional status of local government: subservient to provinces
Official languages: English and French
Number and types of constituent units: ten provinces, three territories
Population, area and per capita GDP in US$ of the largest constituent unit Ontario:
   12,541,400 people
   1,076,395 square kilometres
   GDP per capita $35,400
Population, area, and per capita GDP in US$ of the smallest constituent unit. PEI:
   138,100 people
   5,660 square kilometres
   GDP per capita $24,994
   Exchange rate = .90

Historically, Canada was formed as a confederation of four provinces, one of which was largely French-speaking and the rest English-speaking. French and English remain the official languages of the country, although the francophone population remains largely concentrated in one province (Quebec) and, to some extent, New Brunswick. Most other provinces have a francophone minority. Immigration has been relatively high in Canada (up to 1 percent of the population annually) and has increased the ethnic diversity of the country. There are particularly large Chinese, South Asian, and European populations concentrated in certain areas, and there is a large population of French-speaking immigrants in Quebec.

There is also a sizable population of Aboriginal peoples, consisting of a large number of different ethnic and linguistic groups ranging from the various First Nations (mostly in the provinces) to the Inuit (in the territories). The federal government retains fiduciary responsibility for Aboriginal peoples and is responsible for providing them with public services and protecting various rights that they have acquired through treaties signed with the British Crown.

Canada is a constitutional monarchy in which the monarch is the British queen or king. A federal governor general and provincial lieutenant-governors are appointed by the relevant governments to be the monarch's representatives in Canada. There is a federal parliament and a legislature in each province and territory that is elected by a first-past-the-post voting system. This results in a parliamentary democracy in which a small number of main parties vie for election. Typically, there is a majority party whose leader becomes the federal prime minister or a provincial premier, and whose policies are enacted by majority voting in the relevant legislature. Occasionally, the government is a minority one that has to rely on second or third party support to pass legislation. In practice, one party (the Liberal Party) has dominated the federal Parliament, while often a different party is in power in many of the provinces. The result is a reasonably stable government with elections every four to five years as chosen by the party in power. Local governments are also elected by majority voting, although the party system does not apply there.

All federal laws are passed by Parliament and must also be passed by the Senate, whose members are appointed by the prime minister and serve until age seventy-five. The Senate can hold up most legislation, but only temporarily. Provincial laws are passed by their legislatures and municipal laws by their elected councils, although there is no second chamber in the provinces or municipalities. The executive branch consists of a permanent civil service, organized mainly into line departments whose heads are usually ministers drawn from the elected representatives of the party in power. There is also a supreme court, which is appointed by the prime minister. It is the highest appeal court and rules on the constitutionality of legislation as well as on matters arising from the Charter of Rights and Freedoms, which is a component part of the Constitution.

The legal system is based on a common law system inherited from the United Kingdom, except in Quebec, where civil law is used, reflecting that province's French heritage. There are also many quasi-judicial bodies that serve regulatory functions delegated to them by the federal and provincial governments.

Accountability is achieved largely by periodic elections in all spheres of government. This is aided by a free press and by a tradition of freedom of speech and association that, along with other rights, are codified in the Charter of Rights and Freedoms, which was incorporated into the Constitution in 1982. The federal government and the provinces also have auditors-general, who audit government programs and report to Parliament and the legislatures on whether funds have been lawfully spent and value for money has been obtained. All governments also have financial management and accountability systems. Citizens are protected by the Charter of Rights and Freedoms as well as by human rights tribunals that oversee human rights legislation, freedom of information legislation, privacy commissioners, and ombudsmen. There is also a federal language commissioner responsible for reporting on the enforcement of official language requirements.

THE STRUCTURE OF GOVERNMENT AND DIVISION OF FISCAL POWERS

The Constitution sets out fundamental obligations with which governments must abide and imposes limits on legislation. Obligations include those imposed jointly on the federal government and the provinces to provide minimum levels of basic public services, to pursue equality of opportunity, and to foster economic development. In addition, the federal government is committed to providing equalization payments to the provinces so that they can provide "reasonably comparable levels of public services at reasonably comparable levels of taxation."[1] Limits on legislation include the requirement that laws satisfy the Charter of Rights and Freedoms and some minimal requirement not to interfere with interprovincial trade.

Federal and provincial legislation is restricted by the division of powers set out in the Constitution. The latter lists a number of powers that are exclusively federal, such as defence, international trade, criminal justice, money and banking, international waterways, unemployment insurance, bankruptcy, and divorce. The federal government can also use any form of taxation it chooses, and it is free to spend as it sees fit and to borrow and lend. Other areas are shared between the federal and provincial governments, including immigration, agriculture, and pensions, although only in the former two is the federal government paramount. More generally, the federal government is allowed to legislate as required for "peace, order and good government,"[2] and it has the power to disallow provincial legislation, although this has rarely been used. The provinces have the residual powers (i.e., those not assigned to either government). Exclusive provincial powers listed in the Constitution include health, education, social services, civil and property rights, administration of justice, highways, and matters of a local nature. There are two areas of formally shared jurisdiction (agriculture and immigration) and several others that, in practice, are also shared (e.g., environmental protection and higher education). Table 2 summarizes the expenditure responsibilities of the orders of government, and Table 3 indicates the breakdown of spending by function and order of government.

Provinces can raise revenues for their own purposes using "indirect taxes," although in practice this has been widely interpreted to include virtually any tax, except that aimed at taxing non-residents. The provinces also own the natural resources within their borders and can manage and tax them as they see fit. This has turned out to be a very important feature of the Canadian federation and one that has led to intergovernmental conflicts. Provinces have unfettered control over their own budgets, including the ability to borrow and lend.

Table 2
Legislative responsibility and actual provision of services by different orders of government

Legislative responsibility (de jure)	Public service	Actual allocation of function (de facto)
Federal	Trade and commerce	Federal
Federal	Unemployment insurance	Federal
Federal	Banking and currency	Federal
Federal	Postal service	Federal
Federal	Census and statistics	Federal
Federal	Defense and foreign affairs	Federal
Federal	Shipping and offshore	Federal
Federal	Bankruptcy	Federal
Federal	Patents, copyrights	Federal
Federal	Indians	Federal
Federal	Citizenship	Federal
Federal	Marriage and divorce	Federal
Federal	Criminal law and penitentiaries	Federal
Federal and provincial	Pensions	Federal and provincial
Federal and provincial	Immigration	Federal
Federal and provincial	Agriculture	Federal and provincial
Provincial	Administration of justice	Provincial
Provincial	Civil and property rights	Provincial
Provincial	Public lands and natural resources	Provincial
Provincial	Health	Provincial
Provincial	Licensing	Provincial
Provincial	Municipal institutions	Provincial
Provincial	Incorporation of companies	Provincial
Provincial	Local services	Local
Provincial	Education	Provincial and local
Provincial	Social welfare	Provincial and local

Table 3
Direct expenditures by function and level of government

Function	Federal (%)	State or provincial (%)	Local (%)	All (%)
Defence	100	0	0	100
Debt servicing	53.2	42.1	4.7	100
General administration	44.0	27.3	28.7	100
Law and order	55.4	23.1	21.5	100
Economic services	26.9	47.7	25.4	100
Social services	57.6	37.1	5.3	100
Health	21.0	77.7	1.3	100
Education	5.3	52.6	42.1	100
Subsidies				100
Total	37.4	45.1	17.5	100
Local public services[1]	0.0	0.0	100.0	100

1. Local public services include: primary and preschool education, secondary education, public health, hospitals, urban highways, urban transportation, drinking water and sewerage, waste collection, electric power supply, fire protection, public order and safety, police.

Municipal governments are entities of provincial governments, and their powers flow from provincial legislation. They are responsible for local matters, such as local policing, water, sewage and garbage, local roads, and recreation. They often participate in the delivery of provincial services, such as welfare and education. Local governments rely on property taxes and user fees and have the freedom to set their own tax rates. They are also able to borrow and lend, although there may be some restrictions on infrastructure investments and on their ability to borrow to finance them. Table 4 shows the sources of revenue by source and order of government.

The division of powers accords well with best-practice principles.[3] National public goods are assigned to the federal government; local public goods are decentralized. The provinces are responsible for public services and targeted transfers delivered to citizens, while the federal government retains responsibility for major social insurance transfers. Both orders of government have access to the main taxes so that a degree of revenue-raising autonomy can be achieved. Expenditure programs that affect provincial residents but have some spillover effects are shared responsibilities. The federal government has the ability to make transfers to the provinces to close any vertical fiscal gap between expenditure responsibilities and revenue raising, and the same applies to the provinces with respect to their municipalities.

Table 4
Tax assignment for various orders of government

	Determination of			Shares in revenue (%)			
	Base	Rate	Tax collection and administration	Federal	State/province	Local	All orders
Federal							
Income tax	Federal	Federal	Federal	64.7	35.3	0	100
Consumption tax	Federal	Federal	Federal	45.3	54.7	0	
Payroll tax	Federal	Federal	Federal	68.6	31.4	0	
User fees	Federal	Federal	Federal	24.4	23.3	52.3	
State or provincial							
Income tax	Federal	Provincial	Federal	64.7	35.3	0	100
Consumption tax	Provincial	Provincial	Fed & prov	45.3	54.7	0	
Payroll tax	Federal	Provincial	Federal	68.6	31.4	0	
Resource tax	Provincial	Provincial	Provincial	0	100	0	
Health premium	Provincial	Provincial	Provincial	0	100	0	
Property tax	Provincial	Provincial	Provincial	0	2.2	97.8	
User fees	Provincial	Provincial	Provincial	24.4	23.3	52.3	
Local							
Property tax	Provincial	Local	Provincial	0	2.2	97.8	100
User fees	Local	Local	Local	24.4	23.2	52.3	

Table 5 indicates the size of the vertical fiscal gap between the federal-provincial and provincial-municipal governments. There are, however, some anomalies. Provincial ownership of natural resources leads to significant horizontal imbalances. Provinces also have the authority to tax business income and capital, despite the fact that these are mobile tax bases. They also have the right to levy taxes on inheritances, but these have disappeared, in part due to interprovincial tax competition. In addition, provinces have the authority to regulate both securities markets and labour markets, and this has the potential to create inefficiencies in internal markets.

While this assignment of responsibilities contributes to the efficient delivery of public services, it also has the potential to create inefficiencies and inequities within the federation. Both can occur if decentralized fiscal responsibilities leave provinces with large disparities in their ability to provide public services and if provinces exercise their fiscal responsibilities in a way that leads to very different levels of public services and different degrees of social protection. Indeed, both spheres of government share responsibility for equity, although some of the major policy instruments for achieving equity are in the hands of the provinces. Moreover, there is a

Table 5
Vertical fiscal gaps

	Total revenue collected (in current US$ million – 2005)	Total revenue available, including net transfers for that level of government (in current US$ million – 2005)	Expenditures (in current US$ million– 2005)
National	181,466	182,044	142,764
Subnational			
State/provincial	172,087	211,367	203,988
Local	38,464	45,737	47,595
All orders	392,018	439,148	394,347

fairly strong national consensus that common levels of social programs should be provided across the country.[4] Indeed, social citizenship in the form of minimum standards of social services like health, education, and welfare are regarded as one of the more important functions of governments, even more so than the progressivity of the tax system. As a result, the role of government as a vehicle for social protection is given much more emphasis than are other government roles, such as defence and infrastructure spending, and the majority of government spending can be interpreted as contributing to redistributive objectives.

The fact that both spheres of government share responsibilities for national equity and efficiency, while the provinces control many of the important policy instruments, leads to the federal government's exercising some influence over provincial program design. This is largely done using spending power – that is, federal grants to the provinces and territories.[5] This is a powerful way for the federal government to influence provincial policies, notwithstanding the fact that provinces enjoy exclusive legislative jurisdiction in such areas as health, education, and social services. The federal government uses transfers to equalize the capacity of the provinces and territories to provide public services and to influence the design of some services so as to achieve basic national standards.[6] A by-product of this is that the federal government occupies relatively more of the tax room than do the provinces, and this contributes to its ability to induce tax harmonization among governments in income and sales taxation.

The federal government is also able to influence provincial decisions through moral suasion, given that federal and provincial officials are in constant negotiations. As well, there are federal-provincial agreements in various areas that contribute to policy harmonization. Some of these are multilateral, such as the Agreement on Internal Trade and the Social Union Framework Agreement. Others are bilateral, such as agreements on immigration and child tax credits between the federal government and individual provinces. The tax harmonization agreements covering corporate, personal, and sales taxes are also bilateral in nature, although common templates apply to all provinces that choose to participate.

Naturally, conflicts and situations of disharmony arise between the federal government and the provinces regarding fiscal issues. This is inevitable in a setting in which (1) both spheres of government share some common goals, (2) both have access to similar broad tax bases, and (3) both act independently. Three main sources of fiscal conflict arise. The first results from the fact that the federal government uses its spending power to influence provincial government program design by putting conditions on federal-provincial transfers. The federal government argues that it needs to use its spending power in this way to ensure that provincial social programs take account of national equity and efficiency objectives. The provinces argue that the imposition of conditions violates the spirit of the Constitution, which assigns exclusive legislative authority to the provinces in such areas as health, education, and welfare. There can be no clear resolution of this conflict, although it can be minimized by the federal government attaching only broad, general conditions to its grants, which in recent years has been the case. The Social Union Framework Agreement was negotiated between the federal and provincial ministers to manage the use of the federal spending power, requiring, among other things, that the federal government give advance notice before it is used.

The second source of fiscal conflict concerns the appropriate balance between the revenue and expenditure responsibilities of the federal and provincial governments. The provinces have argued that there is a vertical imbalance in the sense that the level of federal-provincial transfers is too low given the amount of tax room that the federal government has pre-empted relative to its expenditure responsibilities.[7] To the extent that such an imbalance exists – and the federal government has disputed that it does – there are two types of remedies. One is to turn more tax room over to the provinces by reducing federal tax rates and allowing the provinces to increase their rates. The other is to increase the size of transfers. The provinces disagree as to which remedy is preferable. Some, like Quebec and Alberta, favour turning over tax room; others, such as the Atlantic provinces, favour more transfers. In 2003, the provincial and territorial governments joined together as the formal Council of the Federation to promote intergovernmental cooperation. In 2005, the council established the Advisory Panel on Fiscal Imbalance to recommend ways to restore fiscal balance. Its recommendations included an enhanced equalization system and further transfers from the federal government for social programs.[8] However, the provinces were unable to achieve a consensus on the recommendations of the panel.

The third source of conflict involves horizontal fiscal imbalances. As the federation has become more decentralized, fiscal disparities among provinces have increased. This has traditionally been addressed by equalization transfers, but these have come under increasing strain in recent years. The rapid rise in oil and gas prices resulted in large disparities between provinces that have significant oil and gas deposits and those that do not. This increased the cost and the volatility of the equalization program, and the federal government responded by fixing the total transfer and its rate of growth over time. To address the issue, the federal government established the Expert Panel on Equalization and Territorial Formula Financing to advise it on the future design of the equalization program, including whether an arm's-length advisory commission should be established. The panel reported in June 2006 and recommended that a ten-province equalization standard be used that includes one-half of resource revenues.[9] The federal government is expected to announce its preferred resolution to the fiscal imbalance in its 2007 budget.

Another issue is that of the asymmetric treatment of different subnational governments. Various forms of asymmetry have evolved. The fiscal transfer arrangements with the territories differ considerably from those applying to the provinces. Because of their sparse populations and harsh northern conditions, the territories incur a much greater cost with regard to delivering public services than do the provinces. This is recognized by levels of transfers that are significantly higher on a per capita basis than are those made to the provinces. Unlike with provincial transfers, which are based on revenue-raising capacity, transfers to the territories are based on expenditure requirements. Another area of asymmetry occurs between Quebec and the other provinces. Quebec chose to opt out of certain federal-provincial transfers in return for differential tax room. In addition, Quebec chose not to join the federal public pension scheme but to run its own; and it chose not to join the tax harmonization arrangements for the personal and corporate income taxes but to administer its own. In the case of the value-added tax (VAT), Quebec has a special agreement with the federal government whereby the province administers the tax both for itself and for the federal government. Quebec also has special arrangements for immigration. These asymmetries do not constitute special treatment for Quebec because virtually all of the special arrangements that apply to Quebec are available to the other provinces as well, but they have chosen not to adopt them. These asymmetries reflect the unique nature of Quebec relative to the rest of Canada, it being the historical home of the French language, culture, and institutions.

Local governments have considerable independence over public services of a local nature, and they have the authority to determine their own levels of revenue. They are, however, subject to varying degrees of provincial oversight with regard to some of their operations. They must abide by provincial planning rules, and, in some cases, they are involved in administering provincial spending programs. They also face some borrowing restrictions. They rely on provincial transfers for a significant proportion of their spending, and these transfers are typically provided on an equalizing basis. As do the provinces, local governments sometimes argue that they face an imbalance between their spending responsibilities and their revenue-raising capacity. This has led to concern about the fiscal plight of the cities, inducing the federal government to make some direct fiscal transfers to them, bypassing the provinces.

Particular issues of accountability arise where large cities rival provinces in population and economic size. These issues have been magnified by the fact that some provinces have unilaterally amalgamated neighbouring cities into larger units and, in some cases, have created an additional tier of metropolitan governments responsible for region-wide policies such as transportation and policing (e.g., Toronto and Montreal). These amalgamations were intended to improve the efficiency and equity of local service provision but were often controversial. In the case of Montreal, in 2003 a change in provincial government enacted a law that enabled localities to separate from the amalgamated city.

Finally, while issues of national equity have played an important role in guiding the design of Canadian intergovernmental fiscal arrangements, the efficiency of the national economy has been a consideration as well. Efficiency in the internal economic union has been addressed in four main ways. First, the Constitution contains a provision that precludes provinces from interfering with interprovincial trade in goods and restricts them to using direct taxes on their residents. These are relatively weak provisions. The interprovincial trade article does not apply to services or factors of production. Furthermore, the courts have interpreted the restriction on direct taxation in a generous way, with the result that provinces can levy almost any kind of tax. Second, the federal government has used its spending power to induce provinces not to impose mobility restrictions on entitlements for social programs. This has been quite effective in the cases of social welfare and health. Third, federal-provincial tax harmonization agreements have been relatively effective in harmonizing federal and provincial income tax bases and, to a lesser extent, sales tax systems. Experience indicates that, in order to be effective, the federal government needs to retain a significant share of the tax room in these areas. Finally, and potentially most important, the federal and provincial governments have negotiated the extensive and detailed Agreement on Internal Trade, which covers a wide variety of areas, including procurement, labour market regulation, investment, and policies that affect the flow of goods and services across provinces. On paper, this agreement appears to be very comprehensive and should facilitate efficiency in the internal economic union. In practice, however, it has been relatively ineffective, largely owing to a weak dispute-settlement mechanism. Nonetheless, it represents an agreement that could be strengthened in the future. There remain some significant barriers to interprovincial transactions in areas such as regulation of the professions, workplace rules, capital market regulation, and procurement.

FISCAL FEDERALISM AND MACROECONOMIC MANAGEMENT

Fiscal decision making is highly decentralized, with the federal and provincial governments exercising independent legislative discretion with respect to their own fiscal policies. The aggregate size of provincial budgets is comparable to that of the federal government, so responsibility for fiscal policy is inevitably shared. Given the nature of budgetary decision making – especially its norms of secrecy – federal and provincial fiscal policies are not coordinated. Nonetheless, they are interdependent in the sense that the tax bases are common, and federal transfers to the provinces can affect provincial budgets. Indeed, a common complaint of the provinces is that federal changes to provincial transfers sometimes occur unexpectedly, which makes provincial budgetary planning difficult. A problem that arises in this context is that, because budgetary objectives are often relatively short-term and because federal-provincial transfers are budgetary items, changes in federal-provincial fiscal relations may not always take longer-term consequences for the federation into account.

Despite this, the federal government does pursue an active fiscal policy, using taxation, expenditures, and transfers to pursue macroeconomic goals, including employment, growth, and debt control. The larger provinces, which perceive that they have some influence over economic activity within their borders, also use fiscal policy instruments for that purpose. But to the extent that provincial governments are reluctant to use deficits to stimulate activity, the possibility exists that provincial fiscal policies can be pro-cyclical rather than anti-cyclical.

The extent of independence of decision making in all the orders of government leads to a high degree of accountability to their electorates. Moreover, this fiscal independence has precluded soft-budget constraint problems, which arise when fiscal transfers respond to the financial needs of recipient governments.[10] This problem is averted because the bulk of transfers are formula-driven and are based on factors that are independent of government control. Fiscal discipline applies to federal, provincial, and local governments through a combination of political accountability and capital market discipline. Some provinces have enacted legislation that restricts the use of deficit financing. Such legislation is self-imposed rather than enacted by the federal government or embedded in the Constitution.

Monetary policy is the constitutional responsibility of the federal government and is delegated to the central bank – the Bank of Canada. The bank enjoys virtual independence in its policies, although there is constant contact between the minister of finance and the governor of the bank. The bank takes its primary goal to be price stability and uses inflation targeting to determine its policies. It takes as given the debt and borrowing choices of federal and provincial governments, which are chosen independently. There is no Canadian equivalent of the European Union's Growth and Stability Pact limits on member-country deficit finance. No doubt this has the potential for complicating the conduct of monetary policy, and concern has sometimes been expressed about the consequences for some regions of a single national monetary policy, when different regions might be experiencing very different rates of inflation and unemployment. However, there have been no attempts to decentralize decision making and advice over monetary policy, such as is the case in the United States, with its system of twelve federal reserve banks.

ISSUES IN REVENUE-RAISING RESPONSIBILITIES

All spheres of government collect significant amounts of own-source revenues and are responsible for the size of their budgets. The proportion of provincial expenditures financed by own-source revenues has been gradually increasing for several decades, both because provinces have been occupying more and more of the tax room and because their expenditure responsibilities have been rising more rapidly than has the level of federal-provincial transfers.

The federal government has the constitutional right to raise tax revenues by any mode of taxation. It obtains most of its revenues from three broad-based tax sources: personal income taxation, sales taxation, and payroll taxation. The income tax is progressive, although the capital income of various assets is sheltered (e.g., pensions and housing), and is complemented by a corporate income tax that is partly integrated with it. The sales tax is a very comprehensive VAT called the Goods and Services Tax (GST). Payroll taxes are earmarked for social insurance programs (pensions and unemployment insurance). The federal government obtains lesser revenues from excise taxes, trade duties, lotteries, and user fees. Notably, there is no tax on inheritances, although capital gains are deemed to be realized on death. Inheritance taxation was turned over to the provinces decades ago, and it was gradually competed out of existence – a classic case of tax competition. Moreover, there are no direct taxes on resource revenues, although these generate income and sales tax revenues.

The provinces also use the same three broad-based taxes. Their income taxes are similar in structure to the federal one, but sales tax structures vary widely from province to province. Some have adopted a VAT, others have retail sales taxes on goods, and one has no sales tax. Payroll taxes are sometimes used for funding specific social insurance programs and sometimes for supplementing general revenues. Provinces also levy corporation income taxes and capital taxes. Like the federal government, they obtain revenues from specific excise taxes, gambling, user fees, and other lesser sources. A significant source of their revenues comes from taxes and charges imposed on natural resources. Royalties and the sale of licences are used in the case of oil and gas, and mining income taxes apply to minerals of various sorts. Fees are also obtained from renewable resources such as timber. In some cases, especially hydroelectricity, provincial Crown corporations are used to generate profits for general revenues.

Tax harmonization arrangements exist with respect to some tax types that are shared by the federal and provincial governments. In the case of the income tax, harmonization is achieved by tax-collection agreements negotiated between the federal government and individual provinces. These agreements follow a common template and are open to all provinces. In the case of the personal income tax, the provinces must abide by the federal tax base but are allowed considerable discretion with respect to choosing their rate structures, including both the size of tax brackets and the use of tax credits. They have full discretion over the level of provincial tax rates and, therefore, over the amount of revenue they will raise. The provinces have used this discretion fully, so that different tax rates apply in different provinces, as do different rate structures. Indeed, Alberta has opted for a flat-tax system. The provinces must also abide by a common allocation formula, which, in the case of the personal income tax, allocates income to the provinces on the basis of a taxpayer's province of residence on 31 December of each tax year. In return for agreeing to join the tax-collection agreements, a single tax-collection authority – the Canada Revenue Agency – applies for both the federal and provincial income tax. Only one province (Quebec) has not joined the personal income tax collection agreements, choosing to operate its own personal income tax system.

A parallel tax-collection agreement system applies for the corporation income tax. Those provinces that participate agree to accept the federal tax base, but they are allowed full discretion to determine the provincial tax rate. A common allocation formula applies based on an average of a corporation's revenues and payrolls in each province. For participating provinces, the federal government acts as the tax-collecting authority and bears the costs. Three provinces do not participate in corporate tax collection agreements (Alberta, Ontario, and Quebec). Together, they account for over three-quarters of corporate income, which would seem to restrict the usefulness of corporate tax harmonization. However, these provinces have in fact designed their corporate tax bases to be similar to the federal base, and they abide by the same allocation formula.

Two comments should be made on the income tax harmonization system. The first is that the tax collection agreements are a federal government initiative, and it seems clear that, in order to sustain them, the federal government needs to maintain some minimum share of the income tax room. As the share of federal personal income tax room gradually dwindled over the post-Second World War period, the provinces brought increasing pressure to bear to loosen the conditions that applied to them. Indeed, some threatened to leave the agreements. In response to this pressure, the system was changed significantly in the 1990s, from one in which the provinces had to abide by the federal rate structure and could only choose a surtax rate to apply to federal tax liabilities to one in which they could choose their own rate structures (within some limits).

The second point concerns the possibilities of tax competition. Despite the predictions of economic reasoning, there seems to have been little tax competition in the income tax area, apart from the mentioned tendency to reduce income tax progressivity. For example, there appears to have been little competition driving provincial corporate tax rates down. There may be various reasons for this, including implicit cooperation among provincial governments. Some observers have also argued that the existence of a strong equalization system that has put provinces on a more equal fiscal footing may have reduced the impetus for tax competition, especially since the consequences of a competitive reduction in tax rates to attract larger tax bases would, to a great extent, be offset by reduced equalization payments.[11] Despite the wide discretion that provinces have to set tax rates, relative tax rates across provinces do not deviate from the average by significant amounts, with the exception of Alberta, whose tax capacity is well above average due to its oil and gas wealth.

Harmonization of sales taxes is much less complete, and this no doubt partly reflects the difficulty that exists in both operating and harmonizing a VAT in a decentralized setting with no border controls. Two such arrangements exist. The first involves a federal sales tax harmonization agreement with New Brunswick, Nova Scotia, and Newfoundland and Labrador. Under this agreement, there is a single federal and provincial VAT with one rate, called the Harmonized Sales Tax (HST), which replaces both the federal GST and provincial sales taxes. Revenues raised on behalf of the three provinces are allocated to them in accordance with estimates of their aggregate consumption. This arrangement can be seen as essentially a revenue-sharing agreement, although the three provinces together can influence the rate of revenue sharing (i.e., that component of the HST tax rate that reflects the provinces' common rate).

The second such agreement involves the federal government and Quebec, whereby the provincial sales tax – the Quebec sales tax (QST) – is harmonized with the federal GST. In this case, the tax is collected by the Quebec government both for itself and for the federal government. The main problem with administering such arrangements concerns properly accounting for cross-border transactions using the standard VAT invoice-and-credit approach. This is handled by using the so-called deferred payment method, whereby imports of intermediate goods into the province are not initially subject to the QST but become liable once the first sale occurs within the province. This method seems workable when only one province is involved, but it remains to be seen how easily such a system would work if several provinces set up VATs with different tax rates. At the very least, compliance would be complicated.[12]

Other provinces have been reluctant to abandon their retail sales taxes in favour of VATs despite the economic arguments for doing so. Partly, this is because VATs are unpopular, given that they include services in their bases. The provinces also seem to fear that they would lose considerable discretion over sales-tax policy if the most feasible method of harmonization was the HST version, whereby individual provincial tax rates could not be chosen.

It is significant to note that, for those taxes that provinces alone collect, especially resource taxes, there is no harmonization. Indeed, resource taxes come in very different types, depending both on the resource and on the province. This can be taken as a reflection of how difficult it is to coordinate policies horizontally without the federal government acting as facilitator or initiator.

Local governments rely on two main sources of own revenues – property taxes and user charges – with the latter increasing in importance. They have discretion for setting their own tax rates. Sometimes the province also uses the property tax by applying a province-wide tax that is used to finance services like education. Alternatively, a portion of property taxes may be earmarked for education, with the rate being set by the province or by a special education authority. Where metropolitan or regional governments exist, they may also be allowed to set their own property tax rate alongside that of local governments.

Property taxes are harmonized within all provinces. The property tax base is the market value of properties (including both land and buildings), and it is assessed using standard assessment principles in all provinces. Local governments are then able to apply their own property tax rates to this common base. Separate tax rates typically apply to residential and commercial properties. Most provinces have a system of equalizing the fiscal capacities of local governments, with ability to raise property tax revenues being an important determinant of equalization. Moreover, the federal-provincial equalization scheme includes property taxes as one of the bases subject to equalization, including both provincial and local components.

Conflicts similar to those between provinces and the federal government arise between local governments and the province. There may be discontent over the extent of horizontal equalization – for example, between high-fiscal capacity urban areas and low-fiscal capacity areas – with the former resenting the relatively high property tax rates that result from such equalization of, say, education financing. Equally important is the allegation of vertical imbalances between the province and the local governments. Just as the provinces complain that the federal government does not provide sufficient transfers, given the division of tax room and the relative expenditure responsibilities, so the local governments claim that their transfers from the province are insufficient. In fact, property tax levels are high in Canada compared with what they are in other OECD countries, and cities argue that this tax burden makes it difficult for them to attract and retain businesses.

The financing of services to First Nations falls outside the normal federal structure. There are more than six hundred First Nations communities, most of which are quite small, located in remote areas, and have little revenue-raising capacity. The federal government is responsible for providing public services for them, including those that would otherwise fall into provincial jurisdiction. Many Aboriginals choose to live away from their reserve communities, typically in urban areas. They, too, tend to be relatively poor and dependent on the state for income and services, which are provided by the provinces. Members of First Nations on reserves are exempt from paying federal or provincial taxes as a result of past agreements that have become federal acts of Parliament. Federal financing of First Nations is much more hands-on than are transfers to the provinces, which tend to be in blocs and with only general conditions attached. In the case of First Nations financing, transfers are highly discretionary and specific to particular uses, such as schools, health care, housing, and welfare. Even where the First Nations assume some administrative responsibility for delivering the programs, they remain accountable to the federal government for how the funds are spent. The amount that they receive depends on local circumstances, including costs and the ability to raise own-source revenues. This gives rise to potential incentive problems. In the past, commentators have argued that local accountability, good governance, and quality of services could all be enhanced if the transfer system for First Nations were similar to those that apply to the provinces and/or municipalities and if local Aboriginal communities were given more discretion in providing services for themselves. The problem is how to build up the capacity for self-administration and self-government – goals that are widely accepted. It is a typical chicken-and-egg problem, not unlike what one encounters in considering the case for decentralization in developing countries.

FISCAL EQUITY AND EFFICIENCY CONCERNS AND INTERGOVERNMENTAL FISCAL TRANSFERS

Canada is a large, diverse nation with provinces that differ in their geography, their natural endowments, and the extent of their economic development. The decentralization of public service provision and revenue-raising responsibilities inevitably gives rise to disparities in fiscal capacity. Decentralization also affects, as well as reflects, differences in the extent of commitment to national equity objectives, including those that are written into the Constitution. Managing decentralization has been a challenge to the Canadian federation – one that has become increasingly important as the provinces have become more and more self-sufficient.[13]

There are two main sources of significant fiscal disparities in the Canadian federation, one independent of decentralization and the other an integral part. The first results from the fact that the provinces own the natural resources within their borders and have the right to tax them as they see fit. The provinces differ considerably in their ability to raise revenues from natural resources. The most important source of resource-based fiscal disparity is that arising from oil and gas deposits, which are highly concentrated in Alberta and, to a lesser extent, British Columbia and Saskatchewan. There are also oil and gas reserves on federal lands in the territories and off the east coast. In both cases, the resources are rightfully owned by the federal government. However, the federal government has essentially turned over the offshore resources to the provinces of Nova Scotia and Newfoundland and Labrador, and there is a possibility that it will turn them over to the territories as well.

The disparities generated by oil and gas revenues are enormous. Alberta's per capita revenue-raising capacity is over 50 percent higher than that of the next highest province. This poses a conundrum for the federal government. By the Constitution, it is committed to making equalization payments to the provinces to overcome these fiscal disparities; however, in the case of resource revenues, it does not have direct access to them, so affordability is an issue. As a result, oil and gas revenues have never been fully equalized. This is anomalous because other types of resource revenues that give rise to fiscal disparities are equalized, including provincial mining taxes and timber revenues. However, in the case of hydroelectricity rents, which can also create large disparities, equalization is minimal. This is because provinces with significant resources of this type (i.e., Quebec and Manitoba) have tended to exploit them through provincial Crown corporations that dissipate at least part of the rents as lower prices to provincial users.

The second main source of disparities comes from differences in per capita incomes among provinces. These have been fairly persistent, with the large province of Ontario, located in the manufacturing heartland, leading the way, and the five most eastern provinces lagging behind. The sizes of fiscal disparities arising from this source depend on the extent of fiscal decentralization: the more provinces rely on their own revenues, the greater the fiscal disparities. The federal government, unlike in the case of natural resources, has the potential to equalize fiscal disparities arising from differences in per capita income across provinces because it has access to taxes on income or their equivalent. Nonetheless, decentralization makes it more difficult for the federal government to fulfill its equalization objectives because disparities become larger while its own tax room decreases.

Fiscal disparities can also arise on the expenditure side because of differences in the need for public services and differences in the cost of delivering them. There is limited evidence about the magnitude of such differences, although there is reason to believe that they are not as large as they are on the revenue-raising side. That is because differences in costs and need tend to offset each other. Provinces that have the highest need because of the demographic structure of their populations or the number of long-term unemployed also tend to be the ones that have the lowest cost of service delivery. Perhaps the most significant differences in need apply between urban and rural areas. However, there is not a systematic difference among provinces with regard to the extent to which they are urbanized.

There remains a significant vertical fiscal gap, despite the extent of decentralization of revenue raising to the provinces. This fiscal gap serves three purposes. First, it enables the federal government to retain a large share of tax room in the income and sales tax fields, thereby facilitating tax harmonization. Second, a vertical gap is needed to finance the equalization transfers that are the cornerstone of federal-provincial fiscal arrangements. Moreover, as I have mentioned, the larger the vertical fiscal gap, the smaller the need for equalization. Finally, the vertical gap enables the federal government to use conditional transfers to influence provincial social program design. Whatever the validity of these arguments for a vertical fiscal gap, there still remains a conflict over whether there is a vertical imbalance – that is, whether the size of transfers is appropriate, given the revenue raised by the federal government relative to its own expenditure responsibilities.

The form of the system of fiscal transfers is relatively simple. There are two main federal-provincial transfers, comprising about one-quarter of the federal budget. One is the equalization system; the other is the system of social transfers. Equalization payments are unconditional transfers from the federal government to those provinces whose revenue-raising capacity is below a national norm. A representative tax system (RTS) approach is used. For each of the many revenue sources used by the provinces (thirty-three in number), each province's per capita equalization entitlement is calculated using a simple formula: $E = t(B - b)$, where t is a national average of all provincial tax rates used for this revenue source, b is the province's per capita tax base, and B is the per capita tax base used for five representative provinces. This is repeated for each province and each revenue source. Then each province's aggregate equalization entitlements are obtained by summing up its entitlements from all revenues sources. Those provinces with positive aggregate entitlements receive a transfer equal to their entitlements. Those with negative aggregate entitlements receive nothing. Thus, equalization brings the revenue-raising capacity, using standard tax bases, up to the five-province standard by ensuring that, if they applied the national average tax rate, their revenues would be comparable to the five-province standard.

This formula-based RTS system has come under heavy criticism in recent years. The provinces argue that a ten-province standard (which would include all provinces) should be used. This would bring Alberta into the standard and increase all equalization entitlements considerably. The federal government, however, worries about the fact that it will have no discretion over the total equalization payments it must make or how it will change over time. As a result of this conflict, in 2005 the federal government froze the total entitlement and fixed its rate of growth. It then set up the Expert Panel on Equalization and Territorial Formula Financing (hereafter the Expert Panel) to advise it on an appropriate formula in the future as well as on whether to set up a permanent arm's-length advisory body comparable to the Commonwealth Grants Commission in Australia. The panel's report rejected a permanent commission but did recommend a return to a formula-driven, principles-based equalization system, specifically a ten-province RTS system with partial inclusion of natural resources. Until the federal government decides how to proceed, the existing RTS system applies, but with a fixed limit on total equalization payments.

The second major form of transfers consists of equal per capita transfers to help finance provincial spending on health, welfare, and postsecondary education. The transfer is nominally divided into two components – the Canada Health Transfer (CHT) and the Canada Social Transfer (CST), which encompasses welfare and postsecondary education. This equal per capita transfer system evolved from a system of transfers that was initially based on fifty-fifty cost sharing in health and welfare, along with bloc transfers for postsecondary education. These transfers were initially introduced to induce the provinces to introduce public health insurance and welfare programs. Once they were established, the matching component was deemed not to be necessary.

These transfers have minimal conditions attached. To be eligible for the full amount, provinces cannot impose residency programs on their welfare systems, and their health insurance programs must abide by a series of quite general criteria, including such things as accessibility, affordability, and comprehensiveness. Some of the provinces object to the federal government imposing such conditions on its transfers, arguing that these are areas of provincial competence and that the extent of the transfer as a proportion of provincial spending requirements is not enough to be able to insist on federal conditions. As it stands, there are no institutional arrangements for dealing with such disputes. Of course, federal and provincial officials are in constant contact and negotiation, and they exchange views frequently. But in the end, the spending power is a federal legislative prerogative, and any quasi-autonomous body could only be advisory in nature. Nonetheless, such a body might increase the transparency of decision making by subjecting federal policy to ongoing public scrutiny.

There are various smaller transfers from the federal government to the provinces for specific purposes. These are typically highly conditional and may or may not be matching. Examples include cost-sharing transfers for national highway financing, transfers to enable the provinces to provide services to immigrants, and transfers for worker training and health care reform. These transfers are small compared with equalization and social transfers.

The territories are also eligible for the CHT and CST. However, given the high costs of delivering their public services, they receive special transfers in lieu of equalization. These transfers are based on the historical costs of delivering public services, and they escalate annually. The Expert Panel recommended a formula-driven approach, involving a move to an RTS system similar to that used for equalization but excluding resource revenues.

Provincial-local transfer systems are similar to federal-provincial ones. Many provinces have equalization systems and base them on revenue equalization. Effectively, this means property tax equalization as it is the main source of local revenues. RTS-like formulas are used, except that a distinction is often made among communities of different types (large-small, urban-rural, etc.). There are also other transfers to close the vertical fiscal gap, and these are often conditional bloc grants for areas such as education and welfare, to the extent that these are delivered locally.

The Canadian federal system has generally been regarded as exemplary. There is a high degree of autonomous, decentralized decision making.

This has been supported by effective equalization systems that, taken together with social transfers, enable the provinces to provide comparable levels of services at comparable tax rates. Moreover, the federal government's use of its spending power has been relatively non-intrusive compared with that of other federations, although it remains controversial in Quebec. Yet national standards in program design have been achieved, while at the same time leaving provinces open to choosing program design aspects to suit their own needs and to experiment with new approaches. There remains much debate about the extent of decentralization and the role of federal spending power in provincial jurisdictions. Yet this can be regarded more as healthy debate than as devastating criticism. Fiscal equity is achieved to a considerable degree across Canada, with the outstanding exception of Alberta, with its vast oil and gas wealth. It is probably not feasible to go further in that direction.

The main structural problem that needs to be resolved is the issue of vertical imbalance.[14] The provinces are convinced that, for the past decade, the federal government has cut its transfers to the provinces excessively. While the federal government has succeeded in turning budget deficits into large surpluses, some provinces still face fiscal struggles, especially given the very rapid growth of their expenditure requirements in health care and other areas. The issue is whether to resolve that perceived imbalance by turning over tax room to the provinces or by increasing federal transfers. Those who favour the former approach argue that accountability will be enhanced and that the federal government will no longer be able to interfere with provincial spending priorities and to impose unilateral transfer changes. Those who argue for the latter say that a sizeable vertical fiscal gap is necessary for fiscal equity, for ensuring national standards in social programs, and for maintaining a harmonized tax system.

FINANCING CAPITAL INVESTMENT

Capital investment decisions, like other budgeting decisions, are independently taken by the relevant sphere of government. The federal government is responsible for national infrastructure (e.g., small airports, seaports, and railways) as well as capital expenditures involved in providing services (e.g., defence equipment, buildings, and machines). Capital expenditures are budgetary items that exist alongside current expenditures. There is no separate capital budgeting procedure. Capital financing comes from general revenues or borrowing, although borrowing is not typically earmarked to capital purchases. Large capital purchases are subject to tendering rules that ensure accountability and transparency. There are no restrictions on access to capital markets, whether domestic or foreign. Control comes from the discipline of capital markets themselves as well as from standard political and financial management accountability techniques.

Provinces are free to determine their own capital expenditures and to finance them as they choose. There are no restrictions imposed by the federal government, and it does not provide financial incentives for provincial borrowing. (Unlike in the United States, interest on provincial or municipal debt is not tax deductible in Canada.) The normal forms of accountability apply to provincial capital financing decisions, and there is no pressure to change that.

Local governments have somewhat less independence than do the provinces with regard to their capital purchases and financing. Typically, they have to restrict their borrowing to approved capital purchases rather than being able to borrow freely for current spending purposes. In practice, this system has worked well. There have been no major soft-budget constraint problems in local governments, and accountability for capital purchases is effective for both financial markets and electorates.

In recent years, there has been concern that an "infrastructure deficit" has developed, especially in the cities. New mechanisms have been explored for finding the finance to address these infrastructure needs. One innovation has been the use of private-public partnerships to finance and operate new infrastructure, especially in the transportation area. Moreover, the federal government has been looked to as a possible source of finance for provincial and municipal infrastructure.

FISCAL FEDERALISM DIMENSIONS OF THE PUBLIC MANAGEMENT FRAMEWORK

All orders of government enjoy autonomy in their public administration. The federal government has a permanent civil service in which members are career civil servants. Political appointments are restricted to political positions, such as ministerial advisors and staff. The federal government does, however, have considerable authority of appointment to quasi-judicial and judicial bodies. Federal judges are appointed by the federal government, and Supreme Court judges are appointed by the prime minister. The heads of administrative tribunals and Crown corporations are also appointed.

Provincial governments have dedicated civil services, completely independent of the federal civil service. The federal government plays no role in provincial administration. Provincial governments also appoint all provincial judges and all heads of provincial Crown corporations, tribunals, and the like. The local governments also have their own public employees, hired by them and quite independent of the federal or provincial civil service. The provincial government does not interfere in municipal hiring and firing. The result is a set of independent civil services in all spheres of government. It is generally the case that civil servants are very competent and behave with a high level of integrity. Corruption is not regarded as being a problem.

THE WAY FORWARD

As the Canadian federation evolves, demands are being placed on the system to adapt. Fiscal decentralization combined with the rapid growth in demand for the public services provided by provinces has brought with it the prospect of fiscal imbalance, both vertical and horizontal. This prospect also extends to municipal governments and to self-governing First Nations communities, where the need is often greatest. Relations among governments have become strained as each sphere of government seeks to define its own role in the federation. Such soul-searching is not new and, in the past, has always been met by revised fiscal arrangements and tough but amicable negotiations. The question is whether such accommodation will be reached as readily in the future, given the relatively rapid changes now being encountered.

Strains in the federal system frequently stem from two fundamental conflicts that characterize the Canadian federation. The first arises because, while the Constitution gives provinces exclusive legislative responsibility in the important areas of health, education, and welfare, the federal government shares a constitutional commitment to providing essential public services of reasonable quality and to promoting equal opportunities for all Canadians. Given that the public services most critical for fulfilling this commitment are provincial legislative responsibilities, the only feasible policy instrument available to the federal government is its spending power.

The second conflict arises because provinces own the natural resources within their borders and have the right to tax them as they see fit, while, at the same time, the federal government has a constitutional commitment to making equalization transfers so that all provinces have sufficient revenues to provide reasonably comparable levels of public services at reasonably comparable levels of taxation. Given that a substantial source of fiscal disparity among provinces comes from natural resource endowments, fulfillment of the equalization commitment would seem to require violation of the provincial ownership of revenues from these natural resources. Many sources of dispute revolve around the appropriate compromise between these fundamental conflicts.

Recent events and trends have put considerable strain on the system. First and foremost, the federal government, faced with an unsustainable debt situation, reduced its expenditures precipitously. Federal program expenditures fell from 15.7 percent of GDP in 1993–94 to 11 percent in 2000–01 (although they rose subsequently to 12.6 percent in 2004–05). Particularly hard hit were cash transfers to the provinces for social programs. These were cut dramatically and were consolidated into a single bloc transfer. This cut occurred with little prior consultation, and the provinces argued that it effectively transferred part of the federal debt onto the provinces. The provinces argue that this has created a fiscal imbalance – that is, that the federal government collects a share of tax revenues that, relative to its expenditures, is too high, especially given the expected high rate of growth of provincial spending responsibilities (e.g., for health care).

The problem of vertical imbalance is exacerbated by a growing horizontal imbalance, which is partly a natural consequence of decentralizing revenue raising to the provinces, but it is made more immediate by soaring oil and gas prices, which have created unprecedented fiscal disparities among the provinces. The federal response to this has been a series of ad hoc measures, including freezing total equalization entitlements, accompanied by the formation of the Expert Panel to advise the government on future equalization arrangements. Some provinces were stung by what they perceived to be unilateral decisions on the part of the federal government, albeit ones made in the shadow of a fiscal crisis. This is especially a concern given the need to deal with rapidly escalating health care costs as well as the imperative to ensure that education and other human capital policies are in place to deal with the challenges posed by globalization.

These same concerns affect municipal governments and First Nations communities. As the country becomes more urbanized, and cities become the focus of economic growth, there is a need to address the fiscal imbalance that is felt by municipal governments so that they can provide the necessary public services to ensure that their citizens are cared for and their businesses are competitive. The financial problems facing Aboriginal communities are even more immediate. These are communities whose residents are among the poorest in the country and which, in many cases, lack basic public services. The challenge here is a matter not just of financing but also of service delivery as the transition is made from a system in which the federal government had a very hands-on approach to one in which the communities themselves are taking on more and more responsibility.

NOTES

1 Section 36 (2), Constitution Act, 1982.
2 Section 91, Constitution Act, 1982.
3 See Teresa Ter-Minassian, ed., *Fiscal Federalism in Theory and Practice* (Washington: International Monetary Fund, 1997); and Ehtisham Ahmed and Giorgio Brosio, eds., *Handbook of Fiscal Federalism* (Cheltenham: Edward Elgar, 2006).
4 See Keith Banting and Robin Boadway, "Defining the Sharing Community: The Federal Role in Health Care," in *Money, Politics and Health Care*, ed. Harvey Lazar and France St-Hilaire, 1–77 (Montreal: Institute for Research on Public Policy, 2004).

5 See Ronald Watts, *The Spending Power in Federal Systems: A Comparative Study* (Kingston, ON: Institute of Intergovernmental Relations, 1999).
6 See Robin Boadway, "The Theory and Practice of Equalization," *CESIFO Economic Studies* 50, 1 (2004): 211–54.
7 Séguin Committee, *A New Division of Canada's Financial Resources* (Québec: Department of Finance, 2002).
8 Advisory Panel on Fiscal Imbalance, *Reconciling the Irreconcilable* (Ottawa: The Council of the Federation, 2006).
9 Expert Panel on Equalization and Territorial Formula Financing, *Achieving a National Purpose* (Ottawa: Finance Canada, 2006).
10 See Jonathan Rodden, Gunnar S. Eskeland, and Jennie Litvack, eds., *Fiscal Decentralization and the Challenge of Hard Budget Constraints* (Cambridge, MA: MIT Press, 2002).
11 See Michael Smart, "Taxation and Deadweight Loss in a System of Intergovernmental Transfers," *Canadian Journal of Economics* 31 (1998): 189–206.
12 See Richard M. Bird and Pierre-Pascal Gendron, "VATs in Federal Countries: International Experience and Emerging Possibilities," *Bulletin for International Fiscal Documentation* 55 (2001): 293–309.
13 See Robin Boadway, "Inter-Governmental Fiscal Relations: The Facilitator of Fiscal Decentralization," *Constitutional Political Economy* 12, 2 (2001): 93–121.
14 Budget 2006, *Restoring Fiscal Balance: Focusing on Priorities* (Ottawa: Finance Canada, 2006).

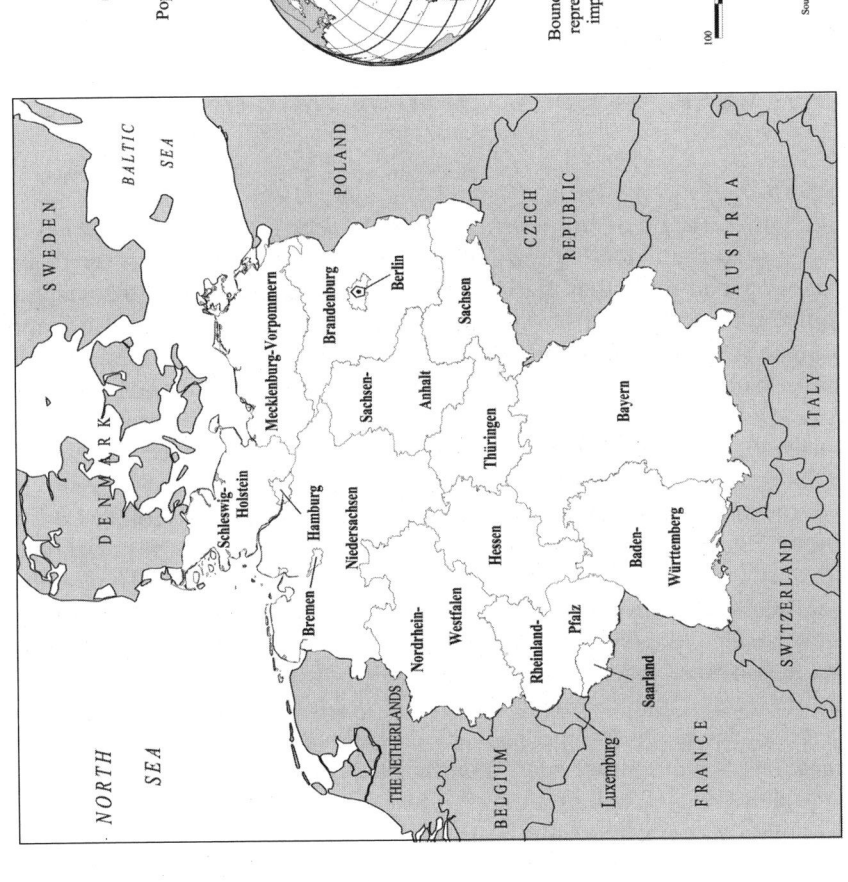

Federal Republic of Germany

LARS P. FELD AND JÜRGEN VON HAGEN

Germany's fiscal federalism is in trouble. In 2003, the city state (*Land*) of Berlin sued the federal government at the Constitutional Court for financial bailout, arguing that Berlin was in extreme fiscal distress from which it could not escape by its own means. In 2005 and 2006 Saarland and Bremen, respectively, followed with similar claims, although they had obtained bailouts from the federal government from 1994 to 2004. As many Land governments have neglected constitutional rules concerning public borrowing for several years, it is only a matter of time before more states (*Länder*) ask for bailouts.

When the system was set up in 1949, the framers of the German Constitution, which is called the *Grundgesetz*, were not aware of the potentially perverse fiscal incentives the fiscal constitution might provide. The Länder lost their tax autonomy with the Weimar Constitution, and the attempts of some Länder, like Bavaria, to obtain higher tax autonomy after the Second World War were not successful.[1] A majority of the Länder favoured a comprehensive system of fiscal equalization in order to provide each Land with the financial means to meet its legal obligations and subsequent spending needs. Without the intervention of the Allies, the fiscal constitution would have allowed the Länder even less influence on tax laws in 1949. However, the Allies were not successful in their attempt to provide the Länder with greater tax autonomy. The involvement of the *Bundesrat* (second chamber of Parliament) in taxation results from the administrative responsibilities the states obtained for the most important (joint) taxes.

Germany's fiscal federalism evolved towards higher cooperation and centralization, culminating in the Great Financial Reform Act of 1969. Soon afterwards, critical assessments argued that this constitutional reform might have gone too far.[2] Further critical discussions emerged in the dawn of the two decisions of the Constitutional Court on the fiscal equalization system in 1986 and 1992. Unification was still unimportant for this case as the decision of 1992 (partly) resulted from the bailout claims by Saarland and Bremen. Thus, the troubles of Germany's fiscal federalism started before unification, although it provided additional problems, as is indicated by the decision of the Constitutional Court on the fiscal equalization system in 1999.

This sequence of events led the political actors in the federal and state spheres to aim at a reform of Germany's federalism in 2001 and to the creation of the Commission for the Modernization of Federal Order in 2003. After one year of deliberations, the commission was, however, unable to agree on recommendations for reforming German federalism.[3] The commission was supposed to suggest a disentanglement of federal and Land responsibilities. Currently, 50.1 percent of all new federal laws require the approval of both chambers of the federal Parliament and, thus, of the Bundesrat, which represents the Länder.[4] Likewise, the Länder are strongly restricted by federal mandates in conducting their own tasks. Thus, neither the federal government nor the Länder have sufficient autonomy to pursue their own policy goals. As the assignment of competencies has constitutional prerogative over the fiscal constitution in Germany, disentanglement is particularly important for German fiscal federalism.

In view of this, the government elected in the fall of 2005 was a grand coalition of Christian Democrats and Social Democrats. They decided in November 2005 to re-enter this reform process with a revision of the compromise that had almost been achieved in 2004 between the Länder and the federal government. In the summer of 2006, the *Bundestag* (first chamber) and the Bundesrat accepted the Federalism Reform Act.[5] It contains a considerable reduction of federal laws that require the consent of the Bundesrat,[6] and it introduces a right for the Länder to deviate from federal law in the areas of administrative institutions and administrative procedures. Moreover, the legislative responsibilities of the federal government and the Länder are revised considerably. With respect to fiscal federalism, the reform is less ambitious. However, the compromise contains the prospect of a second reform step with considerably more changes for Germany's fiscal federalism.

Given these recent reform efforts, the question arises: What is wrong with Germany's fiscal federalism? In order to answer this question, we provide an overview of the components of German federalism and their main advantages and disadvantages. After giving a brief overview of the country, we describe the division of fiscal powers in Germany and relate it to macroeconomic management. Thereafter, we discuss revenue-raising possibilities and intergovernmental fiscal transfers. The final section provides some ideas about the way forward.

OVERVIEW OF THE COUNTRY

The Federal Republic of Germany is a representative democracy with a population of 82.4 million people in 2005 and an area of 357,050 square kilometres.[7] The official language is German. In 2005, 7.3 million people, or 8.8 percent of the population, were foreigners. Immigrants from Turkey make up the largest group, at 1.8 million, which is about as important as are the 1.7 million foreigners from the EU-15.[8] Although there are many people with no religious affiliation living in Germany, by far the largest part of the population is of Christian background. Roman Catholics, at 26.0 million members, and Protestants, at 25.6 million members, cover about one-third of the population each, but the large majority of them are not practising. They are followed by 1.2 million people of Orthodox faith, and 300,000 Free Church followers. About 3.2 million Muslims and 100,000 Jewish people live in Germany.

The Grundgesetz of 1949 legally established two orders of government: federal and state. The Grundgesetz guarantees the existence of the Länder and provides them with a strong constitutional position.[9] It is true that the Grundgesetz allows for changes in the territorial boundaries of states; therefore, some experts of constitutional law have argued that this renders Germany's federalism fictitious.[10] The article in the Grundgesetz regulates the merger of German states as a "new partitioning of the federation's territory." However, because the merger of states is the only area for which a mandatory and binding referendum in all the states involved is established by the Constitution, it must be conceded that the Grundgesetz puts strong emphasis on the sovereignty of those states' citizens and thus also of the Länder themselves. A merger is not accomplished if a majority of the citizens in one Land does not support it.[11]

Local governments do not enjoy the same constitutional status as do the Länder and thus do not form a sphere of their own. Their legal rights and duties are, instead, left to the constitutions of the states. Nevertheless, the Grundgesetz provides the local jurisdictions with strong constitutional rights by obliging the Länder to give the local jurisdictions the right to regulate local community affairs autonomously, including the right of financial autonomy for the local jurisdictions.[12] The Grundgesetz thus establishes Germany as a federation with strong state and local jurisdictions. The robust role of the states and the local jurisdictions is also indicated by a strong administrative decentralization in Germany, whereby locally and regionally elected and responsible representatives as well as local and regional administrations enjoy substantial autonomy. As federal law has constitutional prerogative over state law, and the states' constitutions impose their superiority over any local regulations, this subfederal autonomy is restricted in some ways.[13] These restrictions are important for fiscal federalism.

Table 1
Basic political and geographic indicators

Official name: Bundesrepublik Deutschland (Federal Republic of Germany)	
Population (31.12.2005): 82,438,000	
Area (square kilometres): 357,050	
GDP per capita in US$ (2005): 35,075.34	
Constitution: 1949, written	
Orders of government: Representative democracy	
Constitutional status of local government: Strong	
Official language: German	
Number and types of constituent units: Three levels of government – federal (*bund*), states (*länder*) and local (*gemeinden*)	
Population, area, and per capita GDP in US$ of the largest constituent unit:	
Northrhine-Westphalia (2005) – population: 18,058,105, area: 34,083.52 sq. km., per capita GDP US$33,558.40	
Bremen (2005) – population: 663,000, area: 404.28 sq. km., per capita GDP US$46,161	

Sources: Federal Statistical Office and Statistical Offices of the States

After the creation of Baden-Württemberg by a merger of the Länder Baden, Württemberg-Baden, and Württemberg-Hohenzollern in 1952 and the entry of the Saarland in 1956, Germany consisted of ten states plus West Berlin. In 1991, the five East German Länder of the former German Democratic Republic (GDR) became additional members of the Federal Republic of Germany, thus increasing the number of states to fifteen, while East Berlin was merged with West Berlin to form the sixteenth state. The largest Land is North-Rhine-Westphalia, with a population of 18,058,105, an area of 34,083 square kilometres, and a per capita GDP of $33,558 in 2005. As Germany's per capita GDP is $35,075, North-Rhine-Westphalia is just below average. The smallest Land is Bremen, with, in 2005, a population of 663,000, an area of 404 square kilometres, and a per capita GDP of $46,161.[14] The number of jurisdictions declined considerably, however, first, in a merger wave in the early 1970s, which reduced the number of communities by 63 percent and, second, by unification, which reduced the number of East German communities by about 38 percent. With a larger population, Germany has fewer communities today than does France.

It should be noted that German federalism is historically quite different from the kinds of federalism observed in some older federations, such as Switzerland and the United States.[15] This is partly due to the fact that many existing states were newly created after the Second World War, notable exceptions being Bavaria, Saxony, and the city-states of Hamburg and Bremen. Stefan Oeter argues that another reason for the peculiarities of German federalism is found in the fact that Germany was created in the nineteenth century under Prussian hegemony.[16] Since then, German federalism has been regarded by the public as a mechanism to ensure the influence of regional princes and executives. This is particularly reflected in the nature of the second chamber of Parliament, which resembles the old Bundesrat of the second German Empire (1871–1918). While the old Bundesrat was an assembly of the representatives of the states' (monarchic) executives, the current Bundesrat, according to the Grundgesetz, consists of members of the states' (elected) executives or their representatives.[17] Moreover, since 1871 the basic rationale for Germany's federalism has been the division of functions rather than the performance of actual tasks. The Bismarckian construction was to regulate a number of policy fields jointly but to leave their implementation to the Länder. Legislation and execution were thus divided – a path that has been followed until today. The Grundgesetz lays down the basic principle that the Länder shall execute federal law as their own task.[18]

German politics are organized as a parliamentary democracy with (mainly) proportional representation in the federal and state spheres. Direct elections of mayors in municipalities are the only deviation from that principle. On the one hand, the strong emphasis on parliamentary democracy means that elements of direct democracy are practically non-existent in German political decision making. Only the merger of states provides an exception. At the state and local arenas, a tendency exists for expanding direct democratic decision making, but it is still too weak to exert an important influence on state and local policy making.[19] On the other hand, and more important, the parliamentary system provides the political parties with strong political influence. If representatives want to pursue their political careers, they depend on their parties to put them in secure places on the party lists. Those party lists are more important with regard to winning a seat in Parliament than is success in the constituencies. This leaves Germany with strong parties that can discipline the representatives in the parliaments. The political parties are, however, also deeply rooted in German federalism. They recruit political talents from the local party organizations in the Länder, and those who succeed in the Land sphere have a good chance of obtaining a political post in the federal government.[20] Moreover, party lists are decided within the Land sphere, not within the federal sphere. These recruitment mechanisms do not work only via the Länder. A talented local politician can make it directly to the federal government. Moreover, this holds not only for legislators but also for executives. Success as a state executive serves as a recommendation for the federal government. Since the Second World War, the organization of German politics along these lines has provided for a stable system of (mostly) coalition governments. But it also helps to highlight the bias that leads the main parties and representatives in parliaments and governments to lean more heavily towards a cooperative than a competitive model of federalism.

With respect to Germany's civil law system, it should be noted that judicial oversight by the Constitutional Court restricts representatives in Parliament and the German government and is thus the strongest element of the German separation of powers. As a result, Germany's legal system is also heavily influenced by constitutional and administrative law. The separation of powers is, however, less pronounced between the Parliament and the government (i.e., executive). As the Bundesrat is often controlled by a majority of parties that are in opposition to parties that control the Bundestag, sufficient checks and balances exist outside the judiciary. The judiciary provides for a protection of minorities, but the Constitutional Court also plays an important role in guarding and developing the main constitutional principles of German federalism and, thus, shapes the current state of the country's fiscal federalism.

THE DIVISION OF FISCAL POWERS

The fiscal powers of each sphere of government follow the constitutionally assigned competencies. The latter have prerogative over the fiscal constitution, which, in Germany, is a subsidiary of the basic rules of federalism. According to the Grundgesetz, the Länder have legislative power as long as the Grundgesetz does not assign a legislative competency to the federal government.[21] Such an assignment takes place explicitly in the form of exclusive federal competency according to the Grundgesetz.[22] It also takes place implicitly for the area of concurrent legislation, according to which the Länder only have legislative power if the federal government does not use its legislative power.[23] Put differently and more bluntly, the federal government can acquire legislative competencies under the heading of concurrent legislation whenever it passes a law in a concurrent area. However, the federal government only has jurisdiction in this area if and to the extent that the maintenance of equal living conditions requires it.[24] The Federalism Reform Act will facilitate the use of concurrent legislation by excluding several areas from the requirements of the Grundgesetz.[25] The Länder will instead obtain the right to deviate from federal law in several areas (e.g., environmental law, university access, and university degrees).

The Grundgesetz enumerates the exclusive responsibilities of the federal government.[26] It comprises, among others, the responsibilities for external affairs and defence, citizenship, free movement of persons, immigration and emigration, establishment of a common German market, air traffic, railways, mail and telecommunications, and cooperation between the federal government and the Länder. The Grundgesetz regulates concurrent legislation and enables the federal government to extend its jurisdiction to a much larger catalogue of responsibilities, from the unity of law in different areas to waste disposal, including such fiscally important areas as social welfare, health care, research policy, parts of environmental policy, and the payment and pensions of public employees.[27] In addition, the Grundgesetz establishes the federal right to pass so-called framing legislation, which establishes legislative guidelines in a certain area that must be filled out in detail by the Länder.[28] Prominent examples are the whole legal basis of public employment as well as university education. Framing legislation will be abolished by the Federalism Reform Act, which splits framing responsibilities between the Länder and the federal government. Fiscally most important in this respect, the Länder will have the exclusive responsibility for their civil servants, in particular their salaries and pensions.

Overall, the strong federal role as laid down in the Constitution and the strong emphasis on the equality of living conditions in Germany, together with a historically rooted skepticism about decentralized solutions, have led to Germany's cooperative model of (fiscal) federalism. The range of Land responsibilities is limited because the federal government has used concurrent legislation extensively and thus expanded its responsibilities across time. The federal government also has a strong influence on Land policies, and this is due not only to concurrent legislation but also to framing legislation. Only the latter will be changed by the Federalism Reform Act.

In addition, there are several areas of common financial responsibility. Four areas need to be distinguished. First, there are the common tasks of the federal government and the Länder according to the Grundgesetz (i.e., the construction of university buildings, including university hospitals; research promotion and educational planning; the improvement of regional economic structure for which the expenditure is split fifty-fifty between the states and the federal government; the improvement of agricultural structure, with federal spending at 60 percent; and the protection of the coastline, with federal spending at 70 percent).[29] The Federalism Reform Act abolishes the common tasks involved in the construction of university buildings and replaces the common task of educational planning with a reporting system whose purpose is to observe the performance of the education system within an international context.

Second, there are laws regulating monetary services such as social welfare and housing subsidies for the needy.[30] These laws may establish a financial obligation for the federal government (e.g., as in the case of housing subsidies), but they do not need to do so (e.g., as in the case of social welfare). In both cases, the federal government heavily influences or determines subfederal spending.

Third, there is financial aid that enables the federal government to subsidize state or local services when large investments are involved, macroeconomic stability is affected, or regional differences in economic performance need to be equalized.[31] The Federalism Reform Act introduces the requirement of consent by the Länder in the Bundesrat for federal law in this area and abolishes financial aid for housing construction and local transport. Moreover, financial aid is restricted for certain periods and may only be provided in diminishing amounts across time. Finally, the federal government will be forbidden to shift responsibilities to the local governments.

Fourth, the Länder execute federal tasks for which the federal government does not pay the administrative costs.[32] For example, it pays the direct cost of freeway construction but not the administrative cost in the respective ministries and bureaucratic entities. Finally, it should also be noted that wage bargaining in the public sector is centralized, leaving the Länder with only restricted room for changes pertaining to the salaries and the pensions of their public employees.

The institutions that secure the strong influence of the federal government have come at the price of strong participation by the Länder in national policy making. Across time, an increasing share of federal legislation has required the consent of the Bundesrat. When the interests of the Länder (or their local jurisdictions) are affected by federal legislation, in particular when federal legislation touches the Land administrative competencies, a law requires permission from the Länder in the Bundesrat.[33] Thus, when they act jointly, the Länder have a strong position as a counterbalance in the federal sphere. This institutional environment has led to a "spaghetti bowl" of internal political relations.[34] The federal government cannot decide much without the Länder, while the Länder have only narrow discretion to follow their own policies. Still, the ability of the federal government to pursue autonomous policies in several regulatory areas, and with respect to several spending programs, is higher than is the states' ability to conduct their own expenditure programs. The states' autonomy is restricted to a small number of areas, such as education, culture, law and order, and regional planning – all of which are framed by federal mandates and regulations.[35] Local jurisdictions execute communal services, such as sewerage, sports and recreation, school building, housing, and local road construction.[36] It should be noted, however, that in most areas of government activity, a high degree of vertical integration of functions persists. For example, in health care each sphere of government has a certain amount of responsibility. Even in the areas in which they have autonomy, the Länder have deliberately decided to accept a high level of coordination between each other. In particular, for education policies, the states' executives meet regularly to establish common standards. Otherwise, the states execute the laws decided on by the federal government. German federalism has thus become a typical executive federalism. The Federalism Reform Act will change this assessment somewhat, but less for the fiscally important areas than for regulatory areas.

While the spending side of the different jurisdictional spheres already appears to be heavily restricted, the revenue side is even more so. As is outlined in more detail below, neither the federal government nor the Länder can make any large change of their tax revenue without the agreement of the other side. According to the Grundgesetz, the federal government has exclusive jurisdiction over tariffs, indirect taxes (as long as they are not a common responsibility of federal and state governments or within the exclusive power of local jurisdictions), capital transaction taxes, insurance taxes, and surcharges on income taxes.[37] Since the European Union (EU) obtained the power to change tariffs from the member states in the 1970s, the most important tax sources that the federal government can change without the consent of the Länder are the mineral oil tax, the tobacco tax, the insurance tax, and the surcharges on income taxes. The autonomy of the Länder is even weaker. While the Grundgesetz gives them the exclusive right to obtain the revenues from the wealth tax (which has not been levied since 1996), the inheritance and gifts tax, the car tax, transaction taxes that are not in the power of the federal government or in the common responsibility, the beer tax, and the lottery taxes, the legislation of bases and rates of these tax sources is passed by the federal Parliament as a result of concurrent legislation.[38] The Federalism Reform Act will only assign tax-rate autonomy for the real estate purchase tax to the Länder. The most important taxes as measured by their revenue – namely, the personal and corporate income taxes as well as the value-added tax – are joint taxes, the revenue from which is shared between the federal government, the Länder, and, to a lesser extent, the local jurisdictions. As a result, the states' own-source revenues are far from matching their responsibilities and subsequent spending, and the Länder's tax performance is weak, while tax-base and tax-rate uniformity is ensured across the Länder. The only notable exception to a total tax harmonization in Germany is the local business tax, for which the individual communities and cities can autonomously decide the rates. In addition, the local jurisdictions have autonomy over local property (real estate) taxes, which are of much less importance in Germany, however, than they are, for example, in the United States and Canada.

The relations between the federal and the state governments in Germany are complemented by a very complicated and quantitatively important system of fiscal equalization. After a distribution of the revenue from joint taxes according to an explicit formula, a system of horizontal fiscal equalization sets in that also follows an explicit formula and provides unconditional grants to the Länder. It is strongly egalitarian and lifts the fiscal capacity of all below-average Länder to about 90 percent of the national average. After that, the federal government makes vertical transfers that lift fiscal capacity to 97.5 percent of the national average. Vertical transfers are, to a small degree, conditional. In fact, there are no credible restrictions on state borrowing by the federal government. Germany as a whole is restricted by the EU Stability and Growth Pact. In addition, the Grundgesetz restricts borrowing by the federal government to the Golden Rule amount of investment spending. Similar restrictions apply to Land borrowing but are not enforced by the federal government. In addition, there are several provisions to soften that borrowing restraint. Most notably, borrowing can exceed investment spending if the federal government declares a disturbance of macroeconomic equilibrium.[39]

Although local jurisdictions have a strong constitutional position, they are handmaidens of the Länder. The oversight competence of the Länder is executed in many ways. For example, the Länder control the restriction of local borrowing to their cash flow, although local jurisdictions have a wide range of borrowing possibilities. Moreover, the Länder regulate the provision of local services, although to different degrees, depending on the individual Land. For example, local jurisdictions in North-Rhine-Westphalia are less restricted by Land mandates than are those in Bavaria. Although the local jurisdictions have the power to set the tax rates of the local business tax, the local revenues from autonomous revenue sources do not match local responsibilities. Thus, a similar system of horizontal and vertical fiscal equalization exists and provides additional revenue to the local jurisdictions.

Table 2 summarizes de jure legislative responsibility and actual provision of services by the three different spheres of government. The EU is included in order to show which kinds of responsibilities have been fully adopted by that organization. The shared responsibilities in Germany's federalism that result from the distinction between legislation and execution become obvious (e.g., in health policies that are executed by all three spheres of government, with a predominant federal legislative responsibility). Other functions, like road construction, are split between all three spheres, with federal responsibility for federal roads. But these functions are executed by the Länder, with Land responsibility for Land roads and local responsibility for local roads. This area is even more complicated by the provision of subsidies that induce additional changes in decision-making power.

The shared responsibilities of the three spheres of government on the spending side are evident in Table 3 (calculated according to administrative tasks). Only a few functions are the exclusive responsibility of a particular government (e.g., defence, which is fully a federal responsibility), while local public services I and schools entail no federal responsibility. In the case of science and research, social security, and public enterprises, there is predominant but not exclusive federal responsibility. Similarly, in the case of schools, law and order, and universities, there is predominant but not exclusive Länder responsibility. There are also intermediate cases – for example

Table 2
Legislative responsibility and actual provision of services by different spheres of government

Legislative responsibility (de jure)	Public service	Executive responsibility
Federal/land/local		Federal/land/local
EU	Monetary policy	EU
EU	Customs	EU
Federal	Defence	Federal
Federal	Foreign affairs	Federal
Federal	Citizenship	Federal
Federal	Customs	Federal
Federal	Rail and air transport	Federal
Federal	Post and telecommunication	Federal
Federal	Social security	Federal/Land
Federal	Health including health insurance and local health facilities	Federal/Land/Local
Federal	Social assistance (supplementary welfare)	Federal/Land/Local
Federal	Waste disposal	Local
Federal/land joint task	Regional economic policy	Land
Federal/land joint task	Coastline preservation	Land
Federal/land joint task	Agricultural policy	Land
Federal/land joint task	Publicly funded research	Federal/Land
Federal/land	Environmental protection	Land
Federal/land	Water supply	Local
Federal/land	Sewerage	Local
Land	Law and order	Land
Land	Culture	Land
Land	Schools and education	Land
Land	Universities	Land
Local	Local roads	Local
Local	Sports and recreation	Local
Local	School construction	Local
Local	Public housing	Local

Source: Authors' collection on the basis of legal documents.

Table 3
Direct expenditures by function and sphere of government

Function	Federal (%)	Land (%)	Local (%)	All (%)
Defence	100	0	0	100
Debt servicing	77	19	4	100
General administration	19	29	52	100
Law and order	11	60	29	100
Schools	0	80	20	100
Universities	10	90	0	100
Other education	20	56	24	100
Science and research	72	26	2	100
Social security	65	13	22	100
Health, environment, sports, and recreation	7	40	53	100
Housing, urban development, regional planning	16	47	37	100
Local public services I[1]	0	4	96	100
Subsidies	39	51	10	100
Traffic and communication	44	26	30	100
Public enterprises	63	13	23	100
Total	47	37	17	100
Local public services II[2]	11	53	36	100

Source: Statistisches Bundesamt, Fachserie 14/Reihe 3.1, Finanzen und Steuern, 2002.
1. According to Federal Statistical Office definition, including street lights, sewerage, waste collection, and street cleaning.
2. According to the Forum of Federations definition, approximated as law and order, schools, other education, health environment, sports and recreation, housing, urban development and regional planning, and local public services I.

"other education," health, environment, sports and recreation, housing, urban development, and regional planning, as well as subsidies – for which the largest spending share is that of the Länder. However, to a large extent, either the federal government or local jurisdictions exercise their own responsibilities for these policy areas. It should be noted that local jurisdictions bear the largest share of administrative expenses and are predominantly responsible for local public services I (e.g., sewerage, waste collection, streetlights, and street cleaning). Overall, the federal government accounts for almost half of total government spending in Germany. The Länder spend a bit more than one-third, and the local jurisdictions spend only 17 percent. Local public services II indicate the extent to which the federal and state governments play a fiscal role in local affairs. Still, these figures do not fully capture the extent to which the federal government is able to exercise its influence on state and local policies. The share of 11 percent is certainly an underestimation of its actual influence. Similarly, the local jurisdictions are more heavily restricted by federal and state mandates than even these figures might indicate.

In sum, the division of fiscal powers in Germany establishes a peculiar unitary federal state. With the possibilities of the federal government being able to attract responsibilities and the Länder being compensated by decision-making power in the federal sphere, this system differs from the subsidiarity principle as it is commonly understood; rather, German federalism is governed by strong cooperation between the spheres, leading to a high degree of policy interrelationships and a strong degree of executive federalism. The parallels between the current organization of federalism and the historical form of federalism of Bismarckian times are remarkable.[40]

FISCAL FEDERALISM AND MACROECONOMIC MANAGEMENT

According to the federal stability and economic growth law of 1967, the federal government and the Länder should consider the requirements of macroeconomic equilibrium in their economic and fiscal policy measures so that price stability, high employment, external balance, and adequate economic growth are obtained. Thus, the Länder have macroeconomic responsibilities. Because the European Central Bank conducts monetary policy, the role of the federal government and the Länder is restricted to the other instruments of economic policy, particularly fiscal policy. Moreover, with respect to fiscal policy, the EU Stability and Growth Pact (SGP) aims at a restriction on borrowing by the EU member states. Basically, unless it results from an unusual event outside its control or from a severe economic downturn (defined as an annual fall of real GDP of at least 2 percent), the annual budget deficit of an EU member state is not allowed to exceed 3 percent of GDP. Moreover, member states' public debt should not exceed 60 percent of GDP.

Up to now, the deficit and debt requirements of the SGP have not been divided between the federal and the state governments as a binding agreement. This holds, a fortiori, with respect to an assignment of deficit restrictions between the Länder. However, according to the law regarding the principles of public budgeting,[41] the federal government and the Länder have to fulfill this obligation under the SGP. The Joint

Planning Council on Financial Matters (*Finanzplanungsrat*) has agreed that 55 percent of the allowed public debts may be used by the Länder and municipalities and that 45 percent may be used by the federal government.[42] As this agreement cannot be enforced by the federal government, with the result that the Länder need to be convinced in concrete cases to stick to the rules of the pact, the SGP may impose strong restrictions (and thus high political costs) mainly on the federal government.[43] The Federalism Reform Act will change this. Any sanctions resulting from an application of the SGP will be divided between the federal government at 65 percent and the Länder at 35 percent. The distribution between the Länder is made according to the deficit distribution (at 65 percent) and population (at 35 percent).

The lack of Land autonomy on the revenue side and the strong restrictions on the spending side, which require the Länder to provide a minimum quality of public services, have led the Länder to rely on transfers (as part of the fiscal equalization system) and to use borrowing as the instrument of choice to finance any spending residuals. Indeed, the federal government appears to follow similar strategies, although it can count less on transfers from the Länder. In 2005, the ratio of public debt to GDP in Germany was 67.9 percent. Since 1990, the level of public debt of all German governments together tripled.[44] The federal government bears the largest part of public debt, with 61 percent, followed by the Länder, with 31 percent. In 2005, the share of interest payments in total public spending by the federal government amounted to 14.5 percent, while this share was 8.5 percent for the state and local spheres.[45]

In some Länder, the burden of debt has become so high that they have sued the federal government for a bailout. Already in 1992, the Constitutional Court acknowledged the existence of a situation of extreme fiscal stress for the Saarland and Bremen. The court ruling required the federal government and the other Länder to provide for a bailout, which was provided by the federal government, from 1994 to 2004, in the form of vertical conditional grants mandated to reduce the public debt of these two Länder.[46] Public debt of most Länder (except Bavaria, Baden-Württemberg, and Saxony) has increased tremendously over time. An infamous example is Berlin, which sued the federal government in 2003. Before the Constitutional Court rules on the extant bailout cases, more Länder might well sue for bailouts. The official federal bailout induces the financial markets to let the Länder benefit from the high standing of the Federal Republic of Germany in the financial markets. Although those Länder rated by Standard and Poor's or Moody's may have a slightly lower rating than does the federal republic, it is still far from the one they would have received without a federal bailout. Fitch actually awards all Länder the triple A rating of the federal government.[47]

Some researchers convincingly argue that this bailout provides for soft budget constraints on the Länder.[48] With a soft budget constraint, the marginal benefits exceed the marginal costs of additional spending by the Länder, with the result that they can externalize part of the cost to taxpayers in the other states.[49] As a result, the citizens of a Land can obtain the regionally concentrated benefits of state spending but pay only their share from federal taxation. This provides incentives for excessive spending and deficits.[50] Moreover, by providing a bailout, the federal government induces the Länder's expectations that further bailouts will follow.[51] The Länder adjust their spending and borrowing to these expectations, with the result that it will be difficult to deny bailouts in the future. The 1992 Constitutional Court ruling, in particular, has nourished such expectations. It is thus no surprise that Berlin has followed the former two bailout Länder, Saarland and Bremen, in suing the federal government. In the coming years, other Länder in fiscal trouble will likely follow, particularly when an aging society affects pension liabilities (most Länder have not built notable pension funds).

REVENUE-RAISING RESPONSIBILITIES

As mentioned before, a first reason for the existence of excessive borrowing by the Länder is the lack of autonomy on the revenue side of their budgets. While the German division of fiscal powers requires the Länder to provide public services at a certain quality and level, it leaves some room for them to pursue their own policies. However, the Länder do not have autonomy in setting tax rates or tax bases individually. Their most important revenue sources, the personal and corporate income taxes as well as the value-added tax, are joint taxes and can only be influenced by the Länder collectively via the Bundesrat.[52] The revenue from other tax sources belongs exclusively to the Länder (e.g., inheritance and gift taxes as well as car taxes). Legislation setting the bases and rates for these taxes, however, is passed in the federal sphere, again with the influence of the Länder coming only via the Bundesrat. Thus, taxes in Germany are largely harmonized. Only the local jurisdictions have autonomy to set the rates of the local business and real estate taxes. Tax competition between subfederal jurisdictions may occur only with respect to these two tax sources. This legal situation is reflected in Table 4, in which the revenue shares from the different tax sources are computed on the basis of actual revenue received.

By far the largest share (66 percent) of federal tax revenue thus comes from shared taxes. Of the exclusive federal taxes, only the mineral oil tax and the tobacco tax generate notable revenue. The insurance tax is already less important. Because the federal government does not rely heavily on fees or on grants from other spheres of government, its ability to raise

Table 4
Tax assignment for various orders of government

	Determination of		Tax collection and administration	Shares in Revenue (%)			
	Base	Rate		Federal	Land	Local	All orders
Federal							
Mineral oil tax	Federal	Federal	Federal	100	0	0	100
Tobacco tax	Federal	Federal	Federal	100	0	0	100
Spirits tax	Federal	Federal	Federal	100	0	0	100
Sparkling wine tax	Federal	Federal	Federal	100	0	0	100
Intermediate good tax	Federal	Federal	Federal	100	0	0	100
Coffee tax	Federal	Federal	Federal	100	0	0	100
Insurance tax	Federal	Federal	Land	100	0	0	100
Electricity tax	Federal	Federal	Land	100	0	0	100
Solidarity levy	Federal	Federal	Land	100	0	0	100
State or provincial							
Property (wealth) tax	Joint Federal/land	Joint Federal/land	Land	0	100	0	100
Inheritance tax	Joint Federal/land	Joint Federal/land	Land	0	100	0	100
Real estate purchase tax	Joint Federal/land	Joint Federal/land	Land	0	100	0	100

Table 4
Tax assignment for various orders of government (*Continued*)

	Determination of		Tax collection and administration	Shares in Revenue (%)			
	Base	Rate		Federal	Land	Local	All orders
Motor vehicle tax	Joint Federal/land	Joint Federal/land	Land	0	100	0	100
Betting and lottery tax	Joint Federal/land	Joint Federal/land	Land	0	100	0	100
Fire protection tax	Joint Federal/land	Joint Federal/land	Land	0	100	0	100
Beer tax	Joint Federal/land	Joint Federal/land	Land	0	100	0	100
Local							
Business tax	Joint Federal/land	Local	Land/Local	4.4	15.4	80.2	100
Real estate taxes	Joint Federal/land	Local	Land/Local	0	0	100	100
Shared taxes							
Personal income tax	Joint Federal/land	Joint Federal/land	Land	42.50	42.50	15	100
Interest rebate	Joint Federal/land	Joint Federal/land	Land	44	44	12	100
Corporate income tax	Joint Federal/land	Joint Federal/land	Land	50	50	0	100
VAT	Joint Federal/land	Joint Federal/land	Land	49.50	48.40	2.10	100

Source: Own collection on the basis of legal documents

revenue largely depends on the Länder. In their case, 85.4 percent of their total tax revenue and 64.2 percent of their total revenue are collected from shared taxes. Given that the Länder cannot set the tax rates and bases of exclusively Land taxes and because they do not collect notable fee revenue, they depend on grants and borrowing. This is different from the local governments for which the revenue from the local business tax amounts to 77.9 percent of total tax revenue and 29.3 percent of total local revenue, while the revenue from real estate taxes is 17.4 percent of total tax revenue and 6.5 percent of total local revenue. The local jurisdictions actually use their tax autonomy. The tax-rate surcharges on the local business taxes vary between 200 (legal minimum tax surcharge) and 490 (Munich and Frankfurt), which implies tax rates between 10 percent and (roughly) 25 percent with a uniform tax measure of 5 percent.[53]

Only with respect to the local business tax does tax competition emerge in Germany. There is evidence that local jurisdictions engage in tax-mimicking behaviour, with the result that a reduction of tax rates in one jurisdiction triggers a reduction of tax rates in the other jurisdictions.[54] This evidence might indicate strategic tax setting by the jurisdictions competing with each other. Büttner reports empirical results showing that this kind of tax competition among Germany's local jurisdictions leads to tax-base effects and fiscal externalities. However, Baretti et al. show that the rates of the local business tax increased between 1980 and 1990, thus somewhat contradicting the notion of tax competition and pointing, instead, to a race to the top of local business tax rates.[55]

INTERGOVERNMENTAL FISCAL TRANSFERS

The fiscal equalization system consists of four steps.[56] First, with the exception of revenue from the VAT, tax revenue from the different tax sources in Table 4 is assigned to the Länder. This is particularly important for the personal and corporate income taxes, the revenue of which is distributed according to the residence principle. VAT revenue is allocated per capita. Second, up to 25 percent of the revenue of the VAT is used to increase the fiscal position of the poorer states.

The third step is the horizontal fiscal equalization between the Länder. The Länder with a measure of fiscal capacity below the measure of equalization receive grants from those Länder with a measure of fiscal capacity above the measure of equalization. The measure of fiscal capacity is the sum of all tax revenue minus 12 percent of the more than proportional increase (compared with the average of the Länder) of a Land's tax revenue in the previous year plus 64 percent of local tax revenue in a particular Land. The measure of equalization is derived by calculating the average Land and local tax revenue of the Länder for the whole federation for a single Land using the number of inhabitants. Fiscal capacity of the below-average Länder is thus lifted up to 90 percent of the national average. The redistribution takes place according to a progressive formulary schedule that raises the marginal subsidies to the recipients (and reduces revenue of the donors) from 44 percent to 75 percent. This means that, from an additional euro of tax revenue that a donor Land earns due to, for example, the location of new industry, it must give up seventy-five cents to the recipients. This schedule is associated with the typical adverse incentives on the efforts of the Länder to attract taxpayers.[57] Although the progressivity of the schedule was reduced in the latest reform (in effect since 2005), it is great enough that the incentive problems are still present. To what extent these adverse incentive effects occur empirically is, however, contested between scholars. There is, for example, no conclusive empirical evidence on the efficiency of donor and recipient Länder.

The fourth step in the fiscal equalization system is a vertical grants system. It is asymmetric because only some states receive funds from the federal government. General vertical grants are provided to all financially weak Länder in order to further lift fiscal capacity. Specific vertical grants are provided to the new Länder (to reduce specific burdens due to the separation of the two German states before unification and to deal with high structural unemployment) as well as to ten financially weak and small states to deal with more than proportional costs of political administration ("costs of smallness of a Land").[58] While the grants from the horizontal system are unconditional, the vertical grants introduce conditional grants, at least for some types. For example, the specific vertical grants to the new Länder for a reduction of specific burdens due to the separation of the two German states before unification must be spent for infrastructure and for an increase in local fiscal capacity. This final step in the system leads to an equalization of up to 97.5 percent of average fiscal capacity, thus yielding a strongly egalitarian system of fiscal equalization.

On average, however, the federal transfers to the Länder are not of overwhelming quantitative importance. Only 13.3 percent of total Land expenditures are covered by federal transfers, with a larger weight on capital transfers.[59] As Table 5 shows, the system closes the fiscal gaps between local jurisdictions in particular, but it also eases the cost of social security by mainly burdening the federal government. This look at the vertical fiscal gaps will not, however, suffice to detect the detrimental effects of the fiscal equalization system. One reason why economists strongly criticize this system concerns the negative incentive effects that a progressive redistribution schedule exerts on horizontal fiscal equalization. The implied marginal contribution rates to the fiscal equalization system varied between 60 percent and 100 percent until 2004 and, thereafter, have been reduced only somewhat.[60] However, the most important perverse incentive effect is that fiscal equalization leads to higher borrowing and spending by the Länder. In other words, the system puts a premium on fiscal imprudence.[61]

Table 5
Vertical fiscal gaps

	Total revenue collected (2002) Mill. $US	Total revenue available, including net transfers for that level of government (2002) Mill. $US	Expenditures (2002) Mill. $US
National	346,338	234,867	265,733
Subnational			
Land	227,979	215,967	243,571
Local	96,430	138,257	141,723
Social security	*354,669*	*433,132*	*440,155*
Special purpose associations[1]	*1,872*	*5,063*	*4,989*
All levels	1,027,288	1,027,288	1,096,171

Source: Statistisches Bundesamt, Fachserie 14/Reihe 3.1
1. Finanzen und Steuern, 2002 (specific data provided to the authors).

The advantage of the fiscal equalization system is not only found in the fact that vertical fiscal imbalances are partly closed. Indeed, the East German Länder have relatively low tax-raising powers. The system also provides risk sharing for state budgets, although to what extent risk sharing occurs is contested.[62] There is evidence that fiscal equalization insures state budgets against revenue shocks but not against shocks to regional GDP. In contrast, other reports show a relatively large income-smoothing effect for fiscal equalization. Finally, some estimates indicate that the German fiscal equalization system reduced the cross-sectional variance of income in the West German Länder during the 1970s, 1980s, and 1990s by about 6.8 percent (for an insurance effect that is about the same as that in the United States). Thus, fiscal equalization in Germany appears to smooth income shocks among Länder significantly.

Grants are even more important for the German local governments than they are for the Länder. Including revenue sharing, the local jurisdictions obtain almost 50 percent of their total revenue as grants from other jurisdictions.[63] There are, however, no direct transfer payments from the federal to the local governments. While unconditional grants are larger than are conditional grants to the local governments, the latter are more important at the local than they are at the state level. The Länder run their own fiscal equalization systems, which encompass all local jurisdictions. The incentive effects of the local grants system in Germany have only recently been systematically analyzed. For 1,102 local jurisdictions in Baden-Württemberg, grants have a significant, quantitatively important effect on local spending, but they have only a small effect on borrowing.[64] However, the soft budget constraint problem is more severe for medium-size and large cities than it is for small municipalities. Given that Land oversight of local borrowing is relatively strong, these results are not really surprising. It is more surprising that oversight appears to be less effective in the case of larger cities.

THE WAY FORWARD

German fiscal federalism is characterized by autonomy on the spending side of the budget, which is considerably shaped by mandates from the higher levels of government. The system is burdened by an asymmetry due to the fact that tax autonomy for all spheres of government is even more restricted than is spending autonomy. Neither the federal government nor the Länder can autonomously decide on the tax rates and bases of the most important tax sources. They are forced to decide jointly in the Bundesrat. Only the local jurisdictions have autonomy in setting the local business taxes and real estate tax rates. This institutional framework of cooperative federalism has led to a "spaghetti bowl" of political interrelationships and a strong executive, or administrative, federalism.[65] German fiscal federalism does not, therefore, correspond much with the ideas presented in Oates's decentralization theorem or in his laboratory federalism.[66] The induced soft budget constraint problems associated with the fiscal troubles of some Länder are a logical consequence of the incentives provided by that system. A further bailout will exacerbate the disequilibrium currently governing German fiscal federalism.

There are several possible ways to cope with these problems. Denying a further bailout will lead to a higher variance in how financial markets assess the creditworthiness of the Länder and local jurisdictions. Even timid steps in this direction appear to be politically unfeasible. The only short-term solution will be to impose stronger restrictions on the autonomy of the Länder receiving bailouts. A further reduction in the fiscal autonomy of states will, however, contradict the introduction of tax autonomy as a long-term solution to the disequilibrium in German fiscal federalism. Despite the fact that even a considerable extent of fiscal competition works relatively well in other federations (e.g., Switzerland), a higher tax autonomy for the German Länder is extremely unpopular among Länder officials because they apparently fear pressure from tax competition.[67] The provision of tax autonomy is complicated by the fact that it requires a preceding disentanglement of competencies between the federal government and the Länder. This is because the fiscal constitution is subordinate to the assignment of competencies. However, a disentanglement of competencies will only succeed if it is followed by a reform of fiscal federalism. The recent Federalism Reform Act is a first step in the right direction, but it must trigger the second step – a reform of the fiscal constitution.

NOTES

1. S. Oeter, *Integration und Subsidiarität im deutschen Bundesstaatsrecht* (Tübingen: Mohr Siebeck, 1998).
2. F.W. Scharpf, B. Reissert, and F. Schnabel, *Politikverflechtung: Theorie und Empirie des kooperativen Föderalismus in der Bundesrepublik* (Kronberg/Ts: Scriptor, 1976).
3. See www.bundesrat.de, keyword *Föderalismusreform*.
4. O.E. Geske, "Der Föderalismus in der Bundesrepublik", mimeo, Bonn, 2006.
5. BMF, "Die Föderalismusreform", *Monatsbericht des BMF* (August 2006): 81–90.
6. The scientific service of the Bundestag calculated that, if this reform of federalism had taken place in 1998, the share of these laws would have declined from 55.2 percent to 25.8 percent in the 14th period of legislature and from 51 percent to 24 percent in the 15th period of legislature.
7. Sachverständigenrat zur Begutachtung der gesamtwirtschaftlichen Entwicklung, *Widerstreitende Interessen – ungenutzte Chancen, Jahresgutachten 2006/2007*, Wiesbaden, BT-Drurucksache 16/3450, 506.
8. The EU-15 are Austria, Belgium, Denmark, Finland, France, Germany, Greece, Ireland, Italy, Luxembourg, the Netherlands, Portugal, Spain, Sweden, and the United Kingdom. See Sachverständigenrat zur Begutachtung der gesamtwirtschaftlichen Entwicklung, *Die Chancen nutzen – Reformen mutig voranbringen, Jahresgutachten 2005/2006*, Wiesbaden, CD-ROM version.
9. Grundgesetz, art. 20, Abs. 1.
10. S. Oeter, *Integration und Subsidiarität im deutschen Bundesstaatsrecht* (Tübingen: Mohr Siebeck, 1998). See Grundgesetz, art. 29.
11. Grundgesetz, art. 29, abs. 3.
12. Ibid., art. 28, abs. 2.
13. Ibid., art. 31.
14. See the Federal Statistical Office and the Statistical Offices of the Länder.
15. Oeter, *Integration und Subsidiarität*, 378.
16. Ibid., *Integration und Subsidiarität*.
17. Grundgesetz, art. 51, abs. 1.
18. Ibid., art. 83.
19. A. Kost, ed., *Direkte Demokratie in den deutschen Ländern: Eine Einführung* (Wiesbaden: V.S. Verlag für Sozialwissenschaften, 2005).
20. M. Filippov, P.C. Ordeshook, and O. Shvetsova, *Designing Federalism: A Theory of Self-Sustainable Federal Institutions* (Cambridge: Cambridge University Press, 2004).
21. Grundgesetz, art. 70, abs. 1.
22. Ibid., art. 71.
23. Ibid., art. 72, abs. 1.
24. Ibid., art. 72, abs. 2.
25. Ibid., art. 72, abs. 2.
26. Ibid., art. 73.
27. Ibid., arts 74 and 74a.
28. Ibid., art. 75.

29 Ibid., art. 91a.
30 Ibid., art. 104a, abs. 3.
31 Ibid., art. 104a, abs. 4.
32 Ibid., arts 85 and 104a, abs. 2.
33 P.B. Spahn, "Intergovernmental Transfers in Switzerland and Germany," in *Financing Decentralized Expenditures: An International Comparison of Grants*, ed. E. Ahmand, 103–43 (Cheltenham: Edward Elgar, 1997); and P.B. Spahn and W. Föttinger, "Germany," *Fiscal Federalism in Theory and Practice*, ed. T. Ter-Minassian, 226–48 (Washington, DC: International Monetary Fund, 1997). See also Grundgesetz, art. 84, abs. 1.
34 F.W. Scharpf, B. Reissert, and F. Schnabel, *Politikverflechtung: Theorie und Empirie des kooperativen Föderalismus in der Bundesrepublik* (Kronberg/Ts: Scriptor, 1976).
35 C.B. Blankart, *Öffentliche Finanzen in der Demokratie* 6th ed. (München: Vahlen, 2006).
36 Spahn, "Intergovernmental Transfers."
37 Grundgesetz, arts 105 and 106.
38 Ibid., art. 106.
39 Ibid., art. 115.
40 Oeter, *Integration und Subsidiarität*.
41 *Haushaltsgrundsätzegesetz* 51a, the law on the principles of public budgeting.
42 Decision of 21 March 2002.
43 Wissenschaftlicher Beirat beim Bundesministerium der Finanzen, *Zur Bedeutung der Maastricht-Kriterien für die Verschuldungsgrenzen von Bund und Ländern* (Bonn: Stollfuß-Verlag, 1994).
44 Sachverständigenrat zur Begutachtung der gesamtwirtschaftlichen Entwicklung, *Die Chancen nutzen – Reformen mutig voranbringen, Jahresgutachten 2005/2006*, Wiesbaden, CD-ROM version.
45 Wissenschaftlicher Beirat beim Bundesministerium der Finanzen, *Haushaltskrisen im Bundesstaat* (Bonn: Stollfuß-Verlag, 2005).
46 H. Seitz, "Subnational Government Bailouts in Germany," ZEI Working Paper B20, Bonn, 1999; and J. Rodden, "And the Last Shall Be First: Federalism and Fiscal Outcomes in Germany," mimeo, Department of Political Science, MIT, Cambridge, 2005.
47 Wissenschaftlicher Beirat beim Bundesministerium für Wirtschaft und Arbeit, *Zur finanziellen Stabilität des deutschen Föderalstaates* (Berlin, Bundesministerium für Wirtschaft und Arbeit, 2005).
48 Seitz, "Subnational Government Bailouts"; and Rodden, *And the Last Shall Be First*.
49 D.E. Wildasin, *Externalities and Bailouts: Hard and Soft Budget Constraints in Intergovernmental Fiscal Relations*, unpublished, 1997; and T.J. Goodspeed, "Bailouts in a Federation," *International Tax and Public Finance* 9 (2002): 409–21.
50 J. von Hagen and M. Dahlberg, "Swedish Local Government: Is There a Bailout Problem?" mimeo, University of Bonn, 2002.
51 P. Petersson-Lidbom and M. Dahlberg, "An Empirical Approach for Estimating the Causal Effect of Soft Budget Constraints on Economic Outcomes," mimeo, University of Stockholm and University of Uppsala, 2005.

52 Up until now, tax increases have, however, been initiated by the Bundestag, which had to look for a majority in the Bundesrat.
53 For the exact calculation of the local business tax, see T. Büttner, "Determinants of Tax Rates in Local Capital Income Taxation: A Theoretical Model and Evidence from Germany," *Finanzarchiv N.F.* 57 (2000): 1–26; and T. Büttner, "Local Business Taxation and Competition for Capital: The Choice of the Tax Rate," *Regional Science and Urban Economics* 31 (2001): 215–45.
54 Büttner, "Determinants of Tax Rates"; and Büttner, "Local Business Taxation."
55 T. Büttner, "Tax Base Effects and Fiscal Externalities of Local Capital Taxation: Evidence from a Panel of German Jurisdictions," *Journal of Urban Economics* 54 (2003): 110–28; and C.R. Baretti, R. Fenge, B. Huber, W. Leibfritz, and M. Steinherr, *Chancen und Grenzen föderalen Wettbewerbs* (München: ifo Beiträge zur Wirtschaftsforschung 1, 2000).
56 Spahn, "Intergovernmental Transfers"; and L.P. Feld, *Le degré de décentralisation fiscale en Allemagne: Dépenses, impôts, pression fiscale, dettes*, Report for the Institut de Recherche Européenne en Economie et Fiscalité (IREF) at the University Aix-Marseille, 2003.
57 C. Baretti, B. Huber, and K. Lichtblau, "A Tax on Tax Revenue: The Incentive Effects of Equalizing Transfers: Evidence from Germany," *International Tax and Public Finance* 9 (2002): 631–49.
58 H. Seitz, "Agglomeration und Bevölkerungsdichte – Dünn besiedelte Flächenländer im Finanzausgleich", in *Sonderbedarfe im bundesstaatlichen Finanzausgleich*, ed. M. Junkernheinrich, 136–67 (Berlin: Duncker and Humblot, 2005).
59 Statistisches Bundesamt, Fachserie 14/Reihe 3.1 Finanzen und Steuern, 2004.
60 C. Baretti, B. Huber, and K. Lichtblau, "A Tax on Tax Revenue: The Incentive Effects of Equalizing Transfers: Evidence from Germany," *International Tax and Public Finance* 9 (2002): 631–49; and T. Büttner, "Fiscal Federalism and Interstate Risk-Sharing: Empirical Evidence from Germany," *Economics Letters* 74 (2002): 195–202.
61 For empirical evidence, see Seitz, "Subnational Government Bailouts"; von Hagen et al. "Sub-national Government Bailouts"; J. Rodden, "Breaking the Golden Rule: Fiscal Behavior with Rational Bailout Expectations in the German States," mimeo, Department of Political Science, MIT, Cambridge, 2000; and Rodden, "And the Last Shall Be First."
62 Jürgen von Hagen and Ralf Hepp, "Regional Risk-Sharing and Redistribution in the German Federation," ZEI Working Paper B-15, Bonn, 2000; Kersten Kellermann, "Interregionales Risk Sharing zwischen den deutschen Bundesländern," *Konjunkturpolitik* 47 (2001): 271–91; and Thiess Büttner, "Tax Base Effects and Fiscal Externalities of Local Capital Taxation: Evidence from a Panel of German Jurisdictions," *Journal of Urban Economics* 54 (2003): 110–28.
63 Statistisches Bundesamt, Fachserie 14 / Reihe 3.1 Finanzen und Steuern, 2002.
64 Thiess Büttner and David Wildasin, "The Dynamics of Municipal Fiscal Adjustment," *Journal of Public Economics* 90 (2006): 1105–32.
65 F.W. Scharpf, B. Reissert, and F. Schnabel, *Politikverflechtung: Theorie und Empirie des kooperativen Föderalismus in der Bundesrepublik* (Kronberg/Ts: Scriptor, 1976).

66 W.E. Oates, *Fiscal Federalism* (New York: Harcourt/Brace/Jovanowich, 1972); and W.E. Oates, "An Essay on Fiscal Federalism," *Journal of Economic Literature* 37 (1999): 1120–49.

67 L.P. Feld, *Steuerwettbewerb und seine Auswirkungen auf Allokation und Distribution: Ein Überblick und eine empirische Analyse für die Schweiz* (Tübingen: Mohr Siebeck, 2000); L.P. Feld, "Tax Competition and Income Redistribution: An Empirical Analysis for Switzerland," *Public Choice* 105 (2000): 125–64; L.P. Feld and G. Kirchgässner, "Income Tax Competition at the State and Local Level in Switzerland," *Regional Science and Urban Economics* 31 (2001): 181–213; and L.P. Feld and G. Kirchgässner, "The Impact of Corporate and Personal Income Taxes on the Location of Firms and on Employment: Some Panel Evidence for the Swiss Cantons," *Journal of Public Economics* 87 (2002): 129–55.

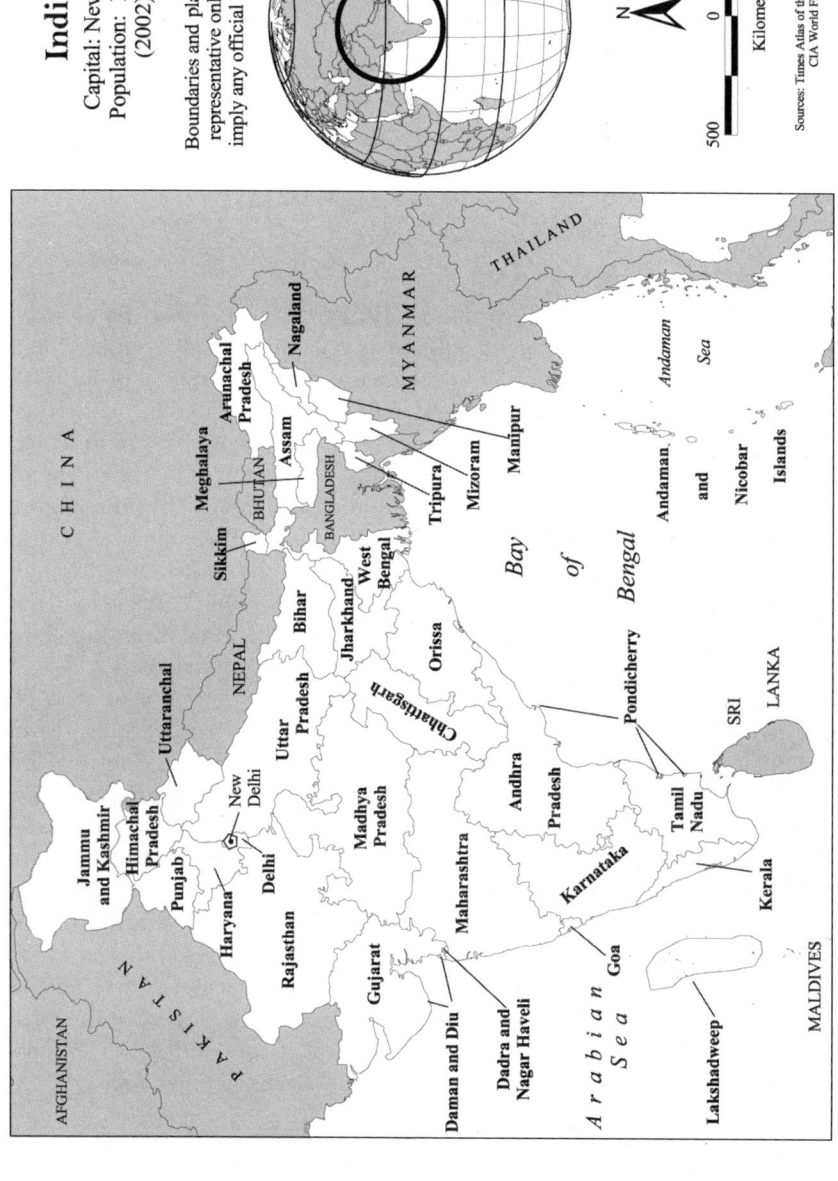

Republic of India

M. GOVINDA RAO

This chapter deals with the evolution and working of Indian fiscal federalism.[1] Many observers characterize India as a "quasi federal" country due to its heavy centripetal bias.[2] The political environment at the time of Independence and the adoption of a public-sector strategy dominated by planned development led to the creation of a multilevel fiscal system with a high degree of centralization. The adoption of market-oriented reforms in 1991 brought out the contradictions between the functioning of markets and the centralized fiscal system. It also underlined the difficulties of subnational governments financing the basic social services and physical infrastructure assigned to them. The growing inequalities in the provision of public services in a market-based environment, leading to sharply widening regional disparities, have also necessitated reforms in intergovernmental transfer systems.

Indian fiscal federalism faces formidable challenges due to economic liberalization and globalization. Creating a competitive environment by providing efficient infrastructure is a major challenge, especially in light of the severe fiscal stress faced by the states. The problem is particularly severe for poorer states. Finding appropriate substitutes for declining customs revenue, reforming the tax systems to enhance revenue productivity while minimizing distortions, and ensuring a common market in the country are important challenges. Designing the transfer system to arrest sharply increasing inequalities in service standards also needs to be addressed sooner rather than later. The emergence of coalition governments at the centre and regional parties in the states, the latter becoming pivotal members of the coalition, and the declining time horizon of political parties and politicians also present serious issues for the functioning of Indian fiscal federalism.

EVOLUTION OF INDIAN FEDERALISM

The Constitution describes India as a "Union of States" and a "Sovereign, Secular, Socialist, Democratic Republic" established to secure justice, liberty, and equality. It is the largest democratic federal republic, inhabited by more than a billion people over an area of 3.29 million square kilometres. Although India attained Independence in 1947, the Constitution was adopted in 1950. The country evolved as a two-tier federation during the first forty years of Independence. In 1992, with Amendments 73 and 74 to the Constitution, the third tier of government – urban and rural local bodies – was given constitutional status.

India is a developing country that, in 2003, had an average per capita income of US$2,890 in purchasing power parity. It ranks 127 among the 177 countries listed in the *Human Development Report 2005* and is nine places lower in per capita GDP (PPP) rank. However, since 1991–92, with economic liberalization, the economy has been growing at 5.5 percent as compared with the 3.5 percent seen in the previous three decades. During 2003–06, India's economy has registered a growth rate of about 8 percent.

An important feature of the Indian economy is its marked diversity. Peoples of several races and religions and speaking 114 languages, eighteen of which are included in the schedule, coexist peacefully with a strong bond of history and culture. Hindi is the official language, but as people in large parts of southern and eastern India do not speak this language, English continues to be a major language. State legislatures may adopt additional languages for official business. The country is predominantly rural, according to the 2001 census, 72 percent of the population live in rural areas.

The country has a three-tier federal structure with governments at the central, regional, and local levels. At the regional level there are twenty-eight states and seven centrally administered territories – two of which have legislatures. Below the state governments, in urban areas there are 96 municipal corporations, 1,494 municipalities, and 2,092 smaller municipalities (called *Nagar Panchayats*). There are 247,033 rural local bodies, of which 515 are at the district level, 5,930 at the block level, and 240,588 at the village level.

There are wide variations in size and economic structure among the states. In 2002, Uttar Pradesh, at 172 million population, was the largest state, and Sikkim, with 0.6 million, was the smallest. The average per capita gross state domestic product (GSDP) for 1999–2002, at Rs 56,599, was the highest in Goa, a small state on the western coast. It was lowest in Bihar, at Rs 6,531, the second largest state in the Gangetic plains in northern India. Due to their small size, low economic base, and strategic location, the eleven small, mountainous states are categorized as "special-category states."

India is a parliamentary democracy with a bicameral legislature. The Seventh Schedule to the Constitution divides legislative, executive, and judicial functions in terms of Union,[3] state, and concurrent lists. The members of Parliament at the centre and the legislatures in the states are directly elected. The upper house of the Parliament – *Rajya Sabha* – is the Council of States, and the members are elected through the electoral

Table 1
Geographical and demographic information

	Variable	Value
1	Official name	India
2	Population (2004–05)-millions	1090
3	Area 1000 sq. km	3287
4	GDP per capita (US$) 2003	2892 (PPP) / Rs. 23222 (NNP) or US$540 Rs. 28636 (GDP) or US$666 (Exchange rate 1 US$ = Rs.43)
5	Constitution: Year and form	1950, Parliamentary democracy, republic
6	Orders of government	Union; State; Local: Urban – municipal Local: Rural – Panchayats (at district, block, and village levels)
7	Constitutional status of local government	Independent, constitutional, recognized local governments after the 73rd and 74th amendment in 1992
8	Official languages	National languages: Hindi and English Official regional languages: 18
9	Number and types of constituent units	28 States; 3682 urban local governments 247,033 rural local governments, of which 515 are at district level, 5,930 at block level, and 240,588 at village level.
10	Population, area, and per capita GDP in US$ of largest unit	Uttar Pradesh Population: 166 million 241,000 sq. km. 10,817 rupees or US$252 Exchange rate: US$1 = Rs. 45.
11	Population, area, and per capita GDP of smallest unit	Sikkim Population: 54,0000 7,000 sq. km. 21,586 rupees or US$502
12	Per capita GSDP (highest)	Goa 55,000 rupees or US$1,279
13	Per capita GSDP (lowest)	Bihar 5780 rupees or US$134

college from each of the states. The Constitution also requires the president of India to appoint a finance commission every five years to review the finances of the centre and the states and to recommend devolution of divisible central taxes and grants to be given to the states for the ensuing five years.

Historical factors have played an important role in the adoption of a centralized federal Constitution in India. There was considerable demand for decentralization at the time of Independence. However, the country needed to hold together in the wake of Muslim majority areas' breaking away to form a new country (Pakistan), and the fissiparous tendency on the part of a number of small principalities contributed to the adoption of a highly centralized and yet federal Constitution. The centralization inherent in the constitutional assignments was strengthened with the adoption of a planned development strategy.

Recent economic and political events, however, have paved the way for a greater degree of decentralization. In the economic sphere, market-based reforms and the more open economic environment have necessitated a greater degree of fiscal decentralization. On the political front, factors such as the end of one-party rule, the emergence of coalition governments at the centre, and the increasing importance of regional parties in the political affairs of the country have resulted in greater decentralization. Furthermore, the amendment of the Constitution in 1992 to give constitutional status to local bodies below the state level has furthered the process.

The first twenty-five years after Independence, the Congress Party, which was at the forefront of the Independence movement, dominated the political architecture of both central and state governments. Leaders of undisputed stature and their commitment to the development and concerns of the people created a dominant one-party rule at both levels. Although this had several positive features, an important consequence was that formal systems of bargaining and conflict resolution did not develop to the desired extent.

The political architecture of the country has undergone four important changes, with significant implications for fiscal federalism. The first is the replacement of the dominance of one-party rule with coalition governments at the centre and in some states. Second, the emergence of regional parties in power in many of the states has led to the focus on a state-centric policy agenda and greater interstate frictions. Third, even as the regional parties dominate the political landscape in some states, their strategic alliance as pivotal members of the coalition at the centre has led to asymmetric arrangements in the functioning of fiscal federalism. Finally, the declining time horizon of political parties and politicians has led to the adoption of populist policies for short-term political gains – "competitive populism" – to the detriment of the medium- and longer-term developmental agenda.

THE STRUCTURE OF GOVERNMENT AND THE DIVISION OF FISCAL POWERS

The Seventh Schedule to the Constitution specifies the legislative, executive, and fiscal domains of the Union and state governments in terms of Union, state, and concurrent lists. There are 97 items in the Union list, 67 items under the state list, and 47 items under the concurrent list. The residual powers are assigned to the centre. The assignment of tax powers follows the principle of separation: they are assigned either to the Union or to the state governments.

In 1992, after the seventy-third and seventy-fourth constitutional amendments, separate schedules (eleventh and twelfth) were created, with twenty-nine items for rural and eighteen items for urban local bodies. The state legislatures are required to devolve functions listed in the schedules to rural and urban local bodies at their discretion. Each of the state governments has devolved powers to levy certain taxes and fees to the local bodies. The states have also instituted a system of sharing their revenues and giving grants to urban and rural local bodies. In addition, a number of central schemes are implemented by the local bodies, and the funds earmarked for this purpose are passed on to them either directly or through the state governments.

The functions required for maintaining macroeconomic stability, international relations, and activities having significant scale economies and, with spillovers, spanning multiple states are assigned exclusively to the centre. Thus, the Union list includes defence, external relations, international trade and commerce, national highways, post and telecommunications, broadcasting, railways and air travel, space, atomic energy, interstate matters, and external borrowing. The functions assigned to the state governments include maintenance of law and order, agriculture, animal husbandry, fisheries, irrigation, urban development, health, water supply and sanitation, intrastate trade, and local self-government. The concurrent subjects include education, health care, the environment (including forestry), electricity, economic and social planning, and all residual matters not included in either the Union or the state lists.

In terms of expenditure implementation, the central government defrays spending on defence; provision and regulation of large infrastructure such as railways, postal service, and telecommunications; and space and atomic energy research. The states have a high share of expenditures on internal security; social and economic services, such as agriculture, animal husbandry, forestry, fisheries, irrigation, and power; and public works. The states' share in expenditure on administrative services is about 68 percent; on social services, 83 percent; and on economic services, about two-thirds. Their role in providing education, public health, and family welfare is close to 90 percent.

Table 2
Indicative legislative responsibility and actual provision of services by different orders of government

Legislative responsibility (de jure)	Public service	Actual allocation of function (de facto)
Union	International trade and commerce	Union
Union	Major minerals	Union
Union	Banking, insurance, and currency	Union
Union	Railways	Union
Union	Postal service	Union
Union	Census	Union
Union	Defence and foreign affairs	Union
Union	Shipping and offshore exploration	Union
Union	Airways	Union
Union		Union
Union	Patents, copyrights	Union
Union	Citizenship	Union
Union	Interstate trade and commerce	Union
Union	Interstate rivers	Union
Union	Banking	Union
Union	Emigration	Union
Union and states	Criminal law and procedures	Union and states
Union and states	Civil procedure	Union and states
Union and states	Marriage and divorce	Union and states
Union and states	Bankruptcy and insolvency	Union and states
Union and states	Education	Union and states
Union and states	Healthcare	Union and states
Union and states	Contracts	Union and states
Union and states	Environment and forests	Union and states
Union and states	Economic and social planning	Union and states

Table 2
Indicative legislative responsibility and actual provision of services by different orders of government (*Continued*)

Legislative responsibility (de jure)	Public service	Actual allocation of function (de facto)
Union and states	Social security and insurance	Union and states
Union and states	Charities and charitable institutions	Union and states
Union and states	Electricity	Union and states
State	Police and public order	State
State	Administration of justice	State
State	Prisons, reformatories etc.	State
State	Public health and sanitation	State and local
State	Agriculture and animal husbandry	State and local
State	Water	States and local
State	Forests	State and local
State	Fisheries	State and local
State	Minor minerals	State
State	Administration of justice, jails, and police	State
State	Civil and property rights	State
State	Public lands and natural resources	State and local
State	Local body institutions (municipal institutions in urban areas and Panchayati Raj Institutions in rural areas)	State and local
State	Water supply and sanitation	State and local
State	Incorporation of companies	State
State	Local services	Local
State	Education	State and local
State	Social welfare	State and local

Table 3
Shares of different levels of government in total expenditures*

Item of expenditure	Centre (%)	States (%)	Total (%)	Percentage of total expenditure
A. Interest payment	53.8	46.2	100	22.7
B. Defence	100	0.0	100	8.0
C. Administrative service	51.6	48.4	100	29.0
D. Social and community cervices	17.3	82.7	100	20.0
i. Education	13.0	87.0	100	10.8
ii. Medical and health	11.2	88.8	100	4.2
iii. Family welfare	20.9	79.1	100	0.6
iv. Others	33.3	66.7	100	4.4
E. Economic services	42.6	57.4	100	23.2
i. Agri. and allied services	38.8	61.2	100	6.6
ii. Industry and minerals	77.9	22.1	100	2.4
iii. Power, irri. flood control	12.6	87.4	100	6.1
iv. Tpt. and communication	47.4	52.6	100	4.4
v. Others	69.5	30.5	100	3.8
F. Others	41.7	58.3	100	5.2
G. Loans and advances	2.1	97.9	100	2.0
Total	42.6	57.4	100	100.0

* There are no reliable estimates of expenditures at local levels. The available information shows that local government expenditure in 2002–03 constitutes less than 10 percent of the total expenditures, or about 2 percent of GDP.

The centralization inherent in the assignments is seen in several ways. The residual powers not listed in the schedule are assigned to the centre. It has overriding powers on items listed in the concurrent list. The centre can change the boundaries of the states or carve out new states from the existing ones (Article 2). In fact, over the years the 14 states and 6 Union territories (in 1947) increased to 28 states and 7 Union territories. The centre can dismiss a state government and impose the president's rule if, in the opinion of the governor of the state, it cannot carry on in accordance with the provisions of the Constitution. The public sector dominated planning strategy, adopted in the initial years of Independence, and central control over major financial institutions have further centralized the functioning of the economic system.

Article 301 stipulates that, "Subject to the other provisions of this part, trade, commerce and intercourse throughout the territory of India shall be free," although Parliament may impose restrictions on this freedom in the "public interest." Thus, the centre is empowered to levy a tax on the interstate sale and purchase of goods. The central government has authorized the states to levy an interstate sales tax subject to a ceiling rate (4 percent), and this is a major impediment to interstate trade. It is proposed that, under the recently initiated value-added tax (VAT) reform, this tax will be abolished to evolve a destination-based VAT. It is to be hoped that this reform will ensure a customs union in the country.

FISCAL FEDERALISM AND MACROECONOMIC MANAGEMENT

Macroeconomic management of the economy belongs primarily to the central government, and external borrowing is entirely a central prerogative. The states can borrow domestically, but if they are indebted to the central government, the latter's permission is required. All states are indebted to the central government; as part of the central plan, assistance is given as a loan. This has meant that, each year, states' borrowings are determined by the Union Finance Ministry in consultation with the Planning Commission and the Reserve Bank of India.

There has been steady deterioration in both central and state finances since the latter half of 1990s. Stagnant revenues on the one hand, and increasing expenditures on account of pay revision, subsidies, and interest payments on the other, have resulted in bulging current budgetary deficits and fiscal deficits, with the latter contributing to an increase in the debt burden. The aggregate public debt in the country steadily increased from 63.7 percent in 1991 to 82 percent in 2004–05. In its review of central and state finances, the Twelfth Finance Commission (TFC) recommended a fiscal restructuring plan that entailed passing legislation to eliminate current deficits by 2008–09 from about 5 percent in 2003–04. It also mandated that the aggregate fiscal deficit of the centre and states should be brought down from 8 percent in 2004–05 to 6 percent in 2008–09. The centre has passed the Fiscal Responsibility and Budget Management Act (FRBMA), and most of the states have also passed fiscal responsibility acts (FRAS).

ASSIGNMENT OF REVENUES

Responsibility for most broad-based and progressive tax handles has been assigned to the centre. The centre also has residual tax powers. Responsibility for some taxes has been assigned to the states as well, but from the viewpoint of revenue productivity, only the sales tax is important. The states collect revenue from excise taxes on alcoholic products, stamps and registration, and taxes on motor vehicles and road transportation.

Table 4
Tax assignment to various orders of Government*

	Determination of			Share in revenue (%)		
Federal	Base	Rate	Collection and administration	Federal	State	All orders
Personal income tax (non-agricultural)	Union	Union	Union	6.5	2.7	100
Corporation income tax	Union	Union	Union	7.8	3.3	100
Union excise duties	Union	Union	Union	18.5	7.8	100
Customs	Union	Union	Union	7.9	3.3	100
Taxes on services	Union	Union	Union	0.87	0.4	100
Total central				41.6	17.4	100
Fees, fines, and charges						
State or Provincial					–	
Tax and land and agricultural incomes	State	State	State		0.6	100
Stamp duties and registration fees	State	State	State		3.3	100
Sales tax	State	State	State		21.5	100
State excise duties	State	State	State		4.8	100
Taxes on transport	State	State	State		3.1	100
Electricity duty					1.3	100
Entertainment tax	State	State	State		0.2	100
Others	State	State	State		1.5	100
Fees, fines and charges					2.0	100
Total					41.0	100
Local*						
Property tax	Provincial	Local	Provincial	n	n	100
User fees on water supply	Local	Local	Local			

* There are no reliable estimates of revenue collected by local governments. The available estimates show that the revenue collected from local governments is not significant. In 2002–03, it constituted about 3 percent of total revenue, or about 0.6 percent of GDP.

On the basis of the principle of separation, tax powers are assigned exclusively either to the centre or to the states. However, exclusivity is only in the legal sense, and this has given rise to anomalous situations. Thus, the centre can levy taxes on production (excise duties), but states can levy taxes on the sale of goods. Similarly, taxes on agricultural income and wealth are in the states' domain, whereas the tax on non-agricultural income is a central prerogative. The states find that taxing agricultural income is not politically feasible. In the event, this has provided an easy means to evade and avoid the personal income tax.

The assignment of taxes on production to the centre and sales tax power to the states has led to the uncoordinated evolution of domestic trade taxes in Indian fiscal federalism. Thus, there is a parallel and uncoordinated domestic trade tax system: the centre levies taxes on production of all manufactured items and the states levy sales taxes. Reform at the central level has transformed manufacturing excise taxes into a VAT on goods at the manufacturing stage. Reform at the state level started only in 2005–06, and cascading sales taxes are being converted into a VAT. This reform will take another few years to complete in order to deal with the complications of interstate transactions. The Union finance minister, in the budget speech for 2006–07, has stated that the country will switch to a coordinated goods and services tax in 2009–10.

The Constitution also recognizes that the states' tax powers are inadequate to meet their expenditure needs; it therefore provides for the sharing of revenues from central taxes. Until 1999–2000, the Constitution provided only for the sharing of personal income tax and Union excise duties; thereafter, all central taxes were included in the divisible pool. In addition to tax devolution, the Constitution provides for grants to aid the states (Article 275). Both tax devolution and grants have to be determined by the Finance Commission (Article 280).

FISCAL IMBALANCES: TRENDS AND ISSUES

Vertical Fiscal Imbalance in India

The constitutional assignment and developments over the years have caused a high degree of vertical fiscal imbalance. The state governments in 2002–03 collected only 41 percent of total current revenues, but their share in total current expenditure was 57 percent. From the revenue sources assigned to them, they could finance only 54 percent of their current expenditures. In other words, the states depend on central transfers to finance about 46 percent of their current expenditures.

Notably, even as the states' revenues have grown faster than have those of the centre, their fiscal dependence on the latter has increased. Although the states' share in raising revenues has increased since the mid-1980s, their expenditure share has increased at an even faster rate. Thus, the states' share in total expenditures increased from 52 percent in 1990–91 to 57.5 percent in 2002–03. However, this does not signify an increase in decentralization because much of the increase was in specific-purpose transfers for which the states functioned merely as implementing agencies of the centre.

Table 5
Vertical fiscal gaps in 2002–03

	Total revenue collected (in million rupees)	Total revenue available, including net transfers for that level of government (in current US$ million, 2005)	Expenditures (in current US$ million, 2005)
National	2,602,080	1,894,782	2,997,842
Subnational			
State/provincial	1,540,040	2,247,338	4,051,943
Local	Na	Na	
All orders	4,142,120	4,145,120	7,049,785

1USD = Rs. 40 (approximate)

Horizontal Fiscal Imbalance

There are seventeen relatively homogenous general-category states, but even these have wide differences in size, revenue-raising capacities and efforts, expenditure levels, and fiscal dependence on the centre. In addition, in terms of economic characteristics, the eleven mountainous states in the north and northeast differ markedly from the rest and, therefore, are designated as "special-category" states. Of the twenty-eight, three states have recently been carved out of three large states.[4]

Analysis of the fiscal indicators of the states brings out important features. First, there are wide interstate variations in revenues in both per capita terms and as a ratio of gross state domestic product. Second, these variations indicate differences in revenue capacity as well as differences in effort. Third, the tax-GSDP ratios in the special-category states are lower in the general-category states, even when their per capita GSDP is higher. This is because, in these states, there is not much economic activity other than that derived from the government. Fourth, although the revenue bases in the special-category states are low, their average per capita current expenditure in 2002–03 was much higher (Rs 5,605) than not only the all-state average (Rs 3,509) but also the average of high-income states (Rs 4,380). Fifth, in the case of general-category states, the fiscal dependence on the centre is high and varies inversely with per capita income. The per capita total (Rs 4,380) as well as development (Rs 2,705) expenditures in above-average per capita GSDP states were higher than were those of the below average-income states (at Rs 1,511 and Rs 2,577) by

45 percent and 42 percent, respectively. Thus, large differences in per capita expenditures have persisted despite equalization.

Interstate disparities in India, even among the general-category states, are not only high but are also increasing. In 1980–81, the per capita GSDP of the richest state, Punjab (Rs 2,674), was about 2.9 times that of the poorest, Bihar (Rs 919). During 1999–2002, the difference increased to 4.3 times with the per capita GSDPs of the richest and poorest states, at Rs 28,039 and Rs 6,539, respectively. Furthermore, per capita income levels tended to diverge sharply after market-based reforms were initiated. An important reason for this has to be found in the inability of the transfer system to offset the fiscal disabilities of poorer states.

INTERGOVERNMENTAL TRANSFERS: EQUITY AND INCENTIVES

Intergovernmental Transfers in India

A notable feature of India's transfer system is the existence of multiple channels. First, there are statutory transfers comprised of tax devolution and grants made on the recommendation of the Finance Commission. Second, the Planning Commission gives plan assistance comprised of grants and loans. However, since 2005–06, only grants are given and the loan component has been discontinued. In addition, various central ministries give specific-purpose transfers for various central schemes with or without matching requirements.

The trends in the relative shares of the three channels of central transfers to states since the fourth five-year plan bring out some interesting features. First, the share of statutory transfers in the total increased to 67 percent during the Fifth Plan but declined thereafter to 62 percent during the Eighth Plan (1992–97). In 2003–04, it was about 59 percent. Second, the proportion of formula-based transfers given by the Finance Commission and the Planning Commission has declined and that of discretionary transfers has increased in recent years. Third, within the Finance Commission transfers, the proportion of tax devolution has been predominant.

Finance Commission transfers Under Article 280 of the Constitution, the president of India appoints the Finance Commission every five years or earlier as deemed necessary. The commission is required to make recommendations on the following:

1 The distribution between the Union and the states of the net proceeds of shareable taxes and the allocation between the states

2 The principles that should govern the grants in aid of revenues of the states out of the consolidated fund of India and the amount to be paid to the states in need of assistance
3 The measures needed to augment the consolidated fund of a state to supplement the resources of rural and urban local governments in the state on the basis of recommendations made by the state finance commissions
4 Any other matter referred to the commission in the interest of sound finance.

With the emergence of the Planning Commission as a dispenser of assistance to meet plan requirements, the scope of the Finance Commission has been confined to meeting the non-plan current expenditure requirements of the states. The approach of the finance commissions to determining transfers consists of (1) assessing the overall budgetary requirements of the centre and states to determine the volume of resources that can be transferred during the period of their recommendation; (2) forecasting the states' own current revenues and non-plan current expenditures; (3) determining the states' shares in central tax revenues and distributing them among the states based on a formula; and (4) filling the post-devolution projected gaps between non-plan current expenditures and revenues with the grants in aid. This is known as the "gap-filling" approach. The latest Finance Commission (twelfth) has made recommendations for the five years beginning April 2005.

Until 1999–2000, proceeds from only two central taxes – the personal income tax and the Union excise duty – were shared with the states. The eightieth constitutional amendment replaced selective sharing with sharing of aggregate revenue from all central taxes. Thus, the Twelfth Finance Commission (TFC) (2005) has recommended the distribution of 30.5 percent of net proceeds of central taxes to be distributed according to the following approach.

Over the years, successive commissions have attempted to improve the degree of equalization in the tax devolution scheme by assigning higher weight to per capita GSDP. Yet population has continued to receive the largest implicit and explicit weight, although the last commission significantly reduced the explicit weight for this factor. Equally important are the unreliability of the tax effort and the index of fiscal discipline. In a tax system that is predominantly origin-based there can be significant interstate tax exportation, and the tax effort indicator ignores this phenomenon. Besides, there are a number of other factors in addition to per capita GSDP that determine the taxable capacity of a state. Equalization has been further blunted by the fact that the parliamentary resolution requires the commissions to use the 1971 population figures in the transfer formula whenever it is used for interstate distribution to provide an incentive for population control.

The approach outlined above has been subjected to some important criticisms. First, none of the finance commissions assessed the overall resource position and requirements of the centre on any objective basis. Second, the transfers made by the finance commissions were not designed specifically to offset the fiscal disadvantages of the states arising from their lower revenue-raising capacity and the higher unit cost of public services. While the tax devolution is determined on the basis of general economic indicators, grants are given on the basis of projected post-devolution budgetary gaps. The introduction of a backwardness factor in tax devolution has had the effect of equalization, but the transfer system is not specifically targeted to fiscally disadvantaged states. Finally, it is argued that the gap-filling methodology has led to both inequity and disincentives for fiscal management in the states.

The critical element in the finance commissions' methodology is the projections. These are calculated by taking the base year actual collections (or their estimates) of own-source revenues and the non-plan revenue expenditures of the states, standardizing them, and projecting them using normative growth rates determined according to the fiscal restructuring plan. The gap thus estimated between projected revenue receipts and non-plan expenditures was first filled by the tax devolution, and the remaining gap was filled by grants.

This gap-filling methodology has been criticized on two grounds. First, in taking the base-year expenditures, the methodology did not take note of the differences in the existing levels of services. The effect of the "tyranny of the base year" was to perpetuate the existing interstate differences in expenditures. The low-income states with a low resource base (even after the transfers) and, hence, low expenditures could not get transfers commensurate with their fiscal disability. In other words, the relevant base should have been fiscal capacity and expenditure needs, not actual revenues and non-plan revenue expenditures. Therefore, it is argued that the methodology has failed to offset the fiscal disabilities of poorer states.

The second important criticism concerns perverse incentives. The methodology is characterized as "fiscal dentistry." It is argued that the finance commissions' practice of filling projected budgetary cavities has adverse incentives for tax effort and expenditure economy. In fact, to a large extent, deterioration in state finances is attributed to the gap-filling approach followed by the finance commissions.

The criticism of the gap-filling approach has led to modifying the terms of reference of the Ninth Finance Commission so that it follows a "normative approach." The commission estimated cost functions in order to measure the expenditure needs of the states. However, the subsequent commissions thought that this approach was too difficult to adopt and continued with the gap-filling approach. The TFC has tried to impart incentives to some extent by linking debt write-off to states that have shown reductions in their revenue deficits. The equity element built into the tax-devolution formula, the assessment of revenues and expenditures, and upgraded grants for education and health care are supposed to take care of equity, although these factors may not entirely offset the fiscal disabilities of low-income states.

Plan transfers The assistance given by the Planning Commission is comprised of both grants and loans. In earlier years, both the volume and the loan-grant component were project-based; however, since 1969, the assistance has been allocated on the basis of a formula devised and occasionally modified by the National Development Council (NDC). The prime minister presides over the NDC, while central cabinet ministers, the deputy chairman and members of the Planning Commission, and the chief ministers of the states are represented on it. At present, 30 percent of the funds are kept apart for the special-category states and are distributed among them on the basis of plan projects, which it is up to them to formulate. Until 2004–05, assistance to these states was given in the form of 90 percent grants and 10 percent loans. The 70 percent of the funds available to the general-category states is distributed with 60 percent weight assigned to population, 25 percent to per capita GSDP, 7.5 percent to fiscal management, and the remaining 7.5 percent to special problems. In the case of these states, until 2004–05, the grant component of the assistance was 30 percent and the remainder was given as loans. However, the TFC recommended the discontinuation of central loans to states, and, from 2005 to 2007, central assistance for plans consisted only of grants, and the states were required to raise the balance of resources from the market.

Assistance to the central schemes The third component of transfers – assistance to the central schemes – is given for specified purposes with or without matching provisions. There are more than two hundred schemes at present, even after a number of schemes were consolidated in 2005–06. These transfers have attracted the sharpest criticism due to their discretionary nature and the conditionality attached to them. They accounted for about 40 percent of total plan assistance and for about 14 percent of total current transfers in 2000–01.

Equalizing Effect of Intergovernmental Transfers

Analysis of intergovernmental transfers shows a fair degree of interstate redistribution. Transfers vary inversely with the level of per capita state domestic product (SDP). The progressivity of the transfer system is mainly due to the equalizing element in Finance Commission transfers. The elasticity of Finance Commission transfers with respect to GSDP is −0.796. In contrast, equalization in the grants for state plan schemes and centrally sponsored schemes is not significant. Thus, while the transfer system as a whole has an equalizing impact, it does not fully offset the shortfall in fiscal capacity and cost disabilities.

Fiscal Transfers from State to Local Governments

Fiscal transfers to local governments in urban and rural areas are comprised of (1) the grants recommended by the Central Finance Commission, which are given to states and passed on to local bodies; (2) state government grants to local bodies based on the recommendation of the state finance commissions; (3) grants for implementing some of the centrally sponsored schemes received either through the state governments or directly from the central government; and (4) funds that state departments give to the local bodies for implementing state schemes.

Each state is required to appoint the State Finance Commission (SFC) every five years to make recommendations on the transfers to be made to urban and rural local bodies. However, the experience of decentralization, which has been undergone by various states, does not bring much cheer. The states are reluctant to devolve revenue and expenditure powers. Some have devolved functions, functionaries, and finances, but the functions have been encapsulated in terms of schemes, and local bodies do not have flexibility or autonomy in expenditure implementation. Despite transferring the employees to local governments, the former are not accountable to the latter. Some states have yet to constitute SFCs; in some, SFCs are yet to submit reports; and in some of those in which reports have been submitted, the state governments have not accepted the recommendations. Furthermore, local bodies have very little enforcement capacity through which to raise revenues.

The volume of transfers is inadequate mainly because the states themselves have been facing a severe financial crunch, and there is a general reluctance to pass on functions as well as funds. The distribution is not conducted in any systematic, scientific manner. Often it is conducted on a lump-sum basis to local bodies at the village level irrespective of their capacity or need. In fact, after the state government has deducted the cost of electricity at the source, very little is available to local bodies for actual spending.

Rural local bodies collect hardly any revenues. The only important rural tax is the property tax, but its enforcement is so poor that very little revenue is actually collected. Of course, these generalizations are simplistic, and there are states where local bodies play more active roles than what has been portrayed here, but they are the exception rather than the rule.

Thus, despite creating an enabling environment more than fourteen years ago, fiscal decentralization below the state level has not brought much joy. Several reasons may be given for this. Forcing decentralization from a centralized situation cannot be carried out according to the implementable rules. It cannot be carried out de novo; rather, it has to be calibrated from the existing situation in a democratic polity. And that can only happen gradually. In the Indian case, employees cannot simply be transferred to implement the schemes. Then there are problems of capacity building at the local level, and the issue of elite capture is also important. All these factors need to be resolved. The issue of local government finance itself deserves a separate chapter.

FINANCING INFRASTRUCTURE AT THE STATE LEVEL: LOANS

For the states, borrowing is an important source of infrastructure financing. Until 1987–88, government savings on the part of the states contributed to financing capital expenditures. Since then, however, with increasing negative savings borrowing is used to finance not only capital expenditures but also a significant part of current state expenditures. In 1998–99, for example, only one-half of the states' borrowing was used to finance capital expenditure.

The states' liabilities consist of central government loans, market borrowings, a share of small savings collections, and provident funds and deposit accounts. Outstanding loans from the central government constitute 60 percent of the states' liabilities. These loans used to be given mainly for financing the plans. However, since 2005–06, on the recommendation of the TFC, the central government has ceased giving plan loans to states, and the latter are required to gain access to market loans.

Commercial banks are required to maintain 35 percent of their lendable resources in stipulated assets, and subscriptions to state government bonds constitute a part of the statutory liquidity ratio (SLR) requirement. Thus, the investible resources of the banking system are preempted for government consumption and investment. Interest rates on government bonds had been significantly below market rates; however, financial-sector reforms initiated since 1991 have gradually aligned interest rates on government bonds with market rates.

IMPORTANT CHALLENGES TO INDIAN FISCAL FEDERALISM

Indian fiscal federalism is faced with a number of important challenges. Some of these arise from inherent shortcomings in policies and institutions; others arise from the changing economic and political environment.[5] Any forward-looking reform agenda has to not only recognize the basic shortcomings in the system but also to examine and identify the challenges that are faced in the emerging political and economic situations. This section summarizes the various challenges confronting Indian fiscal federalism.

Deterioration in State Finances

As mentioned above, some of the challenges faced in Indian fiscal federalism arise from the inherent shortcomings of the system. One such problem arises from the steady deterioration in the fiscal health of the states. This has macroeconomic implications as the aggregate revenue deficits of the states during 2000–03 averaged more than 3 percent of GSDP, and aggregate fiscal deficits were estimated at more than 5 percent of GSDP. In addition, there are deficits in public enterprise accounts, and power-sector deficits alone amount to about 1.4 percent of GSDP. The severity of fiscal stress can have microeconomic implications as well. It can severely affect efficiency in resource allocation by under-providing for the creation and maintenance of physical infrastructure and social development.

Increasing fiscal imbalances in state budgets have been a matter of concern. Every finance commission subsequent to the ninth has been asked to draw up a fiscal restructuring plan to phase out the deficits, to create surpluses in the revenue account, and to contain the fiscal deficits. In fact, the TFC was asked to draw up a restructuring plan "by which the governments, collectively and severally, may bring about restructuring of public finances restoring budgetary balance, achieving macro-economic stability and debt reduction along with equitable growth" (Report of the Twelfth Finance Commission, p. 2). While the focus of all these attempts has been to reduce the deficits, fiscal stress manifests itself in different ways, depending on the response to the situations. This includes, besides reduction in deficits, compression in spending on basic public services.

Even considering deficit measures to infer the severity of fiscal imbalances in states, from the viewpoint of policy intervention, it is important to analyze revenue and fiscal deficits in individual states. Analysis shows three main factors. First, in varying magnitudes, there has been a sharp deterioration in fiscal deficits in every single state. Second, there has been a marked deterioration not only in the quantity of deficits but also in their quality. During 2000–03, current budgetary deficits accounted for almost two-thirds of the states' fiscal deficit, whereas in 1993–96, they accounted for less than one-fourth. Third, curiously, there is no association between the per capita income levels of the states and the severity of their fiscal problems as measured by revenue and fiscal deficits. Contrary to the general impression, the revenue and fiscal deficits are not higher in poorer states.

Thus, there is no significant correlation between revenue and fiscal deficits, on the one hand, and per capita GSDP, on the other. The poor fiscal performance in the two poorest states, Bihar and Uttar Pradesh, was not seen in terms of high deficits but, rather, in terms of low levels of spending on social and economic services. While the middle- and high-income states could finance higher expenditures by borrowing from avenues available to them, including borrowing from public enterprises and creating special-purpose vehicles to borrow additional resources, the poorer states simply compressed their expenditures.

Increasing Inequalities in States

In the aftermath of economic reforms following the crisis in 1991, there has been a significant acceleration in the economic growth of the country; however, at the same time, there has been a significant increase in interstate inequalities. The correlation coefficient between the level of per capita incomes and their growth rates was 0.331 during 1991–2004. Economic liberalization and the opening up of the economy during the 1990s seem to have benefited the states with a stronger manufacturing base and better access to markets than they have those that are predominantly agricultural.

Another interesting feature of the pattern of growth is that the relative positions of the lowest and highest per capita income states have not changed. Bihar continues to be the lowest per capita income state, and Punjab has continued to hold the top spot among the non-special-category states (excluding the small state of Goa). The index of per capita NSDP (all India: 100), which was 60 in Bihar in 1980–81, declined to 35 in 2000–01, whereas the index in Punjab increased from 171 to 263 during the same period.

Transition from Plan to Market

Another set of challenges arises from the transition from plan to market. Market-based reform entails applying the market principles of resource allocation. These call for reforms in federal fiscal policies and institutions.[6]

Centralized planning involves controls on prices and outputs, which cause regional redistribution of resources in unintended ways. Besides, planning also involves allocation of resources according to plan priorities. As the economy is liberalized and resources are allocated according to market principles, such implicit transfers and distortions will be minimized. Nevertheless, the production structure and the stock of capital created by past investments will continue to affect resource allocations.

Restrictions on the free movement of goods and factors create resource distortions as well. In the past, these restrictions were a part of the centralized planning regime and partly the result of supply management in a scarcity hit economy. Ensuring a nationwide common market is an important objective. In India, violations of common market principles have also arisen from the physical barriers erected to administer taxes on the interstate sale of goods. The interstate sales tax is a tax on exports from one state to another. In addition, urban local bodies in some states are allowed to levy *Octroi* – a tax on the import of goods into the local area for consumption, use, or sale – so that resources get distorted in unintended ways. The consequence of all this is to segment the economy into several tariff zones.

Globalization and Fiscal Federalism

Closely related to the above is the challenge arising from globalization. Liberalization of international trade and the flow of international capital entail a number of important initiatives that adversely affect states' fiscal systems. Given the predominance of states in providing social services and their co-equal role in providing physical infrastructure, providing efficient infrastructure to ensure competitiveness for domestic manufacturers requires large investments. In the given environment, this is feasible only when the private sector is effectively involved. Enabling private-sector functioning in strategic areas requires significant changes not only in policies but also in setting up the edifice of the regulatory system.

Another aspect of the opening up of the economy is the loss of revenue from customs. This is a challenge faced all over the world, and, although not entirely adequate, the VAT has often been employed to substitute revenue loss from reducing import duties. In the Indian context, however, the power to levy VAT rests with the states. Not surprisingly, liberalization of imports and reduction in the customs tariff since 1991 resulted in the loss of revenue by more than 2 percentage points of GDP in 2001–02 compared with 1991–92. Further liberalization of imports will cause a further decline in the ratio. Given the need to provide efficient infrastructure, improving the revenue productivity of the domestic tax system in order to replace revenue loss from customs remains an important challenge.

Globalization brings with it greater international mobility of capital and skilled labour, and the challenges of taxing them can be daunting. The problems of transfer pricing and difficulties in taxing e-commerce are only two examples of this. The recent initiative of creating several special economic zones results in providing several tax shelters and further segmenting the economy. As it is, the tax system in India suffers from a narrow base, with several exemptions and tax preferences. Tax administration will have to gear up to meet greater complexities in taxing mobile capital and labour.

Challenges to Fiscal Federalism from the Changing Political Environment

The most important challenge to Indian fiscal federalism comes from the changing political environment. The one-party rule at the centre and in the states for over one-quarter of a century after Independence did not help to evolve the rules and conventions in conflicting situations. With the polarization of political parties and competitive relationships between the centre and many of the states, both vertical and horizontal conflicting relationships have emerged. The resolution of these conflicts will continue to be a major challenge in the years to come.

Another important political development is the emergence of coalition governments at the centre and regional parties in the states. The coalition of disparate parties with differing ideologies makes it difficult to forge consensus on major policy issues. When regional parties become "pivotal" members of the coalition, they tend to extract various concessions – political and economic – and this can result in a discretionary rather than in a rule-based intergovernmental system. The asymmetric treatment of various states could have long-term implications for the stability of Indian federalism.

The discussion on the political environment is not complete without referring to the declining time horizon of political parties and politicians. In the last parliamentary elections, only 32 percent of the candidates were re-elected. With a low probability of getting re-elected, the political parties prefer to pursue policies with short-term electoral gains over long-term developmental requirements. This has adverse effects on reforms in policies and institutions.

REFORMING FEDERAL FISCAL ARRANGEMENTS IN INDIA: THE WAY FORWARD

The preceding analysis brings out the important features of federal fiscal arrangements in India and highlights a number of shortcomings. It also attempts to identify important factors that, due to the changing economic-political environment, are affecting the functioning of the intergovernmental fiscal system. Reforms in fiscal federalism will continue to be a central theme in ensuring efficient public service provision and in creating an enabling business environment.

Reforms in fiscal federalism should encompass both policies and institutions. They have to deal not merely with the factors internal to the intergovernmental fiscal system but also with those that were created by the political and economic environment. Some of the reforms should be carried out in the short term, while others will have to be explored in the medium and long term.

Reforms in Tax Systems

The starting point of reform is the tax assignment system itself. For many reasons, it is preferable not to separate income tax powers on the basis of the origin of the income. At the same time, there are successful cases of states exercising concurrent personal income tax powers by allowing them to piggyback their tax on central levies. This will provide an important tax handle to the states. Of course, the transfer mechanism will have to provide a correction to the skewed resource distribution that could arise from this.

Coordination in the consumption tax system is equally important. From the viewpoint of tax harmonization, the goods and services tax (GST) at the central level, with separate central and state components, would be appropriate. However, this can be achieved only with the willing cooperation of the states, which does not seem feasible in the medium term. The feasible option in the medium term would be to allow separate central and state VATs. This would require reassigning the taxation of services – to enable the states to levy the destination-based retail GST. There are problems surrounding assigning services with interstate scope to states, but resolution of these may not be entirely satisfactory. Nevertheless, a compromise solution has to be found.

Equally if not more important is the issue of phasing out taxes on interstate sales. This is also important from the viewpoint of removing impediments to internal trade and establishing a common market in the country. On the same note, it is also possible to abolish *Octroi* and to empower the urban local governments to levy an additional rate on the VAT on purchases within municipal jurisdictions. This would further remove impediments and provide much needed resources to municipalities. Reforms are also necessary to remove restrictions on the movement of goods within the country under the Essential Commodities Act.

Reforms in the Transfer System

The most important reform of the intergovernmental fiscal arrangement that is required would be in the transfer system. To begin, it is necessary to have clarity in the roles of the Finance Commission and the Planning Commission. This was the recommendation made by the Administrative Reforms Commission almost forty years ago. Given the constitutional position of the Finance Commission, the reform could involve converting it into a professional body with a qualified permanent secretariat and entrusting the grant-giving function entirely to it. It could even administer the specific-purpose transfers on the centrally sponsored schemes of the various ministries. The Planning Commission could be entrusted with the task of developing the physical infrastructure in the country and, until such time as the primary debt market develops, could provide concessional loans to poor and smaller states. This measure would help make it possible to view the budgets of the states in a holistic manner.[7]

The Finance Commission will also have to change its approach and methodology. It will have to evolve a formula-based transfer system that is simple, equitable, and that does not involve disincentives. One way to go about doing this would be to base tax devolution on disability in taxable capacity and provide a larger amount of grants to equalize standards in primary education and health care.

Indeed, the reforms in centrally sponsored schemes should focus on rationalizing them and consolidating them, reducing them from the current two hundred-plus schemes to just about a dozen. Rationalization of schemes would help to ensure minimum levels of these services in all the states.

Fiscal Consolidation

One of the important reasons for the fiscal stress at the state level during the 1990s was the decline in the ratio of central transfers to GDP. A large part of the decline of over 1 percent of GDP was in tax devolution, which was mainly due to declining customs. Although, every five years, the finance commissions will consider the sharing of taxes afresh, the difficult fiscal situation at the centre constrains any appreciable increase in transfers in the near future. The problem is compounded by the fact that there would be further decline in the revenue from important duties as the economy is opened up, and, more important, taxing mobile capital and skilled labour in a globalizing environment would pose difficulties.

The ultimate solution to the fiscal problems lies in fiscal consolidation at both the central and state levels. The TFC has worked out the magnitude of adjustment required to achieve a sustainable fiscal situation. This would require increasing the tax revenue-GDP ratio by about 2 percentage points, increasing non-tax revenues by about 1 percentage point, and reducing revenue expenditure by about 1.5 percentage points. This is a priority area, and, unless there is overall fiscal consolidation, reform of intergovernmental finance will not be meaningful and effective.

Local Government Reform

An important area that has concerned policy makers in India is the poor and declining standards of public service delivery. Constitutional amendments to empower local governments have failed to make them effective, and lack of participation in their functioning, particularly in rural areas, is a major concern. Empowerment of local government is meaningful only when people's stake in local government is enhanced. One important way to do this would be to make concerted efforts to reform local tax systems in order to raise larger amounts of local resources for development. Equally important is the need to consolidate the various schemes implemented by local governments to impart flexibility. And it is necessary to make employees accountable to the *panchayats*. Reform in this area is possible only if the information on revenues, expenditures, and other economic variables in different *panchayats* is collected and used for policy. This is also necessary in order to design an appropriate transfer system at the local level.

Making Intergovernmental Institutions Effective

One of the major problems confronted by Indian fiscal federalism is the absence of an effective mechanism for conflict resolution as conflicts are likely to intensify within an environment of intense intergovernmental competition. This has been amply demonstrated by the river water disputes. Conflicts can be vertical (between different levels of government) or horizontal (between different units within the same level). Indeed, it is necessary to make institutions such as the National Development Council (NDC) and the Inter-State Council more effective in order to ensure greater cooperation among governmental units. This issue has gained importance with the emergence of a coalition government at the centre, with regional parties in power in the states, and with regional parties becoming pivotal members of the coalition at the centre.

While both the NDC and the Inter-State Council have done commendable work in the past, it is necessary to bring them to centre stage in regulating intergovernmental competition. In fact, often the Inter-State Council, which is a constitutional institution, is not involved in tasks that it should legitimately be undertaking. The most important example is the inter-state tax harmonization and introduction of the VAT. The entire reform is calibrated by the Empowered Committee of State Finance Ministers, which is totally outside the Inter-State Council. The issue of resolving interstate conflicts will intensify with the phasing out of the interstate sales tax and with the introduction of a system to relieve the tax paid at the state of origin as goods are taken to the destination state.

Notwithstanding the weaknesses, it must be noted that the system of intergovernmental fiscal arrangements in India has served well for over fifty years. It has achieved significant equalization over the years, instituted a workable system of resolving the outstanding issues between the centre and the states and among the states, and adjusted to changing requirements. It has thus contributed to achieving a degree of cohesiveness in a large and diverse country. No doubt this analysis brings out several areas in need of reform; what is important, however, is that the system is eminently amenable to reform.

NOTES

1 Analyses of Indian federalism are available in the two volumes on Global Dialogue on Federalism brought out by the Forum of Federations. See Akhtar Majeed, "Republic of India," in *Constitutional Origins, Structure, and Change in Federal Countries*, ed. John Kinkaid and G. Alan Tarr, 180–208 (Montreal: McGill-Queen's University Press, 2005); and George Mathew, "Republic of India," in *Distribution of Powers and Responsibilities in Federal Countries*, ed. Akhtar Majeed, Ronald L. Watts, and Douglas M. Brown, 155–80 (Montreal: McGill-Queen's University Press, 2006).
2 For a detailed analysis of the circumstances leading to the centripetal bias in the Indian Constitution, see A.K. Chanda, *Federalism in India* (London: George Allen and Unwin Ltd., 1965).
3 I use the terms "Union" and "centre" interchangeably.
4 The three new states are Jharkhand (carved out of Bihar), Chattisgarh (carved out of Madhya Pradesh), and Uttarachal (carved out of Uttar Pradesh). While the first two states have continued as general-category states, the last one is considered to be a special-category state.
5 Reforms in federal fiscal policies and institutions in the context of the emerging economic environment are analyzed in M. Govinda Rao and Nirvikar Singh, *Political Economy of Federalism in India* (New Delhi: Oxford University Press, 2005).
6 For a detailed discussion on the changes in the framework of fiscal federalism required in developing and transitional economies, see M. Govinda Rao, "Fiscal Federalism in Planned Economies," in *Handbook in Fiscal Federalism*, ed. Etisham Ahmad and Georgio Brosio, 212–28 (Cheltenham, UK: Edward Elgar, 2006).
7 For a more detailed analysis of the role of finance and planning commissions, see M. Govinda Rao and Nirvikar Singh, *Political Economy of Federalism in India* (New Delhi: Oxford University Press, 2005); and Nirvikar Singh and T.N. Srinivasan, "Indian Federalism, Globalization and Economic reform," in *Federalism and Economic Reform in a Globalizing Environment*, ed. T.N. Srinivasan and Jessica Wallace, 258–82 (Cambridge, UK: Cambridge University Press, 2005).

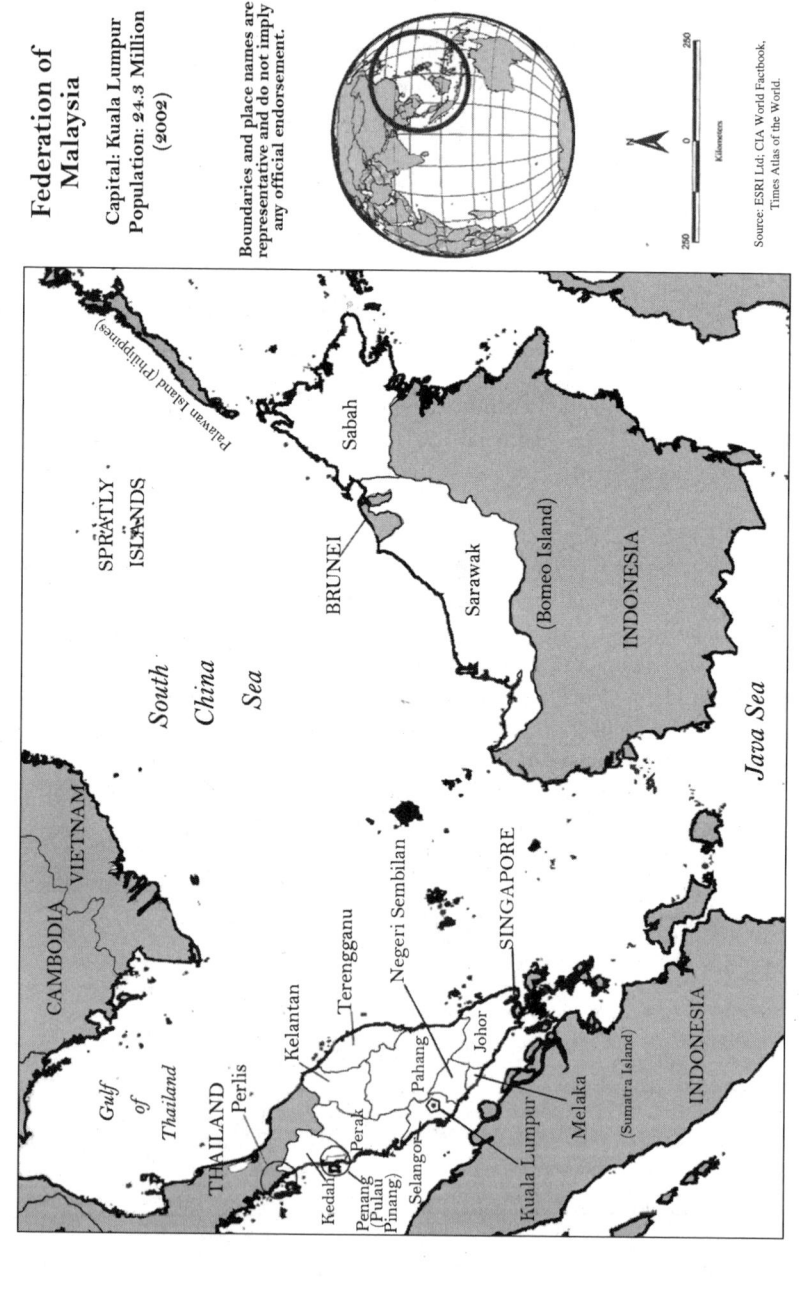

Malaysia

SHANKARAN NAMBIAR

This chapter presents an overview of the manner in which federalism is practised in Malaysia. Malaysia adopted a centrally dominated federal system because it was believed that such a system accorded well with national planning. Malaysia has progressed tremendously since the framing of the federal system. The initial reasoning behind the original intentions of such a system may no longer be valid, principally because of the level of development that has been achieved. However, it appears that the dominant central role is retained because it affords the central government a great measure of control over the state governments. It can be argued that this enables the central government to pursue its national agenda without being distracted by the individual demands of the states. A second possible reason is that a centralized system allows the ruling party, through the central government, to ensure that a system of reward and punishment is preserved. This leads to state governments run by the ruling party or its component parties being favoured in terms of fiscal allocations, while those ruled by the opposition parties are disfavoured. Two issues are at stake here. First, political considerations are intertwined with development and fiscal issues. Second, the central government's aspirations take precedence over the needs of the states.

The next section provides a broad overview of Malaysia's geographical location as well as some of its main indicators. This is followed by a discussion of the structure of the government. Following a brief outline of the governmental system, I outline the division of fiscal powers, mentioning some of the areas of conflict that arise from this division. The third section addresses the issue of how fiscal policy is employed in the context of macroeconomic management, while the fourth section discusses how responsibilities for raising revenue are split between the central government and the states. The fifth section attends to the role of intergovernmental transfers within the context of equity and efficiency. This is followed by a section on the respective roles of the central and state governments with respect to capital investment. Subsequently, I discuss some issues relating to public management, after which I attempt to indicate the way ahead.

OVERVIEW

Malaysia is, in part, a peninsula that lies to the south of Thailand and is surrounded by the South China Sea to its east and the Straits of Malacca to its west. This part of Malaysia is referred to as Peninsular Malaysia, or West Malaysia. The states of Sabah and Sarawak constitute East Malaysia and are both a part of the island of Borneo. West Malaysia, which is at the tip of mainland Southeast Asia, is separated from East Malaysia by the South China Sea. West Malaysia consists of the states of Kelantan, Terengganu, Pahang, Johor, Melaka, Negeri Sembilan, Selangor, Perak, Kedah, Penang, and Perlis. Malaysia is a federal state comprised of thirteen states and three federal territories (i.e., Kuala Lumpur, Putrajaya, and Labuan).

In all, Malaysia is made up of a landmass of 329,736 square kilometres, with East Malaysia accounting for 198,154 square kilometres. Sarawak, with 124,445 square kilometres, is the larger of the two states in East Malaysia; Sabah accounts for 73,709 square kilometres. Malaysia has a population of about 25 million people, with the vast majority (94 percent) being Malaysian citizens. Malaysia is a multi-ethnic country, the bulk of the population being Malays (65 percent). Chinese account for about 25 percent of the population, and Indians are a small minority at 7.7 percent. The rest of the population is made up of members of indigenous tribes and Eurasians as well as those of Cambodian, Thai, and Vietnamese ethnic descent. In Peninsular Malaysia, the Malays, Chinese, and Indians are the dominant ethnic groups, a situation that differs from that in East Malaysia, where non-Malay indigenous people form the majority of the population. Malays and Chinese jointly constitute a little less than half the population in East Malaysia.

Aside from this ethnic division, the Constitution defines a category known as the "Bumiputera." The Bumiputera are defined to include all ethnic Malays as well as those who have at least one parent who is a Malay and who participates in the Malay culture. By definition, Malays are Muslims. This is because the legal system does not generally allow conversion out of Islam, which would be deemed an act of apostasy. The indigenous tribes are also considered to be Bumiputera. This category has important implications, as we shall discover later in our discussion. It must be stated at this point that the critical importance that is given to the Bumiputera in the country's policy space is due to the racial riots that erupted in May 1969. In large part, these riots were supposed to have been triggered by the economic disadvantage experienced by the Bumiputera. They gave rise to the New Economic Policy, which was aimed at correcting ethnically linked income disparities and helping those who had been excluded from economic participation.[1]

Malaysia gained Independence from the British in 1957. Since that time, Malaysia has evolved tremendously, shifting from an economy that was largely agricultural to one that emphasizes industrial development. In 1970, the country's gross domestic product (GDP) (in current prices) was RM11.83 billion (about US$3.2 billion), and it rose to RM487.38 billion (about US$132.3 billion) in 2005. Concomitant with the increase in GDP, the level of GDP per capita has also increased. GDP per capita was RM18,652 (US$5,084) in 2005 as against RM1,087 in 1970. Malaysia can now be characterized as a country that is dependent on export-oriented manufacturing rather than on agriculture.[2] Agriculture, which used to contribute about 39 percent of GDP in 1961, accounted for only 8 percent (at constant prices) of GDP in 2005. Manufacturing, which had a share of 9 percent of GDP in 1961, more than doubled its share to 19.6 percent in 1980 and stood close to 32 percent in 2005. The share of the services sector in GDP has been growing steadily over the years, rising from 42.5 percent in 1961 to almost 58 percent in 2005.

The growth rates that Malaysia has been experiencing since Independence are consonant with the shift in sector emphasis. Strong export-led growth is in large part responsible for the remarkable growth rates that the country has experienced.[3] In the 1970s, the average growth rate was 7.5 percent. The average annual growth rate dropped to about 5.8 percent in the 1980s, rising again to an average of 7.1 percent in the 1990s. During the 1997/98 Asian financial crisis, real GDP growth dropped to recessionary levels, only to recover subsequently. Between 2000 and 2005, the average growth rate was 5.2 percent, although in 2000 the growth rate reached 8.5 percent.

The macroeconomic numbers are testimony to Malaysia's sound trade and investment policies as well as to its prudent macroeconomic management, which have produced a resilient economy that is able to withstand external shocks. The government in Malaysia is optimistic about the country's achievements, especially its resolve to achieve developed country status by the year 2020. This vision was encapsulated as a policy statement by the previous prime minister, Mahathir Mohammad, and has been referred to as Malaysia's Vision 2020.

THE STRUCTURE OF GOVERNMENT AND DIVISION OF FISCAL POWERS

In 1956, the Reid Commission was formed with the express purpose of making recommendations for a "federal constitution" for the Federation of Malaya. This commission recommended a federal state. The Constitution of 1957 was a revision of the Reid Report Draft Constitution. As recommended by the Reid Commission, the Constitution of 1957 granted strong powers to the centre; the states were equal in their status vis-à-vis each other but not to the centre; and the center was envisaged as controlling all essential matters.[4] There have been changes in the composition of the federation since Independence. In 1963, Sabah, Sarawak, and Singapore were included in the federation, necessitating an amendment to the Constitution. A subsequent amendment to the Constitution was necessary in 1966 to accommodate Singapore's decision to leave the federation.

Malaysia is a constitutional monarchy that upholds parliamentary democracy.[5] The Parliament is bicameral, consisting of the House of Representatives (*Dewan Rakyat*) and the Senate (*Dewan Negara*). The Senate is a non-elected upper house, and the House of Representatives is an elected lower house. The Senate is composed of sixty-nine members. Each of the thirteen states appoints two senators, and the king, on the advice of the prime minister, appoints forty-three senators. Clearly, the representatives from the states are outnumbered by those who are federally appointed. The king, or *Yang di Pertuan Agong*, heads the Parliament and has a five-year term. He is appointed from the Conference of Rulers, which is established by the Constitution. The Conference of Rulers is made up of the hereditary rulers from nine states in Peninsula Malaysia and the governors (*Yang di Pertuan Negeri*) of Penang, Melaka, Sabah, and Sarawak, which do not have rulers. The governors do not play a part in the appointment of the king but are appointed by him every four years.

The Constitution of Malaysia divides the authority of the federation into its legislative, judicial, and executive authority.[6] In consonance with the notion of federalism, the separation of power occurs in the federal and state spheres. Federal executive authority (or the power to govern), under Article 39 of the Constitution, lies in the office of the king, but can be exercised by the Cabinet headed by the prime minister. The prime minister and the Cabinet are responsible to the King. Judicial power, as stated in Article 121(1) of the Constitution, is vested in the Federal Court, the High Courts (the High Court of Malaysia and the High Court of Borneo), and the Subordinate Courts, which consist of the Sessions Courts, Magistrates' Courts, and Penghulu's (or village headman's) Courts. The states do not have courts of their own; and they do not have their own constitutions.

The legislative authority, or the power to make laws, raise taxes, and authorize expenditures, is distributed between the federal and state governments. The Ninth Schedule of the Federal Constitution lists the division of legislative powers between the federal and state governments. Legislative power is vested in the federal Parliament. In the states, executive authority rests with the rulers (for the nine states) and governors (in the case of

Penang, Melaka, Sabah, and Sarawak), who are the ceremonial heads. Each state has an executive council (EXCO), and this is the equivalent of the Cabinet in the state sphere. Elections for membership in the EXCO are held every five years. The EXCO is chaired by the *Menteri Besar*, or chief minister. The position of chief minister applies to the states of Penang, Melaka, Sabah, and Sarawak; all other states have *Menteri Besars*. Each state has its own legislature, or state legislative assembly, which is formed by members who are elected every five years.

The Ninth Schedule of the Constitution details the distribution of legislative powers and responsibilities between the federal and state governments. There are three lists that have been drawn out: a federal list, a state list, and a concurrent list. The federal list includes items such as external affairs, defence, internal security, civil and criminal law, and administrative justice. The following matters are also under the federal list: (1) trade, commerce, and industry; (2) shipping, navigation, and fisheries; (3) communication and transport; and (4) medicine and health. Those matters that have been categorized as being under the purview of the states include Muslim affairs and customs, native laws and customs, agriculture and forestry, local government, local public services, boarding houses, burial grounds, markets and fairs, and the licensing of theatres and cinemas. Finally, the concurrent list includes social welfare, scholarships, town and country planning, drainage and irrigation, housing, culture and sports, and public health.

The states, as provided for by the federal Constitution, have jurisdiction over local government. Local government can be divided into rural district councils and urban centres, with city councils and municipalities falling under the latter category.[7] Regardless of the type of local government (i.e., rural or urban in character), all local governments perform the same functions. State governments, which are elected every five years, have the mandate to appoint the presidents who head the various councils (district, city, or municipal). Similarly, the councillors are also appointed positions. These appointments are for a period of three years, subject to reappointment if deemed suitable by the state governments. The councils operate through a committee structure, with the state governments establishing executive or other committees that are chaired by the council president.

State governments have to deal with three problems. First, they have to contend with the problem of credibility. Although the state legislature is elected, the members of the local councils are not elected representatives. Since 1965, local councils have not been elected. This was a consequence of the Emergency (Suspension of Local Government Elections) Regulations (1965) and the Emergency (Suspension of Local Government Elections) Amendment Regulations (1965). Being appointed, local councils do not have the credibility that goes with having passed through an electoral process. As far as the lower layers in the government hierarchy are concerned, they are fraught with the problem of credibility, something that weakens state governments.

Second, local council members are accountable to their respective political parties rather than to their constituencies. With the present arrangement, when there is a conflict of interest between the needs of the citizens in various constituencies and the overall goals of the federal government, it is more likely that the federal agenda will prevail. Taking note that the ruling party is a coalition of several ethnically based parties, with the dominant party being the United Malay National Organization (UMNO), this does not rule out the possibility that UMNO's agenda will ultimately hold sway. Doing away with a system of elections for membership into the local councils means that UMNO's members exist in a state of tension as to whether their loyalties should rest with party leaders or the members of the public.

Third, matters are more distressing when one considers the manner in which the federal, state, and concurrent lists are delineated. It is undeniable that items such as external affairs, defence, federal citizenship, criminal and civil law, and internal security should fall directly under the scope of the centre. However, an examination of the state list reveals that it is extremely restrictive. Aside from areas such as local government and public services, state government machinery, and state works and water, there is little that is within the ambit of the state to direct the nature or course of its own development. Native law, cadastral land surveys, and libraries and museums are among the other issues over which the state has control. Clearly, those areas that are under the state list are either those that only the state can handle (such as local government and state works) or those that are of little interest to the centre (such as land surveys, libraries, and museums). Substantial issues are either directly determined by the centre or are done concurrently.

It is disconcerting that the state has no control over crucial issues that have a bearing on its developmental progress. Important issues such as communication, transport, education, and health are entirely beyond the scope of the state. This restricts its ability to exercise its influence over these matters, leaving the economic development of states very much to the discretion of the centre. Penang, for instance, has long complained about its worsening traffic congestion and the need for a second bridge linking it with the mainland. Penang had to wait for the Ninth Malaysia Plan (9MP) to make federal allocations for the improvement of transportation within the island as well as for the provision of a second bridge to connect it to Peninsular Malaysia.

Refusing to allow the state governments to decide on education is another instance of the centre's reluctance to distribute power and responsibilities to the states. There are reports that some schools in rural areas and on plantations are poorly equipped and maintained. One conjectures that, if state governments had been responsible for education, then assistance might have been more forthcoming. Besides, it would have been easier to pressure state governments on the performance of schools if they were a state affair. Rather than grant some autonomy over education to the states, the centre has been keen to use education as an instrument to garner votes in the general elections. As part of its campaign for the last two general elections, the ruling party, Barisan Nasional (BN), has promised to build a university for Kelantan, which is ruled by the opposition party, *Parti Islam SeMalaysia* (PAS), or Pan Malaysian Islamic Party. This promise will be fulfilled because BN regained some control in Kelantan in the last general elections. While BN is composed of three dominant parties that represent the three major ethnic communities in Malaysia, PAS is an Islamic party that has built its campaign on returning Malaysia to an Islamic state and institutionalizing Islamic law. The plan to allocate funds to Kelantan for the establishment of a university has been announced in the 9MP. This clearly indicates that development considerations are sometimes relegated to secondary status, with political leverage being accorded primacy.

The central government seems to be unwilling to decentralize its powers to the states. This may be because of the historical origins of Malaysia's Constitution. As mentioned earlier, the Reid Commission Report was the forerunner to the Constitution. The Reid Commission argued for a federal state with a strong central bias. While the power of the states in areas like land could be tolerated, it was felt that the centre should be in a position to avoid any actions from the states that might interfere with the national planning process. In regard to financial relations, the Reid Commission thought that financial autonomy could be achieved by reducing the range of responsibilities that should be accorded to the states and ensuring that they would be provided with compulsory grants from the centre. This, perhaps, has led to the concentration of power enjoyed by the central government. It is easy to see why the historical roots for the strong central bias are still being maintained.

The present system is, arguably, a system that allows the BN to maintain its hold over the state governments. Under this system, it is possible to punish those states that are led by opposition parties, while rewarding those that are led by the BN.[8] The tight control that is exercised by the central government ensures that the state governments must rely on the centre for the implementation of development projects. It also encourages the central government to check the growth of opposition parties, as was seen in the case of the promised allocations for building a university in Kelantan. If, for example, the central government were to support the founding of a university in a PAS-dominated state, this would amount to signalling that PAS, a theocratic party, could succeed in achieving the needs of its constituency. This would spark greater interest in PAS as a viable political alternative, something that threatens UMNO, which claims to support the rights of the Bumiputera.

The fiscal issues relating to petroleum production also illustrate the bias that can be exercised by the central government.[9] The 1974 Petroleum Development Act stipulates that 5 percent of the royalty on the gross value of petroleum output should go to the government of the oil-producing state, 5 percent to the federal government, 20 percent to cost recovery, and 21 percent (for profits) to the producer company. The remaining 49 percent should go to Petroliam Nasional Berhad (Petronas), a company established by Parliament through the Petroleum Development Act (Article 144). However, there are only three petroleum-producing states: Terengganu, Sabah, and Sarawak.

The fiscal issues relating to petroleum production give rise to several points of contention. Through the Petroleum Development Act, all states are bound by law to give Petronas sole rights for oil and gas exploration in their respective territories. This implies that state governments have no mandate to initiate or develop the oil industry in their own states; and they do not have any right to participate in the gains accrued from profits obtained in this industry, beyond the 5 percent that is due to them as stipulated by the act. The act states that only Petronas is vested with the power to explore for oil and gas and to develop all aspects of the industry relating to petroleum and its products, including all downstream activities. Further, Petronas is only answerable to the prime minister (not to the state governments). The relative exclusion of the oil-producing states from the fiscal benefits accruing from oil in their own states is compounded by the fact that they have no jurisdiction whatsoever over Petronas. The fiscal monopoly that the centre wields over the oil-producing states abundantly illustrates that the federal government is interested in increasing the concentration of powers and responsibilities of the centre.

The three oil-producing states – Terengganu, Sabah, and Sarawak – do not emerge among the richer states in Malaysia. In fact, on the basis of a number of economic indicators, these three states do not fare well. In terms of the incidence of poverty, two of the three states perform poorly. Sabah has the highest incidence of poverty in Malaysia, while Terengganu is the third poorest state in the country. In terms of the development composite index, all three states are classified as less developed states. States like Penang, Selangor, and Kuala Lumpur (a federal territory) obtain a score of about 139 on average, whereas Sabah, Sarawak, and Terengganu obtain an average of 120 on the development composite index. In spite of these disparities, the federal government has not been inclined to allocate revenues from oil production and its related activities for the development of these states. The fact that equity considerations are ignored under centre-state fiscal relations is highlighted by an incident in 2001, when the federal government ordered Petronas to forgo royalty payments to the state of Terengganu. Terengganu, in response, filed a suit against Petronas because, by law, it was owed 5 percent of revenue. This occurred when Terengganu was under the rule of PAS.

The foregoing discussion raises several areas of conflict. First, the areas that are designated to the states are fairly limited. The limitation arises both in terms of scope of autonomy and control and in terms of the sources of revenue. Second, political considerations take precedence over state determination of areas of priority for development. Consequently, the complaint resides in the fact that development considerations are subject to national agendas, relegating states to the status of passive recipients of federally allocated funds. Third, this passive status does not take into account disparities in horizontal differences in equity (i.e., the attempt to smooth out interstate differences in equity does not occupy a central objective in the federal government's agenda). The pattern of budgetary allocations for state expenditures appears to be aimed neither at eradicating interstate differences nor at accounting for economic deprivation. Thus, we note that states that are less developed are not accorded a special status as far as allocations for expenditure are concerned. Even more problematic is the issue of arbitrarily denying a state its due reward for resources obtained from its territories when such returns substantially added to the federal government's revenues.

FISCAL FEDERALISM AND MACROECONOMIC MANAGEMENT

In most areas, there is a great deal of centralization with regard to fiscal policy. It is not only fiscal policy that is concentrated in the hands of the centre but also budgetary allocations. In keeping with these observations, it is not surprising that the part of macroeconomic management that is covered by fiscal policy is also concentrated in the hands of the federal government and its respective agencies. This tendency was apparent in the aftermath of the 1997/98 financial and economic crisis, and it is a clear indicator of the powers that the centre amasses and executes in the implementation of fiscal policy.

An examination of the fiscal policy response to the financial and economic crisis clearly indicates that the federal government took complete control over the fiscal measures that were employed in response to the crisis. In almost all cases, the measures involved fell exclusively under the federal list. Clearly, the participation of the states in fiscal remedies to the crisis was severely limited.

Table 1
Basic geographic and political indicators

	Geographic
Location	Southeastern Asia, peninsula bordering Thailand and northern one-third of the island of Borneo, bordering Indonesia, Brunei and the South China Sea, south of Vietnam
Area	Total: 329,750 sq km Land: 328,550 sq km Water: 1,200 sq km
Population	24,385,858 (July 2006 est.)
Ethnic	Malay: 50.4% Chinese: 23.7% Indigenous 11% Indians 7.1% Others 7.8%

	Government
Government type	Constitutional monarchy Note: Nominally headed by paramount ruler and a bicameral Parliament consisting of a non-elected upper house and an elected lower house; all Peninsular Malaysian states have hereditary rulers except Melaka and Pulau Pinang (Penang); those two states along with Sabah and Sarawak in East Malaysia have governors appointed by government; powers of state governments are limited by federal constitution; under terms of federation, Sabah and Sarawak retain certain constitutional prerogatives (e.g., right to maintain their own immigration controls); Sabah holds 25 seats in House of Representatives; Sarawak holds 28 seats in House of Representatives
Legislative	Bicameral Parliament, or *Parlimen*, consists of the Senate or Dewan Negara (70 seats; 44 appointed by the paramount ruler, 26 appointed by the state legislatures) and the House of Representatives, or Dewan Rakyat, (219 seats; members elected by popular vote to serve five years) Elections: House of Representatives Election results: House of Representatives
Judiciary	Federal Court (judges appointed by the paramount ruler on the advice of the prime minister)

The degree of centralization over the use of fiscal measures is not surprising. The division of fiscal powers and responsibilities centralizes powers in the hands of the federal government. The concurrent list, which presents matters over which the centre and states have room for cooperation, is limited to matters such as social welfare, town and country planning, housing, public health, drainage, and irrigation. With those important areas over which the state has exclusive control being limited to issues that include local government, land, state government, and local public services, it is obvious that the states have a very restricted mandate over the fiscal matters that determine their well-being.

ISSUES IN REVENUE-RAISING RESPONSIBILITIES

The Malaysian Constitution is the definitive guide to federal-state relations, and in spirit it seeks to provide a framework where powers and responsibilities are shared between central and state governments. Although the federal and state governments are supposed to complement each other, this has not been borne out in practice. States, especially those run by the opposition parties, have frequently complained of the narrow role that is allotted for them in fiscal matters. In spite of the federalist nature of the Constitution, there has been an increasing tendency to centralize fiscal powers.

The Constitution clearly divides the sources of revenue to which federal and state governments have access. The federal government has access to direct taxes such as income tax, property and capital gains taxes, and estate duties. Other revenue sources that come under the domain of the federal government include indirect taxes such as import, export, excise, and stamp duties; sales, service, and gaming taxes; and taxes on betting, sweepstakes, lotteries, and the like. Non-tax revenue – such as road taxes, licences, and service fees – also accrues to the federal government.

The states, by comparison, have less flexibility in raising revenues as they are restricted to import and excise duties on petroleum products, export duties on timber and other forest products, and the excise duty on toddy. Other sources of revenue include income from forests, lands and mines, and entertainment duties. States also gain their revenue from non-tax sources such as licences and permits, royalties, service fees, commercial undertakings, receipts from land sales, and rents on state property. Earnings from federal grants, *zakat*,[13] and other Islamic sources of revenue count among the sources of revenue for the states.

The Constitution provides the federal government with exclusive powers to institute and collect all taxes and non-tax revenues. Yet, on considering the division of revenue sources between centre and state, one cannot help but be struck by the asymmetry that exists between the two entities.[14] The division of revenue sources between the centre and the states unarguably indicates that the sources of revenue are highly centralized, with the bulk accruing to the federal government. Given this state of affairs, the fiscal independence of states cannot be assured. Notwithstanding the fact that Malaysia is a small country, there are still valid reasons why a greater degree of fiscal decentralization should be forthcoming. First, it gives greater flexibility and autonomy for the states to determine their respective economic agenda. Second, more fiscal decentralization would also spur greater efficiency and accountability among the states, and this would encourage better governance. Third, decentralization would also reduce political patronage. Fourth, the federal government could concentrate on its role as overall coordinator rather than on its present function, which has it assessing plans and implementing projects for all the states. There are two areas in which the federal government is well poised to serve: (1) coordinating policies and the institutional frameworks across states and (2) ensuring that interstate fiscal transfers are carried out in order to ensure interstate equity.

The available evidence does not seem to indicate that the federal government is in any way inclined to decentralize powers for the collection of tax revenues. In absolute terms, the total consolidated state government revenues for all the states in Malaysia have been rising from 1985 to the present period. Yet, on average, the rate of growth of state government revenue has been declining in recent years.[15] The average annual rate of growth of state government revenue between 1995 and 2000 was about 4.9 percent. However, the average rate of growth of consolidated state government revenue from 2000 to 2005 declined to approximately 2.5 percent, indicating that the state governments' capacity for revenue collection has diminished. This declining trend is not observed for the rate of growth of federal government revenue. The average annual growth of federal government revenue between 1995 and 2000 was about 4.4 percent, but between 2000 and 2005 it was approximately 14.4 percent. Obviously, the state and federal governments are not subject to the same set of circumstances. The trends seem to indicate that those sources of revenue open to the federal government are growing, while those open to the state governments are declining.

As far as the sources of revenue for the local governments in Peninsular Malaysia are concerned, the general provisions are enshrined under Part 3, Section 39 of the Local Government Act, 1976. Similarly, in Sabah, revenue for local government is governed by the Local Government Ordinance, 1961; and in Sarawak the same is guided by the Local Authority Ordinance, 1948. Local government revenues are composed of taxes, rates, rents, fees, fines, and property income.[16] Local authorities also obtain their revenue from grants and contributions from the federal and

Table 2
Malaysia: Summary of federal and state government functions

	Federal		State
1	External affairs	1	Muslim laws and customs
2	Defence	2	Land
3	Internal security	3	Agriculture and forestry
4	Civil and criminal law and the administration of justice	4	Local government
5	Federal citizenship & alien naturalization	5	Local public services; boarding house, burial grounds, pounds and cattle trespass, markets and fairs, licensing of theatres and cinemas
6	Federal government machinery	6	State works and water
7	Finance	7	State government machinery
8	Trade, commerce, and industry	8	State holidays
9	Shipping, navigation, and fishery	9	Inquiries for state purposes
10	Communication and transport	10	Inquiries for state purposes, creation of offence and indemnities related to state matters
11	Federal works and power	11	Turtles and riverine fishery
			Supplementary list for Sabah and Sarawak
12	Surveys, inquiries and research	12	Native law and custom
13	Education	13	Incorporation of state authorities and other bodies
14	Medicine and health	14	Ports and harbours other than those declared federal
15	Labour and social security	15	Cadastral land surveys
16	Welfare of aborigines	16	In Sabah, the Sabah Railway
17	Professional licensing		
18	Federal holidays; standard of time		
19	Unincorporated societies		
20	Agricultural pest control		
21	Publications		
22	Censorship		
23	Theatres and cinemas		
24	Cooperative societies		
25	Prevention of and extinguishing fires		

Table 2
Malaysia: Summary of federal and state government functions (*Continued*)

Shared functions	Additional shared functions for Sabah and Sarawak
1 Social welfare	17 Personal law
2 Scholarships	18 Adulteration of foodstuff and other goods
3 Protection of wild animals and birds; national parks	19 Shipping under fifteen tons
4 Animal husbandry	20 Water power
5 Town and country planning	21 Agriculture and forestry research
6 Vagrancy and itinerant hawkers	22 Charities and charitable trusts
7 Public health	23 Theatres, cinemas and places of amusement
8 Drainage and irrigation	
9 Rehabilitation of mining land and land which has suffered soil erosion	
10 Fire safety measures	
11 Culture and sports, housing	

Source: Malaysia, Constitution of Malaysia, Ninth Schedule (Article 74, 77) on "Legislative Lists."

state governments. The Ministry of Housing and Local Government has a classification of the sources of income for all local authorities. The six categories of income that it has laid out include (1) assessment rates, licences, and rentals; (2) government grants (inclusive of road grants); (3) car parking charges; (4) planning fees; (5) compounds, fines, and interest income; and (6) loans from higher levels of government or financial institutions.

The sources of revenue, as defined by the various legal provisions, have not been modified over the years to take into account the changing realities that confront local governments. This has created vertical imbalances between the state governments and local authorities. One of the complaints from local authorities is that the assessment of property taxes, an important source of revenue, can only be increased subject to approval from the respective councils and state governments – something that involves a complicated political process. Similarly, a change in the annual value, or the value-added (selling price), of property requires a re-evaluation of the properties under question – a process that, once again, requires a lengthy exercise. Both these changes are difficult to bring about. As a consequence, the rating percentages have remained stagnant. Although the Local Government Act stipulates the ceiling rate of an assessment tax at 35 percent of the annual value of a property, or 5 percent of the value added, this is not executed in practice. Local authorities have refrained from imposing the maximum possible rating percentage. The average national percentage that is effectively implemented by the local authorities in Malaysia is about 9.8 percent, which is way below the maximum rate that can be imposed. Local authorities also face restrictions on the rates that they can effectively charge because any attempt to raise the rates will attract a great deal of censure from political quarters. In fact, local authorities find it difficult even to collect outstanding dues on assessment taxes, with many local councils in Selangor having as much as RM20 million (US$5.4 million) payable to them in arrears.

Another important source of revenue for local governments is licences and permits. These are revenues that are obtained from the licences and permits extended to small establishments such as photography shops, hawkers, provision shops, pawn shops, goldsmiths, restaurants, and launderettes. The revenue obtained through this source is a direct result of the local governments' attempts to control and regulate the operation of these businesses. Again, these businesses are typically small, and any attempt to raise the rates that are extended to them will in all likelihood have strong political repercussions. The local governments are fully aware that an increase in licence and permit fees will only adversely affect small traders and entrepreneurs, without resulting in significant gains in marginal revenue. Nor will such an exercise serve any distribution objective; it will only lead to a loss in political popularity.

State governments in Malaysia have a limited space within which to manoeuvre the collection of fiscal revenues. The sources that have been allotted to them are fairly restricted, causing a high frequency of deficits among many state governments. Both these phenomena, in turn, result in an unfavourable degree of dependence on the federal government for funds. The only respite that is available to some states is the availability of revenues due to petroleum royalties or the taxes arising from forestry products. Most states are endowed neither with petroleum nor forest products, implying that they are mainly dependent on the federal government for support. Aside from those states that are highly industrialized and enjoy a high level of urbanization, state sources of fiscal revenue are limited.

There are problems of horizontal imbalances across the states; there are also problems of vertical imbalances within states. The sources of revenue available to local governments are limited, causing local authorities difficulty in raising funds. Those sources that can be tapped for further tax revenue (e.g., assessment taxes, licences, and permits) are those that are most sensitive as tapping them would act against distribution concerns and incur the political wrath of a significant section of the electorate.[17]

FISCAL EQUITY AND EFFICIENCY CONCERNS AND INTERGOVERNMENTAL FISCAL TRANSFERS

In view of the high level of centralization that characterizes the Federation of Malaysia, it is worthwhile discussing how the federal government perceives questions of equity and efficiency. Of course, these issues are addressed through the intermediary of intergovernmental fiscal transfers as it is possible to level equity imbalances between states through transfers. This necessitates a review of the federal government's position and record on fiscal transfers in order to demonstrate how it addresses these pressing questions.

The states in Malaysia traverse a range of poverty and per capita income levels as well as stages of development. The geographical area that they cover varies too. These distinctions invite differences, and fiscal transfers from the federal government to the state governments ought to bridge these differences. Indeed, an important function of the transfer mechanism ought to be an attempt to seek to support the less advantaged states. Equally, states are in different stages of development and so have different development needs, be they in the area of infrastructure, education, or health care. Daunting as the task may be, the federal government should be expected to be sensitive to the equity imbalances and development needs of the states. This is all the more important in a country like Malaysia, where, given the limited powers and sources of revenue to which the states have access, there is considerable dependence on the federal government.

Aside from reducing equity imbalances across states, intergovernmental fiscal transfers also enable local authorities to perform their obligatory duties. In Malaysia, intergovernmental fiscal transfers include launching grants, annual equalization grants, development project grants, road maintenance and drainage grants, and balancing grants. Launching grants are funds that are provided to the state governments for restructuring their local authorities, usually with the objective of providing service extensions or infrastructure development. This type of grant is calculated on the basis of land area and population.

The annual equalization grant (AEG) is used to compensate or equalize the difference between the fiscal capacity (FC) (i.e., revenue sources) and fiscal need (FN) (i.e., expenditures) of local authorities. The federal government provides the grant to the local authorities in Peninsular Malaysia in conformity with the State Grants (Maintenance of Local Authorities) Act, 1981. Sabah and Sarawak are not privy to this facility because they are governed by their own local government acts and ordinances. The AEG is calculated on the basis of the fiscal need and fiscal capacity of local authorities. Fiscal need is calculated on the basis of the total population of the local authority, population density, geographic size of the local authority area, socio-economic development rate of the local authority, and poverty rate. The Ministry of Housing and Local Government calculates fiscal capacity employing the formula: FC = 1/2 {(8.9% × Annual Value) + Administrative Revenue}.[18] The fiscal residuum, FR, is the difference between FN and FC (i.e., FR = FN − FC). The federal government does not undertake to pay the full amount of the FR but, rather, gives 15 percent of the FR as the annual equalization grant. To extend the entire FR as a grant would place a heavy burden on the federal government's finances.

The development project fund, which, again, requires the approval of the Ministry of Housing and Local Government, is extended for the implementation of socio-economic projects. The influence that the states have with regard to determining these lies in their right to propose projects that are appropriate to their needs; however, the decisions are centrally determined. Of course, these projects have to be in line with the national agenda. Local authorities are expected to use these funds for infrastructure development, social facilities, and the beautification of areas that lie within their jurisdiction. Other projects for which these funds can be used include maintenance of recreation parks, purchase of equipment and machinery, and sanitary endeavours. If there is a basic thrust to the use of the development funds, it is towards uplifting the Bumiputera community, especially with regard to the development of Bumiputera entrepreneurship and the growth of the Bumiputera industrial community. Two other categories of grants are provided for the maintenance of roads and drains.

Poverty provides one indicator of the manner in which fiscal transfers should be made, if the objective of intergovernmental transfers is aimed at promoting equity among states. Selangor is one of the states with a low incidence of poverty, which was about 2.5 percent in 1995. Wilayah Persekutuan (Federal Territory) had a lower incidence (0.7 percent) in the same year. Other states with low incidences of poverty are Penang (4.1 percent) and Johor (3.2 percent). By contrast, Kelantan (23.4 percent), Terengganu (23.4 percent), and Sabah (26.2 percent) had high rates of poverty.

Using a different criterion, Kelantan, Kedah, Sabah, and Perlis are the four states with the lowest per capita GDP. Kelantan and Kedah are consistently at the bottom of the ranking list with regard to both criteria, but Sabah and Perlis are not. Terengganu was one of the states with a relatively high per capita GDP in 1995, although the incidence of poverty in this state was less comforting. Those states that performed well in terms of per capita GDP included the Federal Territory, Terengganu, Selangor, and Penang.

The evidence on federal government grants suggests that Sarawak, Sabah, Johor, and Kedah have been receiving the highest grants, with Sabah and Sarawak receiving grants far in excess of the other states. This ranking of preference suggests that all is not in order as the incidence of poverty does not appear to be a dominant factor in deciding the distribution of grants.

Table 3
Federal government development expenditure: A functional classification[1]

Period	Total (RM million)	Defence and security	Subtotal	Economic services						
				Agriculture and rural development	Trade and industry	Transport	Public utilities	Others	Subtotal	
1995	14,051	2,888	6,440	1,360	1,218	3,151	654	57	3,513	
1996	14,628	2,438	7,693	1,182	1,212	4,530	733	36	3,984	
1997	15,750	2,314	7,501	1,105	1,285	3,578	1,496	37	4,919	
1998	18,103	1,380	9,243	960	3,227	3,062	1,968	26	5,783	
1999	22,614	3,122	8,969	1,088	2,798	2,893	1,850	340	6,936	
2000	27,941	2,332	11,639	1,183	3,667	4,863	1,517	408	11,076	
2001	35,235	3,287	12,725	1,394	4,830	5,042	1,092	367	15,384	
2002	35,977	4,333	12,433	1,364	3,474	5,401	1,808	387	18,043	
2003	39,353	6,029	13,793	1,620	3,456	7,354	920	443	17,707	
2004	28,864	4,133	11,851	2,881	1,201	6,630	945	193	10,260	
2005	30,534	4,803	14,957	2,482	3,221	7,660	1,481	112	7,450	

Source: Monthly Statistical Bulletin, December 2006
1. Data at state level disaggregation is generally not available. Thus, comparable data on expenditure by function at state level is not included.

However, on the basis of per capita GDP, Sabah and Kedah do deserve the treatment that they have been accorded. At any rate, it is difficult to justify why Johor and Sarawak should top the list for federal government grants. Sarawak, it should be remembered, is a recipient of petroleum royalties and taxes derived from forestry products, and Johor is a state that ranks well in terms of various development indices.

There are complaints that the federal government does not undertake its responsibility of resolving horizontal imbalances in a transparent or equitable manner. Development allocations, made over the five-year plan periods, reflect some biases. Penang's development allocation is extremely high and completely out of proportion in light of its small geographical area. In terms of area (allocation per 1,000 square kilometres), Sabah, Sarawak, and Pahang fared poorly. To some extent, the attention that Pahang deserves has been redressed in the Ninth Malaysia Plan (9MP), with this state receiving 15 percent of the total federal government's development allocation; but Sarawak is neglected under this plan, having been allocated only 1.2 percent of the total allocation.

Table 4
Malaysia: Summary of federal and state government revenue

Federal	State
Tax revenue	*Tax revenue*

1 Direct taxes
  i Income tax
     Individuals
     Companies
     Cooperatives
     Petroleum tax
     Development tax
  ii Taxes on property and capital gains
     Real property gains tax
     Estate duty
	1 Import and excise duties on petroleum product and export duties on timber and other forest products for Sabah and Sarawak, excise duty on toddy for all states
	2 Forests
	3 Lands and mines
	4 Entertainment duties

2 Indirect taxes
  i Taxes on international trade
     Export duties:
     palm oil, petroleum
     Import duties:
     tobacco, cigars, and cigarettes,
     petroleum, motor vehicles, surtax
     on imports
  ii Taxes on production and
    consumption
     Excise duties: heavy fuel oils,
     Petroleum, spirits, motor vehicles
     Sales tax
     Service tax
  iii Others
     Stamp duties
     Gaming tax
     Betting and sweepstakes
     Lotteries
     Casino
     Pool betting duty
	Non-tax revenue
	and non-revenue receipts
	1. Licences and permits
	2. Royalties
	3. Service fees
	4. Commerical undertakings, water, gas ports, and harbours
	5. Receipts from land sales
	6. Rents on state property
	7. Zakat, fitrah, and Bait-ul-Mal, and similar Islamic religious revenues
	8. Proceeds, dividend, and interests
	9. Federal grants and reimbursements

Non-tax revenue and non-revenue receipts 1 Road tax 2 Licences 3 Service fees 4 Fines and forfeitures 5 Interests 6 Contribution from foreign government and international agencies 7 Refund of expenditure 8 Receipts from other government agencies 9 Royalties	

Little that is innovative is being done to correct vertical imbalances. The state and local governments have very limited powers available to them. This continues to be a nagging problem as the costs of development projects, maintenance and repair, and provision of public services have kept rising, yet the state and local governments do not have the tax room to raise revenues. Many of the sources of revenue that are available to the state and local governments are unable to yield higher revenues in that any attempt to raise them will trigger political dissatisfaction. To make matters worse, there has been a tendency to shift away from the provision of grants towards the extension of loans to state governments. This is likely to result in the more developed states having the resources to develop further and to provide better public services than the less developed states.

FINANCING CAPITAL INVESTMENT

The federal government has, according to the powers vested in it by the Constitution, the right to determine those items that it deems necessary for capital investment. Capital investment for these items is budgeted in the five-year plan documents under the category of development expenditure. Typically, the five-year plans allocate expenditure on specified items to the various states. However, the annual national budget determines the actual payment that is made to the states. In other words, although central government spending is allocated within the format of a five-year plan, transfers are carried out on an annual basis. Financing for these projects, as far as domestic sources of financing are concerned, comes from direct and indirect taxes as well as from non-tax revenue. Tax and non-tax revenues are not the only sources of finance. The federal government finances its capital expenditure through domestic borrowing; it also takes loans from bilateral lenders and multilateral institutions. Direct taxes are the major contributor to federal government revenue. However, in recent years the rate of growth of direct taxes has been decreasing because the government has been making attempts to provide a more competitive tax structure, with the intention of attracting investors to Malaysia. The rate of growth of indirect taxes has been exceeding that of direct taxes. Non-tax revenue, on average, contributed about 20 percent of total federal government revenue over the Eighth Malaysia Plan (8MP) period (2001–05).

Non-financial public enterprises (NFPFEs) are the public entities in Malaysia that incur the largest capital expenditures. NFPEs include Petronas (National Petroleum Company), Sarawak Electricity Supply Corporation (SESCO), and Tenaga Nasional Berhad (National Energy Company). The federal government makes development allocations for the capacity expansion of these companies, as it did during the 8MP period, accommodating the expansion of the national grid and upgrading transmission lines so as to meet the growing demand for electricity. This, as well as several large-scale petrochemical projects that Petronas had launched, were major objects of capital expenditure. A source of contention is the fact that the financial statements of these NFPEs are not always open to public scrutiny, Petronas being a prime example. Consequently, there is no transparency in the financial standing of such entities – an unfortunate instance of poor governance, especially when public funds are at stake.

The Local Government Act, 1976, empowers local governments with the legal standing to borrow. This borrowing can be done through mortgages, overdraft facilities from private banks, and issues of stock and debentures. Local governments can also borrow from state and federal governments. Although in theory the local authorities could borrow from a wide range of sources, in practice they have been limited to the federal government. This is because the local authorities require the approval of the respective state governments, and these have been rather conservative in their choice of sources of finance.

To summarize, the federal government has complete control over the items requiring capital investment that affect the nation as a whole, including such items as expenditure on defence, education (public universities and schools), and infrastructure (ports, airports, bridges, and dams). The financing of these items of capital investment goes through the normal budgetary process. Since the 1980s, the federal government has increasingly resorted to privatization as a way of reducing its fiscal burden. Privatization in this context has not been untainted as there have been accusations of crony capitalism at work; and, at any rate, economic considerations such as efficiency have not been the guiding principle in the privatization process. Further, the process of public procurement has not been as transparent as it should be, throwing the principles of accountability, transparency, and efficiency to the wind.

The narrowness of the list of areas in which the states can exercise power through capital investment diminishes the power of the states. The states are stripped of their autonomy over issues that would best be left in their hands. This, by implication, ignores local preferences. Because state matters that would imply significant capital investment are really decided by the centre, the federal government's powers are reinforced and concentrated. We need to be reminded that issues such as transportation, education, and health, for instance, are on the federal list. For those matters that require state funding, the states, where possible, finance their own capital expenditure; otherwise, the states seek the indulgence of the federal government. Local authorities must obtain the endorsement of local agencies (such as the Department of Public Works), which, with the support of the state government, is forwarded to the Ministry of Finance for approval.

FISCAL FEDERALISM DIMENSIONS OF THE PUBLIC MANAGEMENT FRAMEWORK

There are civil servants who attend to the duties that are associated with the offices of the federal, state, and local governments. Civil servants who work in the federal and state governments are quite distinct with regard to the recruitment processes that they have to go through. Those who wish to serve in the federal government have to be selected for training by the Malaysian Administrative and Diplomatic Service. An officer who is selected for appointment by a particular level of authority remains there for the duration of his career.

Individual states are responsible for staffing their local authorities, which have the power to recruit their own staff. The power to discipline and dismiss staff also lies within their ambit. Occasionally, senior civil service staff from the centre are seconded to local governments as council presidents. The recruitment process for employment in local government is by no means unorganized; rather, it is based on the principle of merit and seeks to appoint on the basis of intellectual ability, professional or technical expertise, and integrity. Subsequent to selection by the relevant board, the appointment is not made until appropriate clearance is obtained from the state government, the treasury, and the Public Service Department. A frequent complaint that is voiced against the selection of civil servants both in the local and federal governments involves the racial bias that seems to be attached to the selection process as the vast majority of officers are Bumiputera. The government has responded to this complaint by stating that the non-Bumiputera have not shown an interest in civil service positions.

It cannot be denied that, in so far as the administrative machinery is concerned, there is some interference from the federal government in running local government. The public management apparatus at the district level is headed by the district officer, who is usually a federal government appointee – a civil servant who is a member of the Administrative and Diplomatic Service. The only states that make appointments for the district position from their own state civil service are Sabah, Sarawak, and Kelantan. The appointment of district officers by the federal government is a critical move because all projects targeted at the district level have to be discussed at various committees, and these are often chaired by the district officer. This ensures that the federal government's interests prevail.

There have been veiled comments that there is some degree of corruption among government officers. The government's response to these remarks has been to expose those officers guilty of corruption to the Anti-Corruption Agency. The present prime minister, Abdullah Badawi, has launched a campaign against corruption and, in so doing, has reiterated a stand that the previous prime minister, Mohammed Mahathir, undertook early in his career: to pursue a "clean, efficient, and honourable" administration. The collapse of national trunk roads and cracks in school buildings have also led to some speculation about the system of awarding government contracts and the subsequent monitoring of projects.

The civil service is not the premier choice of employment that it was prior to the 1980s. Government officers and civil servants themselves complain of salary scales that do not reflect present market conditions. There is also much dissatisfaction with the fact that promotions are slow and not always based on merit and performance.

THE WAY AHEAD

Although Malaysia is a federation, much needs to be done to achieve a greater modicum of decentralization. As it stands, the division of powers and responsibilities is heavily in the hands of the centre; and while that is not without some advantages, the arguments in favour of more decentralization are urgent and compelling. One of the more pressing issues that centralization has not addressed very successfully is the question of equalization, because, on the one hand, a small number of states have achieved a respectable level of development; on the other hand, there are a number of less developed states. The federal government does not seem to have had much success in identifying and addressing these imbalances because, repeatedly, it allocates funds to states in a manner that is not sensitive to geographical size, incidence of poverty, or level of development. It is possible that a more decentralized fiscal system would handle issues of this sort without being distracted by factors such as ethnic origin and political loyalty.

Some issues, such as education, health care, and transportation, are intrinsically more suited for consideration by the states than are others. If there were concerns that decentralizing decision making on these issues would result in policies that are at odds with national policies, then an approach that involves the federal government playing the role of coordinator could be taken. At any rate, to persist with a centralized approach would mean long time lags, bureaucratic inefficiencies, and a loss in effectiveness in serving the local populace.

More urgently, it is necessary for the federal government to explore ways in which the sources of revenue open to the state governments are enlarged. This can be done in two ways: (1) through the devolution of powers to the state and (2) through the introduction of non-conventional sources of taxation. With regard to the latter, it is possible for the state governments to lease state land, trade in emissions, or levy road congestion charges. The devolution of fiscal powers to the states is a more straightforward affair and must be seriously considered.

Efforts must also be made to improve the efficiency and effectiveness of civil servants and personnel employed in government offices. This requires a system that can demand greater accountability and efficiency from officers employed in the federal and state governments. There have been attempts to upgrade the salaries of certain sections of government personnel. This has been done by increasing the bonuses due to them and by providing for increments in salaries that are commensurate with performance. Despite these arrangements, their productivity has not increased, and this suggests that a system that is based on productivity needs to be introduced.[19]

ACKNOWLEDGMENT

I would like to thank Anwar Shah, John Kincaid, Suresh Narayanan, and two anonymous referees for comments on earlier versions of this chapter. The usual disclaimer holds.

NOTES

1 For useful discussions on the NEP, see K.S. Jomo, "Malaysia's New Economic Policy and National Unity," *Third World Quarterly* 11, 4 (1989): 36–53; and R. Klitgaard and R. Katz, "Overcoming Ethnic Inequalities: Lessons from Malaysia," *Journal of Policy Analysis and Management* 2, 3 (1983): 333–49.
2 For a discussion of Malaysia's economic transformation, see K.S. Jomo, *Growth and Structural Change in the Malaysian Economy* (London: Macmillan, 1990).
3 See M. Ariff and H. Hill, *Export-Oriented Industrialisation – The ASEAN Experience* (Sydney: Allen and Unwin, 1985).
4 For background on the history and political processes of federalism in Malaysia, see B.H. Shafruddin, "Malaysian Centre-State Relations by Design and Process," in *Between Centre and State: Federalism in Perspective*, ed. B.H. Shafruddin and I.A.M.Z. Fadzli, 2–28 (Kuala Lumpur: Institute of Strategic and International Studies of Malaysia, 1988); and B.H. Shafruddin, *The Federal Factor in the Government of Peninsular Malaysia* (Singapore: Oxford University Press, 1987).
5 For a thorough discussion of the structure of government in Malaysia, see R.S. Milne, *Government and Politics in Malaysia* (Boston: Houghton Mifflin Co., 1967).
6 See Government of Malaysia, *Federal Constitution* (Kuala Lumpur: Government Printers, 1988).
7 For an understanding of how local governments function in Malaysia, see S.N. Phang, *Sistem Kerajaan Tempatan di Malaysia* (Kuala Lumpur: Dewan Bahasa dan Pustaka, 1997).

8 See K.S. Jomo and C.H. Wee, "The Political Economy of Malaysian Federalism: Economic Development, Public Policy and Conflict Containment," *Journal of International Development* 15: 441–56.
9 See K.S. Jomo and C.H. Wee, "The Political Economy of Petrol Revenue under Malaysian Federalism," paper presented at the Workshop on Human Rights and Oil in South East Asia and Africa, organized by the Berkeley Centers for African Studies and Southeast Asia Studies, University of California, Berkeley, 2003.
10 See S. Nambiar, "Malaysia's Response to the Financial Crisis: Reconsidering the Viability of Unorthodox Policy," *Asia-Pacific Development Journal* 10, 1 (2003): 1–23.
11 See S. Narayanan, "Towards Economic Recovery: The Fiscal Policy Side," paper presented at the MIER 1999 National Outlook Conference, Kuala Lumpur, December 1998, and V. Vijayaledchumy, "Fiscal Policy in Malaysia," Bank of International Settlements Papers 20, 2003.
12 See M.H. Piei and T. Tan, "An Insight into Macroeconomic Policy Management and Development in Malaysia," in *Rising to the Challenge in Asia: A Study of Financial Markets*, Asian Development Bank (Manila: Asian Development Bank, 1999).
13 *Zakat* refers to a compulsory levy on each Muslim who has wealth equal to or greater than a minimum, referred to as *Nisab* (which is approximately US$1,400 per year).
14 See S. Wilson and S. Mahbob, "Decentralisation and Fiscal Federalism in Malaysia," in *Malaysia's Public Sector in the Twenty-First Century*, ed. S. Mahbob, F. Flatters, R. Boadway, S. Wilson and E.S.L. Yin, 146–64 (Kuala Lumpur: Malaysian Institute of Economic Research, 1997).
15 See K.S. Jomo and C.H. Wee, "The Political Economy of Malaysian Federalism," Discussion Paper No. 2002/113, United Nations University/Wider, 2002.
16 For a comprehensive overview of revenue raising and the local government, see S.N. Phang, *Financing Local Government* (Kuala Lumpur: Universiti Malaya, 1997).
17 For some recommendations on sources of revenue for local government, see Setapa Azmi, "Study on the Development of Government Bond Markets in Selected Developing Member Countries: The Case of Malaysia," paper presented at the Asian Development Bank Conference on Local Government Finance and Bond Market Financing, Asian Development Bank, Manila, 19–21 November, 2002.
18 See Ministry of Housing and Local Government, *Laporan Program/Projek Pembangunan Jabatan Kerajaan Tempatan dan Kedudukan Kewangan*, September 1995.
19 No data on vertical fiscal gaps is available for Malaysia. For this reason, I was unable to include the appropriate table.

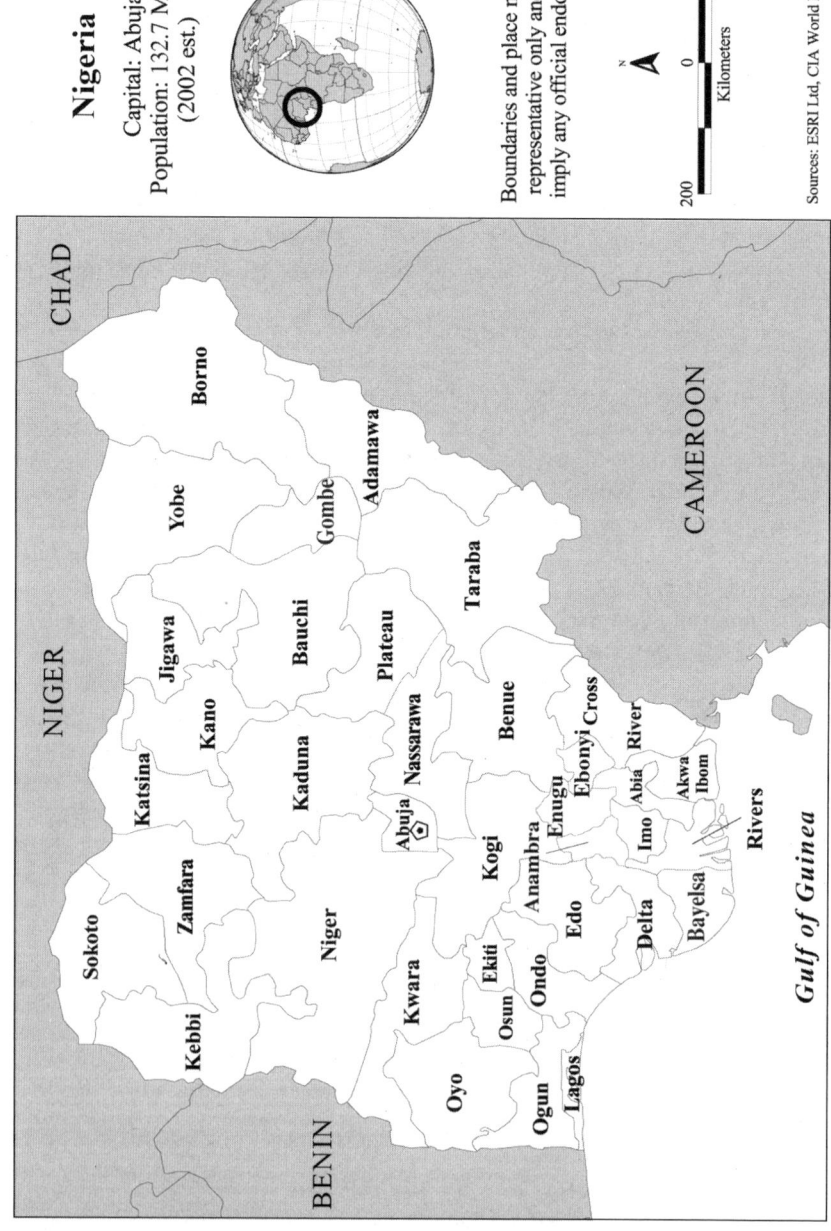

Federal Republic of Nigeria

AKPAN H. EKPO

Nigeria has a population of about 130 million people.[1] It consists of over 250 ethnic groups and over 100 languages. The official language is English; the major ethnic groups are the Hausa, Ibo, and Yoruba located in the north, east, and west of Nigeria, respectively. At Independence in 1960, these three groups held sway in these regions, hence, minority ethnic groups agitated for the creation of more states in order to break the yoke of the dominant three. The country's fiscal federalism is predicated on economic, political, constitutional, local, and cultural developments. From three regions in 1960, the country grew to four regions in 1963. During the civil war of 1967–70, the country was carved into twelve states. By 1976, the states increased to nineteen, and by 1987 they increased to twenty-one. In August 1991, the number of states increased to thirty, and a separate Federal Capital Territory (FCT), Abuja, was created in place of the old capital of Lagos. By October 1996, six additional states were created, bringing the total number to thirty-six. At present there are also 774 local governments. The country exports oil and the GNP per capita in 2003 stood at US$441. Nigeria operates a three-tier type of government (federal, state, and local).

The country runs a presidential system of government akin to that of the United States, with a bicameral legislature, a senate, and a house of representatives at the centre. In each state, there exists a house of assembly. The local governments have their councils. Members of all houses at the three tiers of government are elected during a general election. There are several political parties. However, two parties – the People's Democratic Party and the All Nigeria Peoples' Party – are dominant. The People's Democratic Party is the party in power, and it controls twenty-seven states in the Federation. It has been in power since the return to democratic rule in 1999 and won re-election in 2003. The All Nigeria Peoples' Party controls seven states, mainly in the north, while the Alliance for Democracy and the All Peoples Grand Alliance control one state each in the southwest (Lagos) and southeast (Anambra), respectively.

There are three branches of government: executive, legislative, and judiciary. The executive and legislative arms are elected along party lines. The Nigerian Constitution does not provide for independent candidature. The judiciary is made up of several tiers of courts, culminating in the Supreme Court. The Federal Appeals Court entertains appeals from the Federal High Courts and the State High Courts.

The FCT, Abuja, also has its own High Court, as do the states in the Federation. The Customary and Sharia Courts, the Magistrate Courts in the states, and the FCT run almost parallel to the system of High Courts. The judges and magistrates of the Customary and Magistrate Courts are learned in modern law, while those of the Sharia Courts, found mainly in the north, are learned in Islamic law.

Following years of military rule, the new presidential system faces a series of challenges. The introduction of Sharia law by some Muslim states in the north was the first problem for the new administration. There has been a rise in ethnic/sectional militant groups, such as the O'dua Peoples Congress in the southwest, the Movement for the Actualization of the Sovereign State of Biafra (MASSOP) in the southeast, and the numerous militant groups in the oil-producing Niger Delta Area.

The growth rate of Nigeria's economy was about 3.5 percent in 2001–03. It relies heavily on crude petroleum, which provides about 90 percent of foreign exchange. The country was heavily indebted but recently obtained debt relief from the Paris Club. About two-thirds of the country's debt has been "forgiven," while the remaining one-third is to be paid in two installments.

The aim of this chapter is to examine the practice of fiscal federalism in Nigeria, paying attention to issues such as the structure of government, macroeconomic management, revenue-raising responsibilities, and challenges that will result in a better fiscal federalism for the country.[2] The analysis confirms that, for Nigeria's fiscal federalism to remain robust, the diverse ethnic groups must be willing to live together in a context of fairness and equity.

THE STRUCTURE OF GOVERNMENT AND DIVISION OF FISCAL POWERS

Nigeria operates a federal structure of government. The 1999 Constitution guarantees the existence of the federating units. The functions of the federal government are listed in the Exclusive List, while those of the states are in the concurrent list; where conflict exists, the exclusive functions of the federal government dominate.

The Constitution of the Federal Republic of Nigeria recognizes three tiers of government: federal, state, and local. The Constitution spells out the assignment of functions and areas of fiscal jurisdiction among the various units of the Nigerian federal system.

The current 1999 Constitution, in Section 4 (Second Schedule), indicates the Exclusive Legislative List, consisting of the responsibilities on which only the federal government can act, and the Concurrent Legislative List, on which both the federal and the state governments can act. In addition, Section 4 (7a) assigns the so-called residual functions to state governments. These are functions not specified either in the Exclusive List or the Concurrent Legislative List. Section 7 (5) (Fourth Schedule) of the Constitution provides for the establishment of local government councils with responsibilities set out in the Fourth Schedule of the Constitution.

Regarding the structure of government as defined in the Constitution, it is necessary to note the following:

- The Constitution lumps both expenditure responsibilities and revenue-raising functions together in its assignment of functions.
- The assignment of functions is generally the outcome of several constitutional conferences that the country has had over the years, while details of the assignment of revenue-raising functions are usually left to be determined by the various Fiscal Commissions, which usually follow each constitutional conference.
- The assignment of functions in Nigeria has remained more or less constant since the country's Independence in 1960, starting with the 1963 Constitution up to the current 1999 Constitution.
- It is necessary to examine the underlying principles behind the assignment of functions in Nigeria.

FISCAL FEDERALISM AND MACROECONOMIC MANAGEMENT

The major institutions driving economic policy include the Federal Ministry of Finance and the Central Bank of Nigeria. The Central Bank is responsible for monetary and exchange rate policy, while the Ministry of Finance oversees fiscal policy. In theory and practice, it is important that coordination exists. Hitherto in Nigeria there was no coordination between the Ministry of Finance and the Central Bank. In recent times, particularly from the year 2000, there seems to be coordination between the two.

Over the years, the problem with the economy has been persistent budget deficits. This economic phenomenon exists not only at the centre but also at the subnational government levels (state and local governments), where it also creates problems for the wider economy. Hence, there is the need for fiscal coordination at all levels.[3]

The Central Bank of Nigeria is independent with regard to the conduct of monetary policy and the maintenance of price stability. The law establishing the Central Bank guarantees that independence. However, the governor of the Central Bank informs the president about monetary, credit, and exchange rate issues. The independence of the Central Bank can be anchored on the recent example of bank consolidation, which required all banks to raise their capital to 25 billion naira. This policy has met no resistance from the presidency.

The Central Bank's mandate goes beyond ensuring price stability: as part of the federal government's economic team, it participates effectively in the overall management of the economy. The government's present economic reform program, known as the National Economic Empowerment and Development Strategy (NEEDS), was conceptualized, formulated, and is now being implemented with the full participation of the Central Bank.[4]

The Central Bank has been struggling to reduce the inflation rate to the single-digit level in order to ensure a positive real interest rate. In addition, the bank is concerned with reducing the cost of funds in order to stimulate investment. The economy operates a managed float exchange rate regime. These issues form part of a broad macroeconomic framework for managing the Nigerian economy.

It was mentioned earlier that, if the assignment of functions in a federal system is discussed from the point of view of the major functions of government, the federal/national government would be in a better position to perform its stabilization function. Yet the federal system has inherent destabilizing characteristics due to the existence and fiscal perversity of subnational governments. For instance, periods of excess oil revenue, when the economy is likely to be overheated, call for spending restraint. However, with increased revenue, the state and local governments usually increase their spending. During downturns, when efforts should be geared towards increasing spending, state and local governments are often forced to cut back on their spending, thereby compounding the problem of macroeconomic management at the national level.

Fiscal Responsibility Act

To improve the management of the economy at all levels of government, the federal government has proposed the Fiscal Responsibility Act. It aims at committing all tiers of government to effective, disciplined, and coordinated budgetary planning, implementation, and reporting. One of the major features of the act is that it institutionalizes a stabilization strategy to save windfall oil revenues in order to smooth consumption during periods of decline in oil revenues. Other features are purposeful investment of the windfall; reduction in fiscal deficits through the provision of guidelines against over-borrowing and incurring unjustified debts; standard formats for reporting and evaluating budgetary goals and performance; guidelines to stem the culture of indiscipline, waste, and corruption in public finance in order to improve transparency and accountability; and establishment of high standards of financial disclosure and public access to information on government finances. The Fiscal Responsibility Bill has gone through the various stages in the houses of Parliament and will soon become law.

Stabilization Fund

The concept of the Stabilization Fund, also referred to as the National Reserve Fund, or the Excess Crude Account, was introduced at the national level to moderate the impact of up and down swings in oil revenue on aggregate spending in the economy. It aims at creating a special holding account, whereby surpluses in oil revenue during periods of rising oil prices would be set aside and utilized during periods of fall in oil revenue in order to keep government spending stable. There is no doubt that the stabilization concept would be a useful tool in macroeconomic management. However, from past experiences, the problem was not with the idea of a reserve fund but, rather, with how it was managed and eventually utilized. The states had complained of their non-involvement in decisions on how the fund was to be utilized. Indeed, the federal government, especially during the military era, unilaterally utilized the fund however it pleased. Apparently, the federal government tended to confuse the Stabilization Fund with the establishment of the Contingencies Fund provided for in Section 83 of the Constitution. While the Contingencies Fund is also meant for urgent and unforeseen expenditures, its major characteristic is that it is to be established out of the federal government's own money, unlike the Stabilization Fund, which is established with monies belonging to all the governments of the Federation. In 2001, the Contingencies Fund stood at N4.8 billion. It increased to N5.3 billion in 2002.[5]

It is also important to point out that the Supreme Court did not rule in April 2002 against the concept of the Stabilization Fund but, rather, against how it was funded (i.e., deducting it as a first charge on the Federation Account before the account is shared among the owners, the three tiers of government).[6] In addition, it is important to establish proper ownership of the Stabilization Fund, whereby the contributions to it would be proportional to the relative shares of the different tiers of government in the Federation Account. This would ensure that each tier of government is fully aware of its share in the Stabilization Fund when it comes to disbursement. It would also reduce the temptation on the part of the federal government to see the fund as an additional source of revenue for its own use.

For now, the federal government controls the Stabilization Fund. In 2001, the Stabilization Fund stood at N6.4 billion; it increased to N7.5 billion in 2002 and to N10.4 billion in 2005. In 2005, state governments received a total of N1.5 billion from the stabilization fund.[7]

Borrowing and Taxation

Items 7 and 59 of the Exclusive Legislative List of the Constitution confer on the federal government exclusive rights over borrowing monies within and outside Nigeria for the purposes of the Federation or the state, and major taxes, including taxation of income, profits, and capital gains, respectively. But it does not appear that the federal government has ever had a firm grip on controlling borrowing by the various governments, including itself, especially in terms of the timing, purpose, and monitoring of the use of loans. It is hoped that, with the better management of available resources envisaged by the Fiscal Responsibility Act, there will be a reduction in deficit financing and, consequently, a reduction in public debt, at both national and subnational levels. At present, subnational governments can only obtain external loans with the approval of the federal government.

However, taxation has not proved to be a useful tool in managing aggregate spending in the economy. Outside corporate income tax, income tax has been of limited use in controlling spending in an economy dominated by oil revenues.

ISSUES IN REVENUE-RAISING RESPONSIBILITIES

This section discusses the assignment of expenditure responsibilities and the assignment of revenue powers.

Assignment of Expenditure Responsibilities

If political authority is divided among the different levels of government, then there is a need to determine the appropriate functions to be performed by each level. Ideally, two factors may influence the allocation of functions among the different levels of government. These are the geographic range of spillover effects, or benefits from collective action, and economies of scale. With respect to the geographic range of benefits, each function should be assigned to that level of government that coincides in size with the group that benefits from that activity. This implies that the national/central (federal) government would provide those services that benefit the whole national population, while state and local governments would provide those services whose benefits are more divisible geographically. A federal arrangement enables the federating units to take advantage of economies of scale due to the fact that some functions could be performed more efficiently (in terms of lower unit cost) by the national government than by lower levels of government.[8]

The allocation of functions among federating units is more of a political than an economic exercise, and there may be no stated principles underlying such allocation in the Nigerian Federation. However, it is not unreasonable to infer that considerations of the extent of the benefit region (externalities) of government services and economies of scale must weigh heavily in the decision to allocate some functions to the federal government and others to state and local governments. Hence, those functions whose benefit region covers the entire country and/or that can be more efficiently performed at a national level have been assigned to the federal government. These include national defence, external relationships, banking, currency, coinage and legal tender, and weights and measures.

Functions whose benefit areas are more local than national but with the possibility of spillover effects – such as antiquities and archives; electric power; industrial, commercial, or agricultural development; scientific and technological research; and university, technological, and postprimary education – are on the Concurrent List. Finally, functions that are purely local in character in the sense that the benefits accrue, in the main, to limited geographic areas within the country, are usually assigned to local authorities. Such functions include the establishment and maintenance of cemeteries, markets, motor parks, public conveniences, refuse disposal, and construction and maintenance of local roads and streets. Table 3 contains a summary of the assignment of expenditure responsibilities in Nigeria.

It is also conventional to discuss the assignment of functions in a federal system from the point of view of the major functions of government – namely, allocation, distribution, and stabilization. At the theoretical level, it has been argued that the central government would be in a better position to perform the distribution and stabilization functions. Discussion of the allocation function is not all that simple because it depends on a number of factors, one of which is the division of functions between the private and the public sectors of the economy. The other types of publicly produced goods that are involved – private goods, impure public goods, and pure public goods – depend on the degree of market failure in their provision. For instance, it is questionable whether public production of a private good such as electricity and its placement under the federal government can still be justified on the basis of the failure of the market system to provide for such goods. In other words, not all publicly produced goods are public goods, and even in the case of pure public goods, as noted earlier, there is a distinction between national public goods whose spatial incidence covers the entire nation and local public goods whose spatial incidence is limited to particular geographic areas.

Table 1
Basic political and geographic indicators

Official name: Nigeria
Population: 129.9 million
Area (square kilometres): 923,768.64 square kilometres
GDP per capita in US: $493.2 (2004)
Constitution: 1999 (presidential)
Constitutional status of local government: By election (third tier of government)
Official language English
Number and types of constituent units: federal, state, local governments, municipal governments
Population, area, and per capita GDP in US$ of the largest constituent unit – not available.
Population, area, and per capita GDP in US$ of the smallest constituent unit – not available.
Currency: Naira = 100 kobo
Federal capital: Abuja

Assignment of Revenue (Tax) Powers

A proper understanding of the basis of the allocation of tax powers requires a brief review of the evolution of the division of tax powers in the Nigerian federal system. Between 1914 and 1946, Nigeria operated a unitary system of government. With the creation of regional authorities in 1946, there was a need for some formalization of the fiscal relationship between central and regional authorities. Hence, the 1947 Constitution identified two sources of revenue for the regional authorities. One was "declared revenue derivable from within the region and the other was non-declared revenue, consisting of block grants from central revenue."[9] Within this framework, therefore, some of the issues that had to be resolved were the division of tax powers between central and regional authorities and the criteria for declaring any revenue source as regional.

The first Fiscal Commission, the Phillipson Commission, appointed in 1946, set out very stringent conditions for declaring any revenue source regional. For instance, "regional revenue sources would have to be essentially local in character for easy assessment and collection; regionally identifiable; and have no implications for national policy."[10] With these stringent conditions, it became obvious that very few revenue heads (taxes) would qualify as regional (now states and even local governments). The obvious implications would be that the revenue sources that would qualify as regional or subnational would be inadequate for the performance of subregional functions.

Thus, although both the Phillipson Commission and most of the subsequent commissions saw the merit of the principle of maximum independent revenue for the regions (now states) and, subsequently, local governments, they all ended on a pessimistic note about the scope for the enlargement of the tax jurisdiction of lower-level governments.[11]

We discuss briefly tax powers in Nigeria. Because of the limited scope for manoeuvreability already noted, there has been very little change in the allocation of tax powers over the years. The only notable exception was the reverse transfer of the legal aspects of the capital gains tax, personal income tax, and sales tax (now value-added tax) from state governments to the government of the Federation. It became obvious that these taxes do not fully satisfy the conditions required for them to be declared truly state taxes. The major sources of revenue – import duties, mining rents and royalties, petroleum profit tax, corporate income tax, excise duties and value-added tax, and personal income tax (legal basis only) – come under the jurisdiction of the federal government. The administration and collection is conducted by the states, which also retain the proceeds for their own use. One consequence of the concentration of revenue-taxing powers in the federal government is the dependence of lower-level governments on federal sources of funding but not on the federal government. The other is the imbalance between the functions constitutionally assigned to state and local governments and the tax powers available to them.

FISCAL EQUALITY AND EFFICIENCY CONCERNS AND INTERGOVERNMENTAL FISCAL TRANSFERS

There is no doubt that fiscal arrangements are a consequence of a federal structure. However, the kinds of fiscal arrangements in place ought to affect the nature of the federal structure. The fundamental problem becomes how to devise a federal structure that would be conducive to national and equitable allocation of the country's resources among the different tiers of government so as to reduce intergovernmental and intergroup tensions. Other problems in the country's fiscal arrangement include power sharing and the consequent imbalance between the expenditure responsibilities assigned to the different levels of government and the tax powers available to them, state and local government dependence on federal sources of funding, and the concentration of spending powers on the part of the federal government.

Consequently, the government faces the challenges of vertical and horizontal fiscal gaps and how to overcome them. There is no systematic pattern of providing grants to lower levels of government. Where grants are provided, they follow an ad hoc pattern. The federal government makes vertical and horizontal allocations to lower levels based on a formula, which remains a subject of contention. Budget deficits are prevalent in the country's federal system. The Nigerian Constitution established a Revenue Mobilization Allocation and Fiscal Commission (Section 153) with powers to review and recommend revenue-sharing rules in the Federation (Section 162).

Table 2
Nigeria: Legislative responsibility and actual provision of services by different orders of government

Legislative responsibility (de jure)	Public service	Actual allocation of function (de facto)
Federal	Education (tertiary and secondary)	Federal and state
Federal/state	Education (primary)	Local
Federal/state/local	Health	Federal, state, and local
Federal	Defence	Federal
Federal/state	Law and order	Federal
Federal and state	Fire services	State

The following section considers issues of power sharing and imbalance between assigned responsibilities and tax powers, revenue allocation, and the method used to channel allocations to local governments.

Power Sharing and Imbalance between Assigned Responsibilities and Tax Powers

In a federal structure, it is normal for each order of government to be given adequate resources to enable it to discharge its responsibilities. In practice, this does not run all that smoothly. Often, one order of government may end up with more financial power than it actually needs, while another may have less than it needs.

The fiscal arrangement in Nigeria is characterized by excessive concentration of fiscal powers in the federal government. Invariably, there is a lack of correspondence between the spending responsibilities and the tax powers and revenue resources assigned to different levels of government. The federal government is the "surplus unit" and the state and local governments are the "deficit units."[12] The allocation of tax powers centre on administrative efficiency and fiscal independence. The efficiency criterion insists that a tax be assigned to that order of government that will administer it efficiently (at minimum cost), while fiscal independence requires that each order of government raise adequate resources from the revenue sources assigned to it in order to meet its needs and responsibilities. Concerning tax powers, the efficiency criterion often conflicts with the principle of fiscal dependence. In Nigeria, weighting has always been in favour of the efficiency criterion, which allows for the concentration of taxing powers in the hands of the federal government.

The effect of concentrating tax powers in the federal government is the dependence of state and local governments on federal sources of funding, which is often confused with dependence on the centre. The federal government is assigned to administer the most lucrative sources of revenue because it is perceived to be in a better position to administer those taxes efficiently. Thus, the federal government administers those taxes on behalf of all the governments of the Federation. Hence, the federal government has no more right over the monies it collects than do the state and local governments. It follows that, in sharing the revenues collected by the federal government on behalf of itself and the other tiers of government, it is not correct to assert that the lower levels of government depend on the centre. In fact, the federal government is not constitutionally assigned to collect such revenues.[13]

Revenue Allocation

With respect to the reassignment of functions, since the federal government is the "surplus" unit, this would entail shifting functions from state and local governments to the federal government. However, given the principles that guide the allocation function, such reassignment of functions might necessitate assigning the functions that would otherwise be more suitable for lower-level governments. Nevertheless, there were some attempts in the past to shift some functions from the state governments to the federal government. For instance, as a result of its access to more elastic sources of revenue in the 1970s, the federal military government shifted such functions as university education and primary education and, to some extent, television and radio broadcasting and major newspapers from state and local governments to itself. On shifting tax powers from the surplus unit to the deficit units, given the principles that guide the allocation of tax powers in the Nigerian system, any realignment of tax powers to lower-level governments to match their expenditure responsibilities might entail transferring to state and local governments tax sources that they lack the capacity to administer.

In the Nigerian context, therefore, it would appear that the most viable option for remedying the problem of imbalance between the functions and the tax powers assigned to the different tiers of government is to make adjustments in the revenue-sharing formula. This issue is explored further below in the discussion of public revenues and unresolved issues that revolve around revenue allocation in Nigeria.

The Federation Account

Section 162 (1) of the current Constitution stipulates that the Federation shall maintain a special account to be called "the Federation Account" into which shall be paid all revenues collected by the federal government. Section 162 (2) of the Constitution makes provisions for sharing the Federation Account among the three tiers of government, as already noted.

Before the Resource Control Suit,[14] the areas of contention with respect to the Federation Account had to do with non-payment of some revenues collected by the federal government into the account and some deductions from the account before sharing among the three tiers of government. The Supreme Court decision declared both actions of the federal government illegal. However, the controversy over the deductions from the Federation Account, the so-called Special Fund, still rages. Prior to the Supreme Court verdict, 7.5 percent of the Federation Account was set aside and distributed as follows:

Federal Capital Territory	1.0%
Stabilization	0.5%
Derivation	1.0%
Development of mineral-producing areas	3.0%
General ecology	2.0%

The sum set aside as the Special Fund and its allocation to various heads has changed over time.[15]

The current debate on the Special Fund tends to confuse the need for funding some activities with who foots the bill. Taking the Federal Capital Territory (FCT) as an example, no one can fault the case for its development. However, there is also the need to develop the thirty-six state capitals, especially those in the newer states. Some of the state capitals still have the characteristics of a rural setting and need to be developed. As a matter of fact, there is a compelling reason for dispersing the high population centres concentrated around Lagos and Abuja to other parts of the country. Therefore, the development of state capitals points to a way out. If one accepts the case for the development of state capitals, which must be funded by state governments, there is no reason why the federal government could not fund the development of the FCT out of its resources, especially considering the proportion of the Federation Account that goes to the federal government.

It should be noted that, when the Supreme Court, in its landmark decision of April 2002, voided the distribution of the Federation Account to the Special Fund, the federal government, by presidential order, simply transferred the Special Fund to the federal government's share, thereby increasing it from 48.5 percent to 56 percent. This modification to the Revenue Allocation Act was unsuccessfully challenged at the Supreme Court by the state governments in January 2003. The court ruled that the president had the constitutional powers to make such an alteration to an act.

Often the case of funding the FCT from the Federation Account hinges on the often misinterpreted Section 299 of the Constitution. It states that "the provision of this constitution shall apply to the Federal Capital Territory, Abuja, as if it were one of the States of Federation." However, subsequent Section 299 (a) elaborates on "the constitution applying to FCT as if it were one of the states of the Federation" to mean that, just as in the case of states, the legislative powers, executive powers, and judicial powers are invested in the House of Assembly, the governor of the state, and the courts of the state, respectively. These powers in the case of the FCT are vested in the National Assembly, the president of the Federation, and the courts established for the FCT, respectively. Moreover, the First Schedule of the Constitution, Part 1, lists the states of the Federation without any mention of Abuja.

A further concern is that ecological disaster could occur anywhere in the country. Each level of government should have contingency plans to ameliorate the effects of such disasters. This would imply that the federal government, whose territory is the whole country, should also make provisions for intervening when disasters occur in the country, especially in those cases where the lower-level government may not be able to cope with the situation. It is also expected that, when the resource control controversy is finally settled, more resources will be under the control of mineral-producing areas to enable them to handle the development problems of their areas.[16]

Vertical Revenue Allocation

A lingering problem of vertical revenue allocation in Nigeria is how to devise a rational and equitable allocation of the country's resources among the different tiers of government that would minimize intergovernment and intergroup tension and promote national unity and development. The federal government has been allocated a large proportion of the Federation Account relative to the states and local governments. Of interest here is whether the federal government's retention of the lion's share of the Federation Account could be justified on the basis of the relative weight of the functions assigned to it. Alternatively, the federal share might reflect a legacy of past thinking, which, in the absence of a viable private sector, perceived a leading role for the federal government in the field of economic development.

Weight of Federal Government Functions

Claiming that the share of the federal government is based on the weight of functions assigned to it does not tell the whole story. Indeed, many of the Fiscal Commissions had justified the assignment of more than 50 percent of the Federation Account to the federal government on that basis.[16] Yet, there is no indication of the basis for assigning both quantitative and qualitative weights to such functions. For instance, with today's costs, the whole of the federal budget may not be enough to "adequately" fund the various arms of the armed forces (military, navy, and air force). Moreover, it is important to bear in mind that the allocation of functions in a federal set-up does not necessarily connote an ordering of such functions in terms of the preferences of the people for whom the services are provided. The relative development of the private sector and the current emphasis on private sector-led development strategy imply that the federal government should move to limit its role to the regulatory aspects of some functions and to engage less in actual production. For example, the post office and NITEL may not be needed with the proliferation of private courier services and GSM operators.[17] Moreover, the current policy of privatization should reduce the expenditure responsibilities of the federal government, which could reduce its funding of public monopolies. These developments may lead to taking another look at the weight of federal functions and, by implication, the federal government's share in the Federation Account. One thing that is certain is that an appropriate balance is yet to be struck in the use of revenue allocation to correct the imbalance between functions and tax powers assigned to state and local governments.

Federal Presence in the States

Perhaps the concentration of fiscal powers in the federal government would have been less objectionable if that government were expending its resources equitably for the good of all the components of the Nigerian Federation. "Federal presence" refers to the spatial pattern of federal government spending. It has been argued that federal government spending in a particular state would probably influence the relative distribution of state income to a much greater extent than does the direct revenue share received by the state from the Federation Account. Thus, a state that gets little or nothing from the Federation Account but attracts a preponderance of federal spending may, in the final analysis, be at a great advantage.[18]

The disparity in the development of different parts of the country, occasioned by the inequity in the spatial distribution of federal spending in the states, can only heighten intergroup tension. Such preferential treatment of some states violates the principle of equality among lower tiers of government. The current cries of marginalization and the controversy over resource control are cases in point. It is not surprising that some state governments, groups, and individuals are calling for the minimization or elimination of surplus funds in the hands of the federal government. Thus, while there is a need for the centre to be strong enough to maintain the unity of the component units and to give the country a sense of national direction, the essential pluralism of Nigeria must be recognized and respected. A situation in which too much financial power is left in the hands of one order of government tends to encourage prodigality and gross mismanagement of scarce resources on the part of that government, and this does not make for a workable federalism.[19]

Horizontal Revenue Allocation

One reason for intergovernmental transfers is to correct vertical imbalances that arise because the national government retains the major tax bases, leaving insufficient fiscal resources to the lower-level governments to meet their expenditure needs. Another reason for intergovernmental transfers is to correct horizontal imbalances. These may arise due to the fact that some jurisdictions have higher tax bases than do others or have higher (or extraordinary) expenditure needs than do others. The objective of the fiscal transfers is to try to close the gap between the fiscal capacities and fiscal needs of the subunits. The horizontal revenue allocation in Nigeria is, therefore, a sort of unconditional block grant to states and local governments to correct the horizontal fiscal imbalances among them. To what extent do the formulas or principles used for horizontal revenue allocation address the problem of horizontal fiscal imbalances? More fundamentally, what is the extent of horizontal fiscal imbalances among the states and local governments? This question cannot be satisfactorily addressed without some knowledge of the fiscal capacities and fiscal needs of the different subnational units. Although it deserves serious attention, excursion into these areas is outside the scope of this study. Another matter in contention is the formula for horizontal revenue allocation in Nigeria.

The formulas and principles that have been applied for horizontal revenue allocation use population as a factor. This tends to complicate the problem of having an accurate population census in the country as various states and groups accuse one another of manipulating the census figures in order to reap some relative advantage in the use of population as a principle in revenue allocation. In spite of this controversy, the fact still remains that government is about people, development is about people, and, in the end, government is about the welfare of the people. Therefore, population ought to continue to play a dominant role in horizontal revenue allocation in Nigeria.

The case for internal revenue effort is another factor influencing horizontal revenue allocation. Internal revenue effort would encourage the states and local governments to look inward and try to maximize their internally generated revenue potentials. However, using internal revenue effort as a factor runs into serious problems when it comes to operationalizing the concept. The Okigbo Fiscal Commission of 1980 proposed that the ratio of internal revenue to total expenditure be used as a measure of internal revenue effort. The government rejected that proposal, and rightly, too, on the ground that such a measure would unjustly penalize states that raise loans for their approved capital projects; rather, the government substituted the ratio of internal revenue over recurrent expenditure as a proxy for internal revenue effort. Admittedly, this measure is likely to ginger up the lower-level governments to make serious efforts to either increase their internal revenue or to put a lid on their recurrent spending. However, the flaw in the index is that it fails to take into account the fact that internal revenue effort is a function of two factors – taxable capacity and tax effort (including tax rates and efficiency in tax administration). Hence, a state with high taxable capacity but with lower tax rates and inefficient tax administration may still have higher internal revenue or a higher ratio of internal revenue to recurrent expenditure relative to another state with lower taxable capacity but higher tax effort. There is, therefore, an urgent need to devise a better index of tax effort. And, until such an index is devised, the weight currently given to internal revenue effort in horizontal revenue allocation should be very minimal.[20]

Land mass terrain was surreptitiously introduced into the history of revenue allocation in the 1980s, when the Shagari Administration used it to break the alliance between the Unity Party of Nigeria, the Great Nigerian Peoples Party, and the Peoples Redemption Party at the Joint Committee of the Senate and the House of Representatives. The Joint Committee was appointed to reconcile the differences between the two bodies in their recommendations on revenue allocation. With the introduction of land mass at the Joint Committee meeting, states that stood to gain from its inclusion abandoned the alliance and voted with the ruling National Party of Nigeria. The recommendations of the Joint Committee were successfully challenged in court, in that they were presented to the president for assent without reference to the National Assembly, which set up the Joint Committee. Another reason had to do with the controversy that it was likely to generate. Land mass, as a principle of revenue allocation, was expunged from the recommendations of the Joint Committee that were sent to and approved by the National Assembly and subsequently signed into law. However, during the subsequent military regimes, landmass and terrain found their way back into the revenue allocation formula, without being thrown open to national debate (as is the case with most principles). Until that is done, the weight assigned to the principle of land mass and terrain should be greatly reduced.

Perhaps derivation as a principle of revenue allocation, or what has now come to be known as "resource control,"[21] is the most controversial issue in revenue allocation in Nigeria. The derivation principle has been criticized as being capable of generating intergroup tension in a federation that strives for the unity of the component parts. This is because derivation tends to make the rich richer and the poor poorer. Not only was derivation the dominant principle of revenue allocation in the 1950s and 1960s but it was also vehemently defended by the power blocs that benefited from it. It was even defended on equity grounds – that the area from which the bulk of revenue is obtained should receive some share of the revenue beyond what other areas receive.[22]

Under military rule, and as the source and base of revenue changed, the principle of derivation became insignificant. The recently concluded National Political Reform Conference on resource control pointed to the fact that the appropriate weight to be given to the derivation principle in revenue allocation in Nigeria is yet to be determined.[23]

We strongly believe that emphasis on derivation encourages states and local governments to exploit their natural resource endowments. A situation in which groups clamour for recognition as states and local governments, without any regard for the sustainability of such units and mainly because they expect to be funded out of the Federation Account, does not make for true federalism.

Oil-Producing Areas and Resource Control

Crude oil production has been the most important economic activity in the Nigerian economy since the early 1970s. Its impact is not limited to the fact that it contributes almost 90 percent of Nigeria's total foreign exchange earnings but also includes the fact that the national budget is predicated on the expected annual production and price of crude oil. Therefore, crude oil is the primary engine for national economic growth and development. It is, thus, quite reasonable to expect that the areas producing the nation's crude oil would be very highly compensated for what is taken from them as well as for the devastation of the land engendered by the exploration process.

The Niger Delta region suffers from near total neglect by both the federal government, which claims ownership of the oil, and the multinational companies, which actually exploit the oil reserves. It is a picture of wanton environmental degradation of all types – land (despoliation of farmlands), water (destruction of fishing areas and sources of drinking water), and air (release of many pollutants causing diseases in humans, animals, and plants). The devastation and degradation suffered by the oil-producing areas are indications of the extraordinary expenditure needs of those areas that ought to be addressed by intergovernmental transfers. The federal government's intervention through the Niger Delta Development Commission (NDDC) is a welcome development. However, enough weight ought to be given to derivation to enable the state and local governments of the oil-producing areas to handle their developmental problems according to self-determined needs and priorities. The minimization of the derivation factor over the years – from the earlier 50 percent, to 1 percent, and now 13 percent – affects oil exploration and production, and it seems both unjust and unfair.

Channeling Allocations to Local Governments

Section 162 (5)–(6) of the 1999 Constitution says that the local government share of the Federation Account is to go to local government councils as follows:[24]

- The amount standing to the credit of local government councils in the Federation Account shall be allocated to the states for the benefit of their local government councils on such terms and in such manner as may be prescribed by the National Assembly.
- Each state shall maintain a special account to be called the "State Joint Local Government Account" into which shall be paid all allocations to the local government councils of the state from the Federation Account and from the government of the state.

On payment into the State Joint Local Government Account from the government of the state, Section 162 (7) of the Constitution provides that each state shall pay to the local government councils in its area of jurisdiction such proportion of its total revenue on such terms and in such manner as may be prescribed by the National Assembly. A number of issues still remain unresolved with respect to channeling to local government councils amounts standing to their credit from the Federation Account and from the government of the state. The local government councils complain that not all the amounts due to them from the Federation Account are paid into the State Joint Local Government Account. They complain that state governments find all sorts of reasons to make deductions before the payment of Federation Account proceeds into the Joint Account and that, contrary to Section 162 (7) of the Constitution, hardly any state governments paid the stipulated percentage of their internally generated revenue into the Joint Account.

Another problem that arises with respect to the channeling of revenues to local governments relates to the apparent contradiction between Section 162 (5) and Section 162 (8) of the Constitution. Section 162 (5) states that payment to local government councils should be as prescribed by the National Assembly. Section 162 (8) states that "the amount standing to the credit of local government councils of a state shall be distributed among the local government councils of the state on such terms and in such manner as may be prescribed by the House of Assembly." Thus, while the National Assembly prescribes the manner of payment of the proceeds of the Federation Account into the State Joint Local Government Account, the method of the distribution of amounts in the Joint Account to the local governments is to be determined by the House of Assembly of the state. A strict interpretation of these provisions is that the House of Assembly of the state is free to use, in the allocation of the Joint Account to the local governments, an entirely different set of principles from that used in allocating the Federation Account to local government councils. An obvious implication is that no local government council is in a position to legitimately compare what it receives from the Joint Account with what was due to it from the Federation Account. Even more frightful is the concern that some state governments may abuse this freedom and indulge in politically motivated discrimination in the allocation of the proceeds of the Joint Account among the local governments under their jurisdictions.

In an apparent attempt to resolve the problem of channeling resources to the local government councils, the National Assembly enacted the Monitoring of Revenue Allocation to Local Government Act, 2005. This act provides for the establishment of a body to be known as the State Joint Local Government Account Allocation Committee, whose purpose is to:

- ensure that allocations made to local government councils in the state from the Federation Account and from the state concerned are promptly paid into the State Joint Local Government Account;
- ensure that the funds paid into the State Joint Local Government Account under paragraph (a) of this section are distributed to the local government councils in accordance with the provisions of the 1999 Constitution of the Federal Republic of Nigeria and any law made on behalf by the House of Assembly of the state; and
- monitor the payment and distribution of the funds mentioned in paragraphs (a) and (b) of this section so as to ascertain the actual amount paid to each local government.

The monitoring process can detect divergence between total payments into the Joint Account and total payments to local government councils. However, it cannot legitimately detect divergence between allocations to individual local governments from the Federation Account and their receipts from the Joint Account. This is because different principles are used for payments from the Federation Account into the Joint Account and for the distribution of the Joint Account to the local governments. It is evident that intergovernmental fiscal arrangements in Nigeria have several challenges to overcome, particularly with regard to transfers from both the centre and state governments to local governments. In order to overcome some of these challenges, in 1989 the federal government established the Revenue Mobilization, Allocation, and Fiscal Commission.

Revenue Mobilization, Allocation, and Fiscal Commission

The Revenue Mobilization, Allocation, and Fiscal Commission is the federal government agency that determines the revenue-sharing formula, pending approval by both houses of Parliament. The commission was established in 1989 by Decree No. 49 and was inaugurated in 1990 in order to bring some sanity to the problem of revenue sharing in Nigeria. The commission was not effective during the military era because the government ignored its advice on revenue-sharing formulas. The situation changed in 1999, when the Constitution defined the membership of the commission as consisting of a chairperson and one member from each state of the Federation and the Federal Capital Territory, Abuja. The members were to be individuals who, in the opinion of the president, were persons of unquestionable integrity with requisite qualifications and experience.

The commission has the power:

- to monitor the accruals to and disbursement of revenue from the Federation Account;
- to review, from time to time, the revenue allocation formulas and principles in operation to ensure conformity with changing realities: "Provided that any revenue formula which has been accepted by an Act of the National Assembly shall remain in force for a period of not less than five years from the date of commencement of the Act";
- to advise federal and state governments on fiscal efficiency and methods by which their revenue can be increased;
- to determine the remuneration appropriate for political office holders, including the president, vice-president, governors, deputy governors, ministers, commissioners, special advisers, legislators, and the holders of the offices mentioned in Section 84 and Section 124 of the Constitution; and
- to discharge such other functions as are referred to the Commission by this Constitution or any act of the National Assembly. (See 1999 Constitution of the Federal Republic of Nigeria, 147–48.)

The Commission does make recommendations on vertical and horizontal revenue allocations for the country. However, it is not uncommon for such recommendations to be adjusted by the federal government in its favour. Between January 1990 and June 1992, there were five revisions to the revenue allocation formula.

Table 3
Nigeria: Direct expenditures by function and level of government

Function	Federal (%)	State or provinces (%)	Local (%)	All (%)
Defence	100	–	–	100
Debt servicing	100	–	–	100
General administration	70	20	10	100
Law and order	85	10	5	100
Economic services	80	15	5	100
Social services	70	20	10	100
Health	60	30	10	100
Education	60	20	20	100
Subsidies	NA	NA	NA	NA
Total				100
Local public services	NA	NA	NA	NA

Table 5 shows changes in vertical revenue allocations between 1992 and 2002. A notable change in the recent vertical revenue-sharing formula is the increase in the allocation to the local governments from the previous 15 percent to 20 percent to enable them to cope with funding primary education. In addition, as a result of the Supreme Court judgment on resource control, allocations to the Special Fund out of the Federation Account were declared illegal. However, in redistributing the Special Fund, the federal government appropriated 82.4 percent of the 7.5 percent of the fund, while only 17.6 percent was redistributed to the states (9.6 percent) and local governments (8.0 percent). This resulted in a phenomenal increase in the federal government's share of the Federation Account, from 48.5 percent to 54.68 percent.

FINANCING CAPITAL INVESTMENT

The federal, state, and local governments finance capital projects through budgetary allocation; there is no law barring governments from raising invisible funds through the capital market. A few states, for example, Akwa Ibom, have floated bonds to finance selected projects. Federal government development stocks – long-term bonds – were introduced in 2003. This instrument deepens the financial market and encourages the government to source its long-term financing needs from the capital

Table 4
Nigeria: Tax assignment for various orders of government

	Determination of shares in revenue (%)						
Federal	Base	Rate	Tax collection and administration	Federal (%)	State/ province (%)	Local (%)	All others (%)
Import duties	Federal	Federal	Federal	100	–	–	100
Company income tax	Federal	Federal	Federal/state	70	25	5	100
Withholding tax on companies	Federal	Federal	Federal/state	100	–	–	100
Petroleum profit tax	Federal	Federal	Federal	100	–	–	100
Capital gains tax	Federal	Federal	Federal	NA	NA	NA	NA
Minus rents & royalties	Federal	Federal	Federal	100	–	–	100
Stamp duties	Federal	Federal	Federal/State	NA	NA	–	NA
Value-added tax (VAT)	Federal	Federal	Federal	100	–	–	100
Education tax	Federal	Federal	Federal	100	–	–	100
Personal income tax (except members of the armed forces, Nigerian police, residents in Abuja, staff of the Ministry of Foreign Affairs, and non-residents)	Federal	Federal	Federal/State	80	20	–	100
State							
Entertainment	State	State	State	NA	NA	NA	NA
Road taxes (motor vehicle and driver's licences)	State	State	State	NA	NA	NA	NA

Table 4
Nigeria: Tax assignment for various orders of government (Continued)

Federal	Determination of shares in revenue (%)			Federal (%)	State/ province (%)	Local (%)	All others (%)
	Base	Rate	Tax collection and administration				
Pools, betting, and lotteries Gaming taxes	State	State	State	–	–	–	–
Land registration	State	State	State	–	–	–	–
Survey fees	Federal	Federal	State	–	–	–	–
Development levies	State	State	State	–	–	–	–
Property taxes	State/federal	State	State/local				
Local							
Market and trading licences and fees	Local	Local	Local	NA	NA	NA	NA
Motor park dues	Local	Local	Local	NA	NA	NA	NA
Marriage, birth, and death	Local	Local	Local	na	na	na	na
Registration fees				–	–	–	–
Bicycles, truck, canoe, and wheel barrow fees	Local	Local	Local	–	–	–	–
Public convenience, sewage, and refuse disposal fees	Local	Local	Local	–	–	–	–
Signboard and advertisement permit fees	Local	Local	Local	–	–	–	–

Table 5
Nigerian fiscal gaps

	Total revenue collected / Total expenditures								Total revenue available			
	2001	2002	2003	2004	2001	2002	2003	2004	2001	2002	2003	2004
National/federal (billion naira)	1427.5	1606.1	2011.6	2638.2	797.0	716.8	1023.2	1234.6	1018.0	1018.2	1226.0	1377.3
States (million naira)	573.5	670.0	855.0	1114.0	278.8	245.6	309.7	557.1	596.9	724.5	921.2	1125.0
Local (million naira)	171.5	172.2	370.2	468.3	48.8	47.4	158.5	172.6	171.4	170.0	361.8	461.0

Source: Computed from Central Bank of Nigeria, *Annual Report and Statement of Accounts*, various issues.

market.²⁵ The proposed fiscal act intends to provide guidelines limiting lower levels of government from foreign borrowing, except when they obtain approval from the federal government.

PUBLIC MANAGEMENT FRAMEWORK

The Federal Civil Service Commission is charged with the responsibility of hiring staff for the federal civil service. This commission cannot influence the hiring and firing of staff at lower levels of government. However, each tier of government has its own Civil Service Commission, and they are autonomous with regard to the hiring and firing of staff. It is very unusual for the federal government to undermine the authority of subnational governments in the area of employment matters.

Corruption is a serious matter in Nigeria. Transparency International lists Nigeria as one of the most corrupt countries in the world. Corruption produces distortions in the economy. Reasons postulated for corruption within the economy include low wages and salaries, greed, and a primitive accumulation instinct. Other forms of corruption include nepotism, tribalism, and favouritism. During the military era, there was no concerted effort to fight corruption. However, the present democratic experiment, which commenced in 1999, has demonstrated some seriousness in fighting corruption, despite the inherent constraints.

In fighting corruption the economy is seen as one. In other words, there are three tiers of government but one economy; therefore, the government agencies charged with fighting corruption cut across all tiers of government.²⁶ Two prominent agencies are responsible for eradicating corruption: the Independent Corrupt Practice Commission (ICPC) and the Economic and Financial Crimes Commission (EFCC). The EFCC has spread its net over top government functionaries, such as state governors, members of Parliament (federal and state), and even the inspector-general of police. It is interesting to note that, recently, the former inspector-general of police was brought to court and jailed for embezzling public funds. The general opinion is that these anti-corruption agencies are moving in the right direction, and it is anticipated that their efforts can be sustained.

THE WAY FORWARD: CONTEMPORARY ISSUES IN NIGERIAN FISCAL FEDERALISM

Given the dependence of all tiers of government on centrally collected revenue, especially the rent from oil and gas production, the most contentious and controversial issue in Nigerian fiscal federalism is the competing demands of each tier of government for a larger share of revenue.

Historically, the federal government, especially under successive military regimes, has retained the lion's share of federally collected revenue. However, with the return of civil democratic rule in 1999, the states, especially in the resource-rich Niger Delta region, have been agitating for a greater share of national revenue.

The Nigerian Constitution makes provision for periodic review of the sharing rules to reflect changing economic and social realities. However, there has been no such review since the 1999 Constitution came into force. Therefore, agitation for a greater share of the so-called "national cake" has continued unabated.

The Constitution provides for derivation to be given a weight of not less than 13 percent in the sharing formula. Advocates of resource control in the Niger Delta region have continued to press for raising this floor to at least 25 percent.

There have also been controversies about the way the federal government operates the Federation Account. In its ruling in April 2002, the Supreme Court settled the issue of illegal and unconstitutional deductions from this account. However, the federal government continues to operate this account, disregarding the Constitution and the Supreme Court's ruling. For example, the federal government continues to divert revenues meant for the Federation Account into so-called dedicated accounts such as the Nigerian National Petroleum Corporation (NNPC) expenditure account and the excess crude oil revenue account.

From these illegal accounts, the federal government proceeds to undertake unappropriated and unbudgeted expenditures. For example, recently the Revenue Mobilization Allocation and Fiscal Commission alerted the nation to the fact that the federal government had utilized the funds in the excess crude revenue account to pay Paris Club debts without authorization from the National Assembly. This happened in spite of the fact that these revenues belong jointly to all tiers of government in the Federation. In addition, some states and all local governments do not owe any Paris Club debt.

The federal government has similarly withdrawn money from these accounts to pay for the development of independent power plants, located solely in the southern part of the country, without appropriation from the National Assembly. The president himself admitted in a letter to the National Assembly that he withdrew funds from the excess crude revenue account to pay for the completion of the National Population Census. However, if constitutional federalism is to be protected and promoted and democracy itself is to be sustained in the country, this throwback from the decade of military dictatorship must be discontinued.

Flowing from all this is the contentious issue of who is the custodian of the Federation Account. The federal government has, to all intents and purposes, conducted itself not as just the custodian but also as the owner of the Federation Account. This claim was, however, not sustained in the judgment of the Supreme Court in the case of Lagos State versus the federal government.[27] The court held that the federal government has not been conferred with the powers of custodian and trustee to this account and, therefore, cannot proceed to operate it in any manner as it deems fit. The Constitution does not confer on the president the right to withhold funds meant for any government in the Federation.

It was in order to avert the illegal operations and unconstitutional acts of the federal government with respect to the operation of the Federation Account that the National Political Reform Conference recommended the creation of the position of accountant general of the Federation. This position is separate from the accountant general of the federal government and is to be responsible for the maintenance and operation of the Federation Account.

The National Political Reform Conference

The recently concluded National Political Reform Conference further cements the notion that perhaps the Nigerian Federation is still fragile. It was widely reported that South-South delegates (i.e., those from the Niger Delta region) staged a walkout at the conference over the proposed marginal increment of the weight assigned to the derivation principle from 13 percent to 17 percent. The South-South delegates had demanded 50 percent. Despite the walkout, the conference concluded its deliberations and presented its report to the president, who, in turn, presented it to a joint session of the House of Representatives and the Senate. It is evident that the Conference could not agree on the issue of resource control. The heated debate on resource control and some unpleasant pronouncements on the matter by some delegates highlight the fundamental problems in Nigeria's fiscal federalism.

Another burning matter concerns political power sharing among the different levels of government and the six geo-political zones. For federalism to work, the federating units must agree on some workable formula for sharing power. Power sharing should include which zone is going to account for the position of president. The same agitation is found both at the state and local government levels with regard to governors and council chairs, respectively.

The main purpose of the National Political Reform Conference was to discuss and find solutions to burning issues affecting Nigeria. While there were broad agreements on such areas as the economy, foreign policy, education, youth, and gender, the discordant voices on resource control and power sharing, among others, are reminders of the fragility of Nigeria's federal system. It should also be noted that the conference had no constitutional or statutory mandate to implement its decisions. Perhaps this explains why the president submitted the report to both houses of Parliament. It is hoped that the National Assembly will deliberate on the report and implement those aspects of the recommendations that will benefit the country.

CONCLUSION

There is no doubt that the practice of fiscal federalism in Nigeria has generated contentious issues, particularly around factors that would ensure an equitable and stable revenue allocation among the three levels of government. These factors include, among others:

- adopting a uniform derivation principle;
- giving adequate weight to the equality of states;
- giving special attention to the development of areas producing natural resources; and
- sharing revenue based on the responsibilities of each tier of government.

If Nigeria is to remain a federation, then meaningful dialogue and compromises ought to guide deliberations aimed at reducing the tensions emanating from the practice of fiscal federalism. This would help to guarantee the sustained implementation of reforms.

NOTES

I wish to acknowledge the comments of the referees, particularly Chichi Ashwe and John Kincaid. Their suggestions have improved this chapter; however, the usual disclaimer applies.

1 This is an estimate. See the Nigerian government's website: <http://www.nigeria.gov.ng>. A national census was conducted in April–May 2006; the results are still expected.
2 There are several studies of Nigeria's fiscal federalism. For example, see Adedotun O. Phillips, "Four Decades of Fiscal Federalism in Nigeria," *Publius: The Journal of Federalism* 21 (1991): 103–11; John Kincaid and G. Allan Tarr, eds., *Constitutional Origins, Structure, and Change in Federal Countries* (Montreal: McGill-Queen's University Press, 2005), 240–75; and B.O. Nwabueze, *Federalism in Nigeria under the Presidential Constitution* (Lagos: State Ministry of Lagos, 2002), 4–55.
3 Izevbuwa Osayimwese and Sunday Iyare, "The Economics of Nigerian Federalism: Selected Issues in Economics Management," *Publius: The Journal of Federalism* 21

(1990): 89–101. See also Akpan H. Ekpo, "Fiscal Federalism: Nigeria's Post-Independence Experience, 1960–90," *World Development* 22 (8): 1129–46.
4   Central Bank of Nigeria, *Annual Report and Statement of Accounts* (Abuja: Central Bank of Nigeria, 2004). See <www.cenbank.org>.
5   Ibid.
6   Selected states – notably Akwa Ibom, Rivers, Cross River, and so on – had challenged the federal government's introduction of the on-shore and off-shore oil dichotomy for the purposes of revenue allocation. They also urged, among other demands, that the federal government pay the 13 percent derivation. The Supreme Court ruling touched on several matters, including the Stabilization Fund. See Udeme Ekpo, *The Niger Delta and Oil Politics* (Lagos: International Energy Communications, 2004), 159–241.
7   Central Bank of Nigeria, *Annual Report and Statement of Accounts*, 156–61.
8   G.F. Mbanefoh, "Federalism and Common Property," *Guardian*, 20 February 1993, 13.
9   A. Adedeji, *Nigerian Federal Finance* (London: Hutchinson Educational, 1969).
10 P.N.C. Okigbo, *Nigerian Public Finance* (London: Longmans, 1965).
11 Ibid.
12 G.F. Mbanefoh, "Nigerian Fiscal Federalism: Assignment of Functions and Tax Powers," seminar organized by RMAFC, Enugu, 21–23 April 1992. See also Akpan H. Ekpo, *Fiscal Theory and Policy: Selected Essays* (Lagos: Somaprint, 2005).
13 Ibid.
14 The "resource control" suit refers to the attempt by some states to control resources in their jurisdiction by using the courts; it also implies their having more than a fair share (through the sharing formula) of mineral resources by emphasizing participation in the exploitation of such resources. At present, the formula allows 13 percent for derivation. When the states took the federal government to court, the latter was not even adhering to the 13 percent provided for in the Constitution.
15 Akpan H. Ekpo and Enamidem Ubok-Udom, eds., *Issues in Fiscal Federalism and Revenue Allocation in Nigeria* (Ibadan: Future Publishing, 2003).
16 Ibid.
17 NITEL is the government-owned telecommunications company. GSM operators in the country now include Vmobile, MTN, and Globacom. See G.F. Mbanefoh and Akpan H. Ekpo, *Review of Constitutional Provisions and Fiscal Federalism in Nigeria*, Abuja: World Bank, 2005.
18 Federal Republic of Nigeria, *Report of the Presidential Commission on Revenue Allocation*, vol. 1, Main Report (Apapa: Government Press, 1977).
19 Akpan H. Ekpo,. "Fiscal Federalism and Local Government Finances in Nigeria," in *Nigerian Economic Society, Fiscal Federalism and Nigeria's Economic Development* (Ibadan: Nigerian Economic Society, 1999).
20 See Mbanefoh and Ekpo, *Review of Constitutional Provisions*.

21 It was expected that an increase in the weight attached to derivation might reduce the tension surrounding the control of petroleum resources by the Niger Delta region.
22 Victor B. Attah, "Fiscal Federalism in Nigeria: A Re-Examination of My Views," remarks made by the Akwa Ibom State Governor during the Roundtable on Global Dialogue on Federalism, Uyo, 29 September 2005.
23 Ibid.
24 Federal Republic of Nigeria, *Constitution of the Federal Republic of Nigeria 1999* (Lagos: Government Press, 1999).
25 See Central Bank of Nigeria, *Monetary Policy Circular* (Abuja: Central Bank of Nigeria, 2004), 1–58.
26 Federal Republic of Nigeria, The Corrupt Practices and Other Related Offences Act, 2000. See also <www.icpcnigeria.com>.
27 On 19 April 2004, the Lagos State Government sued the federal government, challenging the authority of the latter to withhold its statutory allocation to the new fifty-seven local government councils it created. In its ruling the Supreme Court reaffirmed that no one tier of government had more rights than did any other over the Federation Account and that, thus, the federal government could not stop payment to the Lagos state government's existing (not new) councils.

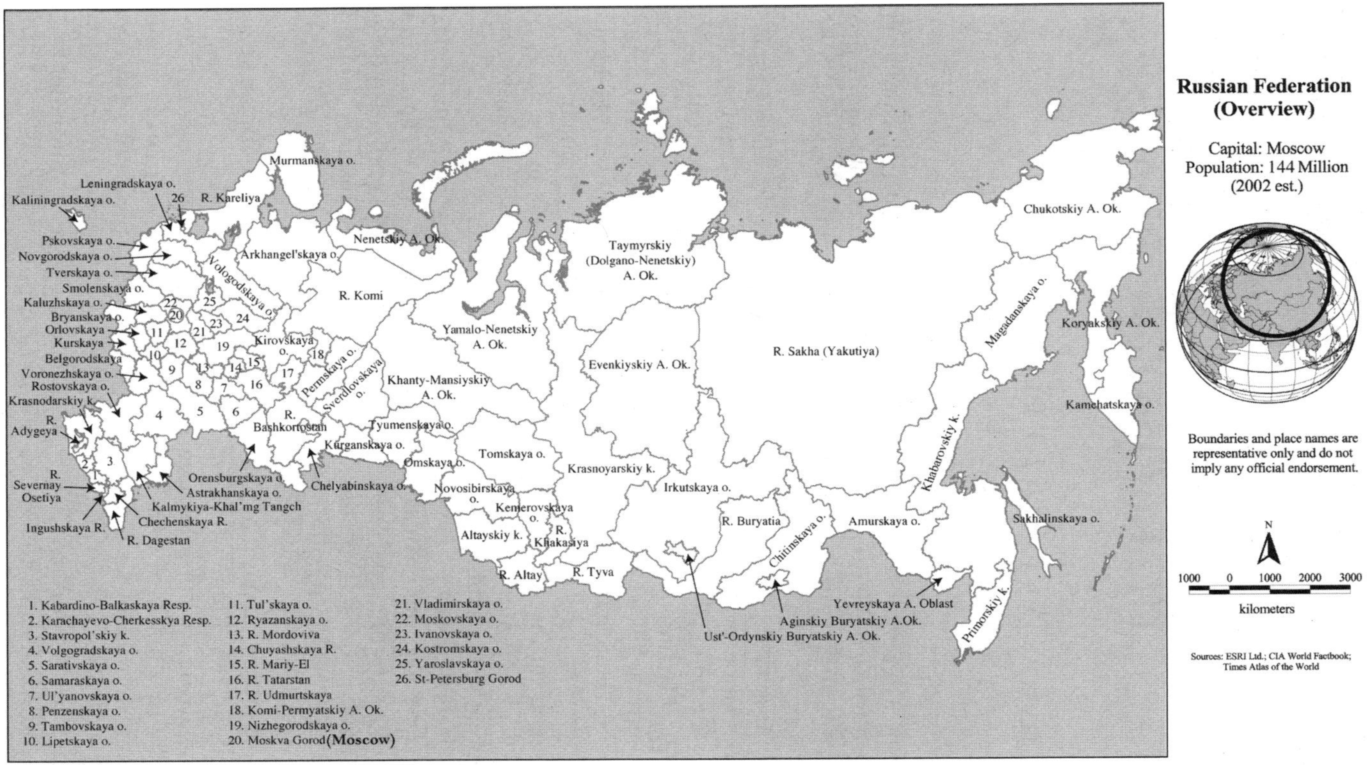

Russian Federation (Overview)

Capital: Moscow
Population: 144 Million (2002 est.)

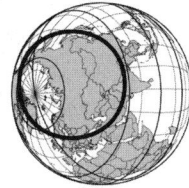

Boundaries and place names are representative only and do not imply any official endorsement.

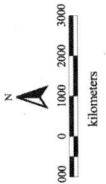

Sources: ESRI Ltd.; CIA World Factbook; Times Atlas of the World

1. Kabardino-Balkarskaya Resp.
2. Karachayevo-Cherkesskya Resp.
3. Stavropol'skiy k.
4. Volgogradskaya o.
5. Saratovskaya o.
6. Samaraskaya o.
7. Ul'yanovskaya o.
8. Penzenskaya o.
9. Tambovskaya o.
10. Lipetskaya o.
11. Tul'skaya o.
12. Ryazanskaya o.
13. R. Mordoviva
14. Chuvashskaya R
15. R. Mariy-El
16. R. Tatarstan
17. R. Udmurtskaya
18. R. Komi-Permyatskiy A. Ok.
19. Nizhegorodskaya o.
20. Moskva Gorod (**Moscow**)
21. Vladimirskaya o.
22. Moskovskaya o.
23. Ivanovskaya o.
24. Kostromskaya o.
25. Yaroslavskaya o.
26. St-Petersburg Gorod

The Russian Federation

ALEXANDER DERYUGIN
AND GALINA KURLYANDSKAYA

Russia is a federative state with a republican form of government. The chief executive is the president, who is elected by direct votes of the people for a term of four years. The same person cannot hold the office of president for more than two successive terms.

The Russian Parliament comprises two chambers: the State Duma and the Council of the Federation. The State Duma has 450 deputies – members of the political parties that successfully passed the 7 percent barrier at elections. Elections to the Duma are based on universal, secret, equal, and direct suffrage for a term of four years. The Federation Council comprises two representatives from each region (subject) of the Russian Federation: one from the legislative and one from the executive branch of power. Depending on the region of the Federation, members of the Federation Council are appointed by either the head of the regional administration or the legislative assembly.

Russia is the world's largest federation, consisting of eighty-six (as of 1 January 2007) regions (see Table 1). The parade of sovereignties in the early 1990s (in the wake of the breakdown of the USSR) reflected the ethnic republics' quest for political and economic independence, which led the existing administrative-territorial units to split up and form the new constituent units of the Russian Federation.

Disparities in climate, population, and development between regions hinder the development of symmetric federal-regional relations, thus making a case for consolidating units of the Federation through mergers. The first practical steps towards consolidation were made in 2004, following an official decision on the merger (effective from 1 December 2005) of Perm Region and Komi-Perm Autonomous District. In the pipeline are Krasnoyarsk Krai with Taimyr and Evenk Autonomous Okrugs, and Kamchatka Region with Koryak Autonomous Okrug. Further

Table 1
Basic political and geographic indicators

Official name	Russian Federation (Russia)
Population	143,474,200
Area	17,075,400 square kilometres
GDP per capita in US$	(2004): 4,214
Constitution	1993, democracy, federation, republic
Levels of government	Federal, regional, and local. Local governments can have one or two tiers; some regions (autonomous *okrugs*) have two tiers of state government
Constitutional status of local government	Separate tier, not part of state government
Official languages	The official language of the Federation is Russian. Ethnic republics have several official languages: Russian plus ethnic language/s. Some ethnic localities within constituent units (regions) also use two official languages.
Number and types of constituent units	There are 21 republics (ethnic autonomies), 48 oblasts, 7 krais, 2 federal cities, 1 autonomous oblast, 7 autonomous okrugs (autonomous districts). The RF Constitution grants equal rights to all constituent units of the federation, disregarding their type.

mergers could hardly be on a mass scale because the merger of a relatively wealthy region with a poorer one would lower the per capita budget revenue of the former, so it would not be easy to sell this idea to residents of wealthier regions.

THE STRUCTURE OF GOVERNMENT AND DIVISION OF FISCAL POWERS

The Russian Constitution establishes two levels of government: state government and local self-government. The state level subdivides into federal and regional, with local self-government, according to the 1993 Constitution, falling outside the system of state power.

The procedure for establishment of regional bodies of state governments is set by federal law according to general principles of the organization of legislative (representative) and executive state government bodies. This law establishes, inter alia, a list of powers of state government bodies and the procedure for conferring powers on the chief executive of a region, whose candidacy is nominated by the president of the Russian Federation and approved by the regional legislative assembly.

Federal law also establishes general principles of organization of self-governance in the Russian Federation. This law was passed in 2003, but it comes into effect in stages and is not expected to become fully effective until 2009.

The Russian fiscal system features three to four tiers, depending on the type of jurisdiction. For state government, it is the federation and region. For local government, it is the city, or municipal district (*raion*), and settlements (*poselenniye*) in a municipal district.

Formally, federal, regional, and local levels of government have designated revenue sources and spending obligations, and each level drafts and approves its own budget. One might see this as evidence of the fiscal autonomy of subnational and local governments. However, this would be incorrect as the upper levels of government continue to rule both the revenue and expenditure arrangements of the lower level governments. Subnational governments do not have transparent mechanisms to determine the total amount of revenues that will be available to them in a forthcoming year, nor do they have the authority to levy taxes other than those established by the Tax Code of the Russian Federation and other federal laws.[1]

The Assignment of Spending and Regulatory Responsibilities

Federal laws govern the expenditure obligations of the subnational governments, although regions and localities (except for the recipients of the equalization transfers) may choose to expand the list of spending obligations established for them by the federal government, if they have their own resources to fulfill them.

The 2000–04 reform of federative relations and local government targeted comprehensive demarcation of expenditure obligations and revenue sources across all levels of government in the Russian Federation, but the result was somewhat disputable. Federal legislation still sets basic requirements to, or details of, expenditure obligations, and each level of government is responsible for the provision of public goods and public services in conformity with the assignment of spending responsibilities. From that perspective, there are no explicitly federal or explicitly regional functions in Russia: decentralization is limited to deciding which level of government would finance the delivery of standard public goods and/or services, but the standards are established by the central government.

In the course of the 2000–04 reform, three categories of government functions were identified: (1) functions that subnational and local

Table 2
Legislative responsibility and actual provision of services by different orders of government

Legislative responsibility	Public service	Actual allocation of function
Federal	Defence	Federal
Federal	Law and order	Federal
Federal	Environment security	Federal and provincial
Federal	Higher education	Federal and provincial
Federal and provincial	Secondary education	Local
Federal and provincial	Health	Federal, provincial, and local
Federal and provincial	Welfare	Provincial
Federal	Tax collection	Federal
Federal	Civilian registry	Local
Federal, provincial, and local	Culture	Federal, provincial, and local
Federal, provincial, and local	Housing services	Local

governments perform and finance from their own resources; (2) delegated functions (i.e., those that governments of lower levels perform and governments of upper levels finance through earmarked transfers); and (3) functions that fall into the category of exclusively federal responsibilities (e.g., national defence [see Table 2]).

In 2005, a new assignment of expenditure responsibilities was enacted, although, for several reasons, this was unsuccessful. One reason for its lack of success is that, due to a dramatic reduction in the political weight of regional governors, the power of regional governments has substantially shrunk. Then, some actual expenditure needs of the regions were overlooked, while a significant number of federal functions performed by the regions remained unfunded (unfunded mandates). These all led to further revisions of the assignment of spending responsibilities in 2005 and 2006.

It is pertinent to note that, given current budget reporting requirements in Russia, a number of federal or regional spending obligations transferred to lower levels of government together with funds are recorded in relevant sector items as expenditures of lower-level governments, while the government that provided the funding reports them as intergovernmental transfers (see Table 3). This is the case, for instance, with regard to social spending obligations such as education (recently

Table 3
Direct expenditures by function and level of government (2006)

Function	Federal (%)	State or provincial (%)	Local (%)	All (%)
Defence	100	0	0	100
Debt servicing	85	13	2	100
General administration	58	22	20	100
Law and order	77	20	3	100
Economic services	36	56	8	100
Social services	46	31	23	100
health	13	69	18	100
education	22	26	52	100
Subsidies				0
Total	54	29	17	100
Local public services*	13	45	42	100

* Local public services include: primary and preschool education, secondary education, public health, hospitals, urban highways, urban transportation, drinking water and sewerage, waste collection, electric power supply, fire protection, public order and safety, police

shifted from the regional to local level of government together with the targeted transfers) and social safety net benefits (transferred from the federal to regional level and then, in part, from the regional to local level). Health care does not include spending on the compulsory medical insurance fund, which stays out of the general budget and has revenues and expenditures that are less transparent.

Monitoring of budget execution is quite thorough. Local governments furnish their financial statements of budget execution to the regions, which, in turn, submit their own plus municipal statements to the federal Ministry of Finance. The Russian Accounting Chamber (the federal financial auditing body) performs comprehensive audits of regional governments that are recipients of federal grants (75 percent of all regions) on top of regular audits of targeted-use grants transferred to regional governments for the implementation of federal mandates. Regions employ the same scheme to monitor local budgets. Monitoring is focused, inter alia, on the match between reported expenditures and the expenditure responsibilities of subnational governments established by federal law.

*The Subsidiarity Principle and Causes of Conflicts
in Intergovernmental Fiscal Relations*

The subsidiarity principle is adhered to only for housing and communal services, education, maintenance of cultural institutions, and health care. Some traditionally local services, such as public transport, roads, fire prevention, and public safety, are funded and provided by regional rather than local governments.

Regional bodies of the federal government also perform a number of local functions. These include law and order and tax collection. According to the Russian Constitution, local self-governments are not authorized to undertake legislative and/or enforcement measures; these functions are assigned to the state. However, the Constitution obliges local self-governments to safeguard public order. The City of Moscow, certain districts of the City of St Petersburg, and the cities of Perm and Saratov did create municipal police units; however, these in fact became part of the federal police, and they report to the Federal Ministry of the Interior rather than to local mayors.

The current system – wherein the assignment of spending responsibilities and the monitoring of budget execution are controlled by the federal government, while spending obligations and budget execution per se are controlled by the subnational governments – often produces clashes of interests. For instance, in 2005 the law on monetization of social benefits was enacted to substitute federally guaranteed in-kind social benefits with cash payments. The provision of these benefits used to be an unfunded mandate imposed on regional governments by federal regulations. Unfortunately, the Ministry of Finance underestimated the amount of social expenditure obligations of the regional governments when allocating monetization grants to the regions. This led to the inability of the regions to implement the new law. In January 2005, pensioners in a number of Russian regions, driven by the loss of their right to use public transportation free of charge, and not having been fully compensated for this with a cash subsidy, picketed highways. The federal government then had to take advantage of the record-breaking surplus of the federal budget in 2005 to substantially increase the size of the compensation transfers to the regions.

Redistribution of state assets between regional and local governments illustrates another type of intergovernmental conflict. Federal regulations prohibit subnational and local governments from holding assets that are not directly involved in delivering the public services assigned to them. Federal law mandates that all such property should be assigned to the government that is responsible for delivering the service; however, it says nothing about compensation or what should be done with the property that is not involved in delivering public services but, rather, is a source of local government revenues. Hence, there are property shuffles between regions and municipalities and desperate activities on the part of local governments to protect property at all costs. Some local authorities have found a solution in selling off (privatizing through shell companies) municipal buildings occupied by regional administrations. Courts are snowed under with claims brought by regions against municipalities and vice versa.

Intergovernmental conflicts resulted in calls to expand the transition period (established for the full implementation of the law on self-governance throughout Russia) and to postpone the implementation of a number of provisions until 2009.

Common Values: Emphasis on Social Services, Military Spending, and Horizontal Equity

Judging by the allocation of consolidated government funding across functions, the most important public goods in Russia are education, pensions, national defence, the social safety net, and law and order. These expenditures account for almost 60 percent of total spending of the fiscal system (including all levels of government but excluding special federal social security funds – the Medical Fund, Pension Fund, and Social Insurance Fund).

Federal transfers to subnational governments constitute about 15 percent of total federal expenditures, making it the third largest expenditure item of the federal government. The largest spending item of the federal government is transfers to the Pension Fund (18.6 percent of total federal expenditures), followed by national defence outlays (16 percent). The budget of the Pensions Fund in FY2005 was $47.5 million, of which $18.1 million consisted of transfers from the federal budget. As for subnational governments, their largest spending category is education, followed by health care and housing and grants for communal services. The purpose of the latter is to compensate providers of housing and utility services for their losses from state-regulated tariffs.

To the common people in Russia, the main function of government at any level is social protection of vulnerable groups, including old-age pensioners, families with children, war veterans, disabled persons, and many others (there are more than 150 categories overall). A special category is the working poor – schoolteachers and doctors in the public sector, whose wages have been the lowest in the country for years. To correct this, the federal government has recently launched "national projects" for education and health care that target increased wages in these sectors and the purchase of modern equipment. However, these projects are not contemplating structural reforms and serve mainly as an additional cash channel.

Channels of Federal Influence on Subnational Policies and Vice Versa

Although the federal government has not officially stated the goals and objectives of intergovernmental fiscal relations, it does have a number of tools that allow it to influence regional fiscal policies either directly or indirectly. The tools for exerting financial influence on the regions include:

1 Earmarked transfers. This is a tool that directly influences regional budget policies (funded mandates). Spending these grants is subject to strict control by the federal authorities, and the share of these grants in total subnational revenues is rapidly growing.
2 Budget loans. Because the Russian banking system is underdeveloped, the federal government budget is often the only source of short-term lending available to subnational governments for covering cash shortages. Until GY2005 the budget loans were interest free. The federal budget provides these loans selectively, although selection criteria are not transparent.
3 Non-formula-based transfers. All regions, including the relatively wealthy Moscow, Tatarstan, and Bashkortostan, receive transfers other than equalization grants. Most of these are capital transfers that are invested in public improvements (e.g., subways, highways, and restoration of historic sites).
4 Timing of transfers. No schedule is fixed for the disbursement of transfers to regions; therefore, the federal government can choose the timing, warranting absolute loyalty on the part of heavily subsidized regions.

Thus, the federal government dictates budget policies to the regional governments, not the other way around. The Federation Council is not instrumental in protecting regional interests: it approves virtually all federal bills that impose unfunded mandates on regional governments and has approved the abolition of a number of regional and local taxes. Furthermore, the council approved the president's initiative to change the council nomination procedure. Formerly, each region of the Federation was represented in the Federation Council by the governor and the speaker of the legislative assembly. Under the new procedure, each region of the Federation is still represented by two council members, but these are nominated either by the governor or the legislative assembly of the respective region and approved by the Federation Council. This new procedure has substantially weakened the council's political influence.

The Legal Status of Local Governments and the Provision of Local Services

According to the Russian Constitution, local self-governance should be implemented throughout Russia. Until recently, however, many localities had no elected self-government, and they were administered through local offices of the regional government.[2]

The new federal law (2003) introduced two levels of local self-governance, including settlements (*poselennyie*), either urban or rural, and municipal districts/urban districts (i.e., cities that combine the functions of a settlement and a municipal district). Furthermore, the entire territory of Russia was divided into municipal districts and urban districts. Territories with low population density may not have a settlement level of government. All these entities are called municipalities, and the total number of municipalities in Russia exceeds 24,000. Federal cities (i.e., Moscow and St Petersburg) have the right to issue their own regulations regarding the organization of local self-governance within their boundaries.

The responsibilities of regional authorities with respect to the organization of local self-governance are limited to procedural matters, such as the establishment of boundaries and the status of municipalities, scheduling first elections, and so on. Federal law strictly defines the scope of local self-governance, although regional governments may delegate some regional functions to local governments, together with the resources to perform them. This does not work in reverse (i.e., local governments do not delegate local functions to regional governments), except when local governments become insolvent. Bilateral agreements on the relocation of functions (together with their associated resources) are possible only between municipal districts and settlements within districts.

Special Features of Providing Local Services in Rural Areas

In Soviet times, collective farms used to be major providers of services in rural areas. Today, most of the former collective farms are joint-stock companies, with 100 percent of the stock held by regional governments, and these companies continue to support villagers in one form or another. The forms of support include providing fodder, seeds, and timber for heating purposes; plowing land in village smallholdings; and so on. In monetary terms, the total cost of services provided by such a farm to local residents may exceed the cost of public services provided to them by the local government. This, of course, does not favour business development. Reports do not capture the actual losses of these farms from the performance of social safety net functions, but it is commonly recognized that their economic inefficiency correlates with the amount of their welfare activities. These successors to collective farms and private smallholdings exist as a symbiosis, and a considerable portion of the subsidies and benefits these farms receive from the government ends up supporting the private smallholdings of their labourers. The low labour capacity of these farms is also attributed, at least partially, to the fact that they continue to provide employment to local residents as a form of welfare support.

Collective farms used to hold most of the communal utilities in rural areas, such as roads and heating systems, and these facilities serviced both the farms and the households. The current ownership of communal utilities in rural areas is mixed: some of them remain in the ownership of former collective farms; others were taken over by local self-governments. Utilities are often subsidized through federal or regional targeted programs. For instance, improvement of local roads is financed through the federal program entitled Modernization of the Transport System. In this program, the federal government transfers funds to regional governments in the form of earmarked capital transfers, and regional governments upgrade the internal roads of former collective farms to bring them into the network of public roads.

Barriers to Trade and Factor Mobility

The Constitution of the Russian Federation guarantees a common economic space; free movement of goods, services, and capital; support for competition; and freedom of entrepreneurship. Nevertheless, barriers to trade between regions do exist and take different forms, such as inspection of goods en route to prevent export of subsidized agricultural products from the region, various charges for entry to a regional/local market, and establishment of onerous sanitary requirements. In the 1990s, regional administrations even levied taxes on imports (primarily, imports of alcohol), but this practice was banned by the federal government.

Since regional authorities have virtually no revenue autonomy, they often set trade barriers for dual purposes: for fundraising and for protecting local producers. In addition, regional authorities use administrative levers to drive out competitors. All this leads to serious market distortions. According to the estimate of the Russian Federation Ministry of Agriculture, removal of barriers in interregional grain trade would have reduced domestic grain prices by 25 percent.

Big cities, such as Moscow and St Petersburg, maintain a system of obligatory residence authorization as a barrier to labour movement in order to protect their citizenry from competition in the labour market and their budgets from additional social expenditures.

ECONOMIC AND FISCAL POLICY COORDINATION

The legislative and executive branches of the federal government design and monitor Russian economic and fiscal policies, including regional ones. The federal government monitors regional development by means of statistical observations and departmental reporting, where regional line ministries report to their federal counterpart ministries. The governors report on the social and economic achievements of their regions at the sittings of the federal Cabinet of Ministers.

Formally, governors have to draft short-, medium-, and long-term programs for the social and economic development of their regions. Unfortunately, a typical regional program establishes no objectives, time frame, or indicators, so it looks more like a political agenda than an action plan.

The revenue autonomy of regional governments is negligible, and their influence on regional fiscal policy is limited to varying the rates of certain taxes (within the limits established by the federal government) and introducing tax exemptions from regional and local taxes. When both regional development and fiscal equalization are regulated by the federal government, the issue of interregional economic and fiscal cooperation is not on the top of the list.

Monetary Policy

The Central Bank of the Russian Federation is responsible for the design and implementation of monetary policy. The bank reports to the State Duma, which appoints the chair of the bank nominated by the president, and members of the board nominated by the chair of the bank. The bank's performance is monitored by the National Banking Council, whose members represent the Federation Council, State Duma, President's Office, Cabinet of Ministers, Central Bank, and regional governments.

Soft Budget Constraints and Fiscal Discipline

Until 2000, soft budget constraints created a serious problem. But since then, federal legislation has established strict limits on regional/local debt and the level of current budget deficits, and subnational over-borrowing has ceased to threaten the stability of the budget system. According to Russian Federation Ministry of Finance surveys, the most common violation of financial discipline on the part of regional finance departments is the presence of overdue liabilities. In 2006, thirteen out of eighty-six regions reported they had overdue liabilities.

The other common breach of financial discipline is excessive remuneration of regional officials. In many regions that are recipients of federal equalization transfers, regional officials get higher wages than do federal officials of the same rank, which is against the federal regulations.

Assignment of Revenue-Raising Powers

Sources of government revenues in Russia are taxes, non-tax collections, and intergovernmental transfers. Earnings from the business activities of subnational governments often accrue to extra-budgetary funds that are controlled by the government but are beyond public control. Regional taxes account for roughly 3 percent of the total revenues of the consolidated budget of the Russian Federation, and the share of local taxes is less than 1 percent. On average, regional and local taxes account for 9 percent to 10 percent of total subnational government revenues. The majority of regional revenues are comprised of federal shared taxes.

Taxpayers pay taxes to governments at all levels through the offices of the Federal Treasury, and the Federal Tax Service administers the collection of all taxes, federal and subnational alike (see Table 4). Neither regions nor municipalities have the authority to collect or monitor the collection of subnational taxes. This sometimes results in under-collection of subnational taxes because the Federal Tax Service, as a federal body, is interested primarily in collecting the taxes that accrue to the federal budget. For the same reason, the collection rate of shared taxes that partly accrue to regional budgets tends to be higher than that of taxes that accrue 100 percent to subnational budgets. Since the majority of subnational governments in Russia levy regional and local taxes at the maximum rates allowed by federal laws, subnational revenue autonomy is limited essentially to the use of regional/municipal assets for generating non-tax revenues. According to official reports, non-tax revenues currently account for about 8 percent of regional/local budgets.

But even if they have no formal tax administration powers, regional and local governments have other means to make businesses pay subnational taxes. Media campaigns, audits and inspections, threats to bring in the audit of the Federal Tax Service or the Prosecutor's Office, and other forms of pressure on taxpayers often serve as effective fundraising tools. In addition, subnational governments often succeed in getting businesses to make in-kind contributions to local communities in exchange for tax breaks, budget loans or budget guarantees, land lease or sale, and other favours.

Issues of Tax Competition

As mentioned above, the tax autonomy of subnational governments is limited to the provision of tax breaks and the establishment of tax rates within the range established by federal laws. The two most important taxes that are regulated by subnational governments in terms of their tax rate are the Enterprise Profit Tax (EPT) and the Business Property Tax

Table 4
Tax assignment for various orders of government (2005)

	Determination of			Shares in revenue (%)			
	Base	Rate	Tax collection and administration	Federal	State/province	Local	All orders
Federal							
Enterprise profits tax	Federal	Federal	Federal	27	73		100
VAT	Federal	Federal	Federal	100			100
Excises on alcohol and alcohol-based products	Federal	Federal	Federal	50	50		100
Excises on gasoline and diesel fuel	Federal	Federal	Federal	40	60		100
Excises on alcoholic products, beer	Federal	Federal	Federal		100		100
Other excises	Federal	Federal	Federal	100			100
MET (fuel gas)	Federal	Federal	Federal	100			100
MET (hydrocarbons, exclusive of fuel gas)	Federal	Federal	Federal	95	5		100
MET (widespread minerals)	Federal	Federal	Federal		100		100
MET (other minerals)	Federal	Federal	Federal	40	60		100
Fee for the use of aquatic biological resources	Federal	Federal	Federal	100			100
Fee for the use of fauna	Federal	Federal	Federal		100		100
Water tax	Federal	Federal	Federal	100			100
Single social tax	Federal	Federal	Federal	100			100
Personal income tax	Federal	Federal	Federal		70	30	100
Tax on inheritance and gifts	Federal	Federal	Federal		100		100
Federal special tax regimes							
Single tax on imputed income	Federal	Federal	Federal	10		90	100

Table 4
Tax assignment for various orders of government (2005) (*Continued*)

	Determination of			Shares in revenue (%)			
	Base	Rate	Tax collection and administration	Federal	State/province	Local	All orders
Single tax levied under an applicable simplified taxation system	Federal	Federal	Federal	10	90		100
Single agricultural tax	Federal	Federal	Federal	10	30	60	100
State or Provincial							
Enterprise property tax	Federal	Provincial	Federal		100		100
Transport tax	Federal	Provincial	Federal		100		100
Tax on gambling business	Federal	Provincial	Federal		100		100
Local							
Personal property tax	Federal	Local	Federal			100	100
Land tax	Federal	Local	Federal			100	100

(BPT). The regional rate of the EPT, one of the largest tax sources of subnational budget revenues, which accounts for some 38 percent of total regional tax revenue, may vary from 13.5 percent to 17.5 percent, and the rate of the BPT varies from 0 to 2.2 percent.

In terms of real economic growth, establishing lower tax rates or granting exemptions from these or other taxes is hardly instrumental because long-term growth depends on investments. Favourable economic and political conditions attract greater investments than do short-term benefits. Besides, federal tax legislation that regulates the taxing powers of subnational governments changes almost every year, and there are no guarantees that low tax rates and/or tax exemptions granted by a regional government would remain in force even one year ahead.

Nevertheless, regions do benefit from setting lower tax rates because lower rates induce businesses to move their headquarters to these jurisdictions and to register as payers of the profit tax. By using transfer prices, such companies turn their headquarters located in domestic offshore zones into profit centres. Although offshore regions report high profits, they do not lose in terms of federal equalization. This is possible because the transfer allocation methodology used by the federal Ministry of Finance relies on economic performance data rather than on actual tax collections. The State Statistical Agency (*Rosstat*) registers economic performance (production) where it actually occurs rather than where production taxes are paid. Therefore, although the drain of businesses from other regions occurs only on paper, it significantly increases regional revenues.

Notable cases of tax competition include the Republic of Mordovia, which, in 2002, granted $700 million worth of tax concessions, whereas in 2002 its revenue-generation capacity (estimated by means of a methodology based on economic performance) amounted to only $130 million. As a region with low per capita fiscal capacity, the republic receives federal equalization transfers and capital transfers for regional development.

The scale of losses that regions can suffer if large taxpayers decide to move the registration of their businesses elsewhere is illustrated by the case of Sibneft. One of the largest oil companies in Russia, Sibneft, whose owner, Roman Abramovich, was the elected governor of Chukotka, set up an affiliated company, Sibneft-Chukotka, specifically for paying taxes in Chukotka. This generated a fourfold growth of regional budget revenues over four years. Later, the new owners of Sibneft refused to continue paying taxes to Chukotka and dissolved the affiliated company. Now they are considering shifting the registration of the parent company, which was originally registered in Omsk Oblast, to the City of St Petersburg. This will reduce the Omsk Oblast budget revenues by 60 percent.

FISCAL EQUITY AND EFFICIENCY CONCERNS

The existing assignment of revenue sources across levels of government creates vertical imbalance in the budget system of the Russian Federation, and this imbalance keeps growing over time. The gap between the richest and the poorest regions exceeds 280-fold in terms of per capita taxes collected. The upper revenue group comprises oil- and gas-producing regions, and the lowest revenue group includes the republics of the Northern Caucasus, whose fiscal capacities are affected by ethnic and/or religious strife, the predominance of the shadow economy, and a rapidly growing population.

Regional fiscal capacities vary dramatically, and so do geoclimatic conditions and distances from centres of production, leading to disparities in energy prices and prices of other inputs and, ultimately, to disparities in the cost of delivery of public services. The difference in the cost of living between the richest and the poorest regions is threefold, disparities in the costs of communal services are twentyfold, and the difference in the length of the heating season across Russian regions is ninefold.

To reduce the fiscal gap, the federal government allocates general-purpose (fiscal equalization) and other transfers to subnational governments. The number of subsidies, subventions, and other transfers that the federal government allocates every year is close to one hundred, as measured by the number of line items under the intergovernmental transfers section of the federal budget. The major types of federal transfers are equalization transfers, gap-filling subsidies, the Compensation Fund, co-financing of social programs, capital transfers, regional finance reform transfers, operating transfers to special territories, ad hoc subsidies, and transfers to closed cities.

Equalization transfers are formula-based, general-purpose grants. The Budget Code – the federal code of laws that govern public spending procedures across all levels of government in Russia – does not restrict the spending of this grant money to any specific purpose. But in reality these transfers are spent primarily on paying the wage bill and go by the name of "wage subsidies" in the parlance of regional finance officials.

Gap-filling subsidies, which were first introduced in 2004, compensate regions for implementation of federal policies leading to regional revenue gaps and/or expenditure increases (see Table 5). In 2004, these subsidies compensated regional governments for the federally mandated increase in wages in the public sector. In 2005, gap-filling subsidies had a three-part purpose: (1) to compensate for losses from changes in the equalization formula; (2) to compensate for revenue gaps caused by the reduction in the regional share in the oil and gas extraction tax, 100 percent federal retention of the water tax, and a 1.5 percentage point reduction in the regional component of the corporate income tax; and (3) to compensate for the devolution of vocational schools and so on. Note that the increase in the minimum wage in 2004 was not included in the list of purposes for allocating gap-filling subsidies in 2005.

Transfers from the Compensation Fund compensate regional governments for implementing federal mandates. These include (1) the rental subsidy granted to certain categories of federal beneficiaries (such as war veterans and victims of irradiation catastrophes), (2) benefits for blood donors, and (3) compensation of regional governments for civil status registration (all three are federal functions).

Co-financing of social programs partially compensates regional governments for a number of social safety net entitlements. In fact, federal laws have introduced most of these entitlements, so they can be interpreted as federal mandates. These include childcare subsidies and subsidies for victims of political repression, distinguished retirees, and individuals who worked in military enterprises during the Second World War. Subsidies for co-financing social safety net programs resemble mirror grants, but they do not create incentives for increasing the regional contribution: the federal government estimates the spending needs of the regions for implementing

Table 5
Vertical fiscal gaps

	Total revenue collected (in current US$ in millions – 2006)	Total revenue available, including net transfers for that level of gov't (in current US$ in millions – 2006)	Expenditures (in current US$ in millions – 2006)
National	273,000	248,000	171,000
Subnational			
state/provincial	106,000	98,000	93,000
local	25,000	58,000	54,000
All orders	404,000	404,000	318,000

federal mandates and transfers funds that cover a certain fixed share of this spending need. If the regions chose to contribute more, this would not make the federal government liable to increase its share in the total funding of social programs.

Capital transfers include transfers targeted for capital investments in the public sector (e.g., construction of schools, hospitals, and information technology). Regional finance reform transfers are awarded to regions through competition for prompt reform of public finance management. Participating regions must submit an action plan and demonstrate successful implementation of the plan in order to win the grant. The World Bank initiated the Regional Finance Reform program in 2000; currently, the World Bank and the federal government co-finance the program.

Operating transfers to special territories are subsidies to Chechnya and regions that have suffered from irradiation. Ad hoc subsidies include the annual Best Run City Award, grants to cities celebrating anniversaries, ad hoc compensation for federal mandates other than those covered elsewhere, and so on. Transfers to closed cities are general-purpose subsidies for military industrial centres as well as research and development centres. The federal government provides direct support to these cities rather than going through subnational governments.

Every year almost half of the total federal transfers (about $6,329 million) goes through the federal Fund of Financial Support to Regions as an equalization allowance for the low-income regions. Each year, sixty-five to sixty-eight regions out of eighty-six receive equalization grants from the federal government. Equalization grants are allocated through two windows. First, 80 percent of the total amount is allocated to all regions whose per capita fiscal capacity before equalization is less than the national average. The greater the difference between the national average and the regional per capita fiscal capacity, the greater the equalization grant allocated to that region. And second, the remaining 20 percent is allocated to the lowest-income regions in order to bring their fiscal capacity up to a certain uniform level.

The government used a formula-based approach for grant allocation to prevent regions from influencing the grant allocation process. Estimation of a region's fiscal capacity is based on value added by economic sectors, ignoring tax migration, a practice that is widely used by businesses. To account for differences in the demand for public services and input costs across regions, per capita fiscal capacities are adjusted by applying expenditure needs indices that account for price, demographic, socio-economic, geographic, climatic, and other objective factors that influence the per capita cost of providing the same public service in different regions.

Estimation of the per capita cost of public services relies, to a large extent, on the judgment of federal experts, which introduces a certain degree of opacity into the equalization formula, even if comprehensive statistical information is available.

Special federal transfers, such as compensation for federal mandates and certain capital transfers (these include subsidies for implementation of the Federal Targeted Program Reducing Disparities in Socio-Economic Development of Regions of the Russian Federation) are also allocated based on transparent formulas. Distribution of grants from the Regional Finance Reform Fund is also transparent, but distributable amounts are rather small.

The allocation of all other transfers remains non-transparent, and strong regions seem to have the power to negotiate the allocation of federal funds in their favour. For instance, the lion's share of federal transfers for implementation of regional development programs ends up in Tatarstan and Bashkortostan, two republics that are in the upper-income group of the regions, ranking fifth and nineteenth, respectively, in per capita fiscal capacity. The two regions used to receive two-thirds of the regional development grant pool, although their combined population is only 5.5 percent of the total Russian population. In total, the federal government allocates about 12 percent to 13 percent of its annual expenditure budget for support to the regions, and these finance about 16 percent of subnational government expenditures in Russia.

Size of the Grant Pool and Allocation of Fiscal Transfers

Different types of transfers are estimated differently, and the size of the total pool of federal grants to the regions is determined as a sum of these different types of transfers. Some types of transfers are adjusted for inflation, and others are not. For instance, for many years, the Best Run City Award has been equivalent to $3 million. By contrast, the size of the fiscal equalization pool is determined every year based on the figure from the preceding year, which is adjusted for inflation and changes in federal tax and budget legislation. Transfers from the Compensation Fund cover 100 percent of the estimated expenditure needs of the regions associated with implementing federal mandates. Apparently, there is no formalized methodology for estimating the need for financing the gap-filling subsidy since this subsidy was used for financing different needs in FY 2004 and FY 2005. Nevertheless, in this case too the Ministry of Finance presumably takes into account the figure from the preceding year.

Fiscal Disparities across Localities

The prosperity of a municipality almost completely depends on the local businesses or, better to say, on the businesses that locate their headquarters in the municipality rather than on the well-being of its citizenry. Therefore, disparities across localities are as dramatic (and even worse) as are those across regions.

The personal property tax generates a minor part of the overall local revenue due to the underdeveloped personal property market. And income tax (paid by employers) accrues to the budget of the locality where the employer is registered as a taxpayer rather than to the locality where the employees reside.

Typically, the presence of a strong and profitable business, such as an oil company or a liquor factory, allows the host municipality to prosper in comparison with its neighbours. The difference in the per capita fiscal capacity of the richest municipality of the region is 1.5 to two times as high as is the average per capita fiscal capacity across all municipalities of the region, and in oil producing regions this gap can be three- to sevenfold.

Most of the rural municipalities fall into the lowest income category as their taxable base is negligible (if they have one at all), and regional transfers generate 80 percent to 90 percent or more of their revenues.

For example, significant disparities across the 290 settlements of Stavropol Krai reflect the tax potential of rural versus urban settlements. The tax base of the former is far beyond that of the latter. Further, urban settlements (small towns) tend to drain labour along with income tax from rural areas.

Fiscal Disparities across Regions as a Matter of Political and Policy Concern

Given the significant variations between regional conditions and development opportunities, the fiscal inequality of regions is often taken for granted and is seen as something that would be impossible to change.

Despite ongoing increases in the volume of federal transfers, inequality between regions continues to grow, which calls for a revision of the equalization policy. The main concern is that the current policy reproduces inequality rather than providing regions with development incentives. So far, policy makers have discussed putting heavily subsidized regions under external financial management, but the first candidates that have been placed under external control are ethnic republics, which makes this issue extremely sensitive.

Allocation of Equalization Transfers and the Degree of the Resulting Equalization

The federal equalization transfers are premised on a formula-based assessment of the regions' fiscal capacity and current expenditure needs. The equalizing exercise results in the reduction of the gap in per capita revenue capacity between the wealthiest and poorest regions from about 100-fold to seventeenfold. The federal government does not take negative transfers from richer regions, but the new law on local self-governance contains provisions that allow regional governments to use negative transfers to equalize the per capita fiscal capacities of local governments.

Two out of five regions in the upper income group – Chukotka and Evenk – receive equalization transfers due to the exceptionally high expenditure needs attributable to their remote northern location.

Other Equalization Instruments

Allocation of equalization transfers is the main, if not the only, equalization instrument used by the federal government. Federal/regional shares in the co-financing of social programs depend, to some extent, on the fiscal capacity of the region in question. A portion of capital transfers is allocated based on a formula that captures the interregional inequalities in per capita availability of communal networks and social facilities, such as schools and hospitals, but this is a relatively small portion of capital transfers. Compensation for federal mandates is based on estimated expenditure needs and does not depend on the per capita fiscal capacity of the regions. In fact, allocation of such compensation enhances the inequality across regions. Direct investments of the federal government could serve as an equalization tool but, in fact, also contribute to inequality enhancement, as is demonstrated by their bias towards stronger regions, such as Tatarstan and Bashkortostan.

Transfers to Local Governments

The share of transfers in local revenues is about 30 percent to 80 percent. The Russian Federation Budget Code requires that regional governments allocate their equalization transfers to municipalities based on the localities' per capita fiscal capacities. However, regions customarily equalize local government capacities in order to maintain the existing social infrastructure. For instance, education expenditure needs are estimated by the number of schools and teachers rather than by the number of schoolchildren.

The Budget Code allows regions to use several equalization windows: one for equalization transfers, one for capital transfers, and so on. The choice of the equalization algorithm is up to the regions. The Budget Code provides for several possibilities: regions may choose to allocate grants from the regional pool to all municipalities (i.e., municipal districts/urban districts and settlements) directly, or they may choose to use a two-step procedure (i.e., to equalize municipal districts/urban districts at the regional level and then allow districts to equalize settlements). The majority of the regions are using the second approach because it means less work for them.

Impact of Fiscal Transfers on Efficiency and Equity of Service Delivery and Interjurisdictional Equity

Federal laws set the requirements and terms for most of the public services delivered by subnational governments in Russia. However, regions differ dramatically in terms of accessibility of services and per capita expenditures.

The diversity of Russian regions resembles the diversity of the countries in the world: there are megacities, oil regions, oriental-type appendages, northern territories with tribal relations, and so on. Equalization of all of those territories is impossible in principle, especially if the same approach is applied to all regions. The federal government's recent efforts to diversify its regional policy show that policy makers are aware of this problem. So far the search for new solutions has tended to focus on strengthening financial controls, including the introduction of external financial management.

CAPITAL FINANCE, PUBLIC MANAGEMENT, AND CORRUPTION

Financing Capital Investment

In the majority of regions in Russia, private business is the major investor in business as well as in social infrastructure development. This is explained not so much by the "good citizen" attitude of businesses as it is by the existence of high entrance fees to regional and/or local markets. Recent scandals around Ikea in Yekaterinburg, Voronezh, and St Petersburg; the Mega Trade Centre in the Moscow region; and so on, testify to this.

Federal capital transfers are a source of about one-fourth of all subnational public investments ($3,111 million out of $12,261 million in 2004).

Only 1.6 percent of subnational investments are financed with bank loans. Increased bond-related liabilities cover 13 percent of subnational investments, and proceeds from sales of regional/local assets add another 8 percent. All these sources cover not more than half of the reported investments of subnational governments. Thus, the conclusion is that at least half of subnational investments are financed from the regions' current own revenues. This has been made possible by the hike in the world oil price.

The market for regional bonds is small, although it exhibits a high growth rate: most of the regions have either issued or redeemed regional bonds in the last two to three years. Moscow and Moscow region's bonds prevail on the market, and, according to expert estimates, they account for more than 70 percent of total sales of regional securities.

The Budget Code restricts subnational borrowing by setting a limit on debt (the allowed debt cannot exceed the regional government's own revenues) and the deficit (the allowed deficit cannot exceed 15 percent of regional own revenue exclusive of proceeds from property sales).

Formally, the Budget Code allows foreign borrowing by subnational governments, but any such borrowing is allowed in Russian rubles only, which effectively prevents foreign lenders from entering this market. Nevertheless, as of the end of the first quarter of 2005 (the most recent data available at the time of writing), the aggregate debt of the subnational governments to international credit institutions was about $230 million.

The Budget Code does not restrict the federal government's borrowing in foreign currency. Subnational governments widely use sublending by the Ministry of Finance as an alternative to foreign borrowing. As of the end of the first quarter of 2005, these loans amounted to about $400 million.

Problems with Financing Capital Investments and Implications for Reform

Most of the federal government's capital expenditures are non-program expenditures that are scattered among regions and individual construction projects, thus giving rise to delays in construction. The federal government finances several thousands of projects, including those of local importance (such as water and gas network utilities).

Another problem with financing capital investments is that spending across levels of government in Russia is shared by type of expenditures – such as operating or capital – rather than by function or service. Subnational governments responsible for service delivery often do not have enough resources to bear the corresponding capital expenditures; instead, these expenditures are undertaken by the higher level of government – federal government in the case of regional functions, regional government in the case of local government functions. A one-year-based budgeting process contributes to the problem as no one can guarantee that financing for a capital construction project that spans several years will continue in the next year. It is hoped that medium-term budgeting, which is being introduced under the current state budget reform, will largely resolve this particular problem.

Fiscal Federalism Dimensions of the Public Management Framework

Many state functions are centralized at the federal level, and the federal government appoints the heads of its territorial branches. Either the regional governor or the legislative assembly of the region appoints the regional chief executive officials. Members of regional legislative assemblies and, until recently, governors were elected by a direct vote of the people and had a fixed term.

After the Beslan school hostage crisis in September 2004, the federal government took more serious measures to concentrate political power. Among the most controversial was the president's bypassing of direct governors' elections in favour of appointing them himself. As a result, governors have become integral to the national executive power, and political centralization has replaced decentralization of responsibilities (although the centralized state now exists in a deconcentrated form).

Corruption and Its Possible Causes

All studies of corruption in Russia agree on one point: the level of corruption is high. Leaving aside such considerations as historical traditions and low civil service wages, one may presume that one reason for the high level of corruption in the regions is the federal equalization policy. The regions tend to report lower revenues and to hide their revenue sources in the shadow economy in order to be able to claim a larger share of the federal equalization grants.

Corruption is also rooted in the unavailability of legal levers that would allow regional and local governments to adjust their revenues to their spending needs. Subnational governments in Russia have very limited tax-raising authority, which drives them into entrepreneurship, especially as they can use their administrative resources to efficiently oust competitors.

Corruption may get even worse thanks to the enactment of the new law on local self-governance. This law does not allow local governments to hold assets that are not directly related to the provision of the public services assigned to them. Local governments have started stripping themselves of such assets and transferring them to hastily created firms that, although not formally government-owned, are in fact controlled by the government.

THE WAY FORWARD

Russian statehood is going through a period of very rapid changes. The vertical line of power has been strengthened considerably under Vladimir Putin, while federalism seems to be growing thin. Is it just another swing of the pendulum or will centralist tendencies stay for good? It is difficult to say because these new developments are somewhat controversial. The new legislation upon which the federal government is working will devolve more state powers to the governors, but the president will continue to appoint those governors. The federal government has already delegated new federal functions to the regions, and it promises to add more. Monitoring of the governors' performance will be exercised by federal inspectors who report to presidential envoys in each of the seven federal districts as well as to the Main Control Department at the Administrative Board of the president.

Thus, Putin's strategy of federalism has become clear. The federal centre appoints regional authorities, delegates the federal functions that are supported with relevant funding, and keeps this spending under strict control. If these earmarked transfers are ever misappropriated and the situation in a region worsens, the president possesses the means to reverse it. There is a potential danger inherent in this strategy. Once the centre has started to exercise control over the execution of federal responsibilities by the regions, it may also be tempted to assume control of regional functions. The danger is quite real because the regions now carry out many additional functions that are not exempt from the federal centre's interference.

How was it possible to turn from decentralization to centralization – that is, to the unitary past? Why did the regions not put up some resistance? One of the explanations is that agreeing with the president's policy in modern Russia warrants a successful political or business career. Another is that, given heavy financial reliance on the federal centre, many governors consider accountability to the president to be more important than accountability to the voters. Besides, the taxable base in Russia's regions is created by businesses, not by citizens, and the governors seek to attract businesses rather than to improve the living conditions of households.

Fixing the assignment of revenue sources and sharing rates across government levels in the Budget Code (2004) as an alternative to annual revisions has lessened the fiscal dependence of subnational governments on federal government budget policies. However, it has not noticeably strengthened the fiscal autonomy of the regions. The same applies to the equalization transfer formula. On the one hand, formula-based transfers make cash flows to the regions more transparent; on the other hand, it is the federal government that devises the formula. Given annual amendments to the formula, the revenues of the regions have not become more predictable. In any case, experts have failed to notice some statistically meaningful correlation between changes in the independent variables describing the economic situation in a region (and its expenditure needs) and the resulting changes in the volume of the equalization transfer.

Today, there is no federal strategy in Russia to further fiscal federalism, and there is no unanimity about the prospects of political federalism. Most experts are of the opinion that subnational governments should have different spending obligations because of disparities in regional development, climate, ethnic traditions, and the like. Therefore, a return to the asymmetrical model of federalism looks almost inevitable. However, the wrapper will be different. In the 1990s, strong regions received additional powers under bilateral agreements with the federal centre, while the model discussed today provides for taking powers away from weaker regions.

Is it valid to say that the efforts to develop intergovernmental fiscal relations in the period between 1999 and 2005 were wasted because fiscal federalism will inevitably die away right after political federalism? Or could steps towards the financial autonomy of the regions be perceived as evidence that federalism is going to stay?

Is fiscal federalism possible without political federalism? And is political federalism possible without some degree of fiscal autonomy? Some experts believe that Russia's present return to a unitary system will not last – that fiscal federalism will pave the way for the further development of political federalism. They point to the greater financial autonomy of the regions due to the revenue sources – however scarce – assigned to them, the formula-driven allocation of equalization transfers, and several federal funds that have been set up to allocate targeted transfers to the regions. Others believe that fiscal federalism and local self-governance are impossible without true revenue autonomy and that fiscal federalism cannot co-exist with a vertical axis of executive power. In other words, the highly centralized authority in Moscow trumps the ability of the regions to exercise any real powers of their own. There is one thing upon which many can agree: in attempting to improve fiscal federalism, the country must not wait for the appearance of an ideal form of federalism.

NOTES

1 For more on revenue autonomy, see Michael Alekseev and Galina Kurlyandskaya, "Fiscal Federalism and Incentives in a Russian Region," *Journal of Comparative Economics* 31 (2003): 20–33; Galina Kurlyandskaya and Natalia Golovanova, "Decentralization in the Russian Federation," forthcoming in *Economic Change and Restructuring*; and Jorge Martinez-Vazquez, Andrey Timofeev, and Jameson Boex, "Reforming Regional-Local Finance in Russia," WBI Learning Resource Series, World Bank, Washington, DC, 2006.

2 For a historical overview of local self-governance in Russia, see Galina Kourliandskaia, Yelena Nikolayenko, and Natalia Golovanova, "Local Governments in the Russian Federation," in *Developing New Rules in the Old Environment: Local Governments in Eastern Europe, Caucasus and Central Asia,* ed. Victor Popa and Igor Munteanu, 161–264 (Budapest: LGI/OSI, 2002); and Irina Starodubrovskaya, *Analysis of Revenues and Expenses of Local Budgets* (Moscow: CEPRA, 2003).

Republic of South Africa

Capital: Pretoria
Population: 43.5 Million
(2002 est.)

Boundaries and place names are representative only and do not imply official endorsement.

Sources: CIA World Factbook; ESRI Ltd;
Times Atlas of the World: UN Cartographic Dept.

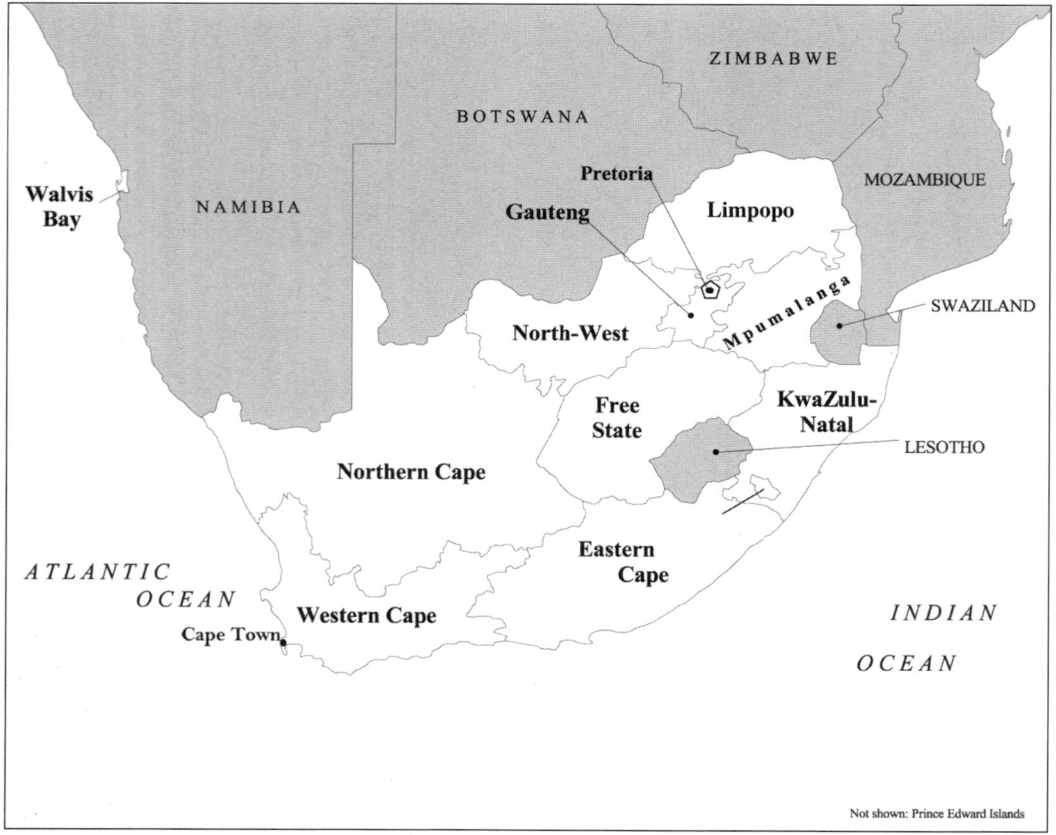

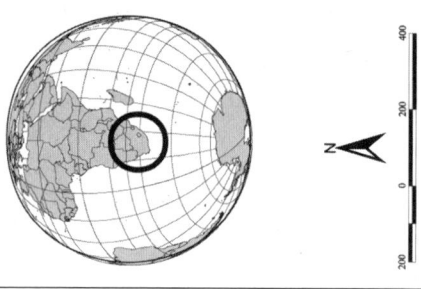

Republic of South Africa

BONGANI KHUMALO
AND RENOSI MOKATE

The Constitution establishes South Africa as a constitutional republic founded on the principles of democracy. There are a number of political parties that are represented in all spheres of the government – national, provincial, and local. Some political parties emerge only during election periods and disappear thereafter. The political landscape is dominated by the African National Congress (ANC), which holds a more than two-thirds majority in the National Assembly. The ANC also controls all of the provincial legislatures and most metropolitan municipalities.

The system of government in South Africa is generally stable, with a clear separation of powers between the executive, the legislature, and the judiciary. However, given that the decentralized system of government has only been in existence for ten years, some aspects of it are still evolving. This is particularly true with respect to the assignment of powers and functions among the three spheres of government and the exercise of those powers where they are concurrent. The government has made significant strides in enacting enabling legislation, which is required for the exercise of powers and functions. However, implementation of such legislation has presented its own challenges. For example, there is uneven distribution of technical and institutional capacity between national, provincial, and local governments in the area of housing. Although the enabling legislation for the exercise of powers in this concurrent area exists in the form of the National Housing Act, implementation in the form of delivery of houses to those that need them has not progressed smoothly.

Provincial government executives are appointed by the premiers who, in turn, are appointed by the president. In the local government sphere, councils are elected by the people and the mayors are elected by the councillors. In all the subnational governments, the majority party has a significant say in the choice of mayor through executive structures.

The Constitution establishes an independent legislature, judiciary, and executive. The executive, which can be loosely referred to as the government at all spheres, is held accountable to the electorate through the relevant legislatures. The National Assembly and the National Council of Provinces are at the national level, the nine legislatures are at the provincial level, and the councils are at the local level. All these legislative institutions have a role in monitoring and ensuring that the government is held accountable to the people through their own institutions, which ensure citizen participation. Over and above these institutions, the Constitution establishes other institutions such as the Human Rights Commission, the Gender Commission, the Constitutional Court, and so on, all of which ensure that the government is held accountable for any violations of the Constitution. All these statutory bodies are independent.

These independent institutions also receive complaints from the general public regardless of race, gender, colour, or creed, and they can influence the activities of the government. For example, where the government fails to deliver on the provisions in the Bill of Rights (Chapter 2 of the Constitution), aggrieved parties can and have challenged the government in the Constitutional Court, where judgments can and have been made for the complainants. The Human Rights Commission has also received complaints from aggrieved parties and made pronouncements in their favour. The media in South Africa are free and, as such, provide a key avenue for keeping the government under scrutiny. Several government corruption scandals that have ended up being investigated were initially exposed by the media.

South Africa has a population of 44.8 million people and a surface area of 1.2 million square kilometres. It has a racially and ethnically diverse society. Its gross domestic product (GDP) was $212.8 billion in 2004, and its per capita gross national income was $3,630. South Africa has a stable macroeconomic environment characterized by moderate growth rates, low inflation, and low interest rates.

THE INTERGOVERNMENTAL FISCAL RELATIONS SYSTEM IN SOUTH AFRICA

The intergovernmental fiscal framework inherited from the apartheid era was one in which the various provinces differed markedly in their economic endowments and administrative capacity. In 1994, following protracted negotiations between the liberation movements and the apartheid government and a series of compromises on both sides, South Africa settled on a democratic, fiscally decentralized, unitary state. The system consisted of nine provinces and more than one thousand municipalities that, in 2000, were reduced to 284. With respect to provinces, the fiscal

Table 1
Basic political and geographic indicators

Official name: South Africa	
Population: 47.4 million people	
Area (square kilometres):	Western Cape = 129,370 sq. km.
	Eastern Cape = 169,580 sq. km.
	KwaZulu-Natal = 92,100 sq. km.
	Northern Cape = 361,830 sq. km.
	Free State = 129,480 sq. km.
	North West = 116,320 sq. km.
	Gauteng = 17,010 sq. km.
	Mpumalanga = 79,490 sq. km.
	Limpopo = 123,910 sq. km.

Total Area = 219,090 sq. km.

GDP per capita in rands (year): R32,483
Constitution: 1996, constitutional democracy
Orders (spheres) of government: National, provincial, and local
Constitutional status of local government: Autonomous sphere
Official languages: English, Afrikaans, IsiZulu, Sesotho, Setswana, isiXhosa, siSwati, isiNdebele, Xitsonga, Tshivenda, and Sesotho sa Leboa
Number and types of constituent units: Nine provinces

Population, area, and per capita GDP in South African rands of the largest constituent unit
Northern Cape

    902,300 people
    361,830 sq. km.
    GDP per capita R32,870

Population, area, and per capita GDP in South African rands of the smallest constituent unit
Gauteng

    9,415,231 people
    17,010 sq. km.
    GDP per capita R43,923
    Exchange rate = .73

decentralization process could be characterized as mainly involving the decentralization of service responsibilities, with limited revenue-raising capacity. Allowing provinces to choose applicable tax rates and tax bases could result in tax competition that would interfere with trade, investment, or migration across provincial boundaries, thus reinforcing economic disparities and potentially creating a highly skewed distribution of wealth and economic activity. In addition, the weak administrative capacity (and institutions) inherited by most of the provinces, especially those that inherited the apartheid legacy of the homelands, and self-governing states meant that disadvantaged provinces would be ineffective in optimizing and maximizing any expanded revenue-raising powers granted by the Constitution. The issue of revenue assignment is discussed in more detail below.

Provinces neither impose nor collect levies on broad-based taxes such as corporate income and profits, personal income, consumption, and trade. Most of the taxes available to provinces are narrow-based and relate to fees levied on motor vehicle licences, gambling, liquor, hospital fees, and tourism. However, the Constitution grants provinces the power, subject to national legislation and national economic policy objectives, to impose other taxes, such as a surcharge on personal income tax and a fuel levy.

By comparison, an interesting feature of South Africa's intergovernmental fiscal system is the degree to which local governments, especially the larger municipalities, have been given revenue-raising powers. This feature provides the country with a mechanism to develop a much more efficient intergovernmental fiscal system than can other lower-income developing countries with similar fiscal systems. Similar to the White Local Authorities (WLAS) under apartheid, the major sources of revenue for local government include taxes, user charges, and private-sector equity in infrastructure provided by local authorities. Although in the aggregate, local government in South Africa raises a substantial amount of own revenue (90 percent of expenditure needs are financed from own revenue), the situation changes drastically when municipalities are viewed individually. For example, some metropolitan municipalities finance as much as 98 percent of their expenditure needs from own revenues, while some small rural municipalities may depend entirely on transfers in the form of equitable share transfers, conditional transfers, and grants from other spheres and institutions.[1]

EXPENDITURE AND REVENUE-RAISING RESPONSIBILITIES

Macroeconomic policy management in South Africa is the function of national government. Financial and fiscal matters of the state are stipulated in Chapter 13 of the Constitution. This chapter establishes the key institutions and roles for dealing with macroeconomic management. The National Treasury, through the minister of finance, has the role of determining and implementing the country's fiscal policy. An independent central bank, the South African Reserve Bank (SARB), has the role of determining and implementing the monetary policy of the country through constant consultation with the minister of finance. The National Treasury, through Parliament, has set the key parameters within which monetary policy is exercised, while the Reserve Bank is responsible for determining the instruments for effecting that policy. South Africa follows an inflation-targeting policy, with the current target for the consumer price index (excluding mortgage rates) set at 3 percent to 6 percent, and it has a floating exchange rate policy. The governor and deputy governors of SARB are appointed by the president of the country after consultation with the SARB board of directors and the minister of finance.

In 1994, South Africa was in an undesirable fiscal condition, with a budget deficit close to 10 percent, inflation hovering around 20 percent, and debt service costs at 4.7 percent of GDP. The priority of Nelson Mandela's government was, thus, to get macroeconomic policy right. This was achieved with significant success through the implementation of a tight fiscal program. The government adopted its national Growth, Employment and Redistribution (GEAR) macroeconomic strategy through extensive consultation with organized labour and business. The stance adopted by the government was that of macroeconomic stabilization, and it has been under implementation for over five years. The main achievements of this strategy have generally been seen in terms of a substantial reduction in the budget deficit to under 2 percent in 2005 (from the 1994 level of over 10 percent), stable inflation at under 6 percent (from around 20 percent in 1994), reduced debt service cost at 3.5 percent in 2005 (from a high of 5.6 percent in 1997), and general stability in subnational budgets.[2]

However, due to the austerity measures that accompanied the strategy of government investment, infrastructure especially suffered. Investment in social services did not grow as quickly as some sections of society expected. Therefore, while access to social services greatly improved, this was achieved mainly through efficiency gains rather than increased investment. The success of the government's GEAR strategy has been tempered by lack of adequate growth in employment. Unemployment currently stands at about 26 percent.

As has already been indicated, macroeconomic policy management is the exclusive function of the national government, and, under times of fiscal austerity, subnational governments must follow the direction of the national government. The impact of the austerity measures in the early years of GEAR was to enforce the same measures at the subnational government levels.

Over the past five years, rapid reforms in the fiscal arena have strengthened tax administration and improved tax buoyancy and public expenditure management. This development has allowed the government to embark on new investments and the rehabilitation of infrastructure as well as to accelerate investment in basic services.

A comprehensive budget reform process has been carried out alongside the overhaul of the intergovernmental system. Key reforms have included the introduction of three-year budgeting. This has introduced certainty on transfers to subnational governments and allows for decentralized budgeting as captured within the Medium Term Expenditure Framework (MTEF) and the Medium Term Budget Policy Statement (MTPBS). It has also transformed a "bean-counting" treasury into a treasury with strong policy assessment capacity, modernized financial management through the Public Finance Management Act and the Municipal Finance Management Act, removed bail-outs/guarantees for provincial municipal debt and the possibility of ad hoc allocations during the financial year, and finally enhanced the development of clear fiscal frameworks for provincial and local governments. The results have been seen in improvements on expenditure management at both the provincial and local government levels.

However, on the revenue side, much work still needs to be done, especially around the issue of revenue forecasting. As the National Treasury has noted, inaccurate revenue forecasting – either in the form of over- or underestimation of receipts – could result in the expansion of unnecessary borrowing or in the inadequate allocation of funds. This could hamper the implementation of crucial socio-economic programs.[3]

Despite budget reforms and the overhaul of the Intergovernmental Fiscal Relations (IGFR) system, many challenges remain. The following sections identify key weaknesses in four dimensions of the IGFR system in South Africa – expenditure assignment, revenue assignment, intergovernmental transfers, and fiscal management – some of which have persisted despite policy reforms. In turn, such weaknesses pose significant challenges for effectiveness and efficiency in the delivery of constitutionally mandated basic services as well as for the transparency and accountability of the IGFR system as a whole. These weaknesses are explored in greater detail below.

Expenditure Assignment

According to public finance theory, a crucial element of fiscal decentralization requires that a clear and concise set of functions, responsibilities, and services be provided by the jurisdiction with control over the minimum geographic area that would internalize the benefits and costs arising from the provision of such services (and other functions). The current assignment of expenditure functions in South Africa, which is closely aligned with the above theory, aims to achieve three main objectives – efficient resource allocation via a responsive and accountable government, an equitable provision of services to citizens in different jurisdictions, and macroeconomic stability and growth.

Expenditure functions that have a national dimension (justice, defence, correctional services, foreign affairs, and tertiary education) as well as macroeconomic and redistributional implications are the primary responsibility of the national government. These expenditures account for around 39 percent of total budgeted expenditure. By contrast, provincial governments account for about 55 percent of total budgeted expenditure but generate less than 6 percent in revenue.[4] Most of the expenditure

Table 2
Legislative responsibility and actual provision of services by different spheres of government

Legislative responsibility (de jure)	Public service	Actual allocation of function (de facto)
National/provincial	Administration of indigenous forests	Provincial/local
National/provincial	Social security and welfare	National/provincial
National/provincial	Agriculture	Provincial
National	Health	National/provincial/local
National	Correctional services	National
National	Defence	National
National	Justice and constitutional development	National
National	Safety and security	National
National	Water affairs and forestry	National
National	Trade and industry	National
National	Transport	National
National	Minerals and energy	National
National	Foreign affairs	National
National	Home affairs	National
National/provincial	Casinos, racing, gambling and wagering, excluding lotteries and sports pools	Provincial
National/provincial	Vehicle licensing	Provincial
Provincial	Ambulance services	Local
National/provincial	Education	National/provincial
Provincial	Libraries other than national libraries	Local
Provincial	Liquor licences	National
National	Museums other than national museums	National
Provincial	Provincial planning	Provincial
Provincial	Provincial recreation and amenities	Provincial
Provincial	Provincial sport	Provincial

Table 2
Legislative responsibility and actual provision of services by different spheres of government (*Continued*)

Legislative responsibility (de jure)	Public service	Actual allocation of function (de facto)
Provincial	Provincial roads and traffic	Provincial
Provincial	Veterinary services, excluding regulation of the profession	Provincial
National/provincial/local	Air pollution	Local
National/provincial/local	Building regulations	National/provincial/local
National/provincial/local	Child care facilities	Local
Local	Electricity and gas reticulation	Local
National/provincial/local	Firefighting services	Local
National/provincial/local	Local tourism	Local
National/provincial/local	Municipal airports	Local
National/provincial/local	Municipal planning	Local
National/provincial/local	Municipal health services	Local
National/provincial/local	Municipal public transport	Local
National/provincial/local	Stormwater management systems in built-up areas	Local
National/provincial/local	Water and sanitation services limited to potable water supply systems and domestic waste-water and sewage disposal systems	Local
Provincial/local	Beaches and amusement facilities	Local
Provincial/local	Billboards and the display of advertisements in public places	Local
Provincial/local	Cemeteries, funeral parlours, and crematoria	Local
Provincial/local	Municipal parks and recreation	Local
Provincial/local	Municipal roads	Local
Provincial/local	Street lighting	Local
Provincial/local	Traffic and parking	Local
Provincial/local	Refuse removal, refuse dumps and solid waste disposal	Local

responsibilities are derived from Schedule 4 of the Constitution, which stipulates that provincial governments are responsible for primary and secondary education, health and welfare services, provincial roads, and local economic development. Local governments account for just over 4 percent of total budgeted revenues and are tasked with the delivery of key basic municipal services such as housing, water, electricity, and sanitation.[5]

Despite the fact that the Constitution sets out clear responsibilities and a solid framework, some matters related to the assignment of expenditure functions continue to remain unresolved. These are the persistent potential for unfunded mandates, a lack of clear delineation of responsibilities when functions are transferred to other spheres of government, and the lack of a detailed and comprehensive framework for the assignment of powers and functions. Unfunded mandates refer to situations in which subnational governments are legally mandated in terms of the Constitution or by policy pronouncement to undertake specific functions but do not receive funds from nationally raised revenues in order to fulfill these functions. This scenario is highlighted in cases where the framework underlying the provision of particular services requires provincial and local governments to implement nationally determined minimum-service standards. However, the funding for the delivery of such services fails to reflect the cost of the service standards, forcing subnational authorities to divert scarce own-revenue funds to meet the standards set.

A clear classification of responsibilities for some functions shared by the different spheres of government is still required. For example, some roads have yet to be classified either as district or local roads. Until such classification is finalized, these kinds of roads may end up not being maintained, a scenario that could hinder improved access to socio-economic infrastructure. Closely linked to the classification issue is the lack of clarity on the nature of transfer of functions – whether assignment, delegation, or agency agreement. Where this occurs, planning and budgeting for service delivery becomes difficult as each type of assignment has its own implications.

Although a draft policy framework for assigning powers and functions to the local government sphere has been developed, the proposals contained in the framework are not comprehensive. They fail to cover all legislation originating in national line function departments. For instance, in the health sector, the national government has yet to specify the range of activities that comprise the environmental health services that should be provided by local authorities. This lack of specificity has necessitated laborious negotiations between local municipalities and their respective district municipalities regarding which entity should bear responsibility for providing environmental health. Another drawback of the draft framework is that it applies only to functions assigned to local governments and excludes shifts/transfers of functions from the national sphere to the provincial

Table 3
Direct expenditures by function and level of government

Function	Federal (%)	State or provincial (%)	Local (%)	All (%)
Defence	100	0	0	100
Debt servicing	100	0	0	100
General administration	44	0	56	100
Law and order	100	0		100
Economic services	100	0		100
Social services				100
health	78.3	21.7	0	100
education	66.1	33.9	0	100
Social development	74.5	25.5	0	100
Subsidies	0	0	0	100
Total				100
Local public services*	0	0	0	100

* Local public services include: primary and preschool education, secondary education, public health, hospitals, urban highways, urban transportation, drinking water and sewerage, waste collection, electric power supply, fire protection, public order and safety, police.

sphere. In the absence of an appropriate framework, subnational governments either initiate legislation to fill gaps or develop policies that could place increased future demands on the country's treasury.

Revenue Assignment

Despite improvements in revenue-sharing arrangements since 1994, there still remain marked differences in revenue-generating capacity across the three spheres of government. The differences stem largely from the structure and assignment of taxation powers allocated by the Constitution to the spheres of government. South Africa's revenue system is based on ensuring fiscal uniformity, harmony, and efficiency. However, the assignment of revenue functions involves lower fiscal autonomy for subnational governments. All broad-based taxes (mainly personal income, corporate, and consumption taxes) are assigned to the national government, while narrow-based/minor taxes (such as motor vehicle licence fees, hospital user fees, and gambling taxes) are assigned to provincial authorities. In comparison, municipalities have greater revenue powers than do provinces as they are assigned property rates and turnover and utility user charges.[66] The collection of most revenue in South Africa is carried out by the South African Revenue Service. Currently, the Revenue Service only collects revenue for the national government, although there is nothing that stops provinces and municipalities from entering into agency arrangements with it so that it can collect on their behalf as well.

The exercise of subnational revenue-raising powers can only be implemented subject to the enactment of enabling legislation by the national government. The enactment of this legislation in South Africa has taken quite a while, although it has happened. The Property Rates Act is currently being phased in and is envisaged to take a period of seven years before it is fully phased in. The Municipal Fiscal Powers and Functions Bill is still being developed, as required in Section 229 of the Constitution, while the Provincial Tax Regulation Process Act only came into effect in 2001. All these pieces of legislation give certain discretion to the national minister of finance and, to some extent, local government with respect to the exercise of revenue-raising powers by subnational governments.

In general, South Africa's intergovernmental fiscal relations are characterized by relative centralization on the revenue side and highly decentralized expenditure responsibilities. Although expenditure on the delivery of social services constitutes about 89 percent of total provincial spending, these services generate very little in terms of revenue. Unable to raise adequate revenue from their assigned taxes, in order to achieve their constitutional mandate, the provinces have come to rely heavily on intergovernmental transfers (or grants), which make up 95 percent of the total revenue utilized at the provincial level.

While subnational governments argue that narrow-based taxes limit their capacity to increase revenue, efficient administration and collection of revenue, especially by provincial governments, remains a significant problem. In most provinces, the major revenue-generating departments – public works, economic affairs, education, health, and transport – lack dedicated and staffed internal revenue collection units. The establishment of dedicated revenue collection units is critical for ensuring that fees for services are adjusted in a timely manner, that due revenues are collected, and that projections or forecasts of revenues are provided to enhance the budgeting abilities of provincial treasuries. Over the past decade, most provinces have rarely adjusted fees and tariffs unless pressured by the national government, and they have continued to collect less revenue.

The inability of provinces to maximize collection of own revenue has reinforced the dependence of the provinces on transfers from the national government, an outcome that affects expenditure in two important ways. First, it imposes a constraint on the provinces' ability to change their expenditure patterns. Thus, the volume of expenditure incurred by each

Table 4
Tax assignment for various orders of government

	Determination of			Shares in revenue (%)			
	Base	Rate	Tax collection and administration	National	Province	Local	All orders
National							
Direct taxes 1. Taxes on Income, profit, and capital gains 2. Payroll taxes 3. Taxes on property	Taxes under direct taxes and indirect taxes are assigned according to 1996 Constitution.	100% determined by the national sphere	Taxes collected and administered by the South African Revenue Service (SARS)	80.8	1.1	18.1	100
Indirect taxes 1. Value-added taxes 2. Excise duties 3. Taxes on international trade and transactions		100% determined by national sphere					
Other revenues 1. Stamp duties and fees.							
State or provincial							
Tax Revenue 1. Casino Taxes 2. Horse Racing Taxes 3. Liqour Licenses 4. Motor vehicle licenses	Tax bases are in line with Section 228 of the 1996 Constitution	1. Review of applicable rates carried out by relevant departments/ provincial treasuries and submitted to the minister of finance for approval.	Relevant line departments in conjunction with the Provincial Treasury.				
Non-tax revenue 1. Sale of non-capital goods 2. Transfers received 3. Fines, penalties, and forfeits 4. Interest income 5. Sale of capital assets 6. Other financial transactions		2. Regarding non-tax revenue, applicable rates and prices wholly determined by provincial authorities					

Table 4
Tax assignment for various orders of government (*Continued*)

	Determination of		Tax collection and administration	Shares in revenue (%)			
	Base	Rate		National	Province	Local	All orders

Local

Revenue
1. Regional levies
2. Property rates
3. User fees (levied on electricity, water, and refuse removal services)
4. Subsidies and grants

Base: In line with municipal fiscal powers and functions outlined in Section 229 of the 1996 Constitution

Rate: With the exception of subsidies and grants (intergovernmental transfers) and allocations from nationally raised revenues, rates on other tax sources 100% determined by local government authorities. However in certain instances, determination of rates on property is done in accordance with the Property Tax Act (2004)

Tax collection and administration: Income collected by revenue departments in specific municipalities.

province depends on the volume of transfers. Second, this dependence means that the national government has significant influence on equity considerations in spending through the structure of the provincial equitable share formula. Encouraging provinces to raise more of their revenue needs could result in provinces' being better able to alter spending in line with their local circumstances and priorities.

Therefore, it is important that the implementation of the Provincial Tax Regulation Process Act, 2001, considers various ways in which the assignment of revenue powers could incorporate appropriate incentives for provinces to raise more of their own revenues and that it direct such revenues towards expenditure programs that support sustainable local economic growth and development. The act was passed as a necessary legislation to enable provinces to exercise their revenue-raising powers, as detailed in

Section 228 of the Constitution. Although most of the provinces have not used the act, recent moves by the Western Cape province to impose a fuel tax and the recent decision by the minister of finance to rescind the regional services levies accruing to local governments have significant implications for both local and provincial fiscal sustainability. These implications make the case that reform of tax assignment at the subnational level is all the more necessary. The regional services levy was a tax levied on the payroll bill of business entities.

Intergovernmental Transfers

Intergovernmental transfers (grants) within South Africa's IGFR fall within two main categories: general purpose grants and specific purpose (conditional) grants. Given that the expenditure responsibilities of the provincial and local governments are extensive but their revenue-raising abilities are minimal, general purpose transfers are intended to reduce fiscal imbalances arising from these asymmetric revenue-raising capacity and expenditure functions. Specific purpose grants are intended to correct interjurisdictional spillovers, meet national redistribution objectives, and achieve specific national priorities and policies concerning services provided by subnational spheres of government.[7] Provinces and local governments receive general purpose grants through the provincial equitable share (PES) and the local equitable share (LES), respectively. Both PES and LES are formula-driven and utilize factors such as population, poverty, and household income and expenditure in determining the per capita share accruing to each province or municipality.[8] Furthermore, the Constitution specifies the criteria that must be taken into account in allocating the equitable share to the three spheres of government. These criteria are listed in Section 214 (2) [a-j] of the Constitution of the Republic of South Africa. General purpose grants can be spent at the discretion of subnational governments.

Since 2000, specific purpose grant allocations to subnational governments, which are allocated on an ad hoc and discretionary basis, have represented a growing share of transfers (see Figures 2 and 3). Over the 2001/02 to 2007/08 fiscal years, growth in conditional grants allocated to local governments averaged over 23 percent compared with the equitable share's average growth of 22 percent. In the case of provinces, and over the same period, growth in conditional grant allocations averaged just over 14 percent compared with the 11 percent recorded for equitable transfers. To a large extent, the increasing importance of conditional transfers reflects the proactive policy stance of the national government and the unsustainable expenditure assignments to subnational governments.

Despite their intended objectives, a number of problems hinder the effective implementation of conditional grant-funded programs. Most notably, the grant system is characterized by a high number of conditional grants, many of which are allocated on an ad hoc and discretionary basis.[9] The ad hoc and discretionary nature of allocations in turn creates unintended, negative consequences. First, aims and objectives tend to be duplicated, and this exerts an unnecessary administrative burden on implementing subnational governments. Second, many grants are poorly designed: they lack clear purpose and either lack measurable outputs or have outputs or conditions that are unreasonable. Third, the ad hoc and discretionary nature of grants makes the transfer system less transparent, an outcome that makes monitoring difficult and that undermines coordination between policy and budgeting. It also enhances budget game playing and confusion regarding accountability.

In addition to the above problems, some research studies have highlighted poor financial and project management skills, a shortage of staff, and inadequate facilities as hindering the smooth spending of conditional grants.[10] Despite the teething problems identified with conditional grants, their use in the South African IGFR system continues to grow. This growth is largely driven by the introduction of new basic services programs, notably, those geared towards HIV/AIDS prevention and treatment, school nutrition, and adult basic education programs as well as infrastructure and institutional capacity-building grants. Conditional grants have also been used to provide for services that are clearly needed (e.g., early childhood education), but where the institutional framework for delivery either needs to be transformed or is not adequately understood and where the cost structure for providing the service needs to be clarified.

FISCAL EQUITY, EFFICIENCY CONCERNS, AND INTERGOVERNMENTAL FISCAL TRANSFERS

South Africa adopted a formula-based approach to the equitable division of nationally collected revenue. This approach was proposed by the Financial and Fiscal Commission (FFC) and takes into account the expenditure needs of subnational governments as determined by the government in general. The FFC is an independent body established under Chapter 13 of the Constitution. Its main function is to make recommendations on the equitable division of nationally raised revenue among the three spheres of government (vertical division) and across provinces and municipalities (horizontal division). The Constitution requires that, before an Act of Parliament affecting the equitable shares is tabled, the minister of finance must indicate how the recommendations of the commission have been taken into account.

The process for the division of revenue starts with the FFC making recommendations that are subjected to consultations and public hearings with the national and provincial legislatures and organized local government. From the government side, these recommendations fit into the process through the Budget Council and Budget Forum. The Intergovernmental Fiscal Relations Act, 1997, established these forums, which consist of the national minister of finance and his nine provincial counterparts (the Budget Council). The Budget Council and organized local government constitute the Budget Forum. These two then make recommendations to the Minister's Committee on the Budget, which, in effect, is a subcommittee of the Cabinet chaired by the minister of finance and makes recommendations to the Cabinet on the final budget allocations. Once the division of revenue is finalized, a Division of Revenue Bill must be tabled to be passed by Parliament. The bill contains memoranda explaining all the formulas used to determine the allocations, which FFC recommendations have been accepted, and whether any have not been accepted and, if not, why not. The payment schedule for transfers is also included. In general, the FFC's recommendations have been accepted by the government. The reason for this is that the FFC has steered clear of making recommendations on actual allocations and, rather, has focused on the principles that should guide the determination of allocations. Its recommendations have also been based on thorough and sound research and analysis, taking into account best practices on IGFR matters.

An interesting aspect of the system as it has evolved is that, while the horizontal division is formula-driven, the vertical division is determined through a political process based on the government's priorities for the medium-term expenditure cycle. The pool of revenue available for sharing among the provinces (and municipalities) is thus predetermined. In the last couple of years, some quarters have raised concerns about the objectivity of the vertical division, especially with respect to the transparency of the issues surrounding the vertical division. The Select Committee on Finance of the National Council of Provinces (NCOP) has asked the FFC to comment on the vertical division. This is in spite of the fact that, in its response to the commission's very first recommendations, the government adopted an approach that implied that the vertical division was a political process and could not be determined through a formula. Whether such an approach might compromise the government's power to determine and resource its priorities is still subject to intense debate.

Once the vertical division has been established, the next step is the horizontal equitable division of revenue among the nine provinces and 284 municipalities. This is followed by other allocations in the form of conditional and unconditional grants to the provinces and municipalities. The intergovernmental fiscal relations system in South Africa is structured in such a way that subnational governments (provincial and local) are mandated to deliver most basic social services. Although in terms of revenue powers, the fiscal autonomy of the provinces is very limited, this is not the situation with local government. Thus, vertical and horizontal imbalances exist due to the nature of the assignment of revenue sources and the vast variation in fiscal capacity, especially in the local government sphere. Generally, subnational governments are empowered to determine their own resource allocation decisions in the context of the government's broad, medium-term, strategic objectives.

Currently, a number of conditional grants flow to provinces and municipalities. Some of these are block grants, while others are specific purpose grants.[11] Generally, conditional grants have been problematic, and a comprehensive review of these grants is currently under way to find out whether they follow an appropriate framework/design. The review is being carried out by both the FFC and the National Treasury (the two institutions are working independently on this review).

The vertical division of revenue among the three spheres of government involves a policy decision that reflects the priorities of the government over an MTEF period.[12] The horizontal division of revenue is formula based and takes into account demographic patterns and broad indicators of need. The provincial equitable share formula is specified as follows: $A = E + H + B + P + EA + I$, where A is the allocation per province, E is the weighted share of the province's school-age population, H is the share of the population of the province without medical aid, B is the share of population for the province, P is the weighted provincial share of population living in poverty, EA is the share of the province in economic activity, and I is an amount allocated equally across provinces for governance costs.

The local government's equitable share formula takes into account basic municipal services, the number of poor households, the fiscal capacity of a municipality, and an allocation for the cost of governance based on the number of poor households in the municipality. The formula is driven by the demographic patterns in the country and captures the need to finance the constitutionally assigned functions of subnational governments.

In general, significant fiscal disparities are driven to a large extent, but not exclusively, by differences in costs and capacity in the production and delivery of public services. These are a matter of policy concern, and mechanisms are being investigated to address them. Recently, there have been comprehensive reviews of the fiscal frameworks of both the provincial and local government levels together with the relevant revenue allocation formulas. The reviews were conducted independently by the National Treasury and the FFC. The outcome of both reviews was that the recommendations of the FFC that were limited to the data that are used for different components in the PES and the structure for the LES were all accepted, although the implementation will be phased in as the relevant data become available. With respect to the LES, the structure that has been adopted is a component-based structure that mirrors that of the PES.

Table 5
Vertical fiscal gaps

	Total revenue collected in millions of rands	Total revenue available, including net transfers for that level of government in millions of rands	Expenditures in millions of rands
National	369,869		283,113
Subnational			
state/provincial	5,663	205,367	204,869
Local	72,900	8,100	86,000
All orders			

In general, the revenue-sharing mechanism ensures that the fiscal gap between revenue and expenditure responsibilities for sub-national governments is reduced. The formula also addresses horizontal disparities within the spheres. However, the South African approach is not an equalization approach but, rather, an equitable sharing of nationally raised revenue.

FINANCING CAPITAL INVESTMENT

It is the government's goal to expand investment and spending on capital to boost economic growth and employment creation and to improve service delivery. The critical question is the assignment of responsibilities between different role players. In particular, the question concerns defining the role that government needs to play in terms of financing capital expenditure. In terms of funding, the government is driven by spending priorities and functional responsibilities that each sphere of government has to meet, taking into account policy changes. This is done through intergovernmental transfers. In the last five years the government has embarked on a program to accelerate investment in infrastructure. The program incorporates what is known as the extended public works program, which requires that infrastructure projects incorporate employment generation by utilizing local people through labour-intensive methods. The beneficiaries must include women and other disadvantaged groups. The extended public works program extends beyond infrastructure programs as it includes other activities, such as home-based care for HIV/AIDS sufferers and so on.

A question that arises relates to how borrowing can be used to finance capital expenditures. In relation to this question, it can be argued that a sound revenue base among governments is crucial before they can start borrowing. The current situation in South Africa is one in which provincial governments have limited borrowing powers, although the Provincial Borrowing Powers of Provincial Government Act has been in place since 1996. Generally, provinces raise an insignificant amount of revenue relative to their expenditure needs. However, local governments raise a substantial amount of revenue relative to their expenditure needs and, therefore, exercise significant borrowing powers.

Increasingly, policy makers realize they need to distinguish among capital investments in the local sphere. Investment in new infrastructure and capital expenditure on maintenance need to be taken into account as discrete components. It is important to ensure that capital investment also takes account of maintenance needs for existing infrastructure. For example, there has been a significant focus on the establishment of new infrastructure to address the backlogs that were created under apartheid. There is a growing recognition that, as new infrastructure was created, not enough attention and resources were provided to maintain already existing infrastructure.

The lack of coordination in planning and implementing large capital investment projects is another matter of concern. For example, the rapid-rail project (Gautrain) is a provincial project, whereby the province of Gauteng will receive some funds from the national government for constructing the Gautrain. However, the implications of the project for the other spheres of government have not been addressed. For example, it will require local government to provide ancillary infrastructure such as feeder transportation and amenities at the stations. This unintended cost for local government has not been taken into account.

The government's role needs to focus on helping those municipalities that are not economically affluent and are therefore unable to raise project financing through the capital markets. It is generally acknowledged that the national government has an important role in terms of financing but that it should not be expected to entirely absorb financing as the specific province needs to take full responsibility. An additional question relates to whether there are mechanisms in place for provinces to consult with the national government before they initiate a large project that has significant national or regional implications. The government is in the process of establishing mechanisms that would guide the process on those issues, particularly as equitable share transfers do not cater to huge investment projects.

In conclusion, it is important to take into account the need to synchronize funds (expenditure versus revenue) with mechanisms to deal with municipalities that have structural problems. It is a fact that municipalities are the source of economic activities. Therefore, there may be a need to review the pool of funds that goes to municipalities in the form of the equitable share. For the provinces, there is a need to align provincial and national priorities on capital expenditure. Finally, there is a need to investigate whether the national government should develop alternative funding vehicles other than intergovernmental transfers and borrowing.

INSTITUTIONAL DIMENSION AND CORRUPTION

Appointments and Termination of Services

All spheres of government have the right to appoint their own personnel without a directive from another sphere. The hiring and firing of staff happens within the context of national legislation such as the Labor Relations Act, 1988, the Basic Conditions of Employment Act, and the Skills Development Act.

Secondment also exists in the system, taking the form of advisory teams in cases of glaring gaps in human resource capacity. Apart from this, at the very senior executive management level (e.g., deputy director generals and director generals/superintendents), secondment also takes place, particularly where there is a dearth of leadership.

Currently, there is a dualistic public service. National and provincial conditions of service are governed in terms of a single law and policy, while the local sphere has its own separate policy and laws regarding conditions of service. Generally, it is felt that municipal employees have access to relatively better conditions of service (remuneration and other allowances) than do employees in the national and provincial spheres. This is particularly true with respect to senior management at the local sphere (e.g., municipal managers).

Despite the dualistic approach, in general the conditions of employment and related matters in South Africa, both in the private and public sectors, are governed by the overarching labour legislation indicated above.

Autonomy at Each Level of Government

Each sphere of government is autonomous and, thus, retains an independent right to hire and fire staff. There is also a separation of powers between the judiciary, the executive, and the legislature.

Nevertheless, there is a systematic process that allows for intervention in one sphere by another and that is governed by law. Sections 100 and 139 of the Constitution enable the national and provincial spheres to intervene in the affairs and the administration of a province (and a municipality) where there is evidence of failure to deliver on mandates. It is important to note that this form of intervention is temporary in nature. However, legislation does permit the intervening sphere to rectify the situation, and, in the case of municipalities, measures may include firing or dissolving a council. This is done on a case-by-case basis, depending on the merits of each scenario.

What often emerges as a potential threat to autonomy, particularly of subnational government, is the issue of unfunded and underfunded mandates. In principle and law (the Division of Revenue Act), funds should follow function. However, in practice this principle is sometimes violated, especially in incidents where the higher sphere lacks trust and confidence in the subnational governments, particularly in their ability to plan, prioritize, and spend resources. It also results from a lack of clear policy frameworks on the assignment of powers and function, especially where such powers and functions are concurrent in nature. This can lead to a lot of frustration within the system. However, a framework for the efficient and effective assignment of powers and function is currently being developed, and it is anticipated that these problems will be dealt with in a more systematic and controlled manner than is found in the ad hoc and discretionary approach that has characterized the system thus far.

A matter related to unfunded mandates involves the fact that, quite often, municipalities have received qualified financial reports in cases where they have borne expenditure for functions that are not assigned to them by the Constitution. Similarly, there are challenges with respect to concurrent functions such as education and health. The national government sets policies, which are often input norms and not output based. Due to the lack of sufficient accuracy in the costing of services, this ultimately results in underfunded mandates. In this way, the autonomy of a subnational government to deliver services based on its own priorities may be largely compromised.

Corruption and the Use of Resources

The Public Finance Management Act (PFMA) and the Municipal Finance Management Act (MFMA) were introduced to repeal the Exchequer Act in order to modernize public financial management and to increase public accountability.

The PFMA has provided a solid background for a good MFMA. The MFMA is considered to be more solid and comprehensive in some areas where the PFMA is silent. The government has indicated a desire to strengthen the PFMA in areas that were not very tight, such as supply chain management. These two pieces of legislation apply to the financial management practices in the provincial and national governments (PFMA) and in local government (MFMA). They empower the authorities to hold public officials accountable, provide checks and balances in the utilization of public funds, and detail sanctions in case of violation of the law, including imprisonment for offences deemed to be very serious.

One of the outstanding pillars of South Africa's IGFR system is the auditor general, who audits government departments and bodies across all three spheres of government. However, the major weakness is that the auditor general's reports are often released a year after the incidents have taken place, thus providing an opportunity for correcting future encounters rather than for dealing with issues as they happen. The audits have also tended to focus too much on financial management issues and the accuracy of financial statements rather than on the overall performance of the government. In the future, however, the audit process will focus more on the performance of state institutions.

By law all government departments and agencies must have internal audit functions. These are aimed at assisting management in identifying weak management systems, which are potential areas for fraud and corruption, and developing corrective systems where risks appear. Significant attention is often given to fraudulent and corrupt activities in the government rather than in the private sector and multinational corporations. The government's other fraud and corruption strategies include toll-free numbers, bodies such as the Scorpions and the National Prosecuting Agency, Anti-Corruption Summits, the Whistle Blowers Act, and the encouragement of the development and implementation of fraud prevention plans.

Oversight

The Constitution establishes the Parliament, which serves an overarching oversight role on government activities and programs. The Parliament has sectoral committees that focus on specific areas (e.g., education, finance, etc.). The National Council of Provinces has committees that mirror those of the National Assembly. In some instances, joint committees are established to increase the effectiveness of the oversight role (e.g., the Joint Budget Committee). One issue that is clear is that a significant amount of work still needs to be done to ensure that legislatures and various committees are able to competently and robustly take departments to task in key areas of failure. This requires, among other things, that the committees be given adequate capacity to undertake rigorous independent research into the activities of the departments. Improving the oversight role of all the legislatures is an ongoing process.

CONCLUSION

South Africa's system of intergovernmental relations is still evolving as the country is still a young democracy. The clarity with which powers and functions are defined in the Constitution safeguards the country against arbitrary reallocations of functions. Nonetheless, there have been some shifts in functions over the past ten years, such as the reallocation of social security grants from the provincial governments to the national government and the reallocation of primary health care from local governments to provincial governments. A framework has been formulated for the effective assignment of functions, and it ensures that the assignment remains true to the spirit of the Constitution and that principles such as funding follows function are adhered to. Issues of public accountability, anti-corruption, and fraud prevention are important elements that are being inculcated within South Africa's democratic system.

NOTES

1 See South African National Treasury, *Intergovernmental Fiscal Review* (Pretoria: South African Government Printers, 2003).
2 See South African National Treasury, *Budget Review 2006* (Pretoria: South African Government Printers, 2006).
3 Ibid.
4 See Financial and Fiscal Commission, Annual Recommendations, Financial and Fiscal Commission, Midrand, 2002.
5 Ibid.
6 Municipalities derive most of their revenue from tariffs on utilities, in particular water and electricity. It is important to highlight that the electricity distribution industry in South Africa is undergoing reform. The reforms will involve a movement away from the current scenario, in which some municipalities distribute electricity to consumers, to a scenario in which an electricity distribution holding company – through regional electricity distributors – will be in charge. The amount of revenue available to originally distributing municipalities may be affected and, therefore, total revenues available to municipalities in the form of surpluses arising from the sale of electricity.
7 W. Oates, *Fiscal Federalism* (New York: Harcourt Brace Javanovich, 1972).
8 Detailed explanations of the revenue-sharing formulas are provided in Annex E of the Budget Review on an annual basis. The explanatory memorandum for these formulas also captures revisions to the input data that occur either as the result of a new census or new survey data, such as data on medical aid to the population with respect to health, data on school enrolments in the provinces, or new poverty data with respect to basic services for the local government.
9 According to the Division of Revenue Act (2005), provincial and local governments administered more than twenty-five grants during the 2005–06 fiscal year.
10 See, for example, A. Hickey, "Provinces Improve Spending on Conditional Grants for HIV/AIDS Health Programs," Budget Brief of the AIDS Budget Unit, Institute for Democracy in South Aftica, 2003.

11 The Division of Revenue Act (the legislation that deals with the allocation and equitable division of nationally collected revenue and is tabled annually with the budget) has very detailed schedules that present the frameworks for the various conditional grants to provinces and municipalities. These grants are classified into specific and general purpose grants and then listed in the appropriate schedules.

12 Main budget revenue includes all revenue less payments made to the revenue pool of the Southern African Customs Union. In 2005/06, this amounted to 12 billion rands. The Southern African Customs Union is the regional grouping that existed during the Apartheid era and includes Botswana, Namibia, Lesotho, and South Africa.

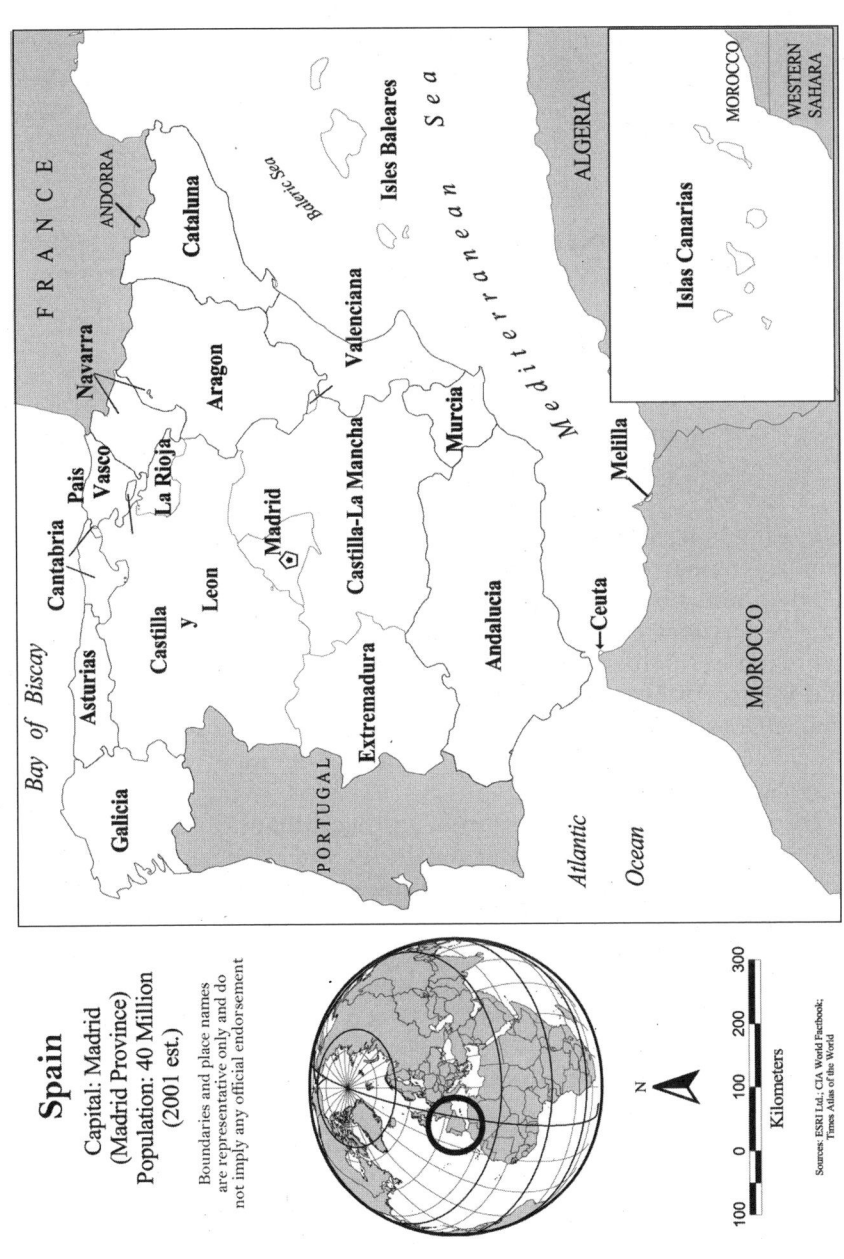

Kingdom of Spain

JULIO LÓPEZ-LABORDA,
JORGE MARTÍNEZ-VÁZQUEZ,
AND CARLOS MONASTERIO*

The Kingdom of Spain, defined in the 1978 Constitution as a parliamentary monarchy, is a unitary country with most of the features of a federation. Currently, Spain's population of a little over 44 million, and its territory covers 505,997 square kilometres, incorporating the mainland in the Iberian Peninsula plus the Balearic and Canary Islands and the North African city-enclaves of Ceuta and Melilla (see Table 1). The official language is Castilian (Spanish), which is co-official with Catalan, Euskera, and Galician in the communities in which these languages originate.

Historically, Spain emerged from a process that involved the unification of different kingdoms and territories and culminated in the later part of the fifteenth century. Its constituent units, often identified with significant geographical and climatic differences, had and continue to have strong cultural identities, including different languages. Spain's historical legacy is crucial in understanding that country's strong demands for self-government and fiscal decentralization. In the last quarter of a century, Spain was transformed from one of the most centralized countries in the world at the time of General Francisco Franco's death in 1975 into one of the most decentralized. Spain's historical legacy is also the fundamental reason that the Spanish Constitution adopted an asymmetric system of intergovernmental finance whereby, as we will see below, two regions (the Basque Country and Navarre) have a fiscal framework that is completely different from that of the rest of the regions. The fast pace of reform displayed by Spain's fiscal federalism is influenced in many ways by these historico-political issues.

Table 1
Basic political and geographic indicators

Official name: Kingdom of Spain
Population: 43,398,190
Area (square kilometres): 505,987
GDP per capita: 20,864 euros (2005)
Constitution: Parliamentary monarchy
Orders of government: Three
Constitutional status of local government: Yes
Official languages: Castilian (Spanish), which is co-official with Catalan, Euskera, and Galician in the communities in which these languages originate
Number and types of constituent units: 17 Autonomous Communities (as the regional governments are called), two Autonomous Cities at the intermediate level, and 50 provinces and 8,109 municipalities at the local level
Population, area and per capita GDP of the largest constituent unit: Andalusia, with a population close to 8 million, an area of 87,597 square kilometres, and a per capita income of 16,196 euros (in 2005)
Population, area and per capita GDP of the smallest constituent unit: La Rioja, with a population of 297,000, an area of 5,000 square kilometres, and a per capita income of 22,326 euros.

The current vertical organization of government includes, besides the central government, 17 Autonomous Communities (as the regional governments are called), two Autonomous Cities at the intermediate level, and 50 provinces and 8,109 municipalities at the local level. The Constitution explicitly recognizes the existence and right to self-governance of local governments and the Autonomous Communities.[1] Although the Autonomous Communities have some regulatory powers over the local governments, the structure of government and the fiscal system is not essentially hierarchical. Local governments have their own sources of revenues and receive transfers directly from the national government in what we may refer to as a bifurcated system of finance. Under this system, the national government deals directly with the intermediate level and the local level governments, and there are minimal fiscal relations between intermediate and local governments.[2] Overall, the very significant decentralization thrust of the past twenty-five years has benefited the intermediate level of government – the Autonomous Communities, which have gone from not existing to representing 36 percent of the consolidated public sector.[3]

The Autonomous Communities are the fastest-growing level of government, with total expenditures financed largely by transfers from the central government and mainly focused on health and education – the two largest components of total public expenditures after pensions.

Meanwhile, local government budgets have continued to represent 13 percent of total expenditures, very close to what they represented at the start of the decentralization process a quarter of a century ago. The fact that the decentralization process has been dominated by the devolution of competences and revenues to the Autonomous Communities has led many observers and political forces in Spain to talk about the need for a "second decentralization," which would be focused on local governments.[4]

The level of political accountability is relatively high as all government representatives are democratically elected and responsible to their respective constituencies. At the same time, there is a significant civil society presence; however, there are no important elements of direct democracy.[5] The Constitutional Court handles disputes between different levels of government. At the national level, there are two dominant political parties positioned at the centre-right and the centre-left, but regional parties, especially in Catalonia and the Basque Country, have played key roles in their regions and as coalition members in the national Parliament.

Over the past twenty-five years of rapid decentralization, Spain enjoyed high rates of economic growth and prosperity, spotted with unusually high rates of unemployment associated with rigidities in labour market institutions. In 2005, GDP per capita was $25,500. Over the same twenty-five-year period, Spain underwent a considerable increase in tax effort. In 1975, total tax revenues as a percentage of GDP stood at less than 20 percent. By comparison, at that time, the average OECD country was collecting 31 percent of GDP in tax revenues. By 2002, Spain had converged upon the OECD average, with total tax revenues representing over 35 percent of GDP. Over the past quarter century, the increases in real GDP and the considerably higher presence of the public sector in the economy allowed a significant jump in the provision of public services at all levels of government.

THE ASSIGNMENT OF RESPONSIBILITIES

The Constitution addresses the fundamental division of responsibilities across different levels of government. Table 2 shows the current assignment of responsibilities.[6] The actual assignment has evolved over the years, with the Autonomous Communities taking on responsibility for the provision of a wide range of public services of a regional-local nature, including most health and education services. For example, the full devolution of health care responsibilities to regional governments took place only in 2002.

An interesting aspect of the devolution of responsibilities in Spain is that it has been asymmetrical. Originally, and mostly for historico-political reasons, only a small group of Autonomous Communities was devolved responsibilities in education and health matters. This led to a distinction between "high-level communities" (i.e., those with a high level of devolved

Table 2
Assignment of responsibilities at different levels of government in Spain

1. Central government
Defence
International representation
Justice
National police
Regulation and economic planning
Financial system regulation
Customs
Income and wealth redistribution
Basic social security legislation and funding
National infrastructure: highways, railroads, and hydraulic river works across more than one Autonomous Community; commercial ports and airports

2. Autonomous Communities (intermediate level)
Education at all levels (primary, high school, and college)
Health
Agriculture
Industry, energy, and mines
Environment
Tourism and domestic trade
Social services
Historical and artistic patrimonial protection and own region's language protection
Housing and territorial arrangement
Regional infrastructures: highways and railroads within the Autonomous Community, sport ports, and sport airports

3. Local governments
3.1 Municipalities
Water supply
Sewerage systems and garbage collection
Public lighting systems
Social protection
Cemeteries
Repair and maintenance of non-university school centres
Parks and public gardens
Street paving

....

Municipalities with more than 50,000 inhabitants
Urban transportation
Local environmental protection

3.2 Provinces
Funds destined to small municipalities for infrastructure and public services
Legal assistance and managerial support to small municipalities
Delivery of services of a super-municipal nature

Source: Authors' elaboration.

responsibilities) and "low-level communities." With time, all Autonomous Communities came to have substantially the same responsibilities, although some minor asymmetries persist (e.g., only some communities have the power to run the prison system and the police). A more permanent manifestation of asymmetrical assignments occurs at the local level, where only municipalities with more than 50,000 people have responsibilities for urban transportation services and environmental protection. In addition, the provinces (the first tier of local government) perform some administration services and conduct infrastructure projects for small municipalities that lack the capacity to do so themselves.

Generally, the assignment of responsibilities follows accepted principles, including subsidiarity. The responsibilities assigned to the national government are for services that benefit the entire national territory (e.g., economic stabilization policy, income and wealth redistribution, international relations, defence, customs, financial system regulation, basic social security legislation and funding, national infrastructure, and transport). Local governments are assigned services with typically local benefit areas, such as water and sewerage, parks, and street lighting. It is notable that none of the education services (e.g., basic education) or health services (e.g., primary health) are assigned at the local level. Although there has been and continues to be considerable discussion about the devolution of more expenditure responsibilities from the intermediate to the local level of government (in particular, basic education), in the context of the "second decentralization" nothing much has been done. It is usually argued that the main roadblock is the very low administrative capacity of many small municipalities. Rather than waiting for the difficult amalgamation of those small municipalities, one possibility that has been discussed involves the adoption of an asymmetric approach, whereby the provinces could be put in charge of providing those services that the smaller municipalities lack sufficient administrative capacity or scale to provide for themselves. In Spain, a cooperative approach among local governments with insufficient scale for the provision of a variety of services has taken root. The cooperative arrangements are known as *mancomunidades*, and they operate as special districts across several local governments to provide water services, garbage collection, tourism, and social services.

The responsibility assignments in Table 2 need to be further qualified. While, in some cases (e.g., regional public works, infrastructure, and transport), the Autonomous Communities exercise their powers freely, in other cases their autonomy is restricted, with varying intensity, by upper-level governments. For example, in the cases of environmental protection and agriculture, European Union (EU) directives determine such matters as minimum environmental quality standards and the kinds of crops that may be grown.[7] However, the most significant limitations occur in the area of

Table 3
Direct expenditures by function and level of government, 2004 (Percent)

Function	Federal (%)	State or provincial (%)	Local (%)	All (%)
General public services	67.0	21.3	13.7	100
Defence	100	0	0	100
Public order and safety	54.9	19.3	25.8	100
Economic affairs	50.8	35.6	13.6	100
Environmental protection	8.3	23.3	68.4	100
Housing and communal services	3.1	24.8	72.1	100
Health	7.7	90.6	1.7	100
Recreation, culture, and religion	24.1	32.2	43.7	100
Education	6.5	89.4	4.1	100
Social protection	87.8	8.4	3.8	100

Source: Ministry of Economics and Finance; authors' elaboration.

social services – specifically health care and education. These are truly co-shared responsibilities. Although the Autonomous Communities have responsibility for delivery and implementation in those areas, the central government has significant regulatory powers with regard to, inter alia, establishing the basic conditions for the provision of the service and the rules governing access to it. These rules typically provide minimum standards nationwide and cannot be altered by the regional governments. However, the Autonomous Communities have the power to enact specific regional laws that are applicable within their territory, the purpose being to improve service provision and so on.

Table 3 presents the distribution of functional expenditures at different government levels.

A significant issue in Spain's fiscal federalism has been the methodology employed to estimate the expenditure needs associated with the devolution of responsibilities to regional governments – the so-called "effective cost method."[8] Fundamentally, this is a historical cost-cum-update index methodology. Because practically all the service responsibilities devolved were previously provided by the central government, the fiscal-financial information available on those costs of provision at the time of devolution has been used to cost the expenditure needs associated with those responsibilities. The methodology suffers from certain well-known problems, not the least of which is obsolescence due to changing conditions (e.g., population changes, the development of technology, etc.). Nevertheless, the effective cost method did provide an effective bridge in the process of devolution and avoided excessive budgetary tensions. The problem lies in the fact that this methodology is, to a certain extent, still being used for the computation of equalization grants and other important operational aspects of the decentralization system, and no clear alternative has yet been developed.

FISCAL FEDERALISM AND MACROECONOMIC MANAGEMENT

Membership in the EU has come to shape in detail Spain's macroeconomic management within a setting of fiscal federalism.[9] Due to Spain's integration in the euro area, the European Central Bank (ECB) is in charge of monetary policy management. The ECB has autonomy from Spain and other member countries in conducting monetary policy, and its actions are guided by the objective of price stability throughout the entire euro area. These arrangements eliminate any possibility of budget deficit financing via monetary emission.

Conducting fiscal policy is also affected by membership in the EU, which, among other things, has encouraged overall fiscal discipline and the coordination of fiscal policy among the different levels of government, especially in the area of public debt management. Spain experienced a period of large deficits and rapid debt accumulation at the central and regional levels from the mid-1980s to the mid-1990s. This followed not only several economic downturns associated with international macroeconomic shocks but also ambitious and not well-disciplined public spending programs. In the mid-1990s, general government gross liabilities as a percentage of GDP had reached – for the first time in Spain's history – the average level of OECD countries. However, this situation improved quite sharply in preparation for Spain's joining the euro zone in the late 1990s. The Growth and Stability Pact and the Protocol on Excessive Deficits established a maximum combined public deficit of 3 percent of GDP and public debt levels not in excess of 60 percent of GDP. These so-called Maastricht criteria were met in time for Spain to join the euro zone. Actually, in recent years, Spain, with Finland, has been the EU country with the best results in deficit control.[10]

As mentioned above, these fiscal restrictions imposed by the EU have forced a strong level of coordination in fiscal policy among all levels of government in Spain. This coordination became a necessity because, while the central government became responsible for the overall deficit of the public sector, it only directly manages half of the total public budget. In 2001, the national Parliament approved the Budgetary Stability Law, which has served as a domestic multilevel government pact of stability. This law has provided the means to distribute the general government's target deficit between the different levels and, at the same time, has toughened the deficit performance of all governments. In fact, during the first stage, between the promulgation of the law in 2001 and its recent reforms, which were approved in May 2006 (and will take effect at the start of fiscal year 2007), the general performance rule was budget balance.

The budget balance rule was duly criticized because it induces a pro-cyclical fiscal policy, especially in the area of investment in capital infrastructure. For this reason, the 2006 amendments to the Budgetary Stability Law emphasize budget balance over the economic business cycle. However, it allows a maximum deficit of 1 percent of GDP during economic slowdowns, while demanding a budgetary surplus during periods of economic expansion.[11] In addition, the amended law allows a permanent deficit equivalent to 0.5 percent of GDP targeted to finance productivity-enhancing investments.[12]

According to the Budgetary Stability Law, the global fiscal objective (deficit or surplus) for the entire public sector is distributed among the different levels of government. It is interesting that, of the maximum combined public-sector deficit of 1.5 percent of GDP, regional governments can accumulate up to 1 percent (with the central government at 0.4 percent and local governments at 0.1 percent), or 75 percent of the entire public sector. Thus, the new law is more generous with the regional governments (i.e., Autonomous Communities), which is a concession to their consent and agreement. However, the amended law also establishes that any regional government that fails to fulfill its deficit objective must present a "financial recovery" plan for the next three years and must get the central government's authorization for any new debt emissions as long as the non-performance situation persists.

Two important intergovernmental institutions are charged with, among other things, the horizontal distribution and negotiation of the deficit target among all levels of government units. These institutions are:

1 The Fiscal and Financial Policy Council (CPFF), which acts as a consultative body linking the central and the regional governments. Its membership includes the central government's ministries of finance and public administrations as well as the finance counsellors of the Autonomous Communities. Regional alliances in the CPFF tend to form more around regional income levels than around political party affiliation. Income levels tend to define who among the regions are the gainers and losers when it comes to the divisive question of the extent and reach of the unconditional equalization grants (or Sufficiency Fund), which are discussed below.
2 The National Commission of Local Administration (NCLA) represents all municipal and provincial governments. The NCLA leads discussions and negotiations with the central government.

ISSUES IN REVENUE-RAISING RESPONSIBILITIES

The system of revenue assignments in Spain is rather complex by international standards. This complexity arises from two sources. First, there are significant differences in the bifurcated revenue assignments at the intermediate and local levels of government, and those two systems need to be discussed separately. Second, the system of revenue assignments at the intermediate level of government is complicated by a very marked asymmetry between two groups of Autonomous Communities. Thus, for the purposes of discussion, it is useful to separate the two types of financing of regional governments from the financing of local governments.

Revenue Assignments of the Autonomous Communities[13]

The Spanish Constitution establishes two basic systems for financing the regional governments – the common regime and the special regime. The common regime applies to all Autonomous Communities with the exception of two: the Basque Country and Navarre. These two Autonomous Communities operate under the special (in Spanish, *foral*, or charter) regime.[14] The two systems introduce a fundamental asymmetry into the financing of regional governments that, fundamentally, benefits the two Autonomous Communities that operate under the special regime.

The common regime. The revenue assignment in the common regime was originally established by the Autonomous Communities Financing Act, 1980 (*Ley Orgánica de Financiación de las Comunidades Autónomas [LOFCA]*), which was comprehensively refurbished in 2001. For this reason, the revenue assignments in the common regime are typically known as the LOFCA system. While LOFCA establishes the basic principles of the system, specific implementation issues as well as disputes are settled within the CPFF, the intergovernmental body discussed above. One of the most important responsibilities of the CPFF has been to assess the evolution of the regional finance system on a regular basis and to recommend any necessary changes. Significant reviews of the LOFCA system took place in 1986, 1992, 1996, and 2001.

Initially (late 1970s and early 1980s), the financing system of the regions in the common regime was based on lump-sum general grants. These grants were calculated to cover the expenditure needs arising from the devolved expenditure responsibilities, using the "net effective cost" method. This approach had several weaknesses. First, it tended to perpetuate whatever differences existed across regions, under the centralized provision of services, before their devolution to the regional governments. Thus, it did not guarantee an equal provision of public services. Second, the complete reliance on grants, as opposed to own taxes, meant that regional governments had practically no revenue autonomy. This blunted the greater efficiency and accountability benefits typically associated with fiscal decentralization.

Both central and regional government authorities commonly agreed to the problems posed by the lack of revenue autonomy. The subsequent evolution of revenue assignments to regional governments can be seen as a continued strategy of gradual corrections to this problem, starting with the tools offered by LOFCA's initial version in 1980.

One side of the strategy consisted of modifying the method used to calculate expenditure needs. In 1986, there was an agreement to replace the net effective cost method with a quantification of regional spending based on indicators that would more accurately reflect the *expenditure needs* of each Autonomous Community. The concept of expenditure needs was identified as the costs each regional government would need to incur in order to provide the same level of public goods and services as did other regional governments. The indicators currently applied, and their relative weights, were last reformed in 2002. Three different sets of indicators are used, respectively, for three blocks of expenditure responsibilities: health services, social services, and other services (including education). Clearly, population is the indicator with the highest weighting in all three groups of responsibilities. However, despite the introduction of these indicators into the quantification of regional expenditure needs, the effective cost has continued to play a decisive role in their determination. This is because all of the regional financing reviews approved by the CPFF have included a "hold harmless provision," such that no regional government can be assigned lower revenues than it had received in the previous period.

The other side of the strategy was to reform revenue assignments properly. Funding of regional governments exclusively on the basis of general purpose grants was abandoned after an initial period and was replaced during 1982–84 with a system consisting of a set of devolved, or "ceded taxes" (*tributos cedidos*), and a general equalization transfer. The latter was first referred to as "revenue sharing in central government taxes" (*participación en ingresos del Estado*) and, since 2002, has been referred to as the Sufficiency Fund (*fondo de suficiencia*). These measures provided regional governments with standard revenue sources, much in line with standard practices in other decentralized countries.

However, until 1997, the ceded taxes could not be categorized by the regional governments as "own taxes" because, besides being introduced at the will of the central government, they were strictly regulated by the central authorities. However, while the regional governments were granted no discretion vis-à-vis the structure of the ceded taxes, in some cases they were put in charge of their administration and collection. Thus, in the initial period through 1997, the ceded taxes should be considered an extension of the tax-sharing system rather than own taxes that provided regional governments with meaningful tax autonomy. Starting in 1997, several degrees of discretion were granted to the regional governments vis-à-vis some of the ceded taxes, allowing the Autonomous Communities to set the tax rate and establish tax credits and allowances. Thus, for the regional governments, the ceded taxes progressively became own taxes.[15] A quite different story involves how the newly gained discretion was actually used or not used by the regional governments. In general, and along the lines of international trends, the Autonomous Communities have reduced their fiscal effort for direct taxes (personal income, inheritance, and gift taxes) and have increased it for indirect taxes (capital transfer tax, stamp duties, and hydrocarbon retail sales tax).

Table 4 provides the current status of ceded taxes with regard to the arrangements for the distribution of revenue collections, the level of government in charge of administration and collection and the discretionary powers granted to the regional governments over that particular tax. From Table 4 it can be seen that many important taxes have been either ceded as own regional taxes (e.g., 33 percent of the personal income tax) or actually shared with regional governments, as in the case of the value-added tax (VAT) and excise duties. The central government has been assigned exclusive authority over the collection, administration, and regulation of corporate income tax, the tax on insurance premiums, import duties, payroll taxes, and non-resident taxes.

The arrangements for the personal income tax deserve a special note because they are not those found in the typical piggyback schemes used by other decentralized countries. The law divides the tax schedule for the personal income tax into a central government schedule and a regional government schedule. The revenue from the central government schedule, which is equal to 67 percent of the total tax, is allocated at the central level, while the regional schedule, which is equal to 33 percent, is allocated to each Autonomous Community. The regional governments may maintain this tax schedule, in which case they will receive 33 percent of the total tax take, or they may increase or reduce the rates, but with the requirement that the rate schedule has to be a progressive tax having the same number of brackets as are found in the central government's income tax. The regional governments may also establish their own tax credits, which would only affect their differential tax take. While many regional governments have changed tax credits, only the Autonomous Community of Madrid has actually modified the tax rate schedule.

Overall, the current level of regional autonomy in the personal income tax is exercised in a coordinated and harmonized fashion with the central government in order to minimize taxpayer compliance costs. The definition of taxable income is common for both central and regional taxes. Taxpayers

Table 4
Current revenue assignments to regional governments

Tax	Sharing of collections (%)		Administration by regional governments		Discretion by regional governments	
	Common Regime	Charter Regime	Common Regime	Charter Regime	Common Regime	Charter Regime
Personal income tax	33	100	No	Yes	Tax schedule and tax credits	Full
Tax on net wealth	100	100	Yes	Yes	Threshold, tax schedule, and tax credits	Full
Inheritance and gift tax	100	100	Yes	Yes	Allowances, tax schedule, tax credits, administration, and collection	Full
Corporate income tax	–	100	–	Yes	–	Full
Non-Resident income tax	–	100	–	Yes	–	Full for permanent establishments
Capital transfer tax, taxes on the raising of capital, and stamp duties	100	100	Yes	Yes	Tax rates, tax credits, administration. and collection	Full, with some exceptions
Gaming taxes	100	100	Yes	Yes	Allowances, taxable base, tax rates, administration, collection, and inspection	Full, with some exceptions
Vehicle excise (registration)	100	100	Yes	Yes	Tax rates	Tax rates, declaration and payment forms and payment periods
Hydrocarbons retail sales tax	100	100	Yes	Yes	Tax rates, administration, collection, and inspection	Tax rates, declaration and payment forms and payment periods

Table 4
Current revenue assignments to regional governments (*Continued*)

Tax	Sharing of collections (%)		Administration by regional governments		Discretion by regional governments	
	Common Regime	Charter Regime	Common Regime	Charter Regime	Common Regime	Charter Regime
Value-added tax	35	100	No	Yes	No	Tax declaration and payment forms and payment periods
Excise duties (alcoholic beverages, tobacco, and petrol)	40	100	No	Yes	No	Tax declaration and payment forms and payment periods
Electricity tax	100	100	No	Yes	No	Tax declaration and payment forms and payment periods
Tax on Insurance Premiums	–	100	–	Yes	–	Tax declaration and payment forms and payment periods

Source: López Laborda, J., Financiación y gasto público en un Estado descentralizado, *Economía Aragonesa*, 24 (2004): 63–82.

need to fill out only one tax return, which incorporates the central and regional income taxes. In the case of the regions under the common regime, the State Tax Administration Agency (AEAT in Spanish) collects and distributes the revenues between the central and regional governments.

Besides the ceded taxes, regional governments subject to the common regime have other sources of financing. First, regional governments may introduce their own regional taxes and surcharges (which are different from the devolved or ceded taxes). For these taxes, the Autonomous Communities have full powers of collection, administration, and regulation. However, the LOFCA imposes strict bounds on the type of taxes regional governments can introduce on their own. Most important, this law prohibits regional governments from using the same tax bases or types of taxes already assigned or used by the central government and municipal governments. The exclusion of cohabitation of the same tax bases at different levels of government explains why regional governments have so far introduced so few genuine regional taxes (basically environmental and gaming taxes) as well as why the revenue collections from this source are so small. Other sources of financing for regional governments under the common regime include equalization grants, known as the Sufficiency Fund, and conditional grants. The nature of these transfers is discussed below.

Of the (non-financial) revenues for the Autonomous Communities under the common regime for 2004, own revenues, including revenues from ceded taxes and those from genuine regional taxes, amount to 34 percent of regional non-financial revenues. Shared taxes represent 21 percent; equalization grants, 24 percent; and conditional grants, 21 percent of non-financial revenues.

The charter system The charter financing system applies to two Autonomous Communities: Navarre and the Basque Country. The financing arrangements for these two regions are called the *Convenio* in Navarre and the *Concierto* in the Basque Country, with both terms referring to the asymmetric conditions incorporated into the two special laws for the two regions: the Economic Agreement between the State and Charter Community of Navarre Act, 2003 (*Ley del Convenio Económico entre el Estado y la Comunidad Foral de Navarra*), and the Economic Agreement with the Autonomous Community of the Basque Country Act, 2002 (*Ley del Concierto Económico con la Comunidad Autónoma del País Vasco*).

In contrast to the common regime, the charter system is not based on the assignment of specific revenues to fund a given level of spending. The chief feature of the charter system is that it provides the two regions concerned with a much higher level of fiscal autonomy than is found in the Autonomous Communities under the common regime. Both the *Convenio* and the *Concierto* basically recognize the capacity of the charter regions to establish and regulate their own fiscal systems, provided that the solidarity principle and the freedom of movement and residence of people and the freedom of movement of goods, services, and capital are all ensured.

In essence, the charter regions are financed exclusively through tax revenues known as "agreed taxes" (*tributos convenidos* in Navarre and *tributos concertados* in the Basque Country). These two regions have wide powers over these revenue sources, which are, in general, considerably greater than are the powers that, under the common regime, have been granted to the Autonomous Regions in the form of ceded taxes.[16]

In most cases, the charter regional governments have full power over the agreed taxes. The only taxes that are currently outside the charter regime list of agreed taxes are import duties and payroll taxes for social security (see Table 4).

In contrast to the revenue assignments for regional governments under the common regime, the charter regions have full powers over all personal and corporate income taxes. The finance departments of the charter regions also have control over the administration of the main indirect taxes, the VAT, and excise duties.[17] However, for indirect taxes the charter regions have no regulatory powers, mainly because of the restrictions imposed by EU rules governing the harmonization of those taxes.

In practice, the charter regional governments have used their ample discretionary powers to reduce tax burdens within their borders. For example, in the case of the corporate income tax, depreciation allowances are more generous here than they are in the rest of the regions under the common regime; also, tax credits for investment and job creation are higher, while tax rates in general are lower.[18]

The long list of significant taxes fully assigned to the charter Autonomous Communities and the relatively high income levels of these two regions guarantee the full financing of their expenditure needs without any transfers from the central government. In fact, the asymmetric regimes for the Basque Country and Navarre call for negative transfers to be remitted from the regional governments to the central government. These negative transfers are called the "quota" (*cupo*) in the case of the Basque Country and the "contribution" (*aportación*) in the case of Navarre. The rationale for these negative transfers is that the two regions should help finance the cost of public goods provided by the central government throughout the national territory. In contrast to this single payment by the charter regions, the regions under the common regime have several ways of "contributing" to the financing of central government services. The most important of these are the non-ceded taxes collected in their territories (67 percent in the personal income tax, 100 percent in the corporate income tax, 65 percent in the VAT, and so on).

The actual amount of the negative transfers, or quota, is based on a fairly complex formula. The share in the cost of central government services attributable to each charter region is based on an "imputation index," which is basically a relative income function (vis-à-vis the entire national economy). The imputation index is 1.6 percent for Navarre and 6.24 percent for the Basque Country.

Since the central government still collects certain revenues in the charter regions (arising from the "non-agreed" taxes as well as from non-tax revenue sources), and part of central government expenditures are financed through "below the line" deficit financing sources, a distinction is made in the calculations between the "Gross Quota," GQ, and the "Net Quota," NQ. The NQ is calculated as the GQ less all revenues obtained by the National Treasury in the charter regions. The amount of the GQ in the "base" year for charter Autonomous Community *f* is as follows:

$$GQ_{f0} = i_f \cdot G_0 \quad (f = Navarre, Basque\ Country)$$

where i_f is the imputation index for charter Autonomous Community f, and G_0 represents the level of public services provided by the central government in the "base" year. In addition, let us identify the revenues not covered by the financing agreements as TN, and the deficit of the central government by D (note that in the case of a surplus, this variable would simply work in the opposite direction). Finally, the value of the NQ, which is the amount actually transferred by the finance departments of the charter regions to the central government's Ministry of Finance, is given by:

$$NQ_{f0} = i_f \cdot G_0 - i_f \cdot TN_0 - i_f \cdot D_0 = i_f \cdot [G_0 - (TN_0 + D_0)]$$

The quota is not calculated on an annual basis. The calculation methodology is reviewed every five years. For any year t subsequent to the base year, the amount is calculated by applying to the base year value the rate of growth in central government taxes equivalent to the agreed taxes, which is denoted by IE:

$$NQ_{ft} = NQ_{f0} \cdot \frac{IE_t}{IE_0}.$$

Hence, the revenues kept by charter Autonomous Community f in year t are the difference between the revenues actually obtained from the agreed taxes, T_f, and the amount of the quota remitted to the central government:

$$R_{ft} = T_{ft} - NQ_{ft} = T_{ft} - NQ_{f0} \cdot \frac{IE_t}{IE_0}.$$

The discussion above provides a description of the "basic financing model" for the charter regions. But, as in the case of the regions under the common regime, the Basque Country and Navarre also have other sources of revenues with which to finance their expenditures, such as own taxes, surcharges and fees, and borrowing.

An evaluation of the charter system produces a mixed scorecard. This system scores high from the standpoint of the financial autonomy and accountability of subnational governments. In contrast to the still heavy reliance of the regional governments under the common regime on revenue sharing and transfers, the charter regions would appear to finance all their expenditure out of their own revenues. But there is more. In fact, the degree of fiscal autonomy provided by the charter system to the regional governments is unique in the international experience. A similarity can be found in the "single channel" scheme that some Russian regions practised in the early 1990s against the wishes of the federal government, whereby the regions collected on their own all taxes, including those that were supposed to be federal taxes, and negotiated with Moscow a single payment or remittance.[19]

It would be misleading to confuse the degree of autonomy granted to the charter regions in Spain with that existing in the world's most fiscally decentralized countries, such as the United States, Switzerland, and Canada. In those countries, some of the federal taxes may be administered by the subnational governments and then remitted (e.g., Canada and Switzerland), and subnational governments have their distinct separate taxes (e.g., the United States and Canada). But in none of those countries are subnational governments assigned most or all the taxes and then expected to negotiate with the centre a single payment transfer as a contribution to the cost of providing federal services.

The important drawbacks of the charter system emanate from the asymmetric nature of the arrangement vis-à-vis the common regime applied in the rest of the Spanish regions. In the first place, the greater financial autonomy provided by the charter regime provides the means and incentives for asymmetric tax competition between these regions and the regions under the common regime. For example, if a charter region decides to implement tax measures to attract firms from other regions, for the most part the regions under the common regime are unable to react because, for example, they do not have regulatory powers over corporate income tax.

Second, the charter regime may be seen as unfair to the rest of the regions under the common regime. A comparison of the structure of the common and charter financing systems shows that an equal level of tax effort will provide the charter regime regions with higher revenues, while both types of regions have the same expenditure obligations. In other words, the regions under the common regime would need to levy higher tax rates on their constituents to provide the same standard of regional-type public services. An explanation for this difference is that the charter system is designed so that, out of their taxes, the citizens residing in the charter regions fund the cost of regional public goods and, with the quota remittance, the respective share of national public goods. The citizens residing in the common regime regions *also* finance equalization grants (the Sufficiency Fund) to allow those Autonomous Communities with low fiscal capacity or high expenditure needs to provide the same level of regional public goods and services as is enjoyed by the other communities.

Revenue Assignments of Local Governments

Municipal governments have their own revenue assignments separate from those of the regional governments. Local revenues are regulated by the Law on Local Finance (*Ley Reguladora de las Haciendas Locales*), 1988, which was updated in 2004. As in the case of the charter regions, and in contrast to what is practised in the common regime regions, the financing system of local governments is not based on the computation of expenditure needs that then have to be financed with a particular set of revenues.

Five taxes are currently assigned to local governments: property tax, local business tax, vehicle tax, tax on increased property values in urban areas, and tax on construction, facilities, and infrastructure. Of the five local taxes, three are mandatory in all the municipalities: the property tax, the local business tax, and the vehicle tax. The other two taxes – a tax on increases in property value and a tax on construction, facilities, and infrastructure – are optional taxes; it is up to the municipal council whether or not they are introduced.[20] In practice, most municipalities have decided to use these two optional taxes. In general, municipal governments enjoy a high level of autonomy in setting tax rates, allowances, and tax credits for local taxes within the framework of the (centrally issued) law, and they make wide use of these rights. Therefore, it is fair to say that local taxes are truly own municipal taxes.

In the case of the property tax, the Ministry of Finance, through the Office of the Cadastre (*Dirección General del Catastro*), centrally manages the most significant aspect of this municipal tax – the assessment of property values. This is an unsatisfactory situation for many municipalities, especially in the case of large cities, which feel they would be better able to manage the assessment of property values within their borders. Large local governments have at different times asked the central government to let them do their own property assessments. In periods of fast increases in property values, as has been the case since 2000 throughout Spain, the delay in assessed values catching up with real market values has made this problem more acute. This situation has led to expensive emergency revisions of cadastral values in order to increase revenue collections from the property tax. Nevertheless, the typical municipality has proceeded to lower property tax rates after a revised increase in cadastral values. Property tax burdens have become a particularly sensitive issue, and the overall equity of the tax has been increasingly questioned, especially in light of the fact that housing expenditures are proportionally higher for lower-income people and that there are no circuit-breakers for pensioners whose property values have increased quite considerably but whose incomes have not.

With some exceptions (such as property assessments or the register of economic activities), local taxes are administered by the municipal governments. However, in the case of small municipalities lacking administrative capacity and skilled personnel, tax administration is often delegated to the tax agency of the province or the regional government. Despite the significant degree of local tax autonomy, there has not been a considerable degree of tax competition, perhaps with the exception of the anecdotal case of the vehicle tax, where some small municipalities near large cities have bet on the minimum tax rates allowed in order to attract the vehicle rental market.

Another important revenue source for municipalities involves charges based on the straight application of the benefit principle, such as user fees for local services for water, access to municipal sports facilities, and local transport. Other significant sources of revenues for local governments are unconditional transfers, including revenue sharing and tied grants. These are discussed in the next section.

In 2004, own revenue sources represented 60 percent of non-financial revenues. This means that there is a significant level of autonomy and accountability at the municipal level, although there are significant variations in fiscal pressure (and expenditure levels) across municipalities. Shared taxes and grants represent 40 percent of non financial local revenues. The only tax revenue actually received by the provincial government is a surtax on the local business tax raised by the municipalities in the provincial territory.

Table 5 shows the recent changes in non-financial revenues by level of government. Comparing these figures with the evolution of non-financial public expenditures, we can see that the vertical fiscal gap has evolved favourably for the regional governments.[21]

FISCAL EQUITY AND EFFICIENCY CONCERNS AND INTERGOVERNMENTAL FISCAL TRANSFERS

Because Spain's decentralization system works in a bifurcated fashion, without any significant hierarchical relationship between regional and local governments, it is necessary to discuss the system of central transfers to the regions and the system of central transfers to local governments separately.

Transfers to Regional Governments

Regional governments receive general unconditional equalization grants and conditional grants. The main equalization grant for regions subject to the common regime is the Sufficiency Fund.[22] This equalization grant is formula-driven and is generally based on the fiscal gap between the expenditure needs and the fiscal capacity of the regions. The central government computes for each ceded tax a "standard yield" that each regional government should obtain by making the same tax effort as the other regions. To the extent that this aggregate standard yield is less than the region's expenditure needs, the system provides an equalization grant to cover the difference between expenditure needs and fiscal capacity. However, those regions for which expenditure needs are less than fiscal capacity (as measured by the standard yield) are assigned a negative grant and need to remit the "excess" funding to the central government. In summary, the Sufficiency Fund operates as a conventional unconditional equalization grant with a mix of sources of funding, from central government general revenues and from the contributions (negative grants) of the "surplus" regions.

Table 5
Composition of non-financial public expenditures and revenues by level of government (%)

YEAR	Central Government*		Autonomous Governments		Local Governments	
	Expenditures	Revenues	Expenditures	Revenues	Expenditures	Revenues
2001	54.1	80.2	33.0	9.5	12.8	10.3
2002	53.3	70.6	33.6	19.3	13.1	10.1
2003	52.6	69.0	34.1	21.2	13.4	9.8
2004	53.1	67.6	34.4	22.2	12.6	10.2
2005	51.2	67.5	36.0	22.6	12.8	9.9

* Including the social security system
Source: Ministry of Economics and Finance and authors' elaboration.

However, the actual computation of the equalization transfers is unconventional. The following paragraphs describe the most salient features of the methodology used to determine the Sufficiency Fund transfers. The intergovernmental CPFF establishes a "base" year for the system and calculates the expenditure needs of each Autonomous Community, E_{i0}, and the standard yield for the ceded taxes, T_{i0}^*, for that base year. The Sufficiency Fund for the base year, SF_{i0}, is calculated as the difference between expenditure needs and tax capacity from the base year:

$$SF_{i0} = E_{i0} - T_{i0}^*.$$

For relatively richer Autonomous Communities, for which the standard tax yield exceeds expenditure needs (e.g., the Balearic Islands and Madrid), the grant is negative and, as pointed out above, that amount is remitted from the Autonomous Community to the central government.

The most significant twist is that the Sufficiency Fund is not determined annually. For any year t subsequent to the base year, the amounts for the Sufficiency Fund transfers are calculated by applying to the base year results a growth index equal to the rate of growth experienced by the central government (or state) taxes equivalent to the ceded taxes (*Ingresos Tributarios del Estado* [*ITE*]). Therefore, the Sufficiency Fund transfer for the current year t is given by:

$$SF_{it} = SF_{i0} \cdot \frac{ITE_t}{ITE_0}.$$

The effect of this is that the revenue that Autonomous Community i would receive in the current year t (R_{it}) is equivalent to the sum of the actualized Sufficiency Fund and the actual yield from the taxes ceded (T_{it}).

Note that this is different from the "standard yield," which is used only to calculate the Sufficiency Fund in the base year:

$$R_{it} = SF_{it} + T_{it} = SF_{i0} \cdot \frac{ITE_t}{ITE_0} + T_{it}.$$

The reliance of the equalization system on the computations of expenditure needs for a base year creates some serious issues. It seems correct to assert that, at the base year, the equalization system and the rest of the regional financing system guaranteed that all Autonomous Communities under the common regime had the funds required to finance all the service responsibilities devolved at a reasonably equal level. However, the same cannot be said for subsequent years. The actual level of equalization may gradually be weakened over time because, although the Sufficiency Fund evolves at the same rate for all Autonomous Communities, the measure of expenditure needs and the standard tax yield are likely to evolve at different rates. This is, in fact, what actually occurred in the early years of the application of the current system, when population growth was unevenly spread across the Autonomous Communities.

The system provides two instruments to correct this problem, although, so far, neither has been applied. First, the law requires periodic analysis of the impact of demographic changes in the Autonomous Communities on their expenditure needs. Second, because health care and education are defined as basic public services, with service standards fixed by the National Parliament (the catalogue of guaranteed sanitary benefits in health and obligatory education until the age of sixteen, and so on), the financing system is conceived to ensure that the regions have the necessary resources for their provision. Regional governments may receive additional funding to guarantee provision if the annual increase in public system users exceeds 3 percent of the increase in the national average. This additional funding would take the form of specific purpose grants or Basic Public Services Equalization Grants (*Asignaciones de Nivelación de Servicios Públicos Fundamentales*). Should these grants again be allocated to the same Autonomous Community within a five-year period, then the Sufficiency Fund must be adjusted to reflect the substantial change in expenditure needs of that regional government.[23]

In addition to the equalization grants, under the overall objective of reducing regional disparities in income and wealth, the regions receive conditional grants that are intended to foster regional development. Examples of this type of grant are the Inter-territorial Compensation Funds (*Fondos de Compensación Interterritorial [FCI]*) and several grants from the EU budget, such as the European Regional Development Fund (ERDF).

Transfers to Local Governments

The current transfer system for local governments was last updated in 2004. It provides municipalities with unconditional grants that come directly from the central government's Ministry of Finance. Although the system of unconditional grants is ultimately enacted in a law from the National Parliament, the substance of that law is elaborated in a process of negotiation between the Ministry of Finance at the central level and the Spanish Federation of Municipalities and Provinces (FEMP), which represents all local governments.

The funds are distributed according to different formulas, which differentiate between large cities and medium and small municipalities.[24] In the case of the larger cities (those with a population exceeding 75,000 inhabitants),[25] the transfer is composed of two components. The first component involves revenue sharing on a derivation basis on three types of central government taxes: the personal income tax (with a sharing rate of 1.6875 percent), the VAT (with a sharing rate of 1.7897 percent), and excise taxes (with a sharing rate of 2.0454 percent).[26] The second component is the Complementary Fund (*Fondo Complementario*), which was added in the last reform of the transfer system to hold these municipalities harmless. For the base year, the Complementary Fund is calculated as the difference between the amount previously received in transfers[27] and the revenue sharing (calculated as in the first component). For any year t subsequent to the base year, the Complementary Fund is calculated by applying to the base year a growth index equal to the increase in central government taxes (ITE).

For all other municipalities, medium and small, the amount of the transfer fund, referred to as "sharing in central government revenues" (*participación en ingresos del Estado*), is distributed according to an index formula with three sets of variables: population, with an assigned relative weight of 75 percent; the inverse of the tax capacity, with a relative weight of 12.5 percent; and fiscal effort, with a relative weight of 12.5 percent. The pool of funds is adjusted every year according to the rate of growth in ITE.[28]

This transfer system has been criticized from different angles.[29] For example, the distinction between the large municipalities and the rest lacks a clear rationale and transparency. In addition, this system lacks flexibility vis-à-vis the new problems faced by the country, such as the massive increase in the number of immigrants in some parts of the national territory, which has resulted in considerable increases in municipal (and regional) expenditures for social protection.[30] Several equity issues have arisen because of the out-migration from rural and mountain areas and the need to maintain facilities and services in those areas as well as in urban areas, which have much higher population densities. In addition, it is only in a very indirect manner that the transfers to the local governments pursue an equalization objective.

The provincial governments benefit form a transfer scheme that is similar to that applied to large cities and that has the same two components: the Complementary Fund and revenue sharing on the personal income tax (at a rate of 0.9936 percent), VAT (with a sharing rate of 1.0538 percent), and excise taxes (with a sharing rate of 1.2044 percent).

SUMMARY AND THE WAY FORWARD

Spain has undergone a fast and deep process of decentralization since the late 1970s, thereby becoming one of the most decentralized countries in the world. This decentralization process, however, has been uneven. There has been more meaningful decentralization on the expenditure side than on the revenue side of subnational budgets. The regional governments (Autonomous Communities) currently represent 36 percent of total public spending, while local governments represent close to 13 percent. Together, these subnational governments play a fundamental role in the provision of the public goods and services that are closest to the lives of citizens and that most affect their welfare. For some observers, central government intervention in many areas that are the responsibility of subnational governments remains too high, reducing effective subnational autonomy.[31] Nevertheless, overall, at least from the expenditure side of the budget, Spain has many of the features of many other federal systems, although formally it continues to be identified as a unitary country.

In comparison to other highly decentralized systems, the relative importance of local governments within the subnational public sector in is low. Largely, this is because, in Spain, the responsibility for all education services, including primary and secondary education, is assigned at the regional level. However, the respective roles of regional and local governments have not been completely sorted out. There continue to be repeated calls from many quarters in the country to strengthen expenditure and revenue assignments to local governments and to proceed with a "second decentralization" reform process, following the mostly successful one involving regional governments. Many small municipal governments, with less than an optimal scale, represent the most important obstacle to going forward with these reforms.

The decentralization of tax sources has lagged behind expenditure responsibilities. However, this is not to say that, in Spain, subnational government revenue autonomy is very low. As we have seen, own revenues currently represent between 35 percent and 55 percent of total revenues among regional governments under the common regime, while in the case of the two regions under the charter regime, almost all of their revenues could be interpreted as own revenues. In the case of local governments, revenue autonomy is higher than it is for regional governments under the common regime: their own revenues represent more than 60 percent of total municipal revenues. However, accountability and, generally, more fiscally responsible behaviour can be strengthened by increasing revenue autonomy and decreasing the dependence on tax sharing and transfers of subnational governments, especially in the case of regional governments under the common regime.

There are two fundamental options for increasing regional revenue autonomy. The first is to continue the current approach by increasing the allocated share of ceded taxes and raising or allocating normative powers over certain taxes such as the personal income tax, excise duties, or even, at some later date, the VAT.[32] A second option would be to introduce completely separate taxes for regional governments cohabitating the same tax bases as the central government. In this approach, regional governments would have their own personal income tax, excises, or even a VAT or corporate income tax; legislative or normative power over these taxes could be regulated by national laws or could be left entirely up to the regional parliaments. This approach is essentially the one used in Canada and the United States.[33] The reform of the current revenue assignments would create the necessary fiscal or tax space for regional governments to introduce their own taxes. A system of separate taxes has some similarities with the current system of ceded taxes, but there are also important differences between the two. Perhaps the most significant difference is that, in the case of ceded taxes, the central government designs backup tax rates (*tarifas supletorias*) for the regional governments' use in case the latter do not design their own. This arrangement has, de facto, provided regional governments with few incentives to exercise their tax autonomy, and, to a large extent, it transforms ceded taxes more along the line of revenue sharing than along the line of real own taxes. Regional governments have found it much more attractive to bargain with the centre over the level of the ceded tax (for example, 50 percent rather than 33 percent) than to increase their own rates in order to raise any additional needed revenues. The use of the ceded tax scheme has helped to obscure regional government accountability. It may also be possible, along the same lines, to introduce some new taxes or to strengthen some existing ones at the regional level, such as in the case of environmental taxes, where some Autonomous Communities have already established an incipient presence.

An additional dimension of revenue autonomy involves tax administration. Greater involvement of the Autonomous Communities in tax collection and management is an avenue that several regional governments that are revising their Autonomy Statutes are currently considering. There have been discussions and plans drafted to strengthen the regional governments' tax administration agencies; in some cases, the regional administrations would be put in charge of collecting all taxes in their own regions, including central government taxes, whether in partnership with the central tax administration agency or on their own. This would reproduce the arrangement currently in place in the two charter regions of Navarre and the Basque Country. Rolling out this model to the rest of the regions (i.e., those under the common regime) could bring increased interregional equity; it could also fragment the administration of the most important taxes, with losses in efficiency and likely increases in compliance costs. It is also argued that the complete decentralization of tax administration would increase the political risk of disintegration. A separate tax administration for separate taxes (personal income tax, etc.) at the central and subnational levels is another option.

Vertical imbalances remain an issue. Subnational governments have continued to complain about the lack of sufficient funding and to demand (and frequently receive) additional funding from the central government. Beyond the issues of whether subnational governments have been assigned adequate autonomous tax sources and how much they have been predisposed to use them (which is clearly quite decisive in resolving any issue of vertical imbalances), we note two things: first, after using an effective cost method, all regional expenditure responsibilities have been devolved by mutual agreement between the regional and central governments; second, it has not been shown that the evolution of central and subnational government revenues has resulted in any vertical imbalance that has been to the detriment of the subnational governments.

The incentives and behaviour of the subnational and central governments further muddle the issue of vertical imbalances. On the one hand, subnational governments have had the incentive to continue to behave strategically by asking for more revenue sharing and thus seeking to spread the costs of their spending decisions to all citizens in the country (rather than accepting the political cost of increasing the taxes paid by those residents in their own territory). This is just one more manifestation of the common pool problem. More important, it reflects the fact that, ultimately, subnational governments in Spain have been operating under a soft-budget constraint: the central government sees itself as directly implicated in the delivery of certain regional services, such as health and education, as well as certain local services. On the other hand, the central government has, in certain expenditure programs, sometimes taken de facto decisions involving unfunded expenditure mandates to the subnational governments. On other occasions, the central government has undertaken tax reforms that have had a significant impact on the revenues of these governments (e.g., reducing the yield of certain subnational taxes) without compensation or counterbalancing measures.

Horizontal fiscal imbalances will continue to exist in the near future. The current system of intergovernmental finance provides a reasonable level of equalization among regions under the common regime. However, the current formula for estimating the fiscal capacity and expenditure needs of different regions is in need of an overhaul. The funds dedicated to equalization and, therefore, the appropriate degree of equalization continue to be matters of hot debate in Spain. This is ultimately a political decision, with positions naturally taken according to who benefits and who pays. Beneficiary regions support a high level of equalization on the grounds of solidarity, while those regions with the highest fiscal capacity point to the disincentive and efficiency effects of high levels of equalization. Also, as we mention above, the system of local transfers continues to be the target of a variety of criticisms.

Transfer funding issues have been affected by the expansion of the EU to include ten new member states from Central and Eastern Europe, and this raises other issues for regional financing. Most important, this expansion implies the loss of European Structural Funds and other funds aimed at regional development, which currently benefit quite a few of the poorer Autonomous Communities.

The asymmetric treatment of common regime and charter regime regions is a thorny issue. The Constitution permits the existence of two financing systems with very different structures. However, the Constitution does not seem to allow for the results of the two systems to differ – that is, for Autonomous Communities with the same expenditure responsibilities to provide different levels of public services, depending on whether they receive funding under the common regime or the charter regime. Despite the interregional inequity implied by this situation, few new ideas have been proposed to address it, other than possibly replicating the charter regime in all regions. This would be far from desirable not only for the central authorities but also for anyone concerned with efficiency and equity. A desirable stopgap measure would be to make all regions, including charter regions, participate in the financing of the equalization grant system.

NOTES

* Financial support by the Spanish Ministry of Education and Science, Projects MEJ-04-SEJ2004-08253 (Carlos Monasterio) and SEJ2006-4444 (Julio López-Laborda and Jorge Martínez-Vázquez) is gratefully acknowledged.
1 The Autonomous Communities are highly diverse in terms of size, population, per capita income, and other factors. The largest is Andalusia, with a population close to 8 million, an area of 87,597 square kilometres, and a per capita income of 16,196 euros (in 2005). The smallest is La Rioja, with a population of 297,000, an

area of 5,000 square kilometres, and a per capita income of 22,326 euros. There are also large variations in size among municipalities, which range from large modern cities to very small rural municipalities.

2   There is an exception to this general principle in the case of the two Autonomous Communities with the "special regime" (Navarre and the Basque Country), in which municipalities – and, in the Basque Country, its own regional government – are financially dependent on the first tier of local government (i.e., the provinces).

3   From a different perspective, the Autonomous Communities represent more than 50 percent of general government employment.

4   See F. Pedraja, J. Salinas, and J. Suárez-Pandiello, "Financing Local Governments: The Spanish Experience," in *Tax Reform in Spain: Accomplishments and Challenges*, ed. J. Martínez-Vázquez and J.F. Sanz (Cheltenham: Edward Elgar, 2007).

5   Provincial deputies, at the first tier of local government, are not directly elected but are designated by the municipal councils. The provincial deputies select one of their own as president of the Provincial Council.

6   This section and some other parts of the chapter draw upon J. López-Laborda and C. Monasterio, "Regional Governments: Vertical Imbalances and Revenue Assignments," in *Tax Reform in Spain: Accomplishments and Challenges*, ed. J. Martínez-Vázquez and J.F. Sanz (Cheltenham: Edward Elgar, 2007).

7   For environmental policy, EU norms establish air and water quality standards, delimiting regional government as well as municipal responsibilities (n.b., municipal governments receive financial support from regional governments to meet these responsibilities).

8   For a discussion of this methodology, see J. López-Laborda and C. Monasterio, "Regional Governments: Vertical Imbalances and Revenue Assignments," in *Tax Reform in Spain: Accomplishments and Challenges*, ed. J. Martínez-Vázquez and J.F. Sanz (Cheltenham: Edward Elgar, 2007).

9   See P. Drummond and A. Mansoor, "Macroeconomic Management and the Devolution of Fiscal Powers," IMF Working Paper 2/76, 2002, on the general problem of macroeconomic management with a federal setting.

10 From 2001 to 2004, there was balance in the fiscal sector as a whole, and in 2005 it registered a surplus equivalent to 1 percent of GDP.

11 For the period 2007–09, a deficit will be allowed if the real growth rate of the economy is below the potential growth rate of 2 percent. For real rates of growth in the economy between 2 percent and 3 percent of GDP, budget balance will be required; for rates of growth above 3 percent of GDP, a budget surplus will be required.

12 The general fungibility of budgetary funds deprives this distinction on the causes of the deficit of any real economic meaning.

13 See C. Monasterio, "El laberinto de la financiación autonómica," *Hacienda Pública Española* 163 (2002): 157–85, for a general discussion of autonomous financing.

14 There are some other minor deviations from the common regime in the case of the Autonomous Community of the Canary Islands, which, due to its geographical location, receives special treatment. However, the Canary Islands are typically

treated as part of the common regime. The two North African cities of Ceuta and Melilla also have a special status, which falls halfway between the position of a municipality and an Autonomous Community.

15 The standard assumption in the fiscal federalism literature is that some minimum degree of discretion over the structure of the tax is required (e.g., ability to change the tax rate) before we can consider it to be an own subnational government tax. See, for example, R. Bird, "Threading the Fiscal Labyrinth: Some Issues in Fiscal Decentralization," *National Tax Journal* 46 (1993): 207–27.

16 In the case of the Basque Country, tax autonomy is granted to the three provinces, or "Historical Territories," of Álava, Guipúzcoa, and Vizcaya. The "agreed taxes" in the Basque Country are administered and collected at the provincial level, with the regional government playing only a coordinating role. In this manner, the Autonomous Community is basically financed by transfers from the provincial governments. Note that this is not the case for Navarre because there the provincial and regional levels overlap perfectly.

17 The case of VAT and excise duties is quite complex. The tax yield collected by the regional governments is adjusted on the basis of estimates of consumption by the residents of each Autonomous Community. See I. Zubiri, *El Sistema de Concierto Económico en el contexto de la Unión Europea* (Bilbao: Círculo de Empresarios Vascos, 2000) for a complete explanation of these steps.

18 Some of the measures taken by the charter regional governments have been stricken by the European Court and by the Spanish Supreme Court because they were construed to represent public support of activities distorting economic competition. See I. Zubiri, *El Sistema de Concierto Económico en el contexto de la Unión Europea* (Bilbao: Círculo de Empresarios Vascos, 2000), 212–25.

19 See C. Wallich, ed., *Russia and the Challenge of Fiscal Federalism* (Washington, DC: The World Bank, 1994).

20 In its "Fiscal Regulations," the plenary session of the municipal council must decide, before the start of the fiscal year, which taxes are approved for implementation and within which margins, as specified by law. There is a third optional municipal tax on luxury expenditures, and this covers the use of hunting and fishing grounds. This tax has little revenue significance.

21 Data regarding vertical fiscal gaps was not available for Spain.

22 As we have seen above, the two regions under the charter regime receive no equalization grants. Actually, in their case, there is a negative transfer from these two regions to the National Treasury.

23 Special guarantees have been established for health care funding, including guaranteed increases that are at least equal to the rate of growth of GDP. In addition, revenue collections from the hydrocarbon retail sales tax, levied at the regional level, are formally tied to health (and environmental) spending.

24 See F. Pedraja, J. Salinas, and J. Suárez-Pandiello, "Financing Local Governments: The Spanish Experience," in *Tax Reform in Spain: Accomplishments and Challenges*, ed. J. Martínez-Vázquez and J.F. Sanz, (Cheltenham: Edward Elgar, 2007).

25 This group also includes the capital cities of all provinces and the capital cities of the Autonomous Communities regardless of their population size.
26 The allocation of revenues from consumption taxes is based on indirect methods that approximate relative levels of consumption expenditures.
27 This transfer used to be computed in a similar manner to the transfer system that, since 2004, has been used by the rest of the municipal governments.
28 The system of transfers for tourist municipalities with populations over 20,000 involves the two systems just described.
29 See, for example, F. Pedraja and J. Suárez-Pandiello, "La última reforma de la participación municipal en los tributos del estado. Un analisis cualitativo," *Papeles de Economía Española* 100 (2004): 77–92.
30 See I. Joumard and C. Giorno, "Getting the Most out of Public Sector Decentralisation in Spain," OECD *Economics Department Working Paper* 436 (2005): 8, 20.
31 See, for example, C. Viver Pi-Sunyer, "Finalmente, una amplia autonomía de baja calidad," *El País*, 6 September 2003.
32 This appears to be the route chosen by the regional governments (such as Catalonia) currently rewriting their regional constitutions (Autonomy Statutes) and negotiating with the central government.
33 Note that, fundamentally, the two Spanish regions under the charter regime have this sort of formal authority. In the charter arrangement, as in the common regime, there is no cohabitation of tax bases; however, in this case, the central government does not raise any of the taxes used by the regional governments. We should also note that this potential new arrangement could provide the basis for addressing the current asymmetry in revenue assignments between the regions in the common regime and those in the charter regime.

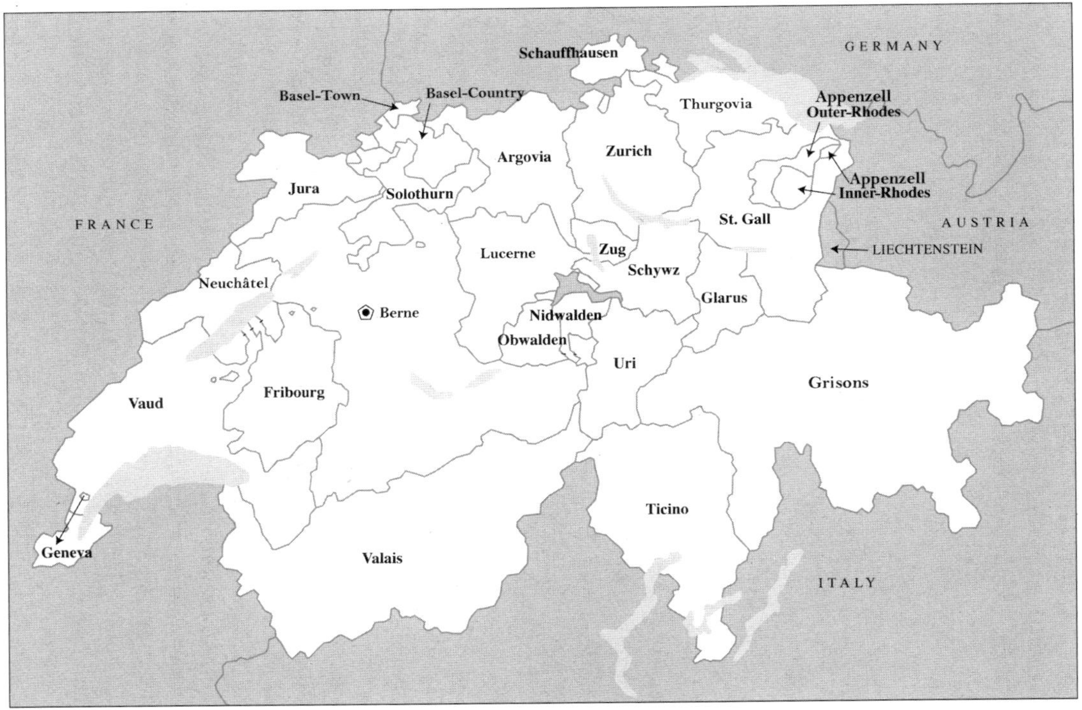

SWITZERLAND

Capital: Bern
Population: 7.2 million (2002 est.)

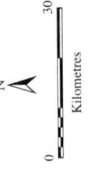

Swiss Confederation

GEBHARD KIRCHGÄSSNER

Switzerland is a rather small country; nevertheless, it has an extensive federal structure. Nowhere else do states, or cantons, of such tiny size have such extensive political and fiscal autonomy and power. Moreover, nowhere else do the people have such extensive direct political rights. There are possibilities for initiatives and referenda in all three spheres of government: local, canton, and federal. In the last twenty years, about 50 percent of all referenda worldwide have taken place in Switzerland.

The extensive fiscal autonomy of the cantons has two consequences. First, as it implies fiscal responsibility, there exist in the cantons special constitutional and statutory rules to enforce sustainability of canton (and local) public finances. Fiscal referenda as well as the so-called debt breaks play a prominent role. Second, the strong fiscal competition arising among the cantons endangers the coherence of the country. Thus, a fiscal equalization system is needed. This chapter places special weight on the peculiarities of the Swiss federal fiscal system, which are alien to most other federal systems: the fiscal referenda, debt breaks, and strong tax competition as well as the (rather complicated) system of corporate income taxation in the cantons, along with the (new) fiscal equalization system.[1]

The twenty-six Swiss cantons are the basic constituent polities of the country.[2] They all have, for example, their own income and property taxes; in 2002 the federal share of all income and property tax revenue was only about 21.5 percent. The cantons are free to decide not only on the tax rates but also on the tax schedule as well as on how progressive these taxes are. In deciding this, however, the governments and the parliaments of the cantons are not autonomous as they have to ask the citizens whether or not they accept changes in the tax law.

Although Switzerland is small, with a land area of 41,284 square kilometres and a population of 7.3 million people, its constituent parts are

Table 1
Basic political and geographic indicators

Official Name	Swiss Confederation
Population	7.3 million
Area	41,284 square kilometres
GDP per capita in US$	37,465 (2002)
Constitution	Republic, first Constitution 1848, current Constitution since 2000
Constitutional status of local government	Autonomy guaranteed in the canton Constitutions
Official Languages	German, French, Italian, Romansch
Number and types of constituent units	26 cantons
Population, area, and per capita GNP in US$ of the largest constituent unit	1.3 million, 1,728.9 square kilometres, 39,319 (Zurich)
Population, area, and per capita GNP in US$ of the smallest constituent unit	14,700, 172.5 square kilometers, 26,873 (Appenzell Inner-Rhodes)

remarkably different. It has four official national languages along with the corresponding cultures: 63.7 percent speak (Swiss) German; 20.4 percent, French; 6.5 percent, Italian; and 0.5 percent, Romansch. The remaining 9 percent speak various other languages.[3] Because German and French are the dominant languages, public officials are expected to understand both.

Language is not the only area of diversity. The Swiss population also adheres to different religions: 41.8 percent are Roman Catholics; 35.3 percent are Protestants; 4.3 percent are Muslims; 3.4 percent are adherents of other religions; and 15.4 percent have no religion or did not answer the corresponding question. Moreover, 20 percent of the population are foreigners.[4] This is a higher percentage than is found in any other country in Europe (except some very small countries such as Monaco). Thus, Switzerland, as a nation, lacks cultural, linguistic, and religious homogeneity; it is a nation shaped by the resolve of its citizens, a "nation of will" (*Willensnation*), and it is well aware of its many diversities.

This holds for the modern federal system, which was founded in 1848 but has roots going back to the thirteenth century. Although there was a first treaty between the three primary cantons – Schwyz, Uri, and Unterwalden – in 1273, the official founding date of Switzerland is 1291. However, the Swiss nation was strongly affected by Napoleon and came together in 1848 after a short civil war between the Protestants and Catholic separatists, *the*

Sonderbundkrieg, in 1847. That Switzerland has survived and did not split up according to linguistic divisions in the second half of the nineteenth century (when its neighbours, Italy and Germany, created their national states) is presumably due to its rather decentralized federal structure. The other key ingredients that constitute the Swiss nation are its direct democracy and its political neutrality in international affairs.

The cantons vary greatly in size and in population density. The average canton has about 280,000 people, but population sizes range from 14,700 in Appenzell Inner-Rhodes to 1.3 million in Zurich. The average population density is 178 people per square kilometre. Compared with some other European countries, such as Belgium and the Netherlands (as well as with the United Kingdom and Germany), this might not seem to be very high. However, Switzerland's internal differences are quite large. In Zurich, the population density is 723 persons; in Uri, a canton consisting almost entirely of mountains and valleys, it is thirty-six persons per square kilometer.[5] Basle-Town, with 190,700 inhabitants in its thirty-seven square kilometres, has a population only a little under that of the geographically largest canton, Grisons, whose 191,200 inhabitants are spread across 7,106 square kilometres and 150 valleys. Thus, some areas are rather densely populated, especially in the "Mittelland," a relatively narrow tract that runs from Lake Geneva to the Lake of Constance. North and west of the Mittelland are the Jura Mountains, to the south and east are the Pre-Alps and the Alps. Large parts of these mountain areas are unproductive and, correspondingly, quite sparsely populated (e.g., the canton of Uri).

The record of Swiss economic growth during the last fifteen years has been rather bad; Switzerland has had the lowest average growth rate of all OECD countries. Nevertheless, it is still a rather rich country. Based on current exchange rates, Switzerland lags behind Luxembourg and Norway as the third richest country in the world, but it is ahead of the United States, Denmark, and Ireland. Based on purchasing power, its record is not so splendid, as gross domestic product (GDP) per capita is higher in the United States and Ireland, and gross national investment per capita is higher in the United States. Even so, ranking fourth or fifth in the world is still very good.[6]

Inside Switzerland, however, there are strong economic discrepancies. In 2002, gross national product (GNP) per capita was US$49,774 in Zug but US$23,188 in the Jura.[7] The discrepancies are even stronger with respect to GDP. In 2001, the average Swiss GDP per capita was US$37,456, with the canton Basle-Town being 106 percent above, and the canton Appenzell Inner-Rhodes being 47 percent below, the national average.[8] Such large discrepancies create tensions in the fiscal system.

THE STRUCTURE OF GOVERNMENT AND THE DIVISION OF FISCAL POWER

The basic constituents of Switzerland are the twenty-six (twenty-five) cantons that founded the federal state in 1848.[9] Article 3 of the federal Constitution states that they "are sovereign insofar as their sovereignty is not limited by the federal Constitution; they shall exercise all rights which are not transferred to the Confederation." The Confederation has authority only in those areas in which it is empowered by the federal Constitution (e.g., foreign affairs, defence, customs, and monetary policy). Tasks that do not expressly fall within the scope of the Confederation are handled by the cantons.

Each canton and half-canton has its own constitution, parliament, government, and courts.[10] The canton parliaments have between fifty-eight and two hundred seats, while the canton governments have five, seven, or nine members. All of these are directly elected by the people at the ballot box, with the exception of the canton Appenzell Inner-Rhodes, where they are elected by the canton general assembly (*Landsgemeinde*), which convenes every year in April.

All the cantons are divided into municipalities, of which there are at present 2,760. Their number is tending to diminish as some municipalities are merging. Around one-fifth of these municipalities have their own parliament; in the other four-fifths, decisions are taken by direct democracy in a local assembly. In addition to the tasks entrusted to them by the Confederation and the canton – such as the population register and civil defence – local authorities also have specific responsibilities of their own with regard to, inter alia, education and social welfare, energy supply, road building, and local planning. To a large extent, these powers are self-regulated. The scope of municipal autonomy is determined by the individual cantons and, therefore, varies widely. However, given the autonomy for local government provided in the canton constitutions, neither the cantons nor the federal authorities have the right to interfere with local decisions. The only exception occurs when the financial situation of a local community deteriorates seriously. When this happens, the local budget has to be approved by the canton government.

The federal Constitution assigns specific tasks to the Confederation; all other matters are canton responsibilities.[11] However, there are many shared responsibilities. This applies to situations in which the federal government has legislative responsibility but the cantons execute the legislation (e.g., motorways are built by the cantons as ordered and financed by the federal government). However, joint responsibility applies also to areas such as education. This is a canton task, which means that the cantons are, in theory, responsible for all the universities. However, there are two federal universities: the two Swiss Federal Institutes of Technology in Zurich and Lausanne. Moreover, research is a federal task, which is mainly financed by the Swiss National Science Foundation located in Berne. This foundation also finances research conducted in the canton universities. Further, the federal government gives subsidies to the canton universities, depending on the number of students enrolled. Finally, the federal government tries to develop a consistent national university policy, although the canton ministers of education and, therefore, the canton governments have to agree to it. Nevertheless, due to its large role in financing universities, the federal government has a large impact on decisions that are formally in the domain of the cantons.

University policy reveals another specific trait of the Swiss system. The majority of the cantons are far too small to have their own university. In addition to the two federal institutes, ten cantons have universities, all of which are public, and students' fees are rather low. To finance the universities, the cantons have agreed among themselves that the canton from which a student comes has to pay a certain amount of money to the canton in which he or she is studying. So part of the financial burden of the universities is spread across the country without the intervention of the federal government. Such inter-canton cooperation is to be enforced by the new system of fiscal equalization described below.

The possibilities for the national government to interfere with canton or local policies are quite limited. This creates problems, as there are many areas in which the Confederation is in charge of strategic (and legislative) matters but the cantons are in charge of operational or executive matters. If the cantons do not behave appropriately, the federal government has hardly any means to force cooperation. This is relevant, for example, in environmental policy. By way of illustration, if the Confederation sets limits for the emission of some pollutants, and if these limits are violated in certain areas, there is hardly anything the federal government can do about it. It cannot, for example, force the canton governments by withholding grants or revenues from tax sharing or by any other fiscal means. This situation is known as the "implementation deficit" (*Vollzugsdefizit*) and is seen as a problem in Swiss politics.

The other side of the coin is that the cantons (and local communities) do not have much say in national politics; the national government and Parliament are free to take decisions – subject always to the will of the people. Whenever the Constitution is to be changed (a question that usually comes up several times a year), the people have to be asked to approve the change. Furthermore, whenever there is a new law or a change in a law, Swiss citizens only have to collect 50,000 signatures to get a referendum.

Table 2
Legislative responsibility and actual provision of services by different orders of government

Function	Legislative Responsibility	Execution
International relations	Federal	Federal
Defence	Federal	Federal
Monetary policy, customs	Federal	Federal
Postal services, telecom, mass media	Federal	Federal
Railway, aviation	Federal	Federal
Atomic energy	Federal	Federal
Water power	Federal	Federal
National roads	Federal	Canton
Trade, industry, labour legislation	Federal	Canton
Agriculture	Federal and canton	Federal and canton
Civil and criminal law	Federal and canton	Federal and canton
Police	Canton	Canton
Churches	Canton	Canton
Education (secondary schools, universities)	Canton	Canton
Taxes	Federal and canton	Federal and canton
Social security	Federal	Canton
Environmental policy	Federal	Canton
Cantonal roads	Canton	Canton
Local roads	Local	Local
Local public transport (in cities)	Local	Local
Local gas, electricity and water supply, waste	Local	Local
Primary schools	Local	Local
Public care	Local	Local

Source: Wolf Linder, *Schweizerische Demokratie: Institutionen, Prozesse, Perspektiven* (Berne: Haupt, 1999), 140; with reference to Jürg M. Gabriel, *Das politische System der Schweiz* (Berne: Haupt, 1990), 97.

Table 3
Direct expenditures by function and level of government (percentages)

Function	Federal	Canton	Local	All
Defence	90.8	4.8	4.4	100
Debt servicing	59.6	23.0	17.4	100
General administration	20.7	38.3	41.0	100
Law and order	9.3	65.7	25.0	100
Economic services	41.1	36.1	22.8	100
Social services	20.6	48.3	31.0	100
Health	1.0	57.8	41.2	100
Education	13.7	54.3	32.0	100
Subsidies	41.7	35.4	22.9	100
Total	31.4	41.6	27.0	100
Local public services	5.2	51.5	43.2	100

Switzerland does not have a constitutional court with the power to declare that a law passed by Parliament violates the federal Constitution; the Federal Supreme Court in Lausanne functions as a constitutional court only for the cantons (i.e., it has the power to declare canton laws unconstitutional). There is, of course, the upper chamber of Parliament, which was modelled after the US Senate, and in which each canton has two members. These are representatives of the people of the canton, not of its government or parliament. That is why conferences comprised of the presidents and also of other members of the canton governments (e.g., those who are responsible for education) have been created. Such conferences have two purposes: first, they decide about arrangements between the cantons in areas in which the cantons have sole responsibility but need some coordination; second, they represent the interests of the cantons in political discourse in the national arena.

If, in making a new law, the Confederation interferes too much with the cantons' interests, the cantons can launch a referendum if at least eight of them demand it. The first such referendum was held in May 2004, when the cantons opposed a tax reform that would have changed the base for the taxation of owner-occupied houses and apartments. The referendum was successful, and the reform was rejected. Since then, the federal finance minister has been much more hesitant to mingle with issues that touch canton interests.

FISCAL FEDERALISM AND MACROECONOMIC MANAGEMENT

Monetary policy is a strictly federal issue, although, in practice, the responsibility for this is delegated to the Swiss National Bank (SNB), which is located in Zurich and Berne. The SNB has been quite independent for some time – a situation that was recognized by the Swiss central bank law, which became effective in 2004. The SNB's main objective is to ensure price stability, but "in so doing, it shall take due account of the development of the economy."[12] After the breakdown of the Bretton Woods system in the 1970s, SNB policy, until 1999, focused on the quantity of money. However, as this was considered to be one of the factors contributing to the low growth of the Swiss economy in the second half of the 1990s, the SNB's strategy since 2000 has been to attempt to keep the rate of inflation between zero and 2 percent.

The SNB's main goal, price stability, is generally conceded to have been very effectively achieved. Switzerland has one of the most stable currencies in the world. From 1980 to 2004, the average inflation rate was 2.29 percent, compared with 2.23 percent in Germany and 2.93 percent in the United States, two other countries whose central banks also have a very high respect for price stability. This is also reflected in the development of the exchange rate. Since 1974, when the Swiss franc began floating against all other currencies, there was an appreciation against the German mark of nearly 40 percent until 1998 and an appreciation against the American dollar of about 140 percent until 2004.

As Switzerland is a small country, the scope for fiscal policy is limited, although it is exclusively a matter for the federal government. Even large federal deficits, as seen in the 1990s, hardly provide an impulse to the Swiss economy. Quite recently, there have been some tentative attempts to create some coordination between the federal government and the cantons,[13] but these did not go farther than initial discussions. Indeed, considering the great budgetary independence of the cantons, it is hardly conceivable that there will be effective coordination.

Every canton is responsible for its own fiscal discipline. In 1981, the conference of the canton ministers of finance edited the *Handbook of Public Budgeting* (Vol. 1),[14] which contains a model for canton budgets. According to Article 2, the principle of a balanced budget has to be observed. This is stated more concretely in Article 4, according to which the current budget has to be balanced in the medium term, and in Article 18, which demands that canton-accumulated debt has to be cut back in the medium term, whereby "medium term" means within about ten years. Today, such rules can be found in nearly all canton constitutions and in the corresponding budget laws. The cantons are obliged to balance their budgets over the business cycle and also to cut down accumulated debt. All this did not prevent canton debt from increasing considerably during the 1990s, partly because of the low economic growth rate. Canton real debt increased by about 106 percent (in real terms) from 1990 to 2002, but the development varied from canton to canton.[15] For example, St Gall and Fribourg showed only modest increases in their public debt over that period; Vaud's debt increased considerably; and Geneva's increased dramatically. In 2002, Geneva's a public debt per capita was US$26,865, which was 418 percent of the average canton debt in the country.

FISCAL REFERENDA

A special feature of the canton constitutions, in contrast to the Swiss federal Constitution, is the existence of a fiscal referendum.[16] If it is mandatory and the outlay for it exceeds a certain limit, the canton's citizens have to be asked whether they agree to the project in question. This is also the case if the referendum is optional and if a given number of signatures are collected. The limit that is specified can be different for non-recurring expenditures and for recurring expenditures. With the exception of Vaud, all cantons have such a referendum.[17] Because the citizens know that sooner or later they will have to pay for the projects that are carried out by the canton or local community, this acts a restraint on overly ambitious projects.

Take St Gall as an example. There, fiscal referenda are optional for recurring expenditures of more than US$179,000 and for non-recurring expenditures of more than US$1.79 million. They are mandatory for recurring expenditures of more than US$893,000 and for non-recurring expenditures of more than US$8.93 million. In relation to the budget, which in 2002 was about US$2.06 billion, these limits amount to 0.009 percent or 0.043 percent, respectively, for current expenditures, and 0.09 percent or 0.43 percent, respectively, for non-recurring expenditures. These limits are rather low. In order for an optional referendum to take place, four thousand signatures have to be collected within a thirty-day period. This corresponds to about 1.5 percent of the electorate.[18]

However, the existence of the fiscal referendum combined with the regulations for a balanced budget were insufficient to prevent public debt from increasing. Therefore, partly because they had carried debts for longer periods than had the others, eight cantons introduced new instruments within the past ten years in order to limit deficits: St Gall (1994), Fribourg (1994), Solothurn (1995), Appenzell Outer-Rhodes (1995), Grisons (1998), Lucerne (2001), Berne (2002), and, the last one for the time being, Valais (2002).[19] These regulations are, in some cases, in canton constitutions, although they are usually in canton budget laws.

St Gall may again be used as an example.[20] The rules require the current budget to be "balanced" – defined as a maximum permissible deficit of 3 percent of the "simple tax revenue," which at the moment is about 60 percent of total tax revenue.[21] Whenever a deficit is expected, the tax rate is supposed to be adjusted in order to keep within this limit. Moreover, if there are no savings available, the deficit is transferred to the budget of the year after the next year. In turn, whenever there is a surplus (e.g., because of an economic upswing), the money has to be saved and/or utilized for additional depreciations. Tax rates cannot be reduced if these savings do not amount to seven times the maximum allowable deficit. In addition to considerations regarding the current budget, there are considerations relating to the capital budget, which is used for financing public investment. The rule is that investment projects up to US$2.98 million have to be included in current budgets, while the debt principal of projects between US$2.98 and US$5.95 million has to be paid back within five years, and of projects above US$5.95 million within ten years. These depreciations (as well as the interest payments) have to be included in the current budgets. Thus, such projects cannot lead to a long-run debt increase. It is possible to raise debt in order to buy shares of firms (e.g., of the canton banks), but there must be returns as compensation.

Thus, the citizens of St Gall can – within the boundaries of the federal Constitution – authorize necessary expenditures in relation to the tasks the canton has to perform. With respect to revenue, they decide all constitutional and statutory rules, especially regarding the different taxes as well as the tariff scales (including the progression of the direct taxes) but not about the tax rates. The authority for the latter lies with the canton parliament, although that authority is restricted by the regulations described above, which oblige the canton to build up savings to a certain level before tax rates can be reduced. This rather unusual requirement means that surpluses are built up in "good" years and can be used to cover (to a certain extent) deficits created during "bad" years. This institutionalizes anti-cyclical fiscal policy in the cantons without leading to an increase in public debt.[22] This is remarkable, as it is usually assumed that anti-cyclical fiscal policy can only be conducted successfully by the federal government; the medium and lower levels of government are generally thought to be pro-cyclical.[23] Swiss canton experience shows that, with the appropriate culture and institutions, this does not have to be the case.

The combination of direct democratic expenditure restrictions, quasi-automatic revenue adjustment, and the build-up of savings has proved to be successful. In 2002, for instance, St Gall's public debt per capita was $US2,346; only Schwyz, Zug, Argovia, and the two Appenzells had lower public debt.

As mentioned above, today there are similar rules in seven other cantons. Solothurn and Grisons, for example, also accumulate savings in order to equalize revenue fluctuations over the business cycle. In Appenzell Outer-Rhodes, the rule is that no deficit is allowed in the budget once there is an accumulated deficit that exceeds 5 percent of the canton and local tax revenue budgeted for the current year.[24] This rule is intended to force the government to build up reserves in good times and to eliminate structural deficits.[25] While Fribourg also strives for a budgetary balance over the business cycle, the regulation is even stricter with respect to balancing the annual budget. The tax rate has to be increased as soon as the deficit in the proposal for the current budget exceeds 3 percent of total revenue.[26]

The experience of these cantons has also been positive. In Fribourg, debt per capita rose from US$2,069 in 1990 to US$3,165 in 2002 – that is, it rose by only 46 percent (in real terms), far below the average for the Swiss cantons (92 percent). The other cantons that have had debt brakes for more than five years also performed well in this respect.

So much for the evidence of the available case studies.[27] An alternative to case evidence is provided by econometric studies that investigate whether cantons and local communities that use such instruments have, ceteris paribus, lower deficits and debts than do those of other cantons and local communities.[28] Investigations show that cantons with a fiscal referendum have significantly lower expenditure and revenues than do other cantons. However, because the reduction is stronger for revenue than for expenditure, the deficit is significantly higher. Correspondingly, the public debt is also higher, although the corresponding coefficient is not significantly different from zero. Fiscal constraint leads to somewhat lower expenditure but higher revenue. This leads to a significantly lower deficit and also to significantly lower debt.

Whenever a local community has a mandatory fiscal referendum that requires it to raise additional public debt, this leads to significantly lower expenditure and revenue and, especially, to lower public debt. The estimated impact on the deficit is also negative but is not statistically significant.[29] As for the cantons, the debt brake leads to somewhat lower expenditure and somewhat higher revenue, which leads to a significantly lower deficit. The estimated impact on the local public debt is also negative, although not significantly so.

Thus, for the cantons as well as for the local communities, the combination of the fiscal referendum and the debt brake has a stabilizing effect on public finances. This does not necessarily lead to a lower tax ratio, but it does lead to a lower deficit and lower public debt. To that extent, the St Gall model can be seen as an example of institutionalized arrangements resulting in sound public finances, as described by the finance minister of this canton.[30]

PUBLIC REVENUE

A special feature of the Swiss fiscal constitution is the substantial autonomy of the cantons not only on the expenditure side but also on the revenue side of the budget.[31] The main progressive taxes on personal and corporate income are state and local taxes. The cantons have the basic power to tax income, wealth, and capital. The municipalities can levy a surcharge on canton taxes. The federal government relies mainly on indirect (proportional) taxes, a value-added tax, and specific consumption taxes, such as the mineral oil tax. There is, however, a small but highly progressive federal income tax, which amounted to 29 percent of total federal tax revenue in 2002, while the cantons and municipalities rely on income and property taxes for about 46 percent of their total current revenue and 90 percent of their tax revenue. The federal income tax has a maximum marginal rate of 13.2 percent and an average rate of 11.5 percent. Owing to a basic tax exemption, the highest 3 percent of income taxpayers pay about 50 percent of the revenue of the federal income tax. Thirty percent of this tax is paid back to the cantons.[32] The federal government can also rely on a source tax on income from interest, the so-called *Verrechnungssteuer*, which has a rate of 35 percent. While there is no federal or canton deductibility of personal income taxes paid to the cantons or localities, there is a tax deductibility in the case of corporate income taxes.

The tax burden varies considerably between the cantons and, in some cantons, also between the municipalities. In the index of the burden of personal taxes for the year 2003,[33] there were huge discrepancies between "rich" cantons, like Zug and Schwyz, and "poor" ones, like Obwalden, Uri, and Jura. It seems obvious that such discrepancies demand a fiscal equalization system. The current system is apparently not able to sufficiently equalize the situations. This is the reason a new system is to be implemented, which – it is hoped – will be effective from 2008 onward.

Strong tax competition takes place in Switzerland. Investigations show that the proportion of rich people in a canton is significantly influenced by the canton's tax rate.[34] Choice of canton for residence often depends, for high-income earners, on the amount of income tax they would have to pay. Social transfers are less influential for the choice of residence. Thus, fiscal competition consists of tax competition rather than of transfer competition, and tax competition is stronger for self-employed than it is for dependent employees and retirees. Among local communities, the effects of tax competition are even stronger than they are for cantons.

From an international perspective, the Swiss tax burden is low compared with other locations in Europe and the United States. This holds even for the higher-tax Swiss cantons. In terms of the index of the effective average tax rate for people with an annual income of US$170,000,[35] the burden is considerably lower in the low-tax cantons.

Table 4
Tax assignments for various orders of government

	Determination of base	Determination of rate	Collection and administration	Shares in revenue (percentages)		
				Federal	Canton	Local
Federal						
Direct federal income tax	Federal	Federal	Canton/local	70.0	30.0	0.0
Withholding tax	Federal	Federal	Canton/local	90.5	9.5	0.0
Capital transfer tax	Federal	Federal	Canton/local	100.0	0.0	0.0
Value added taxes	Federal	Federal	Canton/local	100.0	0.0	0.0
Excise taxes	Federal	Federal	Canton/local	100.0	0.0	0.0
Import duties	Federal	Federal	Canton/local	100.0	0.0	0.0
Traffic duties	Federal	Federal	Canton/local	100.0	0.0	0.0
Agriculture duties	Federal	Federal	Canton/local	100.0	0.0	0.0
Steering taxes	Federal	Federal	Canton/local	100.0	0.0	0.0
Gambling house taxes	Federal	Federal	Canton/local	100.0	0.0	0.0
Patents and concessions	Federal	Federal	Canton/local	100.0	0.0	0.0
Fees for legal acts	Federal	Federal	Canton/local	100.0	0.0	0.0
Hospital fees	Federal	Federal	Canton/local	100.0	0.0	0.0
User fees, services	Federal	Federal	Canton/local	100.0	0.0	0.0
Other	Federal	Federal	Canton/local	100.0	0.0	0.0
Canton						
Personal income taxes	Canton	Canton/local	Canton/local	0.0	54.9	45.1
Property taxes	Canton	Canton/local	Canton/local	0.0	55.3	44.7
Corporate income taxes	Canton	Canton/local	Canton/local	0.0	55.6	44.4
Capital taxes	Canton	Canton/local	Canton/local	0.0	60.6	39.4
Real estate taxes	Canton	Canton/local	Canton/local	0.0	26.5	73.5
Property gain taxes	Canton	Canton/local	Canton/local	0.0	53.8	46.2
Property transfer taxes	Canton	Canton/local	Canton/local	0.0	72.2	27.8
Heritage and gift taxes	Canton	Canton/local	Canton/local	0.0	91.5	8.5
Motor vehicle taxes	Canton	Canton	Canton	0.0	100.0	0.0
Amusement taxes	Canton	Canton/local	Canton/local	0.0	31.8	68.2

Table 4
Tax assignments for various orders of government (*Continued*)

	Determination of base	Determination of rate	Collection and administration	Shares in revenue (percentages)		
				Federal	Canton	Local
Dog taxes	Canton	Canton/local	Canton/local	0.0	25.6	74.4
Other property and expense taxes	Canton	Canton/local	Canton/local	0.0	76.0	24.0
Patents and concessions	Canton	Canton/local	Canton/local	0.0	84.5	15.5
Fees for legal acts	Canton	Canton/local	Canton/local	0.0	76.4	23.6
Hospital fees	Canton	Canton/local	Canton/local	0.0	44.4	55.6
User fees, services	Canton	Canton/local	Canton/local	0.0	26.5	73.5
Other	Canton	Canton/local	Canton/local	0.0	49.2	50.8

Table 5
Vertical fiscal gaps

	Total revenue collected	Total revenue available	Expenditures
National	44,512,121	35,951,574	38,806,603
Subnational	74,278,429	82,838,976	84,893,416
Canton	45,729,651	49,771,186	51,447,276
Local	28,548,778	33,067,790	33,446,140
All orders	118,790,550	118,790,550	123,700,019

Corporate income taxes in Switzerland also vary considerably among the cantons. From anecdotal evidence, it is known that two tax havens are in or close to Switzerland – the small country of Liechtenstein, which forms an economic union with Switzerland, and Zug. Taking the value of the (weighted) average for Switzerland as 100, the index of the tax burden of corporate income and capital taxes varied in 2003 from 49.0 in Schwyz to 141.7 in Grisons.[36]

Again, from an international perspective and compared with other OECD countries, Swiss taxes are comparatively low. In terms of the effective average tax rates,[37] only Ireland has average tax rates as low as Zug. Thus, with respect to personal as well as company taxation, at least some Swiss cantons have a very strong position in international tax competition.

By contrast, the Swiss system of corporate income taxation appears to be quite complicated, partly because of the canton and local competencies. All in all, capital may bear seven different taxes: the corporate income tax on profits, the capital tax, the federal source-tax on interest and dividend income, an emission charge, the property tax, the church tax, and – in some cantons – a minimum tax if revenue from corporate income tax does not reach a certain amount. Estimates place the taxation of profits and capital-induced administrative costs at about US$8,300 per firm per year.[38] This amount is about 40 percent of the average administrative costs that small and medium-size firms bear due to public regulation and accounts for about 3 percent of their investment in equipment.

Three characteristics are fundamental to the taxation of corporate income:

1 In many cantons, the tax on profits follows a progressive tax schedule according to the rate of return on capital. The federal government has levied a proportional tax on corporate profits since the tax reform act of 1998. Seven cantons already had a proportional tax rate before that reform, while Geneva introduced it after the reform.
2 In addition to taxation of profits according to the rate of return on capital, capital is taxed separately by all cantons. In most cases, a proportional rate is used. The federal government abolished its tax on firms' capital in 1998.
3 The Swiss corporate income tax is similar to the corporate income tax in the United States. Profits are taxed at the corporate level and again at the shareholder level as dividend income.

A particular feature of corporate income taxation in Switzerland is the fact that holding companies are taxed at lower rates or, in some cantons, not at all. This is to avoid double taxation of the profits of parent and affiliate companies. However, generous tax exemptions for holding companies provide incentives for profit shifting on the part of firms. Zug is supposed to owe its economic wealth to such a policy. In addition, nearly all cantons, with the notable exceptions of Zug and Argovia, have special tax holidays for "newly founded" firms. These holidays are restricted by the federal tax-harmonization law of 1993 to ten years at the most. "Newly founded" may mean anything from the construction of new firms or affiliates to the relocation of companies that, for years, have been located in other cantons.

Given the large differences in tax burdens among Swiss cantons, double-taxation agreements between cantons and profit allocation rules for firms with plants in different cantons play a non-negligible role. Between Swiss cantons, an exemption system is used exclusively. If, for example, a firm resides in Zurich and has a subsidiary in Zug, Zurich exempts the profits earned in Zug from taxation in Zurich. Moreover, profit allocation between both cantons is regulated by a kind of formula apportionment. There is no unique, harmonized formula apportionment rule for all cantons, and this leaves room for a large variety of such rules between cantons. Payroll, capital, or sales are used as a basis for calculating profit shares. For example, the profits of retail firms are usually allocated according to sales, while the profits of manufacturing firms are allocated according to capital and payroll (capitalized by 10 percent). Given that capital is taxed in addition to profits and that profits are taxed on the basis of rates of return on capital, it is not only profit allocation rules that are used but also capital allocation rules.

Due to the small size of the country and its subfederal units, corporate taxpayers can easily move to places with low tax burdens and respond to canton tax differentials accordingly. The exemption system basically provides an incentive for tax-induced relocation, while profit-sharing rules, in the sense of a kind of formula apportionment, reduce incentives for profit shifting. Moreover, the differences in canton legal and accounting systems are not so substantial as to render the relocation of firms difficult. All in all, firms may have sufficient fiscal incentives to relocate between cantons. In addition, formula apportionment might not work well enough to completely prevent the occurrence of profit shifting. Thus, tax competition for mobile capital in Switzerland may take place either through relocation of real capital, leading to subsequent changes in economic activity, or through profit shifting among cantons.

What are the effects of tax competition on the location of firms and on employment? Corporate and, in particular, personal income taxes have a stronger impact on the canton distribution of firms than they do on employment.[39] This provides some indirect evidence for the existence of profit shifting among cantons and/or for smart tax management on the part of firms located in one canton only. This holds despite several incentives provided by inter-canton tax laws, such as the tax exemption system and formula apportionment.

FISCAL EQUITY AND THE EQUALIZATION SYSTEM

As explained above, fiscal competition in Switzerland leads to huge differences in the tax burden, as well as in the economic potential, between the different cantons (and, in some cantons, between the different local communities). Nevertheless, redistributive (progressive) personal income taxes are canton and local taxes first and federal taxes second. There is considerable redistribution within cantons and local communities.[40] This clearly contradicts the usual textbook wisdom, which says that, in a federal polity, redistribution should be undertaken by the federal government.

The Swiss post-tax income distribution is somewhat more unequal than is such distribution in other European countries, especially the Scandinavian and Benelux ones; however, it is in the same range as that of the southern European countries and the United Kingdom and Ireland.[41] Thus, the special design of the Swiss federal system does not inhibit income redistribution comparable to that of other European countries. The main reason for this is the existence of an institutional framework that ensures that high-income people also have to contribute. Further:

1. The federal income tax is highly progressive, and 30 percent of the revenue is paid back to the cantons, one part of it directly and the rest via the fiscal equalization system.
2. There is a federal source tax of 35 percent on interest and dividend income.
3. The federal government upholds the first pillar of the old-age pension system, which is financed on a pay-as-you-go basis and is highly redistributive. Contributions are proportional to labour income (without any limit), but the maximum pension is about US$1,200 for singles and about US$1,800 for couples. Today, about 60 percent of all senior citizens receive the maximum pensions, and the share receiving these is increasing.
4. There is a fiscal equalization system.

Besides these arrangements, it is possible that direct democracy also helps to secure the system. Whenever the people themselves decide public issues, especially issues in relation to the tax burden, they are more prepared to accept the decisions and to contribute their share. There is clear evidence that tax evasion is lower when the people have more direct political rights.[42]

As mentioned in the introduction, there are large discrepancies between the Swiss cantons: we have some small and very rich cantons, like Zug, Nidwalden, and Schwyz, and we have others that are relatively poor. The rich cantons spend more money per capita than do the poor cantons, but they are nevertheless able to have – ceteris paribus – lower tax rates. Moreover, the discrepancies have increased in the recent past. In order to keep the country together, a system of fiscal equalization necessary.

The existing fiscal equalization system is highly inefficient and, therefore, is currently being reformed. The reform, which is expected to be effective beginning in 2008, consists of four elements:[43]

1. Some tasks and financial responsibilities that are, at present, the joint responsibility of the Confederation and the cantons will be separated. However, some tasks will still be common responsibilities.
2. New kinds of collaboration between the federal and canton governments and new kinds of financing will be introduced. The traditional

system of matching grants will be replaced by a system in which the cantons get all the financial means that are necessary for those tasks for which the Confederation controls strategic issues and the cantons control implementation. Objectives for these tasks will be fixed and described in an intergovernmental contract.

3 There will be new forms of collaboration between the cantons, with cost compensation. If some cantons agree to collaborate on tasks they cannot perform by themselves (e.g., because they are too small), and if their activities have benefits for other cantons, the federal government can require reluctant cantons to participate if at least half of the cooperating cantons ask for such an intervention. The idea is to prevent free-rider behaviour.

4 The fiscal equalization system (in the narrow sense) will be reformed. The new system consists of three building blocks. First, there will be revenue equalization. Its objective is to provide at least 85 percent of the average financial means for all cantons. About 70 percent of the US$1,445 million the "poor" cantons will get will be provided by the Confederation, and the remaining 30 percent will be provided by the "rich" cantons. Second, there will be a cost equalization scheme, financed by the Confederation: about US$165 million for geo-topographic burdens and another US$165 million for socio-demographic burdens. Third, there will be a "cohesion fund." The idea behind this fund is that "no canton with a weak financial capacity which today benefits from equalization, should suffer from worse conditions in the new scheme."[44] Two-thirds of this fund's money will come from the Confederation and one-third from the cantons. There will be full payment for the first eight years, and then a decrease of 5 percent each year for twenty years. Thus, this transition fund will exist for twenty-eight years.

The main difference between the old and new systems is twofold. First, there will be more division of power between the different spheres of government, and there will be a stricter correspondence between the tasks the cantons have to perform and their financial means. Second, the incentives for the cantons to care about their own tax base by, for example, attracting new firms will be strengthened. Thus, there is hope for efficiency gains that might eventually lead to a reduction of the tax burden.

The Swiss people accepted the constitutional changes necessary for this reform in November 2004.[45] In the meantime, the corresponding law passed the parliament and will be effective in 2008.

There are also fiscal equalization systems within the cantons. They are, as usual in Switzerland, very different between the cantons. Some are rather strict, while others, like the one in Schwyz, allow huge discrepancies within the canton.

FINANCING CAPITAL INVESTMENT

Some cantons have nearly zero debt, while others have considerable debt. This is also true for local communities. The main rationale for public debt is capital investment. However, for some cantons there are special reasons for their recent debt problems: insolvency of the canton bank due to risky investments (as in Berne and Solothurn), and the challenge posed by undercapitalization of public pension funds (e.g., Vaud and Geneva).

There are two main ways in which the cantons can borrow: (1) from the public by issuing bonds and (2) from commercial banks by obtaining loans. The municipalities have a third source: the Emission Centre of the Swiss local communities. This is a cooperative that currently has 928 local communities as members. It was founded in 1971, a time when it was difficult for local communities to get loans from Swiss commercial banks. Cantons as well as local communities can also get loans from foreign banks, and some of them do so. They are, however, not allowed to issue bonds outside of Switzerland.

What happens if a canton or local jurisdiction violates fiscal discipline and incurs excessive debt? How realistic is it for that canton to hope that it will be bailed out by the upper federal or canton government? How credible is the statement that such a bailout would not take place? It is difficult to believe that a canton or a local community could go bankrupt. Moreover, Switzerland (like every other country) does not have explicit bankruptcy rules or laws for such situations.

The federal Constitution provides each of the administrative levels in the country with an adequate financial basis. Cantons retain tax autonomy with respect to personal as well as corporate income and property taxes. In theory, there is no reason why a canton should ever find itself in a financial crisis. The cantons can increase tax revenue, should this be necessary. In fact, since 1848, there has never been a situation in which the federal government has needed, or been asked, to intervene financially. It must, however, be pointed out that the alternatives to raising tax revenue, and the expectations regarding what they have to contribute to national tasks, varies by canton. The problems that arise from this situation have to be addressed by the fiscal equalization system described above. This will prevent the country's being divided into much richer and much poorer communities (provided all parties continue to address problems with reasonableness) while maintaining the incentives that encourage the cantons to take care of their own tax base. If this objective can be met by the fiscal equalization system, there is no reason why different cantons should not take different approaches to debt. And their varying indebtedness will be reflected in their different ratings in the capital market.

The picture is somewhat different for the local communities. In principle, they also have a sufficient tax base to perform their tasks. However, if a local community is highly indebted or actually goes bankrupt, as happened in the case of the community of Leukerbad, first of all the private banks (and individuals who hold the relevant bonds) have to at least partially depreciate their credits. However, the canton is responsible for supervising the situation. In the case of Leukerbad, the banks blamed Valais for having violated this duty and took the canton to court. However, the Federal Supreme Court in Lausanne decided that the canton was not responsible,[46] so there was no bailout. On the other hand, the bankruptcy of Leukerbad signalled the importance that ratings have in this market, and this induced higher interest rates for cantons and local communities with less sound finances.

In most cases, however, at least if a financial crisis is foreseeable, cantons intervene long before attempts to reach a settlement are necessary. For example, if the financial situation of a local community in St Gall deteriorates to the point where it has to be included in the canton fiscal equalization system, it loses its sovereignty to some degree. While the system allows the canton to prevent the local community from going bankrupt by simply pooling resources, the local communities have a strong interest in their sovereignty. This being the case, they do what they can to avoid such a situation.

Of course, in federal countries, local community irresponsibility in fiscal policy can never be totally excluded. The Swiss example shows, however, that, with appropriate institutional rules, the bailout problem can be solved satisfactorily and that federalism does not have to encourage irresponsible behaviour on the part of subfederal communities.

FISCAL FEDERALISM DIMENSIONS OF THE PUBLIC MANAGEMENT FRAMEWORK

In Switzerland, agencies of the federal government are never involved in canton or local appointments, and there are no federal government restraints on subnational hiring and firing. Nor is there an elite federal service that is appointed and rotated through subnational positions in the cantons. Consequently, canton and local governments have full autonomy in hiring and firing personnel. Within the restraints of the federal Constitution, the cantons and local communities have full autonomy and flexibility in the exercise of executive powers. There are no avenues open to the federal government for undermining local autonomy.

Since the 1990s, New Public Management (NPM) instruments and structures have been developed and implemented by all three orders of government. It started with pilot projects: the first was launched in 1993, while the bulk of them were started between 1995 and 1998. In recent years, evaluations of these projects have shown that they provide incentives for the administration to reduce costs and to take the interests of the clients more into account. Despite some ongoing discussions about its effectiveness, NPM is currently fairly widespread among Swiss cantons and local communities.[47]

There is, of course, some corruption in Switzerland, but it plays an extremely marginal role. According to the Corruption Perception Index of Transparency International, in 2004 Switzerland ranked seventh out of 146 countries.[48] So there is neither great concern about corruption in Switzerland nor any special policy in relation to it.

THE WAY FORWARD

As mentioned in the introduction, Switzerland is a rather small federal country, which nevertheless has strong tax competition between the cantons. This causes problems as it creates strong divergences between cantons as well as between local communities. There are relatively poor cantons with a high tax burden and relatively rich cantons with a low tax burden. To keep the country together while preserving canton tax sovereignty, a new fiscal equalization system is being implemented. In a few years we will see whether this will meet expectations or whether there will be a need for additional measures to reduce the discrepancies in Switzerland.

However, another development could cause problems in the future. In 2004, Schaffhausen introduced regressive personal income taxes for high incomes; the marginal tax rate is considerably lower for incomes above US$650,000 than it is, for example, for incomes of US$150,000. Consequently, at a certain point, the average tax rate also declines. In December 2005 Obwalden introduced a similar scheme. So we see increasing competition for high-income earners. The Federal Court decided that the new tax law of Appenzell Outer-Rhodes was against the Federal Constitution; thus, it had to be abolished once more.

Yet, even for very high-income earners, the tax load in Schaffhausen will still be higher (and in Obwalden hardly lower) than it is in Zug and Schwyz, which have a progressive tax schedule but, up until now, have been the cantons with the lowest tax burden. Thus, it is doubtful whether Schaffhausen and Obwalden (and perhaps also other small cantons that follow their strategy) will really be able to attract enough high-income people from other cantons to balance losses from reductions in the tax rate. It may be a zero-sum game between these cantons, with few spillovers to other cantons and, therefore, few effects on Switzerland as a whole;[49] instead, regressive income tax schedules might increase the incentives for tax evasion for those who have lower incomes but have to pay relatively more taxes. This could, in the long run, deteriorate the fiscal situation of the Swiss cantons, which – at least until today – have not suffered from a race to the bottom with respect to income and property taxes.

However, there is a clear race to the bottom with respect to inheritance taxes. In the last fifteen years, several cantons completely abolished these taxes for direct descendents. This is problematic in so far as these taxes are – from an economic point of view – less harmful than are, for example, labour or capital income taxes.

Finally, from time to time, there are proposals to reduce the number of cantons in order to have larger cantons with less divergent structures. This would, of course, reduce many problems. For example, there would be no need for fiscal equalization between the cantons as the necessity for such a system arises mainly from the asymmetries between cantons. However, all attempts to merge various cantons have failed because voters have rejected them.[50] As Swiss citizens have a strong commitment to direct political rights, and as the cantons are deeply rooted in the consciousness of the population, the chance for any merger between them is extremely low.

NOTES

1 For a description of the Swiss Federal System, see also Nicolas Schmitt, "Swiss Confederation," in *Constitutional Origins, Structure, and Change in Federal Countries*, ed. John Kincaid and Alan Tarr, 347–81 (Montreal and Kingston: McGill-Queen's University Press, 2005); and Thomas Fleiner, "Swiss Confederation," in *Distribution of Powers and Responsibilities in Federal Countries*, ed. Akhtar Majeed, Ronald Watts, and Douglas M. Brown, 265–94 (Montreal and Kingston: McGill-Queen's University Press, 2006).
2 Switzerland consists of twenty "full cantons" and six "half cantons." With respect to fiscal matters, there are twenty-six cantons with twenty-six different fiscal constitutions.
3 These data refer to the year 2000. See Bundesamt für Statistik, ed., *Statistisches Jahrbuch der Schweiz* (Zurich: Verlag Neue Zürcher Zeitung, 2005), table 1.5.1.1, p. 111.
4 Ibid.
5 The most densely populated canton is Basle-Town, with 5,045 persons per square kilometre.
6 The data are for 2004. Source of the data: OECD, <http://www.oecd.org/dataoecd/5/29/36463741.xls>, viewed 2 October 2006; and World Bank <http://devdata.worldbank.org/data-query/>, viewed 2 October 2006.
7 See Bundesamt für Statistik, ed., *Statistisches Jahrbuch der Schweiz* (Zurich: Verlag Neue Zürcher Zeitung, 2005), table 4.5.1, p. 249.
8 No official GDP data are available for the cantons. The data provided are estimates made by Basel Economics.

9 In 1848, Switzerland consisted of nineteen "full cantons" and six "half cantons." The last canton, the Jura, was founded in 1979 (earlier, it had been part of the canton Berne).
10 The six half-cantons are Basle-Town and Basle-Country, Appenzell-Inner-Rhodes and Appenzell Outer-Rhodes, and Obwalden and Nidwalden. Basle, Appenzell, and Unterwalden were split into the six half-cantons for historical reasons. However, the only difference between them and other cantons is that they have only one member in the upper chamber of the Swiss Parliament and have only half the weight in constitutional referenda and initiatives.
11 For the assignment of powers among the different levels of governmental, see Tables 2 and 3. See also Fleiner, "Swiss Confederation."
12 Art. 5 of the Federal Act on the Swiss National Bank.
13 See Yves Ammann, "Quelques réflexions à propos des règles de politique budgétaire," Staatssekretariat für Wirtschaft, Wirtschaftspolitische Grundlagen (WP), Diskussionspapier No. 13, May 2002.
14 See Thomas Stauffer, *Instrumente des Haushaltsausgleichs: Ökonomische Analyse und Rechtliche Umsetzung* (Basel: Helbing und Lichtenhahn, 2001), 83ff.
15 Source of the data: Eidgenössische Finanzverwaltung, *18 Öffentliche Finanzen der Schweiz* (Bern/Neuchâtel: Bundesamt für Statistik, 1990), 52; ibid., 2002, 74.
16 At this point there is no fiscal referendum at the federal level, but the Constitution limits the maximum rates of the federal income tax and the value-added tax; any change needs a constitutional referendum. Moreover, up until 2004, with respect to those two taxes, the taxing power of the federation was only given to it based on a clear constitutional time limit.
17 See the overview in Georg Lutz and Dirk Strohmann, *Wahl – und Abstimmungsrecht in den Kantonen* (Bern: Haupt, 1998), 151.
18 See Alexander Trechsel and Uwe Serdült, *Kaleidoskop Volksrechte: Die Institutionen der direkten Demokratie in den schweizerischen Kantonen 1970 – 1996* (Basel: Helbing und Lichtenhahn, 1999), 330ff. To calculate these figures in US dollars and to make them independent from short-run exchange rate fluctuations, average purchasing power parity-values for the period from 2000 to 2004 are used.
19 Actually, in 1994 St Gall merely codified a practice that had been operative since 1929. For a detailed description of the different regulations, see Stauffer, *Instrumente des Haushaltsausgleichs*, 85ff.; and Verfassungsrat des Kantons Basel-Stadt, "2. Zwischenbericht der Verfassungskommission Finanzverfassung: Einführung einer Schuldenbremse"(Basel, 5 March 2002 [B/Nr. 503]). Attempts to introduce similar regulations are currently under way in other cantons as well (e.g., Berne and Zurich). Whether they will be successful remains an open question. Not all such attempts have been successful in the past. In the canton of Vaud, for example, such a proposal was rejected in 1998.
20 See Art. 82 of the canton constitutions and, especially, Arts. 61 and 64 of the "Staatsverwaltungsgesetz." A detailed description of these institutions in the canton St Gall is given in Peter Schönenberger, "Institutionelle Massnahmen zur

Verschuldungsbegrenzung im Kanton St Gallen" (Vortragsmanuskript, Dornach, 31 März 1995). See also Stauffer, *Instrumente des Haushaltsausgleichs*, 86ff.

21 The "simple tax revenue" is the basis for the income and property tax revenue; actual revenue is given by the simple tax revenue times a multiplier in the sense of a surcharge (called "tax foot"), which is currently 115 percent.

22 James M. Buchanan and Richard E. Wagner, *Democracy in Deficit: The Political Legacy of Lord Keynes* (New York: Academic Press, 1977); and James M. Buchanan and Richard E. Wagner, "The Political Biases of Keynesian Economics," in *Fiscal Responsibility in Constitutional Democracy*, ed. James M. Buchanan and Richard E. Wagner, 79–100 (Leiden/Boston: Martinus Nijhoff, 1978). Buchanan and Wagner stated that the transition from balanced budgets to a counter-cyclical policy that allows for deficits during recessions in order to dampen economic fluctuations leads to a huge increase in public debt.

23 A classical reference is the following: "It remains to note that responsibility for stabilisation policy has to be at the national (central) level. Lower levels of government cannot successfully carry on stabilisation policy on their own for a number of reasons. This is obviously the case for the unitary state, where fiscal decentralisation is limited to the provision of local public goods. But it also holds for the federation." See Richard A. Musgrave and Peggy B. Musgrave, *Public Finance in Theory and Practice*, 4th ed. (New York: McGraw-Hill, 1984), 515.

24 Art. 9, Finanzhaushaltsgesetz des Kantons Appenzell Ausserrhoden of 30 April 1995.

25 See Ernst Buschor, Klaus Vallender, and Thomas Stauffer, *Kommentierter Entwurf für ein Finanzhaushaltsgesetz des Kantons Appenzell Ausserrhoden, ausgearbeitet für die Finanzdirektion des Kantons Appenzell Ausserrhoden* (St Gallen: Institut für Finanzwirtschaft und Finanzrecht an der Hochschule St Gallen, 1993), 12ff.

26 Art. 38 (3), Gesetz vom 25. November 1994 über den Finanzhaushalt des Staates, Kanton Freiburg. This rule goes back to the Finanzhaushaltsgesetz des Kantons Freiburg of 1960. This law had similar regulations in Art. 5. As in St Gall, the law from 1994 did not create a really new situation. See Stauffer, *Instrumente des Haushaltsausgleichs*, 93.

27 Such instruments are also used in many local communities. We restrict the discussion, however, to the canton case studies.

28 See Lars P. Feld and Gebhard Kirchgässner, "The Political Economy of Direct Legislation: Direct Democracy and Local Decision Making," *Economic Policy* 33 (2001): 329–67; and Lars P. Feld and Gebhard Kirchgässner, "Does Direct Democracy Reduce Public Debt? Evidence from Swiss Municipalities," *Public Choice* 109 (2001): 347–70. See also the corresponding results in Christoph A. Schaltegger, "Budgetregeln und ihre Wirkung auf die öffentlichen Haushalte: Empirische Ergebnisse aus den US-Bundesstaaten und den Schweizer Kantonen," *Schmollers Jahrbuch* 122 (2002): 369–413.

29 For the impact of the fiscal referendum on local debt, see also Feld and Kirchgässner, "Does Direct Democracy Reduce Public Debt?"

30 Peter Schönenberger, "Institutionelle Massnahmen zur Verschuldungsbegrenzung im Kanton StGallen," *Vortragsmanuskript*, Dornach 31 (März 1995): 1.
31 For the assignment of taxes among the different government levels, see Table 4.
32 This is the main reason for the fiscal gaps between the federal and subfederal levels shown in Table 5.
33 See Bundesamt für Statistik, ed., *Statistisches Jahrbuch der Schweiz* (Zurich: Verlag Neue Zürcher Zeitung, 2005), table T18.2.2.3.1, p. 773.
34 Gebhard Kirchgässner and Werner W. Pommerehne, "Tax Harmonization and Tax Competition in the European Union: Lessons from Switzerland," *Journal of Public Economics* 60 (1996): 351–71; and Feld and Kirchgässner, "Does Direct Democracy Reduce Public Debt?"
35 See Christina Elschner and Robert Schwager, *The Effective Tax Burdens on Highly Qualified Employees* (Heidelberg: Physica, 2005), 5.
36 See Bundesamt für Statistik, ed., *Statistisches Jahrbuch der Schweiz* (Zurich: Verlag Neue Zürcher Zeitung 2005), table T18.2.2.3.1, p. 773.
37 See Elschner and Schwager, *Effective Tax Burdens*, 5.
38 Milad Zarin-Nejadan, Die Besteuerung der KMU in der Schweiz *Die Volkswirtschaft* 70 (February 1997): 56–59.
39 Lars P. Feld and Gebhard Kirchgässner, "The Impact of Corporate and Personal Income Taxes on the Location of Firms and on Employment: Some Panel Evidence for the Swiss Cantons," *Journal of Public Economics* 87 (2003): 129–55.
40 According to Lars P. Feld, "Tax Competition and Income Redistribution: An Empirical Analysis for Switzerland," *Public Choice* 105 (2000): 125–64, excluding the redistributional impact of the Swiss pension system, two-thirds of the redistribution occurs at the subfederal levels. See also Lars P. Feld, *Steuerwettbewerb und seine Auswirkungen auf Allokation und Distribution: Ein Überblick und eine empirische Analyse für die Schweiz* (Tübingen: Mohr [Siebeck], 2000).
41 See Anthony B. Atkinson, "Income Distribution in Europe and the United States," *Oxford Review of Economic Policy* 12 (1996): 15–28.
42 See Werner W. Pommerehne and Hannelore Weck-Hannemann, "Tax Rates, Tax Administration and Income Tax Evasion in Switzerland," *Public Choice* 88 (1996): 161–70; and Lars P. Feld and Bruno S. Frey, "Trust Breeds Trust: How Taxpayers Are Treated," *Economics of Governance* 2 (2001): 87–99.
43 For a more detailed description of the new system, see Bernard Dafflon, "Federal-Cantonal Equalisation in Switzerland: An Overview of the Present System and Reform in Progress," University of Fribourg: BENEFRI Centre for Studies in Public Sector Economics, Working Paper 356, updated version, May 2004.
44 P. Siegenthaler and P. Wettstein, "Finanzausgleich – alle können Gewinner sein: Entgegnung an den Finanzdirektor des Kantons Zürich," *Neue Zürcher Zeitung* 182 (2001): 13. Cited by Dafflon, "Federal-Cantonal Equalisation," 45.
45 Even the people of the canton Zurich accepted the new system, despite the fact that Zurich has to pay more into it in the future. Zürich, on the other hand, largely benefits from the new fund to compensate socio-demographic burdens.

46 Decisions 2C.1/2001, 2C.4/1999, 2C.4/2000, and 2C.5/1999, 3 July 2003. See Charles B. Blankart and Achim Kleiber, "Wer soll für die Schulden von Gebietskörperschaften haften?" in *Perspektiven der Wirtschaftspolitik*, ed. Christoph A. Schaltegger and Stefan C. Schaltegger, 137–50 (Zurich: VDF, 2004), 137–50.

47 For the development and effects of NPM, see Stefan Rieder and Luzia Lehmann, "Evaluation of New Public Management Reforms in Switzerland: Empirical Results and Reflections on Methodology," *International Public Management Review* 3 (2002): 25–42; Kuno Schedler, "... and Politics? Public Management Developments in the Light of Two Rationalities," *Public Management Review* 5 (2003): 533–50.

48 See <http://www.transparency.org/cpi/2005/cpi2005.sources.en.html>, viewed 21 November 2005. There is, moreover, no indication that some cantons are more corrupt than others.

49 Due to the construction of the new system of fiscal equalization described above, such a policy cannot be used to get more out of (or to pay less into) this system.

50 This is contrary to mergers of local communities. There have been quite a lot in recent years, and this has reduced the number of local communities from 2,915 in 1990 to 2,760 today. However, in many of these cases, the cantons provided financial incentives in order to induce the citizens to accept the merger.

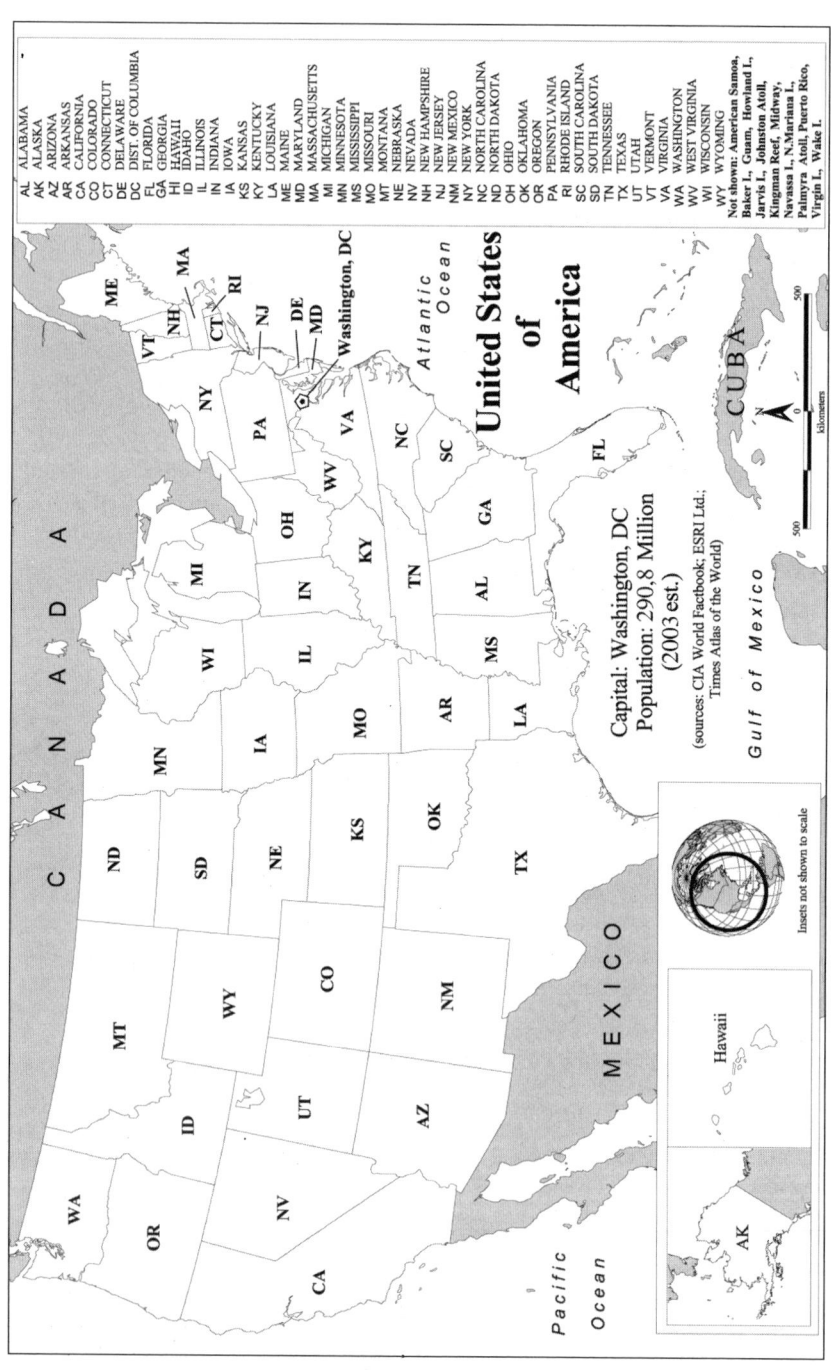

The United States of America

WILLIAM F. FOX

The United States has operated as a federal country for more than 200 years.[1] Even so, discussion of fiscal federalism, and federalism more generally, attracts less attention in the United States than it does in many other federal countries. Deliberations focused on such issues as tax and expenditure assignment, intergovernmental transfers, and equalization seldom receive serious critical discussion in the political, media, or general public arenas. This may be a sign that many people believe that the system is working pretty well and does not require serious reform. An alternative interpretation is that many issues are perceived as being more important. In any event, the topics in this chapter receive much more attention from analysts than they do from the general public.

Two major themes run throughout this chapter. First, the federal role in the US intergovernmental structure has expanded over the past seventy-five years, although not through a major change in the responsibilities undertaken by state and local governments; instead, the federal government has increasingly imposed limitations on the financing sources available to state and local governments and has mandated the ways in which many services are provided. Second, the ever more open economy, both across states and across the world, has limited the ability of state and local governments to generate revenues through their traditional sources. And the national government, which controls interstate commerce, has been unwilling to enable state and local revenue generation.

THE UNITED STATES: A THUMBNAIL SKETCH

The population of the United States was estimated to be 296.4 million people on 1 July 2005, an 18.5 percent increase since 1990 (Table 1). The population is 68.5 percent non-Hispanic white, 13.4 percent black or African-American, 13.2 percent of Hispanic origin, and 4.9 percent other. The

Table 1
Basic political and geographic indicators

Official name:	conventional long form: United States of America conventional short form: United States abbreviation: US or USA
Population:	296,410,404 in 2005
Area:	total: 9,631,420 sq km land: 9,161,923 sq km water: 469,497 sq km note: includes only the 50 states and District of Columbia
GDP per capita (year)	$42,022 in 2005 (current $)
Constitution:	Constitution-based federal republic 17 September 1787, effective 4 March 1789
Constitutional status of local government:	Each state has its own constitution similar to that of the national Constitution. Laws made in individual states cannot conflict with the national Constitution or national laws.
Official languages:	There is no official language at the federal level, but some states have specified English. Languages spoken in the USA: English 82.1%, Spanish 10.7%, other Indo-European 3.8%, Asian and Pacific Island 2.7%, other 0.7% (2000 census)
Number and types of constituent units:	50 states and 1 district
Population, area and per capita GDP of the largest constituent unit:	California 2005 Population: 36,132,147 Total Area: 423,970 sq km GDP per capita: $44,886 in 2005 (current $)
Population, area and per capita GDP of the smallest constituent unit:	Wyoming 2005 Population: 509,294 Total Area: 253,336 sq km GSP per capita: $53,843 in 2005 (current $)

Sources: US Census Bureau, Bureau of Economic Analysis, CIA World Fact Book.

ethnic mix is changing rapidly as people of Hispanic origin have accounted for about 40 percent of the nation's population growth since 1990. The country is geographically large, comprising 9.6 million square kilometers.

The US government structure is composed of one federal government, fifty states, and 87,525 local governments (in 2002). In addition, the District of Columbia, the US capital, is an autonomous city. The states have a median population of nearly 4.2 million, but they vary widely in geographic and population size. For example, California is the most populous state, with 36.1 million people, and exceeds Texas, the second most populous state, by 13.5 million people. At the other extreme, seven states have fewer than 1 million people, with Wyoming having the fewest people, at 506,500 inhabitants.

The states have powers that are independent of the federal government, and they delegated limited powers to the federal government through the US Constitution. The Tenth Amendment to the Constitution reiterates that the states retain all powers not delegated to the federal government. State constitutions and statutes are the primary determinants of local government structure, which means wide differences exist across the country. Counties are the basic unit of local government in many states, and the 3,034 counties cover the geographic space of the United States. There are an additional 35,933 subcounty general-purpose governments, which are normally called cities, towns, or townships. These general-purpose subcounty governments house 82.5 percent of the US population. The number of general-purpose governments has grown slowly from the 34,009 governments that existed fifty years ago, although the number has not risen over the past ten years.

There are 48,558 special-purpose districts. Some of these districts have the same boundaries as do the counties in which they are located, but most do not. Special-purpose districts are created to undertake only one or a few responsibilities; indeed, 91 percent perform only one function. Special-purpose districts are local governments created to deal with such issues as, for example, education, hospitals, fire protection, housing, water supply, sewerage, highways, air transportation, economic development, flood control and drainage, and soil conservation. The largest number of special-purpose districts occurs with regard to education (15,014), followed by fire protection, water supply, housing, drainage and flood control, and soil and water conservation. The number of school districts fell dramatically because of mergers, reorganizations, and so forth during the 1950s and 1960s, declining from 67,355 in 1952 to 15,781 in 1972. School districts have continued to decline slowly since 1972. Other special-purpose districts, by contrast, have nearly tripled, growing from 12,340 in 1952 to 35,032 in 2002.

Local governments differ radically in population size. Ninety-one counties have more than 500,000 people, while 671 have fewer than 10,000 inhabitants. Municipal and township governments also vary dramatically in size. More than 25,000 have fewer than 2,500 residents, and 61 have more than 300,000 people. The total population of municipal and township governments with fewer than 25,000 people is only 10.7 million, about 3 percent of the US population.

HISTORY OF US FEDERALISM[2]

During the country's first 140 years, there was strong confidence that the private sector and private institutions more broadly could deal with public issues. State governments dominated the very small government structure that characterized the United States during this era. Public service delivery, regulatory control, and taxation by state governments and their local governments were perceived as sufficient. The federal government's role was very limited, except during major wars, including the US Civil War and the First World War, but the pattern always involved a reversion to a smaller prewar federal government. Narrow interpretations of the federal role by both the judiciary and political forces upheld this pattern.

The Great Depression in the 1930s, followed by the Second World War and then the Korean War, created sustained centralizing forces that lasted for the next forty to fifty years. The greater central role existed for so long that it still has not been fully reversed. The courts interpreted the constitutional basis for the federal role much more broadly during this time. Federal finance of a wide range of programs, including Medicaid (health care for low-income individuals), Medicare (health care for the aged), Social Security, and large grant programs for state and local governments, was begun, although some of these specific programs did not start until the 1960s.

The last several decades have witnessed a more balanced federal system, although federal influences remain strong in many areas that have traditionally been in the purview of state and local governments. Shannon gives three explanations for the current federal environment.[3] First, middle-class voters, who dominate the political landscape, will not be sufficiently conservative to move the United States back to where state governments dominate. The population appears to have grown more conservative, and, although there is talk about states' rights, the demand for federal expenditures for defence, security, and other purposes precludes a significant fall in federal spending relative to GDP. Citizens have become accustomed to certain government expenditures and would not be comfortable with a move back to the very small federal (and overall) government structure that existed prior to the Great Depression.

Second, middle-class voters are unlikely to prefer movement back to a larger federal role. Confidence in the federal government's ability to deal with many of the large problems facing the United States has waned. Various crises can precipitate a greater federal role for a period of time, such as the relatively strong support for defence and national security that was stimulated by international terrorism, but the pendulum will probably swing back to a more balanced role between the federal and state and local governments.

Third, going forward, Shannon expects "middle-of-the-road" federalism, with neither the federal government nor the states dominating the government structure. Having said this, the political forces in place could result in slow trends towards either the federal or state governments' playing a larger role. A good bet is that state and local governments will remain the dominant service providers but that the federal government's influence will remain significant (and could become even greater).

ASSIGNMENT OF SERVICE RESPONSIBILITIES

What is true of many countries is also true of the United States: summarizing the relative service delivery roles played by the federal, state, and local governments is not simple because many services have been unbundled, with each arena of government taking responsibility for different components. Data on expenditures and revenues tell part of the story but fail to explain fully the nuances of the intergovernmental relationships. This section summarizes the expenditure responsibilities, while the following section summarizes the revenue structure.

The federal versus state/local role is generally based on history and practice, and most service delivery is not specifically articulated in the US Constitution.[4] Table 2 illustrates the levels at which services are generally assigned. The assignment of service responsibilities at the state versus the local level can vary widely across states based on constitutional and statutory provisions, making generalizations difficult. Some state constitutions provide specific assignments. For example, many state constitutions assign responsibility for education to state governments, but even here every state except Hawaii either assigns or delegates most provision of primary and secondary schools to local governments. The national, state, and local governments frequently share responsibility, at least to some extent, for delivering most services. The federal government generally plays a much smaller overall role in direct service delivery than do the state and local governments, but the federal government often has important influence over service delivery. Federal grants, loans, and cost sharing that come with various restrictions, as well as federal laws and regulations, are frequently used to leverage federal priorities far beyond the narrow area in which the funding is provided.

Federal mandates are also used to assert federal priorities over state and local governments. Unfunded federal mandates can be an important source of expenditure growth for state/local governments. Congress enacted legislation in 1995 requiring the federal government to determine the costs of such mandates, whether by congressional or administrative action, but the costs are seldom financed directly by the federal government. Gallo examines the act and applauds the increased supply of information, but she questions the long-term effect on federal decisions as the legislation is narrowly constructed.[5] The Center for Budget and Policy Priorities estimated that unfunded federal mandates cost the states $73 billion more than was provided between 2002 and 2005 in the areas of election reform, No Child Left Behind education reform, and education of disabled children.[6]

In fact, what are often termed mandates by the states come in two general forms. In some cases, Congress, using its control over interstate commerce, directly requires state or local governments to provide certain services in certain ways. Restrictions on drivers' licences and voter registration are examples. But a number of areas, such as constitutional rights, are specifically excluded from the unfunded mandates legislation. Alternatively, Congress may link conditions to grants, and state/local governments may argue that these are mandates. However, the legislation does not regard conditions on grants to be mandates. The No Child Left Behind legislation is probably best characterized as an example of the latter type of mandate. Federal influence over state behaviour is more likely to come through grants than through direct requirements, and what is listed as a mandate may be *changes* in federal programs that can be costly to subnational governments, in part, because they alter the financing relative to the pre-existing conditions.

The system generally follows the subsidiarity principle, with decisions made at the level of government closest to the people, because the system of government was created with strong state governments and a relatively weak national government. As noted above, the balance of power has shifted dramatically over the years as a result of large growth in federal revenues that are often used to encourage particular state/local behaviour, court rulings that have expanded the federal role relative to the state/local role, and congressional legislation based on expansive interpretations of constitutional provisions, such as the interstate commerce clause.

The national government has exclusive responsibility for several services, including national defence (although state militias exist), international affairs, and the postal service. Shared federal, state, and local responsibility exists for a number of services, including the judiciary, police, environmental protection, parks, and economic regulation, with each level having different responsibilities. For example, with environmental issues, the federal government often has responsibility for interstate regulatory issues while states have responsibility for more localized concerns. State and local governments have nearly exclusive responsibility for a number of services, including fire, education, libraries, solid-waste management, sewerage, water supply, and transit. As noted above, the federal government has an important influence on service delivery, even with these "exclusive services."

Data can provide some evidence on the service-delivery assignments. Interestingly, the US Bureau of the Census provides detailed data on state and local expenditures but does not provide comparable data on federal expenditures.[7] However, the census provides employment data for the federal, state, and local governments, and this can give some indication of service-delivery responsibility.[8] Local governments employ about five-eighths of the 18.2 million public-sector non-military workers in the United States.

Table 2
Legislative responsibility and actual provision of services by different levels of government

Legislative responsibility (de jure)	Public service	Actual allocation of function (de facto)
State/local	Higher education	State/local
State/local	Primary/secondary education	State/local
Federal	Defence	Federal
Federal/state/local	Police	Federal/state/local
State/local	Fire	Local
Federal/state/local	Corrections	Federal/state/local
Federal/state/local	Health/hospitals	Federal/state/local
State/local	Solid waste	Local
State/local	Sewerage	Local
State/local	Water	Local
Federal	Postal service	Federal
Federal/state/local	Parks and recreation	Federal/state/local
Federal/state/local	Highways	State/local

The majority of local government workers are employed in education, particularly in elementary and secondary schools. States employ nearly one-fourth of total civilian government workers, while the federal government hires the remaining one-eighth.

Exclusive responsibility can be seen in areas where the government has 100 percent or 0 percent of expenditures (see Table 3). For the federal government, examples include defence, the postal service, and space research. The shared roles in the judicial, police, corrections, health and hospitals, parks, natural resources, and air transportation services are readily apparent. Much of health care is provided through the private sector, but public-sector hospitals and clinics are also common, and regulatory responsibility is vested in all three orders of government.

The federal and state governments share responsibility for social insurance. The federal government is responsible for the Social Security pension program and the Medicare program. States provide food stamps, Medicaid, and the major welfare program, Temporary Assistance for Needy Families (TANF). However, the federal government finances TANF (through a block grant) and food stamps and provides between one-half and three-fourths of Medicaid costs (through a matching grant). States are

Table 3
Direct expenditures by function and level of government, percentages

Function	Federal	State or provincial	Local	All
Defence	100.0	0	0	100
Interest	65.7	13.8	20.5	100
General administration	40.0	25.9	34.1	100
Law and order				100
Economic services				100
Social services				100
Health	66.8	14.5	18.7	100
Education	4.4	26.4	69.2	100
Subsidies				100
Total	45.7	24.4	29.9	100
Local Public services[1]	8.7	27.0	64.2	100

1. Let "local public services" include: primary and preschool education, secondary education, public health, hospitals, urban highways, urban transportation, drinking water and sewerage, waste collection, electric power supply, fire protection, public order and safety, police.

mostly responsible for administering these programs, but service provision is tightly constrained by federal rules. States have varied to some degree in their Medicaid and TANF programs but must obtain a waiver from federal rules in order to do so. Experimentation by the states with these programs is generally regarded as a good laboratory for identifying better ways, often defined as lower-cost ways, of structuring them.

Water, electricity, gas supply, and sewerage are exclusive state and local responsibilities, although the federal government plays some regulatory and fiscal roles in all of these fields (such as through water quality standards established by the US Environmental Protection Agency). The public sector produces the services in some cases, and the private sector does so in others. State or local governments continue to provide regulatory oversight in places where the private sector produces the services, but most of the employment for delivering these services would not be reflected in Tables 2 and 3.

Overlap and confusion in service delivery responsibilities arise both horizontally between local governments and vertically across levels of government because it is not always transparent which government is accountable or should be responsible for service delivery, although the problems are not generally egregious. The response by all governments to Hurricane

Katrina in 2005, the most severe hurricane to strike the United States in many years, is an excellent example. Elected federal, state, and local officials are all pointing the blame at each other, with the federal government, rightly or wrongly, being perceived by many citizens as having failed the most severely. One possible outcome is that the federal government may effectively become responsible for responding to many localized emergencies that might have been better undertaken by the states.

Individuals who do not fully understand that they are paying separately imposed federal and state income taxes is another source of confusion that can limit accountability for specific taxes. Individuals might wish to voice complaints about service delivery but might not be able to readily determine which office or which government to contact. Overlapping service delivery also occurs, and this leads both to confusion and to potentially higher costs. For example, there is likely to be confusion over environmental regulation at the federal versus state levels. Also, it may be unclear to citizens whether federal, state, county, or city law enforcement officials are responsible for certain tasks.

TAX ASSIGNMENTS

Federal, state, and local governments overlap considerably in their use of revenue sources (see Table 4). The US Constitution imposes relatively few limitations on taxation at the US federal (Article 1 Section 8) and subnational government levels. A prohibition against taxing exports from a state is the only notable explicit restriction in the US Constitution on state taxing authority. The US Constitution of 1788 formerly required direct federal taxes to be apportioned equally across the states, but the Sixteenth Amendment to the Constitution was ratified in 1913 so that an income tax could be imposed consistently across the states.[9] Implied restrictions also arise. The prohibition against state taxes distorting interstate commerce arises from the dormant commerce clause and is a very significant limitation on the ability of states to tax. The inability of one government to impose tax on another government came from an 1819 Supreme Court decision.[10] Federal limitations on state and local taxation are discussed in more detail in the next section.

State constitutions also include some restrictions on states' taxation powers, with the major limitation being that state constitutions cannot impose restrictions that run counter to the national Constitution. In turn, states determine, either statutorily or constitutionally, the authority of local governments to levy taxes. For example, several states have limited the annual growth rate in assessments for property tax purposes.

The federal government raises just over one-half of both total tax revenue and total revenue (see Table 5 for total revenues). A limited form of specialization has developed by tax source, though each order of government uses multiple tax sources. The federal government specializes mostly in the individual income tax, which raises more than 80 percent of federal tax revenue. The federal income tax also collects about 80 percent of total US income taxes. In addition, the federal government collects almost all insurance-trust revenue.

Property taxes are used almost exclusively by local governments and generate nearly three-fourths of local revenues. Most local governments with taxing authority can levy property taxes, although there are frequently some state controls and regulation over the base and rate. Specifically, property tax is often thought of as the main source of education finance, with non-education special districts using the tax much less than school districts. The role of property taxes in local finance has slowly diminished over time; as some states have given local governments tax alternatives and the role of states in financing education has risen. Thirty-four states allow local sales taxes, and thirteen permit local income taxes, which are often wage taxes rather than broad-based income taxes. The heavy reliance on property taxes has generated considerable controversy in a number of states, particularly when property values have risen rapidly (as has occurred in recent years). For example, in 1994 Michigan lowered local property taxes and replaced the revenues with a 2 percent increase in the state sales tax. New Jersey, Texas, and a number of other states are currently debating alternatives for changing local school financing by reducing reliance on the property tax.

On average, states have more balanced tax structures than do the federal or local governments. States raise an approximately equal amount of revenue from sales and individual income taxes. Forty-one states impose a broad-based income tax, and forty-five levy a general sales tax. States are the predominant users of sales taxes and motor vehicle licence taxes, and they are the heaviest users of selective sales taxes.[11] Averages fail to reflect clearly the diversity that exists across states. New Hampshire has neither a broad-based income tax nor a sales tax. Oregon raised 70.0 percent of its state tax revenue with the individual income tax in 2004, while nine states raised essentially no revenues from this tax.[12] Tennessee and Washington State generate more than 60 percent of their collections from the sales tax, while five states raise no revenues from the tax. State and local governments collect almost all user fee revenue, which is consistent with the greater service delivery role played by these governments.

States differ radically in their capacity and willingness to raise tax revenues. Figure 1 illustrates the wide variation across states in capacity to raise tax revenues, using per capita personal income as a proxy for capacity. Per capita income in the highest-income state, Connecticut, is 88 percent higher than in the lowest-income state, Mississippi. Cost-of-living

Table 4
Tax assignment for various levels of government

	Determination of		Tax collection and administration	Shares in revenue (%)			
	Base	Rate		Federal	State	Local	All levels
Federal							
Personal income	Federal	Federal	Federal	100			100
Corporate income	Federal	Federal	Federal	100			100
Gasoline[1]	Federal	Federal	Federal	100			100
State or Provincial[2]							
Personal income	State	State	State		0		100
Sales	State	State	State		0		100
Gasoline	State	State	State		0		100
Property	State	State	State/local		0		100
Motor Vehicle Licence	State	State	State		0		100
Alcohol/tobacco	State	State	State		0		100
User fees	State	State	State		0		100
Local[3]							
Property	State/local	Local	Local		0	100	100
Sales	State/local	State/local	State/local		0	100	100
Personal income	State/local	State/local	State/local		0	100	100
Excises	State/local	State/local	State/local		0	100	100
User fees	State/local	State/local	State/local		0	100	100

1. Shared through grants.
2. Often shared by individual state laws.
3. Practices differ widely by state.

differentials probably explain some of the differences in income (no reliable cost-of-living index exists for all states), but significant real income differences exist as well.

Wide differences exist in the extent to which states raise taxes from their own resources. States and their local governments are best combined for cross-state comparisons because of differences in the relative service delivery roles played by states versus local governments across the country. Figure 2 shows that the average state collected 10.4 percent of personal income in taxes during 2002 (the most recent year for which local tax revenue data are available), but the collections varied from 13.1 percent in New York to 8.4 percent in Tennessee and New Hampshire. Per capita tax collections vary even more because there is a positive correlation between per capita income and taxes as a share of personal income. For example, New York has the fourth highest per capita income and Tennessee has the thirty-fifth highest. New York collects $4,684 per capita in taxes, 114 percent more than Alabama (forty-first highest in per capita personal income).

Disparity in the capacity of local governments to raise revenues is significant in every state. For example, New Jersey, the third highest state in terms of per capita personal income, reports that household income varies from $93,432 in Somerset County to $33,858 in Cumberland County – a nearly threefold difference.[13] Similarly, local governments vary widely in the extent to which they choose to tax themselves. For example, the property tax rate imposed in New Jersey varies about 2.5-fold across counties. Relatively poor Camden County has a median effective property tax rate of 3.49 percent, while relatively wealthy Cape May County imposes a median effective rate of 1.37 percent.

FEDERAL LIMITATIONS ON STATE FISCAL ACTIVITIES

The US Constitution imposes two basic constraints on state and local government fiscal actions. First, states are prohibited from discriminating against interstate commerce. This limitation arises from the dormant commerce clause because it is not explicitly mentioned in the US Constitution.[14] Second, states are prohibited from taxing international trade. The limitation on taxation of international trade does not arise as a frequent issue, although it was widely discussed a decade ago when some states sought to use a worldwide unitary approach to tax corporate income. In addition, the US Constitution supersedes the state constitutions when conflicts arise between them.

Limitations arising from states' inability to distort interstate commerce are imposed both by federal court limitations on state actions and by congressional legislation. The US Constitution gives Congress control over interstate commerce, which means that congressional legislation can define when states violate interstate commerce. Many examples of congressional and judicial constraints on states exist, but only a few are given here. No effort is made to describe the long string of court rulings and legislative actions related to interstate commerce. The constraints on state governments almost always prevent states from taking advantage at the expense of other states. There are cases where national and potentially state policies may cause the home state to be disadvantaged relative to others, and the courts have generally ignored these effects.

The US Supreme Court has ruled that states can only require vendors with physical presence in the state to collect the state's sales tax, the largest average state tax source.[15] This limitation allows easy tax planning because vendors can purposely sell into a state from remote locations and avoid the compliance responsibility as well as the tax burden (which is either a legal burden of the vendor or the consumer, depending on the state in question). Combined state and local sales tax rates can be as high as 11 percent, so this can be an important advantage for remote vendors. As a result, rapid growth of Internet and mail-order-based transactions has cost states a significant share of sales tax receipts, amounting to about $19.2 billion in 2006.[16,17]

State taxation of corporate income is increasingly difficult, at least in part because of increasing globalization.[18] States that tax corporate income apportion the corporate tax base for multistate firms. Court rulings have also established the environment within which state corporate income taxes are collected. For example, in 1977 the US Supreme Court set up a framework for determining when a corporation's income can be taxed in any given state.[19] Specifically, the Supreme Court ruled that state taxes must be (1) on activity sufficiently connected to the state, (2) fairly apportioned across states, (3) nondiscriminatory, and (4) related to state services provided.[20] A federal circuit court ruling in 2004 has attracted considerable attention because it potentially would have prevented states in the sixth circuit from adopting many types of tax incentives, specifically incentives that lower a firm's tax burden when it expands in the incentive-granting state but not when it expands the same activity in another state.[21] The US Supreme Court ruled that the plaintiff did not have standing to bring the case to court, but the issue is likely to reappear somewhere for reconsideration by the court system.

The US courts have in some cases also required state and local governments to provide non-residents with equal access to services. Thus, residents can move from one state to another and, within thirty days, can gain access to services such as education, welfare, and health care for the poor. This appears to have limited the extent to which some state and local governments are willing to expand delivery of certain services.

Congressional legislation can preempt state or local governments from imposing taxes in cases where Congress believes that state or local taxation would distort interstate commerce. Such legislation has been important in some cases, and the Federation of Tax Administrators (an association of state revenue departments) has identified twenty-eight examples of preemption.[22] For example, Congress passed the Internet Tax Freedom Act in 1998 and has extended it twice, most recently until 2007. The legislation prevents states from imposing discriminatory taxes on the Internet. It also precludes states from taxing charges for access to the Internet. If interpreted narrowly, the latter does not represent significant foregone revenues for the states, but states continue to be concerned that firms will bundle activities together and define the entire set as access, resulting in a much larger revenue loss. Further, Congress has not acted to require remote vendors to collect the state sales tax, as limited by the *Quill* case, despite the admonition by the Supreme Court in its *Quill* opinion to address the issue. "Temporary" legislation enacted by Congress decades ago (Public Law 86–272) precludes states from collecting corporate income taxes from firms whose only relationship with the state is to solicit for the sale of tangible personal property. This legislation offers significant opportunities for tax planning and results in "nowhere income" – income not taxed by any state.

Congress currently has several pieces of legislation before it that address many of these same issues. For example, legislation has been proposed to (1) allow states to tax corporate income only when firms have physical presence in the state, (2) make the Internet Tax Freedom Act permanent, and (3) allow states to require remote vendors to collect the sales tax on their behalf in cases where the states have simplified their sales tax. Congress seems unlikely to enact any of this legislation during the next year or two because of the different political perspectives within the business community and between the state and local governments and the business community.

Strong constitutional restrictions preventing state discrimination against interstate commerce serve the country well in terms of allowing an unfettered economic union. Labour, capital, and trade are freely mobile both inside the country and, at least from the state and local perspectives, outside the country. While encouraging the mobility of resources helps develop a seamless economic union, state and local governments face significant challenges in raising tax revenues in a very mobile environment. The country continues to grapple with how tax structures should be designed to keep impediments to the open economy small. Similarly, the country still has to determine the best ways for states to raise tax revenues in a very open/mobile economy.

Intergovernmental Financial Relationships

Federal and state governments have independent control over their tax bases and rates, given the limitations described above. The flexibility afforded to local governments varies across states. Governments are not required to coordinate their tax bases or rates, and differences exist in the tax bases used by every state and by the national government. Similar or identical bases are more common for local governments within states, but wide differences exist in some cases. For example, Colorado allows local governments to set their own local sales tax base. In some other states, such as Virginia, the state sets the local sales tax rate and base, making the tax more like a grant program.

Federal, state, and local tax structures are often intertwined, despite their legal and constitutional independence. Most states require individuals and corporations to begin calculation of their income taxes with some variant of the federal definition of taxable activity. For example, thirty-seven states start calculation of their individual income tax base using federal definitions, twenty-seven employ federal adjusted gross income (income before exemptions and deductions), and ten use federal taxable income. Having said this, federal law allows states to piggyback their income tax on the federal income tax, but no state has chosen to do so. State estate and inheritance taxes are also linked to the federal estate tax, although the latter is being phased out over a number of years.

The relationships between federal and state and local personal and corporate income taxes extend to administration as well. Each state has its own tax administration but relies heavily on federal audits and databases to assist in collection.

The institutional linkages between tax bases mean that tax policy decisions made by one level of government frequently have implications for other levels. There is scant evidence that these vertical externalities are given serious consideration when policy decisions are made. The federal government has made numerous tax policy changes in recent years by changing tax bases (frequently narrowing them) and lowering tax rates. Accelerated depreciation provisions and a production credit for manufacturers are two recent corporate income tax base changes. Nonetheless, many national officials (including Larry Summers, former secretary of the US Treasury) have said that they did not consider effects on state and local governments when decisions were made on federal policy.

In many cases, because of the lost revenues, states choose not to conform to federal policy changes. In other cases, states have defined their tax base using the federal legislation that existed at a particular point in time, and the state legislature must act to bring the state tax into conformity with new federal legislation. But, decoupling from the current federal provisions raises compliance costs. For example, nineteen states have chosen not to conform to the production credits that were part of the American Jobs Creation Act passed by Congress in 2004. The result is that firms must calculate their corporate tax liability using different provisions across states and between the state and federal governments.[23] The burdens from tax provisions that differ across the states can be expected to continue growing as the economy opens up to even greater international and interstate activity.

Vertical competition between governments may also exist, and it is an empirical question as to how one level of government responds to policy decisions at another level. The notion is that imposition of a tax by one level of government reduces the tax base available for other governments.[24] The affected local governments could either raise their rate to offset the revenue loss or lower their rate because the tax is less productive. Research has yet to reach a solid conclusion regarding the direction of these relationships. Some evidence suggests that states tend to raise their gasoline and tobacco tax rates in response to federal increases,[25] suggesting that states raised their rates to offset the base decline. Also, research on the US individual income tax has found that states tend to increase their personal income and their sales tax rates in response to federal income tax rate increases.[26] However, there has been too little research to reach a firm conclusion on how federal tax changes affect the states.

Horizontal relationships between states or between local governments can also be important, both in terms of how revenues are distributed across governments and how the governments compete for the tax base. States have considerable flexibility in how they structure their taxes, and this can increase compliance costs. One example of this is the way that revenue from the major state taxes (i.e., individual income, corporate income, and sales) is distributed across states in those cases where the taxpayer or the activity crosses state boundaries. Personal income tax revenue from wages is generally distributed between states based on where the income is earned.[27] Non-labour income is taxed in the state of residence. Sales taxes are due in the state where the goods and services are to be enjoyed or used – that is, on a destination basis. This is normally presumed to be the place where possession of the goods takes place.[28] Corporate income taxes are distributed by formula, although formulas differ significantly across states.

These general approaches suggest much more uniformity than is present in practice as the details of each tax tend to vary by state. As a result, compliance burdens are increased for firms or individuals that operate in multistate environments. Indeed, the US Supreme Court ruling in the *Quill* case was based on the notion that remote vendors, complying with the taxes of many state and local governments, bear higher burdens than does a domestic firm in a single state. Little reliable evidence exists on the compliance burden.

States also cooperate in collecting taxes. Many states participate in compacts with other states to share information on issues such as compliance. The Multi-State Tax Commission is one such organization that also conducts audits of some multistate taxpayers.

More than forty states, in an extraordinary act of cooperation, worked together over the past six years to create the Streamlined Sales and Use Tax Agreement (SSUTA).[29] On 1 October 2005, nineteen states signed on as initial members by enacting the legislation that was developed through the process. The SSUTA is intended to simplify the sales tax and structure it on a destination basis so that states are better able to collect their sales taxes on remote transactions. The SSUTA is a wonderful example of state cooperation, but cartels of this type are difficult to develop and hold together, even when the related structures represent good tax policy (which is generally true of the SSUTA).

INTERGOVERNMENTAL GRANTS

As in nearly every country, the national government finances much more expenditures and services than it delivers. Intergovernmental transfers from the federal government have generally followed the historical pattern of federalism. Federal grants were very small in the early years of the United States, but grants for capital purposes (and, to a lesser extent, for other uses) rose rapidly during the Great Depression of the 1930s, particularly when measured as a share of federal outlays. Grants declined during the centralizing period of the Second World War but afterward proceeded to rise nearly continuously as a share of GDP and of outlays until the late 1970s.[30] Grants fell as a share of GDP and of federal outlays during the initial period of what was described above as balanced federalism through the early 1990s. Grants have risen again over the last fifteen years and, in 2003, were the greatest share in history of both GDP (3.6 percent) and federal revenues (17.9 percent).

Over 600 grant programs exist for state and local governments. The grants are provided in many different forms, including project, categorical, and block grants. Some have matching components and others are structured through formulas. Still, except for a few specific areas, the overall federal-to-subnational intergovernmental grant system is relatively small compared with what we see in US history or in many other countries.[31] As described below, the recent rise in grants has been focused on a narrow set of areas, particularly health care. There is no form of general revenue sharing, although a limited revenue-sharing program existed from 1972 through 1986. The federal intergovernmental grant system is primarily intended to provide a degree of equalization across people, not to equalize subnational government service delivery, with most of the money intended to support low-income people.

The composition of federal grants has changed radically in recent years. Grants to state and local governments for redistribution to individuals have risen, and other types of grants have fallen. In fact, grants for capital and other state and local purposes are the lowest share of GDP (around 1.2 percent) since the late 1960s, while grants for individuals have risen to 11.4 percent of GDP. The rapid rise in health care costs, and therefore in the Medicaid program, has been the driving force behind the growth in transfers for people.

The amount of transfers is decided annually by congressional decisions. However, some programs, such as Medicaid and TANF, have been established as entitlements (with carefully established eligibility requirements), and the basic structure is changed infrequently. Total federal grants in 2003 were $387.3 billion, which represented about 22.0 percent of total state and local revenue. State governments received 88.5 percent of these transfers, but some of the grants are subsequently forwarded to local governments. Two major categories of grants – health and income security – representing more than two-thirds of grant funds, are primarily transferred to state governments so that they can be further transferred to individuals. These funds are transferred as grants because state and local governments administer the programs. Medicaid grants were $160.8 billion of the health-grant programs, and income security is primarily composed of family assistance, housing, and child nutrition. A degree of equalization is built into these programs through the specific grant structures,[32] and this can indirectly influence states' ability to deliver other programs. Strong support for equalizing programs does not exist across states, despite the wide differences across the United States in taxable capacity.[33]

The other large grant categories, transportation and education, are more likely to support state service delivery, but these programs generally do not have strong equalization components. Rather than being "entitlement" payments, the specific amounts are often determined through the annual budget process or by agency decisions. Grant programs are often discretionary at the national level. The interstate highway system is funded with shared federal and state grants. The federal government normally finances 90 percent of the construction cost and the states finance 10 percent. Both governments rely on gasoline taxes that are levied per gallon of gasoline to finance their expenditures.

States have sought to leverage federal grants in a number of ways, as can be evidenced by the Medicaid program. First, some states appear to claim a wide range of expenditures as being appropriate for the Medicaid program and, thus, eligible for the federal matching grant. Second, states have sought to provide their matching component through various creative means. For example, Tennessee created a "services tax" on hospital health care during the early 1990s and used this revenue to finance the state's share of the Medicaid program. Hospitals made the payments but received the money back in Medicaid revenues, allowing the state to draw down the federal funds with no state share. The federal government disallowed this scheme based on the argument that the state was not in fact matching the federal grant, but other states have sought to use similar funding sources in subsequent years. These schemes are generally disallowed.

State and local income, sales (taxpayers can deduct either their income or sales tax but the sales tax deduction was available only during tax years

Table 5
Vertical fiscal gaps, 2003/04

	Total revenue collected (US$000)	Total revenue available, including net transfers for that level of gov't (US$000)	Expenditures (US$000)
National	1,798,093,000	1,798,093,000	1,900,743,000
Subnational	1,464,058,004	1,889,740,590	2,260,330,261
State/provincial	799,442,877	1,194,055,987	1,016,469,065
Local	664,615,127	1,094,729,372	1,243,861,196
All levels	3,262,151,004	4,086,878,359	4,161,073,261

Author's calculations from http://www.whitehouse.gov/omb/budget/fy2005/pdf/hist.pdf and http://www.census.gov/govs/estimate/0400ussl_1.html.

2004 and 2005), and property taxes are deductible expenses in determining federal individual income tax liabilities. Various interpretations are given to the linkage that this establishes between the federal and state and local governments, one of which is that deductibility is a form of grant to the state and local governments, although it may be better seen as a tax expenditure. Deductibility lowers the cost of paying state and local taxes, but it only saves the average federal income taxpayer about 5 percent of the total liability for these taxes.[34] Some political conservatives oppose deductibility, arguing that it subsidizes government and thereby encourages larger government. In any event, the benefits to state and local governments are poorly targeted to achieve particular objectives.

State Grants to Local Governments

States often provide grants and shared taxes to local governments. State government grants to local governments are nearly of the same magnitude as federal grants, totalling $370.6 billion in 2003.[35] However, some of these grants may be the pass-through of federal grant funds. Federal and state grants together provide 40.6 percent of local government revenue. In addition, shared tax revenue in some states is probably not included in these grant funds, depending on the specific accounting arrangements. In Tennessee, for example, approximately 7 percent of state tax revenue is shared with local governments through a wide range of mechanisms. Some portion of most taxes is shared with local governments, using either situs based distribution of the revenues or some type of formula. Sharing of gasoline tax and state sales tax revenues comprises most of the distribution.

The dominant state transfer program in nearly every state is for financing primary and secondary education. The specific grant structure differs across states, but similarities exist in the basic design. A number of states build the grant around ensuring that local governments have sufficient resources to deliver an adequate level of education. Some degree of equalization is usually built into the grants, along with incentives to achieve certain objectives (such as to meet class-size expectations). Equalization is frequently based on both the capacity to raise revenues locally and the expenditure needs in the community.

State constitutions often have provisions indicating that the state will provide education, although local governments are usually the providers. These provisions have led to court suits in about half the states, based on the argument that the state is not ensuring that equal education is being provided in all local jurisdictions. The suits have been upheld in many states, although in some cases the courts have ruled that the state constitution does not establish a requirement that education be provided equally or adequately across the state. States, such as Texas and Tennessee, have lost multiple cases based on different aspects of equalization.

MACROECONOMIC MANAGEMENT

US government agencies have exclusive control over monetary policy and predominant influence over fiscal policy, although state and local governments undertake some fiscal policy actions. No mechanism exists for coordinating the fiscal policies of federal, state, and local governments.

The Federal Reserve (FED) conducts monetary policy in the United States. An independent board composed of seven members who are appointed by the president and confirmed by the US Senate manages the FED. Board members are appointed for nine-year terms (presidents are elected for one four-year term and may succeed themselves once) and may be reappointed for additional terms. The FED Open Market Committee oversees the direction of monetary policy. The committee is composed of the seven members of the Board of Governors and five presidents from the twelve regional Federal Reserve Banks. The FED appears to see price control as its major goal but is free to consider other goals, such as economic growth and currency exchange rates. Maintaining stable growth appears generally to play a strong secondary role as a policy goal. States have no authority to print money or to engage in monetary policy.

The national executive and legislative branches make most fiscal policy decisions. The national government has full control over its budget composition, expenditure levels, tax levels, and extent of debt. The national deficit was $415.2 billion in 2005, equal to 3.3 percent of GDP.

States also control their budget composition, expenditure levels, and tax levels as described above. Forty-nine states have either constitutional or statutory requirements that their operating budgets be balanced, which would appear to limit their capacity to undertake fiscal policy. However, states have many means of sidestepping the balanced budget requirements, and state economic development policies may have greater potential to influence economic activity than has traditionally been expected.[36] The federal government has no balanced budget requirement and, as noted above, has been running significant deficits in recent years.

State and local governments borrow primarily for capital projects, but they have also borrowed for operating purposes (despite the balanced budget limitations), as is illustrated by California's borrowing $15 billion in recent years. In most cases, state and local governments use debt without any explicit intent to influence macroeconomic conditions. State and local government long-term debt totaled $1.81 trillion in 2003, up 7.5 percent from the previous year.[37] The use of debt has grown at a compound annual rate of 5.8 percent since the early 1990s. Local governments rather than states hold most of the debt (61.5 percent). Almost all of the debt (97.8 percent) is long term, and 38.1 percent of the long-term debt is guaranteed with the "full faith and credit of the government." The remaining 61.9 percent is not guaranteed and often has a specific revenue source pledged for repayment. The debt is used mostly for a wide range of capital projects, with 23.8 percent being public debt, where the revenues were used to finance private-sector activities. Much of the debt is used for construction of schools.

The federal government effectively subsidizes state and local debt since the interest earned on these securities is exempt from the federal personal income tax. Proposals to make the interest taxable are raised from time to time, often based on the argument that the exemption costs the Federal Treasury more than it benefits it. President Bush's Tax Reform Panel did not recommend eliminating the exemption of state and local interest payments.[38]

In terms of macroeconomic management, state and local governments have been much more aggressive in using the tax code to pursue economic development strategies that are linked to individual businesses or economic sectors than in using fiscal policy. State and local governments provide concessions for the sales, property, corporate income, and individual income taxes to recruit businesses. In some cases, the concessions are available to any firms meeting specific characteristics, which are often specified in terms of firm size, industry, or location. In other cases, the concessions are specific to individual firms. Governments also offer a range of spending incentives, such as training, infrastructure, free land, or site development. The greatest attention has focused on incentives offered by state and local governments to recruit automobile plants.

Each level of government is normally left to its own resources to accommodate the effects of cyclical macroeconomic slowdowns. Two cases in the past several decades where the national government stepped in to assist states during fiscal stress can be noted. The first involved loans to a number of state unemployment insurance systems during the very strong economic downturn of the early 1980s. Most states are precluded by constitution or statute from carrying shortfalls across fiscal years, and a series of loans were made to rescue unemployment insurance programs that were in serious fiscal difficulty. Second, Congress provided $20 billion to states during 2003 and 2004 to soften the blow of the sharp downturn in tax revenues experienced by many states between 2001 and 2003.[39] In addition, states often have rainy day, or budget stabilization, funds to help smooth over economic transitions. These funds are generally relatively small, amounting to much less than 5 percent of expenditures.[40] Local governments seldom have rainy day funds, but they do have year-ending balances that can, to some degree, serve a similar role.

CONCLUSION

The US system of federalism has evolved over the years in response to various economic, political, and international forces, and the likely scenario is that it will continue changing in future years. The major shift has been towards a much larger role for the national government relative to that which existed in the first two-thirds of the country's history. Having said this, general service delivery responsibilities and major own-source revenue categories across levels of government have not changed radically during the last thirty to forty years and, in many cases, for much longer.[41] Instead, the changes are more subtle in terms of growing limitations that the national government places on state and local governments' ability to raise revenues and increased mandates on the ways in which they deliver services. Forecasting the future is always fraught with risks, but the most likely outcome is for the national role to remain strong and more likely to expand than to contract.

The growing degree of economic mobility, both around the world and within the United States, poses the greatest threat and largest issues for state and local governments. In particular, the forces arising from mobility (such as greater difficulty in monitoring taxable activities, easier tax planning, and greater tax competition) significantly limit the ability of state and local governments to raise revenues using some of their traditional sources. Raising revenue is particularly problematic since US Constitutional rulings leave much of the control in the hands of Congress. Congress has been reticent thus far to enable the states to levy effective taxes, particularly because it receives political benefits from narrowing the capacity of state and local taxation without suffering from the revenue consequences of its actions. Effectively, this means that Congress has paid relatively little attention to the sustainability of state and local fiscal systems, while focusing on national political issues and national revenue systems.

NOTES

1 Other chapters on the United States of America in the series "A Global Dialogue on Federalism" include Ellis Katz, "United States of America," in *Distribution of Powers and Responsibilities in Federal Countries*, ed. Akhtar Majeed, Ronald L. Watts, and Douglas M. Brown, 295–321 (Montreal and Kingston: McGill-Queen's University Press, 2006); and G. Alan Tarr, "United States of America," in *Constitutional Origins, Structure, and Change in Federal Countries*, ed. John Kincaid and G. Alan Tarr, 381–408 (Montreal and Kingston: McGill-Queen's University Press, 2005).
2 This section draws heavily from John Shannon, "Middle Class Votes Bring a New Balance to U.S. Federalism," the Urban Institute, The Future of the Public Sector, Policy Note no. 10 (February 1997).
3 Ibid.
4 The power of the US Congress to deliver national services beyond a narrowly set of enumerated authorities was articulated in an early court decision (*McCulloch v. Maryland* [1819]). This opinion also limited the states' ability to tax the national government.
5 See Theresa Gallo, "History and Evaluation of the Unfunded Mandates Reform Act," *National Tax Journal* 57 (2004): 559–70.
6 See Iris Lav and Andrew Brecher, "Passing Down the Deficit: Federal Policies Contribute to the Severity of the State Fiscal Crisis," Center for Budget and Policy Priorities, 18 August 2004.
7 Federal expenditure data are available through the White House Office of Management and Budget, but developing the data in a manner consistent with the census data is a daunting task.
8 Federal employment shares may be somewhat understated because the federal data are for full-time employees and the state and local government data are for full-time equivalent workers. Thus, part-time federal employment may be excluded.
9 This amendment may have been instrumental in allowing the role played by the federal government to grow relative to state governments because it dramatically expanded the federal government's ability to generate resources.
10 In *McCulloch v. Maryland*, 17 US 316 (1819) the Supreme Court established the doctrine of intergovernmental tax immunity.
11 Selective sales taxes are excises that are generally levied on oil, tobacco, and alcohol products. The rates are normally, but not always, imposed at unit rates. The federal government levies the tax on various oil products.

12 Also, New Hampshire and Tennessee raise small shares of their tax revenue with income taxes on interest and dividend income.
13 See Annual Report, New Jersey Department of Taxation, 2003.
14 The United States Constitution gives Congress the power to regulate interstate commerce but does not explicitly say what states can do in the absence of congressional action. The dormant commerce clause refers to the Constitutional limitation on the inability of states to impose taxes on interstate commerce. It is termed "dormant" because the limitation is implied by other aspects of the Constitution rather than being explicitly provided for in the Constitution. See Walter Hellerstein and Jerome Hellerstein, *State Taxation*, 3rd ed. (Warren, Gorham, and Lamont, 1998 [supplemented semi-annually]).
15 *Quill v. North Dakota*, 112 US 298 (1992).
16 All sales-taxing states levy corresponding use taxes that require the buyer to remit the tax if it was not collected by the vendor. Individuals have extremely poor compliance with the use tax. Businesses are more responsive to the use tax, but non-compliance is still more than 25 percent.
17 See Donald Bruce and William F. Fox, "State and Local Tax Revenue Losses from E-Commerce: Estimates as of July 2004," *State Tax Note* 33 (2004): 511–18.
18 See William F. Fox and LeAnn Luna, "State Corporate Tax Revenue Trends: Causes and Possible Solutions," *National Tax Journal* 55 (2002): 491–508.
19 *Complete Auto Transit Inc. v. Brady* 430 US 274 (1977).
20 See Hellerstein and Hellerstein, *State Taxation*.
21 *Cuno v. Daimler-Chrysler, Inc.*, 386 F.3d 738 (6th cir. 2004).
22 Federation of Tax Administrators, June 2003.
23 See http://www.taxadmin.org/fta/rate/B-2505.html
24 Other relationships could also exist, such as leader/follower responses or demonstration effects.
25 See Timothy Besley and Harvey Rosen, "States' Responses to Federal Tax Setting: Evidence from Gasoline and Cigarettes," *Journal of Public Economics* 73 (1998): 383–98.
26 See Alex Esteller-More and Albert Sole-Olle, "Vertical Income Tax Externalities and Fiscal Interdependence: Evidence from the US," *Regional Science and Urban Economics* 31 (2001): 247–72.
27 This is achieved by the residence state giving a deduction for income taxable in the work state.
28 Some states have traditionally taxed services based on the place of production.
29 The SSUTA was formed primarily as a state response to the Supreme Court ruling in the *Quill* case and in light of the rapidly growing extent of cross-border shopping.
30 See http://www.whitehouse.gov/omb/budget/fy2006/hist.html.
31 For some comparisons across countries, see Richard M. Bird and François Vaillancourt, "Fiscal Decentralization in Developing Countries: An Overview," in *Fiscal Decentralization in Developing Countries*, ed. Richard M. Bird and Francois Vaillancourt, 1–48 (Cambridge: Cambridge University Press, 1998).

32 For example, Medicaid is a matching program with the state contribution inversely related to state per capita personal income.
33 See Daphne A. Kenyon and John Kincaid, "Fiscal Federalism in the United States: The Reluctance to Equalize Jurisdictions," in *Finanzverfassung im Spannungsfeld zwischen Zentrslstaat und Gliedstaaten*, ed. Werner W. Pommerehne and George Ress, 34–56 (Baden-Baden: Nomos Veglagsgesellschaft, 1996).
34 This benefit is only available to people who itemize certain expenditures when calculating their federal income tax liability rather than using the standard deduction.
35 See the US Bureau of the Census at http://www.census.gov/govs/estimate/03sloous.html
36 See William F. Fox and Matthew Murray, "Intergovernmental Aspects of Growth and Stabilization Policy" in *Intergovernmental Fiscal Relations: Perspectives and Prospects*, ed. Ron Fisher, 241–288, (Boston: Kluwer Press, 1997).
37 See US Bureau of the Census, Census of Governments.
38 See http://www.taxreformpanel.gov/final-report/
39 See William F. Fox, "Three Characteristics of Tax Structures have Contributed to the Current State Fiscal Crises," *State Tax Notes* 29 (2003): 375–83.
40 See Corina Eckl, "States Broaden the Scope of Rainy Day Funds," National Conference of State Legislatures, 21 February 2006.
41 Perhaps the largest change is that state reliance on the individual income and sales taxes has tended to grow, and dependence on selective sales taxes has tended to fall.

Comparative Conclusions on Fiscal Federalism

ANWAR SHAH[1]

Fiscal federalism is concerned with the public finances of the various orders of government in a federal system. Federal countries differ a great deal in their choices – specifically, how the division of fiscal powers is allocated among various orders and the associated fiscal arrangements. Further, some aspects of fiscal arrangements, such as intergovernmental fiscal transfers, resulting from these choices can be subject to periodic review (e.g., the five-year sunset clause in Canada) and redefinition in order to adapt to changing circumstances within and beyond nations. Changes in these arrangements may also occur simply as a result of how various constitutional provisions and laws are interpreted by courts (as in Australia and the United States) or by various orders of government, as in all federal countries. In recent years, these choices have come under significant additional strain from the great changes arising from the information revolution and the emergence of a "borderless" world economy. This chapter reviews the practice of fiscal federalism in twelve case study countries and highlights the findings and lessons from these experiences.

Section 1 of this chapter provides a general discussion of the fiscal federalism features of selected federations. This is followed by comparative reflections on the division of fiscal powers in section 2. The allocation of spending and regulatory responsibilities is discussed, and attention is paid to issues in revenue-raising responsibilities, including the financing of capital investments. Issues in macroeconomic management and economic coordination are discussed in section 3. Section 4 highlights the practice of intergovernmental fiscal transfers and pays special attention to transfers whose purpose is to reduce regional fiscal disparities. A final section draws some general conclusions from these experiences.

Comparative Conclusions 371

1 SALIENT FEATURES OF SELECTED FEDERATIONS

The twelve federations (of these Spain and South Africa have unitary constitutions but are considered quasi-federations in practice) reviewed in this book represent a diverse sample in terms of demographics, level of economic development, affinity with stylized models of federalism, and features of fiscal federalism. In our sample, Switzerland is the smallest and the second richest federation with a population of 8 million and a per capita GDP of $37,465 (2002). India is the largest and poorest federation, with a population of 1.1 billion and a per capita GDP of $666 (2004) (see table 1). The sample federations also present diverse models of federalism. Australia, India, and Russia bear affinity to the layer-cake model of dual federalism, with a strong national-government role in the federal system. Under such a model, the responsibilities of the federal and state governments are distinct and separate, and there is a hierarchical relationship among the various orders of government, with the federal government at the apex. In India, the federal government has the residual powers and paramountcy on the shared rule, and it can even change state boundaries. Both Spain and Malaysia can be characterized as asymmetric layer-cake models of dual federalism. In Spain, Navarre and the Basque country and, to a lesser extent, the states of Sabah and Sarawak in Malaysia enjoy autonomous status and are treated more equally than are other constituent units of the federation. Canada, Switzerland, and the United States resemble the coordinate-authority model of dual federalism. Under the coordinate-authority model of dual federalism, states enjoy significant autonomy, and local governments are simply creatures of the states with a limited or no direct relationship with the federal government. Germany and South Africa embody features of cooperative federalism with interdependent (hierarchical) spheres of government, but in these countries the federal government assumes an almost exclusive role in legislative authority for policy and standards, and the intermediate order primarily acts as the implementing agent. Nigeria has a three-tier hierarchical system with a strong federal government. Brazil, by contrast, presents itself as a cooperative-federalism model with three independent spheres of government. Brazil, India, Nigeria, and South Africa have constitutionally recognized local governments, whereas in all other federations local governments are creatures of the regional (province/state) governments.

Countries with a federal form of government vary considerably in terms of federal influence on state governments. Such influence is very strong in Australia, Germany, India, Malaysia, Nigeria, Russia, Spain, and South Africa; it is weak in Brazil, Canada, Switzerland, and the United

Table 1
A comparison of selected fiscal systems

Selected indicators	Australia	Brazil	Canada	Germany	India	Malaysia	Nigeria	Russia	Spain	South Africa	Switzerland	United States
2004 Population (million)	20	184	32	82	1090	24	130	144	40	47	8	296
Area (000 sq. km.)	7687	8512	9985	357	3288	330	924	17075	505	1223	41	9631
2004 GDP per capita (US$000)	32	4	35	33	0.7	5	0.5	4	24	5	37 (2002)	42
Character of federalism*	Dual LC	Cooperative, independent	Dual CA	Cooperative interdependent	Dual CA	Dual LC, asymmetric	Cooperative, interdependent	Dual LC	Dual LC asymmetric	Cooperative interdependent	Dual CA	Dual CA
The character of fiscal federalism	2-tier centralized	3-tier decentralized	2-tier decentralized	2-tier centralized integrated	3-tier centralized	2-tier centralized	3-tier centralized	2-tier centralized	2-tier centralized	3-tier centralized	2-tier decentralized	2-tier decentralized
Local government constitutional status	No	Yes	No	No	Yes	No	Yes	No	No	Yes	Yes	No
Actual state control of local government	Strong	Weak	Strong	Strong	Strong	Strong	Strong	Strong	Strong	Strong	Strong	Varies from fairly strong to fairly weak
Range of local government responsibilities	Limited	Extensive	Extensive	Limited	Limited	Limited	Limited	Limited	Limited	Limited	Extensive	Extensive
Federal/interstate equalization performance	Strong; revenue and expenditure	Fair	Strong; revenue disparities reduced	Strong; revenue and some expenditure	Fair	Fair	Fair	Fair	Fair	Fair	Fair	Weak

Table 1
A comparison of selected fiscal systems (Continued)

Selected indicators	Australia	Brazil	Canada	Germany	India	Malaysia	Nigeria	Russia	Spain	South Africa	Switzerland	United States
Output-based conditional transfers	disparities reduced substantially No	Yes	substantially Yes	disparities reduced substantially No	No	No	No	No	No	No	No	Yes
State tax performance	Weak	Strong	Strong	Strong	Fair	Weak	Weak	Fair	Fair	Weak	Strong	Strong
Local fiscal autonomy	Fair	Fair	Strong	Fair	Weak	Weak	Weak	Fair	Fair	Fair	Strong	Strong
Equalization formula	Paternal capacity and need	Implicit and piecemeal	Paternal fiscal capacity	Fraternal fiscal capacity	Implicit and piecemeal	Paternal capacity and need	Implicit and piecemeal	Paternal fiscal capacity	Implicit	Paternal capacity and need	Mixed capacity and need	Implicit and piecemeal
Equalization standard	Implicit	Implicit	Explicit	Explicit	Implicit	Iimplicit	Implicit	Explicit	Implicit	Implicit	Implicit	None
State tax base conformity	Yes	No	Yes	Yes	No	Yes	Yes	Yes	Yes	Yes	No	No
State tax rate uniformity	Yes	Yes	No	Yes	No	No	Yes	No	No	Yes	No	No
State-local gross revenues more or less match responsibility	Yes	Yes	Yes	Yes	No	No	No	No	Yes	Yes	Yes	Yes

Note. * – constitutionally recognized fiscal tiers; LC – layer cake model; CA – coordinate authority model
Source: Author's impressions

States. In the latter group of countries, federal influence over state expenditures is quite limited, and state governments have considerable authority to determine their own tax bases and tax rates (see tables 2 and 3). In centralized federations, conditional grants by the federal government play a large role in influencing the priorities of regional and local governments. In Australia, a centralized federation, the federal government is constitutionally required to follow regionally differentiated policies.

Federal countries also vary according to the process of provincial/ state influence on national policies. In some countries, there is a clear separation of national and state institutions ("executive" or "interstate" federalism) and the two levels interact through meetings of officials and ministers, as in Australia, Brazil, Canada, India, Malaysia, Nigeria, Spain, and Switzerland. In Germany and South Africa, state governments have a direct voice in national institutions; that is, in both these countries, state governments are represented in the second house of parliament – the *Bundesrat* in Germany and the Council of the Provinces in South Africa ("intrastate" federalism). This is to be expected in view of the primacy of national legislation in all functions and the need for state government inputs for such legislation in these countries. Such arrangements, however, limit the autonomy of both the federal and state governments in Germany, creating an indecision trap associated with this "spaghetti-bowl" politics, as suggested by Feld and von Hagen (see chapter on Germany). In Russia, the Federation Council (upper chamber), as envisaged by the Constitution, was expected to have the governor and the speaker of the legislature of each region represented in it. The Constitution has now been amended to have the one executive member nominated by the governor and the one legislative assembly member nominated by the legislative assembly of each region represented in the Federation Council, thereby weakening the regional influence at the centre. This comes in the wake of an important change in the election of governors – no longer directly elected but nominated by Russia's president and appointed by the regional legislature. In Brazil, India, Malaysia, and the United States, regional and local coalitions play an important role in the second chamber of the national legislature. This role may not support the positions taken by states' executives and therefore works to diffuse regional tensions. In Brazil, because all states have equal representation in the Senate, small states in the northeast have a disproportionate influence on the federal system. In Canada, the members of the second chamber are nominated by the prime minister; therefore, the Senate is considered to be more technocratic in its orientation as members are often appointed based upon recognition of their service achievements in government, politics, or business.

Table 2
Fiscal decentralization to provinces/states

Country	Range of provincial/state government responsibilities	Provincial government influence on national policies	National government influence on provincial policies	Provincial/state revenues finance majority of provincial expenditure	Federal-state intergovernmental transfers: Important/unimportant	Predominant emphasis on conditional grants/unconditional grants/tax sharing/revenue sharing	Fiscal capacity equalization	Expenditure needs equalization	Ability to borrow from domestic banks/higher orders of government	Ability to issue domestic bonds	Ability to borrow from foreign banks	Ability to issue foreign bonds	Overall fiscal decentralization to provinces/states
Australia	Extensive	Weak	Strong	No	Important	Unconditional grants and conditional grants	Yes	Yes	Yes	Yes	Yes	Yes	High
Brazil	Extensive	Fair	Fair	Yes	Important	Revenue sharing and conditional grants	No	Yes	No	Yes	No	Yes	High
Canada	Extensive	Strong	Weak	Yes	Important	Equalization and conditional grants	Yes	No	Yes	Yes	Yes	Yes	High
Germany	Extensive	Strong	Strong	Yes	Important	Equalization and conditional grants	Yes	No	Yes	Yes	Yes	Yes	Medium
India	Extensive	Fair	Strong	Yes	Important	Revenue sharing & conditional grants	No	Yes	Yes	Yes	No	No	Medium
Malaysia	Limited	Weak	Strong	No	Important	Revenue sharing	No	Yes	Yes	Yes	No	No	Low

Table 2
Fiscal decentralization to provinces/states (Continued)

Country	Range of provincial/state government responsibilities	Provincial government influence on national policies	National government influence on provincial policies	Provincial/state revenues finance majority of provincial expenditure	Federal-state intergovernmental transfers: Important/unimportant	Predominant emphasis on conditional grants/unconditional grants/tax sharing/revenue sharing	Fiscal capacity equalization	Expenditure needs equalization	Ability to borrow from domestic banks/higher orders of government	Ability to issue domestic bonds	Ability to borrow from foreign banks	Ability to issue foreign bonds	Overall fiscal decentralization to provinces/states
Nigeria	Extensive	Fair	Strong	No	Important	Revenue sharing and conditional grants	No	Yes	Yes	Yes	No	No	Medium
Russia	Extensive	Weak	Strong	No	Important	Equalization and conditional grants	Yes	Yes	Yes	Yes	Yes	No	Medium
Spain	Extensive	Fair	Strong	Yes	Important	Revenue sharing, and conditional grants	No	Yes	Yes	Yes	Yes	Yes	Medium
South Africa	Extensive	Weak	Strong	No	Important	Unconditional grants and conditional grants	No	Yes	Yes	Yes	No	No	Low
Switzerland	Extensive	Strong	Weak	Yes	Important	Equalization and conditional grants	Yes	Yes	Yes	Yes	Yes	Yes	High
United States	Extensive	Fair	Fair	Yes	Unimportant	Conditional grants	No	No	Yes	Yes	Yes	Yes	High

Table 3
Fiscal decentralization to local governments

Country	Local governments are creatures of provinces/states	Range of local government responsibilities	Local government influence on state/provincial policy	Local government influence on federal policy	Local fiscal capacity equalization	Local expenditure needs equalization	Ability to borrow from domestic banks	Ability to issue domestic bonds	Overall fiscal decentralization to local governments
Australia	Yes	Limited	Weak	Weak	Yes	Yes	Yes	No	Low
Brazil	No	Extensive	Weak	Weak	No	Yes	No	Yes	High
Canada	Yes	Extensive	Weak	Weak	Yes	Yes	Yes	Yes	High
Germany	Yes	Extensive	Weak	Weak	Yes	Yes	Yes	Yes	High
India	Yes	Limited	Weak	Weak	No	Yes	No	Yes	Low
Malaysia	Yes	Limited	Weak	Weak	No	Yes	No	No	Low
Nigeria	No	Extensive	Weak	Weak	No	Yes	Yes	Yes	Medium
Russia	Yes	Extensive	Weak	Weak	Yes	Yes	Yes	Yes	Medium
Spain	Yes	Extensive	Weak	Weak	Yes	Yes	Yes	Yes	Medium
South Africa	No	Extensive	Weak	Fair	No	Yes	Yes	Yes	High
Switzerland	Yes	Extensive	Fair	Fair	Yes	Yes	Yes	Yes	High
United States	Yes	Extensive	Weak	Weak	No	Yes	Yes	Yes	High

In some federal countries, constitutional provisions require all legislation to recognize that ultimate power rests with the people. For example, all legislation in Canada must conform to the Canadian Charter of Rights. In Switzerland, a confederation by law but a federal country in practice, direct-democracy provisions empower citizens to hold government to account (e.g., all major legislative changes require approval by referendum). In Malaysia, the Clients' Charter empowers citizens to hold governments to account in the event specified public service standards are not met.

Regional income disparities, however, are significant in most of the case study countries. These disparities are the largest for South Africa and the smallest for the United States.

2 DIVISION OF FISCAL POWERS

Allocation of Spending and Regulatory Powers

The constitutional division of power on the spending and regulatory responsibilities in the case study countries generally conforms to the subsidiarity principle. India, Malaysia, and South Africa are the exceptions, where, responding to historical legacies, a dominant federal role was carved out by the constitution and, in the case of India, further cemented by a centrally appointed unified civil service. The practice in most federal countries, as a result of historical, cultural, and institutional factors and legal-judicial interpretations varies widely, and most federal countries, with the exception of Canada, have allowed a wider federal role than originally envisaged by the framers of the constitution. The original federal role was largely limited to services of national scope such as "peace, order and good government." This role was later expanded due to wars and judicial interpretation of the constitution, as in Australia and the United States; threats of secession, as in India and Russia; issues in combating terrorism and promoting racial equality, as in the United States; natural-resource management and environmental protection, as in Brazil, Nigeria, and the United States; debt management and fiscal discipline, as in Brazil; protection of the indigenous majority, as in Malaysia; or, more commonly, federal use of regulatory or spending powers in order to achieve national objectives in securing a common economic union, as in most of the case study countries. The use of federal regulatory powers often results in unfunded or underfunded mandates, whereas the use of conditional matching grants can lead to fiscal stress for regional and local governments.

The overall role of the intermediate orders of government is the strongest in Switzerland and Canada; fairly strong in the United States, Brazil, and Australia; and relatively weak in other federations, with the weakest

Figure 1
Subnational expenditure as a % of total government expenditure

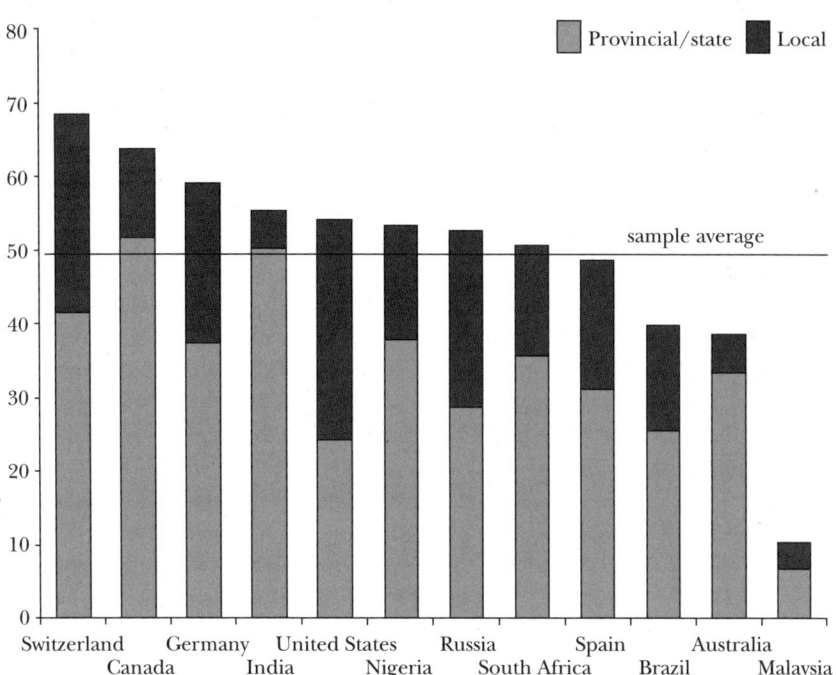

Sources: Various chapters in this volume; *Government Finance Statistics Yearbook* (various issues) Washington, DC: International Monetary Fund.

being in South Africa. However, this role remains large in all the case study countries with regard to the delivery of social and infrastructure services, with the exceptions of Malaysia and South Africa, where such services are centralized. In Canada, provinces have a role in immigration policy and in regulating securities and labour markets, thus creating the potential for inefficiencies in the internal common market.

Local government responsibilities are extensive in Switzerland, the United States, Brazil, and Canada; quite restricted in Spain, India, Russia and Malaysia; and highly constrained in Australia (see figure 1). In Spain, basic education and basic health care are intermediate-order responsibilities. In Russia, several local services, such as public transit, roads, and fire prevention, are regional government functions, whereas local police protection and local tax collection are federal responsibilities. In Australia, local governments play an insignificant role in public service delivery and are primarily responsible for property-oriented services such as garbage collection and street maintenance and cleaning.

Overall, with the exception of Spain, Brazil, Australia, and Malaysia, subnational expenditures in the case study countries account for 50 percent or more of consolidated public expenditures, with state and local governments in Switzerland and Canada accounting for more than 60 percent of such expenditures (see Figure 1).

Shared rule is sometimes a source of confusion and conflict. In Canada, the provinces have attempted to limit the federal spending power in social services by entering into a social union framework agreement with the federal government. In Germany, where the intertwining of federal and state powers is an issue, the Federalism Reform Act, 2006, limits federal laws requiring the consent of the *Bundesrat* (second chamber) to specified areas and also gives states flexibility to deviate from a federal law in its implementation. In Switzerland, ambiguity with regard to shared rule is avoided by having intergovernmental agreements and contracts. In the United States, Russia, and South Africa, unfunded or underfunded federal mandates represent sources of concern for state (province/region) governments.

Allocation of taxing Powers

Taxing powers (tax base and rate determination and tax collection) are highly centralized (75 percent or more central revenues) in Malaysia, South Africa, and Australia; centralized (60 percent to 75 percent of revenues collected by the centre) in Brazil, India, Russia, and the United States; highly decentralized in Switzerland (37 percent of total revenues collected by the centre); and decentralized (40 per cent to 50 percent at the centre) in Canada and Nigeria. Other countries fall in the intermediate range. In Russia, the centralization of tax administration has resulted in a weaker effort in collecting state (regional) and local taxes.

The tax powers of state governments are wide in Switzerland, Canada, the United States, Brazil, and Nigeria and are quite restrained in South Africa, Australia, Spain, and Malaysia (figure 2). Expenditure autonomy as determined by the percentage of expenditures financed by the own-source revenues of states is high in Malaysia, Nigeria, Switzerland, Germany, Canada, and the United States but low in India and Spain (with the exception of the two regions) (figure 3). State tax autonomy (having responsibility for base and rate determination of own taxes) is high in Australia, Canada, Switzerland, the United States, Nigeria, India, and Brazil but constrained in Germany, Spain, Malaysia, and Russia. In the latter countries, states may be given some discretion in setting tax rates but tax-base determination is a federal responsibility. Further, regional governments in Russia do not have revenue autonomy. Taxing e-commerce and mobile factors are important issues imposing limitations on state finances in the United States and India.

Figure 2
Subnational own-revenues as a % of subnational expenditure

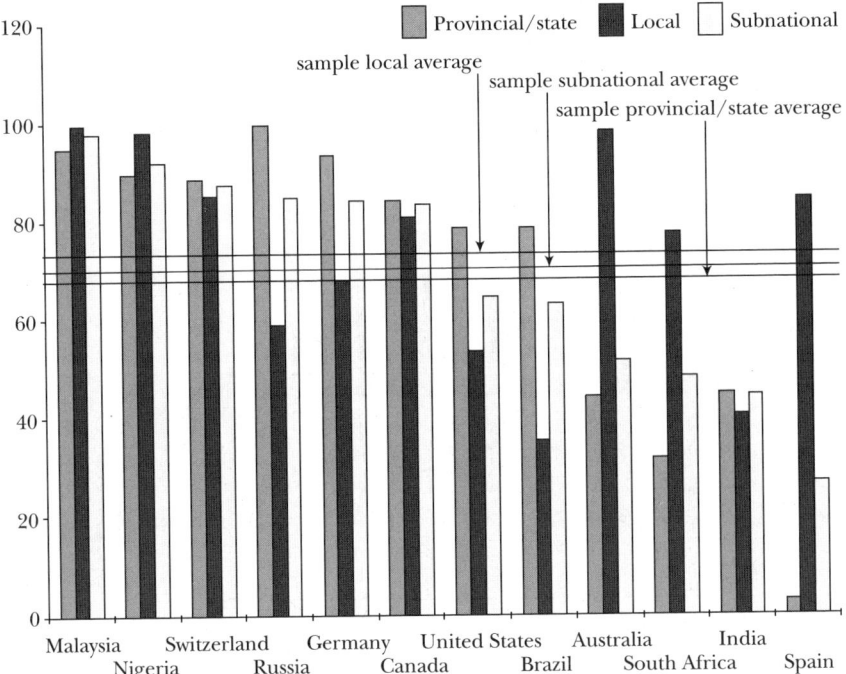

Sources: Various chapters in this volume; *Government Finance Statistics Yearbook* (various issues) Washington, DC: International Monetary Fund.

The income and the sales tax system is harmonized in Australia, Canada, Germany, Malaysia, Russia, Spain, and Switzerland; it is not harmonized in Brazil, India, and the United States. The lack of a harmonized tax system leads to high compliance costs for firms and individuals operating in a multi-state environment. In the United States, the federal Constitution's interstate commerce clause acts as a break against state taxes distorting interstate commerce; in addition, states are prohibited from taxing internal and external trade. In India, on the contrary, taxes on the interstate trade of goods is an important source of state revenues. In Brazil, sales taxation is uncoordinated among the federal, state, and local governments. The Brazilian Council of State Finance Ministers (CONFAZ) has attempted to harmonize the state VATs but with limited success. Fiscal incentives through the state VAT system in Brazil have resulted in fiscal wars among states. In Canada, income tax harmonization was achieved through offering federal incentives to follow a common tax base. Sales tax harmonization through similar incentives had only partial success. Canada also introduced an important innovation in the

Figure 3
Subnational own source revenues resources as a % of total government revenues

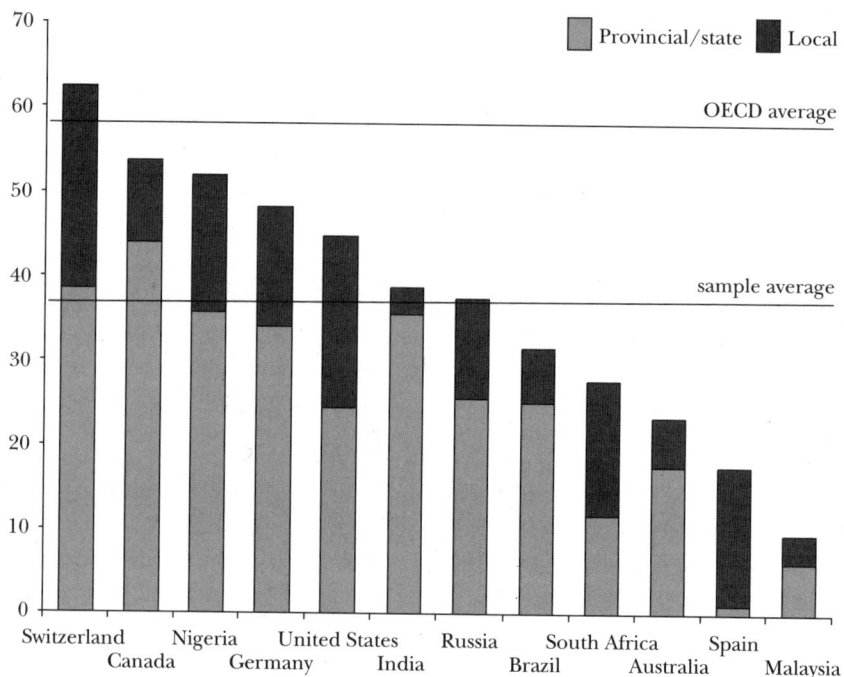

Sources: Various chapters in this volume; *Government Finance Statistics Yearbook* (various issues) Washington, DC: International Monetary Fund.

institutionalization of tax administration by creating an independent agency with oversight by federal and provincial orders and the private sector. In other countries, tax harmonization has been achieved by centralizing tax-base determination and/or tax collection.

The case study countries, with the exception of Nigeria, follow the golden rule principle in borrowing (i.e., borrowing for capital spending only), and they primarily depend on capital-market discipline to restrain such borrowing by state and local governments. In Nigeria, all borrowings by state and local governments require prior federal approval. In Malaysia, local borrowing is subject to state government supervision. Such direct borrowing is typically discouraged; instead, private-sector participation in infrastructure provision is encouraged. In Brazil, external debt requires approval by the federal Senate, and all borrowing is subject to legislated fiscal rules. Several federal countries have special arrangements to assist state and local borrowing for capital projects. In Australia, the Australian Loan Council facilitates such borrowing by making data on public finances available to the capital markets. In Canada, provincial Crown corporations that run on commercial principles assist local borrowing. In the United States, state bond banks (private agencies) collate local borrowing demands and issue bonds for the pooled demand. Also in the United States, interest on such borrowing by state and local governments is deductible against federal income-tax liability – providing a direct federal subsidy for such borrowing. In Switzerland, the Cooperative Centre of Swiss Local Communities provides capital finance to local governments.

There is no evidence of a race to the bottom due to state and local tax autonomy in the case study countries. Most countries do not show any serious tax competition, and where such competition has surfaced – such as in Brazil, Switzerland, and, to a more limited extent, India, Canada, and the United States – it has not resulted in a lower tax effort and lower quality of state and local public services.

In general, taxing powers in the sample countries are more centralized than dictated by fiscal federalism principles. Many factors may have been involved in achieving this result. This may have happened partly because most nations placed a premium on tax harmonization. Also, shifting expenditures downward was politically more feasible than allowing finance to follow function, and state and local politicians were less than enthusiastic about assuming taxing powers but very interested in receiving fiscal transfers from the national government with little accountability to local taxpayers.

Vertical Fiscal Gaps

A downside of over-centralized tax powers with decentralized expenditure responsibility is the creation of vertical fiscal gaps, or the mismatch between revenue means and expenditure needs among state and local governments (see table 4 for details). Vertical fiscal gaps and revenue autonomy in subnational governments remain concerns in those federal countries where the centralization of taxing powers is greater than is necessary to meet federal expenditures and federal fiscal transfers to meet national objectives as this results in extensive use of conditional transfers to exert undue influence on subnational policies. Further, such large gaps create democratic accountability deficits as state and local governments experience the pleasure of spending money without having to justify additional spending to their taxpayers. This is a concern for state governments in Australia, Germany, India, Malaysia, Nigeria, Russia, Spain, and South Africa. In Nigeria, there is a special concern about the central assignment of resource revenues. In Germany, these concerns are prompting a wider review of the assignment problem and a rethinking of the division of powers among federal, *Land*, and local governments. A consensus is yet to be formed on a new vision of fiscal federalism in Germany.

Table 4
Vertical fiscal gaps

Country	Level of government	Revenue share		Expenditure share	Fiscal gap	
		Before transfer	After transfer		Before transfer	After transfer
Australia (2003–04)	National	0.76	0.56	0.61	0.15	−0.06
	Provincial/state	0.18	0.37	0.34	−0.16	0.04
	Local	0.06	0.07	0.05	0.01	0.02
Brazil (2003)	National	0.68	0.55	0.60	0.08	−0.05
	Provincial/state	0.25	0.27	0.26	0.00	0.01
	Local	0.06	0.18	0.14	−0.08	0.04
Canada (2005)	National	0.46	0.42	0.36	0.10	0.06
	Provincial/state	0.44	0.48	0.52	−0.08	−0.04
	Local	0.10	0.10	0.12	−0.02	−0.02
Germany (2002)	National	0.52	0.40	0.41	0.11	−0.01
	Provincial/state	0.34	0.37	0.37	−0.03	−0.01
	Local	0.14	0.23	0.22	−0.08	0.02
India (2002)	National	0.61	0.42	0.45	0.17	−0.03
	Provincial/state	0.36	0.53	0.50	−0.15	0.03
	Local	0.03	0.05	0.05	−0.02	0.00
Malaysia (2003)	National	0.91	0.85	0.90	0.01	−0.05
	Provincial/state	0.06	0.09	0.07	−0.01	0.02
	Local	0.03	0.06	0.03	0.00	0.03
Nigeria (2004)	National	0.48	0.43	0.46	0.02	−0.03
	Provincial/state	0.36	0.40	0.38	−0.02	0.02
	Local	0.16	0.17	0.16	0.00	0.01
Russia (2004)	National	0.63	0.55	0.47	0.15	0.07
	Provincial/state	0.26	0.28	0.29	−0.03	0.00
	Local	0.12	0.17	0.24	−0.12	−0.07
Spain (2002)	National	0.53	0.27	0.51	0.02	−0.24
	Provincial/state	0.29	0.49	0.31	−0.03	0.17
	Local	0.18	0.24	0.18	0.01	0.07

Table 4
Vertical fiscal gaps (*Continued*)

Country	Level of government	Revenue share		Expenditure share	Fiscal gap	
		Before transfer	After transfer		Before transfer	After transfer
South Africa (2002)	National	0.82	0.36	0.49	0.33	−0.13
	Provincial/state	0.01	0.46	0.36	−0.34	0.10
	Local	0.16	0.18	0.15	0.01	0.03
Switzerland (2002)	National	0.37	0.30	0.31	0.06	−0.01
	Provincial/state	0.38	0.42	0.42	−0.03	0.00
	Local	0.24	0.28	0.27	−0.03	0.01
United States (2004)	National	0.55	0.44	0.46	0.09	−0.02
	Provincial/state	0.25	0.29	0.24	0.01	0.05
	Local	0.20	0.27	0.30	−0.10	−0.03

Sources: Various chapters in this volume; *Government Finance Statistics Yearbook* (various issues) Washington, DC: International Monetary Fund.

3 FISCAL FEDERALISM AND MACROECONOMIC MANAGEMENT

Federal fiscal systems aspire to provide safeguards against the threat of centralized exploitation as well as decentralized opportunistic behaviour while decision making remains close to the people. In fact, federalism represents either a "coming together" or a "holding together" of constituent geographic units to take advantage of the greatness and littleness of nations. But federal fiscal systems whose purpose is to accommodate such "coming together" or "holding together" may pose some risks for macro stability. Two main issues raised by the case study countries on this count are (1) fiscal discipline and (2) intergovernmental competition.

Fiscal Prudence and Fiscal Discipline under "Fend-for-Yourself" Federalism

Fiscal lack of discipline among subnational governments is a matter of concern in federal countries in view of significant subnational autonomy combined with an opportunity for a federal bailout. In mature federations, fiscal policy coordination to sustain fiscal discipline is exercised through both executive and legislative federalism as well as by instituting formal and informal fiscal rules. In recent years, legislated fiscal rules have come to command greater attention. These rules take the form of budgetary balance controls, debt restrictions, tax or expenditure controls, and referendums for new taxing and spending initiatives. Most mature federations also specify "no bailout" provisions in setting up central banks. In the presence of an explicit or even implicit bailout guarantee and preferential loans from the banking sector, printing of money by subnational governments is possible, thereby fuelling inflation. Recent experiences with fiscal adjustment programs suggest that, while legislated fiscal rules are neither necessary nor sufficient for successful fiscal adjustment, they can help forge a sustained political commitment to achieve better fiscal outcomes, especially in countries with divisive political institutions or coalition regimes. For example, such rules can be helpful in sustaining political commitment to reform in countries with proportional representation (Brazil) or multi-party coalition governments (India) or in countries with a separation of legislative and executive functions (United States and Brazil). Fiscal rules in such countries can help restrain pork-barrel politics and thereby improve fiscal discipline, as has been demonstrated by the experiences in Brazil, India, Spain, Russia, and South Africa.

Brazil's success with fiscal rules from 2001–07 is particularly remarkable. Germany, however, could not achieve fiscal discipline on the part of the Länder, even with fiscal rules, because the federal Constitutional Court had blessed federal bailouts, thereby creating soft budget constraints for them. A more recent decision (November 2006) by the same court to disallow a requested bailout by Berlin indicates a reversal of such policies. In the United States, fiscal conservatism on the part of states ensures fiscal discipline, but pork-barrel politics in the federal government has not been restrained by fiscal rules. Australia and Canada achieved the same results without having any legislated fiscal rules, whereas fiscal discipline continues to be a problem even though Germany has legislated fiscal rules. The Swiss experience is the most instructive with regard to sustained fiscal discipline. Two important instruments create incentives for cantons to maintain fiscal discipline. First, fiscal referendums allow citizens the opportunity to veto any government program; second, the legal provision enacted in some cantons to set aside a fraction of a fiscal surplus in good times works like a "debt brake" for rainy days (in the United States, these are called rainy-day funds).

Intergovernmental Competition

Competition among state and local governments is quite common in most federal systems. It occurs through lobbying for employment by: generating federal or private-sector projects, including military bases; encouraging domestic and foreign direct investment; providing incentives and subsidies for attracting capital and labour; supplying public infrastructure to facilitate business location; providing a differentiated menu of local public services; offering one-stop windows for licensing and registration; and pursuing endless other ways of demonstrating an open-door policy for new capital and skilled labour. State and local governments also compete among themselves by erecting trade and tariff walls to protect local industry and business. They also try to out-compete each other in exporting tax burdens to non-residents and obtaining a higher share of federal fiscal transfers where feasible.

Preserving intergovernmental competition and decentralized decision making are important for responsive and accountable local governance in federal countries. The Swiss and the American experiences demonstrate the positive impacts of such a competition. "Beggar-thy-neighbour" policies have the potential to undermine these gains from decentralized decision making, as demonstrated by the recent "race to the bottom" experience in Spain and the so-called "fiscal wars" in Brazil and Switzerland. State inheritance taxes have been eliminated through interjurisdictional competition for rich residents in Australia, Canada, and Switzerland. In Switzerland, such competition is further advanced through regressive income tax schedules. Mergers of cantons to abate such competition in Switzerland have been ruled out by referendums. To limit the adverse effects of such competition, a partnership approach that facilitates a common economic union through the free mobility of factors by ensuring common minimum standards of public services, no barriers to trade, and wider information and technological access offers the best policy alternative in regional integration and internal cohesion within federal nations. It is not a matter of "to compete or to cooperate" but, rather, of how to make sure that all parties compete and cooperate but do not cheat.

4 INTERGOVERNMENTAL FISCAL TRANSFERS

In all the case study countries, the federal government collects more revenue than is needed to satisfy its own expenditure/regulatory responsibilities. Such fiscal surplus enables the federal government to use its spending power to pursue national objectives through the use of fiscal transfers. These transfers help achieve national objectives while supporting decentralized decision making. Federal government fiscal transfers finance nearly two-thirds of subnational expenditures in Spain and South Africa and less than 20 percent of such expenditures in Canada, Switzerland, and Nigeria (figure 4). The design of such transfers plays a critical role for efficiency, equity, and accountability in a federal system. Three important objectives of such transfers in the case study countries are (1) bridging

Figure 4
Transfers as a % of subnational expenditure

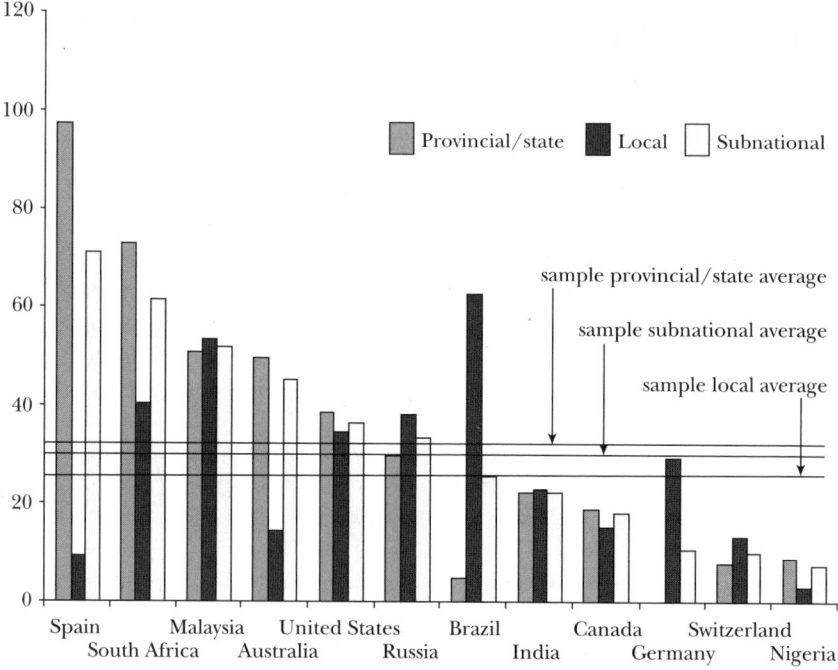

Sources: Various chapters in this volume; *Government Finance Statistics Yearbook* (various issues) Washington, DC: International Monetary Fund.

vertical fiscal gaps, (2) bridging the fiscal divide within nations, and (3) securing a common economic union through establishing national minimum standards in social and infrastructure services. The following paragraphs discuss how these objectives are addressed through fiscal transfers in the case study countries.

Bridging vertical fiscal gaps

Vertical fiscal gaps, at least at the conceptual level, are largely a non-issue in Canada, the United States, and Switzerland because state governments have sufficient fiscal powers to overcome such gaps. In Canada, the federal government used tax abatement as well as incentives for tax-base sharing to overcome such a gap in the past. These vertical gaps represent a significant issue in the remaining case study countries as they have centralized tax administration and constrained state and local taxing powers. To overcome such gaps, general revenue sharing, with a multitude of equalization components, is being used in Brazil, India, Malaysia, and Nigeria. Ironically, in India such revenue sharing uses 1971 population data as the basis for allocating finds among states; in Brazil, state and municipal coefficients are frozen at 1988 levels. Tax-base sharing and tax-by-tax sharing is used in Germany; fiscal need equalization grants are used in Australia, Russia, and Spain (mostly historical expenditures). For most countries in our sample, fiscal transfers reverse the fiscal position of the federal government from surplus to deficit (see table 4).

Bridging the fiscal divide within nations

The fiscal divide within nations represents an important element of the economic divide within nations. Such a divide is a matter of concern in all the case study countries, with the important exception of the United States. In Canada, such a divide is accentuated by provincial ownership of natural resources and soaring oil and gas prices. Fiscal equalization programs, with the objective of enabling constituent units to provide reasonably comparable levels of public services at reasonably comparable levels of taxation, are frequently advocated to overcome such a divide. Such programs are expected to foster goods and factor mobility and help secure a common economic union.

Among the case study countries, Australia, Canada, Germany, Malaysia, Russia, Spain, and Switzerland attempt to address regional fiscal disparities through a program of fiscal equalization. In the United States, there is no federal program because factor mobility has served to bridge fiscal and economic differences to a great extent, although such differences within states remain a matter of policy concern. And, for that reason, state education finance typically uses equalization principles. In Canada, such a program is enshrined in the Canadian Constitution and is termed "the glue that holds the federation together." Such programs in the case study countries are federally financed, with the exception of Germany and Switzerland. In Germany, wealthy states make progressive contributions to the equalization pool, and the poor states receive from this pool. In Switzerland, the new equalization program, effective in 2008, has a mixed pool of contributions from the federal government and wealthier cantons. In Russia, equalization programs conducted by regions for local equalization use the mixed approach.

All the case study countries with an equalization program have some focus on fiscal-capacity equalization. Australia, in addition, has a comprehensive approach to fiscal-need equalization. Spain equalizes fiscal need based on historical expenditures, and both Russia and Malaysia consider partial equalization of expenditure needs based on selected need indicators. The Canadian and German equalization programs use an explicit fiscal-capacity standard of equalization that determines both the total pool as well as allocations across constituent units. Such a principled approach to equalization is desirable as it results in greater transparency and objectivity in allocating equalization payments. All other programs utilize a fixed pool but use allocation formulae to determine allocation across units.

The equity and efficiency implications of equalization programs are a source of continuing debate in most federal countries. In Australia, the complexity introduced by expenditure-needs compensation is an important source of discontent with the existing formula. In Canada, provincial ownership of natural resources is a major source of provincial fiscal disparities, and the treatment of natural-resource revenues in the equalization program remains contentious. In Germany, the applications of overly progressive equalization formulae result in a reversal of fortunes for some rich jurisdictions. Some rich Länder in Germany have, in the past, taken this matter to the Constitutional Court to limit their contributions to the equalization pool. In Spain, the asymmetric treatment of autonomous communities (charter regime) and the rest of the regions (common regime) for equalization purposes is a continuing source of contention. In Brazil, India, Malaysia, Nigeria, Russia, and South Africa, much controversy and debate is generated by the equity and efficiency impacts of existing programs. In Nigeria, arbitrary use of the Federation Account (resource revenue pool) to retire federal debt and revenue-sharing formula components, especially the 13 percent share for derivation component, are sources of concern (especially for the Niger delta region).

*Institutional Approaches to the Design
and Practice of Equalization Transfers*

The case study countries use diverse approaches to institutional arrangements for equalization transfers. These diverse arrangements have been designed to suit the contexts of individual countries. In Spain, Switzerland, Malaysia, Russia, and South Africa, the federal ministry of finance or treasury is responsible for decisions on the total pool and allocation among constituent units. In Brazil, the total pool is determined by the Constitution, and the federal Senate determines the allocation for state and local governments. In Australia, India, and Nigeria (semi-independent), independent grant commissions are entrusted with making recommendations on the formula for allocating such transfers, whereas the total pool is predetermined by legislation. In Canada, intergovernmental forums make the initial determination. These decisions are then endorsed and legislated by the federal Parliament and implemented by the federal Ministry of Finance. In Germany, a federal compact determines the allocation, which is legislated by the federal government and implemented by the Ministry of Finance.

While, on an a priori basis, no one institutional arrangement is preferable to another, experience has shown that independent grant commissions typically opt for greater complexity in designing such transfers, leading to much acrimony and debate. Leaving these decisions to the federal government alone, however, makes such transfers vulnerable to the whims of the regime in power. Intergovernmental forums offer a second-best alternative by having all relevant stakeholders involved in the decisions on such transfers.

Setting national minimum standards through output-based fiscal transfers

Setting national minimum standards in regional-local services serves both efficiency (creating an internal common market) and equity (treating all citizens equally regardless of their place of residence). Such standards can be attained by conditional non-matching grants, in which the conditions reflect national output-based efficiency and equity concerns and there is a financial penalty associated with failure to comply with any of the conditions. Conditions are thus imposed not on the specific use of grant funds but on the attainment of standards in quality, access, and level of services. Such output-based grants do not affect state-local government incentives for cost efficiency, but they do encourage compliance with nationally specified standards for access, quality, and level of services. Properly designed conditional non-matching output-based transfers can create incentives for innovative and competitive approaches to improved service delivery and results-based accountability in the public sector. Input-based grants fail to create such an accountability environment. Although output-based (performance-oriented) grants are best suited to the grantor's objectives and are simpler to administer than are traditional input-based conditional transfers, they are rarely practised in the sample federal countries. Prominent notable exceptions are education and health finance in Brazil, Canada, and South Africa, and highway finance in the United States. The reasons have to do with the incentives faced by politicians and bureaucrats. Such grants empower clients while weakening the sphere for opportunism and pork-barrel politics. The incentives they create strengthen the accountability of political and bureaucratic elites to citizens and weaken their ability to peddle influence and build bureaucratic empires. Their focus on value for money exposes corruption, inefficiency, and waste. Not surprisingly, this type of grant is opposed by potential losers.

In most of the case study countries, with a few notable exceptions, federal conditional grants use input-based conditionality. Such conditionality impairs state and local autonomy and is a source of conflict. Growing use of such grants is a matter of state and local concern in Australia, Germany, Spain, and Russia. Vertical fiscal gaps – differences between the revenue share and expenditure share before fiscal transfers – are very large for provinces in South Africa and states in Australia and India, but these are eliminated by fiscal transfers.

In Brazil and Canada, and to a limited extent in South Africa, education and health transfers focus on output and access-based conditionality. In the Unites States, federal fiscal transfers to state and local governments, with the important exception of highway grants, were in the past predominantly input-based conditional grant programs, although since the 1990s, an emphasis on shifting federal grants towards performance-based criteria is slowly emerging.

5 LESSONS LEARNED AND CONCLUDING REMARKS

The following lessons emerge from these diverse experiences.

- Clarity in responsibilities but periodic joint review is key to the successful working of the fiscal system. As Rudyard Kipling once said, there are 160 ways to design fiscal tiers, and every one of them is right. What matters is that constitutional and legal systems and institutions must provide for mechanisms to build societal consensus for new compacts in view of changing circumstances and be amenable to timely adjustments to implement such compacts.
- Asymmetric federalism arising from symmetric and uniform principles leads to amicable and sustainable outcomes.
- Finance should follow function to strengthen responsiveness and accountability to taxpayers.
- Fiscal rules accompanied by "gate keeper" intergovernmental committees provide a useful framework for fiscal discipline and fiscal policy coordination.
- To ensure fiscal discipline, all governments must be made to face the financial consequences of their decisions.
- Securing a common economic union through unimpeded goods and factor mobility and national minimum standards for social services and infrastructure is the best guarantee for political and economic stability and regional convergence in the long run.
- Institutional arrangements for managing intergovernmental conflicts play an important role in the smooth working of a federal system.
- Properly designed intergovernmental transfers can strengthen results-based accountability and also enhance competition for the supply of public goods, fiscal harmonization, state and local government accountability, and regional equity. Manna-from-heaven transfers or bilaterally negotiated transfers can build transfer dependencies that cause the slow economic strangulation of fiscally disadvantaged regions. All transfers must be open for periodic reviews.

- Societal norms and consensus on the roles of the various orders of government and limits to their authority are vital for the success of decentralized decision making. In the absence of such norms and consensus, direct central controls do not work, and intergovernmental gaming leads to dysfunctional constitutions. Direct-democracy provisions can be helpful in restraining governments.
- A clients' charter with specified standards of services and feedback and redress mechanisms can help strengthen government accountability to citizens.

In conclusion, the federal countries examined in this volume have shown a remarkable ability to adapt and to meet emerging challenges in fiscal federalism. While the challenges they face may be very similar, the solutions they discover and adopt are often unique and local. This represents a remarkable attestation to the triumph of the spirit of federalism in its never-ending quest for balance and excellence in responsive, responsible, and accountable governance. The long march to attain new heights in inclusive governance continues.

NOTES

1 The author is grateful to Professor John Kincaid for helpful comments.

Contributors

ROBIN BOADWAY is Sir Edward Peacock Professor of Economic Theory at Queen's University, Canada. He is a past president of the Canadian Economics Association and editor of the *Canadian Journal of Economics*, and he is currently editor of the *Journal of Public Economics*. He works in the areas of public-sector economics, with special emphasis on tax-transfer policies, fiscal federalism, and cost-benefit analysis. His books include *Public Sector Economics*; *Welfare Economics*; *Canadian Tax Policy*; *The Constitutional Division of Powers: An Economic Perspective*, *Equalization in a Federal State*; and *Intergovernmental Fiscal Relations in Canada*.

ALEXANDER DERYUGIN is the deputy director of the Center for Fiscal Policy, and he is intergovernmental relations team leader. He is supervising and participating in consulting projects covering the assignment of responsibilities across levels of public administration, the assignment of taxes, equalization and special purpose transfers, and tax policy issues in the Russian Federation and former Soviet Union countries. He is also involved in the development of legislation in the intergovernmental fiscal relations sphere and in the computer modelling of transfers and tax assignment formula for the Russian Federation and other CIS countries.

AKPAN HOGAN EKPO was former vice-chancellor, Federal University of Uyo, from 2000 to 2005 and is now pioneer vice-chancellor, Akwa Ibom State University of Technology, Uyo, Nigeria. He is a professor of economics and a member of the Board of the Central Bank of Nigeria. He obtained his PhD in economics from the University of Pittsburgh, Pennsylvania, in 1983. His areas of interest include economic theory and Public Finance. His recent (2005) publications include *Fiscal Theory and Policy: Selected Essays*; and *Macroeconomic Model of the Nigerian Economy*.

LARS P. FELD is full professor of economics, specializing in public economics, at the University of Heidelberg; a member of the Scientific Advisory Board to the German Federal Finance Ministry; research professor at the Centre for European Economic Research, Mannheim; managing editor of the *Perspektiven der Wirtschaftspolitik* of the Verein für Socialpolitik; and Research Fellow of the SIAW-HSG at the University of St Gallen, of CESifo at Munich, and of CREMA at Basel. His research interests include: public economics, public choice, and fiscal psychology. He has published numerous articles on economics.

WILLIAM FOX is the William B. Stokely Distinguished Professor of Business and the director of the Center for Business and Economic Research at the University of Tennessee. He is a past president and recipient of the Steven D. Gold Award from the National Tax Association and former chairman of the Department of Economics at the University of Tennessee. He has held visiting appointments as professor at the University of Hawaii, scholar at the Federal Reserve Bank of Kansas City, and Distinguished Fulbright Chair at the University of Frankfurt, Germany. Fox has served as a consultant in approximately twenty-five countries and more than ten American states.

BONGANI KHUMALO is program manager (fiscal policy analysis) in the Financial and Fiscal Commission. He joined the commission in 1999 as a researcher and worked in various areas, including the design of intergovernmental transfer formulae, the financing of education, the design and implementation of conditional grants, and the assignment of subnational revenue sources. On completing his MSC economics degree, Bongani was offered a lectureship teaching public finance at the University of Zimbabwe (1991–93). In 1994, he moved to Rhodes University in Grahamstown (RSA), where he lectured on public policy in the Department of Economics before taking the position of researcher with the Financial and Fiscal Commission.

GEBHARD KIRCHGÄSSNER is professor of economics and econometrics, and director of the Swiss Institute of International Economics and Applied Economic Research at the University of St Gallen since 1992. His degrees include: Diplomvolkswirt (MA in economics), University of Konstanz, 1973; Dr. rerum socialium (PhD in social sciences) University of Konstanz, 1976; Habilitation, University of Konstanz, 1981; and Habilitation, Swiss Federal Institute of Technology, Zürich, 1982. His fellowships and academic honours include: research fellow, CESifo Network, since 2001; member, German Academy of Natural Scientists, Leopoldina, Section Economics and Empirical Social Sciences, since 2001; and president, European Public Choice Society, 2003–05. His research areas are public choice and public economics, environmental and energy economics, applied econometrics, and methodological foundations of the social sciences.

GALINA KURLYANDSKAYA is the director general of the Center for Fiscal Policy, a Russian NGO that provides technical assistance to central, regional, and local governments in Russia and former Soviet Union countries in the area of fiscal reform and intergovernmental relations. She supervises and participates in consulting and research projects, assigning responsibilities across various levels of government, equalization transfers, unfunded mandates, and public expenditure reviews. Dr Kurlyandskaya is a member of the RF President's Commission on Federative Relations and Local Self-Government.

JULIO LÓPEZ LABORDA is professor of public economics at the University of Zaragoza, Spain. His areas of interest include fiscal federalism, distribution and redistribution of income, and economics of taxation. His recent publications in this area include "Personal Income Tax Decentralization, Inequality and Social Welfare" *Public Finance Review* 2005 (with Jorge Onrubia); and "Regional Decentralization in Spain: Vertical Imbalances and Revenue Assignments" *Edward Elgar* (2007) (with Carlos Monasterio).

JORGE MARTINEZ-VAZQUEZ is professor of economics and director of the International Studies, Andrew Young School of Policy Studies, Georgia State University. He is a member of the Editorial Board of Public Budgeting and Finance, Hacienda Pública Española, and Urban Public Economics Review. His research interests are in the area of public economics, with emphasis on fiscal decentralization, tax policy, and public expenditure management. He has managed fiscal reform projects and worked as an advisor in over forty-five countries. His recent books include *Fiscal Equalization*; *Fighting Corruption in the Public Sector*; *Local Government Finance Reform*; and *Fiscal Reform in Spain*.

RENOSI MOKATE is the deputy governor of the South African Reserve Bank. She was previously the chairperson/CEO of the Financial and Fiscal Commission. Her areas of specialization are development economics, urban economics, and policy analysis. She has held various posts, including those of associate professor of economics at Lincoln University, Pennsylvania, USA; Senior policy analyst, Development Bank of South Africa (DBSA); director, Centre for Reconstruction and Development, University of Pretoria; executive director (group economic and social analysis) at the

Human Sciences Research Council (HSRC); CEO, Central Energy Fund. She is an honorary professor at the University of Pretoria.

CARLOS MONASTERIO ESCUDERO is professor of public finance in the Department of Economics at University of Oviedo (Spain). Professor Monasterio is associate editor of the review Hacienda Pública Española and member of the International Institute of Public Finance and the Association of Local Public Economics. He has been an advisor for the Senate of Spain and the Council of Fiscal and Financial Policy. His research interests centre on fiscal federalism and intergovernmental fiscal relations in Spain as well as performance budgeting and new public management.

ALAN MORRIS is chair of the Commonwealth Grants Commission of Australia. He has wide public-sector experience, having worked at senior levels in federal, state, and territory public services in Australia. He also has considerable international experience and has worked at the International Monetary Fund in Washington, DC, and as executive director of the European Bank for Reconstruction and Development in London. He has provided advice on intergovernmental financial arrangements to a number of developing countries.

SHANKARAN NAMBIAR is a research fellow at the Malaysian Institute of Economic Research. Prior to joining the institute, he was a lecturer in economics. His research interests include technology policy, economic development, and institutional economics. He has published journal articles and book chapters in these areas. He has been engaged as a consultant for the government as well as for international institutions in a wide range of projects in areas such as competition policy, distributive trade, industrial development, international trade, and poverty. He has also been a resource person for capacity-building programs in transition economies in Central and Southeast Asia.

M. GOVINDA RAO is the director of the National Institute of Public Finance and Policy, New Delhi, India. He is also a member of the Economic Advisory Council to the Prime Minister. Dr Rao has a number of additional advisory roles on governance and taxation. His research interests include public finance and fiscal policy, fiscal federalism, and state and local finance. He has published technical articles in a number of reputed journals as well as twelve books and monographs on various aspects of public finance. His recent books include: *Poverty, Development and Fiscal Policy* (2002); *Political Economy of Federalism in India* (2005); and *Sustainable Fiscal Policy for India: An International Perspective* (2006).

Contributors

FERNANDO REZENDE is a professor of public finance and fiscal policy, and director of the Fiscal Studies Program at the Brazilian School of Public and Private Administration, the Getúlio Vargas Foundation, Rio de Janeiro and Brasília. He directed the federal commission on tax reform and fiscal decentralization from 1986 to 1988 and has since been actively engaged in further attempts to reform the Brazilian fiscal system. President of the Brazilian Institute for Applied Economic Research from 1995 to 1998, and special advisor in the Federal Ministry of Development and Trade since 1999, he presently gives technical assistance to the Fiscal Forum of the Brazilian States.

ANWAR SHAH is lead economist and program leader, Public Sector Governance Program, at the World Bank Institute, Washington, DC; member of the Executive Board of the International Institute of Public Finance, Munich, Germany; and a fellow of the Institute for Public Economics, Edmonton, Alberta. Previously, he was responsible for designing provincial fiscal transfers from the Government of Alberta to local governments. Later, at the federal Ministry of Finance in Ottawa, he was responsible for federal fiscal transfers to the provinces, with primary responsibility for the Canadian fiscal equalization program. He has advised the governments of Australia, Argentina, Brazil, Canada, China, India, Indonesia, Mexico, Pakistan, Poland, South Africa, and Turkey on fiscal system reform issues. He co-authored, with Robin Boadway, *Fiscal Federalism: Principles and the Practice* (forthcoming).

JÜRGEN VON HAGEN is professor of economics at the University of Bonn. Previously, he taught at Indiana University and the University of Mannheim. He is a research fellow of the Centre for Economic Policy Research (London), a member of the Council of the German Economic Association and the Academic Advisory Council of the German Federal Ministry of Economics, and a former member of the French National Economic Committee. His publications include over seventy articles on macroeconomics and public economics in leading academic journals, over 130 contributions to other journals and books, and thirty published or edited monographs.

Participating Experts

We gratefully acknowledge the input of the following experts who participated in the making of *The Practice of Fiscal Federalism: Comparative Perspectives.* While participants contributed their knowledge and experience, they are not responsible for the contents of this book.

Mahani Zainal Abidin, National Economic Action Council, Malaysia
Sam Adantia, University of Uyo, Nigeria
Rui Affonso, State of Sao Paulo Water and Sanitation Company, Brazil
Tanya Ajam, University of Cape Town, South Africa
Sunday Akpadiaha, Governor's Office, Nigeria
Eme Akpan, University of Uyo, Nigeria
Otoabasi Akpan, University of Uyo, Nigeria
Haji Mohd Aiseri bin Alias, Office of the State Secretary of Kelantan, Malaysia
H.K. Amamath, National Institute of Public Finance and Policy, India
Mukesh Anand, National Institute of Public Finance and Policy, India
George Anderson, Forum of Federations, Canada
Bernard Appy, Ministry of Finance, Brazil
Erika Araújo, Economic Consultant, Brazil
Mohamed Ariff, Malaysian Institute of Economic Research, Malaysia
Balveer Arora, Jawaharlal Nehru University, India
Linus Asuquo, Ministry of Science and Technology, Nigeria
Edet Attih, Ministry of Health, Nigeria
Fabrício Augusto de Oliveira, Fundação João Pinheiro, Brazil
Amaresh Bagchi, National Institute of Public Finance and Policy, India
Simanti Bandyopadhyay, National Institute of Public Finance and Policy, India
Nirmala Banerjee, Sachetna, India
Gary Banks, Productivity Commission, Australia
Raoul Blindenbacher, Forum of Federations, Canada/Switzerland
Robin Boadway, Queen's University, Canada

Participating Experts

Henner-Jörg Boehl, Member of Parliament, Germany
O.P. Bohra, National Institute of Public Finance and Policy, India
Malcolm Booysen, Government of South Africa, South Africa
Canisius Braun, Cantonal Governments Conference, Switzerland
Kenneth Brown, National Treasury, South Africa
Jim Brown, The Council of State Governments, United States
Tomás Bruginski de Paula, State of Sao Paulo Company for Partnerships of the Ministry of Finance, Brazil
Andrei Burenin, State Duma of Russian Federation, Russia
Michael Butler, Public Sector Policy Analysis, Canada
Bruce Campbell, Canadian Centre for Policy Alternatives, Canada
Luis Caramés Viéitez, University of Santiago de Compostela, Spain
Raimundo Eloy Carvalho, Department of Federal Revenue, Brazil
Antoni Castells Oliveres, Government of Catalunya, Spain
Lekha Chakraborty, National Institute of Public Finance and Policy, India
Pinaki Chakraborty, National Institute of Public Finance and Policy, India
Don Challen, Department of Treasury and Finance, Australia
Ian Chalmers, Australian Local Government Association, Australia
Diwan Chand, National Institute of Public Finance and Policy, India
Rupak Chattopadhyay, Forum of Federations, Canada
Diana Chebenova, Forum of Federations, Canada
Kamalasen Chetty, Winelands District Municipality, South Africa
Chan Huan Chiang, Universiti Sains Malaysia, Malaysia
Mita Choudhury, National Institute of Public Finance and Policy, India
Indrani Roy Chowdhury, National Institute of Public Finance and Policy, India
José Augusto Coelho Fernandes, Confederaçao Nacional da Indústria, Brazil
E.M. Coleman, Finance, Mpumalanga, South Africa
Thomas J. Courchene, Queen's University, Canada
David Crawford, National Competition Council, Australia
Eugenia Cuéllar Barbeto, Financial Coordination for Autonomous Communities, Spain
Erzol D'Souza, Indian Institute of Management, India
Izzuddin bin Dali, Ministry of Finance, Malaysia
Wilson Baya Dandot, Chief Minister's Department, Malaysia
Paul Darby, Conference Board of Canada, Canada
Malti Das, Government of Karnataka, India
Donald Dennison, Next New Brunswick, Canada
Alexander Deryugin, Center for Fiscal Policy, Russia
Santiago Díaz de Sarralde Miguez, Institute of Fiscal Studies, Spain
Navroz Dubash, National Institute of Public Finance and Policy, India
Harley Duncan, Federation of Tax Administrators, United States
Asa Ebieme, Ministry of Culture and Tourism, Nigeria
Festus Egwaikhide, University of Ibadan, Nigeria

Participating Experts

Reiner Eichenberger, University of Fribourg, Switzerland
Edet Ekanem, Daily Trust, Nigeria
Glory Ekong, Newsday Publication, Nigeria
Akpan Ekpo, University of Uyo, Nigeria
Ime Ekpoattai, Ministry of Rural Development, Nigeria
Isawa Elaigwu, Institute of Government and Social Resource, Nigeria
Okon Emah, Ministry of Commerce and Industry, Nigeria
Okpongkpong Enobong Kubiat, Ministry of Economic Development, Nigeria
Saul Eslake, Australia and New Zealand Banking Group Limited, Australia
Dominique Faessler, Europartners, Switzerland
Patrick Fafard, Intergovernmental Affairs, Privy Council Office, Canada
Klaus Feiler, Senatsverwaltung für Finanzen, Germany
Lars P. Feld, University of Marburg, Germany
Angela Fernandez, Secretaria do Tesouro Nacional, Brazil
Wolfram Försterling, Staatskanzlei Nordrhein-Westfalen, Germany
William Fox, University of Tennessee, United States
Robert Gagné, École des Hautes Études Commerciales, Canada
Vyacheslav Gaizer, Government of Komi Republic, Russia
Brian Galligan, University of Melbourne, Australia
Subhash Garg, Government of Rajasthan, India
Sol Garson Braule Pinto, Federal University of Rio de Janeiro, Brazil
Otto-Erich Geske, Staatssekretär a.D., Germany
Gene Gibbons, Stateline.org, United States
Michael Gooda, Cooperative Research Centre for Aboriginal Health, Australia
Anjali Goyal, Government of India, India
Paul Grimes, Department of Treasury, Australia
Fátima Guerreiro, Secretariat of Finance of Bahia, Brazil
Kristi Guillory, The Council of State Governments, United States
Theresa Gullo, Congressional Budget Office, United States
Manish Gupta, National Institute of Public Finance and Policy, India
Prabhu Guptara, Wolfsberg Platform for Business and Executive Development, Switzerland
Merl Hackbart, University of Kentucky, United States
Ulrich Haede, Europa-Universität Viadrina, Germany
Jürgen von Hagen, Zentrum für Europäische Integrations-forschung, Germany
Abd Rahman bin Haji Imam Arshad, Office of the State Secretary of Pahang, Malaysia
Tengku Razaleigh Hamzah, Former Finance Minister, Malaysia
Jim Hancock, University of Adelaide, Australia
Jan Harris, Department of Prime Minister and Cabinet, Australia
Jamaludin bin Hasan, Office of the State Secretary of Pulau Pinang, Malaysia
Luiz Carlos Jorge Hauly, Camara dos deputados, Brazil
Clifford F Herbert, Percetakan Nasional Malaysia Berhad, Malaysia

Participating Experts

Ana Herrero Alcalde, National University for Distance Education, Spain
Anton Hofmann, Bayerische Staatskanzlei, Germany
Rainer Holtschneider, Staatssekretär a.d., Germany
Rudolf Hrbek, University of Tübingen, Germany
Gottfried Huba, Staatskanzlei Rheinland-Pfalz, Germany
Anna Hughes, Australian Local Government Association, Australia
Albert Igudin, Ministry of Finance of Russian Federation, Russia
Dorothy Jaketa, Local Government and Housing, South Africa
P.R. Jena, National Institute of Public Finance and Policy, India
Musalmah Johan, Malaysian Institute of Economic Research, Malaysia
Alcides Jorge Costa, National Treasury Secretariat, Brazil
Jaya Josie, Financial and Fiscal Commission, South Africa
Azidin Wan Abdul Kadir, Malaysian Institute of Economic Research, Malaysia
Ajit Karnik, University of Bombay, India
Abigail Karos, Forum of Federations, Canada
Christian Kastrop, Bundesministerium der Finanzen, Germany
Beth Kellar, International City/County Management Association, United States
Alexandra Kenney, Lafayette College, United States
Bongani Khumalo, Financial and Fiscal Commission, South Africa
Andreas Kienemund, Bundesministerium der Finanzen, Germany
John Kincaid, Lafayette College, United States
Gebhard Kirchgässner, University of St. Gallen, Switzerland
Michael Kleiner, Staatsministerium Baden-Württemberg, Germany
Vladimir Klimanov, Institute of Public Finance Reforms, Russia
Lee Cheok Kua, Gerakan Belia Bersatu Malaysia, Malaysia
Galina Kurlyandskaya, Center for Fiscal Policy, Russia
Mala Lalwani, University of Bombay, India
Kobi Lambert, Akwa Ibom Investment and Industrial Promotion Council, Nigeria
Aleksey Lavrov, Ministry of Finance, Russia
Silke Leßenich, Ministerium der Finanzen, Germany
Edilberto Lima, Câmara dos deputados, Brazil
Elayne Yee Siew Lin, Malaysian Institute of Economic Research, Malaysia
Wolf Linder, University of Bern, Switzerland
Maurício Estellita Lins Costa, Presidência da República, Brazil
Bruce Little, Former Globe and Mail Journalist, Canada
Ian Little, Department of Treasury and Finance, Australia
John Litwak, World Bank, Moscow Office, Russia
Alberto López Basaguren, University of País Vasco, Spain
Guillem Lopez Casasnovas, Pompeu Fabra University, Spain
Julio López Laborda, University of Zaragoza, Spain
Javier Loscos Fernández, Institute of Fiscal Studies, Spain
Doug MacArthur, Simon Fraser University at Harbour Centre, Canada
L. Ian MacDonald, Institute for Research on Public Policy, Canada

Participating Experts

David MacDonald, Forum of Federations, Canada
Cristina MacDowell, Escola de Administração Fazendária, Brazil
Nadejda Macsimova, State Duma of Russian Federation, Russia
Sulaiman Mahbob, Integrity Institute of Malaysia, Malaysia
Mohd Razali bin Mahusin, Office of the State Secretary of Johor, Malaysia
Akhtar Majeed, Hamdard University, India
Debdatta Majumdar, National Institute of Public Finance and Policy, India
Gcobani Mancotywa, First National Bank Public Sector Banking, South Africa
S.K. Mandai, National Institute of Public Finance and Policy, India
O.P. Mathur, National Institute of Public Finance and Policy, India
Ginigene Mbanefois, University of Ibadan, Nigeria
David McLaughlin, Council of the Federation, Canada
Irina Medina, State Research Institute of System Analysis of the Account Chamber of Russian Federation, Russia
Peter Meekison, University of Alberta, Canada
Anthony Melck, University of Pretoria, South Africa
Mónica Melle Hernández, Ministry of Public Administration, Spain
Gilmar Mendes, Supreme Federal Tribunal, Brazil
Marcos Mendes, Senado Federal, Brazil
Hans Meyer, Humboldt-University, Germany
John Milne, Capitol Management, United States
Stanislav Mironov, Government of Astrakhan Oblast, Russia
Sergey Miroshnikov, Ministry of Regional Development of Russian Federation, Russia
Peter Mischler, University of Fribourg, Switzerland
Jorge Khalil Miski, Ministry of Finance/National Treasury Secretariat, Brazil
Sergey Mitrohin, Russian Democratic Party "Yabloko," Russia
Modise Moatlhodi, First National Bank Public Sector Banking, South Africa
Mustapa bin Mohamed, National Economic Action Council, Malaysia
Renosi Mokate, Financial and Fiscal Commission, South Africa
Gugu Moloi, Umgeni Water, South Africa
Mônica Mora, Institute for Applied Economics, Brazil
Alan Morris, Commonwealth Grants Commission, Australia
Walter Moser, Federal Tax Administration, Switzerland
Hiranya Mukhopadhyay, Asian Development Bank, India
Rinku Murugai, World Bank, India
Carlos Mussi, Organização das Nações Unidas, Brazil
Suresh Narayanan, University of Malaysia, Malaysia
Gautam Naresh, National Institute of Public Finance and Policy, India
Ramon Navaratnam, The Sunway Group, Malaysia
Neva Nhlanhla, Congress of South Africa Trade Unions, South Africa
James Nkoana, University of Cape Town, South Africa
Phang Siew Noi, University of Malaya, Malaysia

Alain Noël, Université de Montréal, Canada
Aleksey Novikov, Standard and Poors Russia, Russia
Nsudoh Nsujoh, University of Uyo, Nigeria
Festus Odoko, Central Bank of Nigeria, Nigeria
Donatus Okon, Ministry of Finance, Akwa Ibom State Government, Nigeria
Nice Okure, Akwa Ibom Investment and Industrial Promotion Council, Nigeria
Juan José Otamendi García-Jalón, Financial Coordination for Autonomous Communities, Spain
Ramlan bin Othman, Office of the Chief Minister of Selangor, Malaysia
Aris bin Othman, Malaysian Airports Holdings Berhad, Malaysia
James Overly, The Washington Times, Nigeria
André Luiz Barreto de Paiva Filho, Ministério da Fazenda, Brazil
Rita Pandey, National Institute of Public Finance and Policy, India
Luciano Patrício, Ministério da Fazenda, Brazil
David Peloquin, Secretariat to the Expert panel on Equalization and Territorial Formula Financing, Canada
Ramón Pérez Pérez, Ministry of Public Administration, Spain
Jeffrey Petchey, Curtin University of Technology, Australia
Myron Peter, Financial and Fiscal Commission, South Africa
Marcelo Piancastelli, Institute for Applied Economics, Brazil
Tatiana Pogorelova, Government of Stavropol Krai, Russia
Paul Posner, U.S. Government Accountability Office, United States
Sergio Prado, Sao Paulo State University at Campinas, Brazil
Jennifer Prince, The Treasury, Australia
Adroaldo Quintela, Secretariat for Federative Affairs, Brazil
José Roberto R. Afonso, Banco Nacional de Desenvolvimento Econômico e Social e Camara dos Deputados, Brazil
Vyacheslav Ragozin, Government of Republic of Karelia, Russia
Indira Rajaraman, National Institute of Public Finance and Policy, India
Subba Rao, Economic Advisory Council to the Prime Minister, Government of India, India
Govinda Rao, National Institute of Public Finance and Policy, India
Kavita Rao, National Institute of Public Finance and Policy, India
S.K Rao, College of India, India
Bhujanga Rao, National Institute of Public Finance and Policy, India
V.I. Ravishankar, World Bank, India Office, India
Odoukpo Regina Oliver, Ministry of Economic Development, Nigeria
Ross Reid, Government of Newfoundland, Canada
Wolfgang Renzsch, University of Magdeburg, Germany
Fernando Rezende, Getulio Vargas Foundation Rodolfo Tourinho, Brazil
Maureen Riehl, National Retail Federation, United States
Jürgen Rinne, Mitarbeiter der SPD-Fraktion im Deutschen Bundestag, Germany
Horst Risse, Sekretariat des Bundesrates, Germany

M. Elvira Rodríguez Herrer, Spanish Congress, Spain
José Antonio Roselló Rausell, Government of the Balears Islands, Spain
Saiful Azhar Rosly, Malaysian Institute of Economic Research, Malaysia
Jesús Ruiz-Huerta Carbonell, Institute of Fiscal Studies, Spain
Kubah Saleh, National Youth Council of Nigeria, Nigeria
Javier Salinas Jiménez, Institute of Fiscal Studies, Spain
Ismail Md Salleh, International University College of Technology Twintech, Malaysia
I.V.M. Sarma, University of Hyderabad, India
Tony Saviour, Nigerian Television Authority, Nigeria
Upinder Sawhney, Punjab University, India
Christoph Schaltegger, Federal Tax Administration, Switzerland
Robert Searle, Commonwealth Grants Commission, Australia
Kala Seetharam Sridhar, National Institute of Public Finance and Policy, India
Helmut Seitz, Technische Universität Dresden, Germany
Tapas Sen, National Institute of Public Finance and Policy, India
Bethuel Sethai, Financial and Fiscal Commission, South Africa
Anwar Shah, World Bank Institute, United States
Enid Slack, University of Toronto, Canada
Alba Solà Pagès, University of Barcelona, Spain
Joaquim Solé-Vilanova, University of Barcelona, Spain
John Spasojevic, Commonwealth Grants Commission, Australia
Dan Sprague, The Council of State Governments, United States
Christine Steinbeiß-Winkelmann, Bundesministerium der Justiz, Germany
Carl Stenberg, University of North Carolina at Chapel Hill, United States
France St-Hilaire, Institute for Research on Public Policy, Canada
Syed Unan Mashri bin Syed Abdullah, Office of the State Secretary of Kedah, Malaysia
Stepan Titov, World Bank, Moscow Office, Russia
Jose Manuel Tránchez Martín, National University for Distance Education, Spain
Ibia Trenchand Okon, Ministry of Finance, Akwa Ibom State Government, Nigeria
Ilya Trunin, Institute for the Economy in Transition, Russia
David Tune, The Treasury, Australia
Bernard Turgéon, Quebec Ministry of Finance, Canada
Iniobong Udoh, Nigerian Television Authority, Nigeria
Monday Udoka, Bureau of Cooperative Development, Nigeria
Thorsten Uehlein, University of St. Gallen, Switzerland
Ebebe Ukpong, Ministry of Economic Development, Nigeria
Umana O. Umana, Ministry of Finance, Nigeria
Okon Umoh, University of Uyo, Nigeria
Enubong Uwah, National Youth Council, Nigeria
Uwatt B. Uwatt, University of Uyo, Nigeria
Renato Villela, Institute for Applied Economics, Brazil

Renuka Viswanathan, Planning Commission, Government of India, India
Jüergen von Hagen, Zentrum für Europäische Integrationsforschung, Germany
Pang Teck Wai, Ministry of Industrial Development, Sabah, Malaysia
Roger Wilkins, Government of New South Wales, Australia
Jim Wright, Department of Treasury and Finance, Australia
Galina Yudashkina, Government of Russian Federation, Russia
Andrei Yurin, Ministry of Finance of Russian Federation, Russia
Zainal Aznam Yusof, Government of Malaysia, Malaysia
Farah Zahir, World Bank, India Office, India
Florian Ziegenbart, Universität Tübingen, Germany

Bibliography

Advisory Panel on Fiscal Imbalance. 2006. *Reconciling the Irreconcilable.* Ottawa: The Council of the Federation.

Afonso, José Roberto Rodrigues, and José Serra. 1999. "Federalism in Brazil." Paper for the Forum of Federations Conference in Mont Tremblant, Quebec, Canada.

Ahmad, Ehtisham, and Giorgio Brosio, eds. 2006. *Handbook of Fiscal Federalism.* Cheltenham, UK: Edward Elgar.

Ahmad, Ehtisham, and Vito Tanzi. eds. 2002. *Managing Fiscal Decentralization.* London and New York: Routledge.

Alexeev, Michael, and Galina Kurliandskaya. 2003. "Fiscal Federalism and Incentives in a Russian Region." *Journal of Comparative Economics* 31: 20–33.

Alm, James, Jorge Martinez-Vazquez and Sri Mulyani Indrawati, eds. 2004. *Reforming Intergovernmental Fiscal Relations and the Rebuilding of Indonesia,* Northampton, MA: Edward Elgar.

Ammann, Yves. 2002. "Quelques réflexions à propos des règles de politique budgétaire." Bern: Staatssekretariat für Wirtschaft, Wirtschaftspolitische Grundlagen (WP), Discussion Paper No. 13 (May).

Andreeva, E., and N. Golovanova. 2003. "Decentralization in the Russian Federation." Mimeo., Center for Fiscal Policy, Moscow. <http://english.fpcenter.ru/themes/english/materials-document>.

Baily, Stephen J. 1999. *Local Government Economics: Principles and Practice.* London: Macmillan Press.

Banting, Keith, and Robin Boadway. 2004. "Defining the Sharing Community: The Federal Role in Health Care." In *Money, Politics and Health Care,* ed. Harvey Lazar and France St-Hilaire, 1–77. Montreal: Institute for Research on Public Policy.

Barati, Izabella, and Akos Szalai. 2000. "Fiscal Decentralization in Hungary." Center for Public Affairs Studies, Budapest University of Economic Sciences.

Bardhan, Pranab. 2002. "Decentralization of Governance and Development." *Journal of Economic Perspectives* 16 (4): 185–205.

Baretti, C., B. Huber, and K. Lichtblau. 2002. "A Tax on Tax Revenue: The Incentive Effects of Equalizing Transfers: Evidence from Germany." *International Tax and Public Finance* 9: 631–49.

Baretti, C., R. Fenge, B. Huber, W. Leibfritz, and M. Steinherr. 2000. *Chancen und Grenzen föderalen Wettbewerbs*. Ifo Beiträge zur Wirtschaftsforschung 1, München.

Besley, Timothy, and Harvey Rosen. 1998. "States' Responses to Federal Tax Setting: Evidence from Gasoline and Cigarettes." *Journal of Public Economics* 73: 383–98.

Besley, Tim, and Stephen Coate. 2003. "Central versus Local Provision of Public Goods: A Political Economy Analysis." *Journal of Public Economics* 87 (4): 2611–37.

Bird, Richard, and Francois Vaillancourt, eds. 1998. *Fiscal Decentralization in Developing Countries*. New York: Cambridge University Press.

Bird, Richard M., and Pierre-Pascal Gendron. 2001. "VATs in Federal Countries: International Experience and Emerging Possibilities." *Bulletin for International Fiscal Documentation* 55: 293–309.

Bird, Richard M., Robert D. Ebel, and Christine I. Wallich, eds. 1995. *Decentralization of the Socialist State*. Washington, DC: World Bank.

Bird, Richard M., and Thomas Stauffer, eds. 2001. *Intergovernmental Fiscal Relations in Fragmented Societies*. Bale-Geneve-Munich: Hellbing and Lichtenhahn.

Blanchard, Olivier, and Andrei Shleifer. 2001. "Federalism with and without Political Centralization: China versus Russia." Special issue. IMF Staff Papers 48, 171–9.

Blankart. C.B. 2004. *Öffentliche Finanzen in der Demokratie*. 5th ed. München: Verlag Vahlen.

Blankart, Charles B., and Achim Kleiber. 2004. "Wer soll für die Schulden von Gebietskörperschaften haften?" In *Perspektiven der Wirtschaftspolitik*, ed, Christoph A. Schaltegger and Stefan C. Schaltegger, 137–50. Zurich: Blackwell Publishing.

Blindenbacher, Raoul, and Abigail Ostien Karos, eds. 2006. *Dialogues on the Practice of Fiscal Federalism: Comparative Perspectives*. Kingston and Montreal: McGill-Queen's University Press.

Blindenbacher, Raoul, and Arnold Koller. 2003. *Federalism in a Changing World: Learning from Each Other*. Montreal and Kingston: McGill-Queen's University Press.

Boadway, Robin. 1992. *The Constitutional Division of Powers: An Economic Perspective*. Ottawa: Economic Council of Canada.

– 1996. "Review of 'The Uneasy Case for Equalization Payments' by Dan Usher." *National Tax Journal* 49 (4): 677–86.

– 2001. "Inter-Governmental Fiscal Relations: The Facilitator of Fiscal Decentralization." *Constitutional Political Economy* 12 (2): 93–121.

– 2002. "The Vertical Fiscal Gap: Conceptions and Misconceptions." Paper presented at "Canadian Fiscal Arrangements: What Works, What Might Work Better," Winnipeg, Manitoba, 16–17 May.

- 2004. "The Theory and Practice of Equalization." CESifo *Economic Studies* 50 (1): 211–54.
Boadway, Robin, and Anwar Shah. 1994. "Economic Foundations of Intergovernmental Fiscal Arrangements." Paper presented at the Workshop on Federalism, Departmento de Economia Aplicada, Universidad de Valladolid, Madrid, Spain, October.
- 1994. "Fiscal Federalism in Developing/Transition Economies: Some Lessons from Industrialized Countries." *National Tax Journal* Proceedings issue (April): 64–71.
- 1995. "Fundamentos economicos de los Acuerdos Fiscales Intergubernamentales". In *La Financiacion De Las Comunidades Autonomas. Analisis y Orientacion Desde el Federalismo Fiscal*, ed. Joaquin Romano Velasco, 95–130, Salamanca, Spain: Junta de Castilla y Leon.
- Forthcoming. *Fiscal Federalism: Principles and Practices.* New York: Cambridge University Press.
Boadway, Robin, and Anwar Shah, eds. 2007. *Intergovernmental Fiscal Transfers.* Washington, DC: World Bank.
Boadway, R., and P. Hobson. 1993. *Intergovernmental Fiscal Relations in Canada.* Toronto: Canadian Tax Foundation.
Boadway, R., and P. Hobson, eds. 1998. "Equalization: Its Contribution to Canada's Economic and Fiscal Progress." Policy Forum Series 36, John Deutsch Institute for the Study of Economic Policy, Queen's University, Kingston.
Boadway, Robin, Sandra Roberts, and Anwar Shah. 1994. "The Reform of Fiscal Systems in Developing and Emerging Market Economies: A Federalism Perspective." Policy Research Working Paper 1259, World Bank, Washington, DC.
- 2000. "Fiscal Federalism Dimension of Tax Reform in Developing Countries." In *Fiscal Reform and Structural Change in Developing Countries.* Vol. 1, ed. G. Perry, J. Whalley, and G. McMahon, 171–2000. London: Macmillan.
Bolton, Patrick, and Gerard Roland. 1997. "The Breakup of Nations: A Political Economy Analysis." *Quarterly Journal of Economics* 112, 4 (November): 1057–89.
Bolton, P., G. Roland, and E. Spolaore. 1996. "Economic Theories of the Breakup and Integration of Nations." *European Economic Review* 40, 3–5 (April): 697–705.
Bomfim, Antúlio, and Anwar Shah. 1994. "Macroeconomic Management and the Division of Powers in Brazil: Perspectives for the Nineties." *World Development* 22 (4): 535–42.
Boothe, Paul, and I. Kryvoruchko. 2004. "Do Federal Transfers Stabilize Regional Government Revenues? Evidence from Australia and Canada." *Public Finance and Management* 4 (4): 11–25.
Bowman, A.O., and R.C. Kearney. 1990. *State and Local Government.* Boston, MA: Houghton Mifflin Company.
Brennan, G. and J.M. Buchanan. 1980. *The Power to Tax.* New York: Cambridge University Press.

Breton, Albert. 2006. "Modeling Vertical Competition." In *Handbook of Fiscal Federalism*, ed. Ehtisham Ahmad and Giorgio Brosio, 86–105. Cheltenham, UK: Edward Elgar.

Brillantes, Alex B., Jr., Simeon A. Llago, Celenia L. Jamig, Bootes Esden, eds. 2004. *Decentralization and Good Urban Governance*. Manila: University of the Philippines.

Bruce, Donald, and William F. Fox. 2004. "State and Local Tax Revenue Losses from E-Commerce: Estimates as of July 2004." *State Tax Note* 33: 511–18.

Buchanan, James. 1965. "An Economic Theory of Clubs." *Economica* 32: 1–14.

Buchanan, James M., and Richard E. Wagner, eds. 1978. *Fiscal Responsibility in Constitutional Democracy*. Leiden/Boston: Martinus Nijhoff.

– 1978. "The Political Biases of Keynesian Economics." In *Fiscal Responsibility in Constitutional Democracy*, ed. James M. Buchanan and Richard E. Wagner, 79–100. Leiden/Boston: Martinus Nijhoff.

Bundesministerium der Finanzen, 2006. "Die Föderalismusreform." *Monatsbericht des BMF* (August): 81–90.

Burki, J.S., and G. Perry, eds. 2000. *Decentralization and Accountability of the Public Sector*. Washington, DC: World Bank.

Buschor, Ernst, Klaus Vallender, and Thomas Stauffer. 1993. *Kommentierter Entwurf für ein Finanzhaushaltsgesetz des Kantons Appenzell Ausserrhoden, ausgearbeitet für die Finanzdirektion des Kantons Appenzell Ausserrhoden*. St. Gallen: Institut für Finanzwirtschaft und Finanzrecht an der Hochschule St. Gallen.

Büttner, T. 2000. "Determinants of Tax Rates in Local Capital Income Taxation: A Theoretical Model and Evidence from Germany." *Finanzarchiv*, Finance Canada N.F. 57: 1–26.

– 2001. "Local Business Taxation and Competition for Capital: The Choice of the Tax Rate." *Regional Science and Urban Economics* 31: 215–45.

– 2002. "Fiscal Federalism and Interstate Risk-Sharing: Empirical Evidence from Germany." *Economics Letters* 74: 195–202.

– 2003. "Tax Base Effects and Fiscal Externalities of Local Capital Taxation: Evidence from a Panel of German Jurisdictions." *Journal of Urban Economics* 54: 110–28.

Büttner, T., and D.E. Wildasin. 2006. "The Dynamics of Municipal Fiscal Adjustment." *Journal of Public Economics* 90: 1105–32.

Casella, Alessandra, and Bruno Frey. 1992. "Federalism and Clubs: Towards an Economic Theory of Overlapping Political Jurisdictions." In *European Economic Review, Papers and Proceedings* 36: 639–46.

Celestino, A.B. 2002. "Malaysia: Does it Really Need Decentralization?" In *Decentralization and Power Shift: An Imperative for Good Governance*, ed. A.B. Brillantes, Jr. and N.G. Cuachon, 121–30. Manila: Asian Resource Center for Decentralization.

Chanda, A.K. 1965. *Federalism in India*. London: George Allen and Unwin.

Congleton, Roger, Adreas Kyriacou, and Jordi Bacaria. 2003. "A Theory of Menu Federalism: Decentralization by Political Agreement." *Constitutional Political Economy* 14: 167–90.

Courchene, Thomas J. 1986. *Economic Management and the Division of Powers.* Toronto: University of Toronto Press.
– 1993. "Globalization, Institutional Evolution and the Australian Federation." Paper prepared for the Federalism Research Center Seminar entitled Federalism and the Economy: International, National and State Issues, Canberra, 12 April.
– Forthcoming. "Macrofederalism: Some Exploratory Research Relating to Theory and Practice." In *Microfederalism,* ed. Anwar Shah. Washington, DC: World Bank.
Cremer, Jacques, and Thomas R. Palfrey. 2002. "Federal Mandates by Popular Demand." *Journal of Political Economy* 108 (5): 905–27.
Crook, Richard C., and James Manor. 1998. *Democracy and Decentralization in South Asia and West Africa.* Cambridge: Cambridge University Press.
Dafflon, Bernard. 2004. "Federal-Cantonal Equalisation in Switzerland: An Overview of the Present System and Reform in Progress." University of Fribourg, BENEFRI Centre for Studies in Public Sector Economics, Working Paper No. 356, updated version (May).
de Figueiredo, Rui, J.P. Jr., and Barry R. Weingast. 2005. "Self-Enforcing Federalism." *Journal of Law, Economics and Organizations* 21: 103–35.
Desai, R.M., L.M. Freinkman, and I. Goldberg. 2003. "Fiscal Federalism and Regional Economic Growth. Evidence from the Russian Federation in the 1990s." World Bank Policy Research Working Paper 3138, September.
Diaz-Cayeros, Alberto. 2006. *Federalism, Fiscal Authority and Centralization in Latin America.* New York: Cambridge University Press.
Diaz-Cayeros, Alberto, Kenneth M. McElwain, Vidal Romero, and Konrad A. Siewierski. 2002. "Fiscal Decentralization, Legislative Institutions and Particularistic Spending." Working Paper, Department of Political Science, Stanford University.
Drummond, P., and A. Mansoor. 2002. "Macroeconomic Management and the Devolution of Fiscal Powers." *IMG Working Paper* 02/76.
Eckl, Corina. 2006. "States Broaden the Scope of Rainy Day Funds." National Conference of State Legislatures, 21 February.
Eid, Florence. 1996. *Agency Theory, Property Rights, and Innovation in the Decentralized Public Sector.* Cambridge, MA: Department of Urban Studies and Planning, Massachusetts Institute of Technology.
Ekpo, Akpan H. 1994. "Fiscal Federalism: Nigeria's Post-Independence Experience, 1960 – 90." *World Development* 22 (8): 1129–46.
– 1999. "Fiscal Federalism and Local Government Finances in Nigeria." In *Fiscal Federalism and Nigeria's Economic Development,* Proceedings of the 1999 Nigerian Economic Society Annual Conference Ibadan.
– 2005. *Fiscal Theory and Policy: Selected Essays.* Lagos: Somaprint
Ekpo, Akpan H., and Enamidem Ubok-Udom. 2003. *Issues in Fiscal Federalism and Revenue Allocation in Nigeria.* Ibadan: Future Publishing.
Elazar, Daniel J., 1980. "The Political Theory of Covenant: Biblical Origins and Modern Developments." *Publius: The Journal of Federalism* 10: 3–30.

Emenuga, Chidozie. 1993. "Nigeria: In Search of Acceptance Revenue Allocation Formula." In *Nigerian Economic Society: The National Question and Economic Development in Nigeria*, Nigerian Economic Society, Ibadan.

Esteller-More, Alex, and Albert Sole-Olle. 2001. "Vertical Income Tax Externalities and Fiscal Interdependence: Evidence from the US." *Regional Science and Urban Economics* 31: 247–72.

Federal Republic of Nigeria. 1977. *Report of the Presidential Commission on Revenue Allocation*. Vol. 1: *Main Report*. Apapa: Government Press.

– 1999. *Constitution of the Federal Republic of Nigeria 1999*. Lagos: Government Press.

Feld, L.P. 2000. *Steuerwettbewerb und seine Auswirkungen auf Allokation und Distribution: Ein Überblick und eine empirische Analyse für die Schweiz*. Tübingen: Mohr Siebeck.

– 2000. "Tax Competition and Income Redistribution: An Empirical Analysis for Switzerland." *Public Choice* 105: 125–64.

– 2003. *Le degré de décentralisation fiscale en Allemagne: Dépenses, impôts, pression fiscale, dettes*. Report for the Institut de Recherche Européenne en Economie et Fiscalité (IREF) at the Marburg (Lahn): Philipps-Université de Marbourg.

Feld, L.P., and Bruno S. Frey. 2001. "Trust Breeds Trust: How Taxpayers Are Treated." *Economics of Governance* 2: 87–99.

Feld, L.P., and Gebhard Kirchgässner. 2001. "Does Direct Democracy Reduce Public Debt? Evidence from Swiss Municipalities." *Public Choice* 109: 347–70.

– 2001. "Income Tax Competition at the State and Local Level in Switzerland." *Regional Science and Urban Economics* 31: 181–213.

– 2001. "The Political Economy of Direct Legislation: Direct Democracy and Local Decision Making." *Economic Policy* 33: 329–67.

– 2003. "The Impact of Corporate and Personal Income Taxes on the Location of Firms and on Employment: Some Panel Evidence for the Swiss Cantons." *Journal of Public Economics* 87: 129–55.

Filippov, M., P.C. Ordeshook, and O. Shvetsova. 2004. *Designing Federalism: A Theory of Self-Sustainable Federal Institutions*. Cambridge: Cambridge University Press.

Finance Canada. 2006. *Restoring Fiscal Balance: Focusing on Priorities*. Ottawa: Finance Canada.

Fisher, Ronald. 2007. *State and Local Public Finance*. Boston: McGraw-Hill.

Fleiner, Thomas. 2006. "Swiss Confederation." In *Distribution of Powers and Responsibilities in Federal Countries*, ed. Akhtar Majeed, Ronald Watts, and Douglas M. Brown, 265–94. Montreal and Kingston: McGill-Queen's University Press.

Fox, William F. 2003. "Three Characteristics of Tax Structures Have Contributed to the Current State Fiscal Crises." *State Tax Notes* 29 (6 August): 375–83.

Fox, William F., and LeAnn Luna. 2002. "State Corporate Tax Revenue Trends: Causes and Possible Solutions." *National Tax Journal* 55: 491–508.

Frey, Bruno S., and Reiner Eichenberger. 1999. *The New Democratic Federalism for Europe: Functional, Overlapping, and Competing Jurisdictions*. Cheltenham, UL: Elgar.

Gabriel, Jürg M. 1990. *Das politische System der Schweiz*. Bern: Haupt.

Garnaut, R., and V. Fitzgerald. 2002. Background Paper, *Review of Commonwealth-State Funding Final Report August 2002*. Melbourne.

Geske, O.E. 2006. "Der Föderalismus in der Bundesrepublik." Bonn. Mimeo.

Goodspeed, T.J. 2002. "Bailouts in a Federation." *International Tax and Public Finance* 9: 409–21.

Government of Canada. 2006. *Achieving a National Purpose: Putting Equalization Back on Track*. Expert Panel Report on Equalization and Territorial Formula Financing, Department of Finance, Ottawa.

– 2006. *Restoring Fiscal Balance in Canada: Focusing on Priorities*. Ottawa: Department of Finance.

Hatfield, John William. 2006. "Federalism, Taxation, and Economic Growth." Stanford University Graduate School of Business Research Paper No. 1929.

Hellerstein, W., and J. R. Hellerstein. 1998. *State Taxation*, 3rd ed., New York: Warren, Gorham, and Lamont (supplemented semi-annually).

Hirsch, Werner. 1964. "Local versus Area-Wide Urban Government Services." *National Tax Journal* 42: 331–9.

Huther, Jeff, and Anwar Shah. 1998. "Applying a Simple Measure of Good Governance to the Debate on Fiscal Decentralization." Policy Research Working Paper 1894, 1998, Washington, DC: World Bank. <http://imagebank.worldbank.org/servlet/WDScontentServer/IW3P/IB/2000/02/24/000178830_98111703530240/Rendered/PDF/multi_page.pdf>.

Inman, R.P. 2003. "Transfers and Bailouts: Enforcing Local Fiscal Discipline with Lessons from US Federalism." In *Fiscal Decentralization and the Challenge of Hard Budget Constraints*, ed. J. Rodden and G. S. Eskeland, 35–83. Cambridge, MA: MIT Press.

– 2005. "Financing Cities." NBER Working Paper 11203, National Bureau of Economic Research, Cambridge, MA.

Inman, R.P., and D.L. Rubinfeld. 1992. "Fiscal Federalism in Europe: Lessons from the United States Experience." *European Economic Review* 36: 654–60.

– 1996. "Designing Tax Policy in Federalist Economies: An Overview." *Journal of Public Economics* 60: 307–34.

– 1997. "The Political Economy of Federalism." In *Perspectives on Public Choice Theory*, ed. Dennis C. Mueller, 73–105. New York: Cambridge University Press.

– 1997. "Rethinking Federalism." *Journal of Economic Perspectives* 11: 43–64.

Jomo, K.S., and C.H. Wee. 2002. "The Political Economy of Malaysian Federalism." Discussion Paper No. 2002/113, United Nations University/Wider.

– 2003. "The Political Economy of Malaysian Federalism: Economic Development, Public Policy and Conflict Containment." *Journal of International Development* 15: 441–56.

– 2003. "The Political Economy of Petrol Revenue under Malaysian Federalism." Paper presented at Workshop on Human Rights and Oil in South East Asia and Africa, organized by the Berkeley Centers for African Studies and Southeast Asia Studies, University of California, Berkeley.

Jones, Mark P., Pablo Sanguinetti, and Mariano Tommasi. 2000. "Politics, Institutions, and Fiscal Performance in a Federal System: An Analysis of the Argentine Provinces." *Journal of Development Economics* 61 (2): 305–33.

Joumard, I., and C. Giorno. 2005. "Getting the Most out of Public Sector Decentralisation in Spain." OECD Economics Department Working Paper No. 436.

Joumard, I., and P.M. Konigsrud. 2003. "Fiscal Relations across Levels of Governments." OECD Economic Studies No. 36, Paris.

Katz, Ellis. 2006. "United States of America." In *Distribution of Powers and Responsibilities in Federal Countries*, ed. Akhtar Majeed, Ronald L. Watts, and Douglas M. Brown, 295–321. Montreal and Kingston: McGill-Queen's University Press.

Kellermann, K. 2001. "Interregionales Risk Sharing zwischen den deutschen Bundesländern." *Konjunkturpolitik* 47: 271–91.

Kenyon, Daphne, and John Kincaid, eds. 1991. *Competition among States and Local Governments: Efficiency and Equity in American Federalism*. Washington, DC: Urban Institute Press.

– 1996. "Fiscal Federalism in the United States: The Reluctance to Equalize Jurisdictions." In *Finanzverfassung im Spannungsfeld zwischen Zentrslstaat und Gliedstaaten*, ed. Werner W. Pommerehne and George Ress, 34–56. Baden-Baden: Nomos Veglagsgesellschaft.

Khalilzadeh-Shirazi, J., and Anwar Shah, eds. 1991. *Tax Policy in Developing Countries*. Washington, DC: World Bank.

Kincaid, John, and G. Alan Tarr, eds. 2005. *Constitutional Origins, Structure, and Change in Federal Countries*. Montreal: McGill-Queen's University Press.

King, David. 1984. *Fiscal Tiers: The Economics of Multi-Level Government*. London: George Allen and Unwin.

– 1992. *Local Government Economics in Theory and Practice*. London: Routledge.

King, David, and J.P. Owens. 1994. *Fiscal Federalism in Economics in Transition*. Paris: OECD.

Kirchgässner, Gebhard, and Werner W. Pommerehne. 1996. "Tax Harmonization and Tax Competition in the European Union: Lessons from Switzerland." *Journal of Public Economics* 60: 351–71.

Knight, Brian. 2004. "Legislative Representation, Bargaining Power, and the Distribution of Federal Funds: Evidence from the US Senate." NBER Working Paper No. 10385, National Bureau of Economic Research, Cambridge, MA.

Kost, A., ed. 2005. *Direkte Demokratie in den deutschen Ländern: Eine Einführung*. Wiesbaden: VS Verlag für Sozialwissenschaften.

Kourliandskaia, Galina, Yelena Nikolayenko, and Natalia Golovanova. 2002. "Local Governments in the Russian Federation." In *Developing New Rules in the Old Environment: Local Governments in Eastern Europe, Caucasus and Central Asia*, ed. Victor Popa and Igor Munteanu, 1161–264. Budapest: LGI/OSI.

Kurlyandskaya, G. 2005. "Equalization Transfers to Subnational Governments in the Russian Federation." Center for Fiscal Policy. <http://english.fpcenter.ru/themes/english/materials-document>.

- 2004. "Fiscal Federalism Reform in Russia: Clarifying Expenditure Assignments." World Bank, Washington, DC, May. <http://english.fpcenter.ru/themes/english/materials-document>.
Lav, Iris, and Andrew Brecher. 2004. *Passing Down the Deficit: Federal Policies Contribute to the Severity of the State Fiscal Crisis.* Center for Budget and Policy Priorities: Washington, DC, August 18.
Lazar, Harvey, Hamish Telford, and Ronald L. Watts, eds. 2003. *The Impact of Global and Regional Integration on Federal Systems.* Montreal and Kingston: McGill-Queen's University Press.
Levaggi, R. 2002. "Decentralized Budgeting Procedures for Public Expenditure." *Public Finance Review* 30: 273–95.
Linder, Wolf. 1999. *Schweizerische Demokratie: Institutionen, Prozesse, Perspektiven.* Bern: Haupt.
Litvack, Jennie, and Jessica Seddon, eds. 1999. "Decentralization Briefing Notes." WBI Working Papers in collaboration with PERM Network, Washington, DC, World Bank.
Lockwood, Ben. 2002. "Distributive Politics and the Benefits of Decentralization." *Review of Economic Studies* 69: 313 – 38.
López-Laborda, J. 2004. "Financiación y gasto público en un Estado descentralizado." *Economía Aragonesa* 24: 63–82.
Lutz, Georg, and Dirk Strohmann. 1998. *Wahl-und Abstimmungsrecht in den Kantonen.* Bern: Haupt.
Majeed, Akhtar, Ronald L. Watts, and Douglas M. Brown, eds. 2006. *Distribution of Powers and Responsibilities in Federal Countries.* Montreal and Kingston: McGill-Queen's University Press.
Martínez-Vázquez, Jorge and J.F. Sanz, eds. 2006 *Tax Reform in Spain.* Cheltenham, UK: Edward Elgar.
Martinez-Vazquez, Jorge, Andrey Timofeev, and Jameson Boex. 2006. *Reforming Regional-Local Finance in Russia.* WBI Learning Resource Series. Washington, DC: World Bank.
Martinez-Vazquez, Jorge, and Bob Searle. 2006. *Fiscal Equalization: Challenges in the Design of Intergovernmental Transfers.* New York: Springer.
Mathew, George. 2006. "Republic of India." In *Distribution of Powers and Responsibilities in Federal Countries*, ed. Akhtar Majeed, Ronald L. Watts, and Douglas M. Brown, 155–80. Montreal: McGill-Queen's University Press.
Mbanefoh, G.F. 1986. *Military Presence and the Future of Nigerian Fiscal Federalism,* Faculty Lecture Series No. 1, Faculty of the Social Sciences, University of Ibadan, Ibadan.
- 1992. "Nigerian Fiscal Federalism: Assignment of Functions and Tax Powers." Paper presented at the National Seminar on Revenue Mobilization, organized by the Revenue Mobilization, Allocation and Fiscal Commission, Enugu, 21–23 April.
- 1993. "Federalism and Common Property." *Guardian,* 20 February, 13.

– 1993. "Unsettled Issues in Nigeria's Fiscal Federation and the National Question." *Nigerian Economic Society: The National Question and Economic Development in Nigeria.* Proceedings of the 1993 Annual Conference of Nigerian Economic Society.
Mbanefoh, G.F., and Akpan H. Ekpo. 2005. *Review of Constitutional Provisions on Fiscal Federation in Nigeria.* Abuja: World Bank.
McLure, Charles E., Jr. 1993. "Vertical Fiscal Imbalance and the Assignment of Taxing Powers in Australia." Stanford, CA: Hoover Institution.
– 2000. "Tax Assignment and Subnational Fiscal Autonomy." *Bulletin for International Fiscal Documentation* 54: 626–35.
Mikesell, John. 2002. *Fiscal Administration: Analysis and Applications for the Public Sector.* Belmont: Wadsworth Publishing Company.
Milne, R.S. 1967. *Government and Politics in Malaysia.* Boston: Houghton Mifflin Co.
Monasterio, C. 2002. "El laberinto de la financiación autonómica." *Hacienda Pública Española* 163: 157–85.
Musgrave, Richard. 1983. "Who Should Tax, Where, and What?" In *Tax Assignment in Federal Countries*, ed. Charles McLure, Jr., 2–19. Canberra: Australian National University Press.
Musgrave, Richard A., and Peggy B. Musgrave. 1984. *Public Finance in Theory and Practice.* 4th ed. New York: McGraw-Hill.
Narayanan, S. 1998. "Towards Economic Recovery: The Fiscal Policy Side." Paper presented at the MIER 1999 National Outlook Conference, Kuala Lumpur, December.
Nwabueze, B.O. 2002. *Federalism in Nigeria under the Presidential Constitution.* Lagos: Lagos State Ministry of Justice.
Oates, Wallace E. 1969. "The Effects of Property Taxes and Local Public Spending on Property Values: An Empirical Study of Tax Capitalization and Tiebout Hypothesis." *Journal of Political Economy* 77: 957–71.
– 1972. *Fiscal Federalism.* New York: Harcourt Brace Jovanovich.
– 1998. *The Economics of Fiscal Federalism and Local Finance.* Cheltenham, UK: Edward Elgar.
– 1999. "An Essay on Fiscal Federalism." *Journal of Economic Literature* 37: 1120–49.
– 2005. "Toward a Second-Generation Theory of Fiscal Federalism." *International Tax and Public Finance* 12: 349–73.
OECD. 1997. *Managing across Levels of Government.* Paris: OECD.
Oeter, S. 1998. *Integration und Subsidiarität im deutschen Bundesstaatsrecht.* Tübingen: Mohr Siebeck.
Okigbo, P.N.C. 1965. *Nigerian Public Finance.* London: Longmans.
Olson, Mancur. 1969. "The Principle of Fiscal Equivalence: The Division of Responsibilities among Different Levels of Government." *American Economic Review* 59 (2): 479–87.
Osayinwese, Izevbuwa, and Sunday Iyare. 1991. "The Economics of Nigerian Federalism: Selected Issues in Economic Management." *Publius: The Journal of Federalism* 21: 89–101.

Pedraja, F., and J. Suárez-Pandiello. 2004. "La última reforma de la participación municipal en los tributos del estado. Un analisis cualitativo." *Papeles de Economía Española* 100: 77–92.

Petersson-Lidbom, P., and M. Dahlberg. 2005. "An Empirical Approach for Estimating the Causal Effect of Soft Budget Constraints on Economic Outcomes." University of Stockholm and University of Uppsala. Mimeo.

Phang, S.N. 1997. *Financing Local Government*. Kuala Lumpur: Universiti Malaya.

– 1997. *Sistem Kerajaan Tempatan di Malaysia*. Kuala Lumpur: Dewan Bahasa dan Pustaka.

Phillips, Adedotun O. 1991. "Four Decades of Fiscal Federalism in Nigeria." *Publius: The Journal of Federalism* 21: 103–11.

Piancastelli, Marcelo. 2006. "The Federal Republic of Brazil." In *A Global Dialogue on Federalism*. Vol. 2: *Distribution of Powers and Responsibility in Federal Countries*, ed. Akhtar Majeed, Ronald L. Watts, and Douglas M. Brown, 66–90. Montreal and Kingston: McGill-Queen's University Press for the Forum of Federations.

Picton, Mark, and Peter B. Dixon. 2003. *Issues Involving Modeling by COPS of the Efficiency Effects of Commonwealth State Funding: Report to Queensland Treasury*. Victoria: Centre of Policy Studies, Monash University.

Pommerehne, Werner W., and Hannelore Weck-Hannemann. 1996. "Tax Rates, Tax Administration and Income Tax Evasion in Switzerland." *Public Choice* 88: 161–70.

Prado, Sergio, Waldemar Quadros, and Carlos Cavalcanti. 2003. *Partilha de Recursos na Federação Brasileira*. São Paulo: FUNDAP.

Prud'homme, Remy, and Anwar Shah. 2002. "Centralization vs Decentralization: The Devil is in the Details". Paper presented at the Seminario Internacional Federlismo Fiscal no Mercosul: Os desafios da Integracao Regional, Porto Allegre, Brazil, 26–27 June.

Qian, Yingyi, Gerard Roland, and Barry Weingast. 1997. "Federalism as a Commitment to Preserving Market Incentives." *Journal of Economic Perspectives* 11 (4): 83–92.

Rao, Govinda M. 2006. "Fiscal Federalism in Planned Economies." In *Handbook in Fiscal Federalism*, ed. Ehtisham Ahmad and Georgio Brosio, 224–39. Cheltenham, UK: Edward Elgar.

Rao, Govinda M., and Nirvikar Singh. 2005. *Political Economy of Federalism in India*. New Delhi: Oxford University Press.

Reich, Richard. 1991. *The Work of Nations*. New York: Alfred A. Knopf.

Rezende, Fernando, and José Roberto Afonso. 2006. "The Brazilian Federation, Facts, Challenges and Perspectives." In *Federalism and Economic Reform: International Perspectives*, ed. Jessica Wallack and T.N. Srinivasan, 143–88. New York: Cambridge University Press.

Rezende, Fernando, and Sol Garson. 2006. "Financing Metropolitan Areas in Brazil: Political, Institutional, Legal Obstacles and Emergence of New Proposals for Improving Coordination." *Revista de Economia Contemporânea* (Rio de Janeiro) 10 (1): 21–45.

Rieder, Stefan, and Luzia Lehmann. 2002. "Evaluation of New Public Management Reforms in Switzerland: Empirical Results and Reflections on Methodology." *International Public Management Review* 3: 25–42.

Riker, W. 1964. *Federalism: Origin, Operation, Significance*. Boston, MA: Little-Brown.

Rodden, J. 2000. "Breaking the Golden Rule: Fiscal Behavior with Rational Bailout Expectations in the German States." Department of Political Science, MIT, Cambridge. Mimeo.

– 2005. "And the Last Shall Be First: Federalism and Fiscal Outcomes in Germany." Department of Political Science, MIT, Cambridge. Mimeo.

Rodden, Jonathan, Gunnar S. Eskeland, and Jennie Litvack, eds. 2002. *Fiscal Decentralization and the Challenge of Hard Budget Constraints*. Cambridge, MA: MIT Press.

Rodrik, Dani. 1998. "Why Do More Open Economies Have Bigger Governments?" *Journal of Political Economy* 106 (5): 997–1032.

Rosen, Harvey S., ed. 1988. *Fiscal Federalism: Quantitative Studies*. Chicago: University of Chicago Press.

Sachverständigenrat zur Begutachtung der gesamtwirtschaftlichen Entwicklung. 2005. *Die Chancen nutzen: Reformen mutig voranbringen, Jahresgutachten 2005/2006*, Wiesbaden, CD-ROM.

Salmon, Pierre. 2006. "Horizontal Competition among Governments." In *Handbook of Fiscal Federalism*, ed. Ehtisham Ahmad and Giorgio Brosio, 61–85. Cheltenham, UK: Edward Elgar.

Schaltegger, Christoph A. 2002. "Budgetregeln und ihre Wirkung auf die öffentlichen Haushalte: Empirische Ergebnisse aus den US-Bundesstaaten und den Schweizer Kantonen." *Schmollers Jahrbuch* 122: 369–413.

Scharpf, F.W., B. Reissert, and F. Schnabel. 1976. *Politikverflechtung: Theorie und Empirie des kooperativen Föderalismus in der Bundesrepublik*. Kronberg/Ts: Scriptor.

Schmitt, Nicolas. 2005. "Swiss Confederation." In *Constitutional Origins, Structure, and Change in Federal Countries*, ed. John Kincaid and Alan Tarr, 347–81. Montreal and Kingston: McGill-Queen's University Press.

Seabright, P. 1996. "Accountability and Decentralization in Government: An Incomplete Contracts Model." *European Economic Review* 40: 61–89.

Séguin Committee. 2002. *A New Division of Canada's Financial Resources*. Québec: Department of Finance.

Seitz, H. 1999. "Subnational Government Bailouts in Germany." ZEI Working Paper B20, Bonn.

– 2005. "Agglomeration und Bevölkerungsdichte: Dünn besiedelte Flächenländer im Finanzausgleich." In *Sonderbedarfe im bundesstaatlichen Finanzausgleich*, ed. M. Junkernheinrich, 137–67. Berlin: Analytica.

Serra, José, and José Roberto Afonso. 1999. "Federalismo Fiscal à Brasileira: Algumas Reflexões." *Revista do BNDES* (Rio de Janeiro) 6 (12): 3–30.

Shafruddin, B.H. 1987. *The Federal Factor in the Government of Peninsular Malaysia*. Singapore: Oxford University Press.

Shafruddin, B.H., and I.A.M.Z. Fadzli, eds. 1988. *Between Centre and State: Federalism in Perspective*. Kuala Lumpur: Institute of Strategic and International Studies in Malaysia.

Shah, Anwar. 1988. "Capitalization and the Theory of Local Public Finance: An Interpretative Essay." *Journal of Economic Surveys* 2 (3): 209–43.

– 1989. "A Capitalization Approach to Fiscal Incidence at the Local Level." *Land Economics* 65 (4): 359–75.

– 1989. "A Linear Expenditure System Estimation of Local Fiscal Response to Provincial Transportation Grants." *Kentucky Journal of Economics and Business* 2 (3): 150–68.

– 1991. *The New Fiscal Federalism in Brazil*, Washington, DC: World Bank

– 1991. "Perspectives on the Design on Intergovernmental Fiscal Relations." World Bank Policy Research Working Paper 726, Washington, DC: World Bank.

– 1992. "Empirical Tests for Allocative Efficiency in the Local Public Sector." *Public Finance Quarterly* 20 (3): 359–77.

– 1994. "A Fiscal Needs Approach to Equalization Transfers in a Decentralized Federation." Policy Research Working Paper 1289, Washington, DC, World Bank.

– 1994. "Perspectives on the Design of Intergovernmental Fiscal Relations in Developing/Transition Economies." In *Intergovernmental Fiscal Relations and Macroeconomic Management in Large Countries*, ed. Gupta, S.P., Peter T. Knight, Roberta Waxman, and Y. Wen, Proceedings of an EDI (World Bank) Seminar, 1–68. New Delhi: Allied Publisher Limited.

– 1994. *The Reform of Intergovernmental Fiscal Relations in Developing and Emerging Market Economies*. Washington, DC: World Bank.

– 1995. "Intergovernmental Fiscal Relations in Canada: An Overview." In *Macroeconomic Management and Fiscal Decentralization*, ed. Roy Jayanta, EDI Seminar Series, 233–55. Washington, DC: World Bank.

– 1995. "Theory and Practice of Intergovernmental Transfers." In *Reforming China's Public Finances*, ed. Ehtisham Ahmad, Gao Qiang, and Vito Tanzi, 215–34. Washington, DC: International Monetary Fund.

– 1996. *Fiscal Federalism in Pakistan: Challenges and Opportunities*. Washington, DC: World Bank.

– 1996."On the Design of Economic Constitutions." *Canadian Journal of Economics* 29 (1): 614–18.

– 1996. "A Fiscal Need Approach to Equalization." *Canadian Public Policy* 22 (2): 99–115.

– 1997. *Balance, Accountability, and Responsiveness: Lessons from Decentralization*. Washington, DC: World Bank.

– 1997. "Econometric Analysis and Public Policy: The Case of Fiscal Need Assessment – A Reply." *Canadian Public Policy* 23 (2): 209–11.

– 1997. "Federalism Reform Imperatives, Restructuring Principles and Lessons for Pakistan." *Pakistan Development Review* 36 (4): 499–536.

- 1997. "The Quest for the Right Balance and Responsive and Accountable Governance: Lessons from Decentralization Experience." Paper presented at the World Bank Conference on Evaluation and Development (1–2 April 1997), Washington, DC.
- 1998. "Balance, Accountability, and Responsiveness: Lessons about Decentralizations." Policy Research Working Paper Number 2021, World Bank, Washington, DC.
- 1998. "Fostering Fiscal Responsive and Accountable Governance: Lessons about Decentralizations." In *Evaluation and Development: The Institutional Dimension*, ed. Robert Picciotto and Eduardo Wiesner, 83–96. Washington, DC: World Bank.
- 1998. "Indonesia and Pakistan: Fiscal Decentralization – An Elusive Goal?" In *Fiscal Decentralization in Developing Countries*, ed. Richard M. Bird and Francois Vaillancourt, 115–51. Cambridge: Cambridge University Press.
- 1999. "Fiscal Federalism and Macroeconomic Governance: For Better or Worse?" In *Fiscal Decentralization in Emerging Economies: Governance Issues*, ed. K. Fukusaku and L. de Mello Jr., 37–54. Paris: OECD.
- 1999. "Governing for Results in Globalized and Localized World." *Pakistan Development Review* 38 (4): 385–431.
- 1999. "Review of Comparing Federal Systems in the 1990s by R. Watts." *Canadian Public Policy* 25 (1): 152–3.
- 2001. "Interregional Competition and Federal Cooperation: To Compete or to Cooperate – That Is Not the Question." Paper presented at the International Forum on Federalism in Mexico entitled Local and Global Challenges, Veracruz, 14–17 November.
- 2002. "Globalization and Economic Management." In *Public Policy in Asia: Implications for Business and Government*, ed. Mukul G. Asher, David Newman, and Thomas P. Snyder, 145–73. Westport, CT: Quorum Books.
- 2003. "Fiscal Decentralisation in Transition Economies and Developing Countries: Progress, Problems and the Promise." In *Federalism in a Changing World – Learning from Each Other: Scientific Background, Proceedings and Plenary Speeches of the International Conference on Federalism 2002*, ed. R. Blindenbacher and A. Koller, 432–60. Montreal and Kingston: McGill-Queen's University Press.
- 2004. "Financing Capital Investment for Urban Public Services." In *Decentralization and Good Urban Governance*, ed. Alex Brillantes, Jr., Simeon A. Llago, Celenia L. Jamig, Bootes Esden, 111–22. Manila: University of the Philippines.
- 2004. "Fiscal Decentralization in Developing and Transition Economies: Progress, Problems, and the Promise." World Bank Policy Research Working Paper 3282, Washington, DC, World Bank.
- 2005. "Fiscal Decentralization and Fiscal Performance." World Bank Policy Research Working Paper 3786, Washington, DC, World Bank.
- 2005. "A Framework for Evaluating Alternate Institutional Arrangements for Fiscal Equalization Transfers." World Bank Policy Research Working Paper Series 3785, Washington, DC, World Bank.

- 2005. "Fiscal Decentralization in Developing and Transition Economies: An Overview. In *Decentralization and Local Governance*, ed. L.C. Jain, 164–221, New Delhi: Orient Longman.
- 2006. "Comparative Reflections on Emerging Challenges in Fiscal Federalism." In *Dialogues on the Practice of Fiscal Federalism: Comparative Perspectives*, ed. Raoul Blindenbacher and Abigail Ostien Karos, 40–5. Kingston and Montreal: McGill-Queen's University Press
- 2006. "Corruption and Decentralized Public Governance." In *Handbook of Fiscal Federalism*, ed. Ehtisham Ahmad and Giorgio Brosio, 478–98. Cheltenham, UK: Edward Elgar.
- 2006. "Corruption and Decentralized Public Governance." World Bank Policy Research Working Paper Series 3824, Washington, DC, World Bank.
- 2006. "Fiscal Decentralization and Macroeconomic Management." *International Tax and Public Finance* 13 (4): 437–62.
- 2007. A Framework for Evaluating Institutional Arrangements for Fiscal Equalization Transfers. In *Fiscal Equalization: Challenges in the Design of Intergovernmental Transfers*, ed Jorge Martinez-Vazquez and Bob Searle, 141–62. New York: Springer.
- 2007. "Citizen-Centered Local Governance: Strategies to Combat Democratic Deficits." *Development* 1: 1–9.
- 2007. "A Practioner's Guide to Intergovernmental Fiscal Transfers." In *Intergovernmental Fiscal Transfers*, ed. Robin Boadway and Anwar Shah, 1–53. Washington, DC: World Bank.
- 2007. Rethinking Fiscal Federalism. *Federations* 6 (1): 9–11.

Shah, Anwar, ed. 2005. *Fiscal Management*. Washington, DC: World Bank.
- 2006. *Local Governance in Developing Countries*. Washington, DC: World Bank.
- 2006. *Local Governance in Industrial Countries*. Washington, DC: World Bank.
- 2007. *Budgeting and Budgetary Institutions*. Washington, DC: World Bank.
- 2007. *Local Budgeting*. Washington, DC: World Bank.
- 2007. *Local Public Financial Management*. Washington, DC: World Bank.
- 2007. *Participatory Budgeting*. Washington, DC: World Bank.
- 2007. *Performance Accountability and Combating Corruption*. Washington, DC: World Bank.

Shah, Anwar, and Baoyun Qiao, eds. 2006. *Intergovernmental Finance System: A Review of International Experiences*. Beijing: People's Publishing House (in Chinese).
- 2006. *Local Public Finance and Governance: A Review of International Experiences*. Beijing: People's Publishing House (in Chinese).

Shah, Anwar, and Chunli Shen, eds. 2006. *Fiscal Federalism and Fiscal Management*. Beijing: CITIC Publishing House (in Chinese).
- 2006. *Local Public Finance and Governance*. Beijing: CITIC Publishing House (in Chinese).

Shah, Anwar, and Chunli Shen, and Heng-fu Zou, eds. 2006. *Provincial/Regional Disparities in China*. Beijing: People's Publishing House (in Chinese).

Shah, Anwar, and Paul Bernd Spahn. 1995. "Intergovernmental Fiscal Relations in Australia." In *Macroeconomic Management and Fiscal Decentralization*, ed. Roy Jayanta, EDI Seminar Series, 49–72. Washington, DC: World Bank.

Shah, Anwar, and Robin Boadway. 1994. "Fiscal Federalism in Developing/transition Economies: Some Lessons from Industrial Countries." In *Regional and Local Taxation in a Future South Africa*, ed. Riel C.D. Franzsen, 23–37. Pretoria: Centre for Human Rights, University of Pretoria.

Shah, Anwar, and Sandra Roberts.1995. "La Reforma de Los Sistemas Fiscales en Las Economias en Desarrollo y Los Mercados Emergentes – Una Perspectiva Federalista." *Cronia Legislativa*, H. Camara de Diputados Poder Legislativo Federal, Ano iv, Nueva Epoca, Numero Especial-1, Octobre, 11–160.

Shah, Anwar, and Theresa Thompson. 2004. "Implementing Decentralized Local Governance: A Treacherous Road with Potholes, Detours and Road Closures." In *Reforming Intergovernmental Fiscal Relations and the Rebuilding of Indonesia*, ed. James Alm, Jorge Martinez-Vazquez and Sri Mulyani Indrawati, 301–37. Northampton, MA: Edward Elgar. <http://imagebank.worldbank.org/servlet/WDSContentServer/IW3P/IB/2004/07/29/000090341_20040729134144/Rendered/PDF/wps3353.pdf >.

Shah, Anwar, Theresa Thompson, and Heng-fu Zou. 2004. "The Impact of Decentralization on Service Delivery, Corruption, Fiscal Management and Growth in Developing and Emerging Market Economies: A Synthesis of Empirical Evidence." *CESifo DICE Report, Journal for Institutional Comparisons* 2 (1): 10–14.

Shah, Anwar, and Tugrul Gurgur, 2002. "Localization and Corruption: Panacea or Pandora's Box?" In *Managing Fiscal Decentralization*, ed. Ehtisham Ahmad and Vito Tanzi, 45–67. London and New York: Routledge.

Shah, Anwar, Zia Qureshi, Amaresh Bagchi, Brian Binder, and Heng-fu Zou. 1994. *Intergovernmental Fiscal Relations in Indonesia: Issues and Reform Options.* Washington, DC: World Bank.

Shankar, Raja, and Anwar Shah. 2003. "Bridging the Economic Divide within Nations: A Scorecard on the Performance of Regional Development Policies in Reducing Regional Income Disparities." *World Development* 31 (8): 1421–41.

Shannon, John. 1997. "Middle Class Votes Bring a New Balance to US Federalism." The Urban Institute, the Future of the Public Sector, Policy Note No. 10, February.

Smart, Michael. 1998. "Taxation and Deadweight Loss in a System of Intergovernmental Transfers." *Canadian Journal of Economics* 31: 189–206.

Snoddon, T. 2003. "On Equalization and Incentives: An Empirical Assessment." School of Business and Economics, Laurier University, Waterloo, Working Paper 06-EC, May.

South African Government Treasury. 2004. *Budget Review.* Pretoria: South African Government Printers.

South African National Treasury. 2003. *Intergovernmental Fiscal Review 2003.* Pretoria: South African Government Printers.

– 2006. *Budget Review*. Pretoria: South African Government Printers.
Souza, Celina. 2005. "Constitutional Aspects of Federalism in Brazil." In *A Global Dialogue on Federalism*. Vol. 1: *Constitutional Origins, Structure and Change in Federal Democracies*, ed. John Kincaid and G. Alan Tarr, 76–102. Montreal and Kingston: McGill-Queen's University Press for the Forum of Federations.
Spahn, P.B. 1997. "Intergovernmental Transfers in Switzerland and Germany." In *Financing Decentralized Expenditures: An International Comparison of Grants*, ed. E. Ahmad, 103–43. Cheltenham, UK: Edward Elgar.
Spahn, P.B., and W. Föttinger. 1997. "Germany." In *Fiscal Federalism in Theory and Practice*, ed. T. Ter-Minassian, 226–48. Washington, DC: IMF.
Srinivasan, T.N., and Jessica Wallace, eds. 2005. *Federalism and Economic Reform in a Globalizing Environment*. Cambridge, UK: Cambridge University Press.
Starodubrovskaya, Irina. 2003. *Analysis of Revenues and Expenses of Local Budgets*. Moscow: CEPRA.
Stauffer, Thomas. 2001. *Instrumente des Haushaltsausgleichs: Ökonomische Analyse und Rechtliche Umsetzung*. Basel: Helbing und Lichtenhahn.
Stepan, Alfred. 1997. "Toward a New Comparative Analysis of Democracy and Federalism: Demos Constraining and Demos Enabling Federations." Coréia do Sul. Mimeo.
Stigler, George. 1957. "The Tenable Range of Functions of Local Government." In *Federal Expenditure Policy for Economic Growth and Stability*, ED. US Congress, Joint Economic Committee, 167–76. Washington, DC.
Tarr, G. Alan. 2005. "United States of America." In *Constitutional Origins, Structure, and Change in Federal Countries*, ed. John Kincaid and G. Alan Tarr, 381–408. Montreal and Kingston: McGill-Queen's University Press.
Tiebout, Charles. 1956. "A Pure Theory of Local Expenditures." *Journal of Political Economy* 64 (5): 416–24.
Ter-Minassian, Teresa, ed. 1997. *Fiscal Federalism in Theory and Practice*. Washington, DC: International Monetary Fund.
Trechsel, Alexander, and Uwe Serdült. 1999. *Kaleidoskop Volksrechte: Die Institutionen der direkten Demokratie in den schweizerischen Kantonen, 1970–1996*. Basel: Helbing und Lichtenhahn.
Treisman, Daniel, 1996. "The Politics of Intergovernmental Transfers in Post-Soviet Russia." *British Journal of Political Science* 26 (3): 299–335.
Varsano, Ricardo. 1997. "A Guerra Fiscal do ICMS: Quem Ganha e quem perde." IPEA Discussion Paper, Brasília.
– 1999. "Subnational Taxation and Treatment of Interstate Trade in Brazil: Problems and a Proposed Solution." ABCD-LAC Conference, Valdivia, Chile.
Verwaltungsrat des Kantons Basel-Stadt. 2002. "Zwischenbericht der Verfassungskommission Finanzverfassung: Einführung einer Schuldenbremse." Basel, 5 März (B/Nr. 503).
Vijayaledchumy, V. 2003. "Fiscal Policy in Malaysia." Bank of International Settlement Papers, No. 20.

Von Hagen, J., M. Bordignon, M. Dahlberg, B.S. Grewal, P. Pettersson-Lidbom, and H. Seitz. 2002. "Sub-National Government Bailouts in OECD Countries: Four Case Studies." Inter-American Development Bank Research Network Working Paper R-399.

Von Hagen, J., and M. Dahlberg. 2002. "Swedish Local Government: Is There a Bailout Problem?" University of Bonn. Mimeo.

Von Hagen, J., and R. Hepp. 2000. "Regional Risk-Sharing and Redistribution in the German Federation." ZEI Working Paper B-15, Bonn.

Wallich, C., ed. 1994. *Russia and the Challenge of Fiscal Federalism.* Washington, DC: World Bank.

Watts, Ronald. 1999. *Comparing Federal Systems.* Montreal and Kingston: McGill-Queen's University Press.

− 1999. *The Spending Power in Federal Systems: A Comparative Study.* Kingston, ON: Institute of Intergovernmental Relations.

Weingast, Barry. 2006. "Second Generation Fiscal Federalism: Implications for Decentralized Democratic Governance and Economic Development." Discussion draft, Hoover Institution, Stanford University.

Wellisch, D. 2000. *Theory of Public Finance in a Federal State.* Cambridge: Cambridge University Press.

Whalley, John. 1999. "Globalization and the Decline of the Nation State." Paper presented at the First International Conference of Federalism, The Forum of Federations, Mont Tremblant, Quebec, 6–7 October. Wildasin, D.E. 2004. "The Institutions of Federalism: Toward an Analytical Framework." *National Tax Journal* 57: 247–72.

Wissenschaftlicher Beirat beim Bundesministerium der Finanzen. 1994. *Zur Bedeutung der Maastricht-Kriterien für die Verschuldungsgrenzen von Bund und Ländern.* Bonn: Stollfuß-Verlag.

− 2005. *Haushaltskrisen im Bundesstaat.* Bonn: Stollfuß-Verlag.

Zarin-Nejadan, Milad. 1997. "Die Besteuerung der KMU." In der Schweiz, *Die Volkswirtschaft* 70 (2): 56–9.

Zhuravskaya, Ekatherina V., 2000. "Incentives to Provide Local Public Goods: Fiscal Federalism, Russian Style." *Journal of Public Economics* 76 (3): 337–68.

Zodrow, G., and P. Mieszkowski. 1986. "Pigou, Tiebout, Property Taxation, and Underprovision of Local Public Goods." *Journal of Urban Economics* 19: 356–70.

Zubiri, I. 2000. *El Sistema de Concierto Económico en el contexto de la Unión Europea.* Bilbao: Círculo de Empresarios Vascos.

Index

Aboriginal peoples (Canada), 100, 115
accountability: Australia, 47; Canada, 101, 109; Spain, 290, 311
Advisory Panel on Fiscal Imbalance (Canada): 107–8
African National Congress (South Africa), 263
Agreed taxes (Spain), 301
Agreement on International Trade (Canada), 110
Alberta: flat-tax system, 111; tax harmonization, 113; tax room, 107
American Jobs Creation Act, 2004 (USA), 359
American local government (USA): borrowing, 365; Congressional legislation re taxes, 357–8; exclusive responsibilities, 350, 351, T351; federal policy impact re tax bases, 359; horizontal relationships, 360; profile, 347; property tax, 354; revenue-raising disparities, 364–6; role of, 15; social service delivery, 350, 351–2, T351; shared responsibilities, 350, 351–2, T351; state grants, 363–4; tax structure, 356, T355; vertical competition, 360
American states: administration of federal programs, 351–2; borrowing, 365; budgets and expenditures, 365; compliance costs and state tax systems, 359, 360; Congressional legislation re taxes, 357–8; the Constitution and revenue-raising, 366; education grants, 364; exclusive responsibilities, 350, 351, T351; federal policy impact re tax bases, 359; federal subsidy re state debt, 365; gasoline/tobacco tax rates and vertical competition, 360; global/national economic issues, 366; grants for health, income security, transportation, 361–2; horizontal relationships, 360; incentives to industry, 365; limitations on fiscal activity, 356–61; limited tax powers, 353; macroeconomic management, 365; non-residents' access to services, 357; piggy-backed income tax, 359; powers, 359; property taxes, 354; revenue and Internet/mail order impact, 357; revenue-raising challenges, 358; sales tax on destination basis, 360; service delivery, 349–53, T351, T353; shared responsibilities, 350, 351–2, T351; special-purpose districts, 347; state constitutions and tax powers, 353; Supreme Court and state tax laws, 357; tax assignment, 353–6, T355; taxation of corporate income, 357; tax bases/rates, 358–9; tax collection cooperation, 360–1; taxes as deductible expenses, 362–3; tax structures, 354–6, T355; utilities responsibilities, 352; vertical competition, 359–60; vertical fiscal gaps, T363
annual equalization grants (AEG) (Malaysia), 194–5
anti-cyclical fiscal policy (Switzerland), 327
asymmetric layer-cake models of dual federalism, 371
auditor general: Canada, 101; South Africa, 284
Australia, Commonwealth of, 5, 6, 44; accountability bodies, 47; banking policy, 53; borrowing, 52–3, 67; Cabinet, 46; central bank, 53; changing federal/state

responsibilities, 44–5; Commonwealth Grants Commission, 36, 49, 58, 62, 64, 65; constitution, 44, 47; division of powers, 50, T51; equalization issues, 58–63, 64–5; expenditure assignments, 50, T51; federal override where concurrent powers, 50; financing capital investment, 67; fiscal powers, division of, 48–52; former customs and excise duties, 48–9; grants, 49; GST/HCC grants, 56; horizontal fiscal equalization, 57–60, 63–4; income taxes, 49; intergovernmental transfers, 49–50, 56–7, 61–2; macroeconomic authority, 52; macroeconomic management, 45–52, 52–53; monetary policy, 53; National Competition Policy, 62–3; national objectives (SPPs), expenditures re, 50, T52; profile T46; public sector borrowing, 52–3; public sector debt, 48; public sector management, 67–8; public sector revenue, T54, 55–6; responsibilities, 44; revenue raising responsibilities, 53–5; social security/health care transfers(grants), 62; specific purpose payments (SPPs), 49, 61; strings-attached funding, 56; structure of government, 45–7; tax assignment, 53, T54, 55; taxation powers, GST collection, 53; tied grants, 56–7; untied transfers, 57–60; vertical imbalances, 55–6, T56, 68–70

Australian Loan Council, 52–3

Australian local government, 44, 47; federal/state transfers (grants), 66–7; powers and role, 65–6; revenue powers, 66; tax powers, 53, T54, 55

Australian states/territories, assessed need, 59; conditional payments (SPPs), 61–2; economic/financial policy authority, 52; equalization, 63, 64; equalization basis (rationale), 58–60; financial arrangements, 48–50; financial assistance grants, 49; Goods and Services Tax (GST) and federal/state relations, 49–50; GST/HCC grants, 56; government expenditures, 50, T51; growth rates, 47; macroeconomic policy participation, 52; Ministerial Council of Treasurers, 52; powers and responsibilities, 44; parliaments, 46; profile, 45, T46; public sector revenue share, T54; "relativities," 59–60; reliance on federal transfers (grants), 52; tax bases, 55; tax collection powers, 53, T54, 55; tax competition, 55

autonomous communities (Spain): assignment of responsibilities, 290, 292–4, T291; asymmetric responsibilities, 290, 292; charter profile, 289; revenue assignments, 296–304; shared responsibilities, 293; tax administration, 300, 311–12. *See also* Spanish subnational governments

Autonomous Communities Financing Act, 1980 (Spain), 296

beggar-thy-neighbour policies, 20, 28, 38, 55, 387

Belgium, 6

Bill of Rights (South Africa), 264

block grants, 25; Nigeria, 212; South Africa, 279

Boadway, Robin, 11, 395

borrowing powers: Australia, 67; Germany, 135; Malaysia, 199; Nigeria, 210; Russia, 256–8; South Africa, 281; Switzerland, 336–7; systems compared, 382–3; United States, 365

Brazil, 6; Central Bank, 82; conflicts over functions, 78, 80; dual fiscal regime, 76, 94–5; expenditure assignments, 77–81, T78; Fiscal Responsibility Law (FRL), 82–3, 92, 93–4; formula-based general-purpose transfers, 25; general-purpose transfer issues, 32; fiscal federalism, 81–4; fiscal powers, division of, 77–81, T78–9; horizontal fiscal imbalances, 91; inequality issues, 75, 76, 77; inflation, 81; inflation-targeting regime, 82; local governments, role of, 15; profile, 74–5, T75; public debt, 82, 83; public savings, 92–3; revenue-sharing system, 88–92; shared responsibilities, 77–8; social contributions, 76, 77; structure of government, 77–81; taxing powers, 84, 87, T85–6; transfer formulas in constitution, 36; value-added tax (VAT), 79, 80, 84; vertical disequilibria, 88, T89

Brazilian subnational governments: autonomy, 78, 80–1, 84; capital investment, financing, 92–3; conflicts between state and municipal governments, 80; council of state finance ministers, 80; debt-refinancing contracts, 83; federal government influence on policies of, 81; fiscal discipline, 83; fiscal war, 87; horizontal fiscal imbalances, 91; imbalances in states' political representation, 75–6; influence on

Index 429

national policies, 81; local governments, 80–1, 371; managing internal affairs, 93; mixed origin-destination principle, 84, 87; revenue-sharing system, 88–92; state taxing powers, 84, 87, T85–6; symmetric arrangements among, 80; value-added tax (VAT), 84
budget reform (South Africa), 267–8, 278
Budgetary Stability Law (Spain), 294–5
Business Property Tax (Russia), 247, 249

Canada, 5, 6; capital investment, financing, 120–1; central bank, 12, 111; conflicts within the federation, 122; decentralized decision-making, 99, 110–11, 116 122; division of fiscal powers, 102–10; equity, 105–106, 116–20; efficiency, national government, 109–10; federal-provincial agreements, 106–107; federal-provincial committees, 36; First Nations, 100, 115–16, 122; fiscal conflicts, 107–108; fiscal discipline, 111; fiscal disparities, 116–17; government structure, 102–10; horizontal imbalances, 105, 108; income tax, 111–12; infrastructure deficit, 121; local governments, 15, 104, 109, 114; metropolitan areas, 109; monetary policy, 111; municipal governments, 104, 109; natural resources, 102, 105, 116–17, 122, 123; per capita incomes, 117, 118; profile, 99–102, T100; public management framework, 121; sales tax, 111; tax-collection agreement systems, 112–13; tax competition, 113; tax harmonization, 106, 112, 113–14; territories, 106, 108, 119; transfer payments, 106, 107, 108, 117–20, 122; vertical fiscal gap, T105, 117–18, 119, 123
Canada Health Transfer (CHT), 118, 119
Canada Social Transfer (CST), 118–19
Canadian Charter of Rights and Freedoms, 101; limits on legislation, 102
Canadian federal government: fiscal powers, 102, T103, T104, T105; influence on provincial policies, 106–107; sources of revenue, 111–12
Canadian provinces: capital investment, financing, 121; conflicts with local governments, 115; federal government's influence on, 10–107; federal transfer payments to, 106, 107; fiscal powers, 102, T103, T104, T105; ownership of natural resources, 102, 112; sources of revenue, 112

Canadian subnational governments: asymmetric treatment of, 108; division of powers, 102, T103, T104, T105; local, 104, 109, 114, 121; municipal, 104, 105, 109; provincial, 102, 104, 105; provincial-local transfer payments, 119; shared responsibility for social programs, 105–6; sources of conflict among, 115; sources of revenue, 112–15; territories, 106, 118, 119
capital investment, financing: Australia, 67; Brazil, 92–3; Canada, 120–1; Malaysia, 198–9; Nigeria, 225, 229; Russia, 256–8; South Africa, 280–2; Switzerland, 336–7
ceded taxes (Spain), 297–8, T299–300, 301
central bank: Australia, 53; Brazil, 82; Canada, 12, 111; and monetary policy, 12; Nigeria, 207, 208; Russia, 246; South Africa, 266–7; Spain, 294; Switzerland, 12, 325
Central Finance Commission (India), 168
centralized decision making: administrative and compliance costs, 10; and efficient provision of public services, 9–11; and unitary form of government, 4
charter system (Spain): 301–4
Chechyna (Russia), 7
China, 4
coming together view of federalism, 4
common regime (Spain), 296–301
Commonwealth Grants Commission (Australia), 49, 58, 62, 64, 65
Commonwealth of Independent States (CIS), 7
Community Development Block Grants (USA), 25
Compensation Fund (Russia), 251
competitive model of federalism, 6
Complementary Fund (Spain), 309
conditional grants: Brazil, 90; Canada, 119; in centralized federations, 6; compensating for benefit spillovers, 31; defined, 25–6; Länder grants, 144; matching provisions, 26; non-matching, 30–1; open-ended, 26; output-based vs. input-based, 31; South Africa, 276–7, 278–9; Spain, 306. *See also* grants; intergovernmental transfers
confederal form of government, 7
constitutional division of fiscal powers (Canada), 102, T103, T104, T105
Contingencies Fund (Nigeria), 209
cooperative authority model of dual federalism, 5, 371

cooperative federalism, 5–6, 371
coordinate authority approach to dual federalism, 5
correspondence principle, 8
Council of Australian Governments, 48

debt, country comparison, 382–3
decentralization theorem, 8
decentralized systems: in Canadian federation, 99, 110–11; in federal form of government, 4–5; grants to eliminate fiscal inequity resulting from, 28–30; and provision of public services, 9–11; Spain, 288, 290, 310
Denmark, 7
derivation principle (Nigeria), 220–1
Deryugin, Alexander, 395
developing countries, revenue-sharing agreements, 21
development grants (Malaysia), 194, 195–6, 198
differential net fiscal benefits (NFBs), 10
dual federalism, 5; coordinate authority approach to, 5; layer-cake model of, 5

earmarked grants: Brazil, 81; Russia, 251
economic stabilization by national government, 11–13
economies of scale, and centralized decision making, 10; Nigeria, 210, 211
efficiency: assignment of tax revenues, 20; Canada's national government, 109–10; and expenditure assignment, 10; and government structure, 16, 19, T17–18; and instruments of intergovernmental finance, 21–37; and local service provision, 26–32; Nigeria, 214–15, 217–18
Egypt, 4
Eichenberger, Reiner, 8
Ekpo, Akpan Hogan, 395
Elazar, Daniel J., 4
Enterprise Profit Tax (Russia), 247, 249
equalization programs/transfers, 28–9; Canada, 108, 116–20; grants for, 29–30; institutional approaches to design and practice of, 390–1; Malaysia, 194–6, 198; Russia, 251–3, 255–6, 259; Spain, 306–8; Switzerland, 334–5
equity: and government structure, 16, 19, T17–18; horizontal (regional), 10; and instruments of intergovernmental finance, 21–37; and local service provision, 26–32

European Central Bank, 138, 294
European Charter of Local Self-Government, 25
European Union, 7, 308; tariff restrictions re Germany, 134
European Union Stability and Growth Pact (SGP); German borrowing, 135, 139
executive federalism, 6
expenditure assignment, 9–13; Australia, 50, T51; Brazil, 77–81, T79; Canada, 102, T104; compared, 378–80; economic stabilization, 11–13; efficient provision of public services, 9–10; fiscal efficiency, 10; Germany, 135, 136, 138, T136, T137; India, 156, 159–60, T157, T158; monetary policy, 11–13; Nigeria, 210–12; preservation of the internal common market, 11; provision of quasi-private goods, 11; redistributive role of public sector, 10–11; regional (horizontal) equity, 10; Russia, 238, 240, T240; South Africa, 268, 271–2, T272; Spain, 293–4, T293, T297; spending power, 13; subnational expenditures as percentage of total government expenditure, T379; Switzerland, T34
Expert Panel on Equalization and Territorial Formula Financing (Canada), 108, 118

federal form of government, 4–7; coming together view of, 4; decentralized decision making, 4–5; direct-democracy provisions of, 6; fiscal policy coordination, 12–13; and monetary policy, 12
federal influence on subnational governments, 6, 371, 374; holding together view of, 4; market-preserving model, 7
Federal Reserve Bank (FED) (USA), 364; FED Open Market Committee, 364
federalism: asymmetric form of government, 6–7; confederal form of government, 7; coming together view of, 4; competitive model, 6; cooperative model, 5–6; and corruption, 39; dual model, 5; federal form of government, 4–7; fiscal, *see* fiscal federalism; holding together view of, 4; market-preserving model, 7; review of basic concepts, 3–7; unitary form of government, 4
Federation Account (Nigeria), 215–17, 230–1
Federation of Tax Administrators (USA), 357

Index

federations, constitutional divisions of powers, 3–7
Feld, Lars P., 396
finance, instruments of intergovernmental, 21–37
Finance Commission (Pakistan), 37
Financial and Fiscal Committee (South Africa), 277
First Nations (Canada), 100, 122, 123
fiscal decentralization compared: to local governments, T377; to provinces/states, T375–6
fiscal discipline: Australia, Brazil, 183; Canada, 111; countries compared, 385–6; Germany, India, Malaysia, Nigeria, Russia, 240, 246; South Africa, Spain, 294–5; Switzerland, 325–6
fiscal equivalency, principle of, 8
fiscal federalism: allocation of responsibilities, 9–21; cooperative German model, 132–3; current German issues, 126–7; decentralization theorem, 8; expenditure assignment principles, 9–13, T14; federalism and regional equity, 37–8; fiscal equivalency, 8; home rule, 7–8; intergovernmental finance instruments, 21–37; local governments, roles and responsibilities, 15–19; monetary policy, 11–13; subsidiarity principle, 8; tax-assignment principles, 19–21; theoretical grounds for, 7–8
Fiscal and Financial Policy Council (CPFF) (Spain), 295, 296
fiscal inefficiency, and grants, 29
fiscal inequity, and grants, 29
fiscal need, and the assignment of tax revenues, 20
fiscal prudence. *See* fiscal discipline
fiscal relations, designing institutions for, 35–7; South Africa, 268
Fiscal Responsibility Act (Nigeria), 208–9
Fiscal Responsibility and Budget Management Act (FRBMA) (India), 160
Fiscal Responsibility Law (FRL) (Brazil), 82–3, 92, 93–4
fiscal systems compared, 371, 374, 378, T372–3
formula-based representative tax system (RTS) (Canada), 118
Fox, William, 396
France, 4
free-rider problem, 8

Frey, Bruno, 8
functional, overlapping, and competing jurisdictions (FOCJ), 8

Gallo, Theresa, 349
general-purpose transfers, 25; from states/provinces to local governments, 32; South Africa, 276–7. *See also* grants; intergovernmental transfers
German Länder: autonomy, 133, 140, 146; bailout, 139, 140,146; control of local governments, 135, 145–6; European Union requirements, 134; exclusive tax powers, 134; and federal "framing" legislation, 132; fiscal powers, 131, T136, 137–8; joint responsibilities with federal government, 132–3; macroeconomic responsibilities, 138–40; public debt, 138; shared taxes, 140, T141, T142; states mergers, East Germany entry, 129; tax assignment, 140, 143, T141, T142; tax authority and Federalism Reform Act changes, 134; tax autonomy, 134; tax harmonization, 134; transfers, 139; typical executive federalism, 133; valued-added tax (VAT) and revenue assignment, 143
German local governments: Länder-controlled grants (transfers), 145–6; revenue sources, 143; role of, 128–9; tax assignment, 140, 143, T141, T142; taxing powers, 134
Germany, Federal Republic of, 5, 6; autonomy issues, 133, 146; borrowing, 135; constitution and federal-state powers, 128; cooperative fiscal federalism, 132–3; current fiscal federalism issues, 126–7; equalization system, 143–4, 145; EU deficit/debt requirements, 138; EU and federal taxing powers, 134; exclusive federal responsibilities, 131–2; exclusive taxing (revenue) powers, 134; executive federalism, 133; expenditure assignment, 135, 136, 138, T136, T137; federal-provincial committees, 36–7; federalism, peculiarities, 129–30; Federalism Reform Act, 131, 132, 133; federal-state common financial responsibilities, 132–33; fiscal policy, 138–40; fiscal powers, division of, 131–8, T136, T137; grants (transfers), vertical transfer system, 144, T145; harmonized tax powers, 134; horizontal equalization, 143–4; Joint Planning Council on Financial

Matters, 139; profile, 128–31, T129; public services and levels of government, T136; revenue (tax) powers/sources, 134, 140, T141, T142; revenue sharing and fiscal equalization, 134; shared responsibilities, 135, T136; shared taxes, 140, T141, T142; structure of government, 128–30; transfers (grants), unconditional, 134–5; as unitary federal state, 138; value-added tax (VAT), 143
globalization: local governments' role in, 19; and regional inequalities, 37
government, forms of: confederal, 7; federal, 4–7; unitary, 3–4
grants: capital, 31–2; compensating for benefit spillovers, 31, 134–5; guidelines for designing, 26–8; formula-based, 25; general-purpose transfers, 25; lessons from international practice, 32, T33, 34; local priorities, influencing, 31; matching provisions, 13, 26; national minimum standards, setting, 30–1; objectives for, 28–9; open-ended, 26; positive principles for, 34–5; regional stabilization, 31–2; specific-purpose transfers, 25–6; transfer dependencies, 29–30; transfers to avoid, 32, 34; types of, 25–6; vertical fiscal gaps, bridging, 28–30. *See also* conditional grants; earmarked grants
grants commissions, and systems for supplying grants, 36
Growth, Employment, and Redistribution (GEAR) macroeconomic strategy (South Africa), 267

harmonized tax systems compared, 381–2
hierarchy in layer-cake model of dual federalism, 5
holding together view of federalism, 4
home rule, 8
horizontal competition, and fiscal federalism, 38–9
horizontal (regional) equity, 10
Human Rights Commission (South Africa), 264

implementation deficit (Switzerland), 322
income tax harmonization compared, 381
independent spheres model of cooperative federalism, 6
India, 5, 6; boundary/dismissal power, 159; budget deficits, 160; Central Finance Commission, 168; centralization and planned development strategy, 155; centralized federal constitution, historical factors, 155; coalition governments, 173; commercial bank resources, 169; common market principles, violations, 172; concurrent powers, 153, 156; constitution, 152, 153, 155, 156, 162; decentralization, 155; division of powers, 156–60, T157, T158; equalization and intergovernment transfers, 167–8; expenditure assignment, 156, 159–60, T157, T158; federal (Union) powers, 156; finance commissions, 155, 162, 164, 165, 166; fiscal federalism, 155, 160, 169–73; formula-based vs. discretionary transfers, 164–7; globalization and e-commerce tax issues, 172; government structure, 153, 155, 156–60, T157, T158; grant system reform options, 174–5; GST reform options, 174; intergovernment transfers, 164–7; international trade/capital flow liberalization, 172; macroeconomic management, 160; market-based reform, 171–2; Planning Commission, 160, 164, 167; profile, 153, T154; public service provision assignments, T157; reform options, 173–6; Reserve Bank of India, 160; revenue assignments, 160, 162, T161; specific purpose transfers, 164; statutory transfers, 164; tax assignment, 160–2, T161, 174; transfer principles, 164–7; transfer system reform, 174–5; transfers and state domestic product (SDP), 167–8; Twelfth Financial Commission and fiscal restructuring, 160; Union government's responsibility for transfer schemes, 36; value-added tax (VAT), 160, 162, 172; vertical fiscal imbalance, 162, T163
Indian local government: property tax, 168–9; public service provisions, 156, T158; state transfers to, 168–9
Indian states: borrowing 160, 169; capital expenditures and, 169; concurrent powers, 153, 156; dependency on transfers, 163; economic inequalities, 171; expenditure assignment, 156, T157; fiscal imbalances, 170–1; fiscal responsibility acts (FRAs), 160; horizontal imbalances, 163–4; interstate sales tax, 160, 174; interstate tax power, 159–60; liabilities, 169; per capita incomes, NSDPs, 171; powers, 156, T157;

sales tax power, 160, 161, 162; state finance commissions (SFCs), 168
inflation: Brazil, 81; South Africa, 267; Switzerland, 325
inflation-targeting regime: Australia, 53; Brazil, 82; Canada, South Africa, 266–7
information revolution, and local governments' role, 19
Inman, Robert P., 4, 24
interdependent spheres model of cooperative federalism, 5
Intergovernmental Agreement on the Reform of Commonwealth-State Financial Relations (IGA) (Australia), 49–50
intergovernmental competition, comparison, 386–7
intergovernmental fiscal relations (IGFR) (South Africa), 268, 278, 284
intergovernmental forums for grants programs, 36–7
intergovernmental transfers: bridging gaps, 388–9; compared, 387–92, T388; regional fiscal disparities, 389–90. *See also* grants
internal common market, 11
Internet Tax Freedom Act, 1998 (USA), 357–8
interstate commerce (USA), 381
interstate federalism, 6
investment, and national government, 11
Iraq, 4
Italy, 4

Japan, 4

Kashmir (India), 7
Khumalo, Bongani, 396
Kirchgässner, Gebhard, 396–7
Korea, 4
Kurlyandskaya, Galina, 397

Laborda, Julio López, 397
launching grants (Malaysia), 194
layer-cake model of dual federalism, 5, 371
local finances, tools and issues, 24
local government(s): effective provision of public services, 9–10, 16, 19, T17–18; influence on federal and state governments, 6; regulatory responsibilities compared, 379; roles and responsibilities, 15–19; status in layer-cake model of dual federalism, 5

local services: designing grants for, 26–32; grants for, 25–6, 30–1

macroeconomic management, countries compared, 385–7
Malaysia, 5, 7; Bumiputera, 180, 195; centralized federation, 179, 182, 185, 187, 189; civil service, 200–1, 202; corruption, 200–1; decentralization issues, 185, 190; development expenditures, T196, 198–9; development project fund, 195; division of fiscal powers, 183–7; equity issues, 194–8, 201; federal-state conflicts, 187; financing capital investment, 198–9; fiscal federalism, 187, 189; grant formula, 195; horizontal imbalances, 187, 193, 196; legislative system, 182–3; local government, 183, 190, 192, 193, 199; natural resources, 186; non-financial public enterprises, 198–9; oil and gas, 186–7; political patronage, 179, 185, 190; poverty, 194, 195–6; privatization, 199; profile, 180–1, T188; public management framework, 200–1; public service functions, 183, T191–2; Reid Commission, 181–2, 185; revenue-raising issues, 189–93; sources of revenue, 189–90, 192–3, T197, 201; structure of government, 181–5; tax assignment, 189–90; transfer payments, 194–8; vertical imbalances, 192, 193, 198
Malaysian local government: annual equalization grants, 194–5; borrowing powers, 199; civil service, 200; collecting revenues, 193; credibility problems, 183–4; development project grants, 194, 195; launching grants, 194; licences and permits, 193; local councils, 183–4; property taxes, 192–3; sources of revenue, 190, 192–3; structure, 183; transfer payments to, 194–7, 198; vertical imbalances with states, 192–3
Malaysian state governments: capital investment powers, 199; civil service, 200; collecting revenues, 193; concurrent powers, 183, 184, 189; conflicts with federal government, 187; credibility, 183–4; education issues, 184–5; equity and government transfers, 194–6, 198; horizontal imbalances, 187, 193, 196; jurisdiction, 183, 184; Kelantan, 185; legislative powers, 182–3; oil and gas revenues, 186–7; Penang, 184, 196; political patronage, 179,

185, 190; poverty, 195–6; problems, 183–4; public service functions, 183, T191–2; sources of revenue, 189, 190, T197, 201; tax assignments, 189–90; vertical imbalances, 192–3, 198
marble cake model of cooperative federalism, 5–6
market-preserving federalism, 7
Martinez-Vazquez, Jorge, 397
metropolitan areas: efficient and equitable provision of services, 16, 19, T17–18;
Mexico, 5
mixed origin-destination principle (Brazil), 84, 87
mobile factors, assigning tax revenue from, 20
Monaco, 4
Monastero Escudero, Carlos, 398
monetary policy: Canada, 111; and economic stabilization by national government, 11–13; Nigeria, 207, 208; Russia, 246; South Africa, 266–7; Switzerland, 325
Mopkate, Renosi, 397–8
moral suasion (Canada), 106
Morris, Alan, 398
Municipal Finance Management Act (South Africa), 268, 283
Municipal Fiscal Powers and Functions Bill (South Africa), 273
municipal government: Brazil: 84, 87, 90, Canada, 104, 109, 123; South Africa, 266; two-tier structures for, 16
municipalities: Brazil, 77, 80, 88, 91; Russia, 244, 254; South Africa, 266, 278, 279, 281, 282, 283; Switzerland, 321, 329, 336

Nambiar, Shankaran, 398
National Commission of Local Administration (Spain), 295–6
National Competition Council (Australia), 62
National Development Council (India), 167
national equity, and assignment of tax revenues, 20
national government: designing institutions for fiscal relations, 35–6; economic stabilization, 11–13; and efficient provision of public services, 9–11; preservation of the internal common market, 11; quasi-private goods, providing, 11; redistributive role of, 13; status in layer-cake model of dual federalism, 5

National Monetary Council (Brazil), 82
National Political Reform Conference (Nigeria), 231–2
natural resource royalties: Brazil, 90; Canada, 102, 114, 116–17
new federalism, 4
New Zealand, 4
Nigeria: block grants, 212; borrowing powers, 210; budget deficits, 207, 213; central bank, 207, 208; centralized revenues, 209, 210, 213, 214, 230; civil service, 229; contemporary issues, 229–32; corruption, 229; derivation principle, 220–1; division of powers, 206–7, 214–15; economies of scale, 210, 211; efficiency and taxing powers, 214–15; expenditure assignments, 210–11, 225; Federation Account, 215–17, 218, 230–1; financing capital investment, 225, 229; fiscal gaps, T228; Fiscal Responsibility Act, 208–9; geographic range of benefits, 210–11; horizontal inequity, 213, 218; horizontal revenue allocation, 219–21; internal revenue effort, 219–20; local governments, 222–4; monetary policy, 207, 208; National Political Reform Conference, 231–2; oil revenues, 208, 209, 210, 221–2; Phillipson Commission, 212; power sharing, 231; presidential system, 206; private sector, 218; profile, 205, T212; public goods, 211; public management framework, 229; public service functions, 210–12, T214; revenue allocation, 210–13, 215–17, 219–21, 222; Revenue Mobilization, Allocation, and Fiscal Commission, 224–5, 230; reverse transfer, 213; sources of revenue, 212, 213; Special Fund, 216; Stabilization Fund, 209–10; structure of government, 206–7; system of government, 205–6, 212; tax assignment, 210, 212–13, T226–7; transfer payments, 213, 219–21; vertical gaps, 213; vertical revenue allocation, 217; weighting federal government functions, 217–18
Nigerian local government: allocations to, 222–4; expenditure responsibilities, 210–11; financial dependency of, 215; oil revenues, 208; public service functions, T214; resource ownership, 217
Nigerian states: division of fiscal powers, 207; efficiency, 208; federal presence in, 218–19; financial dependency of, 215; horizontal imbalances, 219–21; internal

Index   435

revenue effort, 219–20; public service functions, 211, T214, 215; regional revenue sources, 212–13; reverse transfers, 213; system of government, 205; tax revenues, 213; transfer payments to, 213–25
Norway, 4

Oates, Wallace, 8; on fiscal equalization, 30
Olson, Mancur, 8
Ontario (Canada): tax harmonization, 113
opting-out (in) arrangements, 7
output-based fiscal transfers, setting national minimal standards through, 391–2
own taxes. *See* ceded taxes (Spain)

Pakistan, 5
patronage, political (Malaysia), 190
personal income tax (Spain), 298, 300, T299
Philippines, the, 4
Phillipson Commission (Nigeria), 212
Portugal, 4
poverty (Malaysia), 194, 195
Property Rates Act (South Africa), 273
Provincial Tax Regulation Process Act, 2001 (South Africa), 273, 275–6
Public Finance Management Act (South Africa), 268, 313
public sector, redistributive role of, 10–11
public services: administrative/compliance costs, 10; decentralizing delivery of, 20–1; economies of scale, 10; effective provision under fiscal federalism, 9–10; expenditure assignments, T14–15; government structure for providing, 16, 19, T17–18; grants to set national minimum standards for, 30–1; private-sector participation, 19; spatial externalities, 10; special-purpose agencies, 16

quasi-private goods, 11
Quebec (Canada), 7; legal system, 101; sales tax, 114; separatism in, 29; tax harmonization, 113; tax room, 107, 108

Rao, M. Govina, 398
referenda (Switzerland), 12, 322, 324, 326–8
regional conflicts, and federal form of government, 5
regional government, efficient and equitable provision of services, 16, 19, T17–18

regional inequities: and fiscal federalism, 37–8; and grants, 29–30; horizontal, 10
regional services, grants to set national minimum standards for, 30–1
regulatory powers, comparison of assignments, 378–80
Reid Commission (Malaysia), 181–2, 185
Reserve Bank of Australia, 53
Reserve Bank of India, 160
responsibilities, overlapping, in competitive federalism model, 6
Revenue Mobilization Allocation and Fiscal Commission (Nigeria), 213, 224–5, 230
revenue sharing, 21; Brazil, 88–92; Nigeria, 213, 214–15
revenue-sharing agreements, 21
revenue-sharing formulas (South Africa), 276, 285n8
Rezende, Fernando, 399
Riker, William H., 5
Russia, 5; barriers to trade, 245; borrowing, 256–8; Budget Code, 255, 256, 257; capital transfers, 252, 255; corruption, 258; division of fiscal powers, 238–45; equalization payments, 252–3, 255–6, 259; equity and efficiency issues, 250–6; expenditure assignment, 238–40, T240; factor mobility, 245; federal influence, 243; financing capital investment, 256–8; fiscal discipline, 240, 246; horizontal inequities, 250–6; intergovernmental conflicts, 241–2; intergovernmental transfers, 242, 251–6; local governments, 243–4, 255–6; mergers, 236–7; monetary policy, 246; operating transfers, 252; policy coordination, 245–50; profile, 236–7, T237; public management framework, 258; public services, 253; regional disparities, 236, 250–1, 252–3, 254–5; regulatory responsibilities, 238–40, T239; rural areas, 244–5; social programs, 242, 251, 255; soft budget constraints, 246; sources of revenue, 247, T248–9, 259; structure of government, 237–8; subsidiarity principle, 241–2; tax assignment, 247, T248–9; tax competition, 247, 249–50
Russian local governments: budget monitoring, 240; expenditure assignments, 238–40, T240; intergovernmental conflicts, 241–2; intergovernmental transfers, 255–6; legal status, 243–4; local services, providing, 243–4; sources of

revenue, 247; tax assignments, T248–9; tax competition, 247, 249–50
Russian regional governments, 237–8, barriers to trade, 245; budget monitoring, 240; equalization allowances, 252–3; expenditure assignments, 238–40, T240; officials' wages, 246; revenue autonomy, 24; sources of revenue, 247; tax assignments, T248–9; tax competition, 247, 249–50

St Gall (Switzerland), 326, 327, 328
seignorage, 12
Shah, Anwar, 399
shared decision making, and federal form of government, 4
Singapore, 4
Social Union Framework Agreement (Canada), 107
South Africa, 4, 5, 6; autonomous government spheres, 282–3; borrowing, 281; budget reform process, 267–8; central bank, 266; centralized revenues, 273, central-local transfers, 32; civil service, 282–3; corruption, 283; decentralized federation, 263, 264–5; division of fiscal powers, 268, 271–2, T269–70; efficiency issues, 277–80; electoral system, 263; equity issues, 275, 277–80; expenditure assignment, 268, 271–2, T272; financing capital investment, 280–2; fiscal discipline, 267; fiscal disparities, 279; fiscal policy, 266–7; general purpose grants, 276; grants, problems with, 277; horizontal imbalances, 265–6, 279; inflation-targeting policy, 266–7; infrastructure, 267, 280–1; intergovernmental fiscal relations system, 264–6, 278–9; intergovernmental transfers, 276–7; legislative system, 264; local governments, 266; monetary policy, 266–7; municipal revenue-raising powers, 266, 272–3; natural resources, 285n6; oversight role, 284; profile, 263–4, T265; public service delivery costs, 279; regulatory responsibilities, 268, 271–2, T269–70; revenue assignment, 272–3, 275–6, T274–5, 277–80; revenue forecasting, 268; revenue-sharing formulas, 276, 285n8; shared responsibilities, 271–2; social services, 267, 277, 278; specific purpose grants, 276–7, 286n11; tax administration, 267; tax assignments, 272–3, 275–6, T274–5; tax collection, 273; unemployment in, 267; unfunded mandates, 271, 283; vertical imbalances, 279, T280
South African Reserve Bank, 266–7
South African subnational governments: autonomy of, 282–3; borrowing powers, 281; corruption, 283; deficit target, 294–5; electoral systems, 263; equity issues, 277–80; fiscal autonomy, 272–3; fiscal discipline, 267–8; fiscal imbalances, 279; intergovernmental relations, 264–6; intergovernmental transfers to, 276–7; local expenditure assignments, 271–2; municipal aid, 281–2; National Council of Provinces, 284; provincial expenditure assignments, 268, 269; provincial regulatory responsibilities, T269–70; public service, 282; revenue-raising powers, 266, 272–3, 275–6; sources of revenue, 266; tax assignments, T274–5
Spain, 4; agreed taxes, 301; ceded taxes, 297–8, T299–300; central bank, 294; charter system, 301–4, 313; common regime, 296–304, 313; Complementary Fund, 309; cooperative *mancomunidades*, 292; division of powers, 290, 292–4, T291; equalization grants, 306–8; equity issues, 309–10; expenditure assignments, 293–4, T293, 297; fiscal discipline, 294–5; fiscal policy, 294–5; grants, 296–7, 306–10; horizontal imbalances, 313; intergovernmental fiscal transfers, 306–10, 313; local governments' revenue assignments, 304–6, T307; macroeconomic management, 294–5; municipal governments, 304, 305–6, 309; negative transfers (quota), 302–3; personal income tax, 298, 300, 302; political accountability, 290; profile, 288, 290, T289; property taxes, 305; public services, 296; regional revenues, 296–304, 306–8, 311; regulatory responsibilities, T291; revenue assignments, 296–304, 311; revenue-raising issues, 296–306; revenue-sharing formula, 302–3; structure of government, 289; Sufficiency Fund, 306–8; tax administration, 300–1, 311–12; tax assignments, 297–8, 300–4; vertical imbalances, 312
Spanish subnational governments: asymmetric treatment of, 313; autonomous communities, *see* autonomous communities (Spain); charter system, 301–4; horizontal imbalances, 313; local government

Index

responsibilities, 292, T291; local government revenue sources, 289, 304–6; regional revenues, 296–8, 300–304, 311; tax administration, 311–12; transfers to local governments, 309–10; transfers to regional governments, 306–8; vertical imbalances, 312
spatial externalities, and centralized decision making, 10
special-purpose agencies, public service delivery, 16
special-purpose transfers, 25–26; South Africa, 276–7
specific purpose payments (SPPs) (Australia), 49, 61
spending power. *See* expenditure assignment
spillover effects (Nigeria), 210, 211
Stabilization Fund (Nigeria), 209–210
state government, status in layer-cake model of dual federalism, 5
Stigler, George, 7
Streamlined Sales and Use Tax Agreement (SSUTA) (USA), 360–1
strings-attached funding (Australia), 56
subsidiarity principle, 8; Brazil's expenditure assignments, 77, T78; United States, 350
Sufficiency Fund (Spain), 306–8
Sweden, 4
Swiss cantons: autonomy of, 322, 337; borrowing, 336–7; collaboration between, 335; debt, 326–8, 336–7; equalization system, 333–5; exemption system, 332–3; expenditure assignments, T324; expenditure limits, 326–7, 328; fiscal discipline, 325–6, 336–7; horizontal discrepancies, 320, 329, 332–3, 334; income tax, 329, 331–3; inter-canton cooperation, 322; post-tax income distribution, 334; profile, 318, 319, 320; referenda, 12, 322, 324, 326–8; regulatory responsibilities, 321–2, T323; revenue equalization, 335; savings, 327, 328; shared responsibilities, 321–2; sources of revenue, 329, 331–3, T330–1; sovereignty of, 321; tax assignments, 329, 331–3, T330–1; tax competition, 329, 333
Swiss National Bank, 325
Switzerland, 6; borrowing, 336–7; central bank, 12, 325; communes, role of, 15; corporate income taxes, 331, 332, 333; corruption, 338; division of fiscal powers, 321–4; economic growth, 320; equity issues, 333–5; exemption system, 332–3; expenditure assignment, T324; federal system, 319–20; financing capital investment, 336–7; fiscal discipline, 325–6, 327, 336–7; fiscal policy, 325–6, 327; governmental autonomy, 322–3; horizontal discrepancies, implementation deficit, 322; income tax, 329; inflation, 325; local governments, macroeconomic management, 325–6; monetary policy, 325; municipalities, 321, 329, 336; personal income taxes, 333; post-tax income distribution, 334; profile, 318, 320, T319; profit sharing, 332–3; public debt, 326–7, 328, 336–7; public management framework, 337–8; public services, T323; regulatory responsibilities, 321–2, T323; revenue sources, 329–33; St Gall, 326, 327; savings, 327, 328; structure of government, 321–4; tax assignments, 329, 331–3, T330–1; tax burden, 329, 331–2, 333; tax competition, 329, 333; university policy, 322

tax assignment, T22–3; administrative feasibility of, 20; compared, 380–83; conflicts re, 78; decentralizing, 20; and economic efficiency, 20; and fiscal need (revenue adequacy), 20; principles of, 19–21, T22–3; subnational own revenues as a percentage of subnational expenditure, T381
tax-base determination, 21
tax-base sharing, 21
tax competition, 383; Canada, 113; Russia, 247, 249–50; systems compared, 381
tax harmonization (Canada), 106–7, 109, 112, 113–15
tradable goods, assigning tax revenues from, 20
trade, and national government, 11
transfer dependencies, 29–30
Turkey, 4
two-tier structures for metropolitan governance, 16

unfunded mandates (South Africa), 271, 283
Union of Soviet Socialist Republics (USSR), 7. *See also* Russia
unitary form of government, 3–4, 371; and monetary policy, 12
United Kingdom, 4
United Nations, 7

United States of America (USA), 5, 6, 7; administration and federal/state tax systems, 359; borrowing, federal, 364; compliance burdens and *Quill* case, 360; compliance costs, horizontal competition, 360; Congress and interstate commerce, 356; the constitution and amendments, 353, 356; constitutional limitations on taxation, 353; direct service delivery, 349; expanding federal system, 348–9; Federal Reserve (FED), 364; federal service exclusive responsibilities, 350; federalism, history of, 347–9; fiscal policy, 364; government structure, 346–7; Hurricane Katrina and service delivery overlap, 352–3; income tax power, 354; intergovernment financial relations, 358–61; intergovernment grants, 349, 350, 361–4; intertwined federal-state tax structures, 359; macroeconomic management, 364–6; mandates and service delivery, 349–50; Medicaid, 348, 351, 362; middle-class voters, 348; middle-of-the-road federalism, 348; monetary policy, 364; "nowhere" (untaxed) income, 358; President Bush's Tax Reform Panel, 365; profile, 345–7, T346; public sector hospitals, regulatory responsibility, 351; service assignment and data, 350; service assignment and delivery, 349, 350, 352–3; service delivery influence, 349; shared responsibilities, 350, 351–2; social security/Medicaid/welfare programs, 348, 351; subsidiarity principle, 350; tax assignment, 353–6, T355; tax bases/rates, 358–9; vertical competition, 359–60; vertical fiscal gaps, 363. *See also* American local government; American states

universities (Switzerland), 322
user charges, 20

vertical fiscal gap, 28–9, 383, T384–5
vertical fiscal imbalance, 21, 28
Von Hagen, Jürgen, 399

Weingast, Barry, 7

Zurich, school communities in, 8